Poetics and Praxis, Understanding and Imagination

Edited by Arthur F. Kinney

Poetics and Praxis, Understanding and Imagination

The Collected Essays of O. B. Hardison Jr.

The University of Georgia Press *Athens & London*

Athens, Georgia 30602

Designed by Walton Harris
Set in 10/12 Sabon by Books International
Printed and bound by Braun-Brumfield, Inc.

The paper in this book meets the guidelines for permanence and durability of the Committee on Production Guidelines for Book Longevity of the Council on Library Resources.

Printed in the United States of America

01 00 99 98 97 C 5 4 3 2 1

Library of Congress Cataloging in Publication Data

Hardison, O. B.
Poetics and praxis, understanding and imagination : the collected essays of O.B. Hardison, Jr. / edited by Arthur F. Kinney.

p. cm.

Includes bibliographical references and index.
ISBN 0-8203-1819-1 (alk. paper)
1. English literature—Early modern, 1500–1700—History and criticism. 2. Imagination. 3. Poetics. I. Kinney, Arthur F., 1933– . II. Title.
PR423.H37 1997
809—dc20 95-39534

British Library Cataloging in Publication Data available

Contents

Acknowledgments

We gratefully acknowledge the following publications in which some of these essays first appeared:

"In Praise of the Essay," *Wilson Quarterly* 14 (Autumn 1990), 54–65. An earlier version appeared in the *Sewanee Review* 96 (1988), 610–32, reprinted in *Essays on the Essay: Redefining the Genre*, ed. Alexander J. Butrym (Athens: University of Georgia Press, 1989), 11–28.

"Aristotle and Averroes" published as "The Place of Averroes' Commentary on the *Poetics* in the History of Medieval Criticism," *Medieval and Renaissance Studies* 4, ed. John Lievsay (Durham: Duke University Press, 1970), 57–81.

"The Orator and the Poet: The Dilemma of Humanist Literature," *Journal of Medieval and Renaissance Studies* 1 (1971), 33–44.

"Blank Verse before Milton," *Studies in Philology* 81 (1984), 253–74.

"The Two Voices of Sidney's *Apology for Poetry*," *English Literary Renaissance* 2:1 (1972), 83–99, reprinted in *Sidney in Retrospect*, ed. Arthur F. Kinney and the Editors of *ELR* (Amherst: University of Massachusetts Press, 1988), 45–61.

"Three Types of Renaissance Catharsis," *Renaissance Drama*, n.s. 2 (1968), 3–22.

"Tudor Humanism and Surrey's Translation of the *Aeneid*," *Studies in Philology* 83 (1986), 237–60.

"Perspective and Form in Petrarch," published as "Petrarch and Modern Lyric Poetry," *Studies in the Continental Background of Renaissance English Literature* (Durham: Duke University Press, 1977), 29–41.

"*Amoretti* and the *Dolce Stil Novo*," *English Literary Renaissance* 2:2 (1972), 208–16.

"Logic Versus the Slovenly World in Shakespearean Comedy," *Shakespeare Quarterly* 31 (1980), 311–22.

"The Dramatic Triad in *Hamlet*," *Studies in Philology* 57 (1960), 144–64.

"Myth and History in *King Lear*," *Shakespeare Quarterly* 26 (1975), 277–42.

"Speaking the Speech: Shakespearean Dialogue" published as "Speaking the Speech," *Shakespeare Quarterly* 34 (1983), 133–46. Originally the keynote address Hardison delivered as president of the Shakespeare Association of America.

"Shakespeare on Film: The Developing Canon," *Twelfth Annual Comparative Literature Symposium* (Lubbock: Texas Tech University, 1979), 131–45.

"Milton's 'On Time' and Its Scholastic Background," *Texas Studies in Language and Literature* 3 (1961), 107–22.

"*In Medias Res* in *Paradise Lost*," *Milton Studies* 17 (Pittsburgh: University of Pittsburgh Press, 1983), 27–42.

"Politics and Beauty," *Soundings* 58:1 (1975), 1–13.

"Dada, the Poetry of Nothing, and the Modern World," *Sewanee Review* 92 (1984), 372–96.

"Great Walls and Running Fences," *Sewanee Review* 94 (1986), 384–417.

"A Tree, a Streamlined Fish, and a Self-Squared Dragon: Science as a Form of Culture," *Georgia Review* 40 (1986), 369–403. Reprinted in *The Pushcart Prize XII*, ed. Bill Henderson (New York: Pushcart Press, 1987), 322–42.

"The Disappearance of Man," *Georgia Review* 42 (1988), 679–713.

Preface

"We live in a world of changes and shadows," O. B. Hardison Jr., wrote in 1990, "a world where the real dissolves as we reach for it and meets us as we turn away. It is a world of mazes and illusions and metaphors, and idols and stairways that proceed upward and downward to infinity." The remark first appeared in the essay "Binding Proteus" (1988), one of many he contributed to *Sewanee Review* in his later years. That essay was reprinted in *Essays on the Essay: Redefining the Genre* edited by Alexander J. Butrym (1989) and then revised considerably as "In Praise of the Essay" for the autumn 1990 *Wilson Quarterly*. Clearly this work—the only one Hardison reprinted this way—was singularly important to him. Initially a scholar of classical, medieval, and Renaissance poetics and poetry, later a visionary writer of cultural history, and always a practitioner of conceptual intertextuality, he designed this statement, which escaped revision, to pay homage to those who most shaped his own understanding of man's condition and achievement: Plato and Aristotle, Shakespeare and Milton, Montaigne and Bacon, Heisenberg and Kant. In his final published essay, Hardison was fashioning the poetics of his own life's work.

Throughout his extraordinarily productive life, Hardison's primary form for thinking and writing was the essay. He used it to explore, meditate, instruct, persuade, and provoke. His books—such as *Toward Freedom and Dignity* (1972), *Entering the Maze* (1982), and *Disappearing through the Skylight* (1989), posthumously nominated for the National Book Award and recipient of the *Los Angeles Times* Book Award for 1991—were in part assemblages of earlier essays. When he died suddenly in 1990 at the age of 61, he left sixteen file drawers crammed with essays which he was carefully writing, rewriting, and reordering, apparently planning a retrospective collection of his work. "In Praise of the Essay" tells us why he so cherished the form: it challenged him; it teased him into thought; it made him wrestle with the implications and consequences of what he was saying. "More than any other literary form," he writes, "the essay, like Proteus, resists all efforts to contain it. . . . It is tough, infinitely adaptable, and ubiquitous." For a student of literary tradition such as Hardison, the essay had a respectable pedigree, yet it was also a form stubbornly inconclusive and contingent, filled with the mysteries of its own potentiality. "The chief characteristic of Proteus is elusiveness. If there is no genre more widespread in modern letters than the essay, there is also no genre that takes so many shapes and that refuses so successfully to resolve itself, finally, into its own shape."

One hallmark of Hardison's writing is his grounding of the present and future in the past; another is his use of one culture as the perspective on another.

> The word "essay" comes from Old French *essai*, defined by [Eric] Partridge as "a trial, an attempt." From this meaning comes English "to essay" in the sense of "to make a trial or an attempt," as Emerson's statement, "I also will essay to be." The word also comes into English via the Norman French *assaier*, "to assay," meaning to try or test, as in testing the quality of a mineral ore.
>
> German has two words for essay, *Abhandlung*, a "dealing with" something, and *Aufsatz*, a "setting forth."

If so—if the essay is either analytic or expository—Hardison characteristically refused to choose: he made certain his essays, often in the form of expositions, were nevertheless, at root, firmly analytic. The research, learning, and labor behind and beneath an apparent explanation is deep and wide: it can be seen, on a second reading, in his careful selectivity and his deft expressions.

He combined the styles of his predecessors, too, as well as their forms. "Montaigne's essays are associative, discursive, informal, meandering, and slovenly." Bacon's "are aphoristic, staccato, assertive, hortatory, abrasive." Hardison liked both: his informal expressions echoed Montaigne's in their near-chattiness; his need to order (or repeat, or enumerate) his points took its cue from Bacon. Like them both, however, he was anti-Ciceronian, scornful of elaboration, of "art for art's sake." In this he was (with them) at one with Cato: "I would have the subject predominate, and so fill the imagination of him who listens that he shall have no remembrance of the words." For Hardison, practicing *ars celare artem*, "art that conceals art," was also work: each of his files contains several drafts of any single essay, some of them overlined and corrected until they are nearly impenetrable. Like Montaigne and Bacon, Hardison's "lack of artifice is an illusion created by years of effort" in which he places reason in the service of imagination, because only the imagination carries the understanding past the mundane and the known to other, richer ends.

Hardison's essays, especially the earlier ones growing out of his classes in poetics, poetry, and drama, initially share with Bacon "the magisterial method," providing a "rhetoric of assurance" born of an "empiricism [that] offers an escape from uncertainty." But, like Bacon, Hardison soon learned that such analyses and expositions, if too fixed, became idols, providing and promulgating "received knowledge" that "crumbled when it was put to the test." Reason and knowledge had to be accompanied by the sense of uncertainty that Hardison first discovered in the work of Sir Thomas Browne (following Plato): "Me thinks there be not impossibilities enough in Religion for an active faith. . . . I love to lose myself in a mystery, to pursue my reason to an *Oh Altitudo*. . . . I learned of Tertullian, *Certum est quia impossible est.*" Such consolation or reward, Hardison knew, could also be frightening. "The terror—or the malaise—of the world makes people want to be spectators, but as Werner Heisenberg has shown, spectators are always tangled up in the things they are observing." So was Hardison, reveling in not being exempt. Rather, he agreed with the Joseph Addison of *Spectator* paper 420: "The Understanding, indeed, opens an infinite Space on every side of us, but the Imagination, after a few faint efforts, is immediately at a stand, and finds her self swallowed up in the immensity of the Void that surrounds it." This, though, was the imagination of the poet—Shakespeare's poet's eye, "with its fine frenzy rolling"—and the imagination of the scientist who sees silicon men succeeding carbon man. For Hardison, reason and understanding need imagination and the void just as poets need a poetics. Attempting to bind Proteus throughout his life, Hardison, in his writings, implicitly and explicitly attempted to show how knowledge and the void, like observation and metaphor, were necessarily, and wonderfully, symbiotic.

O. B. Hardison Jr., appeared on the cover of *Time* magazine on May 6, 1966, as one of America's "great teachers." "Boyish enthusiasm sits poorly on a professor," they wrote inside under the heading "Renaissance Man," "but an urgency and eagerness that transcend enthusiasm can be gripping. At the University of North Carolina, in Chapel Hill, English Professor Osborne Bennett ("O. B.") Hardison, Jr., 37, wears scuffed shoes, drooping socks and chalk-streaked jacket, goes everywhere accompanied by a kindly dog named Poppo, and makes literature an urgent affair." The writers continued, "Hardison, says Neil Forsyth, a graduate student from Britain, 'understands more of Aristotelian thought than anybody who taught me Aristotle at Cambridge.' When one of Hardison's lectures on Milton and the Puritan period ended, Forsyth adds, 'I wanted to stand up and cheer.'" Contagion was always his method in teaching, as his infectious spirits inform each of his essays. "The teacher's own personal enthusiasms can be a powerful stimulant," he wrote in 1982 ("Teaching Literature to Undergraduates"); "It is seldom mentioned that education at its best is exhilarating and that the excitement often lasts a lifetime" ("Education for Utopia," 1985).

His own lifetime was a crowded one. Educated at the University of North Carolina at Chapel Hill (B.A., 1949; M.A., 1950) and the University of Wisconsin (Ph.D., 1956), he taught at the University of Tennessee and Princeton before returning to Chapel Hill (1957) where in 1967 he was promoted to Professor of English and Comparative Literature. From 1969 to 1983 he served as the third director of the Folger Shakespeare Library in Washington, D.C., transforming a scholarly retreat into a cultural center.

He began fellowships for graduate students and doubled the number of readers who did research there each year; he established the Folger Institute with advanced lectures and seminars for college teachers as well as students; in founding there a number of public programs—the Folger Theater, the Folger Consort, the PEN/Faulkner Awards, a poetry reading series, the Anne Hathaway Gallery—he increased the annual number of visitors from thirty thousand to two hundred thousand; he also expanded the rare books collection by twenty-thousand volumes and built an $8.5 million addition to the library, retiring the debt before his departure. Then, the scholar and teacher in him never really subsiding, from 1984 until his death he served as University Professor of English at Georgetown University. Other honors were given him in abundance. He was a member of Phi Beta Kappa, a Fulbright Fellow to Rome, and a Guggenheim Fellow. He was awarded the Doctorate in Humane Letters at eight institutions of higher learning. He was president of the Renaissance Society of America and president of the Shakespeare Association of America. He won the Nicholas Salgo Award for Distinguished Teaching in 1968; he was named a trustee of the University of Detroit in 1970; and he was the John F. Kennedy Memorial Visiting Fellow to New Zealand in 1980. Governments recognized him as well as universities: in 1974 the Italian government decorated him as Cavaliere Ufficiale della Republica Italiana, and in 1983 the British government awarded him the Order of the British Empire.

Throughout, his published work—his extended teaching—continued unabated. There were books like *The Enduring Monument: The Idea of Praise in Renaissance Literary Theory and Practice* (1962, 1972), *Christian Rite and Christian Drama in the Middle Ages* (1965, 1983), and *Prosody and Purpose in the English Renaissance* (1989). With Samuel H. Beer and John Simon he edited and supervised eighty-four titles in the Crofts Classics from Aeschylus to Wordsworth; with George Garrett and Jane R. Gelfman he edited four volumes of film scripts; with Leon Golden he edited a student text of *Aristotle's Poetics* and of *Classical and Medieval Literary Criticism*; with Jerry Mills he edited *The Forms of Imagination*; and with Alex Preminger and Frank Warnke *The Princeton Encyclopedia of Poetry and Poetics*. He oversaw the Goldentree Bibliographies and sat on the editorial board of several journals—*Studies in Philosophy*, *Milton Studies*, *English Literary Renaissance*, and the *Journal of Medieval and Renaissance Studies*—and from 1980 until his death he was an editorial adviser for *The Collected Works of Erasmus* for the University of Toronto Press.

But if his life was full, it was not scattered. The purpose of his writing and editing was education of a particular kind: "What is needed," he wrote in 1984, "is a form of education that orients students to their culture" ("The Hard Core Curriculum: *Realpolitik* for the Liberal Arts"). Culture for him meant the fusing of poetics, as in Aristotle and Averroes; the fusing of forms, as in the works of the orator and the poet; and the intertextuality of poets, as in Dante and Spenser, or Horace and Sidney. His works show a mastery of incidental quotation, swift but telling analogy, and memorable lines: "The spirit of classical comedy is linear"; medieval drama is "often crude, obvious, and ridiculous"; "It is a pity [Milton] did not know Surrey's translation [of the *Aeneid*] because in spite of the help he received from the dramatic blank verse of Marlowe and Shakespeare, he had to make many of Surrey's discoveries about heroic blank verse all over again." He was often, at heart, a structuralist, and in one essay ("Criticism and the Search for Pattern," 1961), he located four organizing methods in literary work: the triad, the character spectrum, antinomy and typology, only to complicate them the moment he sketched them out. These strengths are the strengths of his essays as well as his classroom lectures and his book-length studies. "They reflect not only careful scholarship but vast learning," one scholar recently commented. "Hardison's range is in itself something to behold. He knows not simply a little about a great many subjects but a great deal. He writes with exceptional grace and lucidity, and he has the rare ability to make very complex arguments clear without any substantive loss. . . . Hardison always keeps his larger argument in the foreground but he also has the essayist's talent for the telling observation along the way. The fox and the hedgehog coexist happily in his work." Nor did the encroachment of a computer revolution—which he once likened to the Christian revolution in the Hebrew world—daunt his energy or excitement. "Advances in machine speech-recognition may soon make reading the oddity of a cultural moment rather than a condition of civilization," he wrote near the end of his life, yet "there is still an honorable place in literary studies for a kind of Sephardic humanism resting on faith that the Holy Land of subjects and centers and presences may eventually be reclaimed from the Sultans of Synchrony."

In a memorial service in Washington, D.C., in August 1990, his friend Willard Wirtz, former secretary of labor, noted that O. B. Hardison "ordained gaiety." His personality, like his work, was characterized by creativity, accessibility, and whimsy. According to Wirtz, only O. B.'s computer, with which he was spending increasing time, "had a database and retrieval system that matched his own." Father Timothy Healy added that Hardison had a "savage refusal for abstractions," instead teaching even in conversation with ideas "rooted in common sense." He knew the scholar's isolation and the teacher's public mission. In both, he met the tumult of life with a neatness of thought and with persistent and restless interrogation. He also had "uncommon decency and kindness," his Georgetown colleague, the poet Anthony Hecht, remarked at the same service, adding, "Those who were not in awe of him were probably not aware of his accomplishments."

The present collection of essays is a selection of representative works from throughout his career—from his earliest works to those completed but still unpublished at the time of his death. They all benefit from the intensity and acuity of his thought: one of the most commonly shared memories of family and friends alike is a portrait of O. B. quietly studying in the midst of a whirlwind of activity, as when he frequently prepared his essays hunched over the kitchen table while any or all of his six children played and shouted about him. Then and there, as elsewhere, he made essays and poems (*poeta*, from Greek *poiein*, to make) such as "Pro Musica Antiqua," the title poem from his second volume of poetry (1977; the first was *Lyrics and Elegies*, 1958), which shares the ideas and the wit of many of the essays included in this volume:

Listen to the music.
Listen to the sound of the krummhorn, the rebec,
The vielle, the virginal, the viola da gamba,
The scraping and twanging celebration of order.
It is all in the best possible order.
It streams up through the air of your house
And it is like summer,
A kind of sunlight slanting through the dust
Of almost empty air.

Throw away the dictionary.
Live where you are.
If the sackbut palls,
Bang on a pianoforte.
Limber up drums,
Unleash saxophones, let everything run wild.
Have voices, too, whole choruses of voices,
Doing the Nibelungenlied by ear.

This is the way it should be. Your house should be music.
Welcome it, hold on to it, sweat, let it pour into you
Like an old god making demigods with mortals.
Hold on until your every motion is dance.
Having received, enlarge.
When you let go, you will snore in C major.

As in so many of the poet's essays here, the initial idea leads to a catalogue of observations, propelled by a passion that takes the writer (and us) past the present to an *Oh altitudo* that surpasses all expression. Music, like art and writing, thus serves as a metonymy for the way we think and know.

As a teenager at St. Alban's, O. B. Hardison did not plan to become a teacher, a poet, or a writer: he wanted to be an astronomer imagining, he told a reporter on the Washington *Post* in 1989, "a finite but unbounded universe—if you went far enough in one direction you'd come back to where you started." His interest in science was inspired by Heisenberg, whose uncertainty principle Hardison thought at once was "hugely important. According to this, if you choose to observe nature in one way, you rule out observing it in another. So two observers see different natures. And both are correct. For the observer shapes things being observed. This was the first suggestion to me that nature has disappeared. And then in the 1950s, the Kinsey report on male sexuality had a long preface on how the interviewer shapes the information being derived—for instance how he's dressed. The fancy silk tie, the blue jeans would elicit different information." After St. Alban's, he spent a year "hanging out" at Berkeley, joined student movements and turned toward the humanities. They sustained him through college, graduate school, and the early years of teaching. But in 1965, studying medieval drama, "I came back to science in a weird way." The received theory he studied argued that "drama had evolved in a Darwinian way, evolving from a single-cell organism, 'Quem Quartis'—a teeny, tiny play. It was the first modern play." This is because, according to Hardison, "Darwinism was applied to social theories, history, architecture and fashion." So the drama, too, evolved into more complicated forms, "meaning better—arriving at Shakespeare as the equivalent in drama for *homo sapiens* in biology." But his own research into the history of drama showed no such simple evolution at all. Facts and dates revealed no correlation between complexity and time. When he "exploded the old theories, it was like a revelation."

The lesson Hardison took from his research was not that the history of the humanities was independent of the history of science but, "if you wanted to escape the stereotypes, the prison house of unstated assumptions," inseparable from it. So he began to locate connections or analogies between the humanities and sciences, determined to prove C. P. Snow wrong by proving there were not two cultures, but only one. From studying first science and then art, he progressed to studying both, as an overall history of culture. It was not easy. "The basic paradox of culture is that we cannot exist without it, but as it shapes us, it encloses us." The struggle to escape such imprisonment led Hardison back to history once more: if he could not escape his culture, his understanding of it would shift mastery to him. The search, given another name, would be called education.

And thoughts of education, worked out in many speeches as well as essays in the 1970s and 1980s, began at the beginning, with Socrates. "According to Socrates in Plato's *Republic,* education is the process of learning truth. It frees the individual from bondage to illusions—from the myriad superstitions, mythologies, and prejudices that imprison the ignorant. The result is wisdom, which is a combination of self-confidence and humility. The most famous words of Socrates are probably his admission: 'The only thing that I know is that I do not know'" ("The Future of Liberal Arts: A Humanist's View," 1985). Yet wisdom is not only received knowledge tempered by experience, but for the poet and humanist, the power of the imagination as well, a lesson he discovered in Kant. "Kant taught that the imagination is the most basic human faculty. It is born with each individual, and each individual possesses it in equal measure. It is, essentially, the faculty for making comprehensible impressions out of the welter of inner and outer data transmitted to the mind by the senses." According to Kant, he continued, "experience is a construct of the imagination, and aesthetic response occurs when we contemplate experience for itself rather than for its use or its relation to some abstract system of ideas" ("The Promises of Humanistic Education: Can They Be Kept?" 1973). It is the imaginative leap of understanding, of risk, of discovery, that is shared by the poet, the philosopher, and the scientist; it is their shared *art*. And "Art is committed by its nature to the exploration of otherness. As it does this, and as it communicates to its audience, the otherness is assimilated and becomes familiar. It is no longer strange or frightening. Instead it can be accepted for what it is. Its real values emerge, and its imaginary trappings gradually fade into the air" ("Art as Freedom," n.d.). Committed, exploratory art neither eliminates nor falls victim to imagination, but with the help of the imagination pushes back a part of the mystery and illuminates part of the darkness. And "This is the way it should be."

> Welcome it, hold on to it, sweat, let it pour into you
> Like an old god making demigods with mortals.
> Hold on until your every motion is dance.
> Having received, enlarge.

That is the purpose and final end, too, of the essays assembled here.

Arthur F. Kinney
Washington, D.C.
Amherst, Massachusetts

Part 1

Introduction

In Praise of the Essay

The ancient god Proteus knew the secrets of the past and the future. Those who would learn them were required to bind him with chains before asking their questions. When bound, Proteus would change into all manner of shapes to escape. Menelaus visited Proteus when becalmed at Pharos and forced him to reveal the fates of Agamemnon and Odysseus. Aristaeus, a shepherd of Tempe, was told by his mother Cyrene to visit Proteus when Aristaeus's bees were dying. As Vergil announces in the *Georgics,* she advised: "The more he turns himself into different shapes, the more you, my son, must hold on to those strong chains."

Writing an essay on the essay is appropriate in an age that delights in strange loops and Gödelian recursions and that has announced, more often perhaps than it really needs to, that every art form is first and foremost a comment on itself. More than any other literary form, the essay, like Proteus, resists all efforts to contain it.

Let me put one card on the table immediately. There is a rumor going about that the essay is an endangered species. There have even been calls to "save the essay," as if it were a sensitive species on the point of extinction. Nothing could be more absurd. The essay is tough, infinitely adaptable, and ubiquitous. It has more in common with the German cockroach than with the Tennessee snail darter. The analogy has hidden relevance. The cockroach is a primitive creature. It appears very early on the evolutionary chain. The essay is also primitive. Roland Barthes suggests that, in the evolution of projections of the imagination, it may precede the formation of all concepts of genre.

I recall that the newspapers of my childhood, in addition to printing letters to the editor, regularly paid homage to "literature" by including poems. The poems were often maudlin and sometimes egregious, but they were recognizably poems.

Today, how many poems do you find in the newspaper? Unless you read a paper that comes out once a week in a remote rural county and has a name something like the *Culpeper Eagle,* you do not find a single one. Instead, in any up-to-date newspaper, you find essays. They are called op-ed pieces, and their authors are nationally syndicated. These authors do not need support from foundations. Some earn more in an hour than many Americans do in six months. People read these essays. Today, the essay is one of only two literary genres of which this can be said, the other being the memo.

I return, now, to the myth I have invoked. The chief characteristic of Proteus is elusiveness. If there is no genre more widespread in modern letters than the essay, there is also no genre that takes so many shapes and that refuses so successfully to resolve itself, finally, into its own shape.

Francis Bacon concludes in *The Wisdom of the Ancients* that Proteus symbolizes matter. He adds, "If any skillful servant of Nature shall bring force to bear on matter, and shall vex it and drive it to extremities as if with the purpose of reducing it to nothing," it will assume all shapes but return "at last to itself."

I take heart from Bacon's *Wisdom*. In spite of the danger that the essay may fight back, I propose in the following pages to vex it and drive it to extremities in the hope that by the end it will return to itself and reveal something of its true nature.

The word "essay" comes from the Old French *essai*, defined by Partridge as "a trial, an attempt." From this meaning comes the English "to essay" in the sense of "to make a trial or an attempt," as in Emerson's statement, "I also will essay to be." The word also comes into English via the Norman French *assaier*, "to assay," meaning to try or test, as in testing the quality of a mineral ore.

German has two words for essay, *Abhandlung*, a "dealing with" something, and *Aufsatz*, a "setting forth." Herder's "Essay on the Origin of Speech" is an *Abhandlung*; Martin Heidegger's essay on thingliness—"The Thing"—is an *Aufsatz*. *Abhandlungen* tend to be ponderous and, you might say, Germanic. *Aufsätze* have an altogether lighter touch—a touch, one imagines, like that of Goethe tapping out the rhythms of the hexameter on the back of his Roman mistress.

As far as I have been able to learn, the first use of "essay" to mean a literary composition occurred in the title of the most famous collection of such compositions ever published, Montaigne's *Essais*. If you look for the first English use of the term in this sense in the *Oxford English Dictionary*, you may be surprised at what you find. Instead of a majestic series of entries marching forward from the Middle Ages, you encounter the following statement: "Essay. A composition of moderate length on any particular subject, or branch of a subject; originally implying want of finish . . . but now said of a composition more or less elaborate in style though limited in range. The use in this sense is apparently taken from Montaigne, whose *Essais* were first published in 1580."

In other words, Montaigne invented the term, and the English took it directly from him. Another surprise: In English the term was first used on the title page of the *Essayes* that Francis Bacon published in 1597. It made its second appearance on the title page of John Florio's translation of—you guessed it—Montaigne's *Essayes; or, Morall, Politike, and Militairie Discourses*, published in 1603. Thereafter, the term was applied more and more broadly to any composition that did not fall obviously into some other, better-defined category. It plays the same role in literary criticism that the term "miscellaneous" does in budgeting.

Three historical facts supplement these lexicographical observations. First, the essay did not appear out of nowhere. Montaigne's principal guide in the art of the essay was the Greek writer Plutarch, whose *Opera Moralia* consist of short compositions on topics of general interest, such as the cessation of oracles, whether fish or land animals are more crafty, whether water or fire is more useful, the reasons for not running into debt, and the man in the moon. According to Montaigne, "of all the authors I know, [Plutarch] most successfully commingled art with nature and insight with knowledge." Another writer much admired by Montaigne and more so by Bacon is Seneca, whose unfailingly uplifting letters often come close to being essays.

Second, in spite of this and other precedents, the essay is something new. In the sixteenth century, the standard prose form was the oration. Orations are utilitarian; they seek to accomplish something. As the rhetoric books say, their object is to persuade. Montaigne calls this characteristic the *Hoc age*—the "Do this!"—impulse. To persuade efficiently, orators developed a standard kind of organization called *dispositio. Dispositio* is the literary equivalent of the foregone conclusion.

Montaigne carefully disavows all such advance planning. In the essay "On Education," he quotes with obvious relish the comment of the king of Sparta on a long speech by the ambassadors from Samos: "As for your beginning, I no longer remember it; nor consequently, the middle; as for the conclusion, I do not desire to do anything about it." In "On the Resemblance of Children," he asserts, "I do not correct my first ideas by later ones. . . . I wish to represent the progress of my moods, and that each part shall be seen at its birth." In another context he adds, "I have no other drill-master than chance to arrange my writings. As my thoughts present themselves to my mind, I bring them together." So much for *dispositio.*

As Sir Philip Sidney's *Defence of Poesie* shows, orations can be impressive and informative. They can even, on occasion, be persuasive. There is little room in them, however, for spontaneity. They move ahead with the elephantine thump of the *Abhandlung* rather than the butterfly tango of the *Aufsatz.* The point of orations is not to reveal private feelings but to make things happen.

In fact, the essay is the opposite of an oration. It is a literary trial balloon, an informal stringing together of ideas to see what happens. Let's be frank. From the standpoint of the oration, the essay is feckless. It does not seek to do anything, and it has no standard method even for doing nothing. Montaigne calls essay writing "that stupid enterprise" ("*cette sotte entrepris*"), and when Roland Barthes delivered an oration indicating his acceptance of a chair at the College de France, he apologized for his literary philandering. "I must admit," he said, "that I have produced only essays."

Third fact. Even in its infancy, the essay shows its Protean heritage. Montaigne's essays are associative, discursive, informal, meandering, and slovenly. Being the first of their kind, they ought at least to have become models for what followed, in the same way that even disreputable people—muggers, prostitutes, con men, and so forth—will become models if they are really good at what they do. They did not. Bacon's essays were inspired by Montaigne's but are, if anything, anti-Montaignian. Especially in their 1597 form, they are aphoristic, staccato, assertive, hortatory, abrasive.

This brings us to style.

Morris Croll wrote the classic study of sixteenth-century prose style. He calls Montaigne's style "libertine" and Bacon's "Tacitean." Libertine sentences slither along from phrase to phrase with no proper ending. They are just what you would expect from writing that uses quotations promiscuously and refuses to organize itself. "Tacitean" comes from the name of the Roman historian Tacitus. Tacitus was curt to the point of obscurity, and his name has the same root as English "taciturn." That too is appropriate. In their first edition, Bacon's *Essayes* are curt and businesslike. Not a word wasted. Time is money.

In fact both Montaigne and Bacon were reacting not only against the oration but also against the rhetorical exhibition of the periodic sentence. In the earlier Renaissance, Cicero was the preeminent model for such writing. His sentences make language into a kind of sound sculpture, whose closest English equivalent is found in the elegantly figured prose of John Milton's *Areopagitica.*

Montaigne and Bacon, however, were anti-Ciceronian. In "Of the Education of Children," Montaigne recalls, "At the height of Cicero's eloquence many were moved to admiration; but Cato merely laughed at it. . . . I would have the subject predominate, and so fill the imagination of him who listens that he shall have no remembrance of the words." And again, in "Of Books": "To confess the truth boldly . . . [Cicero's] manner of writing seems to me irksome. . . . If I spend an hour reading him . . . , I find oftenest only wind."

Bacon put the same idea in terms of *res* and *verba*, in terms, that is, of meaning and hot air. In the *Advancement of Learning* he observes that the Ciceronian humanists searched "more after wordes than matter, and more after the choisenesse of the Phrase, and the round and cleane composition of the sentence, and the sweet falling of the clauses . . . than after the weight of matter, worth of subject, soundnesse of argument, life of invention, or depth of judgement."

His style enacts this rejection of humanism. Its harshness is a way of announcing his contempt for Ciceronian flatulence—his commitment to weight of matter rather than to choiceness of phrase.

Does this mean that the early essay abandons rhetoric? Absolutely not. It means, first, that the early essay substitutes one kind of rhetoric for another. Since the new kind of rhetoric is unconventional and thus unfamiliar, it means, second, that the early essay seeks to give the impression of novelty. And since the impression of novelty depends on the use of formulas that are unfamiliar and therefore not obvious to the reader, it means, third, that the early essay seems to create the illusion of being unstudied and spontaneous. It pretends to spring either from the freely associating imagination of the author or from the rigid grammar of the world of things.

There is a formula for such a style: "*ars celare artem*," art that conceals art. Montaigne announces: "The way of speaking that I like is a simple and natural speech, the same on paper as on the lips . . . far removed from affectation, free, loose, and bold." The statement is charming, but it is demonstrably false. Both Montaigne and Bacon revised their essays over and over again. The lack of artifice is an illusion created by years of effort.

I think we have some chains around Proteus. Now let us begin to vex him.

The first edition of Montaigne's *Essais* appeared in 1580. It lacked the present Book III. Another, moderately augmented edition appeared in 1582. A third version, with a new book (incorrectly labeled "Book V") and with major revisions and additions, appeared in 1588. Finally, Montaigne's famous "*fille d'alliance*," Marie de Gournay, issued a posthumous edition in 1595, which with further major changes was the basis of standard editions of the *Essais* until the twentieth century.

The record shows that Montaigne was a familiar type, the literary neurotic who can never let his works alone, even after they are published. In general, as he revised, the self-revelation of the essays became more overt. That is, the more clothes he put on, the more he dressed up, the more he exposed himself as a man of conflicts.

Bacon's first ten essays may be said to initiate literary minimalism. They seem to consist chiefly of sayings from his commonplace book. The Renaissance would have called the sayings "flowers" or "sentences." Bacon's strategy may owe something to the hugely successful collection of aphorisms made by Erasmus—the *Adagia*—but Erasmus could never resist the temptation to gild every aphorism with a commentary. In the first edition of the *Essayes*, Bacon offers his flowers plain.

Like Montaigne, Bacon revised compulsively. By 1625, the ten original essays had grown to fifty-eight plus an incomplete fifty-ninth.

The essays also grew obese over the years. "Of Studies," for example, roughly doubled in size between 1597 and 1625.

Montaigne's revisions made his essays richer. Bacon's revisions seem to me to have been less happy. As his essays enlarge, they lose the taciturnity—the aggressive minimalism—that is the principal source of their power. The sentences become more sequential, more official, more pontifical, more—shall I say it?—like sentences in an oration.

In addition to making the essays more official, Bacon tried to give them philosophical status by suggesting that they were part of the grand philosophical scheme outlined in the *Novum Organum.* By calling his essays "civil and moral," Bacon was proposing them as contributions to the social sciences—specifically, to politics and ethics. In my own opinion, which conflicts with conventional wisdom in this case, the connection of the essays to the program of the *Novum Organum* was an afterthought intended to enhance their dignity.

Whatever the case, philosophy is directly relevant to the early history of the essay. In *Representative Men* Emerson properly calls Montaigne "the skeptic." The first essay that Montaigne wrote is also the longest, most ponderous essay of the lot—Montaigne's *Apology for Raimond Sebond,* which is essay 12 in Book II. Sebond was a late medieval theologian who wrote a *Theologia Naturalis* showing how design in Nature will convince even the most depraved agnostic of the truth of the Christian religion. At his father's request, Montaigne translated it from Latin into French.

Sebond's work is the culmination of a long tradition of pious fatuity about the Book of Nature, and once his father was safely in the ground, Montaigne deconstructed it. The deconstruction was so devastating that by the end, very little basis remained for believing in God, or design in Nature, or in anything else. Shakespeare's Hamlet seems to have read the *Apology,* since he quotes from it when he observes that the earth is a pestilent congregation of vapors and man a quintessence of dust.

When you think about them, Hamlet's quotations are appropriate. Long before Hamlet began questioning the state of Denmark, Montaigne's world had been made problematic by the religious controversies of the Reformation and the collapse of traditional verities. This is what the *Apology for Raimond Sebond* is all about. The St. Bartholomew's Day Massacre, which occurred just eight years before the first edition of the *Essais,* magnified the shock. If Christians who proclaim themselves models of piety can establish their position only by slaughtering those Christians who disagree with them, what evidence is there that reason has any place at all in religion? In short, a world that seemed solid, reasonable, and self-evident had shown itself to be none of the above. There were times when it seemed to Montaigne like a pestilent contagion of vapors. John Donne makes the same point in familiar lines from his first *Anniversary* on the death of Elizabeth Drury:

> And new philosophy calls all in doubt,
> The element of fire is quite put out. . . .
> 'Tis all in pieces, all coherence gone,
> All just supply, and all relation.

Historians argue about whether Montaigne was a fideist or a skeptic. The terms are so close that we need not quibble. The fideist believes that God and His ways are utterly beyond human comprehension and that therefore we must accept whatever law or custom the local tyrant tells us to believe. The skeptic systematically demonstrates that man is deceived both by sense evidence and by reason.

If the skeptics are correct, the proper stance for the philosopher is to doubt everything. This is not nihilism but a reserving of judgment, a determination to be a detached observer rather than a partisan. The Greek term for such detachment is *ataraxia,* which means "calmness" and, by extension, a refusal to become involved. Montaigne explains in the *Apology:* "This attitude of [the skeptics] . . . accepting all objects without inclination and consent, leads them to their Ataraxy, which is a settled condition of life, exempt from the emotions that we experience. . . . They are even exempted thereby from zeal about their own doctrine." At its coolest, ataraxy produces the spectator who views life ironically and refuses to become involved. However, spectators are also outsiders, and for outsiders, detachment sometimes becomes a perverse form of engagement. Hamlet's detachment is announced by his black suit and his refusal to be drawn into the *Gemütlichkeit* of the Danish court. It is closer to despair than to freedom from passion, and its result is not a series of essays enacting the process of self-realization but soliloquies in which the speaker alternates between the thoughts of murder and suicide.

This takes us to the dark outer edge of the early essay. It is a darkness that was acknowledged by Montaigne but one that lies, for the most part, beyond the emotional boundaries he set for himself.

Having been led by his own analysis to doubt the world as he had conceived of it, Montaigne turned inward in the quest for certainty. The basic question of the *Essais* is "What do I know"—"*Que sçais-je?*" This is Montaigne's motto, and as we learn in the *Apology*, he inscribed it under a picture of a pair of scales symbolizing ataraxy—the balancing of alternatives.

Montaigne's innumerable quotations are intended as part of the answer to the question of what we know: André Gide remarks in an often-quoted essay that they are there "to show that man is always and everywhere the same." Unfortunately, the quotations do not show this. As Michael Hall observes, they are inconsistent. Evidently, when you collect several centuries' worth of wisdom on a topic, you do not get a philosophy, you get a chain of contradictory platitudes reminiscent of Polonius's advice to his son Laertes.

Turning inward was no more helpful than consulting the sages. When he turned inward, Montaigne discovered not universality but infinite variety. He was forced to conclude that the self is as various, as elusive, and as many-shaped as the world.

Without fully understanding what he was doing, Montaigne was searching for a central "I"—what Descartes would later call the *cogito*, and as a matter of fact, Montaigne powerfully influenced the Cartesian project. Descartes admitted that we may be dreaming the world, but he insisted that the *cogito* is beyond doubt—so solid, in fact, as to be the rock on which everything else can be built. But Montaigne was more radical than Descartes. He concluded from his inquiry that there is no rock. There is only an endless well-defined shape, namely that of an oration. The initiative method is, by contrast, suggestive. As Bacon explains: "The initiative intimates. The magisterial requires that what is told should be believed; the initiative that it should be examined." Like Montaigne, Bacon was strongly attracted to skepticism. He admitted: "The doctrine of those who have denied that certainty could be attained at all has some agreement with my way of proceeding." Although he argued that empiricism offers an escape from uncertainty, he believed that most of the received knowledge of his age was false—the result of "errors and vanities," which he categorized using the metaphor of Idols: Idols of the tribe, Idols of the cave, Idols of the marketplace, Idols of the theater.

Bacon did not spend much time on religion; perhaps he found it beyond—or beneath—the reach of reason. He never attacked religion, but his heavy-handed condescension resembles thinly disguised contempt. On the other hand, the collapse during the sixteenth century of doctrines that had been accepted as verities for thousands of years fascinated him. The prime example was the toppling of Ptolemaic astronomy by Copernican, but astronomy was only one of many areas in which received knowledge crumbled when it was put to the test. Each failure of a traditional theory was a demonstration of the validity of the theory of Idols.

This kind of skepticism looks forward to a fully developed scientific method. It underlies Sir Thomas Browne's *Pseudodoxia Epidemica*, better known as *Vulgar Errors*, which systematically exposes many superstitions of the sort deconstructed in Montaigne's *Apology*. The *Pseudodoxia* went through six editions in Browne's lifetime. In matters of religion, Browne was a fideist. Montaigne ends the *Apology* with the remark that man "will be lifted up if God by special favor lends him his hand; he will be lifted up when, abandoning and renouncing his own means, he lets himself be upheld by purely heavenly means." Browne writes in *Religio Medici:* "Me thinkes there be not impossibilities enough in Religion for an active faith. . . . I love to lose myself in a mystery, to pursue my reason to an *Oh Altitudo*. . . . I learned of Tertullian, *Certum est quia impossible est.*"

Bacon's dedication of the ten essays of 1597 claims only that they are "medicinable." The dominant meaning is simply that they are useful—they expose various errors and vanities and provide bearings for a world in flux. But the term "medicinable" is a metaphor, and its implications invite comment. According to the metaphor, the reader needs to be cured. In other words, there is some kind of metaphysical plague going around. It is a plague of doubt. Jimmy Carter felt the same thing about twentieth-century America and, in one of his more disastrous orations, called it a malaise. If Bacon had been around, he would have called it a failure of nerve and would have voted for Ronald Reagan. Bacon's essays are intended to be a cure for social malaise. They are medicinable because they distill wisdom gained from life in what Bacon's heirs persist in calling "the real world."

For the same reason, the essays often have the quality of a pep talk by the coach of a losing team. The strategy is to create what might be called a "rhetoric of assurance." Accordingly, in the first edition, the sentences are chiefly commands and assertions. Omission of understood words (zeugma) gives the sentences a telegraphic quality reinforced by the paring away of modifiers, modifying phrases, and subordinate clauses. Further economy is achieved by parallelism and balance. The word order is standard. The speaker knows what he wants to say and says it directly. The main units are set off by paragraph marks—which Bacon uses as we would use "bullets" today. The modern term is appropriate. Bacon wants each sentence to have the force of a pistol shot: "• Reade not to contradict, not to believe, but to waigh and consider. • Some books are to bee tasted, others to bee swallowed, and some few to bee chewed and digested. . . . • Reading maketh a full man, conference a readye man, and writing an exacte man. . . . • Histories make men wise, Poets wittie: the Mathematickes subtle, naturall Phylosophie deepe: Moral grave, Logicke and Rhetoricke able to contend."

The sentences often have an edge of cynicism, of *Realpolitik*, reminding us that Bacon had read his Machiavelli: Ambition is a winding stair; those who marry give hostages to fortune; the stage is more beholden to Love than the life of man; wounds cannot be cured without searching; a mixture of lie doth ever add pleasure.

Is this *Realpolitik* or despair? Whatever it is, the message of the *Essayes* is, "So be it." That's how things are in the real world, and that's how they always will be.

Let us recall one other legacy from Montaigne and Bacon. Both men were authors. Therefore, it follows that, having invented a form, both proceeded to muck it up. As we have seen, neither could let an essay alone once it had been written. This habit is arguably a virtue in Montaigne and not fatal in Bacon, but its implications are ominous. The constant revision implies a change in the conception of the essay from the enactment of a process to something that suspiciously resembles literature—perhaps an oration propped up like a scarecrow on the scaffolding of its *dispositio.*

To turn the essay into literature is to domesticate it—to make it not very different from a letter by Seneca or one of Plutarch's *moralia.* Recall Florio's use of the word "discourse" as a rough synonym for "essay"; the usage is pregnant with future confusion. John Locke's *Essay Concerning Human Understanding* is splendid philosophy. It might even be called an "essay" on the basis of its being an exploration of its subject, but if it is so called, any work of philosophy short of Nietzsche's *Thus Spake Zarathustra* can be called an essay. Its proper title is obviously "discourse," maybe *Abhandlung.*

To turn the essay into literature is also to encourage authors to display beautiful—or delicately anguished, or nostalgic, or ironic, or outraged, or extroverted, or misanthropic—souls, or, alternatively, to create prose confections, oxymorons of languid rhythms and fevered images.

Yet despite all such temptations, the essay has tended to remain true to its heritage. I mean not that essays are products of what you might call "troubled times" but that the essay was born from a moment of profound, even terrifying, doubt, and that its rhetoric has often been adopted by authors who have sensed the power of the forces of dissolution. Matthew Arnold entitled his most famous collection of essays *Culture and Anarchy,* and Joan Didion named her first collection from the apocalyptic image in Yeats's poem "The Second Coming": *Slouching Towards Bethlehem.*

Essays are written on an infinite variety of subjects from infinitely various points of view. However, time and time again, the essay reverts to its original forms—on the one hand to the Montaignian enactment of the process of self-realization in a world without order: "I do not paint [my subject's] being, I paint his passing . . . from day to day, from moment to moment." And on the other hand, to Baconian assertiveness in a world that threatens to reduce assertions to black comedy: "I will do such things . . . what they are, I know not, but they shall be the terrors of the earth."

The eighteenth century approved the idea of cool detachment from the malaise of the times. Addison and Steele are seemingly "men of sentiment" in *The Tatler.* Under the surface, however, lies the old motif of the search for the self. Steele concludes *The Tatler* with the image of the world as labyrinth: "I must confess, it has been a most exquisite pleasure to me . . . to enquire into the Seeds of Vanity and Affectation, to lay before my Readers the Emptiness of Ambition: In a Word, to trace Humane Life through all its Mazes and Recesses." The *Spectator* has even more obvious relations to its ancestry. A spectator is someone who withholds assent—a skeptic, an observer, an outsider. This is exactly the point made by Addison in the introduction to the new journal: "I live in the World rather as a Spectator of Mankind, than as one of the species. . . . I have acted in all the Parts of my Life as a looker-on, which is the Character I intend to preserve in this Paper."

For the most part, *The Spectator* preserves its detachment, but occasionally there is a powerful updraft of emotion. The terror—or the malaise—of the world makes people want to be spectators, but as Werner Heisenberg has shown, spectators get tangled up in the things they are observing. The following comment, from *Spectator* number 420, is directly traceable to the tangling of human motive with the world that science has revealed. It is all the more striking because it is not what you would expect from an eighteenth-century spectator.

> If . . . we contemplate those wide Fields of Ether, that reach in height as far from *Saturn* as to the fixt stars, and run abroad almost to an infinitude, our Imagination finds its Capacity filled with so immense a Prospect . . . [it] puts itself upon the Stretch to comprehend it. But if we yet rise higher, and consider the fixt Stars as so many Oceans of Flame and still discover new Firmaments and new Lights, that are sunk further in those unfathomable Depths of *Ether,* so as not to be seen by the strongest of our Telescopes, we are lost in . . . a Labyrinth of Suns and Worlds, and confounded with the Immensity and magnificence of Nature. . . . Let a Man try to conceive the different bulk of an Animal, which is twenty, from another which is a hundred times less than a Mite, or to compare, in his Thoughts, a length of a thousand Diameters of the Earth, with that of a Million, and he will quickly discover that he has no . . . Measure in his Mind, adjusted to such extraordinary Degrees of Grandeur or Minuteness. The Understanding, indeed, opens an infinite Space on every side of us, but the Imagination, after a few faint efforts, is immediately at a stand, and finds her self swallowed up in the immensity of the Void that surrounds it.

At the beginning of the nineteenth century, the spectator becomes a refugee. Charles Lamb's Elia solves his problems by infantile regression. He is no more ashamed of this habit than Montaigne was of revealing inner monstrosities. Regression is the secret of his modest success. Lamb explains: "The impressions of infancy had burnt into him, and he resented the impertinence of manhood. These were weaknesses; but such as they were, they are a key to explicate some of his writings."

The addiction of Elia to medicinable fantasies undoubtedly objectifies feelings of his creator. Charles Lamb went through a bout of madness himself and lived with a sister who had murdered their mother in a fit of insanity. But the fantasies don't quite work. Reality is always breaking in. In "Dream Children: A Reverie," Elia recalls an interview with two imaginary children named Alice and John. The children ask about their dead mother, also named Alice and also imaginary:

> . . . suddenly, turning to Alice, the soul of the first Alice looked out at her eyes with such a reality of re-presentment, that I became in doubt which of them stood there before me, or whose that bright hair was; and while I stood gazing, both of the children gradually grew fainter to my view, receding, and still receding, till nothing at last but two mournful features were seen in the uttermost distance, which, without speech, strangely impressed upon me the effects of speech: "We are not of Alice, nor of thee, nor are we children at all. . . . We are only what might have been. . . ."

"Dream Children" is affecting, but it is almost literature. Emerson comes closer, I think, than Lamb does to the scope and brilliance—and the breezy solipsism—of Montaigne. Speaking of the achievements of Plato, Shakespeare, and Milton, Emerson creates one of the great literary puns: "I dare; I also will essay to be." Writing an essay is an exercise in self-fashioning.

The sentiment is pure Montaigne. In *Nature*, Emerson expands the image: "Every man's condition is a solution in hieroglyphic to those enquiries he would put on. He acts it as life, before he apprehends it as truth." "Experience" recreates the terror of a problematic world: "Where do we find ourselves? In a series of which we do not know the extremes, and believe that it has none. We wake and find ourselves on a stair; there are stairs below us, which we seem to have ascended; there are stairs above us, many a one, which go upward and out of sight. . . . All things swim and glitter. Our life is not so much threatened as our perception. Ghostlike, we glide through nature, and should not know our place again."

Emerson's title—"Experience"—invokes Baconian empiricism only to reject it. The metaphor of the infinite stair recalls Addison's image of the self "swallowed up in the immensity of the void that surrounds it." It also anticipates the infinite library of Babel imagined in the twentieth century by Jorge Luis Borges.

In the later nineteenth century, the essay underwent a mutation. The prose poem can be defined as literature's revenge on the essay—an essay in which style has become substance. You can see the beginning of the prose poem as early as Sir Thomas Browne's *Urn Burial.* The body of the animal begins to push through the chrysalis with De Quincey's *Confessions*, and it unfurls its iridescent wings and flaps them in Walter Pater's *Renaissance.* But the prose poem appears first in full lepidopteran glory in France: in Baudelaire's *Le spleen de Paris* and Rimbaud's *Les illuminations.* From there it migrates back to the English-speaking world. We are reminded by William Gass's *On Being Blue* of its flight across the vastness of the Atlantic Ocean to the New World.

One other modern development of the genre must be recognized. It is the topical essay—brief, pointed, often amusing, and closely related to a theme, event, or personality of current interest. Bacon's essay "Of Friendship" is a prototype for the form. It did not begin by being topical, but in its final, much-augmented form it commemorates his lifelong attachment to Sir Tobie Matthew. "Of Plantations" is explicitly topical, being a consideration of issues raised by the Virginia colony. The topical essay also owes much to Addison and Steele. That is not surprising, because its native habitat is the newspaper. The Homeric catalogue of its modern practitioners includes Art Buchwald, Mary McGrory, Ralph Kilpatrick, David Broder, Russell Baker, Carl Rowan, James Reston, William Raspberry, Ellen Goodman, and George Will. This catalogue moves us to the present, which is, after all, the main interest of any essay, including an essay on the essay. I suppose most modern essays are Baconian and Addisonian, but the Montaignian essay is still impressively alive.

Much scholarship appears in the form of—you are correct—the critical essay. This, of course, raises the question of what the word "article" refers to. William Gass has solved the problem: "The essay," he writes, "is obviously the opposite of that awful object, 'the article' . . . [whose] appearance is proof of the presence, nearby, of the Professor, the way one might, perceiving a certain sort of speckled egg, infer that its mother was a certain sort of speckled bird."

Speckled birds aside, many of the classic works of our age are essays. I am thinking, for example, of Wallace Stevens's "The Noble Rider and the Sound of Words," Leslie Fiedler's "Come Back to the Raft Again, Huck, Honey," Roland Barthes's "Eiffel Tower," Tom Wolfe's "Kandy-Kolored Tangerine-Flake Streamline Baby," Martin Heidegger's "The Thing," R. Buckminster Fuller's "Grunch of Giants," Werner Heisenberg's "Abstraction in Modern Science," and Robert Nozick's "Fiction," which is a non-fictional essay written by a fictional character who is still asking the Emersonian question: "Must there be a top floor somewhere, a world that is itself, not created in someone else's fiction? Or can the hierarchy go on infinitely?"

Nozick's question seems to me to capture the fascination of the essay for our time. An essay is not an oration or an *Abhandlung* or a prose poem. It is "essaying to be," in Emerson's conceit, and "thought thinking about itself" in Heidegger's. It is the enactment of the process of accommodation between the world and the "I," and thus it is consciousness realizing itself.

A few years ago I wrote a book of essays called *Entering the Maze: Identity and Change in Modern Culture.* The title and subtitle did not take much thought; they seemed inevitable. I might have written a novel. I was never even tempted to do so. To choose fiction is to assert that you know the difference between fiction and fact, while I wanted to dramatize the constant redrawing of the line between the two that is taking place in modern culture. Maybe fiction is possible in societies that change slowly. Maybe that is why the novel was popular in the eighteenth and nineteenth centuries. But who, today, knows the difference between the real, and what was real, and what is not—or not yet—real?

If you think about the novel, you will see that it has taken paths in the twentieth century that lead in the direction of the essay. One kind of novel moves toward a record of hallucinations—I think of Joyce's *Finnegans Wake,* William Gaddis's *The Recognitions,* John Barth's *Giles Goat-Boy.* Another type of novel records a special type of hallucination—a vision of a future presumed to be real—*Erewhon, Brave New World, 1984.* Yet another type aspires to the condition of news, for example, *In Cold Blood.* There is also the tendency, apparently irresistible since Joyce's *Portrait of the Artist,* for novelists to pack their work with essays spoken by characters or by a figure whom, in deference to the fondness of the present age for critical terms, I will label "the intrusive author." Some novels, in fact, seem to consist of almost nothing but essays. Given these tendencies in the novel, why not write essays from the beginning?

But I would like to end with some more challenging notion. I do not think we live in a solid, empirical world of the sort Bacon dangled tantalizingly in front of readers of *The Advancement of Learning* even as he demonstrated that it was an illusion. We live in a world of changes and shadows, a world where the real dissolves as we reach for it and meets us as we turn away. It is a world of mazes and illusions and metaphors and idols and stairways that proceed upward and downward to infinity.

We live at a time much like the sixteenth century. It is a time of immense destructive and constructive change, and there is no way of knowing whether the destructive or the constructive forces are more powerful. It is a time when the world looks like an unweeded garden and doubt is a condition of consciousness. The essay is as uniquely suited to expressing this contemporary mode of being-in-culture as it was when Montaigne began writing the *Apology for Raimond Sebond.*

But what *is* the essay? If there is such a thing as an essential essay—a *real* Proteus—it changes into so many shapes so unlike the real one that it requires an act of faith to believe the shapes merely variations on a single underlying identity. For this reason, of course, Proteus adopted the strategy of change in the first place. People who lack faith will turn away convinced that nothing is there. We, however, will remember the advice of Cyrene: "The more he turns himself into different shapes, the more you, my son, must hold on to those strong chains."

Holding on may be important. If the essay is an enactment of the creation of the self—if we must essay to be—and the essay does not exist, then you might legitimately ask whether that which the essay enacts can be said to exist. The epigraph of the last *Spectator* is from Persius: "*Respue quod non es,*" "Throw away what you are not." It is good advice, but it assumes that, after you throw everything superfluous away, something is left.

If you have bound Proteus and all the changes have occurred, and if he returns to his own shape, he will have already answered your first question: Something is there. But is it? Maybe you are seeing only another counterfeit, another Idol.

That's the way things are, and the essay is the most expressive literary form of our age because it comes closest to being what all literature is supposed to be—an imitation of the real. You can vex the essay and drive it to extremities. Maybe the result will be nothing. Your action will be doubtful, but in the real world, to get a piece of the action, you, however doubtful, must follow the advice: "Hold on."

(1990)

Part 2

Poetics

Aristotle and Averroes

Aristotle's *Poetics* was written between 347 and 322 B.C. In view of the prestige which the treatise now enjoys, it often comes as a surprise to the contemporary student of criticism to learn that after Aristotle's death the *Poetics* disappeared almost without trace from the ancient literary scene. Obviously the text must have been copied during the classical and Byzantine periods; otherwise we would have no manuscripts at all. The influence on all later manuscripts of a single source, the eleventh-century manuscript designated Paris 1741, indicates, however, that the stemma of the *Poetics* is relatively uncomplicated. Evidently there was little demand for the work in antiquity. Efforts to reconstruct the history of the text before the eleventh century have produced tenuous, often contradictory results. The same may be said for efforts to trace the influence of the *Poetics* on post-Aristotelian criticism, such as those made by McMahon, Rostagni, and (most recently) C. O. Brink.[1] If Aristotle's *Poetics* had any influence, it was via two or three intermediaries, which, by warping its thought to fit the prevailing assumptions of rhetorical criticism, obliterated just those qualities that are today considered characteristically Aristotelian. The fragmentary essay *On the Poets* appears to have been far more widely known than the *Poetics*, and Theophrastus, Aristotle's pupil and popularizer, had far more influence on later critical thought than his master.

According to the widely accepted view offered by Joel Spingarn in his *History of Literary Criticism in the Renaissance,*[2] the *Poetics* remained almost unknown from the time of its composition until the early sixteenth century. An abortive effort at translation was made by Giorgio Valla in 1498. Ten years later, in 1508, the Greek text, edited by John Lascaris, was issued by Aldus. The volume in which it appeared was entitled *Rhetores Graeci,* a title which indicates that neither Lascaris nor Aldus sensed the fundamental difference between Aristotle's theory of rhetoric and his theory of poetry. The first passable Latin translation of the *Poetics* was made by Alessandro de' Pazzi (Paccius) and published posthumously in 1536. This translation made the *Poetics* available as a subject for university lectures. Thus during the early 1540s we find Bartolomeo Lombardi and later (after Lombardi's death) Vincenzo Maggi lecturing on the *Poetics* at Padua and Ferrara. Finally, in 1548 Francesco Robortello's *Explicationes* was published, and the *Poetics* gradually came to be considered a prescriptive document. "Laws" of art were discovered in it which became the basis of neoclassical criticism. Lodovico Castelvetro's *Poetica d'Aristotele Vulgarizzata,* published in 1570, is the first commentary to offer something like the famous "law" of the three unities. Adulation of the *Poetics* reached its climax in seventeenth-century France—the notorious "quarrel" over Corneille's *Cid* is a case in point—and continued, though with more moderation, in the eighteenth century. Not until the romantic period was the preeminence of the *Poetics* challenged.

This is a useful preliminary view of the history of the *Poetics.* It is still, perhaps, correct in outline; but as more specialized studies have appeared, the need for revision in details has become increasingly apparent. One of the most important errors made by Spingarn is his failure to do justice to the history of the *Poetics* in the Middle Ages. Although he knew that a work purporting to represent Aristotle's theory of poetry was extant as early as the thirteenth century, he apparently did not have first-hand knowledge of this work and had only a vague notion of its background and content. Thanks to the work of David Margoliouth, Jaroslav Tkatsch, Georges Lacombe, and Bernard Weinberg,[3] we are now in a much better position than Spingarn to trace the history of the *Poetics* and appreciate its significance. The remainder of this paper will concentrate on these two subjects.

I

The version of the *Poetics* that influenced the Middle Ages was not Greek but Arabic. According to the best guesses of Margoliouth and Tkatsch, the source of the Arabic tradition is a Greek manuscript dating before the year 700 and independent of the archetype that is the source of Paris 1741 and its descendents. This manuscript, for example, preserved the word *anonumos* in chapter 1 ($1474^{b}9$), which is missing in the Greek manuscripts. Around the year 900 the Greek manuscript was translated into Syriac by Isac ibn-Hunain. Fragments of Hunain's translation are preserved in the *Butyrum sapientiae*, a thirteenth-century miscellany of philosophic and other lore compiled by Bishop Gregory Barhebraeus, and in the *Dialogues* of Jacob bar Sakko (d. 1241), and are reprinted by Margoliouth in his *Analecta orientalia ad Poeticam Aristoteleam.*[4] The Syriac translation was, in turn, converted into Arabic around 920 by Abu Bishr. It is available in an edition prepared by Fausto Lasinio (Pisa, 1872) and in a Latin translation forming the appendix of Margoliouth's *Poetics of Aristotle,* published in 1911. It has some significance for the reconstruction of the Greek text, although Margoliouth's extravagant claims almost succeeded in discrediting it entirely. Its interest for the historian of criticism, however, is that its vocabulary departs widely from the Greek. It thus initiated the process of assimilating Aristotle by misinterpretation that continued throughout the Middle Ages.

The next phase in the history of the medieval *Poetics* is the result of the adoption by Arab philosophers of a scheme originally formulated by Alexander of Aphrodisias and other late Greek commentators on Aristotle. According to this scheme, Aristotle divided human knowledge (*scientia*, often translated as "science") into four main branches. First come the instrumental sciences of the *Organon*. These are sciences of technique or "faculties," and they have no "content" in the Aristotelian sense of that term. The other three branches, which *do* have content, are the theoretic (including metaphysics, mathematics, astronomy, and physics), the practical (including politics, economics, and ethics), and the productive (including most professions and crafts). It is the *Organon* that is important for present purposes. Today, scholars agree that the *Organon* is made up of six works; namely, *Categories, On Interpretation, Prior* and *Posterior Analytics, Topics,* and *Sophistic Refutations.* To these six books the late Greek commentators and their Arab disciples added the *Rhetoric* and the *Poetics*. The most influential Arab expression of this theory is the *Catalogue of the Sciences* written by Al-farabi in the tenth century. This work was twice translated into Latin during the twelfth century, first by Gerard of Cremona and second by John of Seville.[5] The theory which it proposes may be called the "context theory" of the *Poetics*, since it arises from the context within which Aristotle was thought to have placed his treatise. To include the *Poetics* in the *Organon* is to assert that it is an essay on method, and that the method itself is a "faculty" without "content." Furthermore, since each of the logical faculties was supposed to be distinguished from the others by its use of a unique logical device, the inclusion of *Poetics* in the *Organon* shifted emphasis from "imitation," the key term in the Greek *Poetics,* to the "device" which differentiates poetry from its sister faculties. The result is clearly illustrated in the twelfth-century treatise "On the Division of the Sciences" by Dominicus Gundissalinus,[6] where the parts of the *Organon* are tabulated as follows:

PART	PURPOSE	DEVICE
Categories, On Interpretation, Prior and *Posterior Analytics*	Demonstration	Demonstrative syllogism
Topics	Probable demonstration	Probable (dialectical) syllogism

PART	PURPOSE	DEVICE
Sophistic	Error made to seem truth	False (*errativa*) syllogism
Rhetoric	Persuasion	Enthymeme
Poetic	Imaginative representation	Imaginative (*ymaginativa*) syllogism

This interpretation ignores imitation, plot, characterization, catharsis, and most of the other subjects stressed by Aristotle in favor of an element—the imaginative syllogism—for which the reader of the Greek text will search in vain. It also ignores the moral "purpose" usually attributed to poetry in the Middle Ages, because to bring in moral questions would be to assign a "content" to poetry—in Aristotelian terms, to treat it as a subdivision of "practical science" rather than of the *Organon.* Poetry is "imaginative representation" and its device is "the imaginative syllogism." Gundissalinus does not explain exactly what these terms mean, but their general import is clear enough. "Imaginative representation" is the creation of illusion by means of images, a concept almost antithetical to "imitation." The "imaginative syllogism" is a technique of manipulating language so as to produce the illusion. The term "imaginative" does not mean "of or related to the imagination," but something like "using the figures (or images) of rhetoric." A few scattered comments suggest that Gundissalinus had in mind the figures of exaggeration and understatement, but he leaves the matter somewhat ambiguous.

To return to the Arabic *Poetics,* the next contribution to the tradition after Al-farabi was made by Avicenna (980–1037). Avicenna accepted the idea that the *Poetica* is a logical work and part of the *Organon.* His most important innovation was to divide the *Poetics* into seven sections. This division represents a theory concerning the organization and content of the *Poetics*, and, of course, gives an impression somewhat different from that given by the modern division of the text into twenty-six chapters.

The third and most important Arab student of the *Poetics* was Averroes (Ibn Roshd, 1120–1198). Averroes is considered the greatest of the Arab philosophers of the Middle Ages, and he is also the Arab philosopher who most deeply influenced the Latin West.[7] During his long and active career he wrote commentaries on all of Aristotle's major works, and all but two of these were translated into Latin during the scholastic renaissance of the thirteenth century. Medieval interest in the *Poetics* must therefore be understood as a by-product of scholasticism, and in particular, that phase of scholasticism which was a self-conscious revolt against the earlier, Platonizing tradition of medieval thought.

Averroes wrote his commentaries in three forms. First there is the "great" commentary, in which he quotes a short passage (lemma) from the source, then discusses it, and then proceeds to the next passage. This, incidentally, is why Dante calls him "Averrois che 'l gran commento feo" in the *Divine Comedy* (*Inf.*, IV, 144). Next, there is the "middle" commentary, in which Averroes cites a passage from Aristotle by a brief identifying phrase or sentence, and then proceeds to discuss the whole section associated with the quotation. Finally, there is the "paraphrase" or "analysis," in which Averroes speaks in his own person, explaining, quoting, and interjecting new ideas, so that a "paraphrase" often amounts to an original essay on an Aristotelian topic.

Averroes treated several of Aristotle's works in more than one form. Commentaries in all three forms exist, for example, for the *Posterior Analytics,* the *Physics,* the *de Caelo,* and the *Metaphysics.* The *Poetics*, however, is treated only once and in the form of the "middle" commentary. This should be kept in mind, because the Latin translation is sometimes misleadingly called a "paraphrase."

The absence of a "great" commentary on the *Poetics* is significant. Averroes remarks frequently that much of what Aristotle says applies to Greek poetry and is irrelevant to the Arabs. In fact, large sections of the *Poetics* were unintelligible to him. He had never read Homer, nor had he seen anything remotely resembling a Greek drama. To make sense of the *Poetics* he was forced to interpolate material alien to it, to transpose passages from one section to another, and to omit many passages which the modern reader would consider central. Moreover, he freely substituted references to Arab poetry for the Greek examples provided by Aristotle. His references show a surprising knowledge of Arab poetry from pre-Islamic times to the popular Hispano-Arabic forms of his own day, but they obscure rather than clarify the sense of the original. The product of all this effort is a work which its most loving modern student, Jaroslav Tkatsch, has called "a medley of monstrous misunderstandings and wild fantasies,"[8] but which, for all its limitations, had a significant influence on European criticism.

Two key ideas, both of them foreign to Aristotle, run through Averroes' commentary. The first is the notion derived from Al-farabi and Avicenna that poetry is a branch of logic. The second also owes something to earlier Arab commentaries, but its basic source would seem to be the vocabulary of the Arab translation. This is the idea that poetry can be defined as the art of praise and blame. Praise and blame are rhetorical techniques, explained at length in books 1 and 3 of Aristotle's *Rhetoric.* They are brought into the *Poetics* in chapter 4, where Aristotle asserts the first two forms of poetry were "lampooning verses" and "praises of famous men." Averroes could understand this theory much better than the complex theory of imitation developed in the first three chapters of the

Poetics. Better still, it seemed consistent with what he knew of the history of Arab poetry, whose early forms tend heavily to invective and ecomiastic verse. From this apparent point of contact between the *Poetics* and Arab literary tradition, Averroes moved outward to the genres and function of poetry. Not only did poetry originate in praise and blame, its major forms fall into one or the other category. Epic and tragedy are poems of praise; comedy (by which Averroes means satire) is a form of blame; and ode is a mixed form that employs both techniques. Good poets praise good men in order to lead their readers to virtue, while base poets satirize and vituperate evil men and thus warn against vice. This approach, it should be noted, assigns poetry an ethical function and is incompatible (or, at least, hard to reconcile) with the theory that poetry is a branch of logic. Averroes either failed to perceive the conflict or was indifferent to it, for the two theories exist side-by-side in his commentary, and no effort is made to harmonize them.

Whatever the deficiencies of Averroes' interpretation, his commentary began a long European career in 1256, when it was translated into Latin. The translator was a German monk, Hermannus Alemannus, living in Toledo under the patronage of John, Bishop of Burgos.[9] Hermannus had previously translated the middle commentary on the *Nicomachean Ethics* (1240), and his translation of the commentary on the *Poetics* forms a kind of appendix to his translation of the commentary on the *Rhetoric*. He was one of a number of scholars involved in the first phase of the scholastic recovery of Aristotle, which depended on translations from Arabic rather than the Greek originals. In his preface to the commentary on the *Poetics* Hermannus says that he planned to translate the *Poetics* itself into Latin but had to give up because of the difficulty of the vocabulary. His admission shows that the original was just as obscure to a thirteenth-century European as it was to Averroes.

If the *Poetics* was unintelligible to Hermannus and his contemporaries, Averroes was not. Twenty-three manuscripts of the Hermannus translation survive, and it was printed in 1481, thus becoming the first version of Aristotle's literary theory published during the Renaissance.[10] Its compatibility with medieval critical ideas is attested by the fact that in 1278 William of Moerbeke, Bishop of Corinth, made a remarkably accurate translation from the Greek, which was, however, ignored; William's translation exists in only two manuscripts, both dating from the thirteenth century, and it was not printed until 1953.[11] The obvious moral of this tale is that the late Middle Ages was not prepared to assimilate the *Poetics*. On the other hand, Averroes' commentary was easy to assimilate. The distortions which disconcert the modern reader are the very features which made the work intelligible and attractive to the medieval audience. In effect, it enlisted Aristotle in support of the most characteristic (and most un-Aristotelian) features of medieval poetic theory.

A few quotations from the Hermannus translation will illustrate this point. In a preface referring to both the *Rhetoric* and the *Poetics* Hermannus discusses the placing of these works in Aristotle's system of the sciences:

> That these two books are part of logic no one will doubt who has read the books of Al-farabi, Avicenna, and Averroes, and various others. Indeed, this is quite obvious from this text itself. Nor can one be excused (as some may think) because of the *Rhetoric* of Marcus Tullius Cicero and the *Ars poetica* of Horace. Tully made rhetoric a part of "civil philosophy" and thoroughly treated it from this point of view. Horace, on the other hand, treated poetry as a part of grammar.[12]

This quite explicitly locates the *Poetics* in the *Organon.* To avoid possible confusion, Hermannus cites the two common rival theories of poetry—first, the theory that considered rhetoric and poetry a part of "civil" philosophy, by which he means "practical" or "moral" philosophy; and second, the theory associating poetry with grammar. The first theory, attributed justifiably to Cicero, is the didactic theory, which considers poetry a device of ethical instruction.[13] It is commonplace in medieval criticism, and both Averroes and Hermannus subscribed to it in practice. In his preface, however, Hermannus takes pains to call attention to the difference between it and the allegedly Aristotelian theory, which emphasizes technique rather than content. The second theory, which Hermannus attributes to Horace, leads to emphasis on the prosodic element of poetry. Classical grammar included the study of syllables and quantity, and hence the study of the various poetic meters. According to the grammarians, the difference between poetry and nonpoetry is the use of meter; and the differences between the various poetic genres are the meters themselves. This inverts the normal relation between form and content. Poetry becomes "heroic," for example, by using dactylic hexameter, and only secondarily by narrating the deeds of noble heroes. In the same way, the essence of elegy is the elegaic distich, of satire and comedy, iambic meter, of the ode, lyric strophes, and so forth. The authors collected by Heinrich Keil in the sixth volume of his *Grammatici Latini,* entitled simply *Scriptores de Arte Metrica,* amply illustrate the grammatical theory.[14] Again, Hermannus explicitly rejects the *ars metrica* in favor of the logical theory attributed to Aristotle and justified by "Al-farabi, Avicenna, Averroes, and various others."

The appropriateness of Hermannus's emphasis on the logical "placement" of poetry is apparent from the first section of the commentary.[15] In chapter I of the *Poetics* Aristotle discusses imitation and then moves on to consider the differentiation of poetic genres according to means of imitation. The word *imitatio* appears very infrequently in Hermannus. It is replaced by the phrase *sermo imaginativus*, to which *assimilatio* and *representatio* are often added as synonyms. In the following passage, I have translated *imaginativus* as "figurative" and *assimilatio* as "resemblance," although there are no really adequate English equivalents:

> Aristotle says. . . . Poetic expression is figurative (*imaginativus*). There are three kinds of figuration and resemblance (*assimilatio*), two simple and the third composed of the first two. One of these simple forms consists of the comparison of one thing to another and its use to exemplify the thing, and this occurs in any language through the expressions proper to it, like *quasi* or *sicut* and similar words, called particles of comparison. . . . And in this art this is called "exchange" [*concambium*]. . . . The second type occurs when the comparison is reversed, as when you say "the sun is like this woman" rather than "this woman is like the sun." And the third kind is compounded from these two.[16]

The definition (here somewhat condensed) is entirely foreign to Aristotle. The justification for it is that the identification of poetry and logic requires "imitation" to be interpreted as the use of a technical device. Gundissalinus called this device the "imaginative syllogism." Averroes and Hermannus are much more explicit. The poetic device is comparison, which is subdivided, with the help of hints in *Poetics*, chapter 20, into three parts: (1) simile and metaphor, (2) inverted simile and metaphor, and (3) a "mixed" form which should probably be understood as the proportional analogy. The Aristotelian concept of poetry as an imitation of action, human character, and/or nature is replaced by the concept of poetry as the skillful manipulation of figures of comparison.

This surprising interpretation of imitation had some traceable influence. St. Thomas Aquinas, for example, remarks at the beginning of his commentary on the *Posterior Analytics* that *similitudo*—poetic comparison—is the basic device of poetry.[17] Two centuries later, Savonarola wrote that "without logic no one can be called a poet," and added, "clearly, the syllogism which the Philosopher calls Example is the object of poetic art, just as the enthymeme is the object of rhetoric, induction and the probable syllogism of dialectic, and the syllogism proper the object of the *Prior analytics*."[18] More generally, the notion that poetry is essentially the clever use of figures is certainly compatible with late medieval aureate diction, although it is impossible, so far as I know, to show direct influence.

The relation of poetry to logic continued to be debated until late in the sixteenth century. On the other hand, the theory destined to have the greatest influence on later critics is the one which is dominant in the Averroes commentary. This is the theory of praise and blame. Returning to Averroes' discussion of chapter 1 of the *Poetics*, we find that the initial definition of poetry, offered as a quotation from Aristotle himself, is as follows: "Aristotle says: Every poem and all poetic speech are either blame or praise (*aut vituperatio aut laudatio*). And this is evident from examination of poems themselves, especially the poems which are concerned with matters of choice, either honest or base."[19] The passage is, of course, not in the *Poetics*. Like the definition of imitation, it is an interpolation required to reconcile the text with the presuppositions of the commentator. Unlike that definition, however, it has some Aristotelian precedent. Averroes has transposed the notion that the original poetic forms were encomia and lampooning verses from chapter 4 to chapter 1 and converted it from an observation about primitive poems to a categorical assertion about poetry in general.

The praise-blame theory was attractive to Averroes for two reasons. First of all, it furnished a point of contact between Arab and Greek poetry. Second, it justified poetry by making it an instrument of moral instruction. These ideas are combined in a comment on chapter 2 of the *Poetics,* where, after remarking that the Greeks had many excellent poems of praise, Averroes adds, "Children should be brought up to read those poems which incite and incline one to acts of fortitude and magnificence. In their poems the Arabs treat only these two virtues, although they do not incite to these virtues because they are good in themselves but because they are a means of attaining honor and glory."[20] Averroes is probably thinking of the *quasidah* and is certainly hinting that the native form can be made even more moral than it has traditionally been. Incidentally, this criticism of Arab poets for failing to live up to Aristotle's standards accounts, as we will see, for the last echo of the Averroes commentary in European criticism.

The didactic motive extends throughout the commentary. Consider, for example, the following expansion of Aristotle's discussion of "object of imitation":

> Aristotle says: Those who represent and emulate do so in order to induce others to perform certain voluntary acts and to refrain from certain others. Thus the objects of the representation were necessarily virtues or vices. For all action and all character is concerned with one or the other of these two; namely, virtue or vice. Necessarily, then, good and virtuous men represented good and virtuous characters; and base men, vices and depraved characters. And since all resemblance and representation is for the presentation of the proper and improper or base, it is clear that its object is to encourage goodness and refute vice. . . . And from these kinds of men came praise and blame; that is, praise of good men and rebuke of bad ones.[21]

What Aristotle says, of course, is that the object of imitation is action (*praxis*), not virtue or vice. He then adds that actions are performed by agents (*prattontas*) who are of necessity better than, similar to, or worse than ourselves. This is not a moral exhortation but an analytic statement based on the fact that "practical philosophy" is the division of philosophy devoted to the study of human actions, and within this division, the categories of evaluation are goodness and badness. The commentary distorts Aristotle's position in two ways. First, it makes character rather than action the object of imitation and intensifies the moral overtones of this revision by making virtue and vice the specific qualities of character to be imitated. Second, it again transposes the remarks made by Aristotle concerning the earliest poets from chapter 4 to another context.

The exotic combination of additions, transposed passages, and warped interpretations continues in the later sections of the commentary. According to Aristotle, the *Iliad* anticipates tragedy in its seriousness, its sustained plot, and its emphasis on dialogue, while the *Margites* anticipates comedy by dramatizing "the ludicrous" rather than continuing the earlier Greek tradition of personal satire. Because he knew neither Homer nor Greek drama, Averroes failed completely to understand these distinctions. Homer, he says, "established the first principles of these arts, and there was no one before him whose achievement either in praise or blame had anything worth mentioning."[22] Tragedy is defined simply as the "*ars laudandi,*" while comedy is "*ars vituperandi*"—the art of rebuking "not only everything that is bad, but what is despicable and almost beyond cure; that is, what is base and almost worthless."[23] If this not only misses but inverts Aristotle's thoughts about the geniality that Homer introduced into comic tradition, it also wholly ignores the distinction between dramatic and narrative form. We are reminded here of the medieval habit, illustrated in the work of Dante, Lydgate, and Chaucer among others, of referring to narrative poems as "comedies" or "tragedies." Averroes' commentary did not create this misconception but may well have encouraged it. Benvenuto da Imola, for example, found that the Averroes commentary provided just the theory needed to explain the organization of Dante's *Comedy.*

Needless to say, the confusion of the commentary concerning poetic form produces a woefully distorted interpretation of the six "parts" of tragedy listed by Aristotle in *Poetics* 6. Plot becomes *sermo fabularis;* character *consuetudines,* a category that includes both actions and morals; thought becomes *credulitas;* diction *metrum;* song *tonus;* and spectacle something called *consideratio,* by which Averroes seems to mean the gestures and facial expressions used by orators to emphasize their arguments.[24] Equally characteristic, the concepts of probability and necessity are interpreted morally, with the surprising result that the poet is denied the right to create fictions:

> And it is evident from what has been said about poetic speeches that representations that are based on lies are not proper to the poet's

> work. These are called proverbial tales and exempla like those found in the book by Aesop and similar fabulous writings. It is therefore proper for the poet to speak only of things that either are or can be; such things, moreover, as should be desired or spurned. . . . The poet gives names only to things that exist and at times speaks in universals; and therefore the art of poetry is closer to philosophy than the art of proverbial tales.[25]

Again, reversal is treated not as sudden change in the action of a work but as a shift in poetic technique from praise to blame or vice versa. It is

> the representation of the reverse of what is proposed in praise, so that the soul first rejects and despises the thing imitated, and then is changed from this attitude by imitation of what is praiseworthy. Thus, for example, if one should desire to depict good fortune and fortunate men, he should begin by depicting ill fortune and unfortunate men and then suddenly change to depiction of good fortune and men who have it.[26]

An intriguing problem emerges here. If tragedy is "the art of praise" and is intended to incite men to virtue, should it not avoid the disasters that usually overtake the tragic protagonist? Averroes appears to waver. He recognizes the importance of pity and fear, but his example of an ideal tragedy is the story of Abraham, which ends happily. A little later he adds that "certain poets introduce into their tragedies representation of things through which only *admiratio* is intended rather than fear or sorrow."[27] This is the earliest use that I have found of the term *admiratio* in relation to tragedy. In Averroes it is a positive emotion aroused by the moral excellence of those being praised. In the Renaissance it became a key critical term, but was used in two rather different senses. On the one hand, it can mean "admiration" in Averroes' sense. This usage preserves the tradition that tragedy is based on praise and that its figures should be literally admirable. On the other, it can mean something like awe or wonder at the tragic events and is used by didactic critics like Sir Philip Sidney who teach that tragedy shows the awesome fall of great men because of their moral failings.

As a final example of Averroes' misinterpretation of Aristotle, we can turn to his comments on *Poetics* 12, which deals with the Greek terms used to designate the structure of tragedy—parode, episode, stasimon, and the like. Averroes solves the problem by substituting terms from rhetoric:

> [Aristotle] mentions in this discussion the parts that are proper to Greek poems. Of these, the parts that are found in Arab poems are three. First comes the part that resembles the exordium of rhetoric. It is the part where the Arabs speak of houses and noble buildings and of ruins and remains. . . . And the second is the praise proper; and the

> third is the part that is like the rhetorical conclusion. And this third part is usually either an invocation or petition to the man being praised, or a commendatory section praising the valuable poem itself.[28]

This is an outline of the contents of the classic Arabic ode form, the *quasidah*. Its chief significance, however, is its suggestion that the formulas of rhetoric for organizing speeches are equally applicable to literature. This would doubtless have seemed a gratifying confirmation of what many Latin readers of the commentary already believed. The original passage in the *Poetics*, conversely, would have been as unintelligible to them as to Averroes.

II

Let us now turn from the Averroes-Hermannus commentary to its influence on subsequent criticism. Two kinds of evidence are available. The first is the history of the manuscripts and editions, and the second, references to the commentary by significant critics.

The bibliographical history of the commentary is complex, but this very complexity testifies to its enduring interest. The twenty-three surviving manuscripts range in time from the thirteenth to the fifteenth century, and in location from Spain and France to England, Italy, and even Poland. The manuscripts[29] fall into two distinct families. The first family is by far the larger. Manuscripts of this family usually contain, in addition to the Averroes-Hermannus commentary, translations of Aristotle's *Politics* and *Rhetoric,* and either the *Ethics* or the *Magna Moralia.* Evidently this family stems from an anthology of Aristotelian works on "practical philosophy" compiled toward the end of the thirteenth century. The inclusion of the commentary on the *Poetics* indicates that the users of the manuscript regarded the work as an exposition of the didactic view of poetry—i.e., that they read it in terms of the praise-blame theory rather than the logical theory.

The second family of manuscripts has in common the fact that the commentary on the *Poetics* is included with works on science and logic. It thus reflects the "context theory" according to which the *Poetics* is a part of the *Organon.* The fact that the manuscripts of this family are in the minority does not mean that the "context theory" is insignificant, but it shows that the didactic view was more attractive to medieval writers. This conclusion is confirmed by the way in which medieval and early renaissance critics used the commentary.

The Hermannus translation was not the only translation of the commentary that circulated during the Middle Ages. In 1337 Todros Todrosi, a Jewish philosopher living near Arles in France, translated the Averroes commentary into Hebrew. Several manuscripts of this work are extant, and it became the source for two sixteenth-century Latin translations. That Todrosi also translated Averroes' commentaries on the *Sophistical Refutations* and the *Rhetoric* suggests that he considered the *Poetics* part of the *Organon.*

By the fifteenth century, most of the manuscripts are Italian. This doubtless reflects the migration of Averroists from Paris to Padua and Venice following bitter denunciations of them by St. Thomas Aquinas and his followers. It was at Venice that the Hermannus version was first printed. It appeared in 1481 together with the *Rhetoric* in an edition published by Philipus Venetus. Although not reprinted again in the fifteenth century, it was issued at least five times in the sixteenth, in 1515, 1525, 1556, 1572, and 1600.[30] In addition, two other translations, both from the Hebrew of Todrosi, were issued. The first was made by Abraham de Balmes, a Neapolitan physician. It appeared in 1523, and later as part of the Giunta "Aristotle with Averroes" edition of 1574. The other was made by Jacob Mantinus, physician to Pope Paul III, and appeared in the Giunta "Aristotle" of 1552 and 1562.

The large number of manuscripts, editions, and translations of the Averroes commentary shows that it was read and "in demand" from 1300 to the end of the sixteenth century. Perhaps the most remarkable observation that emerges from this brief review of its history is that Averroes continued to be popular long after the Greek *Poetics* had been edited, translated into Latin and Italian, and minutely analyzed by humanist commentators. We may conclude tentatively that in spite of his failings, Averroes offered a view of poetry that conservative humanists of the sixteenth century were reluctant to abandon.

References to the Averroes commentary begin almost immediately after its translation into Latin. Roger Bacon referred to the translation of "master Hermannus" with qualified approval,[31] and a fourteenth-century manuscript of what appear to be lecture notes on the commentary has recently been discovered by Professor William Boggess of the University of Georgia. So far as I know, however, the first critic to make extensive use of the commentary is Benvenuto da Imola, one of the fourteenth-century commentators on Dante. Benvenuto knew the Hermannus translation well. Confidently claiming "Aristotle's authority" for his definition, he asserts that "it is manifest to whoever contemplates the forces of poetry . . . that all poetic discourse is either praise or blame."[32] Later he cites Averroes rather than Aristotle to support the idea that poetry is morally edifying. Evidently, he considered both writers equally authoritative and did not differentiate between them.

Benvenuto's general acknowledgment is complemented by his analysis of the structure of the *Divine Comedy.* It is, he believes, a poem fully in accord with Aristotle's rules. The *Inferno* is a work based on "blame." It consists of a series of vignettes showing the ugliness of vice and its terrible consequences. It thus warns the reader to reform. After the *Inferno* comes the first of two "reversals" of the sort advocated by Averroes. The *Inferno* stresses unhappiness, the despair of the damned. In the *Purgatory* the tone abruptly changes to hope. The *Purgatory* contains some "blame"; but however wicked, the characters in this section have redeeming qualities which are "praised" by Dante. The second reversal comes at the beginning of the *Paradiso*. Here the tone changes from hope to joyful fulfillment, and the technique from a mixture of blame and praise to unqualified praise of men of preeminent virtue whom the reader is encouraged to emulate. As Benvenuto remarks, "no other poet ever knew how to praise or blame with more excellence. . . . [Dante] honored virtue with encomia and lacerated vice and vicious men."[33]

Although Benvenuto's commentary was known in the sixteenth century, he remains primarily a medieval figure. It is significant that the next critic to be influenced by the Averroes commentary is Coluccio Salutati. Salutati is the most famous of Petrarch's disciples and was regarded during the sixteenth century as a full-fledged humanist. Among his many works, his allegorical interpretation of the life of Hercules, *De laboribus Herculis,* is especially significant. It stands midway between Boccaccio's *Genealogy of the Gods* and the allegorized mythologies of such sixteenth-century writers as Comes (or Conti) and Cartari. The first book of the *De laboribus* is a little "art of poetry," in which Salutati offers a theory that in parts may be accurately described as Averroes expanded and ornamented by examples from the Latin classics. In chapter 2 Salutati attempts to differentiate between rhetoric and poetic. This is difficult because, following Averroes, he believes that the two disciplines share the same "matter"—that is, praise and blame. They are eventually distinguished by the assertion that poetry is (1) in meter (an echo of the *ars metrica*) and (2) employs "imaginative and figurative discourse," an idea derived from Averroes' definition of imitation. Later, the tired classical definition of the orator as *vir bonus dicendi peritus* is reworked to apply to the poet, who is called a *vir optimus laudandi vituperandique peritus*—a perfect man skilled in praise and blame. Even Horace is assimilated into the system. The "delight and instruct" formula from the *Ars Poetica* is explained in the following way: "The reprehension of vice may profit right away, but does not immediately please; praise pleases but does not immediately profit. Therefore blame is primarily for utility, praise for pleasure; although in a secondary way the former may please and the latter profit."[34] As is appropriate for a forward-looking humanist, Salutati compliments modern poets on their ability to "celebrate virtue and criticize vice" in the way prescribed in "[Aristotle's] little book."[35]

Averroistic ideas remained attractive during the sixteenth century, although they were occasionally attacked and more frequently disguised by an increasingly heavy overlay of erudition. Savonarola, Robortello, Segni, Maggi and Lombardi, and Mazzoni all debate the "placing" of poetry among the sciences and all decide that poetic is at least in part a branch of logic. Pietro Vettori was not only aware of Averroes, he edited the commentary for the Giunta "Aristotle" of 1552, eight years before composing his own analysis of the *Poetics.*[36] Almost every one of these writers cites the Averroes commentary directly and with respect, often to buttress his own position. As late as 1575, in fact, Alessandro Piccolomini appealed to "the authority of Averroes which has always had great force with me" to refute Robortello's theory of the origin of poetry.[37] Throughout the sixteenth century, it may be added, the didactic theory of poetry existed side-by-side in rather uncomfortable proximity with more precisely Aristotelian doctrines. The fact is that the *Poetics* was difficult to accommodate to the moralistic attitudes of the humanists, whereas Aristotle as interpreted by Averroes is not only moral but oppressively so. In the early part of the century, before the publication of the great commentaries on the *Poetics,* the problem was not fully understood. Aulo Parrasio, for example, was responsible for the first of many efforts to harmonize Horace with Aristotle. His "Commentary on the *Ars Poetica*" appeared posthumously in 1531. Although one reference in the commentary seems to be to the Greek *Poetics*, the remainder of his allegedly Aristotelian principles are evidently quotations or paraphrases from Hermannus Alemannus.[38] Obviously, such an approach became increasingly difficult as time went by. The tension between didacticism and Aristotelian criticism finally became an open break in Lodovico Castelvetro's *Poetica d'Aristotele Vulgarizzata,* published in 1570. Although Castelvetro himself radically distorted the *Poetics,* his interpretation is free of the influence of Averroes. For this reason, he was viewed with suspicion by his great humanistic contemporary Torquato Tasso. In the *Discorsi del Poema Eroico,* published in 1594, Tasso attacked Castelvetro's rather hardheaded view that praise is irrelevant to heroic poetry. "Without doubt," Tasso wrote,

> Castelvetro erred when he said that praise is not appropriate to the heroic poem, because if the heroic poet were to celebrate virtue, he would have to exalt it clear up to the heavens with his praises. On the other side, St. Basil says that Homer's *Iliad* is nothing but a praise of virtue, and Averroes has the same opinion in his commentary on poetry, and Plutarch too. . . . Therefore, leaving aside the followers of Castelvetro in their ignorance, let us follow the opinions of . . . St. Basil, of Averroes, of Plutarch, and of Aristotle himself.[39]

In the last decade of the sixteenth century, in other words, the most eloquent spokesman of Italian humanism found Averroes not only worthy of citing, but in some respects more truly Aristotelian than the most influential student of the *Poetics* that the age produced.

Tasso was, however, already an anachronism in his own age. The canons of neoclassicism were beginning to harden around the freer poetic of the Renaissance. These canons had little place for the barbarous Latin and benighted scholarship of the Averroes commentary. *Concettismo*, which briefly rivaled neoclassicism in Italy, revived the notion that poetry is a matter of cleverly manipulating figurative language, but its sources are Aristotle himself, not his Arabian commentator. The last unambiguous echo of the Averroes commentary that I have been able to discover is in Thomas Rymer's 1674 preface to his translation of Rapin's *Reflections*. Rymer remembers Averroes not for his theory of poetry, but for his rebuke of Arab poets. "The *Arabians*," says Rymer, "observe but little these laws of Aristotle: yet Averroes rather chooses to blame the practice of his countrymen as vicious than to allow any imputation on the doctrine of his *Philosopher* as imperfect."[40] If this makes Averroes a predecessor of Corneille, Boileau, and Alexander Pope, it also writes finis to the story of his influence on European criticism.

(1970)

The Orator and the Poet: The Dilemma of Humanist Literature

I will begin with an image rather than a text. The image is that of Petrarch standing in the Senatorial Palace on Rome's Capitoline Hill on April 8, 1341. He is garbed in the robe of King Robert of Naples, and he has just been crowned with the laurel—the first such coronation in Rome, it is said, for a thousand years.

During his oration, Petrarch speaks of the love which draws him up the lonely slopes of Parnassus, and of the stimulus which his eagerness to advance the honor of the state provides for the ascent. At this point my scene is an emblem of the relationship which I wish to consider here. It is an emblem of an ideal relationship between power and beauty as complementary means of human betterment—between the robe of King Robert and the laurel of Apollo, the lonely slopes of Parnassus and the civic glory of Rome.

In deference to Petrarch, who is a poet delivering an oration in the Capitoline Palace, I will speak of it as a relationship between the orator and the poet in the typical roles assigned them by humanist rhetorical theory—that is to say, a relationship between the ideal leader who uses language to persuade and the ideal artist who uses language to manifest what Petrarch, in his oration, calls "an inner force divinely infused in the poet's spirit."[1]

Time and again we are told by humanists that their objective is nothing less than the total reform of human society. Hence the enduring fascination throughout the Renaissance of imaginary states, of the Pastoral Eden of Corydon and Phyllis, of manuals on the education of princes, of courtesy books, and on occasion, of grandiose schemes for political surgery, from the sacred Republic of Cola di Rienzo to the Protectorate of Oliver Cromwell. Time and again, too, we encounter complementary efforts by artists to lift reality to the level of the ideal: in Verrocchio's equestrian statue of Bartolommeo Colleoni, in Holbein's portraits of Francis I and Henry VIII, in Michelangelo's soaring dome for St. Peter's basilica. If there is a tension in these works—a touch of cruelty in the grace of Colleoni, of cynicism in the smile of Francis I, of vanity in the engineering triumph that helped to alienate half of Christendom—we are chiefly aware of it from later history. The artists, we imagine, were passionately sincere.

In the great scheme of reform, the orator occupies the chief position. Demosthenes, after all, was the main pillar of Athenian liberty; and Cicero gained eternal fame by his defense of the Roman Republic. Impatient with the chop-logic, the jargon, and the esoteric theorizing of the schools, humanists looked to the orator to change society and made rhetoric the central discipline in their educational system. How, after all, do you translate the morality of Christ and the ethics of Socrates into social realities? Not through ever more obscure treatises written by professors for other professors, the argument runs, but through addressing mankind at large. The orator speaks in the public forum. His announced object is persuasion, and his instrument is eloquence. Aeneas Silvius writes his friend Adam Mulin in farthest England:

> I read your letter with great eagerness and wondered that Latin style had penetrated even into Britain. It is true that there have been some few Englishmen who have cultivated the eloquence of Cicero, among whom common consent would place the Venerable Bede. . . . Persevere, therefore, friend Adam. Hold fast and increase the eloquence you possess; consider it the most honorable thing possible to excel your fellows in that whereby men excel other living creatures. Great is eloquence; nothing so much rules the world. Political action is the result of persuasion; his opinion prevails with the people who best knows how to persuade.[2]

Eloquence is the power to shape society: "nothing so much rules the world." The curious but familiar emblem of Hercules with chains in his tongue makes the same point. Alexander Ross explains this in his *Mystagogus Poeticus:*

> By Hercules the ancients did not only mean valor and strength of body, but the force of eloquence also; which they did express by that picture of Hercules clothed in a horse skin, armed with a club, with bow and arrows, having small chains, proceeding from his tongue, and tied to the ears of people whom he drew after him; by which they signified how sharp and powerful eloquence is to pierce and subdue the affections of people, and draw them far.[3]

If this makes the idea of power associated with oratory uncomfortably obvious, we have the assurance of the humanists that it is all in a good cause. The end in view is the betterment of mankind, and if men have to be dragged to their own salvation in chains, then so be it. Cato's first requirement for the orator is that he be a good man—a *vir bonus dicendi peritus*—and Crassus, who speaks for the divine Tully in the *De oratore,* insists that whatever else he may or may not know, the orator must be deeply versed in moral philosophy. As a result of the New Dispensation, humanists could claim a sanction far more reliable than Cato. The title of Thomas Wilson's preface to *The Art of Rhetoric* reads, "Eloquence first given by God, and after lost by man, and last repaired by God again."[4] Eloquence, Wilson explains, was the first cause of human civilization, and the earliest orators were instruments of divine will:

> Whereas men lived brutishly in open fields, having neither house to shroud them in, nor attire to clothe their bodies, nor yet any regard to see their best avail, these [i.e., orators] appointed by God called them together by utterance of speech and persuaded with them what was good, what was bad, and what was gainful for mankind. And . . . being somewhat drawn with the pleasantness of reason, and the sweetness of utterance . . . after a certain space they became . . . of wild, sober: of cruel, gentle: of fools, wise: and of beasts, men: such force hath the tongue, and such is the power of Eloquence and reason, that most men are forced, even to yield in that which most standeth against their will.[5]

Like Aeneas Silvius, Wilson considers eloquence a source of power. It is psychological rather than physical power, but it is power nonetheless, for it causes men "even to yield in that which most standeth against their will." Wilson adds the rhetorical question, "What man would not rather look to rule like a lord than to live like an underling: if by reason he were not persuaded . . . to live in his own vocation." Although invisible, the chains are still there.

But it is all in a good cause. No humanist can doubt this without questioning the validity of humanism itself. The orator is a good man, perhaps even an instrument of God. He civilizes, orders, reforms, upholds justice, and from the pulpit leads (or drags) his followers along the road to salvation. The figure of the evil orator, whose tongue drops manna and can make the worse appear the better part, was familiar to humanists; but the evil orator was considered the exception, not the rule. The remedy, as Ben Jonson explained, is for the *vir bonus,* the good man, to study rhetoric as assiduously as the bad man. Rhetorical skills being equal, the orator with truth on his side will be assured of victory.

Though I began with the image of a poet delivering an oration, so far I have said little about poetry. My emblem of Petrarch on the Capitoline Hill suggests that the poet is so closely related to the orator in humanist thought that the two can easily merge into a single figure. In fact, the poet and the orator had already been closely associated in the classical past to which the humanists looked for guidance. The topic, "Is Virgil to be considered an orator or a poet?" was a set piece for late classical *controversiae,* and a lengthy section of book 5 of the *Saturnalia* of Macrobius is devoted to Virgil's rhetorical skill and has the topic "Virgil is as much an orator as a poet."[6] As we know, the practice of reading the poets in the schools to cull out images and *sententiae* for the improvement of prose style was standard in both the classical and the Renaissance curriculum.

But the main point and the chief humanist justification for poetry is that the poet shares the reforming mission of the orator. Cicero's *Pro Archia* explains how Ennius celebrated the Roman people, and the *Aeneid* is a case study in the way that poetry can be used to reinforce the political ideals which also concern the orator. The difference is not one of function but of degree. Colluccio Salutati, disciple of Petrarch and chancellor of Florence, expresses the humanist view with exquisite precision. After defining the orator in the approved Catonian fashion as *vir bonus dicendi peritus,* he defines the poet as *vir optimus laudandi vituperandique peritus*—a perfect man skilled in praise and blame. Poetry, in other words, is a higher form of oratory. It is eloquence, and it is a supreme eloquence.[7]

Given this situation it is not surprising to find that the claims made for oratory are also made for poetry. If the orator can be considered the founder of human society, so can the poet, and on better evidence. The achievements of the *prisci poetae* were celebrated by Boccaccio in books 14 and 15 of the *Genealogy of the Gods* and again by Politian in his poem *Nutricia,* in which poetry is described as the nurse of human civilization. The commonplaces are neatly summarized by the author of *The Art of English Poesie:*

> Poetry was the original cause and occasion of [men's] first assemblies, when before the people remained . . . dispersed like the wild beasts, lawless and naked . . . so as they little differed for their manner of life from the very brutes of the field. Whereupon it is feigned that Amphion and Orpheus, two poets of the first ages, one of them, to wit Amphion, builded up cities and reared walls with the stones that came in heaps to the sound of his harp, figuring thereby the mollifying of hard and stony hearts by his sweet and eloquent persuasion. And Orpheus assembled the wild beasts . . . implying thereby, how by his discrete and wholesome lessons uttered in harmony and with melodious instruments he brought the rude and savage people to a more civil and orderly life, nothing it seemeth, more prevailing or fit to redress and edify the civil and sturdy courage of man than it. And as these two poets, and Linus before them, and Musaeus and also Hesiodus in Greece and Arcadia, so by all likelihood had more poets done in other places and in other ages before them. . . .[8]

Poetry, like oratory, is a source of power. The poet employs "sweet and eloquent persuasion," than which "nothing is more prevailing or fit to redress and edify" mankind. The political role of poetry is objectified in myths depicting its power to convert "rude and savage people to a more civil and orderly life." The *via negativa* of the Middle Ages stressed passivity, meditation, and illumination. It regarded language as a vehicle of transcendence. But the *Aeneid* celebrates the imperial destiny of Rome, and Petrarch's *Africa* attempts to revive that sense of worldly destiny. Both are poems of action intended to arouse action—*praxis*—among their readers. As Sir Philip Sidney explains, "moving is of a higher degree than teaching . . . for as Aristotle sayeth, it is not *gnosis* but *praxis* must be the fruit."[9]

Hercules leads men in chains; the poet leads them with "sweet lessons uttered in harmony"—with the honey on the rim of the medicine cup, the sweet coating of the bitter pill, or, to quote Sidney again, "a medicine of cherries."[10] Poetry is eloquence of the same kind as oratory but of a higher degree. Writing to Sir Walter Raleigh to explain *The Faerie Queene*, Edmund Spenser sets the *Cyropaedia* before Plato's *Republic* because "so much more profitable is doctrine by example than by rule."[11]

II

What the humanists symbolize by their near identification of the orator and the poet is an ideal harmony of power and beauty. It is a seductive ideal which retained its force throughout the Renaissance. But for all his public concerns, Petrarch was happier at Valchiusa than at Parma or Avignon. He preferred the *vita otiosa* to the active life, and the tension between the elements which he sought to combine is clear in his debate with St. Augustine in the *Secretum*. It is equally clear in Sir Thomas More's decision to become a "counsellor of Kings" only a few years after his fictional hero Raphael Hythloday had decisively rejected this course of action, and in Spenser's criticism of Gloriana's court in poems like "Mother Hubberd's Tale" and "Colin Clout's Come Home Againe."

Dulce bellum inexpertis—the ideal is sweet until tested. The case of John Milton, last and perhaps greatest in the proud line of Christian humanists, illustrates both the ideal and the reason for its ultimate failure.

During Milton's youth the gap between power and beauty, between the political commitment of the orator and the human insight of the poet, was already obvious to those with eyes to see. The magic of Elizabeth's reign had died with her. If *The Faerie Queene*—an epic—speaks for the sixteenth century, the seventeenth century typically expresses itself in two quite different forms of literature—in plays like *Volpone, Sejanus, Bussy D'Ambois,* and *The Duchess of Malfi,* which reveal the corruption of power; and in the introspective lyric poetry of Donne, Chapman, and Herbert. The questioning evident in these works is paralleled in the real world by the spreading disenchantment of Englishmen with their political system and their state religion.

For all this, the most important public statement by the young Milton is an impassioned manifesto of humanism. Milton's *Seventh Prolusion* was composed for delivery at Cambridge in 1632. Trinity College is not exactly the Capitoline Hill, and we imagine Milton in an academic gown rather than the robe of King Robert of Naples, but again we have an emblem in which the poet appears as orator. Milton's subject is social reform through learning. The Middle Ages, he says, were condemned to barbarism through ignorance, whereas learning is a solace to the individual, an adornment to social relations, and the best foundation for political power. The latter point is exemplified by the ancients: "there have been only two men who have had possession of the whole circle of earth as heaven's gift . . . : Alexander the Great and [Augustus] Caesar, both of them students of philosophy. Indeed, it is as if they had been divinely provided for humanity as an example of the kind of man to whom the helm and reins of affairs are to be entrusted."[12]

A decade later Milton was not only advocating reform, he was living it as a propagandist for the Puritan revolution. In *The Reason of Church Government* he pauses in his diatribe against the religious establishment to comment on the office of the epic poet. Among other things, its purpose is "to inbreed and cherish in a great people the seeds of virtue and public civility."[13] Two years later the polemicist appears in the more formal role of deliberative orator. His speech is addressed to Parliament, which he honors by comparing it to the ancient Athenian tribunal, the Areopagus. The irony of the fact that *Areopagitica* was delivered to Parliament only in Milton's imagination, and that its proposals were not so much rejected as totally ignored, is underscored by its most famous passage. Petrarch had retired periodically to the *vita otiosa* at Valchiusa; and Milton had spent most of the 1630s reading, meditating, and writing poetry at Horton. In *Areopagitica,* however, he vehemently rejects the idea of the contemplative life: "I cannot praise a fugitive and cloistered virtue, unexercised and unbreathed, that never sallies out and seeks her adversary, but slinks out of the race where that immortal garland is to be run for, not without dust and heat." Poetry, he adds, has a central role to play in the enterprise of reform. The point is illustrated by "our sage and serious poet Spenser, (whom I dare be known to think a better teacher than Scotus or Aquinas,) describing true temperance under the person of Guyon, [bringing] him in with his palmer through the cave of Mammon and the bower of earthly bliss, that he might see and know, and yet abstain."[14] Of so much more profit is doctrine by example than by rule.

Of course, this is commonplace humanist doctrine, even to the contrast between scholastic theorizing and Renaissance eloquence. What is unique is the intensity of Milton's commitment. Earlier humanists had often qualified their reforming zeal with irony, as though they knew in their hearts that their efforts would be ineffectual—that power rests on force, that the orator is more likely to be a politician than a statesman, and that in the real world the poet is usually faced with the alternative of flattering a Nero or retiring to the lonely Parnassus of his own psyche. But Milton is passionately sincere. He is the reformer turned revolutionary. Caught up in a national effort to transform society, he is mesmerized by his vision of the future: "Methinks I see in my mind a noble and puissant nation, rousing herself like a strong man after sleep, and shaking her invincible locks. Methinks I see her as an eagle mewing her mighty youth, and kindling her undazzled eyes at the midday beam; purging and unscaling her long-abused sight at the fountain itself of heavenly radiance."[15]

This is, I think, the high point of Milton's humanism. It is a synthesis of powerful conviction and magnificent eloquence. The form is a prose oration, but the eloquence is in all respects poetic. For a moment (though only in Milton's imagination) the robe of King Robert perfectly sets off the laurels of the poet.

But the mood of exaltation was temporary. Milton was destined to give his sight and a good part of his life to a cause that began as an effort to create a new society, degenerated into a military dictatorship, and ended as a butt of ridicule among its triumphant enemies. *Paradise Lost* is still humanistic in its didacticism—its ambition to justify the ways of God to men—but in it the poet and the orator have become separated. The poet is a blind prophet who turns away from the visible world. Bidding farewell to "the Book of Universal Nature," he cries out to the Spirit:

> So much the rather thou, Celestial light,
> Shine inward . . . there plant eyes, all mist from thence
> Purge and disperse, that I may see and tell
> Of things invisible to mortal sight.[16]

Conversely, the social reformer, the orator, is not a hero but a demon. No passage in *Paradise Lost* is a more explicit reminder of the humanist ideal of eloquence than the following description:

> As when of old some orator renowned
> In Athens or free Rome, where Eloquence
> Flourished, since mute, to some great cause addressed,
> Stood in himself collected, while each part,
> Motion, each act, won audience ere tongue
> Sometimes in height began, as no delay
> Or Preface brooking, through his Zeal of Right.[17]

But the description is bitterly ironic. It is Satan who is preparing to speak. His audience is Eve, and his eloquence will bring about the Fall of Man.

The harsh lesson of the Commonwealth years becomes overt in *Paradise Regained.* There Satan offers Christ the opportunity to do exactly what earlier humanists had dreamed of doing—he offers the power to translate ideals into social realities. "With what ease," Satan remarks,

> Endued with Regal Virtues as thou art,
> Appearing, and beginning noble deeds,
> Might thou expell [Tiberius] from his Throne,
> Now made a sty, and in his place ascending,
> A victor people free from servile yoke.[18]

There is no irony in Christ's reply. It is unambiguous and, from the humanist point of view, profoundly disillusioned:

> What wise and virtuous man would seek to free
> These, thus degenerate, by themselves enslaved,
> Or could of inward slaves make outward free?[19]

Whether you approve of these words or not, they constitute a decisive rejection not only of the temptation but of the ideal of social reform itself. They thus strike at the heart of the humanist belief that the orator and the poet have complementary roles. If society cannot be reformed, then eloquence is useless or worse. It may not be "the first gift of God" as Thomas Wilson believed, but an instrument of hell.

There is a movement in *Paradise Regained* toward a new concept of eloquence. The great public abstractions—Wisdom, Liberty, Justice, the Rights of Man, and the like—begin to sound hollow. Milton's Christ seeks a more intimate communication. This is reflected in the shift from the gorgeous rhetoric of *Paradise Lost,* with its echoes of Homer and Virgil, to the plainer but subtler language of the later poem, which draws not on classical epic but on the Book of Job. The dream of the puissant nation stirring itself from slumber is over. Rome and Athens, symbolizing human glory and human culture, are mirages, seen from a great distance through an "airy microscope." The reality of the poem is not Eden but the desert. The magnificent effort to create a Christian epic has been succeeded, as Professor Martz taught us, by something closer to meditation.[20]

What I want to stress in this account of Milton's rejection of humanism is that it was forced on him by history. As a young man Milton eagerly embraced the humanist program of social reform. In the 1640s he lived its success; and in his later years he lived its failure. His response to this failure was a rejection of the ideal of the orator based on disillusionment with the possibility of meaningful reform. "So shall the world go on," says Michael, summarizing human history for Adam, "to good malignant, to bad men benign." Milton's solution is expressed in traditional Christian formulae. It is the cultivation of what Puritans called the "inner light." In a famous passage Michael uses the term "paradise within" to express the idea:

This having learned, thou hast attained the sum
Of wisdom . . . only add
Deeds to thy knowledge answerable, add Faith,
Add Virtue, Patience, Temperance, add Love,
By name to come called Charity, the soul
Of all the rest: then wilt thou not be loath
To leave this Paradise, but shall possess
A Paradise within thee happier far.[21]

III

A paradise within thee happier far—this we assume is what Petrarch really sought on the lonely slopes of Parnassus when he described the "inner force divinely infused in the poet's spirit." The notion that the quest would advance the glory of the state was an illusion; the Robe of King Robert, an impediment rather than an asset.

During the period that I am discussing, the lesson was existential. It was felt but not adequately conceptualized. It could be put in conventional religious terms, but the vocabulary of Renaissance theology was imprecise. What was needed to shape the experience into a conception was a radical new analysis of experience itself.

The problem encountered by the humanists was, I think, eventually solved. The solution came toward the end of the eighteenth century as a corollary of the "Copernican revolution" in philosophy which Kant describes in his *Prolegomena to Any Future Metaphysic,* and it is characteristic of most later aesthetic systems derived from Kant. It requires us to distinguish once and for all between purposive and nonpurposive judgments, and to assign art to the latter category. Purposive activity is directed toward something beyond itself. This is another way of saying that it is subordinated to the abstract. Conversely, nonpurposive activity is its own excuse for being—a kind of play. It does not subserve abstraction and for this reason is truly human. "To speak the truth," wrote Schiller in his *Letters on the Aesthetic Education of Man,* "man only plays in the full meaning of the word when he is man; and he is only completely a man when he plays."[22]

In the light of this analysis we can understand far better than Milton the source of the recurrent tension in Renaissance thought between action and contemplation, Rome and Parnassus, oratory and poetry. The humanist belief that fusion is possible is simply false. The orator and poet are not cousins—they are not even of the same race. Their functions, in fact, are antithetical. The orator is purposive, committed to abstractions like Goodness, Justice, Liberty. The test of eloquence is action—in Sir

Philip Sidney's words, "not *gnosis* but *praxis*." The error of the humanists was to put poetry in the same category, to treat it as a higher eloquence, a more persuasive goad to action. To the humanist view of poetry we oppose Schiller's flat declaration: "If, after [aesthetic] enjoyment . . . we find ourselves especially impelled to a particular mode of feeling or action, and unfit for other modes, this serves as infallible proof that we have not experienced any pure aesthetic effect."[23]

Here, I think, is the truth toward which Milton was driven by the failure of humanism, but which he could express only in the religious image of the "paradise within thee happier far." The inwardness which Milton sought is the inner structure of experience that Europeans have come to understand and to some extent control through Kant's analysis.

IV

The notion that art must be free of the practical functions for which oratory is responsible is our legacy from Kant and his popularizers. It allows us to recognize that all human activities have their proper spheres, and also that the boundaries of those spheres cannot be overstepped without loss—this, in spite of the fact that in practice they are overstepped constantly, and that in practice the result is a loss.

I have tried to show in this article that humanism began with the ideal of an order in which beauty is sustained by power and power fulfilled by beauty. The goal was never achieved outside of the idealizing world of Renaissance art. It retained its hold, however, throughout the Renaissance. Men spoke and behaved and organized their schools as though the ideal was valid or could be if only enough speeches were made and enough grammar schools founded. Milton was not the last European to be swayed by it, but his life illustrates its inadequacy with particular vividness. In view of the dreams of social reform that seem endemic to our own century—and the reiterated demands that the modern poet use his talents in the service of these dreams—the failure of humanism provides a lesson well worth remembering. Wallace Stevens remarks, "Be an orator but with an accurate tongue, and without eloquence." And there is the adage that so intrigued Erasmus: *Dulce bellum inexpertis.*

(1971)

Blank Verse before Milton

In 1937, George K. Smart, writing in the journal *Anglia,* threw down a small gauntlet. Discussing sixteenth-century blank verse, he announced, "Histories of literature and of prosody universally trace these developments very sketchily, jumping dextrously from Surrey's non-dramatic blank verse to that in the drama *Gorboduc,* and passing on to its use in dramas by Marlowe, Shakespeare, and other dramatists, to return to non-dramatic blank verse with Milton. . . . In addition to being incomplete, this method is misleading, for dramatic blank verse is quite different from non-dramatic, and the two ought not to be considered as one form."[1]

Smart's gauntlet fell with an inaudible clank on the floor of English Renaissance scholarship. In spite of excellent work by scholars such as John Thompson, Howard Baker, Glenn Spiegel, and Coburn Freer, it has been lying there ever since.[2] Covered with rust though it may be, it is a serious challenge. To confront it is to question a good many of our unexamined assumptions about sixteenth-century heroic and dramatic poetry.

I

Current knowledge about the history of sixteenth-century blank verse can be summarized very briefly. The form was, apparently, invented by Henry Howard, Earl of Surrey, for his translation of books 2 and 4 of Vergil's *Aeneid,* dated around 1540. Except for two set pieces by Grimald and a few lines by Norton, this is the only example of the use of blank verse for heroic poetry prior to Christopher Marlowe's translation of book 1 of Lucan's *Pharsalia,* issued posthumously in 1600, which, in turn, is the only use of blank verse for heroic poetry until Milton's *Paradise Lost,* published in 1667. Milton's decision to use blank verse was, in its own turn, such a peculiar one that his printer asked him to explain it in the second issue of *Paradise Lost.* Milton obliged and produced the well-known note on "The Verse" of *Paradise Lost.* In the note, Milton claims that his poem is "an example set the first in *English*" of the use of what is now called blank verse for heroic poetry.[3] Milton, of course, was mistaken; evidently the efforts of Surrey and Marlowe were so obscure in 1667 that he was unaware of them.

Milton recognizes that writers of "*English* Tragedies" used blank verse. He thus makes an emphatic distinction between the dramatic and heroic forms of blank verse. In fact, until the publication of *Paradise Lost* blank verse was considered a dramatic rather than an heroic meter. Although all of the major English Renaissance dramatists use blank verse, the best known heroic poems of the sixteenth and seventeenth centuries used other forms: fourteeners, like Phaer's translation of the *Aeneid* and Chapman's *Iliad,* or decasyllabic couplets, like Chapman's *Odyssey,* and Cowper's *Davideis,* or stanzas, like Spenser's *Faerie Queene* and Davenant's *Gondibert.* Between Surrey and Marlowe, the chief non-dramatic use of blank verse was for elegiac poems: Turberville's six blank-verse epistles from Ovid's *Heroides,* the "complaint of Dives" in Anthony Maundy's *Mirror of Mutability,* the elegaic "scrole" recording the lament of the old man whose corpse is disinterred in the second part of Barnabe Rich's *Adventures of Don Simonides,* and Spenser's elegiac "sonets" in *The Theatre of Voluptuous Worldlings.* One other use of blank verse may be noted. Gascoigne calls his *Steele Glas* "A Satyre written without rime" and cites Lucilius as his precedent.[4]

Gorboduc, which was acted before Queen Elizabeth in 1561/2, is the first English drama in blank verse. Unfortunately, not a line survives from the writings of either Norton or Sackville, its authors, to indicate why they decided to use the form. It seems possible that their decision was independent of most of what had happened in English poetry before they began to write their tragedy. On the other hand, there is evidence that Norton and Sackville were seriously interested in prosody. Norton had reduced brief passages from book 6 of the *Aeneid* and book 4 of the *Georgics* into blank verse in his translation of Calvin's *Institutes* (1561),[5] and would contribute twenty-eight psalms in fourteeners to Sternhold and Hopkins' famous anthology. And after *Gorboduc,* Sackville would contribute two impressive compositions to *The Mirror for Magistrates,* the *Induction* and *The Tragedy of Buckingham,* both in rhyme royal.

Meanwhile, Norton and Sackville were surrounded by a veritable industry of Seneca translations. Nine of the ten tragedies published by Newton in 1581 were translated between 1559 and 1567, all but one (Thomas Nace's *Octavia,* in heroic couplets) in fourteeners. Norton and Sackville must have been aware of these efforts. Thomas Heywood, who translated three of the tragedies, explicitly praises Sackville's "Sonetts" and Norton's "ditties" in the introduction to *Thyestes* (1560).[6] The fact that Norton and Sackville rejected the dominant trend of the period toward fourteeners suggests that their decision to write *Gorboduc* in blank verse was calculated. Deliberate or not, it was ratified in 1566 when Gascoigne and Kinwelmarsh translated Ludovico Dolce's version of *Jocasta,* originally in *versi sciolti,* into English blank verse and ornamented the play with dumb shows in the manner of *Gorboduc.*

II

In the absence of further direct evidence it is helpful to review the context within which blank verse appeared. This context can be established in considerable detail.

Romantic critical theory is organic. It asks how each aspect of a literary work expresses the central value of the work. Humanist critical theory is not organic. It is formal. It divides poetry into genres and prescribes a unique function and a unique decorum for each genre. To the degree that humanist authors were humanists, they rejected the mixed genres and imprecise concepts of decorum of the Middle Ages, and called for a return *via* imitation to the more elevated standards of the ancients. This summons was not, at least overtly, a call for slavish imitation. It was, rather, a summons to a level of expression sufficiently noble to lift society out of its Gothic lethargy. It was, in other words, a call for social reform. The point can be illustrated by any number of humanist documents. After praising "the workes of divers Latines, Italians, and other" Tottel goes on to say that his anthology is published "to the honor of the Englishe tong, and for profit of the studious of Englishe eloquence" and advises detractors of its "statelinesse of stile" to "purge that swinelike grossenesse" of their taste.[7]

Classical doctrine reached England in three ways. In the first place, there were the works themselves. Homer, Vergil, and the Greek and Roman dramatists provided models for humanistic imitation, which is expressed most directly in translation. In the second place, there were the ancient precepts. Here, Horace is the commanding figure, reinforced by a miscellaneous array of aphorisms, commonplaces, and critical platitudes from classical literature, conveyed in the schools through the grammar and rhetoric curriculum. In the third place, there was a growing body of vernacular imitations of classical works. The successful ones were important as precedents. They became, in effect, the real objects of imitation of later authors in spite of the claims of these authors to be imitating Greek and Latin originals, a point especially obvious in the case of drama.

If we turn from doctrine to application, we are confronted with an irreducible fact. Ancient heroic poetry is written in dactylic hexameter, while ancient drama is written, in its non-choric episodes, in irregular iambic trimeter lines, with three units of two feet to each full line. This is a fact with which any sixteenth-century schoolboy would have been confronted as soon as he began reading Vergil, Plautus, Terence, and Seneca. The unique quality of heroic verse on the one hand and of dramatic verse on the other was explained in the grammar curriculum by lessons in what was called the *ars metrica*, which presented the standard classical meters and explanations of how each was adapted to its function.

Although the *ars metrica* is forgotten today, anyone wishing to review it will find a substantial collection of texts in volume 6 of Keil's *Grammatici Latini,* titled simply *Scriptores Artis Metricae.*[8] Renaissance redactions of the *ars metrica* are found, usually under the rubric *prosodia,* in the standard school texts reviewed in T. W. Baldwin's *William Shakspere's Small Latine & Lesse Greeke* (1944) and Derek Attridge's *Well-Weighed Syllables* (1974).[9] The desire to create verse forms complementary to the traditional genres is, in fact, one of the motives behind the movement traced by Attridge. In the second part of *The Mirror for Magistrates* Thomas Blenerhasset remarks of his use of the unrhymed Alexandrine: "It agreeth very well with the *Roman* verse called *lambus,* which consisteth on sixe feete. . . . so proper [is it] for the Englishe toung, that it is greate marvaile that these ripewitted Gentlemen of *England* have not left of their Gotish [i.e., Gothic] ryming."[10] William Webbe seeks "some perfect platforme or *Prosodia* of versifying" in order to win "credite" for the English Muse;[11] and Samuel Daniel argues that Campion's elaborate exposition of meter is unnecessary because "everie Grammarian in this land hath learned his *Prosodia,* and alreadie knowes all this Arte of numbers."[12]

The commonplaces of the *ars metrica* are restated in Horace's *Ars Poetica.* In Ben Jonson's translation:

> The gests of Kings, great Captaines, and sad Warres,
> What number best can fit, *Homer* declares.
> In verse unequall match'd, first soure Laments,
> After mens Wishes, crown'd in their events
> Were also clos'd. . . .
> The *Iambicke* arm'd Archilochus to rave,
> This foot the socks tooke up, and Buskins grave
> As fit t'exchange discourse, and quell the rings
> Of popular noyses, borne to actuate things.[13]

Any Renaissance author who needed a gloss on these lines would have found one ready made in the many annotated editions of the sixteenth century. The popular commentary of Aulo Parrasio (Parrhasius, 1531) explains: "Homer is considered the first poet to have sung the noble deeds of heroes in heroic measure. The measure is called 'heroic' and 'epic' because it is hospitable to a great variety of locutions. . . . It is first in dignity, has ample scope for serious speeches, is preeminent for expressing honor, and is outstanding for its beauty."[14] Parrasio adds that the meter can express many different things, but that Horace warns against using it for presenting "light things" and love and banquets. Francesco Fillipi, commenting on the *Ars Poetica* in 1546, writes a little essay on its prosodic section titled "On the Rhythmic Art." He remarks concerning iambic meter:

> Since comedy and tragedy derive their excellence from characters engaging in dialogue . . . they delight in using this meter for precisely expressing the alternation of speeches, and such speeches work well in performance and arouse the cheers and applause of the audience.[15]

For a Renaissance humanist seeking to express in the vernacular the civilizing vision of ancient art, the problem of heroic expression would therefore have been entirely different from—almost antithetical to—the problem of dramatic expression, and this is true in spite of the fact that Surrey on the one hand and Norton and Sackville on the other chose the same meter, namely, blank verse. As we have seen, the distinction was still significant in 1668 when Milton wrote his note on "The Verse" of *Paradise Lost.*

Since Surrey and Norton and Sackville were thoroughly grounded in Latin literature, they would certainly have known of the prosodic commonplaces of the *ars metrica* and of the Renaissance commentaries on Horace. In both cases, however, Italian influence may also have been important. The Italians led the way in European efforts to imitate the classical forms of the ancients, and the metrical form called *verso sciolto,* which is unrhymed hendecasyllabics, was used in Italy for both epic and tragedy before blank verse appeared in England.

In his *History of English Prosody,* Saintsbury remarks: "It would, of course, be gratuitous futility to argue that, as a matter of fact, Surrey did not take [blank verse] . . . from the Italians, who were then the only nation and language in Europe that had made considerable attempts at it."[16] Who, however, was Surrey's model? The most obvious choice is Giangiorgio Trissino, whose *Italia Liberata dai Goti* is entirely in *versi sciolti.* However, the *Italia* was not published until 1547, and Surrey's *Aeneid* was completed around 1540. Padelford therefore suggests Hippolito de Medici's translation of *Aeneid* 2 in 1539 and Nicolo Liburnio's translation of *Aeneid* 4 in 1534, both of these translations being in *versi sciolti.*[17] Edwin Cassady, in his biography of Surrey (1938), opts for the experiments in *versi sciolti* in the *Opere Toscane* of Luigi Alamanni, dedicated to Francis I and published in 1532 when Surrey was in France.[18] Herbert Hartman, editor of the unique copy of the Day edition (ca. 1554) of Surrey's translation of *Aeneid* 4, argues, conversely, that the invention of blank verse was independent of the Italians and "a product of strictly English humanism."[19]

There appears to be no comparable effort to discover the source of the blank verse of *Gorboduc* in spite of the fact that it was as unprecedented in drama as Surrey's blank verse was in heroic poetry. Here the possibility of Trissino's influence is very strong since his *Sophonisba,* which is the first regular tragedy in any European vernacular and which uses *versi sciolti* for its dialogue sections, was published in 1525. The possibility is increased by the fact that *Gorboduc* uses dumb shows, which were common in Italian tragedy.

Sources aside, one can recover a lively sense of the issues that blank verse presented to a Renaissance humanist by reviewing Trissino's explanations of *versi sciolti.* Commenting on its use in *Italia Liberata* in a dedicatory preface to Charles V, Trissino begins with the quality of *enargia* as described in the treatise *On Style* by Demetrius Phalarion. *Enargia* (vividness) is essential to epic poetry. It is created by the particularizing of descriptions, which requires that the descriptive units be extended to the full length required by the subject. Poetic *enargia* therefore depends on an open verse form (i.e., *versi sciolti*) which does not, like couplets and stanzas, break the descriptions into arbitrary units.[20] Trissino's comment, while brief, clearly points to the use of enjambment and irregular verse paragraphs, and this implication is made explicit in English discussions of blank verse. Thomas Campion, for example, complains in his *Observations in the Art of English Poesie* that stanzas are like Procrustes' treatment of prisoners, "whom, when he had taken, he used to cast upon a bed, which if they were too short to fill, he would stretch them longer, if too long he would cut them shorter."[21] And Milton remarks in his note on "The Verse" that rhyme causes poets "vexation, hindrance, and constraint to express many things otherwise, and for the most part worse than else they would have exprest them," whereas blank verse permits "the sense variously drawn out from one Verse into another."[22] Trissino adds that *enargia* demands the use of "comparisons and similes and images," and in Homer it results in a "marvelous spaciousness" (*meravigliosa larghezza*) as well as a "sonorousness" and an "elevation" of the verse, which, however, Trissino is willing to forego.[23]

Trissino's epic *versi sciolti* are rather flat. However, they do express the qualities that he considers essential to heroic *enargia*—a continuation of descriptions to their proper length, unhindered by the arbitrary divisions of rhyme or stanza, and the use of ornate language at climactic moments. In the sixth book of his *Poetica* (1562), Trissino adds the following comment: "Hexameter verse is splendidly adapted to [heroic poetry] because it is more solid and more elevated than any of the other verse forms, and accepts better than any of the others words, and metaphors, and other figures, as we find first in Homer and later in Vergil. But we [Italians], because our language cannot accept this sort of verse, have chosen the hendecasyllabic which, since it does not have a rhyme at the end, is 'open' (*sciolto*)."[24]

Sophonisba is dedicated to Pope Leo X. In spite of the fact that it uses the same verse form as *Italia Liberata,* the explanation of the form is entirely different. Here Trissino says nothing of *enargia.* Instead, recalling the discussions of iambic trimeter in the *ars metrica* tradition and in commentaries on Horace, he lectures his patron on the natural adaptability of the form to expressing emotion: "I do not think that it can justly be considered a defect that [the tragedy] . . . does not use rhyme, as is commonly done, but is free (*libere*) in many places. . . . [*verso sciolto*] is better and more excellent and perhaps less easy to write than it may be considered to be. And you will see that it is most useful not only in narrations and formal speeches but in the arousal of the piteous emotion that is necessary [in tragedy]. And this is because the speech that arouses such emotion is born from painful emotions, and painful emotion does not express itself in carefully thought-out words; and rhyme, which expresses careful thought, is, in fact, directly opposed to the expression of pity."[25]

To Trissino, in other words, *verso sciolto* is two quite different meters. As epic meter it permits the enjambment and verse paragraphing needed for heroic *enargia*. On the other hand, in drama it expresses the rapid movements and disordered sequences of intense emotion appropriate for dialogue.

It would be possible to extend this survey of humanist theories of prosody almost indefinitely. However, perhaps sufficient illustration has been provided to show that no humanist could conceivably have confused the object of heroic prosody with that of dramatic prosody. From the humanist point of view the two are separate, and although they may use the same form in vernacular languages because of the peculiarities of these languages, as imitations they express the qualities of different meters with different functions.

III

The most sophisticated treatment of the theory of prosody in ancient criticism is found in Aristotle's *Poetics*. The *Poetics* became available in a coherent Latin translation in the 1536 edition by Alessandro Pazzi, and by 1540 it had become the central text for Italian criticism. Whether Surrey or Norton and Sackville were familiar with it is doubtful. They probably were not. On the other hand, the theories of the *Poetics* are echoed, if remotely, in much of the ancient critical theory which they would have known, including the *Ars Poetica,* and it is worth considering Aristotle, if only briefly, before moving back to England.

In chapter 22 of the *Poetics,* Aristotle discusses heroic style.[26] The heroic style requires "strange words and metaphor and lengthened words and everything that goes beyond ordinary diction." Heroic verse—that is, dactylic hexameter—is hospitable to all these forms, but "in iambic verse, because as much as possible it imitates conversation, only those words are appropriate that might be used in prose," a point already made in chapter 4, where Aristotle notes that "iambic is the most conversational of the meters, as we see from the fact that we speak many iambs when talking to each other, but few [dactylic] hexameters, and only when departing from conversational tone." In chapter 24 these ideas are developed further. The heroic meter, he says, "is the stateliest and most dignified meter, and therefore it is especially receptive to strange words and metaphors." Iambic meter, on the other hand, displays "the quality of action," that is, of drama. As Horace would later remark, it is "born for action" (*natum rebus agendis*).

Although Aristotle accepted the chorus, there is good reason to agree with the conclusion of Gerald Else that he considered it an anachronism.[27] Since drama imitates the actions of men and is the mode of imitation in which the author speaks through the characters, it is objectified in speeches. Else believes, again on persuasive grounds, that Aristotle considered iambic meter a useful convention but that its essential quality was its likeness to the prose of ordinary conversation.[28]

Underlying these concepts are two important principles derived from Aristotle's concept of method of imitation, that is, the relation of the poet to the work. Heroic poetry is the expression of the poet in narrative, and hence of the poet's epic voice. It is larger than life in its plot, its music, and its ornament, and it is hospitable to the marvelous and the irrational. Heroic meter expresses the epic voice and through it the other epic qualities. Tragedy on the other hand is an imitation of actions by men. The poet takes no part in it. He has no voice for he objectifies actions through the speeches of the characters. The language of drama should not call attention to itself but should express the motives and emotions of the characters. It should be as close to conversation as possible, and this is why the dramatists chose iambic meter rather than dactylic or trochaic meter. Whether or not Else is correct about Aristotle's openness to the idea of drama in prose, he is pointing in the right direction. Dramatic verse succeeds to the degree that it is not an object in itself but a window through which motive and emotion are visible.

IV

When he decided to translate the *Aeneid,* Surrey was fully aware of the quality of his original. He would have learned about dactylic hexameter in grammar school and would have been exposed to more sophisticated comments on the music of Vergil's line in Renaissance editions of Vergil. Since his decision to use blank verse had no precedent in English poetry, it must have been deliberate. One of his motives was obviously the simple one of imitating the lack of rhyme of his original. Along with this came the freedom to extend each passage to its proper length, which Trissino associated with heroic *enargia.* And along with enjambment and the verse paragraph came the opportunity—at times the necessity—to vary the expression through devices used only infrequently in the poetry of Chaucer and the translation of the *Aeneid* into couplets by Gavin Douglas. These devices are commonplaces in Vergil's Latin. They appear in Surrey's translation as corollaries of his verse form: suspension, inversion, parenthesis, substitution, counterpoint of syntactical against metrical rhythm, and moveable caesura, to name a few of the most prominent. They are called *figurae verborum* in Latin rhetoric and "auricular figures" by Puttenham in *The Arte of English Poesie*.[29] Along with these prosodic strategies came a vocabulary which, if not Latinate, moves in the direction of the "strange words and metaphor and lengthened words and everything that goes beyond ordinary direction" considered proper to epic verse by Aristotle, and is quite different from the homely vocabulary of Gavin Douglas.

The result is best displayed in Hartman's facsimile of the Day edition of book 4, since Tottel edited many of Surrey's most striking effects out of his later (1557) edition of books 2 and 4, but it can be sensed in any edition. It is a new kind of language with a unique melody created by the voice of the epic poet which runs through it and binds it together. At its best it anticipates the verse of *Paradise Lost*.

In spite of his success, few of the references to Surrey after Ascham (1570) suggest direct acquaintance with his translation. Webbe, for example, cites it as an example of quantitative hexameter. Meanwhile, the poets continued to experiment as though nothing had happened. Phaer translated the *Aeneid* into fourteeners, and Chapman used fourteeners for the *Iliad* and heroic couplets for the *Odyssey*. Critics like Webbe and Harvey discussed the possibility of a "reformed" versifying based on quantitative prosody, and experimenters like Stanyhurst, Spenser, Sidney, and Campion attempted to produce examples of the new form. As noted earlier, the only sustained sixteenth-century heroic poem in blank verse after Surrey is Marlowe's translation of the first book of Lucan's *Pharsalia*.

Let us now turn to Norton and Sackville. When they decided to write *Gorboduc* they had three precedents. The first was Latin drama. As we have seen, that precedent called for iambic trimeter, and the critical theory surrounding it explained the meter as one that approximated normal speech. The second precedent might have been Italian drama. If Sackville and Norton were aware of the Italian precedent, they would have known that blank verse is appropriate for drama not only because it is like conversation but also because it is adapted to the rapid ebb and flow of dramatic emotions. The third precedent was English drama. Here all that can be said is that the authors of school dramas such as *Roister Doister* and *Gammer Gurton's Needle* use the fourteener as the closest English equivalent to the relaxed iambic trimeter of Plautus and Terence. If the translations in Newton's Senecan anthology of 1581 are indicative of learned opinion at the time of *Gorboduc,* the fourteener was also considered the best English equivalent of the more formal iambic trimeter of tragedy. Thomas Preston's *Cambises* (written ca. 1561) illustrates the agreement of the playwrights with the translators. The fourteener is a loose meter capable of being broken into stichomythia or strung out for longer speeches. Because it is akin to what is usually called "common meter"[30] it may have seemed "conversational"—that is, like classical iambic meter—to those who used it. Although it is rhymed, its couplets are simple in comparison to the elaborate stanzas of English medieval drama. They are used clumsily, but they allow considerable flexibility. Their main problem is their singsong quality, which overrides the inflections of the speaking voice. They are, at the least, more appropriate for drama than Poulter's measures.

The verse of *Gorboduc* has been damned with faint praise so often that it may seem beyond redemption. Its most remarkable feature, aside from its sudden appearance in 1561, is that it is not verse in the sense that Surrey's *Aeneid* is verse. It is speech. Those who consider it drab may be criticizing it for exactly the quality that led Norton and Sackville to choose it. It does not have the sustained music that is so evident in the best passages of Surrey's *Aeneid,* nor does it have the singsong quality of the fourteener. One can only guess that its attraction was its difference from the fourteener. It did not call attention to itself unless asked, and it did not impose an arbitrary pattern on the development of the dialogue.

To the modern reader the idea that the verse of *Gorboduc* is "natural" or "conversational" may seem improbable. The verse itself is relatively simple. It is regular in its meter, generally end-stopped, loose in its syntax, and straightforward in its vocabulary. But it is served up in interminable formal speeches which seem to have little to do with action.

Although these speeches seem artificial today, they probably seemed entirely dramatic to Norton and Sackville. In the first place, there was the precedent of the long formal speeches in Seneca's tragedies. In the second, there was rhetoric. Rhetoric is, essentially, the theory of how to compose speeches. It provides elaborate formulas for their organization and ornamentation and explains how the formulas are to be used for different kinds of speeches. What is drama if not speeches? The prominence of deliberative and forensic speeches in *Gorboduc* can be traced to the facts that Norton and Sackville were both trained as lawyers and that *Gorboduc* was originally composed for performance before law students at the Inner Temple.[31] The rhetorical quality of the speeches in *Gorboduc* thus expresses a fervent desire on the part of its authors to write drama and their use of the best available theory to insure the success of the effort.

If the execution is weak, the concept is sound. It is the same concept that underlies the great set speeches in Shakespeare. Moreover, in spite of the pervasive influence of rhetoric, the verse of *Gorboduc* occasionally manages to be dramatic by modern as well as by Renaissance standards. The following bit of dialogue from the first scene illustrates both the virtues and the defects of its line at such moments:

Ferrex: My gracious lady and my mother dear,
Pardon my grief for your so grieved mind
To aske what cause tormenteth so your heart.
Videna: So great a wrong and so unjust despite,
Without all cause against all course of kind!
Ferrex: Such causeless wrong, and so unjust despite
May have redresse or, at the least, revenge.
Videna: Neither my son; such is the forward will,
The person such, such my mishap and thine.
Ferrex: Mine I know none, but grieve for your distress.
Videna: Yes, mine for thine, my son. A father? No.
In kind a father, not in kindliness.
Ferrex: My father? Why? I know nothing at all
Wherein I have misdone unto his Grace.[32]

There are end rhymes here that call attention to themselves and hint that at one time parts of the play may have been in stanzas. A strong rhetorical bent is evident which becomes almost overpowering in the long orations of the later acts, but the rhetorical strategies are those that facilitate understanding—parallelism, isocolon, parison, anaphora, and the like—and the play avoids more complex strategies of the extended period. The meter is regular and emphatic. It can be recited so as to emphasize its regularity, but it can also be spoken realistically.

In short, the verse is adapted for performance, and no actor would be satisfied merely to recite it. To perform it, the actors must analyze the situation of the speakers, which means that they have to read it as an expression of motive and emotion. In the example cited above, Videna is presenting her case in a manner calculated to cause maximum shock. Ferrex is at first ignorant, then shocked, and then angry. As the tension builds, the verse becomes more transparent, until in the last two lines it disappears completely.

My father?
Why? I know nothing at all wherein I have misdone unto his Grace.

It is this effect—which is, as Trissino noted in his *Poetics,* quite different from the heroic effect—that the verse of *Gorboduc* seeks to express, even though, as a pioneer work, the play does not fully understand what it is seeking to accomplish and seems wooden to readers used to the verse of *Hamlet* and *The Duchess of Malfi.*

V

To observe that there is a difference during the English Renaissance between epic and dramatic blank verse is only to begin the task of analysis. In English, blank verse is blank verse. No matter how emphatic the difference may be in theory, in practice the epic and dramatic forms are bound to overlap. The overlap is least frequent in comedy, which deals with everyday matters and low life, and most frequent in tragedy, which has essentially the same subject-matter as epic. Campion observes:

> These [quantitative iambic pentameters] are those numbers which Nature in our English destinates to the Tragick and Heroick Poeme: for the subject of them both being all one, I see no impediment why one verse may not serve them both, as it appears more plainly in the old comparison of the two Greeke writers, when they say *Homerus est Sophocles heroicus,* and againe *Sophocles est Homerus tragicus,* intimating that both Sophocles and Homer are the same in height and subject, and differ only in the kinde of their numbers.[33]

Turning to comedy, Campion adds:

> The Iambick verse in like manner being yet made a little more licentiate, that it may thereby the neerer imitate our common talke, will excellently serve for Comedies.[34]

Campion's point of view is typical of Renaissance criticism in that it is based on the assumption of a close relationship between genre and subject matter. Tragedy and comedy are members of the same genre (drama), but the subject matter of tragedy is more elevated than comedy. Epic is also elevated, and therefore epic and tragic verse will resemble each other. At the same time, Homer remains *heroicus* and Sophocles *tragicus.* The epic requirement is that the elevation never become bombast and that, at informal moments, the verse never fall into bathos, as it does, for example, in Milton's disastrous comment on the picnic in the Garden of Eden: "No fear lest dinner cool." *Dormitat bonus Miltonus.* Drama, on the other hand, observes the norm of characters engaged in dialogue. The tragic line should be elevated, but it is dialogue, not narrative. If the elevation is too artificial or is not sustained by a moment of great intensity it becomes undramatic. John Dennis suggests that recognition of this fact was one of Shakespeare's most important contributions to English drama:

> [Shakespeare] seems to have been the very Original of our *English* Tragical Harmony; that is the Harmony of Blank Verse, diversifyed by Disyllable and Trissyllable Terminations. For that Diversity distinguishes it from Heroick Harmony, and bringing it nearer to common

> Use, makes it more proper to gain Attention, and more fit for Action and Dialogue. Such Verse we make when we are writing Prose; we make such Verse in common Conversation.[35]

An excellent illustration of the difference between heroic and dramatic blank verse in the sixteenth century is provided by Marlowe's *Tamburlaine,* which comes as close, perhaps, as any Elizabethan drama to epic in both content and style. In spite of the overlap, however, the norm remains dramatic. At its most elevated the "mighty line" of *Tamburlaine* tends to be natural in its word order and end-stopped in its syntax, with heavy emphasis on parallelism and isocolon, and it generally avoids the complex, sustained periods of Surrey's epic style. In other words, it sounds complex, but it is designed for performance not recitation. It is, nevertheless, artificial. To say that it is "Marlovian" is to say that the poet's voice frequently overrides the voices of the characters. After his initial and spectacular success, Marlowe turned away from it. The style of the *The Jew of Malta, Edward II,* and *Dr. Faustus* is far more restrained than *Tamburlaine,* and in the final soliloquy of *Faustus* the "poetry" is absorbed almost completely by the passion of the dramatic moment.

The norm of Marlowe's epic blank verse is evident in the opening lines of his translation of the *Pharsalia:*

> *Caesars* and *Pompeys* jarring love soone ended,
> 'Twas peace against their wils; betwixt them both
> Stept *Crassus* in: even as the slender *Isthumos*
> Betwixt the *Aegean* and *Ionian* sea,
> Keepes each from other, but being worne away
> They both burst out, and each incounter other:
> So when as *Crassus* wretched death, who stayd them,
> Had fild *Assyrian Carras* walls with bloud,
> His losse made way for Roman outrages.[36]

This is less musical and perhaps cruder than Surrey's blank verse, but the tone may derive from the source, which describes the ugly death throes of a culture rather than its noble beginning. The verse fully expresses heroic *enargia.* It is sustained, ornamental, inverted, filled with strange words and similes, and larger than life.

The verse of the *Pharsalia* contrasts strikingly with the verse of *Tamburlaine.* Consider Tamburlaine's magniloquent self-justification in act I:

> I am a Lord, for so my deeds shall proove,
> And yet a shepherd by my Parentage:
> But Lady, this faire face and heavenly hew,
> Must grace his bed that conquers *Asia:*
> And meanes to be a terrour to the world,
> Measuring the limits of his Emperie

By East and West, as *Phoebus* doth his course:
Lie here ye weedes, that I disdaine to weare.[37]
(I.ii.34–41)

The lines are dramatic in spite of their artificiality. The meter is regular, the thought-units are relatively short, and the structure is loose rather than periodic. When the sentence threatens to become too long, it is cut off by a turn in the action. No one who tries to imagine these lines in performance can miss the speech emphasis required by the fact that Tamburlaine is addressing Zenocrate. The actor cannot merely recite the lines, he must articulate them, and in doing this he further defines the movement implicit in their syntax. The speech begins with a boast: "I am a Lord." It then requires a pause and a gesture that makes Zenocrate a participant even though she says nothing: "But Lady." It ends with another pause required by an action that is only suggested in the speech. Tamburlaine removes his outer garments, throws them on the ground, and turns away with the contemptuous comment, "Lie here ye weedes." This sensitivity to the dramatic qualities of blank verse dialogue seems to increase as Marlowe gains theatrical experience.

An equally striking contrast is evident if one compares a Vergilian passage from Surrey's translation with Marlowe's translation, adapted to performance, in *Dido Queen of Carthage*. Dido's rebuke of Aeneas is a moment in the *Aeneid* when Vergil's music veers to the colloquial, and hence to the dramatic norm, but even in this passage the difference between epic and dramatic expression is evident. In Surrey:

To Italy passe on by helpe of wyndes,
And through the flouds go searche thy kyngdome newe,
If ruthfull Gods have any power, I trust
Amyd the rockes thy hyre thou shalt fynde
When thou shalt cleape full oft on Didoes name,
Wyth buryal brandes I absent shall thee chase
And when cold death from lyfe these lymbes divydes,
My goste shall styll upon thee wayte,
Thou shalt abye and I shall here thereof.
Among the soules below this brute shall come.[38]

This is verse intended to be recited or read. In Marlowe's *Dido,* conversely, one catches glimpses of characters acting and gesturing and of voices continually changing inflection:

Goe go and spare not; seek out *Italy,*
I hope that that which love forbids me doe,
The Rockes and Sea-gulfes shall performe at large,
And thou shalt perish in the billowes waies,
To whom poor *Dido* doth bequeath revenge.

I traitor, and the waves shall cast thee up.
Where thou and false *Achates* first set foot.[39]

VI

As T. S. Eliot observed, Shakespeare seems to progress from a line that calls attention to itself through its strong meter and ornate rhetoric and frequent use of rhyme, to a line that is close to prose. This, however, is a generalization. It must be qualified by the fact that in the mature plays, elevated and rhetorical passages abound for the same reason that they occur in *Gorboduc:* tragedy requires elevated moments. Othello's initial narrative of his exploits, for example, moves toward the heroic and is imbued with the music that provided the title of G. Wilson Knight's famous essay. Yet the Othello music is never there for itself. It is functional. It expresses a quality of character essential to understanding Desdemona's love for Othello, and the speech, when well performed, keeps the music under control. Othello is a dramatic character, never an inspired bard. Later, the Othello music disintegrates, as Knight points out, in the passion of the climactic scenes. The disintegration is objectified by the contrast of the later with the earlier verse.

The norm for Shakespeare's mature style is not the Othello music but the voices of characters expressing motive and emotion. Here, so many examples could be offered that one will have to suffice. It is intended as a defining example only, since a detailed examination of the dramatic quality of Shakespeare's verse would require a separate essay. It is the familiar line that begins Antony's speech to the Roman mob:

Friends, Romans, countrymen, lend me your ears.

The line can be scanned if one considers the first two syllables an iambus:

Friĕnds, Rómăns, cóuntr̆ymén, lĕnd mé yŏur eárs.

Possible, but unlikely.

What could Shakespeare have intended here? The answer defines the gulf between the internal imperatives of heroic and dramatic blank verse. Heroic verse carries its explanation with it. It must, because the reader has only the words on the page. Dramatic verse, on the other hand, exists in several contexts: the context of the plot, the context of the character speaking, the context of the situation on the stage at the moment of the speech, and the context of the actor's interpretation of all the other contexts.

The plot of *Julius Caesar* makes Antony's speech the dramatic crisis of the play. Antony is addressing a mob that has just endorsed the cause of Brutus. The context on the stage is variable because it is determined in part by the set design, in part by the way the director handles the Roman mob, and in part by the actor's sense of what is happening. In this case, the sequence is relatively clear. When Antony begins to speak, the mob is still enthusiastically babbling about Brutus and either indifferent or hostile to Antony.

He tries to speak over the noise. His first word is conciliatory: FRIENDS! Perhaps the mob grows a little more quiet, but perhaps it grows louder and utters a few catcalls and jeers. Antony pauses and tries again in a louder voice, this time reminding the mob of its patriotism: ROMANS!

The sequence is problematic from here on, but one likely result of Antony's appeal is more jeering. He tries again, this time, perhaps, at the top of his lungs: COUNTRYMEN! The word unites the concepts of "friends" and "Romans." It works. The crowd becomes quieter.

Antony now tries a complete sentence: "Lend me your ears." Perhaps there is another pause to let the message sink in. Obviously it does sink in, because by the next sentence the crowd is sufficiently quiet for Antony to begin his oration: "I come to bury Caesar, not to praise him."

This reconstruction is not offered as definitive. There cannot be a definitive reconstruction of even such a simple bit of dramatic speech because every stage production will provide a slightly different set of contexts for it. The point is that the speech cannot be uttered without some sort of reconstruction, and a good reconstruction will explore at least as many aspects of the play as the one just offered. The result has less to do with verse than with the motives and passions of the characters. The single line is so broken up and the inflections so dependent on the specific moment in the unfolding action of the play that there is little possibility of retaining even the suggestion of a metrical scansion in its performance. Moreover, to perform it requires two voices: the voice of Antony and the voice of the mob. Each change in the voice of the mob changes the way that Antony's words are spoken.

This example suggests a generalization. It is because Shakespeare establishes the norm of dramatic speech in the major plays that their moments of lyricism and of sustained eloquence stand out, becoming functional, as in Othello's narrative of his exploits, rather than being absorbed into a general artificiality.

VII

There is a great deal more to be said about heroic and dramatic blank verse in the English Renaissance. Perhaps, however, enough has been said to provide a stopping point, if not a conclusion. The stopping point can be marked by repeating George Smart's statement quoted at the beginning of this paper. "Dramatic blank verse is quite different from non-dramatic, and the two ought not to be considered as one form." After all the necessary qualifications have been made, to recognize the difference is to gain a much deeper appreciation of what each, in fact, is.

(1984)

The Two Voices of Sidney's *Apology for Poetry*

Since Professor Kenneth O. Myrick's study in 1935, nearly all readers and editors of Sir Philip Sidney's *Apology for Poetry* have accepted the idea that it follows the organizational pattern of a legal oration recommended by classical and Renaissance manuals of rhetoric.[1] Sidney's choice of classical form is hardly surprising. Imitation was a hallowed tradition in Renaissance educational literature. The English *locus classicus* for the doctrine, Roger Ascham's *Schoolmaster,* offers a three-stage process for teaching children good Latin style: first, translating a Ciceronian work from Latin into English; second, translating the English back into Latin; and third, comparing the translation with the Latin original. Ascham believed that the habits so inculcated would persist in maturity; as he observes, "This aforesaid order and doctrine of imitation would bring forth more learning and breed up truer judgment than any other exercise that can be used."[2]

Sidney, of course, was no fanatic Ciceronian. Erasmus and, later, Sidney's friend Gabriel Harvey had written against mindless copying of the immortal Tully.[3] As is well known, Sidney was interested in Ramus; and according to tradition, he translated two books of Aristotle's *Rhetoric.*[4] In the *Apology,* Sidney mildly satirizes imitation of Cicero in his reference to "*Nizolian* Paper-bookes"[5]—that is, phrase books like the *Thesaurus Ciceronianus* by Marius Nizolius (1498?–1576), which had become a textbook for teaching imitation of Cicero; and everywhere in the *Apology* Ciceronian elevation is softened by Sidney's wit and his colloquial language. These facts suggest that Sidney took an independent and somewhat eclectic view of rhetorical theory. I will return to this point later. For now, I wish only to observe that the formality of Sidney's *Apology*—its adherence to the pattern of a legal oration—links it with the pre-Aristotelian phase of Renaissance criticism. Barnardino Daniello's *Poetics,* for example, written in 1536, just before the influence of Aristotle's *Poetics* began to be felt, uses the organization of Cicero's *De oratore* as a framework within which to deploy critical doctrine; while John Rainolds' *Oratio in laudem artis poeticae,* the first formal defense of poetry by an English author, is a set speech following the pattern of a rhetorical encomium.[6] The form of Sidney's *Apology* thus associates it with traditional rather than avant-garde critical theory in spite of its famous borrowings from the *Poetics*.

Myrick's analysis of the structure of the *Apology* has, so far as I know, never been questioned. Most classical and Renaissance rhetoricians agreed that an oration should have from five to seven parts. These are the exordium; the narration, or discussion of the background of the matter being considered; the proposition (statement of thesis); the partition; the confirmation (or proof); the refutation; and the peroration. The first four parts—exordium, narration, proposition, and partition—are parts of the introduction. They are usually brief and one or another of them can be omitted at the discretion of the speaker. Aristotle's *Rhetoric*, in fact, rejects the whole system as superfluous, claiming that there are only two essential parts of an oration, an introduction stating the author's thesis and the confirmation, or proof, of the thesis.[7] All rhetoricians agree that the confirmation is the most important part. Refutation is optional, with the qualification that it is especially desirable in a forensic speech, which also can make free use of such *ad hominem* appeals as invective, depreciation, and sarcasm. The peroration balances the introduction by restating the main points and making a final bid for the reader's (or listener's) sympathy.

Obviously, Sidney's *Apology* follows this general pattern. Myrick's application of the pattern, however, is somewhat procrustean. It assumes that Sidney is following Cicero and Quintilian scrupulously, whereas, as we have seen, his view of rhetorical theory was relatively independent. According to Myrick, the *Apology* has a formal exordium, narration, proposition, and partition. The exordium is the story of Signore Pugliano and his horse. The narration is the lengthy section on the history of poetry and the name for poet. The partition comes much later, when Sidney promises "to waigh this latter sort of Poetrie by his works, and then by his partes"(160).

Quite aside from the fact that this analysis produces a mammoth introduction, comprising about one-fifth of the entire *Apology*, it obscures what Sidney is doing. Quintilian's prescriptions for the narration stipulate that "we are to address ourselves constantly to the judge . . . we are to speak in our own person . . . [and] we are to introduce no argumentation."[8] Whether Sidney's comments on the antiquity of poetry are addressed to a judge and are "in his own person" can be doubted. It is obvious, at any rate, that they violate Quintilian's rule about avoiding argumentation. Earlier editors like A. S. Cook and J. Churton Collins never doubted that Sidney's comments were part of his proof; Collins, in fact, began the section that Myrick calls narration with the heading, "first argument in [poetry's] favor—its antiquity."[9] To be fair to Myrick, he recognizes the difficulty and seeks to mitigate it by observing that ancient rhetoric accords a measure of latitude to the narration. But this has the quality of special pleading. It is necessary only because of Myrick's insistence that there must be a one-to-one correspondence between the classical formulas and the *Apology*. The need for special pleading vanishes the moment we recognize Sidney's independent attitude toward rhetoric. If classical sanction is needed, the simplified approach toward organization found in Aristotle's *Rhetoric* provides it.

This is only the first of several problems that crop up as Myrick continues his analysis. As a result, his theory that the *Apology* has the form of a classical oration remains valid, but his outline seems out of focus. As one attempts to bring it into focus, certain new and interesting aspects of the *Apology* begin to appear.

I

The first step in modifying Myrick's outline is to concede that the section on the ancient honors of poets is just what empirical readers have always taken it to be—namely, the first section of Sidney's proof of the excellence of poetry. This reduces the introduction of the *Apology* to the length of two or three modern paragraphs. The anecdote of Signore Pugliano, who praised his horse so vehemently that he shamed Sidney into writing, remains, as Myrick suggested, the exordium. The thesis follows immediately, when Sidney remarks that after hearing Signore Pugliano, he was "prouoked to say something . . . in the defence of that my vnelected vocation, which if I handle with more good will then good reasons, beare with me, sith the scholler is to be pardoned that foloweth the steppes of his Maister" (150–51). The notion that Sidney is a mere tyro in comparison to the masterful Pugliano is amusing and a typical instance of Sidney's *sprezzatura,* but the humor need not obscure the fact that Sidney has directly and simply stated his purpose—to defend the art of poetry. His sentence is, in other words, a rhetorical proposition.

The proposition is followed by a passage that explains the method to be used and the reason why a defense of poetry is needed. The passage is not long, but it provides just the sort of background information proper for a narration and is, interestingly enough, "in Sidney's own person" in the sense of being a statement by the author (in his own person): "I must say," Sidney writes, "that as I haue just cause to make a pittiful defence of poore Poetry, which from almost the highest estimation of learning is fallen to be the laughing-stocke of children; so haue I need to bring some more auaileable proofes: sith the former [evidently, horsemanship] is by no man barred of his deserued credite, [while] the silly latter [that is, poetry] hath had euen the names of Philosophers vsed to the defacing of it, with great danger of ciuill war among the Muses" (151). The reference to "some more auaileable proofes" is an emphatic signal for the transition from introduction to confirmation. The next sentence begins, "And first, truly to al them that professing learning inveigh against Poetry, may iustly be objected, that they goe very neer to vngratfulnes, to seek to deface that which, in the noblest nations . . . hath been the first light-giuer to ignorance, and first Nurse." The word *first* announces the beginning of the confirmation. The reference to poetry as light-giver and nurse neatly identifies the topic that will be the basis of the proof in this section.

If this modest revision of Myrick's outline is acceptable, the *Apology* can be seen to have seven logical units: an introduction, three sections of proof of the excellence of poetry, a section refuting charges against poetry, a section on the current state of English poetry, and a conclusion.

Let us now turn from form to content. Sidney's first major proof of the excellence of poetry is the commonplace idea that it is "the first light-giuer to ignorance, and first Nurse." The classical source for this idea is Horace, who praises Orpheus for having "weaned savage forest tribes from murder and foul living; whence the legend that he tames fierce lions"; and Amphion, the founder of Thebes. It recurs in the earliest humanistic treatise on poetry, books 14 and 15 of Boccaccio's *Genealogy of the Gods,* and can be seen in its most striking form in Angelo Politian's Latin poem *Nutricia,* written under the influence of Florentine neo-Platonism.[10]

Comment on the wisdom of the earliest poets leads naturally to an extended discussion of the words for poet in various languages. As Sidney remarks at the end of the section, the argument is based on "the Etimologie of his [the poet's] names" (158). That is, not only is the substance of the argument highly traditional, but the strategy is also—it is the characteristic medieval strategy discussed by Curtius in his essay "Etymology as a Category of Thought."[11]

Three sorts of "names" are considered. The Indians called poems *areytos,* songs of praise; the Welsh, who are "the true remnant of the auncient Brittons," call their poets *bards.* Most important are the classical titles for the poet, *vates* and *poeta. Vates,* the Roman term, relates the poet to the priest and prophet. "So heauenly a title," Sidney writes, is appropriate to the "hart-rauishing knowledge" contained in poetry (154). Sidney not only agrees that the title is proper, he observes that it explains the "high flying liberty of conceit proper to the Poet, [which] did seeme to haue some dyuine force in it" (154). In other words, poetry is a kind of prophecy. Because it is different in kind from discursive expression, a different language—"high flying liberty of conceit"—is appropriate. Sidney illustrates the point with David's psalms, which reveal "that vnspeakable and euerlasting beautie to be seene by the eyes of the minde, onely cleered by fayth" (155). Without attempting to gloss this passage fully, we can observe that it points toward, if it does not express, an a-logical theory of poetry.

The word *poeta* is derived from Greek *poiein,* to make. Sidney devotes considerable space to it. The concept of making does not lead him, as it did Castelvetro, for example, to the concept of poetry as a rational craft, or *techne,* but in precisely the opposite direction, to the concept of the poet as inspired creator. Sidney begins by distinguishing between poetry and the other human "arts." Every other art, he says, has "the workes of Nature for his principall obiect" (155). Poetry, however, does not depend on nature. "Onely the Poet," he writes, "disdayning to be tied to any such subiection, lifted vp with the vigor of his owne inuention, dooth growe in effect another nature, in making things either better than Nature bringeth forth, or, quite a newe, formes such as neuer were in Nature, as the *Heroes, Demigods, Cyclops, Chimeras, Furies,* and such like: so as hee goeth hand in hand with Nature, not inclosed within the narrow warrant of her guifts, but freely ranging onely within the Zodiack of his owne wit" (156). Having liberated the poet from reliance on nature, Sidney identifies the source of his ability not with reason but with God: "giue right honor to the heauenly Maker of that maker, who, hauing made man to his owne likenes, set him beyond and ouer all the workes of that second nature, which in nothing hee sheweth so much as in Poetrie, when with the force of a diuine breath he bringeth things forth far surpassing her dooings" (157).

There is nothing particularly original in Sidney's arguments. Many of them had been a part of the humanist tradition in criticism since Boccaccio, while others, particularly the emphasis on the suprarational nature of poetry, are colored by the aesthetic theories of the Florentine neo-Platonists. The point is that Sidney's first proof places him squarely in the humanist camp and in direct opposition to the rationalist theories of poetry becoming fashionable in Italy. Poetry is the mother of civilization. It is allied to prophecy. Its language is characterized by "high flying liberty of conceit." It is dependent not on nature but on inspiration. It is suprarational and reveals "unspeakable beauty" seen only by the mind cleared by faith.

Sidney's second major proof is didactic. He observes that didactic poetry can be treated from two points of view, its "works" or social function, and its "parts" or genres.

The section based on "works" seeks to demonstrate that poetry is more successful than other disciplines, especially history and philosophy, in leading man to virtue. The discussion of ancient names for poet was speculative and strongly influenced by neo-Platonism. The discussion of "works" is more practical. It is Platonic, since Plato insisted that poetry, if admitted at all to the ideal republic, should be morally instructive. But the Platonism blends easily with the classical and Renaissance commonplaces of didactic criticism. Emphasis on the divinity of poetry takes second place to its capacity to teach delightfully. In spite of the use of terms from the *Poetics* like *spoudaioteron* ("more serious") and *katholou* ("universal"), Sidney wholly absorbs Aristotle into his didacticism.

Neither Aristotle's aesthetic theories nor the rationalistic tendencies stressed by continental writers like Scaliger and Castelvetro—the need for verisimilitude, the idea of the three unities, the distrust of inspiration, the criticism of exaggerated conceits—enter the discussion at all. From this section of the *Apology* one might conclude that Plato, Aristotle, and Horace were all in complete agreement concerning the function of poetry.

According to Sidney, poetry has a special capacity to move the reader, producing, "not *Gnosis* but *Praxis*" (171). It is highly significant that Sidney does not rule out certain kinds of poetry for being absurd rather than truly moving. His list of examples includes Sophocles and Homer; but it also includes Chaucer's *Troilus,* Dante's *Divine Comedy,* and *Amadis de Gaule,* although Sidney admits concerning the latter that "God knoweth [it] wanteth much of a perfect Poesie" (173). The same genial inclusiveness is allowed the poet in his subject matter. Dante takes in all, "from . . . his heauen to hys hell"; Aesop offers "pretty Allegories . . . vnder the formall tales of Beastes"; mythology offers Tantalus; and the Bible, Dives and Lazarus (166–69). All of these examples represent departures from the norm of imitation of nature, but far from being failures they are offered as examples of successful poetry. In fact, Sidney remarks that historians labor under a special difficulty because, unlike poets, they are "captiued to the trueth of a foolish world" (170).

The third and last of Sidney's major proofs of the excellence of poetry is announced by the sentence "I am content not onely to decipher [poetry] by his works . . . but more narrowly will examine his parts" (175). The "parts" are pastoral, elegy, comedy, tragedy, and heroic, in ascending order of excellence. Lyric, it should be noted, is placed above tragedy and below heroic poetry. This high estimate is based on Pindar, but Sidney also makes the famous reference to the *Ballad of Chevy Chase* here: "I must confesse my own barbarousnes: I neuer heard of the olde song of *Percy* and *Duglas* that I found not my heart mooued more then with a Trumpet" (178).

At the beginning of the section, Sidney touches on a highly controversial issue of Renaissance poetics, the question of mixed genres. "It is to be noted," he says, "that some Poesies haue coupled together two or three kindes, as Tragicall and Comicall, wher-vpon is risen the Tragicomicall. Some in the like manner haue mingled Prose and Verse, as *Sanazzar* and *Boetius.* Some haue mingled matters Heroicall and Pastorall" (175). Sidney's examples are of great interest. The debate over tragicomedy was just beginning. It would become more intense after the publication of Jason de Nores' *Discorso* (1586) and Guarini's *Il Verrato* (1588), and would have far-reaching implications for English critical response in the seventeenth century to Shakespeare and his contemporaries. The reference to Sannazaro and to the mixing of heroic and pastoral has obvious relevance to Sidney's own *Arcadia.* Sidney's conclusion is unequivocal endorsement: "that commeth all to one in this question, for, if seuered [the genres] be good, the coniunction cannot be hurtfull" (175).

Most of Sidney's remarks about individual genres repeat what he has said about the works of poetry. Pastoral, elegy, comedy, and tragedy teach virtue and expose vice. Lyric "giueth praise, the reward of vertue, to virtuous acts" (178) and "rayseth vp his voice . . . in singing the laudes of the immortall God." Heroic poetry "doth not onely teach and moue to a truth, but teacheth and moooueth to the most high and excellent truth" (179). In this category Sidney continues to be eclectic. Homer, Xenophon (for his prose *Cyropaedia*), Virgil, and Ariosto are all brought forward as worthy practitioners of heroic poetry.

The discussion of drama is also conventional. Comedy is defined in the Donatine manner as "an imitation of the common errors of our life" (176). Tragedy is explained in terms not much different from those used by William Baldwin in 1559 in the introduction to the *Mirror for Magistrates*. "High and excellent Tragedy," writes Sidney, " . . . openeth the greatest wounds, and sheweth forth the Vlcers that are couered with Tissue . . . maketh Kinges feare to be Tyrants, and Tyrants manifest their tirannicall humors" (177). Both of these definitions are directly opposed to the analysis of comedy and tragedy found in Castelvetro's commentary on the *Poetics*, which Sidney is usually said to have known well. Castelvetro, for example, considers comedy a way of pandering to the lust, cruelty, and vanity of a depraved audience: and tragedy devoid of moral significance.[12]

Sidney now comes to charges against poetry: first, that poetry is trivial, an entertainment rather than a serious occupation; second, that it is "the mother of lyes"; third, that it corrupts innocent youth; and last, that Plato banished poets from the *Republic*. These are restatements of the charges made by Plato in books 2, 3, and 10 of the *Republic*, although the second—that poetry lies—is expressed in a metaphor borrowed from Cornelius Agrippa.[13] Most of Sidney's answers are familiar from our earlier discussion and need not be repeated here. One answer, however, is new. This is Sidney's reply to the charge of lying. From the earlier arguments, we might expect the commonplace idea that poets conceal the bitter pill of morality under the pleasing sugarcoating of fiction. But Sidney offers something considerably more sophisticated. "The Poet . . . nothing affirmes, and therefore neuer lyeth . . . The Poet neuer maketh any circles about your imagination, to coniure you to beleeue for true what he writes. Hee citeth not authorities of other Histories, but euen for hys eentry calleth the sweete Muses to inspire into him a good inuention" (184–85). This does not deny truth-value to poetry—the appeal to inspiration implies a surer source of truth than that available through the reason. It does, however, deny that poetry is subject to rational verification; and by corollary, that verisimilitude is a significant factor in the success of a poem. In case the reader doubts that this is exactly what he means, Sidney makes his position explicit by applying it to tragedy: "What childe is there," he asks, "that, comming to a Play, and seeing *Thebes* written in great Letters vpon an olde doore, doth beleeue that it is *Thebes?*" (185). In short, Sidney's view of poetic truth, like his references to the divine breath, the superiority of poetry to nature, and the "high flying liberty" of poetic conceits, places him squarely in the humanist camp and in opposition to the Aristotelian and rationalist critics of his own day.[14]

Thus far, the movement of Sidney's argument has been simple and cogent. A short introduction is followed by three sections of defense and a refutation. These sections are unified by their relation to the main subject, and by their use of Platonic, neo-Platonic, and humanist commonplaces.

From the rhetorical point of view, the three sections of proof followed by the *refutatio* represent a neat though by no means extraordinary use of the standard formulae for a forensic oration. If we turn to content, a second organizational principle emerges. Recall that the first proof is etymological, depending on the classical names for poet. The second proof treats the "works" or social effect of poetry, and the third, the "parts" or genres of poetry. I suggest that this pattern is an adaptation of the standard schema devised by Alexandrian critics for the treatment of poetical questions. The schema required that a treatise on poetry be organized under three heads—*poeta, poesis, poema.*[15] Porphyrius, a late classical commentator, maintained that Horace followed this pattern in the *Ars Poetica,* and Porphyrius was regularly quoted by or assimilated into the notes in Renaissance editions of Horace. Another possible source is Scaliger, whom we know Sidney read, and who attempts to correlate the three-part critical schema with the four Aristotelian causes.[16] Whatever the source, however, Sidney would have been familiar with the scheme long before the 1580s and it seems very likely that the three categories of poet, poetry, and poem are reflected in his decision to base the proof of the excellence of poetry in the *Apology* on the etymologies of the poet's name, the general function of poetry, and the function of the individual genres or types of poem.

II

From the critical as well as the rhetorical angle, then, the sequence of three proofs and refutation is a finished argument. The defense of poetry is complete. The case rests. We expect Sidney to move directly to his conclusion, or *peroratio.* Instead, he surprises us by introducing a lengthy passage on the current state of English poetry. The passage clearly does not contribute to the defense of poetry. Its tone is hostile, and if anything, it undermines the defense by suggesting that English poets are guilty of many—if not most—of the charges that the enemies of poetry have levelled against it. Nor is the section required by the schema of *poeta, poesis, poema*. What is its function?

Myrick recognized this problem. His solution is curiously lame. On the one hand, he suggests that the passage on the English poets is a digression and cites a remark in book 2 of the *De oratore* that after the *refutatio* some authorities call for the conclusion or peroration; while others require, before the peroration, a digression for embellishment or amplification. At the same time that he labels the passage on the English poets a digression, however, Myrick argues that "though a digression, [it] is intimately related to the whole argument"; and that "organic unity could hardly be more complete."[17] This is a remarkable exercise in having one's organic unity and eating it too. And how a passage attacking English poetry can be "intimately related" to a defense of poetry is left unexplained.

These questions recur when we analyze the section on the English poets in detail. In the first place, the tone of Sidney's references to poetry so far has been genial. Even poets banned by Plato for traducing religion are let off with the excuse that they were led astray by false religion, whereas the philosophers, "shaking off superstition, brought in Atheisme" (191). In the discussion of English poets, on the other hand, the tone becomes negative, even garrulous. In England, says Sidney, "base men with seruile wits" write poetry; they are so depraved that "by their owne disgracefulnes [they] disgrace the most gracefull Poesie." They are called "bastard Poets" and "Paper-blurrers" (194–95). The reason for their bad reputations is "want of desert," and they "weary" their readers. Is this the same author who praised *The Ballad of Chevy Chase* along with Pindar, and could even find something good to say about *Amadis de Gaule?*

Along with the change in tone, there is a marked change in critical perspective. At the beginning of the section Sidney asks poets to "looke themselues in an vnflattering Glasse of reason"; and while still admitting that poetry is a "diuine gift," he insists: "the highest flying wit [must] haue a *Dedalus* to guide him. That *Dedalus* . . . hath three wings . . . that is, Arte, Imitation, and Exercise. But these, neyther artificiall rules nor imitatiue patternes, we much cumber our selues withall" (195). Earlier in the *Apology* the poet was said to range freely "within the Zodiack of his owne wit," guided by the supra-rational force of inspiration. Now the point of view is reversed. Instead of images of freedom and flight, emphasis is on control and guidance; instead of imagination, "unflattering reason" is to assist the poet, and it is symbolized by the figure of Daedalus, who restrains "highest flying wit" and who (with charitable allowance for the odd metaphor) is equipped with three wings representing "artificiall rules," "imitatiue patternes," and "exercise." Nothing has been said previously about "rules" of art even in passages where Aristotle has been named and quoted; but now they appear as central principles. By the same token, when the term *imitation* has been used, it has meant creation, especially the creation of fictions. Now, however, it is used in the rhetorical sense of "copying the masterpieces." Imitation in the sense of copying is not merely different from Sidney's earlier view, it is irreconcilable with the idea that the poet should range freely "onely within the Zodiack of his owne wit." It is the very sort of imitation advocated in the "*Nizolian* Paper-bookes" which Sidney has earlier satirized.

The comment on the third of the wings of Daedalus is equally surprising. Sidney complains, "where we should exercise to know, wee exercise as hauing knowne: so is oure braine deliuered of much matter which neuer was begotten by knowledge" (195). This is a shrewd anticipation of Bacon's strictures on poetry, but it appears to be a direct contradiction of that passage in which, after remarking that all other arts are subject to nature, Sidney had exclaimed, "Onlye the Poet, disdayning to be tied to any such subiection, lifted vp with the vigor of his own inuention, dooth growe in effect another nature, in making things either better then Nature . . . or, quite a newe, formes such as neuer were in Nature. . . ."

The source of the new attitudes in the *Apology* is obvious as soon as they are noticed. Sidney has abruptly turned from the Platonizing, idealizing tradition of humanist poetics to the critical and rationalistic poetic of neoclassicism that was gaining favor in Italy and France between 1560 and 1580. It is the newer poetic for which the negative tone, the tendency to equate criticism with censuring faults, is characteristic. It is also the newer poetic which tends to treat poetry in relation to rules, reason, and the norm of nature; which is suspicious (or in the case of Castelvetro, openly scornful) of inspiration; and which equates imitation with copying the masterpieces or nature.

As Sidney moves to specific authors and works, the neo-classic flavor of the discussion becomes increasingly pronounced. In the earlier parts of the *Apology* a catholic and inclusive view of literature prevails, which can accommodate *Amadis de Gaule* as well as Homer, and the *Ballad of Chevy Chase* along with Pindar. Now it becomes more exclusive. Chaucer is revered; but he lived in a "mistie time" and "had . . . great wants, fitte to be forgiuen" (196). Spenser is worthy; but "that same framing of his stile to an old rustick language I dare not alowe" (196), because, we are told, archaism was not used by Theocritus, Virgil, or Sannazaro. As for the Brand-X poets of the age, Sidney complains that most of them do not make sense: "let but most of the verses bee put in Prose, and then aske the meaning; and it will be found that one verse did but beget another, without ordering . . . which becomes a confused masse of words, with a tingling sound of ryme, barely accompanied with reason" (196). The norm of reason (not to mention the heresy of paraphrase) is very plain here. Ben Jonson, who sometimes wrote his compositions in prose before turning them into verse, would doubtless approve highly. But where, one wonders, are the "unspeakable beauties" seen only by the mind cleared by faith, not to mention the splendid but notoriously obscure verses of the "unimitable Pindar"?

The remarks on English drama are so obviously neo-classic that they require little comment. In spite of redeeming virtues, *Gorboduc* is "faulty both in place and time, the two necessary companions of all corporall actions" (197). This leads to the doctrine of the unities, which is said to be evident "both by *Aristotles* precept and common reason" (197). Of course, Aristotle does not teach the doctrine of the three unities. Gregory Smith asserts that Sidney "drew direct from Castelvetro" for his theory of the unities.[18] If so, the explicitness of Sidney's formulation of the doctrine is remarkable. Castelvetro's *Commentary* appeared in 1570, only about ten years before the *Apology* was written, and its discussion of the unities is tentative and diffuse. In effect, Sidney has taken an avant-garde critical theory and restated it as though it were a widespread, generally accepted critical commonplace.

The theory, itself, is in direct conflict with Sidney's earlier statements about poetry. It is based on the notion of verisimilitude—the idea that drama must be as close to reality as possible if it is to gain the belief of the audience. But Sidney has already argued that the special excellence of the poet is his freedom to transcend reality—to create "*Heroes, Demigods, Cyclops, Chimeras, Furies,* and such like" which never existed. Moreover, he has approved the whole range of non-realistic poetry from the "Pretty Allegories" of Aesop to the heaven and hell of Dante because of its power to move, to create *praxis,* not *gnosis*, while deploring the plight of the historian who is limited to "the truth of a foolish world." As we have seen, these remarks led Sidney to a denial that verification has anything to do with poetry—"the Poet . . . nothing affirmes, and therefore neuer lyeth"; the poet "neuer maketh any circles about your imagination"; and in respect to tragedy: "What childe is there that, comming to a Play, and seeing *Thebes* written in great Letters vpon an olde doore, doth beleeue that it is *Thebes?*" Clearly, the voice that speaks in these phrases is different from the voice that condemns English dramas for "grosse absurdities" (199) because they violate the unities.

Discussion of drama leads Sidney to consideration of mixed forms. He complains that English plays are "neither right Tragedies, nor right Comedies; mingling Kings and Clownes. . . . So as neither the admiration and commiseration, nor the right sportfulnes, is by their mungrell Tragycomedie obtained" (199). This is quite different in tone and conclusion from the earlier observation, "some Poesies haue coupled together two or three kindes, as Tragicall and Comicall, wher-vpon is risen the Tragicomicall. . . . But that commeth all to one in this question, for, if seuered they be good, the coniunction cannot be hurtfull" (175).

The last topic in the section on English poetry is diction. Concern for purity of diction, hostility toward strained conceits, and emphasis on the norm of nature in language, are characteristic of neo-classic poetic theory from Ben Jonson to Samuel Johnson. Sidney's remarks anticipate this attitude. Earlier, when discussing the poet as *vates*, he praised "that high flying liberty of conceit proper to the Poet." Now he speaks of the "Curtizanlike painted affectation" of English poets (202). The norm of nature is evident in his rejection of imagery based on unnatural natural history: "I think all Herbarists, all stories of Beasts, Foules, and Fishes are rifled vp, that they come in multitudes to waite vpon any of our conceits; which certainly is as absurd a surfet to the eares as is possible" (202–03). A little later, the same norm leads Sidney to question whether the untutored courtier, who follows what he "findeth fittest to nature," is not superior to the professor, who "vsing Art to shew Art . . . flyeth from nature, and indeede abuseth Art" (203). Whatever the merits of these views, they are hard to reconcile with the poet who "disdains subiection" to nature and brings forth things "far surpassing her dooings."

III

Close reading of Sidney's *Apology* leads inevitably, I think, to the conclusion that it speaks in two distinct and discordant voices. The first is the familiar voice of humanist poetics. Its basic debts are to Plato, the neo-Platonists, and Horace, and it is heard most clearly prior to Sidney in the writing of Boccaccio, Politian, Daniello, and Tasso. It results not only in a particular content in the *Apology,* but also to some degree in a particular form—the pattern of the forensic oration, using the *poeta, poesis, poema* schema attributed to Horace. Its tone is affirmative and inclusive. It welcomes classical and medieval poems, mixed forms, allegory and fable, and complex, sometimes obscure diction. Its key ideas are inspiration, the superiority of imagination to reason and nature, and the power of poetry, through its emotional appeal, to cause *praxis* rather than *gnosis.*

The second voice is that of incipient neo-classicism. Its tone is prescriptive, sometimes satiric or openly scornful. It is exclusive rather than inclusive, for it expects the critic to act as a judge, censuring and even excluding work which is flawed. It is suspicious of allegory and complex diction, and it ridicules mixed forms. Its touchstones are the subordination of imagination to reason and nature, the need for artistic "rules," the interpretation of imitation as copying masterpieces, and insistence on verisimilitude—with the corollary of the three unities—in drama.

One cannot, I believe, reconcile the section on the English poets with the main body of the *Apology.* The contradictions of attitude and precept are too fundamental. What we have, in fact, is a single document that reflects the tension in the last quarter of the sixteenth century between an older and a newer understanding of poetry, a tension whose elements are not fully defined in England until the seventeenth century.

Quite possibly, Sidney was unaware of the contradictions in the *Apology*. However, given the organization of the *Apology* and the fact that the neo-classic material is concentrated in a passage that is logically unrelated to the main argument, a few conjectures may be permissible.

In the first place, there seems to be little reason to doubt that the *Apology* was written around 1580–82 as a reply to Stephen Gosson's *Schoole of Abuse*, published in 1579 and dedicated to Sidney without his permission. Between 1579 and 1582 Sidney had leisure for literary pursuits and was in contact with the group of *literati* that Spenser half-facetiously called the Areopagus. The first draft of the *Arcadia* also probably belongs to this period. Since Gosson attacks poetry for immorality and blasphemy, his treatise would have called for a general defense rather than a criticism of English poets for their failure to observe the rules of art, the unities and the like. Thomas Lodge, who answered Gosson in 1579, took this tack, and there is no reason to believe Sidney would not have taken it also.

One further bit of information is relevant. We know that at some time between 1580 and 1586, the year of his death, Sidney went to considerable trouble to recast the original *Arcadia*. The difference between the two versions is striking. The first is a pastoral romance, informal in structure, and mingling prose and verse. Most contemporary scholars agree with Myrick that the second is an effort to make the work over into a heroic poem in prose, a form which Sidney discusses in the *Apology*. In spite of the fact that it is incomplete, the revised *Arcadia* is more formal, more elevated in diction, more didactic in sentiment, and more exemplary than the earlier version. If completed, the work would have had a five-book structure modelled on the five acts of a drama. Whether or not the interest of Sidney's sister, the Countess of Pembroke, in Robert Garnier and French neo-classic drama influenced Sidney is conjectural, but the possibility certainly exists. What is beyond dispute is that during the 1580s there was a change in Sidney's critical outlook which made him dissatisfied with the first *Arcadia*. This dissatisfaction led him in the direction of increased formalism.

It seems probable that the neo-classic material in the section of the *Apology* on English poets is related to this change. If so, we might tentatively speculate that the *Apology*, like the *Arcadia*, was written in two phases. Shortly after 1580, Sidney wrote an answer to Gosson in the form of a "defense" or "apology" for poetry. Its form was that of a forensic oration, and it consisted of introduction, three major proofs, refutation, and peroration. Complementing this traditional form, the argument rested on the traditional commonplaces of humanist poetics. Some time later, Sidney became interested in neo-classic poetics. The newer interest resulted in a critique of contemporary English poetry on grounds foreign to the earlier work. Nevertheless, this critique was interpolated between the refutation and the peroration of the original defense. Before a thorough revision was possible Sidney died, and when the *Apology* was printed the newer material remained incompletely harmonized with the old.

The result is that the *Apology*, as we have it today, speaks in two voices. The first is humanistic in the manner of Boccaccio, Politian, and Tasso; the second, neo-classic in the manner of Scaliger, Castelvetro, and Ben Jonson. The first voice, I think, is the one that speaks the more effectively for the poetry of the Elizabethan period.

(1972)

Three Types of Renaissance Catharsis

During the sixteenth century theories of catharsis were as abundant and as various as they are today. Some Renaissance theories were academic. They are found in critical treatises but have little or no relation to the living drama of the period. Others, among them the most influential, were not even labeled "theories of catharsis" by the writers who formulated them. If we define catharsis functionally as "the effect of tragedy," the most common Renaissance theories are in this category. Evidently, the academic theories served chiefly to display the learning of their bookish inventors, while the non-academic ones had a vital and direct effect on the work of practicing artists.

Among the practical theories, three are sufficiently well defined and influential to warrant more consideration than they have yet received in studies of Renaissance drama. As it happens, all three are found in English Renaissance criticism, and, perhaps more interesting, all are self-consciously utilized by Shakespeare. For convenience, they can be labeled respectively as the moral, religious, and literal theories of catharsis. Although these labels are not used by sixteenth-century writers, the theories themselves are sufficiently distinctive to be easily identified wherever they appear. Since they are all theories about the effect of tragedy and were formulated during what is generally considered the most vital period of English drama, they should have a lively interest not only for readers of Shakespeare, but also for historians and critics of tragedy as a literary genre.

I

The first of the three theories appears in its most obvious form in Thomas Heywood's *An Apology for Actors,* written around 1604. In the course of demonstrating the social utility of plays, Heywood remarks on their capacity for "attaching the consciences of the spectators, finding themselues toucht in presenting the vices of others."[1]

What Heywood means is that tragedies can so move individual spectators that they voluntarily divulge, as he says, "notorious murders, long conceald from the eyes of the world." He is so taken with this effect that he devotes some three pages to illustrating it.

The most lurid of his instances concerns a townswoman of Lynn in Norfolk who attended a play titled *Fair Frances*. It seems that the heroine of this Elizabethan soap opera had "mischieuously and secretely" murdered her husband and was thereafter harassed by his ghost, which appeared "at diuers times . . . in most horrid and fearefull shapes." While watching the avenging ghost, the townswoman of Lynn "suddenly skritched and cryd out Oh my husband, my husband! I see the ghost of my husband fiercely threatning and menacing me." Questioned by other members of the audience, she confessed "vn-urged" that she had murdered her own "real-life" husband. Later, she repeated her confession before a magistrate, by whom she was promptly sent to the scaffold. Heywood adds, "That this is true, as well by the report of the Actors as the records of the Towne, there are many eye-witnesses of this accident yet liuing, vocally to confirme it."[2]

Although Heywood is content to tell the story, the psychology underlying it is plain enough. The perpetrator of an undiscovered crime is troubled by a guilty conscience. He is in torment. Confession, the only way to relieve the pain, is prevented by his fear of the consequences. Seeing the crime enacted on the stage can make the pangs of conscience so intense that the need for relief via confession becomes stronger than the fear of exposure. The confession has two beneficial results. First, a crime is solved and a criminal punished. Society is strengthened, if only minutely, by the clearing up of an injustice. In fact, this is one of Heywood's chief arguments for the social utility of drama. Second, and equally important, confession brings relief to the criminal (or sinner). It is the first step toward moral regeneration. The cathartic value of such a step—the purgation of guilt and fear—is obvious. Confession, as the divines say, is good for the soul. Psychology merely underwrites the religious formula. The criminal who confesses after seeing his crime reenacted on the stage is in the same position as the mental patient relieved of guilt symptoms by recalling (and reliving) the experiences that caused them—a technique that Sigmund Freud aptly called "the cathartic method" when he first began using it in the 1880s. Of course, Freud's method was anticipated by Dostoevsky in *Crime and Punishment* as well as by Heywood.

The idea of moral catharsis presented in *An Apology for Actors* may seem rather crude and simplistic to a modern reader. It is used, however, with remarkable effectiveness in Shakespeare's *Hamlet*. After act 1, it will be recalled, Hamlet suspects Claudius of having murdered his father but is also worried that the ghost who has revealed the murder to him may be lying. At the end of act 2 Hamlet devises a plan to test the ghost's veracity. He explains the plan as follows:

I have heard
That guilty creatures sitting at a play,
Have by the very cunning of the scene
Been struck so to the soul that presently
They have proclaim'd their malefactions;
For murder, though it have no tongue, will speak
With most miraculous organ. I'll have these players
Play something like the murder of my father
Before mine uncle. I'll observe his looks;
I'll tent him to the quick. If 'a but blench,
I know my course.

(II.ii.584–594)

Hamlet is referring to the play titled *The Murder of Gonzago,* which he has modified to bring out its parallels with the story told him by the ghost, and which is actually presented before the Danish court in act 3. Note that Claudius may respond to it in three ways. First, he may simply enjoy it, showing no signs of discomfort. If so, Hamlet evidently plans to delay his revenge or abandon it on the assumption that the ghost lied. Second, Claudius may behave like the townswoman of Lynn and "proclaim his malefactions." Third, he may be strong enough to endure the play without confessing, but his behavior may betray his guilt: "if 'a but blench, I know my course."

In the context of Shakespeare's play, the most desirable of the three possibilities is the second, public confession. The Danish court and people accept the legitimacy of Claudius' rule. Unlike Hamlet and the theater audience, they are not aware that a crime has been committed. They may, in fact, share the suspicion of Claudius, suggested in at least two places (I.ii.108–109; II.ii.248–266), that Hamlet is "ambitious" for his father's crown. If Claudius does not "proclaim his malefactions"—that is, if the court and people are not made aware of the King's guilt—Hamlet's revenge will appear to be a brutal political assassination and the kingdom may be plunged into turmoil. As Rosencrantz remarks, "The cease of majesty / Dies not alone, but like a gulf doth draw / What's near it with it" (III.iii.15–17). Denmark, then, desperately needs the sort of social purification that Heywood (and Hamlet) feel tragedy can provide. The point is neatly underscored by Shakespeare's use of the imagery of disease to characterize Denmark's condition. A confession by Claudius would literally purge the kingdom of the sickness that is destroying it.

Unfortunately, as we all know, Claudius does not confess. This may be because Hamlet lacks faith in his own strategy and spoils the play's effect by his interruptions. At any rate, instead of confessing, Claudius abruptly leaves the hall. To Hamlet this is a clear admission of guilt, and most producers of the play accept his interpretation. On the other hand, the precise way in which Claudius should behave when leaving is ambiguous in Shakespeare's text. The only characters who do not know of the murder and who comment on the King's departure are Guildenstern and Gertrude, and both of them believe that he left in a rage as a result of Hamlet's tactless insults. The fact is that no matter what Hamlet may think and Shakespeare's audience may know, to the members of the court Claudius seems in the right and Hamlet in the wrong. The possibility of a public redress of justice has been lost. We are vividly reminded of this fact during the last scene of the play, when the reaction of the courtiers to Hamlet's attack on the King is the horrified cry, "Treason! treason!" (V.ii.315). Even at the end they are unaware of Claudius' guilt.

But seeing one's crimes enacted in the theater has personal as well as public significance. When Guildenstern informs Hamlet of the King's "choler," Hamlet replies with the brutal pun, "for me to put him to his purgation would perhaps plunge him into far more choler" (III.ii. 297–299). Whatever sense we attribute to Hamlet's word "purgation," he has just made an attempt to "put Claudius to it," and in spite of his momentarily triumphant mood, he has failed. There has been no confession, not even an unambiguous sign of guilt. We may assume that Heywood's gentlewoman of Lynn went to the scaffold with an easy conscience, even as Mistress Anne Frankford in his play *A Woman Killed with Kindness* died in the odor of sanctity. Claudius, on the other hand, feels intensified torment, which vents itself publicly as rage.

The anguish of conscience which the courtiers interpret as rage is movingly revealed in the soliloquy that Claudius utters in the scene following the play-within-a-play. As Claudius attempts to pray, he expresses himself in images of horror and self-revulsion. His offense has the stench of a decaying animal: it is "rank, it smells to heaven!" He, himself, is as vile as Cain, the archetypal criminal: "It hath the primal eldest curse upon't / A brother's murder" (II.iii.37–39). Because the impulse to repent is blocked by the desire to retain the crown, the soliloquy develops as a series of paradoxes expressing bafflement, frustration, and entrapment:

> My stronger guilt defeats my strong intent,
> And, like a man to double business bound,
> I stand in pause where I shall first begin,
> And both neglect.
>
> (III.iii.40–43)

And:

> Try what repentance can. What can it not?
> Yet what can it when one cannot repent?
> O wretched state! O bosom black as death!

O limed soul, that, struggling to be free,
Art more engag'd.

(III.iii.65–69)

In short, instead of cooperating with the tragic therapy like the townswoman of Lynn, Claudius resists it. The result is not catharsis—not a calming of the mind—but, as we might say, an anti-catharsis, an intensification of the perturbations associated with guilt.

II

A second, rather more complex, theory about the effect of tragedy is found in Elizabethan discussions of the requirement that drama observe poetic justice. It is a commonplace of the period that at the end of a drama the characters should be rewarded and punished according to their virtues and vices. William Baldwin wrote of the "tragedies" in the 1559 edition of *A Mirror for Magistrates:* ". . . here, as in a loking-glas, you shall see (if any vice be in you) howe the like hath bene punished in other heretofore, whereby admonished, I trust it will be a good occasion to move you the soner to amendment."[3] And in his *Apology* Heywood applies the same theory to the formal drama that had come into being since *A Mirror for Magistrates:*

> If we present a Tragedy, we include the fatall and abortiue ends of such as commit notorious murders, which is aggrauated and acted with all the Art that may be, to terrifie men from the like abhorred practises. If wee present a forreigne History, the subject is so intended, that in the liues of *Romans, Grecians,* or others, either the vertues of our Country-men are extolled, or their vices reproued, as thus, by the example of *Caesar* to stir souldiers to valour, & magnanimity: by the fall of *Pompey,* that no man trust in his owne strength: we present *Alexander,* killing his friend in his rage, to reproue rashnesse: *Midas,* choked with gold, to taxe couetousnesse. . . .[4]

The belief that the aim of literature is moral instruction—and that it achieves this aim by making the punishment fit the crime—underlies a vast (and often rather tedious) body of homiletic writing from Aesop's *Fables* through the morality plays to *Uncle Tom's Cabin* and beyond. The surprising fact about this belief is that, on the one hand, it is almost universal in Elizabethan criticism, while, on the other, it is often hard to discern in the tragedies of the major Elizabethan playwrights. Marlowe, Shakespeare, Chapman, Webster, and Ford, to name only the most obvious, simply do not write tragedies like those described by Heywood, in which the protagonist exemplifies a neatly labeled moral flaw that the audience is taught to "abhor" by the catastrophe.

Let us file this fact away for future reference. For now, we will merely observe that poetic justice has—like moral catharsis—both social and personal significance. The social aspect is easy to define. Society is obviously strengthened if its members learn, when they visit the theater, to cultivate virtue and shun vice.

The personal aspect is more difficult. Literary history, not to mention countless Grade B movies and television serials, teaches us that poetic justice is a standard formula for popular entertainment. In fact, one of the distinguishing features of much of what has been considered "serious literature" since the Victorian period is that it self-consciously *rejects* poetic justice. Since very few people learn their morality from the theater, the enduring appeal of poetic justice must come from the fact that it satisfies needs that go much deeper than simple moral improvement.

We can begin to get an insight into these needs by recognizing that poetic justice is a conscious or unconscious imitation of ideal justice. Ideal justice, however, is not a legal but a religious concept. It is defined not by jury trials and rules of evidence but by eschatology, and its two defining characteristics are a judge who is omniscient and a judgment perfectly suited to the offense. Shakespeare's Claudius makes the contrast nicely. Having observed that in the real world justice is often imperfect, since "the wicked prize itself buys out the law," he adds:

> But 'tis not so above:
> There is no shuffling; there the action lies
> In his true nature; and we ourselves compell'd
> Even to the teeth and forehead of our faults,
> To give in evidence.
>
> (III.iii.60–64)

The fact that plays emphasizing poetic justice are modeled on—or symbolic of—ideal justice is perhaps sufficiently evident from the quite inhuman assurance with which rewards and punishments are parceled out at their conclusions. It also helps to explain the curious tendency of such plays to end with trials in which the judge is either supernatural, or has supernatural powers, or, at the very least, possesses an unrealistic fullness of knowledge concerning the issues. In the *Eumenides* of Aeschylus, to take an example from Greek drama, the judgment is guaranteed by the fact that the judge is no less a figure than the Goddess Athene herself. Shakespeare's *Measure for Measure* is more typical of modern practice, which likes to cover the supernatural with a veneer of rational "explanation." Shakespeare's Duke of Vienna is definitely human, but he spends most of the play disguised as a friar who is able to share the most private thoughts of the other characters. The result is that when he acts as judge in act 5 he has acquired a quite un-judicial omniscience that enables him to deal out perfect justice, tempered with mercy. Among less sophisticated examples of the arraignment play are Shakespeare's *Merchant of Venice* and Ben Jonson's *Every Man in His Humour.* That such resolutions are universal is shown by almost every episode of the Perry Mason television series. Indeed, the typical ending of a Perry Mason episode exactly parallels what Claudius imagines about the Last Judgment. Each episode ends with a trial, and at the end of every trial, with monotonous regularity, the criminal is overwhelmed by a nightmarish impulse to confess—to "give in evidence, even to the teeth and forehead of his faults."

If poetic justice can be understood as an attempt to imitate or symbolize dramatically the ideal of perfect justice, the satisfaction that it provides is best understood in the same context. Evidently, the satisfaction comes from having one's deepest feelings about what is right confirmed by the action on the stage. Life is imperfect, mysterious, frustrating; it seldom works out as we feel it should. A drama based on poetic justice, on the other hand, offers what life cannot. One says of the villains that "they got what they deserved" and of the hero and heroine, "they were married and lived happily ever after."

Like poetic justice, this reaction is sharply defined in traditional thought about divine Judgment. For better or for worse, the most authoritative version of Judgment in the Christian tradition is the Book of Revelation. In chapter 16, St. John has a vision of angels pouring God's vials of wrath onto the sinful earth. As the third angel empties his vial, he exclaims, "Thou art righteous, O Lord . . . because thou hast judged thus. For they have shed the blood of saints and prophets, and thou hast given them blood to drink; for they are worthy" (Rev. 16: 5–6). In other words, instead of arousing pity, the terrible judgment brings righteous satisfaction. One assumes, of course, that St. John's angels do not take a sadistic delight in suffering. Rather, their satisfaction is a by-product of their vision of the completion of God's plan for measuring out to the wicked exactly what they have merited. As the angel observes, "they are worthy"—they have gotten what they deserved.

This is logically understandable, but it does seem a trifle grim. Therefore we turn with relief to the much more congenial expression of the same idea in Dante's *Divine Comedy.* Here again the poet examines human affairs from a transcendent vantage point, but his presentation of this perspective develops only gradually. As Dante passes through the Inferno, he is as troubled as his reader by the suffering that he encounters. Ironically, the pagan Virgil, his guide, often has to reprove him for excessive pity toward the victims of Christian justice. Gradually, as he ascends toward Paradise, his vision clears. On the third level of Paradise he meets the nun Piccarda, who perfectly expresses the lesson that he—and his readers—are to have learned from the preceding journey, with the single line "In His will is our peace" (*Paradiso*, III, 85). That is, in life, where we see through (or in) a glass darkly, pity is a virtue. If we could see truly, however, the pity would be replaced by the deep peace that comes from knowing the perfection of the whole.

To return now to drama, the spectator watching a play based on poetic justice stands in the same relation to the action on the stage as St. John's angel and Dante's saints stand to the world of experience. The spectator sees the dramatic world as these beings see the human world looking down on it from Paradise. This explains, incidentally, why so little pity is elicited for the villains of melodrama: we know of them all that there is to know, and we enjoy seeing them get their comeuppance just as surely as St. John's angel is pleased by the sight of the wicked being punished. But this implies something about the way in which the dramatic world is presented. If the salient characteristic of everyday experience is mystery, the salient characteristic of drama shaped according to poetic justice is clarity. The playwright obviously cannot make his spectators into angels or saints. Instead, he achieves his goal by making the dramatic world simpler than the world of experience. It is life, as it were, purified—the world as it might appear if we could for once penetrate its obscurity. The result is a sense of satisfaction—a catharsis—that meets a deeply felt, inarticulate, but essentially religious, need.

To follow these ideas in Elizabethan criticism we need go no further than Sir Philip Sidney's *Apology for Poetry,* the most eloquent critical statement of the age. Throughout the *Apology* the idea that poetry should conform to poetic justice is central. Frequently poetry is contrasted with history, which, because it lacks poetic justice, can be confusing and morally injurious. In tragedy, Sidney says,

> . . . if euill men come to the stage, they euer goe out (as the Tragedie Writer answered to one that misliked the shew of such persons) so manacled as they little animate folkes to followe them. But the Historian, beeing captiued to the trueth of a foolish world, is many times a terror from well dooing, and an incouragement to vnbrideled wickednes.
>
> For see wee not valiant *Milciades* rot in his fetters? The iust *Phocion* and the accomplished *Socrates* put to death like Traytors? The cruell *Seuerus* liue prosperously? The excellent *Seuerus* miserably murthered?[5]

Sidney is not content simply to assert the moral superiority of the poet's world to the historian's. He is interested in the nature of this world, and the burden of his comments is that the poet's world has the quality of transcendence. The maker who creates it is momentarily lifted out of himself by divine inspiration. He sees, as it were, with the vision of

St. John's angels or Dante's saints. Our world, says Sidney, is "brasen," but the poet's is "golden." History is "captiued to the trueth of a foolish world," but the poet "disdaning to be tied to any such subiection, lifted vp with the vigor of his owne inuention, dooth growe in effect another nature." And in perhaps the best known passage in the *Apology* Sidney urges his readers to

> . . . giue right honor to the heauenly Maker of that maker, who, hauing made man to his owne likenes, set him beyond and ouer all the workes of that second nature, which is nothing hee sheweth so much as in Poetrie, when with the force of a diuine breath he bringeth things forth far surpassing her dooings, with no small argument to the incredulous of that first accursed fall of *Adam:* sith our erected wit maketh vs know what perfection is, and yet our infected will keepeth vs from reaching vnto it.[6]

Here the religious basis of the idea of poetic justice is made explicit. The poet is godlike—a maker—in creating his work. As he composes, his wit is "erected" and a "divine breath" inspires him. The work that results has a "perfection" that in some way parallels the vision of Adam before the fall—that is, before the darkness of sin closed around man's mind.[7]

Sidney's ideal is noble, but—crude dramatic homilies like Heywood's *Fair Frances* aside—it seems to have little application to major Elizabethan tragedies. Attempts have been made to read Shakespeare's tragedies as homiletic—*Romeo and Juliet* a warning against disobeying parents (the moral of Shakespeare's source); *Macbeth* a warning against ambition; *Hamlet* a warning against vacillation; *Lear* a warning against ingratitude or wrath; and so forth. A serious effort to apply this approach in depth and in terms of Elizabethan psychology was made by Lily Bess Campbell in *Shakespeare's Tragic Heroes: Slaves of Passion.*[8] But all of these efforts, from naïve to sophisticated, seem rather inadequate beside the plays themselves. The problem seems to be that poetic justice as conceived by Heywood and Sidney is the wrong formula for tragedy. It leads to melodrama, and its typical result is not "in His will is our peace" but the smug satisfaction of St. John's angels: "they got what they deserved." Although there is some parceling out of rewards and punishments at the end of *King Lear,* "they got what they deserved" is probably the last thought that Shakespeare wanted to induce in his audience. Indeed, the chief effect of Albany's pious comment at the end of the play—

> All Friends shall taste
> The wages of their virtue, and all foes
> The cup of their deservings
>
> (V.iii.302–304)

is to make him look slightly ridiculous.

The most obvious place for poetic justice and the sort of catharsis associated with it is comedy. As explained by Elizabethan critics, poetic justice requires that no truly good or noble person suffer irrevocable harm and that all but the most villainous be redeemed after chastisement. This is in accord with the religious view of which poetic justice is a symbol. Even the Fall of Man, according to theologians from St. Augustine to Milton, was fortunate—a *felix culpa*—and the classic expression of religious catharsis is spoken by a Christian nun in Paradise in a poem conspicuously labeled "comedy." It is only natural, then, that Sidney's golden world should be most evident in comic dramas. *The Merchant of Venice, Twelfth Night,* and *As You like It* all depend for their effect on unexpected but inspired solutions to the problems of their characters. The qualities of the golden world emerge most explicitly, however, in Shakespeare's romances, which provide the supreme instances of religious catharsis in English drama. It seems quite possible, moreover, that Shakespeare understood both the effect and its religious basis, for in the romances he consistently emphasizes the interplay between supernatural or divine forces and the destinies of the characters. At the end of *The Tempest* Prospero is so much the *deus ex machina* that he has been equated with God by at least one allegorizing critic; and if this interpretation commits the error of converting a symbol into a sign, it remains true that Prospero resolves the problems of *The Tempest* in the manner of the *deus ex machina*—with magic and the assistance of a supernatural agent. But perhaps the most explicit statement of the point is at the end of *Pericles,* when Gower steps forth to interpret the outcome of the play as the completion of poetic justice by providential means:

> In Antiochus and his daughter you have heard
> Of monstrous lust the due and just reward:
> In Pericles, his queen, and daughter; seen,
> Although assail'd with fortune fierce and keen,
> Virtue preserv'd from fell destruction's blast,
> Led on by heaven, and crown'd with joy at last.
> (V.iii.86–91)

III

Heywood's moral and Sidney's religious catharsis lead to worthwhile insights into Elizabethan concepts of drama, but they do not, as we have seen, tell us much about the concepts underlying the major Elizabethan tragedies. Fortunately, we have some extremely suggestive hints on this subject from no less an authority than Shakespeare himself.

Before considering these hints, it will be useful to summarize a recent article on Aristotle's *Poetics* by Professor Leon Golden.[9] According to Golden, Aristotle introduces his theory of catharsis in chapter 4 (not chapter 6) of the *Poetics,* where he asserts that the cause of imitative art is the pleasure it provides. Imitative pleasure, moreover, is not a generalized emotion but a quite specialized one associated with learning. As Aristotle says, "The reason for the delight in seeing a picture is that one is at the same time learning—gathering the meaning of things; e.g., that the man there is such and such [a type]" (1448^{b} 9–12). What he evidently has in mind is that when seeing a properly constructed work of art, the viewer gains a sense of the generic nature of the object represented. This explains why objects that are unpleasant when encountered directly—Aristotle mentions the lower animals and corpses—can bring pleasure when presented in a work of art. Aristotle applies this theory to tragedy in chapter 9 of the *Poetics,* where he differentiates poetry from history. An artistic plot, he says, should be constructed along lines of probability and necessity; and therefore "poetry is something more philosophic and of graver import than history, since its statements are of the nature rather of universals, whereas those of history are singulars" (1451^{b} 5–7).

Tragic catharsis, then, is the result of learning something about the events forming the tragic plot. What we learn is the way the events happened according to necessity and probability, rather than the way they may be set down by the historian, whose job is to record, not necessarily to explain, them. Golden argues that the best translation of Greek *katharsis* is "clarification" rather than "purgation." It occurs at the end of a proper tragedy, and it is enjoyable because it is a form of learning. It is analogous, perhaps, to the pleasure that accompanies the solution of a puzzle; but in tragedy it is much more significant, for it involves the discovery of coherence in a world that usually seems dark and chaotic.

The reason for this foray into the *Poetics* is not to solve the problem of what Aristotle meant, although Golden is undeniably persuasive. It is, rather, to establish a background of ideas sufficient to cope with the sort of catharsis that Shakespeare seems to present in *Hamlet.* Since the first two kinds of catharsis have been labeled moral and religious, the present one can be called "literal" catharsis. It does not require a happy (or sad) ending, a spontaneous confession, or the completion of poetic justice. It requires only that the play be experienced exactly as presented and asserts only that when the play is experienced in this way the spectator emerges with a deepened—and hence pleasurable—understanding of its events.

Let us now turn to the final scene of *Hamlet.* Claudius is dead, but Hamlet, too, is mortally wounded. He forgives Laertes and then turns to the Danish court:

> You that look pale and tremble at this chance,
> That are but mutes or audience to this act,
> Had I but time as this fell sergeant, Death,
> Is strict in his arrest, O, I could tell you—
> But let it be. Horatio, I am dead:
> Thou livest; report me and my cause aright
> To the unsatisfied.
>
> (V.ii.326–332)

We learn several things from these words. First, that the courtiers are terrified by what they have seen. Within a few minutes they have witnessed the murder of the man they considered the rightful king (recall their cry of "Treason! treason!" [l. 315] and have also heard accusations of dire treachery by Laertes and Hamlet. They are "audience to this act" in the sense of having been present while it occurred, but they are not audience to the action of the play as it has unfolded before the spectators in the theater. They are dumb with fear precisely because they do not understand what has happened.

Hamlet makes no effort to console the courtiers. Instead, his chief desire is to tell his story. "Had I but time" is followed by "O, I could tell you" and then, as he feels his life ebbing, his request to Horatio, "report me and my cause aright / To the unsatisfied" (ll. 328–332).

Although untouched by the fear that overcomes the courtiers, Horatio is so shaken by Hamlet's words that he threatens to commit suicide. Hamlet stops him with a second petition:

> O God! Horatio, what a wounded name,
> Things standing thus unknown, shall live behind me!
>
> (V.II.336–337)

With his dying breath Hamlet repeats the petition a third time:

> So tell him, with th' occurrents, more and less.
> Which have solicited—the rest is silence.
>
> (V.II.349–350)

Even though Hamlet is now dead, the theme of "telling his story" continues to dominate the dialogue. As soon as the ambassadors have reported, Horatio requests,

> give order that these bodies
> High on a stage be placed to the view;
> And let me speak to th' yet unknowing world
> How these things came about.
>
> (V.II.369–372)

The theme is repeated in Fortinbras' reply:

> Let us haste to hear it,
> And call the noblest to the audience.
> (V.ii.378–379)

This is followed by a last comment from Horatio:

> But let this same be presently perform'd
> Even while men's minds are wild, lest more mischance
> Or plots and errors happen.
> (V.ii.385–387)

We need consider only the essentials of the preceding lines, but we should take them seriously. A terrible and incomprehensible event has taken place. It has made the courtiers dumb with fear (l. 326); it has induced Horatio to threaten suicide (l. 334); it has filled Fortinbras with "woe or wonder" (l. 355); and it has left men's minds "wild" and ripe for "plots and errors" (ll. 386–387); one strategy and one strategy only is offered to remedy this situation. First Hamlet, then Horatio, then Fortinbras insists that Hamlet's "story" must be told. Furthermore, it must be told "aright" (l. 331) and "with the occurrents, more and less, / Which have solicited" (ll. 349–350)—a statement that may be paraphrased, "with all the circumstances, great and small, that have contributed." Although there is no need to insist on the parallel between telling Hamlet's story "on a stage" before "an audience of the noblest" and producing the play *Hamlet*, the ambiguity of the language points to a fact that is of prime importance. If Horatio tells Hamlet's story "aright" and "with the occurrents, more and less" he can only tell it one way: that is, as closely as possible to the way Shakespeare told it. The fact is that Shakespeare's play is absolute truth as far as our knowledge of the affairs of Denmark is concerned. Given the contract between the dramatist and his audience to make every scene and line count, we must assume that everything in the play is relevant or seemed so to Shakespeare when he wrote it. To omit or change part of the story as Shakespeare told it would be to falsify it by omitting "occurrents," no matter how small, that in some way "solicited" the final result.

Let us pursue this train of thought one step further. What is the anticipated result of telling the story? Hamlet wishes his reputation to be cleared, but Hamlet's reputation is of minor concern to the terrified courtiers. Horatio informs us quite explicitly what the telling of his story is intended to accomplish. It will have two effects. In the first place, it will calm men's "wild" minds. In the second, it will prevent new "plots and errors"—i.e., social upheavals such as the treason of Claudius or the rebellion of Laertes. This is, I take it, a concise and authoritative description of the catharsis to be anticipated from telling the story of Hamlet "with the occurrents, more and less, / Which have solicited."

Furthermore, because Shakespeare places his statements in a context which is fully known, we can understand a good deal about how the effect is created. It is lack of understanding that has made the minds of the Danish courtiers "wild" and ripe for "plots and errors." Terrible events have occurred. Evil seems rife, and the Danish state seems on the verge of plunging into chaos. Telling Hamlet's story will not make up for Hamlet's death (or for that matter for the death of Polonius or Ophelia or Laertes), but, to quote Horatio, it will show "how these things came about" (l. 372). Hearing Hamlet's story will therefore be learning in the most literal sense for the "audience of the noblest" assembled before the stage on which Horatio speaks. Its effect will be to alleviate their fear—fear of the present and even greater fear of the future.

If we step back now we can perhaps catch a glimpse of the kind of catharsis that *Hamlet* offers the spectators in the theater. A tragedy, Aristotle reminds us, is more universal and more philosophical than history. The Danish courtiers confronting the bodies of Gertrude, Laertes, Claudius, and Hamlet stand in the same relation to the dramatic event as do members of the theater audience to human experience as recorded in history or what they accept as history. In good Renaissance fashion, Shakespeare regularly used historical or legendary sources for his tragedies. Sometimes he drew on formal history (*Julius Caesar*), sometimes on legendary history (*Lear*), and sometimes, as in *Hamlet,* he drew on stories from legendary history that had already been embellished by previous artists. Yet Shakespeare was always free with his sources. To say that his changes "made better plays" is, I think, to refer impressionistically to what Aristotle considered an essential characteristic of poetic art and explained in detail. The events presented in the sources are insufficiently clear. They are "singulars" which the poet must reshape in terms of "the universal." This is true even for sources that were already dramatic like the *Ur-Hamlet,* since by definition Shakespeare would not have reworked an earlier play if he had felt that it already said everything necessary.

In moving from source to finished drama, Shakespeare added, compressed, combined, and invented. The result in the great tragedies is an almost perfect coherence of parts. If catharsis can be understood in Golden's sense as "clarification," the theater audience that has attentively followed Shakespeare's version of the Hamlet story is surely experiencing catharsis. Their experience is similar to what the Danish courtiers will feel when they have heard Horatio tell "how these things came about" and the wildness of their minds is calmed. For both groups, the disturbing and frightening singulars of history have been replaced by the universals of poetry.

IV

We have, then, three types of catharsis recognized by Elizabethan critics and embodied significantly in Elizabethan plays. Obviously these types are not entirely unrelated. They all involve calming of mental perturbations, and all of them depend on various ways of using or expressing truth. Moral catharsis achieves purgation of guilt and fear through the device of presenting a dramatic imitation of truth to the guilty party, who then reveals truth itself *via* a confession. As a literary convention, this confession can be (and is) taken as absolute. Goethe's knowledge that the best we can hope for when we try to confess is *Dichtung und Wahrheit*—truth mixed with poetry—is simply irrelevant to the literary convention. The strategy of moral catharsis is neatly summed up in Polonius' advice to Reynaldo: "Your bait of falsehood take[s] this carp of truth."

Religious catharsis also depends on the dramatic use of truth. As we have noted, it has the effect of putting the spectator in the position of one of St. John's angels, and the play in the position of "the world seen as it is." Exposure to this world is therapeutic. That is, the spectator may harbor doubts about the possibility of justice in the actual world and may even fall into the kind of despair illustrated by King Lear's speech on justice:

> Robes and furr'd gowns hide all. Plate sin with gold,
> And the strong lance of justice hurtless breaks;
> Arm it in rags, a pigmy's straw does pierce it.
> (IV.ii.165–167)

Such perturbations are dissipated by the dramatic experience of poetic justice. To say this is to say that poetic justice operates as a form of reassurance. To see valiant Milciades released from his fetters and the cruel Severus put to death violates our knowledge of the singulars of history, but it refurbishes our faith that God does not play dice with the world. Moreover, this is not necessarily escapism. The morally coherent world is not a fiction but an imitation of a world that faith tells us actually exists. Unless we dismiss eschatology as pure superstition (which Renaissance humanists most certainly did not) we must admit with Sidney that it is truer than history. In other words, to a Christian humanist, the play based on poetic justice is not the world as we would like it to be (sentimentalism) but the world as it is or would be if we could penetrate the dark glass that clouds the vision of all but inspired makers.

Recalling Heywood's gentlewoman of Lynn, we can say that moral catharsis restores harmony between the sinful individual and the Divine. Religious catharsis is the satisfaction that comes from experiencing this harmony and sharing in it. Clearly the two are complementary, the negative and positive aspects of a single experience. The individual whose affections are not "in right tune" must experience moral catharsis first. Only after he has set them "in right tune" can he affirm the angelic view provided by poetic justice. Tragedy, as we have seen, tends to emphasize moral rather than religious catharsis. This is because the tragic hero is more likely to be a sinner than a saint, to stand with Claudius at the first stage of the cathartic process. Indeed, Francis Fergusson's much-admired formula for the tragic rhythm—purpose, passion, perception—makes it almost mandatory that the tragic hero begin "out of joint" with the true order of things, suffer because of this, and finally discover (and affirm) this order as a result of his suffering. Comedy, on the other hand, is lighter in tone, and its lightness comes from our secure sense that no matter how bad things may seem, we are sure to approve of their resolution. This is simply to say that we view the comic world in terms of its end, which we know will be justice tempered with mercy.[10]

If we try to relate religious to literal catharsis, we seem to encounter the impasse mapped out by Allen Tate in his distinction between the angelic and the symbolic kinds of imagination. What relation, if any, can there be between the world seen as absolute truth and the world seen as world? Religious catharsis operates in terms of the first perspective, literal catharsis in terms of the second. The first seems to demand a turning away from experience to eschatology; the second gives a detailed treatment of experience "with the occurrents, more and less, / Which have solicited." One demands poetic justice; the other merely offers a clarification, an object lesson in "how these things came about."

The easy solution would be to say that religious and literal catharsis are not relatives but antitheses: that one operates as drama aspires to eschatology, the other as it stubbornly remains tied to history. To take this option would, however, be to miss the implications of the concepts which we have been examining in such detail. The fact is that poetic justice claims to be a clarified vision of reality, not an escape from it, while—by the same token—the literal level of drama is not a copy of history but something more universal and more philosophical. We are dealing not with antitheses but with ideas that converge.

Poetic justice and "the world as world" are only antagonistic in a Platonic or Manichean frame of reference. They are not antagonistic in terms of the Christianity of Renaissance humanists. The possibility of their convergence is no more difficult (though, by the same token, no easier) than Pope's "whatever is is right." From the point of view of Christian humanist poetics, it is our inability to see, our own imperfection, which encourages us to turn away from what is, in our search for what is right. If this is so, then the ultimate function of the dramatist is to make clear the presence of the absolute ("what is right") in the actual ("what is"). In doing this the dramatist provides a clarification that might also be called an illumination. To put it another way, the courtiers assembled to hear Horatio's tale at the end of *Hamlet* will not learn that the characters "got what they deserved." They may, however, learn that things as they are, understood according to probability and necessity, are identical with things as they would be if we could see them clearly. It is the erected wit of the poet that grants this vision. As Milton wrote in his Elegy 6:

> Diis etenim sacer est vates, divumque sacerdos,
> Spirat et occultum pectus et ora Iovem.

(1968)

Part 3
Praxis

Tudor Humanism and Surrey's Translation of the *Aeneid*

One of the more interesting facts about English blank verse is that it was invented. The evidence suggests that it was the result of a self-conscious effort by Henry Howard, Earl of Surrey, around 1540 to create a vernacular English form equivalent to the dactylic hexameter of classical epic and parallel to unrhymed continental forms such as Italian *versi sciolti*.

The background of this effort has been illuminated by the excellent studies of such scholars as Jones, Mason, Hagar, and Richardson.[1] It is part of what can be called the esoteric phase of English civic humanism, in contrast to the exoteric phase. The exoteric humanists saw themselves as part of an international movement bent on restoring universal and timeless cultural values—those of antiquity—through the medium of a universal and timeless language, Latin. Conversely, the esoteric humanists recognized, at least tacitly, that the ideal of a universal culture was artificial and that their real task was to disseminate the values of classical culture in the regional and national cultures defined by vernacular languages. Translation was one obvious way to accomplish this, but the work of translation forced the translators to face up to the difference between ancient and modern languages. In the case of poetry the difference extended beyond grammar and syntax to meter and verse forms.

The unrhymed dactylic hexameter of Greek and Latin epics is quantitative rather than accentual. Claudio Tolomei wrestled with the problem of writing Italian verse according to classical rules in *Versi, Et Regoli de la Nuova Poesia Toscana* (1539)—and thus anticipated the efforts in England of Richard Stanyhurst and Thomas Campion, among others[2]—but the simpler and more appropriate solution was to discover an Italian form that fitted the nature of the Italian language and also had many of the qualities that were more impressive in the verse of Homer and Vergil. Bartolomeo Piccolomini, Luigi Alamanni, Cardinal Ippolito de Medici, and Nicolo Liburnio all experimented with using Italian blank verse—*versi sciolti*—for heroic effects, and they are often cited as direct influences on Surrey's experiment with blank verse.[3]

At this late remove there is no direct way to reconstruct Surrey's motives for deciding to use blank verse in his translation of the *Aeneid*. We know he considered Wyatt his master in English poetry, but we know too that his verse is considerably more modern, in the sense of being more regular, than Wyatt's.[4] In his well-known epitaph on Wyatt, Surrey remarks that Wyatt's hand "taught what might be said in rhyme" and "reft Chaucer the glory of his wit." Both points are apt. In spite of Wyatt's interest in domesticating sophisticated continental forms into English—especially the Petarchan sonnet and *terza rima*—his verse is filled with Chaucerian reminiscences. Conversely, Surrey is conscious of the fundamental difference between his own and Chaucer's verse. This is apparent from the fact that when he invokes Chaucer, his diction and vocabulary have the quality of self-conscious imitation, as in his sonnet beginning "The soote season that bud and bloom forth brings, / With green hath clad the hill and eke the vale." The verse here is pretty enough, but it is noticeably different from Surrey's normal style.

In contrast to Wyatt, then, Surrey appears more cosmopolitan and more conscious that he is beginning a tradition rather than renewing or carrying forward an old one. What he did share with Wyatt was a commitment to improving English by introducing new artistic forms. The object was only partly to modernize the language. It was also to make the language sufficiently expressive to be a vehicle of values typical of other, superior cultures, both ancient and modern, and thereby to elevate the quality of English culture.

In the preface to his famous *Miscellany* of 1557, which includes some forty of Surrey's poems, Tottel remarks, "I exhort the unlearned by reading to learn to be more skilful and to purge that swinelike grossness" of their taste in order to appreciate the models his authors offer of new and more refined kinds of expression.[5] The point is briefly made, but it is more than the blurb of an enthusiastic publisher. It clearly echoes the belief of esoteric humanism that by improving the vernacular it will elevate the culture that uses the vernacular.

More extended versions of the same idea abound in Tudor discussion of literature. In the preface to *The Art of Rhetorique* (1553), for example, Thomas Wilson describes eloquence not as the expression of, but as the source of civilization. It was given by God to Adam, lost at the time of the fall, and only laboriously recovered thereafter. At one time, Wilson observes, "Menne lyved Brutishlye in open feldes, hauing neither housis to shroude them in, nor attyre to clothe their backes." By the force of eloquence, however, they were gradually civilized: "After a certaine space thei became through nurture and good aduisement, of wilde, sober; of cruel, gentle; of foles, wise; of beastes, men. Such force hath the tongue, and such is the power of eloquence. . . . Neither can I see that menne could haue bene broughte by anye other meanes, to lyue together in fellowshyppe of lyfe, to mayntayne Cities, to deale trulye, and willyngelye to obeye one another."[6]

This is clearly in the same key as Tottel's claim that his new style of poetry will purge English readers of "swinelike grossness," and its seriousness cannot be doubted. Roger Ascham takes the same position in *The Scholemaster,* adding that whenever language decays, thought and civil life decay also: "Ye know not what hurt ye do to learning that care not for wordes but for matter, and so make a deuorse betwixt the tong and the hart. For marke all ages: looke vpon the whole course of both the Greeke and Latin tonge, and ye shall surelie finde that, whan apte and good wordes began to be neglected, and properties of those two tonges to be confounded, than also began ill deedes to spring, strange maners to oppresse good orders, newe and fond opinions to striue with olde and trewe doctrine . . . and so vertue with learning is contemned, and studie left off: of ill thoughtes cummeth peruerse iudgments, of ill deedes springeth lewde taulke."[7]

Ascham equates the unclassical Latin of the Middle Ages with what he considered the barbarous religion and philosophy of the same period, and he carries the analysis forward to the decay, as he sees it, of literature when right versifying was replaced by the barbarous and "Gothic" practice of rhyming.[8] The idea is thus supported, as far as Ascham is concerned, by the empirical evidence of history. To give Ascham his due, there is a striking similarity between his argument and Ernst Cassirer's twentieth-century argument that language is a symbolic form—that it shapes conscious thought even as it provides the content of consciousness. Ascham's solution to the problem of a language that debases consciousness, and hence culture, is imitation: "Bicause the prouidence of God hath left vs in no other tong, saue onlie in the *Greke* and *Latin* tong, the true preceptes and perfite examples of eloquence, therefore must we seeke in the Authors onlie of those two tongues the trewe Paterne of Eloquence, if in any other mother tongue we looke to attaine either perfit vtterance of it our selues or skilfull iudgement of it in others."[9]

Such, then, is the context of Tudor efforts to improve the English language by translation, by reform of prose style, and by domestication of new poetic forms. In this larger scheme, heroic poetry is both especially important and especially challenging. Heroic poetry was regarded by almost every critic of the sixteenth century as the noblest kind of poetry. It was about noble characters, and it provided a vision of nobility that could animate and elevate an entire nation. Homer had done this for the Greeks and Vergil for the Romans; presumably vernacular poets could, if they could only find the right words, do the same for modern cultures. Spenser clearly expresses this aim in the "Letter to Raleigh" that explains (or purports to explain) *The Faerie Queen:* "The generall end therefore of all the booke is to fashion a gentleman or noble person in vertuous and gentle discipline."[10] Another, equally powerful expression of the idea is found in Sidney's *An Apology for Poetry:* "By what conceit can a tongue be directed to speak euill of that which draweth with it no lesse Champions than *Achilles, Cyrus, Aeneas, Turnus, Tideus,* and *Rinaldo?* who doth not onely teach and moue to truth, but teacheth and mooueth to the most high and excellent truth; who maketh magnanimity and iustice shine throughout all misty fearfulnes and foggy desires. . . . For as the image of each action styrreth and instructeth the mind, so the loftie image of such Worthies most inflameth the mind with desire to be worthy, and informes with counsel how to be worthy."[11] Heroic poetry, in other words, is not only a civilizing force, it is the most powerful civilizing force that language offers. Milton said it best when he remarked in *The Reason of Church Government* that the object of heroic poetry is "to imbreed and cherish in a great people the seeds of virtue and public civility."[12]

The problem of discovering a form which is complementary to the heroic vision therefore seemed especially urgent to those moved by the ideals of esoteric humanism. The solution was twofold—translation and imitation in original compositions. Surrey took the first route. As we know, however, there was no English verse form available to him remotely comparable to Vergil's dactylic hexameter. Even if one grants that there are moments of heroic elevation in Chaucer's *Knight's Tale,* the changes that had occurred in the English language during the fifteenth century made it impossible for Surrey to reproduce Chaucer's effects. In fact, he probably could understand them only imperfectly. Beyond Chaucer, he had two possible models: Caxton's prose *Eneydos* (1490), which is translated from the French and would have appeared to Surrey both clumsy and false to the original; and Gavin Douglas's translation of the *Aeneid* into decasyllabic couplets, completed in 1513.

It is clear that Surrey drew on Douglas. How much he drew is unclear. Henry Lathrop concludes that he owes Douglas "nothing fundamental or inspiring. Douglas is diffuse, Surrey is terse; Douglas is familiar, Surrey dignified; Douglas is clumsy, Surrey aims at elegance."[13] On the other hand, Florence Ridley, a more recent student of the subject, concludes that Surrey's debt was deep and continuous.[14] Perhaps the best answer is that Surrey consulted Douglas as one might consult a Loeb translation today to check the quality of his own work and to pick up any ideas Douglas might have to offer.

The difference between Douglas and Surrey—and it is an absolutely crucial difference—is that Surrey saw Vergil in terms of style as well as content. He had heard the music of Vergil's hexameters, and he understood how it was created. His achievement is that he invented a new kind of English verse capable of expressing, if not exactly the same music, at least a music of comparable elevation and richness. Roger Ascham believed that the heroic vision could not be expressed in English until an English quantitative verse form had been invented. We know today that

Ascham was mistaken and that in seeking an equivalent rather than a duplicate verse form, Surrey was right.

II

Until the twentieth century Surrey's translation of books 2 and 4 of the *Aeneid* was known chiefly in Tottel's edition of 1557. Tottel's edition is apparently the source of a few scattered references to Surrey's *Aeneid* in the sixteenth century,[15] but the translation had been so completely forgotten by the middle of the seventeenth century that when Milton refers to his use of blank verse for *Paradise Lost,* he boasts that it is "an example set, the first in *English,* of ancient liberty recover'd to Heroic Poem from the troublesome and modern bondage of Riming."[16]

Today two versions of Surrey's *Aeneid* are widely available that are independent of Tottel. Both are of book 4 alone. The most familiar of the versions is that preserved in Hargrave manuscript 205, which dates from the 1560s. This version is reprinted parallel to Tottel's version in the edition (rev. 1928) of Surrey's poems by F. M. Padelford.[17]

The less familiar version is an edition published around 1554 by the printer John Day for William Owen, who was "orator" for Surrey's son, Thomas, Duke of Norfolk. Owen tells us in his preface that the text is based on a manuscript "in the authors owne hande" which has been collated by Owen with two other manuscripts, so that it is "both to the latyn most agreeable, and also best standing with the dignity of that kynde of myter."[18]

"The dignity of that kynde of myter" apparently means "the dignity of heroic meter." Owen is claiming that Surrey's blank verse is the appropriate English equivalent to ancient heroic verse—that is, dactylic hexameter. The term "dignity" may seem a little feeble to the modern reader. It is, however, nothing more than a translation of a common Latin epithet, illustrated, for example, in a comment by Badius Ascensius on epic in his popular edition of the *Ars poetica:* "Et primo loquitur [Horatius] de heroico carmine quod et dignitate et aequitate primum esse constat."[19]

The remark about dignity is supplemented by a comment that reveals much about the state of experimentation in English prosody in the 1550s. The title page of the Day-Owen edition announces that Vergil has been "translated into English and drawne into a straunge metre . . . worthy to be embraced." In other words, Surrey's blank verse was considered "straunge" at least by Owen, his editor, but also worthy of imitation. One's natural instinct is to think, "How odd that Owen should consider blank verse 'strange'." Even though no blank verse had been published by the year 1554, decasyllabic lines, usually joined in couplets or rime royal, had been standard for English narrative poetry since Chaucer and were also commonplace in the early Tudor period. Derek Attridge discusses this problem in *Well-Weighed Syllables* and attributes the word "straunge" to the fact that English readers, trained on classical prosodic rules, lacked a vocabulary for discussing (perhaps even for thinking about) their native accentual verse.[20]

Attridge offers ample justification for this position. As I will suggest later in more detail, however, it is probably not the meter *per se* that made Surrey's translation seem "straunge," but the syntactical strategies developed by Surrey in conjunction with the meter.[21] At any rate, the Owen text survives today in a single copy which is preserved at the Carl Pforzheimer Library in New York. It was reprinted by Professor Herbert Hartman in a limited edition in 1933, and it is to this reprint that I will refer in subsequent comments.[22]

None of the three surviving versions of Surrey's translation is completely trustworthy. Tottel's is the least so. As Henry Lathrop remarks, "All of the early verse printed by Tottel was carefully edited to smooth out metrical irregularities, to correct syntax, and to improve expression according to the taste of the day.[23] Comparison of the three surviving versions shows that Tottel frequently altered syntax, repunctuated, substituted modern for what seemed to him archaic words, and reduced the occurrence of run-over lines by heavy end punctuation and other devices. We are dealing here with the mentality of a pedant rather than a creative artist. It is the same mentality we encounter in George Gascoigne's *Certain Notes of Instruction.*

This is unfortunate, because Tottel's version is the one that is most frequently reprinted. It is a misleading version, and it has helped to create the widespread impression that Surrey's blank verse is "primitive" or "wooden" or "mechanical"—a commendable first effort but unworthy to stand beside later achievements in the form. Tucker Brooke, for example, remarks that "a generation passed before this meter was fully domesticated into England";[24] and C. S. Lewis, ever prepared to justify his description of the early English Renaissance as a "drab age," calls Surrey's verse "too severe, too cold . . . it is Vergil in corsets."[25] Florence Ridley adds, "If one thinks in terms of the resounding majesty of Marlowe, the flexibility of Shakespeare, or the close-textured, effortless movement of Milton, Surrey seems amateurish, awkward, even monotonous."[26]

Are these conclusions valid? To answer that question one needs to examine Surrey's translation in detail, and since it is impossible to examine the whole work in detail, I offer here an examination of a twenty-line passage that is particularly instructive. It comes at the end of book 4 and describes the final agonizing moments of Dido's death on her funeral pyre. This passage has always been recognized as one of the finest passages in the Latin original. It therefore must have posed a special challenge to its translator.

Before we move to the translation, it will be useful to note a few characteristics of the Latin original.[27] Vergil devotes thirteen lines to the description. Since Surrey translates them in twenty lines, one might conclude that he expands the original, as did his predecessor in Vergil translation, Gavin Douglas. If anything, the reverse is true. Discounting elisions, Virgil's thirteen lines of dactylic hexameter have two hundred syllables, whereas Surrey's twenty lines of iambic pentameter have perhaps 210. The numbers point to an important feature of Surrey's translation. It neither expands nor contracts. Instead, it is extraordinarily faithful to the literal sense of the original as well as to the artistic devices through which that literal sense is presented.

Having said this, we need to carry the comparison of English and Latin one step further. Vergil's Latin consists of five units, or periods, each of which has its own highly organized internal structure of sense and sound. Vergil's devices are natural to Latin. Being an inflected language, Latin can deal with word order very freely. They are, however, unnatural in English, which, being uninflected, depends heavily on word order. They include extended participial constructions, inversions of several types, interruptions, and parentheses—in short, all of the devices that we call "Latinate" when they are used aggressively by an English author.

By contrast, artistic English before Surrey is generally loose in structure, paratactic, and hospitable to romance language constructions and words. The first eighteen lines of Chaucer's *General Prologue* provide a good case in point. Examples closer to Surrey include Malory's *Morte Darthur* and Caxton's *Eneydos*—both in prose—and Gavin Douglas's translation of the *Aeneid* into Scots decasyllabic couplets. These works tend to follow standard subject-verb-object word order. The poetry tends to be metrically regular, with syntactical stress complementing metrical stress. In couplets, the poetic unit tends to be the line or the couplet, and there is little enjambment beyond the couplet. The chief use of inversion is to allow lines to end with rhyme words.

When sentences are extended for several lines—as, for example, in Chaucer's *General Prologue*—they tend to be enlarged by addition, with phrases and clauses linked in series by repeated subordinating or coordinating conjunctions and emphasized by parallelism. In the aureate rhetoric popular in late medieval Latin, such strategies are common. Their appearance in English vernacular writing of the same period is therefore probably the result of medieval Latin style as well as the character of Middle English.

That Surrey's translation is a marked departure from this tradition has often been recognized by those who have written on his *Aeneid*. Emrys Jones aptly summarizes the effect of Surrey's strategies: "His aim was to reproduce, as clearly as was consistent with the idiom of an uninflected language, the disposition of sense-masses and the figures of speech of the

Latin. . . . The structural unit in Surrey's unrhymed verse is not the line . . . but the phrase or the clause."[28]

As Jones suggests, the syntax of Surrey's *Aeneid* is Latinate. The translation regularly uses interruption, inversion, and parenthesis. Combined with enjambment, these devices create units different from, and often larger than, the pentameter line. The meter is generally, but by no means always, regular, and there are striking instances of metrical substitution that appear to be inserted for explicitly artistic reasons. Still more important from the point of view of the sound of the verse, all of the devices just mentioned combine to produce a consistent play, or counterpoint, of metrical accent against syntactical—or speech—accent.[29]

In the scansions given below, I have generally followed Jones's suggestive lead. In several instances, a regular metrical scansion is directly followed by an irregular scansion reflecting speech accent as defined by phrase and clause. Often the decision as to which scansion is closest to Surrey's intention must be based on aesthetic criteria which are at last partly subjective. Thus there will be occasions when the reader will be able to suggest alternate (and perhaps better) scansions. This is an intrinsic characteristic of prosodic analysis, and I hope that in such cases the reader will, while differing, grant the possibility of the scansion suggested here. In several cases, however, the criteria are objective. The fact that these cases consistently point to irregular scansion based on speech accent strengthens the case for irregular scansion as a conscious and centrally important feature of Surrey's heroic style.

With these all-too-brief remarks as preamble, let us now turn to the passage from Surrey as it appears in the Day-Owen text:

Almyghty Juno hauyng ruthe by thys (Unit 1)
Of her long paynes, and eke her lyngryng death,
From heauen she sent the Goddesse Iris downe,
The thrallying spiryte and ioynted lymmes to loose.
For that neyther by lot of desteny, (Unit 2)
Nor yet by naturall death she peryshed:
But wretchedly before her fatal daye,
And kyndled with a sodayne rage of flame:
Proserpyne had not yet from her head berefte
The golden heare: nor iudged her to hell.
The dewye Iris thus wyth golden wynges, (Unit 3)
A thousand hues shewyng agaynst the sunne,
Amyd the skyes then dyd she flye adowne:
On Didos heade, where as she gan alyght, (Unit 4)
Thys heare (quoth she) to Pluto consecrate.
Commanded I bereue, and eke thy spiryte unloose
From thys body: and when she had thus sayd, (Unit 5)

With her right hand she cut the heare in twayne:
And therewyth al the naturall heate gan quenche,
And into wynde the lyfe foorthwyth resolue.

The first thing to recognize about this verse is that it has none of the predictability of Chaucer's—or Gavin Douglas's—verse. Its unit is the phrase or clause, not the line or couplet. Sometimes a clause unit corresponds with a line (e.g., l. 18), but usually the phrases and clauses are united by being imbedded in the larger grammatical structure of a periodic sentence that extends over several lines. Note also that grammatical structure is by no means rigidly framed by the line unit, a point illustrated by line 17, in which a sustained period comes to an end in mid-line (the colon). The remarkable and—I suggest unprecedented—flexibility of Surrey's blank verse is essential to reproducing Vergilian rhetoric in English. It also provides a solution to the problem of creating the sustained tone of classical dactylic hexameter, with a norm of seventeen syllables to the line, in an English verse form with a norm of ten syllables per line. The flexibility also eliminates the temptation to contract each Vergilian line into a single blank verse line or expand it into a couplet.

For convenience the major units of the passage from Surrey have been indicated in the right margin. There are five of them, and they correspond exactly to the five units of the Latin original. The first unit is a periodic sentence extending over four lines. The subject of the Latin original (*Iuno omnipotens*—"Almyghty Iuno") is placed first, exactly as in Vergil. It is followed by a participial phrase ("hauyng ruthe") that occupies one and one-half lines and thus creates a considerable separation, or interruption, between the Vergilian subject ("Iuno") and its verb ("sent"). The verb is further distanced from "Iuno" by the adverbial phrase "from heauen" (1. 3), which would follow rather than precede the verb in normal English word order.

At this point we note a departure from Vergil. In Surrey's English, "sent" is immediately preceded by a subject—"she," referring to Juno. If "she" is the subject of the verb, "Almyghty Iuno" in line 1 cannot be Surrey's subject and must be the first two words of a long phrase emulating a Latin ablative absolute for which there is no precedent in Vergil. Why did Surrey make his sentence not less but more complicated—more Latinate one might say—than Vergil? The answer is evident. Taken at face value Surrey's sentence reads "Almyghty Juno . . . she sent." In other words, the "she" is a tautology. The motive for the tautology is obviously clarity.

The length of the interval between "Almyghty Iuno" and its verb is, as we have already remarked, considerable. It is far greater than anything that Surrey's readers would have been used to in English, and the extra subject—"she"—is evidently intended to prevent confusion. A similar strategy is used in lines 11–13 ("The dewye Iris . . . then dyd *she* flye adowne"). The need for such an awkward stratagem helps explain why the title page of the edition refers to Surrey's meter as "straunge." The complex syntax must have made the translation seem "straunge" in the sense of "unfamiliar and difficult" to English readers accustomed to stylistic traditions inherited from Middle English.

Difficult or not, the first period is extended further by another inversion in line 4. The infinitive "to loose" follows its objects in line 4 rather than preceding them. Since the infinitive phrase modifies (or, perhaps, complements) the verb "sent," it completes the sense of the sentence and brings the period to a neat conclusion at the end of the line. We note in passing that Surrey translates Vergil's *Olympo* as "heauen" (1. 3). This is not significant in itself but becomes so if related to the substitution of "hell" for "Stygian Orcus" in line 10, a point discussed below.

Surrey's complex syntactical strategies create a strong rhythm that is contrapuntal rather than complementary to the rhythm of his iambic pentameter lines. The largest unit is the sentence itself, which is four lines, or forty (perhaps forty-one) syllables. Because the sentence is a period, continuity must be sustained. This continuity cuts across the division of the sentence into four equal units separated by pauses encouraged by the line endings. Within the sentence there are sub-units. "Almyghty Iuno," for example, is followed by a caesura, which is followed by two units consisting of fifteen syllables, divided themselves by a pause after the word "paynes." The interplay of speech and metrical stress is further complicated in the second line by the fact that a reading based on syntax tends to convert a regular pentameter line into a line of four stresses balanced in pairs:

x / x / x / x / x /
Of her long paynes, and eke her lyngryng death

versus:

x x / / x x x / x /
Of her long paynes, and eke her lyngryng death

The word "spiryte" in line 4 is also interesting in this connection. Both Tottel and Hargrave give "sprite"—a one-syllable word—here. This regularizes the meter. Perhaps "spiryte" is a misprint, but the same error occurs in line 15 and, in fact, elsewhere in the Day-Owen text. Perhaps the word was pronounced as one syllable in spite of the spelling. If Tottel and Hargrave took the trouble to substitute "sprite" for "spiryte," however, the motive was most probably to iron out the meter, and this strongly suggests they regarded "spiryte" as defective—i.e., as having more syllables than the meter wants.

An argument can be made that the sense of the line is better served by the extra syllable of the Day-Owen text than the neat regularity of Tottel and Hargrave. The phrase "lyngryng death" emphasizes drawn-out torment, and the extra syllable in "spiryte" nicely resonates with that idea:

x / x / x / x / x /
The thrallyng sprite and ioynted limmes to loose

versus:

x / x / x x / x / x /
The thrallying spiryte and ioynted limmes to loose.

Unfortunately, there is insufficient evidence to determine which scansion is right. Whatever the case, since the infinitive at the end of line 4 completes the sense of the sentence, it resolves the syntactical as well as the metrical tension of the period. As we have already noted, Surrey resorts to inversion to force the sentence to end as it does. The word "loose" obviously reinforces the sense of tension released. The technique of adjusting the syntax to permit ending both line and period on a thematic word is a favorite of Surrey's and is evident in lines 10, 13, 16, 19, and 20.

The second unit in the passage is six lines long. Its structure is obscured for the modern reader by heavy punctuation (i.e., the colons in lines 6, 8 and 10), and it is almost necessary to refer to the Latin original to be sure of what Surrey intends.

The sentence consists of a compound adverbial clause of four lines ("For that neyther . . . Not yet . . . But wretchedly . . . And kyndled") modifying the main verbs "berefte" and "iudged." The subject of the sentence ("Proserpyne") occurs in line 9. If we assume that the final *e* of "Proserpyne" is silent or elided with "had," the line can be read as metrically regular until the fourth foot. If it is pronounced, however, the beginning of the line is irregular, and the irregularity has the effect of encouraging an extremely irregular scansion of the line as a whole:

x / x / x / x x / x /
Proserpyne had not yet from her head berefte

versus:

x / xx x / / x x / x /
Proserpyne had not yet from her head berefte

The latter (irregular) scansion calls attention to the subject and thus assists the reader—who, given the length of the introductory adverbial clause, can probably use all the help Surrey can offer at this point. Whether or not this scansion is valid, line 9 is saved from metrical isolation by the enjambment that forces the reader to continue to the object of the verb in the next line: "The golden heare."

The second half of line 10—"nor iudged her to hell"—is associated with the main clause as the second half of a compound predicate (i.e., "not berefte . . . nor iudged"). The colon at mid-line is therefore misleading to the modern reader. It indicates a pause and no more. Surrey's language here is interesting because it departs markedly from the Latin original. Vergil's term for the underworld is "Stygian Orcus" (*Stygioque . . . Orco*). Whether or not the phrase would have seemed poetic to a Roman of the Augustan period, it is artificial out of its Roman context. Roger Ascham and other hard-line English humanists might have fancied it, but I suspect that even in the sixteenth century it would have struck most readers as dead erudition. Surrey's substitution of "hell" is obviously right. If it makes the English translation more grim than the original, that is appropriate too. St. Augustine wrote in his *Confessions* (I, 13) that he wept for Dido when he was an adolescent, but that she was, after all, a debauched woman and a suicide and not worth the tears of a Christian convert, while Dante placed her in the *Inferno* (V, 61–2) as an example of lust along with Paolo and Francesca.

Surrey did not invent but he took full advantage of the lovely Vergilian transition in the next period away from the anguished queen to the descent of Iris, goddess of the rainbow, who receives Dido's soul and thus ends her torment. The transition is made in a unit of three and one-half lines (11–14). Note that the Day-Owen punctuation is misleading. One needs to refer to Vergil's Latin to confirm Surrey's meaning here. The phrase "On Didos heade" is part of the sentence that begins on line 11. "Where as she gan" is *not* part of this sentence in the Latin but is the beginning of a new sentence that extends to "thys body" in line 17.

The subject of the transition sentence ("Iris") is separated from the verb ("flye") by a parenthetical description of the wings of the goddess that occupies all of line 12. The effect of the parenthesis is enhanced by the substitution of a trochee for an iambus in the third foot of the line:

x / x / / x x / x /
A thousand hues shewyng agaynst the sunne

In line 13 the verb is further delayed by the inversion of the position of the adverbial phrase "Amyd the skyes." Since the parenthesis and the inversion obscure the connection between subject and verb, we are not surprised to encounter the device of the second subject used previously in l. 3: "The dewye Iris . . . then did *she* flye adowne" (italics mine).

The fourth unit (the speech of Iris, lines 14–17) begins with "where as she gan." It contains two instructive ambiguities. First, in line 14 the meter calls for a light stress on "where" and a heavy on "as." This makes the words sound like the logical connective "whereas," and, in fact, Hargrave and several modern editions print "whereas" as a single word, producing the meaningless clause, "Whereas she began to alight."[30] Although there is no equivalent for this transition passage in the Latin original, Surrey's meaning is plain enough. "As" is used in the sense of "when." The sentence means something like "Where—when she began to alight—she said." If this is correct, the speech stress here needs to be the opposite of the metrical stress. The caesura comes before "where," not after it, and "where" should receive the heavy stress:

x / x / x / x / x /
On Didos heade, where as she gan alyght

versus:

x /x / / x x / x /
On Didos heade, | where / as she gan alyght

The second ambiguity is more difficult, but fortunately Vergil's Latin solves the problem. In line 15 the word "consecrate" looks like an imperative. The end punctuation (i.e., the period) that follows it makes this interpretation mandatory for the reader who does not consult the original. To read the sentence in this way is to make Iris's statement a command to Dido to consecrate her hair to Pluto. Since Dido is all but dead on the pyre at this moment, the interpretation is strained. The Latin text shows that it is wrong. Vergil's Latin reads as follows: *Hunc ego Diti / Sacrum iussa fero teque isto corpore solvo.* The Loeb editor translates as follows: "This offering, sacred to Dis, I take as bidden."

Hunc ("this") refers to the offering, which is the lock of Dido's hair clipped by Iris as she releases the soul from the body. Surrey simply calls it "Thys heare." *Sacrum* is an adjective meaning "sacred" in the sense of "sacred to Dis," or Pluto. Surrey translates it as "consecrate" in the sense of "consecrated." The word, in other words, is not an imperative but a participial adjective with the normal "-ed" removed by rhetorical "shortening" or syncope. Finally, *iussa* is a participle meaning "bidden" or "commanded" and *fero* is the main verb, meaning "I take," or in Surrey's words, "I bereue."

The Day-Owen punctuation of the passage is therefore erroneous. Instead of ending with a period, line 15 should have no end punctuation or at most a comma. When read with the proper meaning and punctuation, the fourth unit ceases to be confusing and becomes a rich, highly contrapuntal Latinate period. It is beautifully effective in conveying Vergil's tone, but it is—if only because of its success in imitating the Latin—unlike anything that had appeared in the English language before Surrey. I suggest that we confront here with special clarity the extraordinary complexity of Surrey's achievement—an achievement usually hidden under the bland observation that Surrey was the first English writer to use sustained blank verse.

The final unit of the passage under consideration is probably the most famous example in the *Aeneid*—other than *sunt lacrimae rerum*—of Vergil's tone of elevated melancholy. It begins with a sentence of one and one-half lines in which metrical stress plays strongly against the claims of syntax:

x / x / x /
and when she had thus sayd

versus:

x x x x / /
and when she had thus sayd

and:

x / x /
With her right hand

versus:

x x / /
With her right hand

In line 19 the metrical pattern calls for regular iambs and a normal caesura. This is acceptable if the second word in the line is the adverbial compound "therewythal." In fact, several modern versions of Surrey's translation encourage this reading by printing "therewythal" as one word, in the sense, perhaps, of "as this was happening." Again, however, reference to Vergil's Latin provides the correct reading. The Latin reads, *omnis et una dilapsus calor*, translated by the Loeb editor as "And therewith, all the warmth ebbed away." Surrey's "therewyth" corresponds to Vergil's *una,* which means something like "all at once," although, as the Loeb translation shows, "therewith" is an acceptable equivalent.[31] Surrey's "al" is not adverbial. It means "all" in the normal English sense, and it modifies "heate," being the exact equivalent of Vergil's *omnis calor.* The scansion of the line must make this plain. This means rejecting the metrically regular reading, placing a heavy stress on "al," and shifting the caesura from just before "the" to just before "al":

x / x / x / x x / x /
And therewythal | the naturall heate gan quenche

versus:

x / / / x / x x / x /
And therewyth | al the naturall heate gan quenche[32]

The final line of the passage (l. 20) is the second clause of a compound sentence. The two clauses are parallel, with the verb ("gan") being understood in the second. The parallelism is emphasized by the repetition of the conjunction "and" at the beginning of each—rhetorical polysyndeton. The second clause is also metrically regular. The larger movement of the final unit is thus from periodic to loose structure and from metrical irregularity to metrical regularity. The effect of this unit is that of a progressive release from tension and expresses nicely, in a sense enacts, the action being described—the release of Dido from her torment. There is, however, a residue of the earlier Latinate structure. Both lines use verb-object inversion so they can end with the verb. Surrey's purpose is clearly to have both of these lines end with thematic words: "quenche" and "resolue." The final line in Vergil, it should be noted, begins with what Surrey translates as "quenche"—*dilapsus*—and ends with his "resolue"—*recessit.* In other words, Surrey's imitation is, at this point, extraordinarily precise, although he reaches his goal by his own path.

III

Prosodic analysis is sometimes inexact and ambiguous, but it can serve a useful purpose. Applied to the conclusion of Surrey's translation of *Aeneid 4,* it confirms the value of the Day-Owen text in contrast to the Tottel and Hargrave versions. At the beginning, for example, Day-Owen avoids punctuation until the thought is completed. Hargrave, conversely, inserts a comma after "Iuno," thereby cutting the subject adrift from the rest of the sentence. In lines 4 and 16, Tottel and Hargrave substitute "sprite" for "spiryte." As we have noted, this cleans up the meter at the expense of the poetic expressiveness of line 4. It cannot be proved to be an error or a phonetic spelling, but the fact that "spiryte" is the consistent spelling in Day-Owen gives it a valid claim to being correct. Tottel and Hargrave compound their mischief in line 4 by rejecting the word "thrallyng." Hargrave substitutes "striving," which is modern but loses the connotation of imprisonment which is present in "thrallyng." This represents a loss of poetic expressiveness, since Dido's spirit is clearly described as imprisoned in her body and struggling for release. She is, after all, being consumed by the flames of the funeral pyre. Tottel substitutes "throwing" for "thrallyng," and this is simply nonsense.

Another example of poetic dilution comes two lines later where Day-Owens reads "Nor yet by naturall death she peryshed." The Latin equivalent for "not naturall" is *nec merito,* meaning (in the Loeb translation) "not by a death she had earned [i.e., deserved]." Surrey found "naturall" in a gloss by Servius on this passage.[33] Dido's fate, Servius observes, was *nec merito* in the sense that it was a suicide rather than a death by natural causes. But "naturall" threatens to violate the iambic pattern, being three syllables where the meter wants two:

x / x / x x / x / x /
Nor yet by naturall death she peryshed

As has already been noted, Tottel is a metrical formalist. He sees extra syllables as a problem, which he eliminates here by substituting the two-syllable word "kindly." Since "kindly" can mean "of the same family"—hence, very generally, "natural"—in the sixteenth century, the substitution may have seemed ingenious to Tottel, although it seems strained and unexpressive today. Even in the sixteenth century, however, the dominant meaning of "kindly" was "merciful," and "kindly death" would have almost inevitably been interpreted to mean "merciful death," which is possible in English but quite different from Vergil's meaning and also the meaning Surrey derived from Servius.

Having recognized the merits of Day-Owen, we may note briefly that even in the twenty lines here examined the text has demonstrable errors, the comma in line 14 and the period in line 15 being the most obvious. In other words, although Day-Owen is the best sixteenth-century text available, it is by no means perfect. Further study is necessary if we want to be sure of having the best text possible.

IV

To move back now to the larger issues touched on at the beginning of this essay, it is evident from Surrey's shorter poems that he was a student of classical and continental humanist poetry. Both the instruction he received from his tutor John Clerk and the lessons that he learned from the poetry of Sir Thomas Wyatt make it likely that his translation of Vergil was a conscious attempt to introduce the nobility and elevation of Vergil, as well as the story of the *Aeneid,* into English, and that this effort was closely related to the belief of civic humanists that a great culture is impossible without greatness in the use of language. Whatever Surrey thought about Gavin Douglas, he could not have considered Douglas a suitable guide in this effort, and, in fact, he rejected just those elements of the Douglas translation that modern critics like C. S. Lewis consider its most attractive features: its couplets, its regularity, its tendency to make syntactical stress complementary to metrical stress, its generally loose sentence structure, and its colloquial vocabulary. For this reason, the argument that Surrey's *Aeneid* is, as Howard Baker puts it, "Gavin Douglas' version transformed into unrhymed heroics,"[34] seems weak.

To accomplish his purpose Surrey had, in effect, to create a new language. This language is the equivalent in English verse of the Ciceronian style in prose. It is invented specifically to be a vehicle for English heroic style. The decision to use blank verse was merely the first of Surrey's tasks. It was perhaps the easiest of them because the decasyllabic line was already standard in English, and the argument for dropping rhyme had already been made by continental humanists in their defense of *versi sciolti.*

Surrey's most remarkable achievement was what he did with the unrhymed iambic pentameter line once he had selected it. Among the strategies evident even from the brief twenty-line passage considered here are the creation of syntactical units different from the iambic pentameter line, extensive and flexible use of such Latinate devices as inversion and interruption, regular counterpoint of syntactical against metrical stress, and free and expressive use of metrical substitution. All of these strategies are, in turn, combined with a willingness to objectify—again the word "enact" suggests itself—in rhythm and sound the actions being described.

George Wright believes that in Wyatt's poetry "the metrical line and the natural rhythm of the language engage each other in a continuing struggle."[35] Most readers find the result highly expressive and preferable to the regularity of much later iambic verse. On the surface there may seem to be a similarity between the irregularity of Wyatt and that of Surrey's *Aeneid.* The verse forms are, however, quite different. As Wright demonstrates, Wyatt uses the irregular decasyllabic line patterns found by Schick in Lydgate's verse. His versification is thus a continuation of traditional English versification, no matter how unorthodox it sometimes seems.

Surrey's *Aeneid* verse is, conversely, something new to English, being based on imitation of Latin devices. It is in this sense illustrative of what the Elizabethans would describe as "artificial" verse, meaning verse created by the use of conscious artistic formulas. In his search for an equivalent to Vergil's unrhymed, syntactically rich quantitative hexameter Surrey moved away from the Middle English tradition. If the result can be described as "Latinate," the artistic effect is occasionally reminiscent of the free, stress-dominated rhythm of English in its Germanic phase. Perhaps there is a level at which Latinate devices are natural rather than unnatural in English.[36] Whatever the roots from which the language of Surrey's *Aeneid* draws its nourishment, its effect is closer to Vergil than any other English translation of the *Aeneid* before the nineteenth century.

It remains one of the curiosities of the history of English poetry that Surrey's achievement was ignored by his successors. Perhaps Tottel is to blame. At any rate, later efforts to create heroic poetry in English in the sixteenth century use almost every form *but* blank verse—fourteeners, poulter's measure, decasyllabic couplets, quantitative dactylic hexameter, ottava rima, and Spenserian stanzas. Marlowe's fine blank verse translation of book 1 of Lucan's *Pharsalia* is an exception, but it was ignored as completely as Surrey's *Aeneid.* There is no reason to doubt Milton's sincerity when he writes that *Paradise Lost* is "the first [example] in English" to use blank verse for heroic poetry, even though we know he is mistaken. It is a pity he did not know Surrey's translation because in spite of the help he received from the dramatic blank verse of Marlowe and Shakespeare, he had to make many of Surrey's discoveries about heroic blank verse all over again.

(1986)

Perspective and Form in Petrarch

Francis Petrarch has the reputation of being the most autobiographical of poets. His fondness for confession, for the *cri de coeur* and the pageant of the bleeding heart, is evident in all his work—his voluminous correspondence, his imaginary dialogues and letters to ancient authors, his *Triumphs,* and his eclogues. Most especially it is evident in the *Canzoniere,* the collection of lyrics he wrote to describe his love for the lady Laura.

The trouble is that Petrarch was never content to describe his experience and leave it at that. We know that he was in bondage to Laura for twenty-one years and that he spent the rest of his life preoccupied with her memory. Far from concealing his passion, he went to great pains to publicize it to all the world. Yet in the autobiographical *Letter to Posterity,* written at the end of his life, Petrarch dismisses Laura in two blunt sentences:

> I struggled in my younger days with a keen but constant and pure attachment, and would have struggled with it longer had not the sinking flame been extinguished by death—premature and bitter, but salutary. . . . As I approached the age of forty, while my powers were unimpaired and my passions were still strong, I not only abruptly threw off my bad habits, but even the very recollection of them, as if I had never looked upon a woman.[1]

This from the poet who continued to revise his poems to Laura until the time of his death!

Goethe, who wrote what is probably the only honest autobiography before Freud, called it *Dichtung und Wahrheit*—fiction and truth. What makes Petrarch especially puzzling is that nothing he wrote—or almost nothing—exists in its original form. He was a tinkerer, a nitpicker, probably the first fully documented neurotic author in history. Having written something, he could never let it go. His letters, his prose works, and his *Canzoniere* look like autobiography, but the more one studies the evidence of revision, the internal contradictions, and the multiple variants, the less biographical they appear. He revised not only phrases and lines, but whole sequences. The *Canzoniere* seems to be a chronological record of his love affair, but many of the poems that can be dated through their allusions to historical events are obviously out of order. What we have, evidently, is not a chronological sequence but a mosaic of fragments arranged for maximum artistic effect.

According to Ernest Hatch Wilkins, the foremost authority on the subject, the *Canzoniere* went through no fewer than eight different stages dating from 1325, two years before Petrarch met Laura, to 1374, the year of his death. Even the last, beautifully written holograph, now one of the major treasures of the Vatican library, is not absolutely definitive since we have marginal numbers, evidently written after the manuscript was completed, proposing yet another arrangement of the last thirty poems. In Wilkins' words, "It is not a collection made toward the end of his life in a single editorial effort, nor is it a mere gradual accumulation of poems: it is a selective and ordered collection, the fashioning of which, begun in his youth, continued to the day of his death."[2]

To attempt to reconstruct Petrarch's life from his writing is therefore like following a thread through an increasingly dense tangle. Certainties tend to end in a confused body of probabilities, conjectures, and sheer guesses.

If biography is at best frustrating, the alternative is to accept a single text and to deal with it in its own terms as a work of art. This is an important point. Shakespeare's insignificance in the brilliant pageantry of Elizabethan London gave him anonymity, and Petrarch's constant tampering with the records of his life provides almost the same thing. Just as Shakespeare the Stratford burgher disappears behind the text of *As You Like it* or *Hamlet* or *The Winter's Tale,* Petrarch gradually assimilates himself into his work. We know all about the heart that bleeds so profusely in the *Canzoniere* and the Latin poems and letters, but it is not Petrarch's heart. The poems are drawn from Petrarch's experience, but the experience stands apart from his life as objectified experience, experience transformed into the shape of art.

Even the most basic facts about the *Canzoniere* are ambivalent. Was Laura really Laurette de Noves, married (with some historical irony) to Hugues de Sade, mother of eleven children, and dead of the plague in 1348? Or is she a montage of the several women in Petrarch's life, one of them the mother of his two illegitimate children? Or is she, in spite of his vehement protests to the contrary, an allegory of Lady Truth or a symbol of the allure of secular learning and poetry to a man who had almost, but not quite, lived past the Age of Faith, or simply a Freudian dream growing out of the tensions between Petrarch's sexuality and the ideal of celibacy? Did he meet her on 6 April 1327, as he states explicitly in Sonnet 176 and elsewhere, or was it, as he states in Sonnet 3, on Good Friday, 1327, which happened to be 10 April? If on 6 April, did he favor Good Friday because it was on a Good Friday that he felt inspired to write his Latin epic *Africa;* and if on Good Friday, did he sometimes refer to 6 April as the date because Laura died on 6 April 1348, and the two dates created a neat frame within which to place the love affair? Does the *Canzoniere* contain 366 poems because that happens to be the number he composed, or because 365 is the number of time, being the number of days in the year, with the concluding poem, a hymn to the Virgin Mary, taking the sequence out of time into eternity?

At one extreme of art there are the confession and the diary. At the other there is the artifact that exists wholly independently of the artist. The writer of confessions is like an aeolian harp, passively waiting to be played by the winds from the world beyond, or a grubby chronicler of life's commonplaces like Samuel Pepys or James Boswell, or a Pavlovian man, salivating a poem each time the gong of experience is rung. The artisan, on the other hand, is an anonymous craftsman placing gargoyles over the buttresses of Chartres or a being separate from his work, who retires from it, to quote Stephen Dedalus, like God paring His fingernails after completing the six days of Creation.

These polarities are universal. They apply to the art of Petrarch's age for the same reason that men obeyed the law of gravity and behaved in psychological ways long before Isaac Newton and Sigmund Freud were born. If we consider the disappearance of Petrarch the man into his work, it is tempting to consider him as a member of the second group—as an artisan, a forerunner of modern symbolist poets, and hence in the aesthetic tradition. After all, art for art's sake is as old as Eratosthenes, and the notion that the artist is less important than his creation is pervasive in the classical authors whom Petrarch admired. Again, to a whole generation of historians, including Burckhardt and Symonds as well as Walter Pater, the Renaissance was a reaffirmation of the absolute value of the here and now. Beauty—the beauty of landscape, of the nude human body, of artificial creations—is valuable in itself and not because it is a cloudy vision of a more perfect beauty to come.

There is something in this, but it is not a point of view that Petrarch would have understood, much less approved. Officially Petrarch believed with Horace that the purpose of art is to delight and instruct or to delight while instructing or to delight as a means of instruction. Petrarch knew in his heart that there was something more. He referred to this extra *je ne sais quoi* in the oration he delivered when he was crowned laureate in Rome on 8 April 1341 as the mysterious love of art that draws the poet up the difficult and lonely slopes of Parnassus. He knew, too, that poets often speak in blind parables and that the myths of Ovid conceal an ancient wisdom that may have survived in pagan literature from the age before the Tower of Babel. But he never discussed inspiration or the hidden truths of mythology with the enthusiasm of his friend Boccaccio. Evidently his understanding of art was much narrower and more practical than the art itself.

The war between understanding and feeling is clear even in the *Canzoniere*. Is this work the record of a glorious, ennobling love, which is what Petrarch's heart told him, or a series of lyrics about a soul ensnared by lust, which is what his understanding, drawing on a tradition that goes back to St. Augustine and earlier, kept whispering? In Sonnet 47 Petrarch exclaims:

Benedetto sia 'l giorno e 'l mese e l'anno
e la stagione e 'l tempo e l'ora e 'l punto
e 'l bel paese i 'l loco ov'io fui giunto
da' duo begli occhi che legato m'ànno . . .

e benedette sian tutte le carte
ov'io fama l'acquisto, e 'l pensier mio,
ch' è sol di lei, sì ch' altra non v'à parte.[3]

One sonnet later the mood is reversed:

Padre del ciel, dopo i perduti giorni,
dopo le notti vaneggiando spese
con quel fero desio ch' al cor s'accese,
mirando gli atti per mio mal sì adorni,

piacciati omai, col tuo lume, ch' io torni
ad altra vita et a più belle imprese,
sì ch' avendo le reti indarno tese,
il mio duro adversario se ne scorni.

The ambivalence runs through the *Canzoniere*. As we have seen, in the *Letter to Posterity* Petrarch disposes of the whole love affair in a few harsh words: "As I approached the age of forty, . . . I not only abruptly threw off my bad habits, but even the very recollection of them, as if I had never looked upon a woman." It is a baldfaced lie, but as a judgment it is no less severe than the verdict of St. Augustine, who appears in Petrarch's *Secretum* and dismisses both the *Canzoniere* and the hunger for fame that is so much a part of it with a phrase echoing Ecclesiastes—Vanity, vanity, all is vanity.

Nothing is fixed in Petrarch. It is all flux and contradiction; more so the more honest he tries to be, the more deeply he looks into his own heart. He was, I think, a fundamentally restless man. What makes him remarkable is that time after time in his quest for meaning in his life he comes back to a few central moments that are linked, at least in the imaginary world of his art, to symbolic dates and festivals and themes. Other men of his age had intense experiences. Petrarch is unique because he could not let them go. He constantly reexamined them in his prose and poetry and confessional dialogues. Since he was never of the same mind about them, he kept seeing them in a new light, adding new versions to the old or revising what he had already written. In Sonnet 43 he quotes the grim motto of Aeschylus: "Call no man happy until the day he dies." For much of his life Petrarch was miserable or claimed he was. When he was dying he may have found some consolation in the fact that his great work carried the stamp of his latest and presumably his sagest insights; but it is more probable that he died indignant that he would not have time for more revisions.

Long before we come to the final version of the *Canzoniere* it becomes apparent that the two themes between which the poems alternate are the world as illusion and the world as fact. St. Augustine speaks in the *Secretum* for the world as illusion, buttressed by the twin authorities of Socrates and the Bible. Life is a dream, the shadows that play across the walls of a cave or a prison. What we see now in a glass darkly we will later see face to face. Only the invisible world is unchanging. Earthly beauty is a snare, and mortal love is a trap invented by Satan. The Augustinian note is dominant in Sonnet 25:

> Quanto più m'avvicino al giorno estremo
> che l'umana miseria suol far breve,
> più veggio il tempo andar veloce e leve
> e 'l mio di lui sperar fallace e scemo.
>
> I' dico a' miei pensier: Non molto andremo
> d'amor parlando omai, ché 'l duro e greve
> terreno incarco, come fresca neve,
> si va struggendo, onde noi pace avremo;
>
> perché con lui cadrà quella speranza
> che ne fe' vaneggiar sì lungamente,
> e 'l riso e 'l pianto, e la paura e l'ira:
>
> sì vedrem chiaro poi come sovente
> per le cose dubbiose altri s'avanza,
> e come spesso indarno si sospira.

It recurs more powerfully in the sonnets on Laura's death, such as Sonnet 303:

> E' mi par d' or in ora udire il messo
> che madonna mi mande a sé chiamando;
> così dentro e di for mi vo cangiando
> e sono in non molt' anni sì dimesso
>
> ch'a pena riconosco omai me stesso;
> tutto 'l viver usato ò messo in bando;

sarei contento di sapere il quando,
ma pur devrebbe il tempo esser da presso.

O felice quel dì che del terreno
carcere uscendo lasci rotta e sparta
questa mia grave e frale e mortal gonna,

e da sì folte tenebre mi parta,
volando tanto su nel bel sereno
ch' i' veggia il mio Signore e la mia Donna!

The second theme is the one everybody knows and remembers. It is the theme that appealed to Petrarch's imitators, who made it into the central theme of modern poetry. It is the theme of the here and now. Life is important; the fleeting experience of beauty, love, and vitality is important; this particular moment and this particular woman, framed in this particular blend of sunlight and shadow, are important, more important than all the syllogisms of the philosophers and all the pieties of the schoolmen. It is a theme that echoes in Marvell's lines, "But at my back I always hear / Time's winged chariot hurrying near; / And yonder all before us lie / Deserts of vast eternity," and ramifies into the obsessive particularities of Impressionist painting. It explains why Petrarch was fascinated with dates and anniversaries and particular moments of vivid experience:

Era il giorno ch' al sol si scoloraro
per la pietà del suo fattore i rai;
quando i' fui preso, e non me ne guardai
che i be' vostr' occhi, Donna, mi legaro.
(Sonnet 3)

At night Petrarch meditates on death, only to interrupt the flow of commonplaces with a passionate exclamation:

Con lei foss'io da che si parte il sole
e non ci vedess'altri che le stelle,
sol una notte, e mai non fosse l'alba!
(Sestina 1)

He repents, but the stubborn reality of beauty pulls him back to the earth:

Misero me, che volli,
quando primier sì fiso
gli tenni nel bel viso,
per iscolpirlo, imaginando, in parte
onde mai né per forza né per arte

mosso sarà fin ch' i' sia dato in preda
a chi tutto diparte?
Né so ben anco che di lei mi creda.
(Canzone 5)

Her memory haunts him:

Erano i capei d'oro a l'aura sparsi
che 'n mille dolci nodi gli avolgea. . . .
(Sonnet 90)

Even after her death, he remembers and catalogues her particular beauties:

Oimè il bel viso, oimè il soave sguardo,
oimè il leggiadro portamento altero!
Oimè il parlar ch' ogni aspro ingegno e fero
facevi umile ed ogni uom vil gagliardo!

Et oimè il dolce riso. . . .
(Sonnet 267)

In old age, in spite of the invisible reality just beyond his reach, he is still drawn back to the flesh:

Tornami a mente, anzi v' è dentro, quella
ch'indi per Lete esser non po sbandita,
qual io la vidi in su l' eta fiorita
tutta accesa de' raggi di sua stella;

sì nel mio primo occorso onesta e bella
veggiola, in sé raccolta e sì romita,
ch' i' grido: "Ell' è ben dessa, ancor è in vita,"
e 'n don le cheggio sua dolce favella.
(Sonnet 290)

Here I think we are close to the essential Petrarch. Not in poems expressing passion—the Goliards and the Troubadours knew all about passion—but in poems that remain attached to the world and the flesh within the context of other poems reminding us that the third member of the trinity of the world and the flesh is the Devil. This is what makes Petrarch unique. It can be explained only by a kind of chemistry within Petrarch himself. He knew better. He had read St. Paul and St. Augustine and St. Thomas and Dante, and he had learned their lessons. Everything in his heritage testified to the superior reality of the invisible world, but though he tried for a lifetime, he could not deny the reality of what he felt or allow the people and events that caused the feelings to be absorbed into a sponge of neat scholastic abstractions. His view of history is like this. In the *Africa,* Scipio Africanus is a symbol of virtue and patriotism, but there are moments when he is a man living at a particular moment in history rather than a figure in a secular morality play. Laura is far more complex. She moves bewilderingly in and out of the world of abstraction. At times she is Lady Truth misunderstood by a youthful poet whose vision is clouded by his sexuality. At other times she represents the lure of fame and at others the attraction of secular as against religious art. She is distanced further by her involvement in the myth of Daphne changed to a laurel tree, the symbol of poetic fame, when pursued by Apollo, the god of poetry. And if the myth of Daphne absorbs her in a secular allegory, her virtue and her spirituality relate her to the world of angels and of the Virgin Mary. She is all of these things because the habit of mind that Petrarch inherited explained everything by making it into a series of abstractions. Beyond all of these symbols and myths and abstractions, however, she remains the Laura who demolishes myths and abstractions. Not necessarily Laurette de Noves, mother of eleven children, but the Laura of the *Canzoniere* who broke in on Petrarch's world on 6 April 1327 and of whose image he wrote:

Misero me, che volli,
quando primier sì fiso
gli tenni nel bel viso,
per iscolpirlo, imaginando, in parte
onde mai né per forza né per arte
mossa sarà fin ch' i' sai dato in preda
a chi tutto diparte?
Né so ben anco che di lei mi creda.

(Canzone 5)

If Laura had been only a figure out of *The Marriage of Philology and Mercury* Petrarch might have written the *Triumphs* and he would probably be remembered as a talented author "in the school of Dante" or "the school of Guillaume de Machaut." He would not, however, be remembered for what he is: the founder of modern lyric poetry.

Here I need to clarify what I meant by my earlier reference to Petrarch's inner chemistry. Everyone knows that Descartes wrote the basic definition of modern consciousness: *Cogito ergo sum*—I think, therefore I am. Descartes' *cogito* applies nicely to the modern scientific consciousness (probably to the medieval scholastics as well). The essence of this scientific approach is to subsume the particulars of experience under the most general of all abstractions, the abstractions of mathematics. A falling apple is dehydrated to $S = 1/2\ gt^2$. The hooks and deflected paths of the atoms of Democritus are abstracted to quantum mechanics, while a glass of port is reduced to a formula: C_2H_5OH plus minor impurities.

By contrast, the formula for the modern sensibility—our way of experiencing reality as against conceptualizing it—could be summed up as *sentio ergo sum*—I feel, therefore I am. For Wordsworth on Westminster Bridge, London is not a case study in sociology but an experience:

> Earth has not any thing to show more fair:
> Dull would he be of soul who could pass by
> A sight so touching in its majesty. . . .

And for Wallace Stevens, a jar is not simply a small vessel but a potential focal point through which the world can become coherent in human terms:

> I placed a jar in Tennessee,
> And round it was, upon a hill.
> It made the slovenly wilderness
> Surround that hill.

In every way a biographer could list, Petrarch was a child of his age. It was an age of abstraction, and he learned all the formulas. He learned the seven parts of speech and the ten difficult tropes and the names of the nine worthies and the seven deadly sins and the three cardinal virtues and the twelve labors of Hercules and the names of the Attic orators and the myths of Ovid and the date when the world began—all before he left grammar school. Later he learned about the nine spheres and the seven wandering stars, the varieties of disjunctive syllogisms, the four humours, and the signs and influences of the zodiac, and later still he studied Roman and canon law at Bologna, and the wisdom of the Fathers from his own reading.

I stress this context because in order to appreciate the greatness of Petrarch's achievement we need to remember how deeply such formulaic learning was impressed on him. What he achieved was the affirmation of his own irreducible and unabstractable reality—the validity of his inner chemistry—in spite of and, as the lyrics testify, frequently in open defiance of the abstractions that he had been given by his culture to explain it. He refused to allow the *sentio* to be absorbed by the *cogito*. I do not mean that no one before Petrarch had feelings that refused to yield to neat explanations; I mean something more important. I assume that men of Petrarch's time commonly had experiences that could not easily be squared with their concepts of experience. What is remarkable about Petrarch is that he did not dismiss his sense of conflict between the *sentio* and the *cogito* or record it in a single poem and then move on. Instead he made it the center around which his whole life revolved for the nearly fifty years that followed his first sight of Laura in 1327.

The result was a vision of reality surrounded by and threatened by abstractions, but always resisting them, always circling back to the month, the day, the moment of that first meeting, when his life was fundamentally changed. A twentieth-century critic would call it an epiphany. Just as Descartes, having discovered the *cogito,* found he could deduce the created world from it, Petrarch, having experienced a particular beauty at a particular moment, found that it organized his life in the same way that Wallace Stevens' jar organized the slovenly wilderness in Tennessee. To put it differently, Petrarch, having experienced the reality of the *sentio,* was never able to forget it or leave it alone.

Not that he didn't try. The penitential theme in the *Canzoniere* and the endless revisions extending to the effort to reorder the last thirty poems show how hard he tried. The curious thing is that the harder he tried—the more he revised, the more he added orthodoxies and symbols and numerological grace notes, the more he emphasized the reality of the invisible world—the more real the sequence became. As Horace could have told him: *Naturam expelles furca tamen usque recurret*—push Nature out of the front door and she comes in at the back. The point is that nobody before Petrarch had tried so valiantly and persistently to push Nature out of the front door, and consequently in no major poem before the *Canzoniere* does she make such a triumphant and visible entrance at the back.

In spite of himself Petrarch created the first modern homily on the text *sentio ergo sum,* and no version of the *Canzoniere* illustrates the text more persuasively than the final version. In doing this Petrarch created the picture frame within which modern sensibility was destined to view the world.

This is my last point and it is an important one. I use the metaphor of the picture frame to recall the view of art developed by Ernst Cassirer. As a latter-day disciple of Kant, Cassirer regards consciousness as a shaping force, a frame or perspective that influences the way reality is perceived. The particular frame that a society or an individual uses is a symbolic form. The most basic symbolic forms are language and religion. In advanced cultures these basic forms are influenced by science and art. Every art work—every poem—is a symbolic form in that it invites the reader to view experience from a perspective not his own. The effect of symbolic forms can be explained in part, but only in part, because in determining the shape of consciousness they determine the way that experience presents itself to the mind for analysis. This is why at least part of the experience of art is, to use Susanne Langer's term, non-discursive.

Individual poems normally affect individuals. Occasionally, however, a work is created that influences a whole culture. Here we return to Petrarch. Petrarchism and the vogue of Petrarchan imitation extended from the fifteenth to the seventeenth century. It was the dominant mode of European lyric poetry for this period, and most subsequent lyric poetry is indebted to it, although the subject matter shifts from love between man and woman to other kinds of experience. This is another way of saying that the form of consciousness objectified in the *Canzoniere,* which began with Petrarch's first meeting with Laura and was developed slowly and painfully through a lifetime of creative effort, was a discovery so important that it swept Europe. It taught Europeans a new way of responding to experience, which is the same thing as saying that it gave Europeans a new framework within which to live their lives.

In this sense the *Canzoniere* is as much a discovery as the discovery of the New World. We are still living in the reality that Petrarch created. If the *Canzoniere* occasionally seems familiar and even commonplace, this is because even if we have not read it, we have lived it. To read a Petrarch sonnet is like looking into an antique mirror. The image is a little strange, a little distorted, but it is familiar because it is our own image. It was duplicated a thousand times, with endless variations, by the imitators who domesticated it in every European vernacular—in English by Wyatt and Surrey, by Gascoigne and Spenser and Shakespeare and John Donne, among others.

Petrarch is tagged as a love poet in the literary histories. He is a love poet, of course, but love is the subject, not the motive of the *Canzoniere.* The motive is an epiphany, the intense moment of experience associated with 6 April 1327, around which the sonnets—and much of Petrarch's life—revolved. The Renaissance took the motive and the subject matter together. They are both present, for example, in Shakespeare's Sonnet 116:

Love is not love
Which alters when it alteration finds,
Or bends with the remover to remove:
O, no; it is an ever-fixed mark,
That looks on tempests and is never shaken;
It is the star to every wandering bark,
Whose worth's unknown, although his height be taken.

We have the same motive, extended to cover the whole spectrum of human experiences, in romantic poetry. The opening lines of Keats's *Endymion*, for example:

A thing of beauty is a joy for ever:
Its loveliness increases; it will never
Pass into nothingness. . . .
Therefore, on every morrow, are we wreathing
A flowery band to bind us to the earth. . . .

We are reminded of Petrarch's fourteenth canzone:

Da' be' rami scendea,
dolce ne la memoria,

una pioggia di fior sovra 'l suo grembo,
ed ella si sedea
umile in tanta gloria,
coverta già do l' amoroso nembo. . . .

It is perhaps enough for my thesis to stop here with the flowery band that binds us to the earth and the image of Laura covered with the petals of real flowers in a real garden at a real moment in time. I would not object to adding a reference to modern love poetry, but I would prefer out of sheer sentiment to defer until another time a consideration of the *sentio* as it is objectified in the poetry of the wasteland and the city of dreadful night.

(1977)

Amoretti and the *Dolce Stil Novo*

In 1903 John Erskine remarked concerning Spenser's *Amoretti,* "Taking the sonnets as a whole, the critic must find in them the truest sequence of this decade."[1] Recent sympathetic studies by Kellogg, Martz, and Nelson tend to confirm this view without, however, greatly refining it.[2] On the other hand, J. W. Lever considers the sequence markedly disunified. "There would seem," he writes "to be only one way of doing justice to Spenser's sequence, and that is by setting apart those sonnets which evidently belong to an earlier phase and run counter to the general stream of thought and feeling. . . . In all, there are at least some eighteen sonnets best considered apart from the main group." The offending sonnets are all those relating to the scorned lover, which present the lady "not only as proud and disdainful . . . but also as sly, licentious, savage, and guileful."[3] The initial problem, then, is whether the *Amoretti* is best considered a "true sequence" or a rather awkward conflation of two distinct groups of poems.

I will begin with a recent discovery concerning the *Amoretti* by Mr. Alexander Dunlop which has been published in *Notes and Queries.*[4] It is well known that there are seasonal references in Spenser's cycle. Sonnet 4 refers to New Year's, sonnet 22 to Ash Wednesday, the beginning of Lent, sonnet 62 to a second New Year's, sonnet 68 to Easter. The apparent implication of these seasonal references is that the *Amoretti* occurs over a period of about two years. Sonnet 4 begins with the line "New yeare forth looking out of Ianus gate. . . ."[5] Clearly it refers to January 1. The normal date for New Year's in Renaissance England was not January 1, however, but March 25, the Feast of the Annunciation. Spenser's second New Year's sonnet (number 62) comes between the Ash Wednesday sonnet and the Easter sonnet. It therefore seems intrinsically probable that sonnet 62 refers to the March 25 New Year's. If so, the sequence depicts not a two-year courtship, but a continuous courtship extending from January through Easter and beyond. As we know from the *Epithalamion,* Spenser's marriage occurred on June 11, 1594; and the title page of the 1595 volume containing *Amoretti* and the *Epithalamion* describes the poems as "written not long since by Edmunde Spenser." The year in question is therefore almost certainly 1594.

Proceeding on this hypothesis, Mr. Dunlop examines the Lenten group of sonnets more carefully. As we have seen, if sonnet 62 refers to the English New Year's, its date is March 25. Mr. Dunlop points out that if we count forward from sonnet 62, assigning a day for each sonnet, when we reach Spenser's Easter sonnet, number 68, we also reach March 31, which was Easter day, 1594. By the same token, counting backward from sonnet 62 to the Lenten sonnet, number 22, we reach February 13, which was Ash Wednesday, 1594. Finally, taking the Lenten sequence as a unit, we find that it is preceded by twenty-one sonnets and followed by twenty-one. The precise matching of dates (which will work for no year in the 1590s other than 1594) and the neat structural symmetry cannot be coincidental. They reflect a carefully worked out plan which has obvious affinities to the calendrical symbolism that Professor Hieatt has shown to be such a prominent feature of the *Epithalamion.*[6]

Considered purely as a structural device, the calendrical element divides *Amoretti* into three units not unlike the panels of a triptych. The first panel consists of twenty-one sonnets which introduce the reader to the love affair and the conflicts involved in it. The second, corresponding to the central panel, develops concurrently with the Lenten season, culminating in Easter. The third panel contains twenty-one sonnets balanced against the first twenty-one and depicting the fruition of love.

If we consider the content of the first panel, we find two apparently clashing motifs, which I will call the *donna angelicata* and the "cruel fair."

The *donna angelicata* motif is, of course, ultimately Italian.[7] In sonnets of the *stil novo* tradition the Lady is conventionally treated as a paragon of virtue, so pure as to approach divinity. The motif emerges most fully, however, after the lady's death, as, for example, in Dante's *Vita Nuova* and Petrarch's *Canzoniere*. Then she becomes a disembodied spirit—literally *angelicata*, "made into an angel"—who appears to the poet, bringing him visions of the life to come. Most English cycles underplay the *donna angelicata* motif. None treats the death of the lady, and most are too deeply rooted in the here-and-now to rise above clichés about the lady's "divine beauty" or her "heavenly virtue." Spenser is the exception. He underscores the motif heavily. The lady is introduced in his first sonnet as being among the "Angels blessed." In sonnet 3 her beauty is an illumination "the light whereof hath kindled heauenly fyre, / in my fraile spirit by her from basenesse raysed." She, herself, is of "celestiall hew" and "ravishes" the poet's pen. In sonnet 8 she is "full of the liuing fire, / Kindled aboue vnto the maker neere." Her eyebeams do not carry Cupid's darts, but "Angels come to lead fraile mindes to rest / in chast desires on heauenly beauty bound"; while in sonnet 17 the poet says that no artist can express "The glorious pourtraict of that Angels face, / Made to amaze weake mens confused skil: / and this worlds worthlesse glory to embase." As these quotations show, the *donna angelicata* motif receives heavy emphasis. It carries with it suggestions of contempt for the world, since by contrast to the spiritual excellence of the lady, human glory becomes "worthlesse." The earth is "lothsome and forlorne," and the flesh, "drossy slime" (sonnet 13).

The "cruel fair" motif is best understood as the reflex of the *donna angelicata* imagery. The lady's virtue causes her to deny the lover, and the denial, in turn, leads to the anguish of frustrated desire. The lady thus can appear to be proud, capricious, and cruelly indifferent to the suffering she is causing. This motif is also ultimately Italian, but it was thoroughly domesticated in both French and English love poetry of the sixteenth century. Spenser introduces it in his second sonnet, which opens with the complaint, "Vnquiet thought, whom at the first I bred, / Of th'inward bale of my loue pined hart," and ends with an appeal to the "fayrest proud" whose compliance will bring life and refusal death: "Which if she graunt, then liue, and my loue cherish, / if not, die soone, and I with thee will perish." The fourth sonnet relates the pangs of desire to the New Year regarded as a reawakening of the erotic impulse. Cupid (literally, *Eros*) has "long . . . slept in cheerlesse bower" but is about to revive with "wanton wings and darts of deadly power," bringing with him "lusty spring." In the sixth sonnet, because she refuses to grant her favors, the lady is denounced for "rebellious pride"; in the tenth she is called a "Tyrannesse" who delights in "huge massacres"; in the eleventh she is a "cruell warriour"; and in the twentieth she is "more cruell and more saluage wylde, / then either Lyon or the Lyonesse."

Although Professor Lever's attack on the unity of *Amoretti* must be revised for reasons that Dunlop's analysis makes clear, his criticism places in much sharper relief than other studies an important fact about Spenser's sonnets. In the first section of the cycle two antithetical attitudes, both deriving ultimately from the *stil novo,* exist side by side. The juxtaposition is deliberate and violent. It begins as a simple a-b, a-b alternation in sonnets 1 through 4. After this initial statement of the motifs, the alternation becomes more complex, but—and this is the main point—nothing new is added. The twenty-one sonnets of the first section are all elaborations of one of the two motifs—either *donna angelicata* or "cruel fair." Both are responses of the poet to love. On the one hand, he worships the lady as a spiritual being, an angel of light, a Platonic Idea, a paragon to whom the world and the flesh are "drossy slime." On the other hand, he desires her physically, feels pain when she refuses her favors, and accuses her of cruelty, vanity, and a sadistic delight in causing suffering. The opposition embodies a conflict between the claims of the spirit and those of the flesh, and in the first section of *Amoretti* this opposition is static. The poet is divided against himself. Because love involves worship and desire, he can satisfy neither impulse.

Let us now move to the forty-six sonnets comprising the central panel of Spenser's triptych. In these sonnets a change occurs in the poet. Gradually, and with considerable vacillation, the contradictory impulses of the first twenty-one sonnets are reconciled, and the Lenten sequence ends with six sonnets celebrating a love that is simultaneously spiritual and physical. The basis of the new attitude is, of course, the ideal of married love that C. S. Lewis long ago identified as Spenser's distinctive contribution to the tradition of English love poetry.[8] The sonnet in which the new attitude first unambiguously appears is, appropriately, the New Year's sonnet associated with March 25—sonnet 62—and the sonnet in which its meaning is fully revealed is sonnet 68, the Easter sonnet.

It is clearly of the greatest significance that the movement of the poet's emotions from anguished self-division to harmonious affirmation precisely parallels the Lenten season. Lent is a period of change. Its dominant tone in liturgy is sorrow, but this tone is relieved by hints of creative sacrifice, of salvation through divine love. Likewise, the penance associated with Lent has a positive function. By purifying man, it prepares him to share the glories of the Resurrection. In the *Amoretti,* then, the poet's quest for a new understanding of human love moves forward against the background of the Christian search for a new and deeper relation to divine love.

Spenser emphasizes the parallelism. The first quatrain of sonnet 22—the Ash Wednesday sonnet—identifies Lent with penance and then links the religious connotations of the season with the imagery of the *donna angelicata:*

> This holy season fit to fast and pray,
> Men to deuotion ought to be inclynd:
> therefore, I lykewise on so holy day,
> for my sweet Saynt some seruice fit will find.

The close linking of human and divine love looks back to the *stil novo*—especially Dante—and forward, perhaps, to Donne. The seriousness of Spenser's attitude is Italian rather than metaphysical, and is, I feel, more striking—because more suggestive of a genuine religion of love—than Donne's self-parodying irony. The most daring image comes in the last quatrain. Here Spenser equates the sacrifice of the lover's heart with the sacrifice of priests within a "temple fair"—that is, with the Eucharist:

> There I to her as th'author of my blisse,
> will builde an altar to appease her yre:
> and on the same my hart will sacrifise,
> burning in flames of pure and chast desyre.

Although the motifs of the *donna angelicata* and the "cruel fair" continue to appear in the Lenten sequence, the idea of creative sacrifice, of moving through suffering toward a new affirmation, often modifies them. The fire imagery of sonnet 22, for example, gives surprising resonance to the conventional "fire and ice" conceit of sonnet 30, and provides an ironic perspective for the lover's complaint in sonnet 32 that the flames of passion may eventually burn him "to ashes" if the lady remains indifferent. That the tensions persist is shown by sonnets 33 and 44, which lament the conflict between love and artistic creativity. The first of these sonnets, incidentally, is the famous complaint to Lodowick Bryskett that the poet cannot complete *The Faerie Queene* because of "a proud loue, that doth my spirite spoyle."

The moments of despair, however, alternate with moments of hope. Sonnets 39 and 40 celebrate the lady's smile, her first sign of favor. In sonnet 39 the *donna angelicata* imagery is subsumed in a comparison of the effects of the smile to mystic rapture: "Whylest rapt with ioy resembling heauenly madnes, / my soule was rauisht quite as in a traunce." And in 40 the same experience is expressed in natural terms by comparison to the happiness of birds and animals after a storm. Sonnet 61 (corresponding, incidentally, to Palm Sunday) begins as a triumphant *donna angelicata* poem. The lady is "The glorious image of the makers beautie, / My soue-rayne saynt" and is later called, "diuinely wrought, / and of the brood of Angels heuenly borne." It ends, however, with an echo of the old conflict: "Such heauenly formes ought rather worshipt be, / then dare be lou'd by men of meane degree."

As I have suggested, the turning point of the Lenten sequence is sonnet 62, the New Year's poem. The January New Year's sonnet related the changing season to Cupid and erotic love. The March sonnet treats the New Year as a moment of conversion, a turning away from sin and error:

> So let vs, which this chaunge of weather vew,
> chaunge eeke our mynds and former liues amend,
> the old yeares sinnes forepast let vs eschew,
> and fly the faults with which we did offend.

From this point on, the mood of the sequence is wholly positive. Sonnet 63 begins with a reference to a long, arduous process finally nearing completion—"After long stormes and tempests sad assay . . . I doe at length descry the happy shore"—and ends with an image that dazzlingly unites the idea of love's completion with the *donna angelicata* motif of love as salvation: "All paines are nothing in respect to this, / all sorrowes short that gaine eternall blisse." Sonnet 64 celebrates the first kiss through imagery comparing the lady to an ideal garden. Sonnet 65 praises married love as bondage that brings true liberty and a refuge where "spotlesse pleasure builds her sacred bowre."

The image of "spotlesse pleasure" defines the new understanding of love precisely. If *Amoretti* begins with a series of sonnets in which worship and desire, spirit and flesh, stand in painful and sterile opposition, the movement of the Lenten sequence is toward a reconciliation of the two principles; in short, toward what may be called "Eros sanctified." The synthesis is beautifully and fully expressed in Spenser's Easter sonnet. In this sonnet human and divine love are treated as complementary. That is, the lesson of the Resurrection is the holiness of the love of man and woman. The sonnet is all the more remarkable in that its rhetorical form is derived from the collects of the Book of Common Prayer:

> Most glorious Lord of lyfe, that on this day,
> Didst make thy triumph ouer death and sin:
> and hauing harrowd hell, didst bring away
> captiuity thence captiue vs to win:
> This ioyous day, deare Lord, with ioy begin,
> and grant that we for whom thou diddest dye
> being with thy deare blood clene washt from sin,
> may liue for euer in felicity.
> And that thy loue we weighing worthily,
> may likewise loue thee for the same againe:
> and for thy sake that all lyke deare didst buy,
> with loue may one another entertayne.
> So let us loue, deare loue, lyke as we ought,
> loue is the lesson which the Lord vs taught.

We now move, although briefly, to the third panel of Spenser's triptych. In general, the last twenty-one sonnets of the *Amoretti* form a coda in which the poet explores the implications of what he has learned during the Lenten sequence. Sonnet 70 celebrates the lady in a blazon anticipating the *Song of Songs* imagery of the *Epithalamion.* Sonnet 74 associates Elizabeth Boyle with two other Elizabeths who symbolize the benign influence of love on Spenser's life—his mother and his queen. Sonnet 80 inverts the motif of the conflict between love and artistic creativity introduced in the Lenten sequence. Now instead of preventing Spenser from continuing *The Faerie Queene,* love is a source of inspiration. Sonnets 84–86 rebuke unnamed critics for questioning the purity of the poet's love. The last three sonnets lament the absence of the lady. The absence, of course, is temporary—a prelude to final possession in the *Epithalamion.*

What I have said thus far demonstrates, I think, that the *Amoretti* is a unified, intensely dramatic, presentation of the experience of human love in the context of Christian belief. The two key motifs are the *donna angelicata* and the "cruel fair." They are both derived ultimately from the *stil novo,* and Spenser's use of the first one is more conscious and more detailed than in other Elizabethan sonnet cycles. The function of the motifs in the *Amoretti* is not, however, derived from the *stil novo,* and is unique to Spenser. This can be shown by a brief contrast between Spenser and Petrarch.

In Petrarch's *Canzoniere* the "cruel fair" and *donna angelicata* motifs reflect an essentially ascetic attitude toward the world and the flesh. The first motif is associated with Laura in life and reveals that, in spite of his admiration for her virtue, the poet cannot suppress the desire that she arouses. The second is associated primarily with the sonnets to Laura in death. Laura no longer exists as a physical being; she is literally *angelicata*—a spirit who visits the poet, consoles him, and raises his eyes from the darkness of this world to the light of the world to come. In short, in the *Canzoniere,* the two motifs not only *seem* irreconcilable, they *are* irreconcilable. Flesh and spirit are at war. Only by the destruction of one can the other realize itself. For the *stilnovisti* there is no question as to which principle should triumph, and the triumph of the spiritual principle is symbolized by the death of the lady. The moment of her death is thus the moment when the poet begins a new and purer life. As Bertoni writes in his study *Il Duecento,* "The death of the beloved ladies in these writers corresponds . . . to the death of human reason in mystic rapture of the soul, to the death, that is, of Rachel, who died . . . to raise herself to the highest contemplation."[9] Lorenzo de' Medici expressed the same idea more directly in the commentary he wrote for his sonnet cycle *Clizia:* "The beginning of the true life is the end of the life which is not true"; and again, "If love has in itself that perfection which we have already remarked, it is impossible to come to that perfection without dying first."[10]

If we now return to the *Amoretti,* we can see that Spenser's concept of "Eros sanctified" enabled him to use the *stil novo* motifs while avoiding the drastic either/or attitude that made the death of the lady the price of love's fulfillment. Instead of placing the "cruel fair" and *donna angelicata* sonnets in separate sections of his cycle, Spenser begins with a section in which both are included. Their opposition begins to move toward resolution with the Ash Wednesday sonnet (number 22). The climax of the process occurs with sonnet 62, the second New Year's sonnet. It is this moment in the *Amoretti* that corresponds to the transition from the old to the new life in the *stil novo* tradition.[11] The conflict that leads to the death of the lady in the *stil novo* tradition is then triumphantly resolved in Spenser's Easter sonnet which asserts that human love—including passionate erotic love—fulfills the divine plan instead of being antithetical to it. In this connection it is surely significant that the Easter sonnet celebrates not death but rebirth, and that the sonnet begins by addressing Christ as "most glorious Lord of lyfe."

To return to my beginning, both in its intricate design and in its creative use of what were for other Elizabethan poets dead conventions, Spenser's *Amoretti* is precisely what Erskine called it—the truest sequence of the decade of the 1590s. Moreover, almost alone among Renaissance sonnet cycles, Spenser's *Amoretti* celebrates love as a benign life force. It thus looks forward to the great hymn of praise to this force which Spenser offers in the *Epithalamion.*

(1972)

Logic Versus the Slovenly World in Shakespearean Comedy

"Comedy aims at representing men as worse, and tragedy as better than in real life." That is the way Aristotle saw things in the *Poetics*, and twenty-five hundred years later, it is still as logical as most of our other theories of comedy. We know a great deal more than Aristotle, of course. We know the comedies of Menander and Plautus and Terence, of Shakespeare and Ben Jonson and Molière, of Sheridan and Bernard Shaw and Charlie Chaplin, and we have, almost at our fingertips, a five-foot shelf of books dealing with comedy in general and specific authors and comedies in particular.

We also have a smaller shelf of works of deconstruction which question whether the logic of seeing literary works in terms of genres is anything more than the critic's version of the Platonic habit of trying to tidy up an inherently slovenly world—a pernicious habit in that it turns our attention from the things of the world, themselves, to the vanities of the mind. Benedetto Croce argued in his *Aesthetic* that the theory of genres is the "greatest triumph of the intellectualistic error"[1] invented by literary critics, and Martin Heidegger devoted much of his considerable energy to discovering the path that leads out of the mind and back to the thing itself, or, at least, the thingness of the thing insofar as it can survive the trauma of its own perception. The advice of this group of critics, who may be understood as the loyal opposition dedicated to preventing genre critics from playing tennis with the net down, is clear: look at each work individually; do not strap a literary work into a Procrustean bed labeled "tragedy" or "comedy" and proceed to lop off its feet because it doesn't fit the master plan.

Aristotle was probably the only critic before the Romantic period to steer a middle path between the Scylla of Plato and the Charybdis of Martin Heidegger. He was able to do this because his method was deductive. He began with the elements from which drama is constructed—its means, materials, and object—whereas his successors picked up a miscellaneous collection of traditions and empirical observations and shaped them into a canon of rules which they then attempted to impose on the authors who wrote plays and the critics who analyzed, defended, and attacked the plays that had been written. The resulting mix took shape in

Alexandria in the third century B.C. and is best expressed in the *Ars Poetica* of Horace and an assortment of lesser rhetorical and poetic treatises extending from the first to the fourth century A.D. By later standards this native classicism was relatively open, partly because the Romans did not think of themselves as being "classical" or "neo-classical," and partly because Roman literary criticism was not the self-conscious academic industry that criticism became during the Renaissance.

The turning point was the fifteenth century. Under the influence of what historians have called "the revival of antiquity," scholars began to review the legacy of Greek and Roman criticism. Possessed by an all-consuming zeal to recover, analyze, formalize, and complete what they believed the ancients had begun, they produced editions, syntheses, and full-scale treatises on the theory of literature. What had been suggestions in Horace began to be regarded as laws for modern authors; and what had been forms and conventions growing organically out of the conditions of ancient society and drama in Aristophanes, Menander, and Terence became models for imitation backed up by the authority of reason. In fact, because such great authority was accorded to the laws, the ancient models became in themselves suspect when they failed to observe the laws, and a good deal of anguished attention was given to classical plays that violated the ideal unity of time or plot or showed violence onstage or ignored the rules of decorum of character. When Aristotle's *Poetics* was rediscovered after the Latin translation by Alessandro Pazzi in 1536, it was not understood, as it is today, as a supremely original analysis of the nature of literature, but as a confirmation, even a codification, by the master of all philosophers, of the rules that earlier critics had had to piece together laboriously from other sources. This procedure caused numerous misreadings, distortions, and omissions (duly recorded in the two volumes of Bernard Weinberg's *History of Literary Criticism in the Italian Renaissance*), but it brought Aristotle into the neoclassic camp, where he remained until the end of the eighteenth century.[2] It also created a two-hundred-year dilemma for English literary critics.

The reason for this dilemma is historical. Ancient drama flourished until the fourth or fifth century A.D. and then it abruptly vanished along with most of the living social and literary tradition that surrounded it. It was replaced some five centuries later by a new kind of drama growing out of medieval and Christian culture. This drama was unself-conscious. It did not generate much literary criticism, aside from a few sporadic complaints by clergymen that it was indecent and blasphemous. It was a popular drama rather than a formal and literary drama, and its characteristics were quite different from anything that can be found in antiquity, with the possible exception of the sprawling, surrealistic comedies of Aristophanes.

A few of these characteristics may be listed. They are frequently regarded as characteristics of "folk drama" or drama produced by naive popular artists for the illiterate masses. This condescending attitude, however, is mistaken. It illustrates the lingering influence of neoclassic taste, even on critics who reject the system itself. In fact, as a considerable body of scholarship has demonstrated over the last twenty years,[3] medieval drama has its own traditions which are not worse than but simply different from those of classical drama and which are in many ways closer than classical traditions to the deep structure of modern Western culture.

The most obvious characteristic of medieval drama is that it is comic rather than tragic. The earliest medieval dramas depict the visit of the Marys to the tomb of Christ on the morning of the Resurrection. They approach in sadness. Their Master is dead, and they have come to anoint the body. Suddenly an angel appears to announce "He is not dead, He has arisen as He foretold; go, tell the disciples that He has arisen." The moment is what Aristotle would have called a reversal—a *peripeteia.* It changes the mood of the women from sorrow to rejoicing. In their joy they sing the *Allelulia* and then depart to deliver their message to the disciples.

In the formulation of Donatus, a fourth-century critic, the essential difference between comedy and tragedy is that a comedy begins ominously but ends happily, whereas a tragedy begins well but ends in disaster.[4] Although this is not Aristotelian, it is a good rough definition of the basic plot structure of comedy and tragedy as understood during the Middle Ages and Renaissance, and it applies equally to medieval and Renaissance drama. The plot out of which medieval drama grew is thus comic. The point holds for the minute Resurrection play of the tenth century and for the vast cycle plays, extending from the Creation to the Last Judgment, which were popular in England in the fifteenth century.

Another characteristic of the Resurrection play which remained true for later medieval drama, and of medieval narration as well, is that it depends on miracles. It violates the laws of verisimilitude which neoclassical critics insisted had to be observed if a drama was not to be laughed off the stage. By corollary, the Resurrection play combines human and divine characters with an easy familiarity that strains, if it does not violate, the ideal of decorum—the theory that characters should be grouped in categories of social class, sex, nationality, profession, and the like, and that class categories should not be mixed. Decorum is both a genre concept and a plot concept. Tragedies in neo-classic theory were supposed to show the lives of kings and nobles, while comedies were to deal with the lives of middle- and lower-class citizens; tragedies were supposed to avoid characters and dialogue that could be considered obscene, ridiculous, or digressive.

Medieval drama recognized no restrictions either of verisimilitude or of decorum. The initial miracle at the tomb of Christ multiplied during the centuries into a cloud of minor and quasi-miracles ranging from divine intervention by God Himself to pranks by demons to magic tricks to impossible coincidences. By the same token, the mixing of human and divine characters at the tomb of Christ is echoed in later medieval drama by what seems today to be an almost total indifference to the idea of decorum. Kings, clowns, peasants, merchants, Jews, Christians, bawds, shepherds, physicians, knights, and housewives are stirred together in the pot of late medieval drama in a way that is as various, as surprising, as outrageous as life itself. What is more, they often have as little regard for their own inner decorum as an American President recording plots with cronies on tape in the White House.

As for the medieval stories, they are often wildly unprobable, and they move from location to location and from one time to the next with casual abandon. If they observe any laws, the laws are those of the imagination: whatever works with the audience is acceptable. As the modern fondness for cartoons demonstrates, in the proper context almost anything will work.[5]

I do not wish to paint a false picture of late medieval drama. In the most charitable valuation, it is often crude, obvious, and ridiculous in the negative sense of that term. My point is different. It is that medieval drama grew organically from the conditions of Christian and Western culture. It expresses the inner nature of that culture. As it became common throughout Europe, it both revealed to its audiences something of what they were and, at the same time, shaped their understanding of what drama should be. The key elements of this understanding were that drama is comic in structure, open in form, and as various and irrational as society itself. This is to say that, for all its imperfections, medieval drama tended to show the world as it is, not as it should be. It did this partly by imitating life rather than literary models, but even more by symbolizing through its own variety and irrationality the larger irrationality of the world around it; and by symbolizing, through its miraculous reversals of fortune, the Christian belief that the ultimate nature of the world, its ontological nature, is good rather than evil or meaningless.

By the end of the fifteenth century medieval drama was firmly established and enormously popular from Spain to Germany and from Italy to England. At this moment, however, its development was profoundly influenced by the rise of humanism. From the point of view of the humanists, medieval drama was a disaster. Compared to *Oedipus the King* or *Antigone,* the typical medieval drama was formless, illogical, and intellectually insulting. While it might please the ignorant masses, it was wholly unsuitable for the enlightened circles of university and court. In the two European countries where humanism had penetrated the upper classes most successfully, Italy and France, medieval drama was attacked so vehemently that it eventually disappeared. It was replaced by dramas that imitated the ancient models, usually in plots based on ancient history or mythology, and that supplemented direct imitation of models with corrective applications of the rules derived from Renaissance criticism. In Italy the medieval tradition was lost and very little drama of permanent artistic value was created in its place. Italian tragedy of the sixteenth and seventeenth centuries is mostly stillborn, although a few comedies, principally those of Machiavelli and Ariosto, are still effective today. The fact that they are comedies and consequently somewhat less formal than the tragedies of the period may have something to do with their success. In France, sixteenth-century classical drama is equally wooden. It is typified in the tragedies of Robert Garnier, which Sir Philip Sidney's sister the Countess of Pembroke translated in the hope of reforming the English stage. In the seventeenth century French classicism finally produced work of universal power in the theatre of Corneille, Racine, and Molière, but seventeenth-century drama is beyond the scope of the present essay.

In two countries there was less hostility to medieval drama. They are Spain and England, and it is of central importance to the present topic to observe that in both countries dramas were produced that are permanent glories of the Western literary heritage. Each country produced unique kinds of drama—which is to say that the art of Calderón and Lope de Vega is quite different from the art of Marlowe and Shakespeare—but in both countries it was a Christian art, popular, open, and various, and an art that remained sensitive to its medieval heritage.

The case of Spain seems relatively simple. Medieval drama is, among other things, Catholic drama, and Spain was less affected than any other European country by the Reformation. Drama shaped by medieval tradition could be allowed to flourish in the marketplace, while members of the court could edify themselves to their hearts' content with stillborn Italian imports. That this was a conscious choice, made partly on the basis of preference for the "naturalness" of the native dramatic tradition and partly out of the economic necessity of pleasing audiences, is clear from two passages by Lope de Vega. In Lope's play *El Fingido Verdadero,* Giocleciano defends the openness of the native tradition on the basis of its human appeal:

> Give me a new plot which has more invention [than the *Andria* of Terence and the *Miles Gloriosus* of Plautus] though it be lacking in art; for in this respect I have a Spaniard's taste and if you give me the lifelike I care nothing for theory. On the contrary, its inflexibility wearies me and I have observed that they who devote themselves to concentrating on art fail to seize upon the natural.[6]

In his critical treatise on drama, *El arte nuevo de hacer comedias,* Lope's attitude is more ambivalent. He claims to admire the rules of "art" but is forced to ignore them in order to attract audiences:

> Not that I was unaware of the rules; I thank God that even as an apprentice to grammar I had already read the books which treated of these subjects. . . . But I finally found that the plays in Spain at that time were not as their early makers in the world thought they should be written, but as many untutored writers treated them who worked for the public according to its own rude ways, and thus insinuated themselves into favor to such an extent that whoever now writes plays with art dies without fame or reward; for among those who lack fire, custom can accomplish more than reason or force.
>
> It is true that occasionally I have written in accordance with the art that few know, but later when from others I saw proceed monstrous things full of theatrical apparatus, to which the crowd and the women who canonize this sad business came running, I returned to the barbarous manner, and when I have to write a play I lock the rules away with six keys.[7]

In England the historical and dramatic situation seems more complex than in Spain. The Reformation came to England in 1535, but it was only a partial reformation. Henry VIII declared himself the supreme authority for the English church and dissolved the monasteries and the monastic orders, but the church itself remained conservative and open to medieval tradition, including the tradition of Catholic liturgy. There was a great deal of interest in new kinds of drama and in the new critical theories imported from Italy and France, but as H.C. Gardiner has shown, Corpus Christi plays continued to be performed sporadically until the 1560s, when they were either suppressed or abandoned because of the opposition of religious authorities.[8] Plautus and Terence and Seneca were performed at grammar schools and universities and were translated and imitated, but at the same time, wildly improbable comedies drawn from medieval romances like *Sir Clyomon and Sir Clamydes,* and tragedies and histories like *The Spanish Tragedy* and *Arden of Feversham* and *Dr. Faustus,* were box-office hits on the popular stage.

It was out of this fluid and extremely complex mix of traditions that Shakespeare's drama emerged. Two examples show immediately how complex and fluid the situation is for his comedies. His earliest comedy has the key word in its title: *The Comedy of Errors.* The most obvious fact about this play is that it is drawn primarily from two classical sources, the *Menaechmi* and the *Amphitryon* of Plautus. The *Menaechmi* was translated by W. W. (probably William Warner) around 1593 and published in 1594. Shakespeare may have seen this translation in manuscript; but there is no reason to think that he did not consult the Latin text directly. The play is set in Ephesus, a suitable classical location, and its characters appear to be taken from the Sears catalogue of ancient comic types: the tricky servant, the lively courtesan, the indignant husband, the shrewish wife. Mistaken identity, which is the engine that makes the plot move, is also the stock device of the source play the *Menaechmi,* and Shakespeare has taken no improper liberties by creating twin servants as well as twin masters.

As soon as one moves beyond these obviously classical features, however, the image changes. The earliest recorded performance of the play was for the members of Gray's Inn on Holy Innocents' Day, 28 December 1594, in connection with the annual revels of the Lord of Misrule. Although the play was probably performed before 1594 on the public stage, its selection for the revels may tell us something significant about Shakespeare's comic art.

It puts the play in the context of a medieval festival that had survived in Protestant England to the closing years of the sixteenth century and that had as its most essential feature the reversal of all the rules of logic, decorum, and verisimilitude. Compared to the *Menaechmi,* Shakespeare's play is a meandering, absurd, hilarious, and at times insane trip behind the facade of ordinary life. There is a good deal of this quality in the plays of Aristophanes, which Shakespeare probably did not know, but comparatively little in Plautus. Moreover, Shakespeare has given the play a Christian frame plot which he derived from one of the redactions—probably the *Confessio Amantis* of John Gower—of the romantic story of Apollonius of Tyre, which was a favorite in the Middle Ages. Aegeon, the merchant of Ephesus, is under sentence of death by "solemn synods" unless he can pay an impossible fine of one thousand marks. Nothing but a miracle can save him.

By the end of the play, for reasons quite unrelated to the preposterous adventures of his two sons and their servants, the miracle has occurred. The Abbess of the local convent, who has no business being in a Plautine comedy but is certainly a welcome guest at the feast of the Lord of Misrule, turns out to be the long-lost wife of Aegeon. She cures Adriana of her shrewishness, she promises to cure Antipholus of Syracuse of his madness with "wholesome syrups, drugs, and holy prayers" (V.i.104), and she gains the release of Aegeon by revealing her identity. Admittedly the miracle is secular: it is caused by an Abbess, not an angel, and it involves coincidence rather than the explicitly supernatural; but the emphasis on an abrupt reversal of mood from tragedy to joy through a process that flies in the face of common sense is unmistakable. We are dealing with a medieval play dressed up in a toga, not the reverse.

It should be added that the preceding description is not remotely adequate to the play that Shakespeare wrote. This is appropriate. The play is an early effort, but already Shakespeare's dramaturgy has a life that is much larger than a description of its central motives. It regularly and easily expands beyond the limits of its plot to present dimensions of experience that are part of the life of its culture, but not in any obvious sense necessary to its subject. Gargoyles ring medieval cathedrals with impudent irrelevance, and in an analogous way Shakespeare's characters, even in *The Comedy of Errors,* habitually exceed the limits of their own decorum. Adriana, for instance, is a shrew. She has no business being anything but a shrew; but she resists the stereotype. She sounds more like Juliet than Kate in *The Taming of the Shrew* when she senses that her husband is becoming estranged:

> Ah, do not tear away thyself from me!
> For know, my love, as easy mayst thou fall
> A drop of water in the breaking gulf,
> And take unmingled thence that drop again
> Without addition or diminishing,
> As take from me thyself and not me too.
> (II.ii.123–28)[9]

Antipholus of Syracuse, whom Luciana considers her sister's husband, is no less eloquent. He speaks in rhyme, not in blank verse or prose, which is another violation of decorum; and if he is a seducer, he is given a degree of eloquence that borders on the immoral. It is the eloquence of Petrarch and the Renaissance love sonnet, not the Age of Augustus:

> O train me not, sweet mermaid, with thy note,
> To drown me in thy sister's flood of tears!
> Sing, siren, for thyself, and I will dote.
> Spread o'er the silver waves thy golden hairs,
> And as a bed I'll take them and there lie;
> And in that glorious supposition think
> He gains by death that hath such means to die.
> (III.ii.45–51)

Then there is the cook. Nothing quite like the cook exists in classical drama. The whole play stops for the cook, who is drawn from the same current of medieval realism that produced the works of Rabelais and Grobius, given a special immediacy here by allusions to Renaissance geography. "What's her name?" asks Antipholus of Syracuse, who plays Abbott to Dromio's Costello:

Dromio S. Nell, sir; but her name and three quarters—that's an ell and three-quarters—will not measure her from hip to hip.
Antipholus S. Then she bears some breadth?
Dromio S. No longer from head to foot than from hip to hip: she is spherical, like a globe; I could find out countries in her.

Antipholus S. In what part of her body stands Ireland?

Dromio S. Marry, sir, in her buttocks. I found it out by the bogs.

Antipholus S. Where Scotland?

Dromio S. I found it out by the barrenness; hard in the palm of the hand.

Antipholus S. Where France?

Dromio S. In her forehead, armed and reverted, making war against her heir.

Antipholus S. Where England?

Dromio S. I looked for the chalky cliffs, but I could find no whiteness in them; but I guess it stood in her chin, by the salt rheum that ran between France and it.

Antipholus S. Where Spain?

Dromio S. Faith, I saw it not; but I felt it hot in her breath.

Antipholus S. Where America, the Indies?

Dromio S. O, sir, upon her nose, all o'er embellished with rubies, carbuncles, sapphires, declining their rich aspect to the hot breath of Spain, who sent whole armadoes of carracks to be ballast at her nose.

Antipholus S. Where stood Belgia, the Netherlands?

Dromio S. O, sir! I did not look so low.

(III.ii.104–31)

The spirit of classical comedy is linear. It moves forward from episode to episode according to rational principles of necessity or probability, to use Aristotle's terms, and the interest is more in the destination than in the scenery along the road. Its qualities are distilled and purified in the comedies of Machiavelli and Molière. Following Aristotle, the characters of neoclassic comedy tend to be worse rather than better than men in real life, and its image is coolly, sometimes bitterly disillusioned. It presents a neatly-structured world which is the opposite in mood and in detail of the slapstick wonderland of *The Comedy of Errors.*

A Midsummer Night's Dream was probably written within three or four years of *The Comedy of Errors.* It too has a classical setting, the court of Theseus, Duke of Athens, but that is almost its only classical feature. It appears to have been written for a wedding and incorporates both the festive mood and the masque-like action appropriate to Elizabethan (though not to classical) weddings. If *The Comedy of Errors* has a slapstick quality appropriate to feasts of the Lord of Misrule, *A Midsummer Night's Dream* has the more phantasmagoric quality associated with lunacies of love and the midsummer moon. Shakespeare's Theseus is the feudal lord of medieval tradition as found, for example, in Chaucer's *Knight's Tale,* and his faeries are taken directly from English folklore. The closest approach to truly classical drama in the play is the "'tedious brief scene of young Pyramus / And his love Thisby'" (V.i.56–57), which probably owes something to Arthur Golding's translation of Ovid's *Metamorphoses* and which is a burlesque rather than an admiring imitation. It is, as Theseus reads in the program notes, "'very tragical mirth'" (V.i.57). This is certainly not a comment on the whole classical tradition in comedy, but it suggests, at least, that Shakespeare saw an absurd as well as a valid side to the vogue of imitation of the ancients.

In *A Midsummer Night's Dream* the plot mechanism shifts from the impossible coincidences of *The Comedy of Errors* to the explicit magic of supernatural beings. Oberon, Titania, Puck, and their faery retinue are spirits from the invisible world who directly shape the course of the human action. As in *The Comedy of Errors,* however, the frame story involves a law which exposes certain characters "to death," or to "a vow of single life" (I.i.121) which one imagines is as severe as death in the minds of the Shakespearean lovers. The threat is not as ominous as in *The Comedy of Errors,* but it is there in the background and echoes in the recriminations of the lovers in the forest. Lysander and Demetrius, in fact, try to kill each other in a duel. Jan Kott calls attention in *Shakespeare our Contemporary* to the uneasy sense of terror lurking beneath the surface of the characters of Puck, Oberon, and Titania.[10] Not all faery folk, after all, are cute; and there seems to be an ambivalence in the Elizabethen attitude toward them stemming from the memory that they sprang from a pagan rather than a Christian culture and had daemonic ancestors. At any rate, the plot has the familiar comic pattern. At the end of act 4 the lovers are discovered by Theseus. Puck has correctly matched them through his magical herb, but Egeus still demands the full penalty of the law. It is now Theseus' turn to be converted, and he responds immediately:

> Egeus, I will overbear your will,
> For in the temple, by and by, with us,
> These couples shall eternally be knit.
> (IV.i.178–80)

The end of *A Midsummer Night's Dream* is not so much a concluding action as a festive celebration of what has already been concluded, seasoned by the performances of Bottom and his company. The comic movement from sorrow to joy is beautifully objectified in the theme of marriage.

This use of marriage is archetypal, as Northrop Frye and C.L. Barber both long ago pointed out.[11] It touches on the themes of rebirth, fertility, and the reconciliation of generations and is the secular equivalent of the sense of community that follows the celebration of the liturgy. It is, of course, a stock device of Renaissance comedy. Shakespeare did not invent it, but he uses it here and in *The Merchant of Venice* and *The Winter's Tale* with particular effectiveness. As Pyramus and Thisbe die in mirthful sorrow, the human lovers are ushered to their marriage beds with a blessing and something like a lustration:

With this field-dew consecrate,
Every fairy take his gait,
And each several chamber bless,
Through this palace, with sweet peace.
(V.i.404–7)

Shakespeare's *Midsummer Night's Dream* is so perfectly an expression of itself that there is no need to isolate passages showing its differences from classical comedy. Innumerable passages reflect the fact that the play comes from a tradition not available to Plautus and Terence and antithetical to the rules and laws of rationalist criticism. No less a figure than Theseus himself marks the distinction. At the beginning of Horace's *Ars Poetica* there is a famous warning against the excesses of poetic imagination:

Suppose a painter chose to couple a horse's neck with a human head, and to lay feathers of every hue on limbs gathered here and there, or that a woman, lovely above, foully ended in an ugly fish below; would you restrain your laughter, my friends, if admitted to a private viewing? Believe me, dear Pisos, a book will appear uncommonly like that picture, if impossible figures are wrought into it—like a sick man's dreams—with the result that neither head nor foot is ascribed to a single shape, and unity is lost (ll. 1–9).

In fact, Shakespeare put a horse's head on one of his characters and explicitly calls his play a dream. Whether or not Theseus speaks for Shakespeare, he sees the poet not as a calculating fabricator of illusions but as an inspired madman (which is exactly what Horace was warning against):

The lunatic, the lover, and the poet
Are of imagination all compact.
One sees more devils than vast hell can hold:
That is the madman. The lover, all as frantic,
Sees Helen's beauty in a brow of Egypt.
The poet's eye, in a fine frenzy rolling,
Doth glance from heaven to earth, from earth to heaven;
And as imagination bodies forth
The forms of things unknown, the poet's pen
Turns them to shapes, and gives to airy nothing
A local habitation and a name.
(V.i.7–17)

So much for history and for the historical context within which Shakespearean comedy is best understood. At an earlier point I suggested that an accident of history created an impossible dilemma for English critics from Shakespeare's own lifetime to the end of the eighteenth century. The dilemma is that the English critics loved Renaissance drama with their hearts but knew with their heads that it violates all the rules of art. Consequently, a schizophrenic quality pervades the comments by seventeenth- and eighteenth-century critics on Shakespeare and his contemporaries. This schizophrenia first appears in major criticism in the *Apologie for Poetrie* by Sir Philip Sidney. Sidney had the English drama of the 1560s and 1570s in mind rather than Shakespeare, but his comments foreshadowed what was to come. At the beginning of the *Apologie* Sidney praises the wonderful power of imagination. His poet is a *vates*—a prophet whose "high flying liberty of conceit . . . did seeme to have some dyuine force in it."[12] Like the poet who gives names to airy nothings, Sidney's poet scorns nature, and "lifted vp with the vigor of his owne inuention, dooth growe in effect another nature . . . so as hee goeth hand in hand with Nature, not inclosed within the narrow warrant of her guifts, but freely ranging onely within the Zodiack of his owne wit" (p. 104). By the end of Sidney's *Apologie,* however, another point of view is evident. It is the point of view of reason, which insists with Horace that the poet must control his imagination, follow nature, and obey the rules. Instead of imagination, Sidney now praises "unflattering reason" which works through "imitative pattern," "exercise," and "artificial rules" (pp. 136–37). Inevitably, when Sidney turns to drama, the "artificial rules" tell him that the English tradition is woefully deficient. He finds even *Gorboduc,* a relatively classical play, "faulty both in place and time, two necessary companions of all corporall actions" (p. 138). He attacks the mingling of genres in tragicomedy, the mingling of "Kings and Clownes" in all forms of drama, and the "Curtizan—like painted affectation" of the English drama of his own age (pp. 139–43). Clearly, his heart and head were in conflict. Instead of choosing one or the other, he wavered.

Ben Jonson is the first major critic who had to confront Shakespeare, and his ambivalence is notorious. There is an almost Hamlet-like vacillation between love and disapproval in the following comment from *Timber, or Discoveries.*

> I *remember* the Players have often mentioned it as an honour to *Shakespeare,* that in his writing, whatsoever he penn'd, he never blotted out [a] line. My answer hath beene, would he had blotted a thousand: Which they thought a malevolent speech. I had not told posterity this, but for their ignorance who choose that circumstance to commend their friend by wherein he most faulted; And to justify mine owne candor, for I lov'd the man, and doe honour his memory, on this side Idolatry, as much as any. He was indeed honest, and of an open and free nature, had an excellent *Phantsie,* brave notions,

> and gentle expressions, wherein he flow'd with that facility that sometime it was necessary he should be stop'd. . . . His wit was in his owne power; would the rule of it had been so too. Many times hee fell into those things, could not escape laughter; As when hee said in the person of *Caesar,* one speaking to him: *Caesar, thou does me wrong.* Hee replyed: *Caesar did never wrong but with just cause;* and such like, which were ridiculous. But hee redeemed his vices with his vertues. There was ever more in him to be praysed than to be pardoned.[13]

This is so expressive that it can stand for the more extended examples of critical schizophrenia to be found in John Dryden's *Essay on Dramatic Poesy,* Samuel Johnson's preface to his edition of Shakespeare, and a host of lesser essays. Not until the Romantic period—especially in the criticism of the Schlegels and of Samuel Taylor Coleridge—was it possible to accept Shakespeare without anguish or apology.

From one point of view, the ambivalence of critics toward Shakespeare is an instance of the perennial conflict between the romantic and classical, or imaginative and rationalist, views of art. This is a reasonably adequate explanation, but it can be improved in two respects.

First, the conflict is partly artificial. Classical and romantic art grew naturally from different cultures. When they flourished they were both adequate expressions of the way people shaped by these cultures experienced the world. Problems only arose when the classical tradition was lifted bodily out of its native soil and imposed on the art of an entirely different culture.

Second, and more important for what it tells us about Shakespearean comedy, the conflict is at bottom a conflict between the urge of the mind to impose order on an irrational world, and the opposite urge of that world to force its way into the mind and take up residence. The greatest achievement of Shakespearean comedy is its openness to a baffling, refractory, and infinitely fascinating world; and a corollary achievement is its affirmation that the ground of the world is something positive, even benign—perhaps closer to humanity than mere logic can suggest. This achievement is best understood in relation to the heritage of medieval drama.

(1980)

The Dramatic Triad in *Hamlet*

No one who has considered the matter can fail to be impressed with the frequency of the dramatic triad in Shakespeare's mature drama. By dramatic triad I mean an arrangement of three characters, one of whom is the center of interest and in some way placed between the other two and contrasted to them. The dramatic triad first appears in unmistakable form in *1 Henry IV* (1597) and is later used in *Othello* and *The Tempest,* to cite only the most prominent examples. The present paper will briefly define the salient features of the dramatic triad and will then turn to consideration of its significance in *Hamlet.*

I

The dramatic triad is a commonplace in literature. It is difficult to say what source was the major influence on Shakespeare. One of the earliest and most widespread manifestations of the triad is the motif of "the choice of Hercules." This motif can be traced to Xenophon.[1] It was especially popular during the sixteenth century in both literature and the visual arts.[2] The fact that it was often expressed in pictorial form, with Hercules standing at the crossroads between two women symbolizing virtue and vice respectively, suggests that ultimately the triad is simply a visual analogy for moral choice. This would explain both its persistence and its frequency in drama, where the artist must express himself in scenes which have visual as well as verbal meaning.

The close relationship between *1 Henry IV* and the native morality play suggests a second source for the convention. The dramatic triad is implicit in that most venerable form of allegory the psychomachia, and becomes explicit as soon as an Everyman is introduced as the bone of contention between the armies of virtue and of vice. The introduction of Everyman or one of his special aspects such as Youth is characteristic of early-sixteenth-century morality. It is the device whereby the interior conflict between the impulse to good and the impulse to evil is objectified. W. R. Mackenzie has described the most typical version of this pattern as follows: "In the best-known class of Moralities, that in which the human hero is striven for by Virtues and Vices, Man regularly falls from grace, persists in sin during a great part of his life, and is usually reclaimed by virtue at the close of the action, when, in many cases, he has neared the end of his days."[3]

As several scholars have pointed out, this is not far from the pattern of *Othello*.[4] Cyprus is a little world in which Vice (Iago) and Virtue (Desdemona) struggle for the allegiance of the noble but naive Moor. As in the morality play, his virtue is soon corrupted. There is a period of degradation, followed by at least the hint at the end of the play that suffering has brought moral regeneration.[5]

The triadic structure by means of which this action is presented on the stage is consistent with the realistic level of the play and preserves the morality effect of objectifying the forces at work within the mind of the protagonist. At each stage in the action Othello's inner condition is made clear through his relationship with the two subsidiary characters. He is naturally inclined to virtue, the noble primitive rather than the degenerate barbarian. The correlative to this is his Platonic love of Desdemona's virtue:

> Vouch with me, heaven, I therefore beg it not,
> To please the palate of my appetite,
> Nor to comply with heat . . .
> But to be free and bounteous to her mind.
> (I.iii.262–66)

When he falls victim to Iago, his choice of vice is dramatized by the scene where he and Iago kneel on the stage and solemnize their pact with "the due reverence of a sacred vow" (III.iii.461). Later his degeneration is illustrated by his crude abuse of Desdemona (especially IV.ii); and his (possible) regeneration by the fact that he dies on his marriage bed embracing her.

Although *1 Henry IV* preceded *Othello* by at least six years, its use of the triad is the less conventional of the two. The morality form of the dramatic triad stresses choice: the protagonist begins his decline by choosing vice. In the development his fortunes become more and more precarious. Finally, when he is on the verge of complete ruin (i.e., damnation) there is frequently a conversion which is really a second choice, this time of virtue. But Hal is neither Everyman nor that particular aspect of Everyman, the prodigal son. He begins *1 Henry IV* as a sophisticate of virtue. Probably because Shakespeare wanted to avoid even the hint of vice in his portrait of the ideal English king, he dispels the illusion that Hal is a prodigal in the first soliloquy: "I know you all, and will awhile uphold / The unyoked humour of your idleness" (I.ii.218–19).

By insisting on Hal's virtue from beginning to end Shakespeare rules out the triad in its traditional morality form. Yet the Falstaff-Hal-Hotspur triad is the basis for the major effects of the play. This is managed by a change in the relationship of the three figures of the triad. Falstaff and Hotspur are no longer Virtue and Vice battling for the allegiance of Everyman. They are twin vices, a Scylla and a Charybdis, which are equally dangerous to the young prince. While Falstaff strikes at the guts of the Body Politic on the road to Canterbury, Hotspur is preparing to slit its throat on Shrewsbury plain. The two characters define extremes to which Hal could easily succumb. In avoiding them Hal becomes a kind of mean between them.[6]

The existence of the triad in *1 Henry IV* is a matter of fact. Its significance, however, is difficult to assess. It could be a conscious attempt to interpret the dramatic triad humanistically in terms of the Aristotelian notion of virtue as a mean between extremes. Aristotle's theory was a commonplace during the sixteenth century. It was available in translations of the *Nicomachean Ethics* and in countless popular treatises on morality. In the *Book of the Governor,* for example, Eliot wrote that virtue is "... an election annexed unto our nature, and consisteth in a meane. which is determined by reason, and that meane is the verye myddes of two thynges viciouse, the one in surplusage, the other in lacke...."[7] However, there is no way of proving that Shakespeare arrived consciously at the form of the triad found in *1 Henry IV.* It is quite possible and perhaps most natural that he came upon it unconsciously because of his desire to employ the morality tradition while avoiding any imputation on Hal's virtue.

Whatever its source, the triad based on the mean and the extremes is dramatically static. Since the central character is engaged in *avoiding* the extremes rather than choosing them, there can be no choice, no reversal based on character, no dramatic action in the strictest sense of that term.[8] This explains the substitution of pageantry and visual contrast for character development in *1 Henry IV.* The play is a series of exemplary episodes or scenes alternating between Eastcheap and the rebel camp, and culminating in the tableau of the next-to-last scene, when Hal stands victorious between the dead Hotspur on the one hand and the supposedly dead Falstaff on the other.

Use of what I will henceforth call the humanistic triad does not make *1 Henry IV* an inferior drama—it is one of Shakespeare's best. But its effect is achieved through its contrasting scenes (Aristotle's *spectacle*) rather than through a continuously developing plot line traced out by a dominant character (Aristotle's *action*). This is a perfectly legitimate technique; Aristotle himself remarked that "Since the imitation in tragedy is achieved through action, the orderly arrangement of what appeals to the eye must first of all necessarily be an essential part of tragedy" (*Poet.* 6). The great blossoming of the visual arts during the Renaissance—shading off into pageants, allegorical paintings, emblems, and masques—had made Shakespeare's contemporaries sensitive to the possibilities of spectacle. When used functionally, as in *1 Henry IV,* spectacle adds an extra dimension to the drama, a dimension often concealed from the reader of Shakespeare and sometimes neglected in stage productions. In *1 Henry IV* the images of life in Eastcheap constitute a definition of private misrule; while those at the rebel camp define treason (public misrule). But each group of scenes is also played off against the other. Falstaff and his fellow robbers are compared as well as contrasted to Hotspur and his fellow conspirators. By this means surprising similarities are revealed; for example, their bloody-mindedness, their inability to control their passions, their boasting, and above all their complementary views of honor. These parallels help to unify the play, thus saving it from becoming a kind of historical variety show, and also remind us of the philosopher's dictum that extremes tend to meet.

In *The Tempest* the Caliban-Prospero-Ariel triad is obviously central. In this case, however, the subsidiary characters do not appear to embody moral states, as in *Othello* and *1 Henry IV.* It is emphasized that both are amoral (that is, neither virtuous nor depraved in the sense that these terms are applied to human characters). They are presented as part of the condition of life on the island. When controlled they can be useful, but when uncontrolled or directed by a malevolent agent they can be harmful. Dramatically speaking, *The Tempest* tends to be static because Prospero never wavers or makes a real choice, nor is there reversal or discovery in the action which directly concerns him. As in *1 Henry IV* the lack of action is compensated for by spectacle, especially the supernatural characters, the enchantments, and the masque.

The preceding brief review of the dramatic triad suggests its importance in Shakespeare's work after 1597. It is natural to ask whether the triad is significant in *Hamlet,* and, if so, what effect recognition of the triad has on the interpretation of the drama. In answering the first question, it is particularly important to avoid imposing a preconceived pattern on the play. Therefore, in the following section, I will attempt to show, by analysis of the dramatic foils in *Hamlet,* that the dramatic triad is intrinsic to the play. Having demonstrated this, I will then comment on its significance in the interpretation of the play. First it will be helpful to summarize the most important features of the dramatic triad:

(1) The main character stands between two subsidiary characters.
(2) The triad objectifies the inner condition of the main character.
(3) In the humanistic form of the triad the subsidiary characters objectify extremes which are also vices; the main character objectifies a mean which is also a virtue.
(4) The humanistic version of the triad operates by contrasts and is essentially static; the main character must *avoid* the extremes rather than choose them.

II

In *Hamlet* the number of subsidiary characters is quite large. In one way or another most of the younger ones can be interpreted as foils to Hamlet. Three characters, however, stand out because they are in the uncommon position of having lost a father by violent death. Fortinbras is mentioned in the very first scene. At first he plans to invade Denmark in order to reclaim his birthright and avenge his father, slain by the elder Hamlet. Later, to everyone's relief, he abandons the idea. Laertes, conversely, swears vengeance after his father's death and carries his plans to their bloody conclusion. Last, there is Ophelia. Her reaction to her father's death is not to desire vengeance. Rather (accepting provisionally the statements of the gravediggers and priest in V.i) it is suicide. Thus three different reactions are presented to a father's violent death: forbearance, revenge, and suicide. Since these are reactions to the same event which is troubling Hamlet, *a priori* all three characters are foils to Hamlet.

The significance of the three foils is very great but is lost if they are considered separately or if only two are considered and the third omitted. This is because the three alternatives which they objectify are identical to the three alternatives which Hamlet ponders. In other words, they permit Shakespeare to dramatize the different facets of Hamlet's dilemma in three sub-plots showing the consequences of three courses of action which he is tempted to follow.

a. Suicide

Hamlet's first soliloquy (before he knows of the murder) shows him in a state of melancholy bordering on despair. Instead of bountiful Nature, nourished by the unceasing flow of love from the Creator which the Elizabethans inherited from St. Thomas and embellished with the Neoplatonic notion of the *circuitus divinus,* Hamlet sees only the perverse fertility of the unweeded garden (correlative to incest) and human bestiality. Because of the displacement of his inner world he finds the outer one "weary, stale, flat, and unprofitable," an idea reiterated when he tells Rosencrantz and Guildenstern that "the goodly frame of the earth" is "a sterile promontory," and "this brave o'erhanging firmament" a "foul and pestilent congregation of vapours" (II.ii.304–23).

The result of his melancholy is that Hamlet longs for death. This means that he has ceased to be merely a man with a temperamental bias toward extreme sorrow. He is in (or close to) the condition which standard theology of the time called despair. Chaucer's Parson gives a definition of despair which is useful because it is in a tissue of commonplaces: "Now comth wanhope, that is despeir of the mercy of God, that comth somtyme of to muche outrageous sorwe, all somtyme of to muche drede, ymaginynge that he hath doon so muche synne that it wol nat availlen hym, thogh he wolde repenten hym and forsake synne. . . . Which dampnable synne, if that it continue unto his ende, it is cleped synnyng in the Hooly Goost. . . ."[9] Despair was the besetting sin of the sensitive man. It was a crucial temptation for Spenser's Redcross Knight, who was rescued only by the intervention of Una; and for Adam and Eve in book 10 of *Paradise Lost*. Like the Redcross Knight and Milton's characters, Hamlet is powerfully tempted to yield to his despair with the irrevocable act of suicide.

Hamlet's preoccupation with suicide is a recurrent motif in the play. Shakespeare places it first in the soliloquy in act 1:

> O, that this too too sullied flesh would melt,
> Thaw, and resolve itself into a dew!
> Or that the Everlasting had not fix'd
> His canon 'gainst self-slaughter!
>
> (I.ii.129–32)

The death wish is complementary to the inverted image of Nature, and Hamlet returns to it at the end of the soliloquy: "But break, my heart; for I must hold my tongue." The soliloquy thus has the dramatic function of informing us of Hamlet's despair and simultaneously reminding us of the Christian sanctions (the Everlasting's canon) against it.

Almost the same point is made in the soliloquy "To be or not to be. . . ." Essentially Hamlet says that he cannot endure the suffering caused by "despised love," "the oppressor's wrong," and various other slings and arrows of fortune. The solution which tempts him at this point is suicide. He wishes "to die, to sleep," to "shuffle off this mortal coil," and to "quietus make / With a bare bodkin." If, as is often done, Hamlet toys with his dagger during this soliloquy, he becomes almost a living emblem of suicide as depicted in allegorical literature from Skelton's *Magnificence* through the *Faerie Queene*.[10]

It must be emphasized strongly that suicide is *attractive* to Hamlet at this point; that it is a genuine and powerful temptation. Yet despite its attractiveness Hamlet draws back. His motive is perfectly clear: "For in that sleep of death what dreams may come . . . must give us pause"; and "the dread of something after death . . . puzzles the will / and makes us rather bear the ills we have / Than fly to others that we know not of" (III.i.70–82). Again the religious sanctions against suicide are emphasized strongly. Knowing that suicide is a mortal sin, Hamlet fears damnation, and it may be remarked parenthetically that damnation has been vividly dramatized for Hamlet and the audience in the Ghost's speech about his purgatorial prison house.

In the light of the Christian principles referred to in the soliloquy, Hamlet's self-denunciation ("Thus conscience does make cowards of us all") is deeply ironic. Obedience to conscience—refusal to commit suicide—is associated with the pejorative "cowards." We can thus say that Hamlet acts morally by resisting temptation but that he despises himself for doing so.[11]

Suicide then is the first of Hamlet's alternatives. It is presented both as a temptation and as a mortal sin; as an escape from pain and as a way to insure damnation. These conflicting ideas are brought dramatically before the audience in the action relating to Ophelia. Like Hamlet she has lost a father through an apparent murder. Like Hamlet she feels betrayed by someone she loves. Like Hamlet she is mentally disturbed. Here the parallel changes to contrast. Ophelia's grief passes over into unambiguous madness, and finally she commits suicide.

Her suicide, it should immediately be said, partakes of the ambiguity which runs through so much of *Hamlet.* Gertrude's speech at the end of act 4 may be true. Ophelia's drowning may have been accidental. On the other hand the speech seems more intelligible as the sentimental wish-fulfillment of a character too weak to face the truth. I believe, but would not insist, that this is suggested by its artificial lyricism and the fact that it is followed immediately by the harsh but frank prose of the gravediggers: "Is she to be buried in Christian burial that willfully seeks her own salvation?" (V.i.1–2); and "Will you ha' the truth on't? If this had not been a gentlewoman, she would have been buried out o' Christian burial" (V.i.26–28).

What is beyond dispute is that the references to suicide in act 5 could have been avoided. They come as a surprise since there has been no preparation for them in the preceding act. The inclusion of not one but two exchanges of dialogue on the topic (the gravediggers and the priest-Laertes exchange) can have only one purpose. That is to objectify in the action the problem which has troubled Hamlet from his first soliloquy. It is impossible to say how Ophelia really died. This is unimportant beside the fact that her death provides an occasion for reiterating the Christian attitude toward suicide. In effect it reminds the audience that by avoiding the extreme of despair Hamlet has acted the part of the good Christian.

b. Revenge

Ophelia's significance in *Hamlet* is often underrated and therefore needs to be stressed. The fact that Laertes is a foil is universally accepted. Shakespeare even puns on it (V.ii.266). However, its implications are not always realized.

Hamlet is, of course, profoundly moved by the Ghost. As a loyal and loving son he knows that it is his duty to carry out the Ghost's command.

He is also moved by his idea of honor, his hatred of Claudius, and his feeling of having been cheated of the crown. The over-all effect of the interview with the Ghost is to show his resolution: "Haste me to know't, that I, with wings as swift / As meditation or the thoughts of love, / May sweep to my revenge" (I.v.29–31).

Yet even at this moment Hamlet has reservations. As the Ghost leaves crying "remember me" Hamlet begins the conventional revenger's vow. Suddenly his tone changes:

> O all you host of heaven! O earth! what else?
> And shall I couple hell? O, fie! Hold, hold, my heart;
> And you, my sinews, grow not instant old,
> But bear me stiffly up. Remember thee!
> Ay, thou poor ghost. . . .
>
> (I.v.92–96)

Why should he hesitate? It is the word *hell* which makes him apprehensive. Apparently he has not been entirely swept away during the interview by the desire for revenge. He is willing to act but not to place his soul in jeopardy. This interpretation is confirmed by the contrasting attitude of Laertes in a similar situation. According to convention the revenger eschews all moral scruples when he undertakes his mission. Laertes is perfectly true to type:

> To hell, allegiance! vows, to the blackest devil!
> Conscience and grace, to the profoundest pit!
> I dare damnation. To this point I stand,
> That both the worlds I give to negligence,
> Let come what comes; only I'll be revenged
> Most thoroughly for my father.
>
> (IV.v.130–36)

And,

> I'll cut his throat i' the church.
>
> (IV.vii.127)

The contrast between Hamlet's hesitation and Laertes' rashness could hardly be made more pointed.

Hamlet's reservations, which first appear in his vow to the Ghost, reappear more emphatically in the players' scene, and in two ways, one direct and the other oblique. The direct statement is, of course, Hamlet's explanation of the need for the play:

> The spirit I have seen
> May be a devil . . . yea and perhaps
> Out of my weakness and my melancholy . . .

> Abuses me to damn me: I'll have grounds
> More relative than this.
>
> (II.ii.627–33)

In other words Hamlet realizes that Claudius may be innocent. If so, killing him would not be revenge but murder, and Hamlet's soul would be forfeit. Thus fear of damnation becomes important for the second time in our reading of the drama. It has prevented Hamlet from committing suicide. It now causes him to have second thoughts about slaying Claudius.

The problem is a real one though sometimes glossed over by nineteenth-century critics of the play. In Shakespeare's presentation the passion for revenge, intensified by filial love, is balanced against the rational knowledge that some corroboration is necessary to test the single "witness" of the crime. This leads to the second, oblique, way in which Hamlet's reservations are brought before the audience in the player's scene.

The long quotation from "Aeneas' tale to Dido" is usually (though not always) considered an interlude in which Shakespeare pokes fun at the bombast of the older London theatre. It has, however, another more significant function. It describes a blood-thirsty young warrior in black armor ("he whose sable arms,/ Black as his purpose, did the night resemble . . .") who butchers an innocent king while the "mobled" queen cries to the gods in horror. The identification of Pyrrhus and Hamlet is inescapable.[12] In effect the passage is a lurid reflection of the way in which Hamlet feels his revenge would appear if Claudius should ultimately prove innocent. It also objectifies his fear of injuring his mother (hence the later reference, "What's Hecuba to him . . .") and of staining his reputation by an act which would furnish material for a second drama like "Aeneas' tale" in which Hamlet would be the villain. His remark that the players are the "abstract and brief chronicles of the time," and his warning about their "ill report" (II.ii.544–51) reflect this concern for reputation and are echoed in his dying requests to Horatio in act 5.

Immediately after the play Hamlet shows the same exultant willingness to act which he displayed after the Ghost's departure: "I'll take the ghost's word for a thousand pound" (III.ii.297). In the scenes which follow he moves toward the pole represented by Laertes. It is surely significant that these scenes are saturated with references to damnation. Not religion but irreligion causes Hamlet to forego killing Claudius at prayer. His exclamation before visiting his mother is an explicit defiance of damnation:

> 'Tis now the very witching time of night,
> When churchyards yawn and hell itself breathes out
> Contagion to this world: now could I drink hot blood,

And do such bitter business as the day
Would quake to look on.
(III.ii.406–10)

This represents the abandonment of all effort to curb passion by reason. The result is that Hamlet stabs through the arras without even looking behind it. The act is almost an emblem of rashness and the revenge is as wide of the mark as Laertes' revenge in act 5. An innocent man (rash and intruding, true, but nonetheless innocent) is slain. The real culprit is warned. Hamlet has committed exactly the kind of crime which he wanted to avoid. He remarks to his mother, "For this same lord, / I do repent" (III.iv.172–3); and later describes the act to Laertes as "madness" (V.ii.237–50). To complete the disaster, his act leads to the death of his intended ("forty thousand brothers / Could not, with all their quantity of love, / Make up my sum" [V.i.292–4] and ultimately to his own death at the hands of Laertes. Those critics who censure Hamlet for inaction fail to remark that the moment when he does act forms the turning point of the play. In the most literal sense it is Hamlet's action in III.iv, which causes his downfall.

After the slaying of Polonius, Hamlet is sent to England. When he returns he is profoundly changed. No longer does he see himself as an avenger without whom God's justice would fail. Rather he seems willing to place himself in the hands of an overruling providence. In his final speech before the duel he seems to be thinking of his own death rather than revenge. The image of the unweeded garden is reversed in the reference to "special providence"; and the death image has been subtly transformed. It is no longer an image of despair but of calm resignation, almost katharsis: "there's a special providence in the fall of a sparrow. If it be not now, 'tis not to come; if it is not to come, it will be now; if it be not now, yet it will come: the readiness is all" (V.ii.230–34).

Hamlet's second alternative, then, is revenge. But the question of revenge is not presented as simply as in the conventional revenge play.[13] The real possibility of Claudius' innocence, the danger of damnation, the concern for reputation, the questionable nature of revenge under any circumstances, all act as deterrents to the impulse to kill. Let us confess that Hamlet's reasons for hesitation are entirely praiseworthy both in the abstract and in the light in which they are placed in the play.

Just as the first alternative of suicide is objectified by Ophelia, the second alternative is objectified by Laertes. The elder Hamlet and Polonius were both slain under questionable circumstances. Both sons are deeply motivated to seek revenge. Both are certain that they know the murderer. Here the resemblance ceases. Hamlet fears damnation, resists the impulse to act, and seeks verification. Laertes enters the court defying damnation. He makes only a token effort to learn the true reason for his father's death, and is easily swayed by Claudius. Once in the power of Claudius he engages himself to perform acts of unmitigated treachery—acts which are in direct violation of his own code of honor. He deepens his treachery by pretending to accept Hamlet's frank confession: "I do receive your offer'd love like love, / And will not wrong it" (V.ii.262–3). Finally he achieves his revenge. By all standards of the conventional revenge play he should die gloating over his success. However the reverse is true. In a moment of revelation he sees how he has been tricked. He dies begging forgiveness of the man he has killed:

> Exchange forgiveness with me, noble Hamlet;
> Mine and my father's death come not upon thee,
> Nor thine on me!
>
> (V.ii.340–42)

The dramatic point is inescapable. Laertes has yielded to the passion which Hamlet has resisted. In so doing he has placed himself in danger of damnation, as Hamlet's "Heaven make thee free of it!" reminds us. At the very least Laertes dishonors himself and achieves the opposite of what he had intended. Instead of Hieronimo triumphant we are shown a pathetic victim of passion whose last knowledge is of the enormity of his crime.

c. Forbearance

To the alternatives of revenge and suicide Shakespeare adds a third, the alternative of inaction. It is this alternative to which Hamlet inclines except when he slays Polonius. In the typical Shakespearean triad Hamlet would be a sufficient embodiment of the middle alternative, just as Hal was a sufficient embodiment of the mean between Hotspur and Falstaff. But Shakespeare has complicated the pattern by embodying the alternative of inaction in two characters, Hamlet and Fortinbras.[14] Fortinbras too has lost a father. At first he is moved to action (the attack on Denmark), but almost miraculously the ambassadors of Claudius are successful (II.ii). He renounces his plans for invasion and, in effect, takes the course of inaction.

It is clear that the chief difference between the forbearance of Fortinbras and that of Hamlet is one of attitude. Hamlet renounces action imperfectly and is continually tempted to act. Conversely, Fortinbras is always shown at a distance. We never learn of his inner struggles. The effect created by this treatment is idealization. Fortinbras emerges as a man who never swerves or doubts himself once he has renounced his invasion plans. Thus Fortinbras helps to define the ideal position towards which Hamlet is half-consciously striving. This interpretation adds significance to the exchange of roles which occurs in the final scene. In this scene Fortinbras is for all intents and purposes made king, the position which Hamlet would eventually have occupied. Conversely, Hamlet is borne "like a soldier" from the stage and accorded "the soldiers' music and the rites of war" (V.ii.407, 410). The imagery suggests that he occupies the position with which Fortinbras has been identified throughout the play. If we accept Fortinbras as an embodiment of the ideal toward which Hamlet has been striving, the effect of the exchange is to suggest that Hamlet's death is a kind of victory.

III

The dramatic triad which has emerged from our consideration of *Hamlet* is as follows: Laertes (revenge); Hamlet-Fortinbras (forbearance); Ophelia (suicide). This triad is clearly not the morality type of triad found in *Othello*. Making provisional use of the word *objectify*, we can say that Ophelia and Laertes do not objectify a virtuous and vicious course of action respectively. Suicide is certainly not desirable for either Hamlet or Ophelia. The revenge question is not so simple, but there is no doubt that the kind of revenge taken by Laertes is shown to be wrong. Ophelia and Laertes objectify two courses of action which Hamlet must avoid in the same way that Hal must avoid the vices objectified in Hotspur and Falstaff.

In *1 Henry IV* the vices are complementary. They suggest the Aristotelian concept of virtue as a mean between extremes. This is also suggested by the triad in *Hamlet*, although the problem is more complex than in the earlier play. The brother-sister relationship is in itself suggestive of a connection between the kinds of action objectified by the characters. Possibly it began as a convenient means of depriving two characters of a father at one blow. But Shakespeare often makes necessities into virtues, and he often uses family relationships symbolically, as father-daughter in *Lear* or husband-wife in *The Winter's Tale*.

The brother-sister relationship—if one admits that it has any significance at all—merely calls attention to the complementary nature of the actions of the two characters. Both are faced with the same fact, Polonius' death. Both came to grief because they yield wholly to passion. In fact an Elizabethan might have interpreted Laertes' contempt for Christian scruples as a kind of madness only slightly less extreme than Ophelia's. Finally, both objectify forms of surrender before a difficult problem—the surrender of despair and the complementary surrender of action without thought. Both extremes involve death and both have the same penalty, damnation. Shakespeare was not in the habit of playing God, and he does not step forth from behind the scene to assure us that Ophelia and Laertes were, in fact, damned after their deaths. Rather, he uses their action to reiterate the commonplace Christian truth that suicide and rash killing involve the *risk* of damnation.

The complementary courses of Laertes and Ophelia serve to illuminate the psychological as well as the moral issues of the drama, forming a link between the external action and Hamlet's inner struggle. The tendency of Elizabethan psychology, with its hierarchy of reason and the passions, was to identify moral and psychological problems.[15] Ophelia's despair and Laertes' rashness are passions as well as vices. Hamlet's forbearance is not merely reasonable; it is the result of Hamlet's desperate efforts to control his own tendencies to despair and rashness. It is emphasized both externally and internally that this control is exerted by reason. When most despondent Hamlet complains that he is prevented from suicide by "the pale cast of thought" which "sicklies o'er the native hue of resolution" (III.i.84–5). And when most eager to act he condemns "some craven scruple / Of thinking too precisely on the event" (IV.v.40–1). These influences show that he recognizes the influence of reason but resents it. They are the utterances of a man divided against himself. Hamlet's closest approach to self-knowledge prior to the last act is in his confession to Horatio that the ideal man is he who most fully controls his passions:

> . . . blest are those
> Whose blood and judgment are so well commedled,
> That they are not a pipe for Fortune's finger
> To sound what stop she please. Give me that man
> That is not passion's slave, and I will wear him
> In my heart's core, ay, in my heart of heart,
> As I do thee.
>
> (III.ii.73–9)

The dramatic triad in *Hamlet* thus permits a remarkable fusion of inner and outer drama. It is exceedingly rich in implications, but its roots are in the techniques employed by the early-sixteenth-century writers of morality. Externally speaking Hamlet occupies the middle ground between Laertes and Ophelia. Internally speaking he is powerfully tempted by the passions which they define. As we learn from his soliloquies, he needs all the support of his Christian principles to avoid succumbing to them. The world seems blighted; the principle of love corrupted; there is no justice—the only recourse is ending one's suffering with a bare bodkin. But there is the danger of damnation. Likewise a swift attempt to end injustice by destroying its apparent source might result in damnation. Hamlet is held in an agonizing stasis between these alternatives. At the same time, in a final refinement of torture, his intellect, the very source of his scruples, whispers the insidious proposition of the sceptics, "There's nothing either good or bad, but thinking makes it so" (II.ii.256). If this should be true, if there are no moral values, then Hamlet's struggle and his anguish are meaningless.

Much of the feeling of unbearable tension in *Hamlet* arises from Hamlet's efforts to avoid the two extremes to which he is tempted. The fate of the characters embodying these extremes demonstrates the rightness of Hamlet's struggle. His suffering demonstrates the immense difficulty of moral action; and in this *Hamlet* is an accurate imitation of life itself.

IV

In the first section of this paper the dramatic triad was considered primarily as a device for arranging the elements of plot in a meaningful form. In the course of considering Hamlet's dilemma we have noticed certain effects of the triad on the larger design of the play. These may now be examined more closely.

Since the *Hamlet* triad is the humanistic variety, the main character, the character between the two subsidiary ones, begins the play in a position of virtue. His problem is to avoid the extremes. That is, any deviation from the mean will represent a moral failure. Hal is in this position, but he is morally perfect. Apparently he is not greatly tempted by either Hotspur or Falstaff and there is no evidence that he has to struggle to remain virtuous. This makes him seem cold and even hypocritical in his dealings with Falstaff, but neither Shakespeare nor Hal was a sentimentalist who believed in the doctrine of the charming rogue. Hal's parting shot ("fall to thy prayers") was probably considered an act of charity by those who could rise to the height of the Shakespearean argument.

Hamlet, of course, is not perfect. His self-doubt and suffering are evidence of his humanity. His problem, however, is similar to Hal's. He must avoid choice. This is not procrastination, at least not as nineteenth-century critics used the term. To them Hamlet was engaged in avoiding a task which he should have performed. But consideration of the *Hamlet* triad suggests that just the reverse is true. Hamlet's delay is the rational course when opposed to the alternatives of Laertes and Ophelia.

Because of the humanistic nature of the triad, *Hamlet* partakes of the same static quality apparent in *1 Henry IV.* It lacks action in the strict sense. As in *1 Henry IV,* this lack of action is offset by spectacle. In *Hamlet* motion, diversity of scene, numerous minor characters, and sensational elements such as the Ghost and the play-within-the-play divert the audience from the basic lack of action. Although close analysis invariably shows manifold thematic relationships between a given scene and the play as a whole—in fact nowhere in Shakespeare are the interrelationships more numerous and more intricate—the primary effect during a performance is of activity too varied and too dense to be compressed within the normal scope of the drama. This illusion compensates for the lack of choice and reversal.

An important qualification must be introduced here. There is one point at which Hamlet does act.[16] It has already been mentioned in connection with the revenge alternative. It is the moment following the play-within-the-play when Hamlet slays Polonius. The episode has two characteristics not found elsewhere in *Hamlet*. It is based upon choice (in the sense that Hamlet chooses to do something positive rather than to restrain himself from action); and it comes closer than any other action in the play to being a genuine reversal. By this I mean that it is an action directly created by Hamlet. It could not have occurred without him, and he would not have performed it except under the special circumstances pertaining at the time of his interview with his mother. The test of a reversal according to Aristotle is that "it causes the action to veer around in the opposite direction." Surely this is the case after Polonius' death. The King is warned and sends Hamlet to England and probable death. In addition, the train of events is initiated which will lead to Laertes' treachery.

The slaying of Polonius is a genuine action, if "moral choice" is broadened to include the idea of choice as a yielding to passion. This is legitimate. It is a variant of the device employed by a novelist like Flaubert to show that the individual is the slave of his character, if not of outward circumstance. However it robs the Aristotelian concept of some of its force. Part of the greatness of *Oedipus* is the fact that the choices of the protagonist are based on a reasoned and reasonable desire to act justly. The overpowering sense of irony in *Othello* stems from the hero's conviction of moral rectitude, a conviction extending even to his impassioned plea that Desdemona confess and repent before her death. The idea of yielding to passion, no matter how powerful the passion, is less forceful. Therefore, to make the slaying of Polonius the climax of *Hamlet* as well as the turning point would be to diminish the greatness of the play. Hamlet achieves tragic stature by resisting his passions rather than by his momentary failure, no matter how important its consequences.

Recognition of this fact further illuminates the structure of the play. Since Hamlet's need is to avoid choice, the climax is neither a choice nor an action resulting from choice. It is the moment in the play when Hamlet reconciles himself to the Christian principles which he has, in fact, observed during most of the drama. This point is reached in the speech on the fall of the sparrow. In accepting providence, Hamlet does more than resign himself to the inevitable. He is freed at last from the burden of self-doubt which he has carried in the earlier part of the play, and he is freed of the burden of action. Forbearance need not be either cowardice or rationalization, and the performance of final justice is no longer dependent on a single frail human being. These ideas are implicit in Hamlet's speech, but they are underscored in the biblical passage which it alludes to:

> . . . do not fear those who kill the body but cannot kill the soul; rather fear him who can destroy both soul and body in hell. Are not two sparrows sold for a penny? And not one of them will fall to the ground without your Father's will. But even the hairs of your head are numbered. Fear not, therefore; you are of more value than many sparrows (MATT. 10:28–31).

When Hamlet begins the fencing match, then, he is at peace with himself. His first act is to confess his faults and ask forgiveness of Laertes. Only when circumstances—the death of Gertrude, the poisoned sword, the confession of Laertes—force him to act does he do so. At this point he is no longer an avenger but an instrument of the providence which he has just affirmed.[17] His dying thoughts are not of satisfied revenge but of the imperative need to make known the justice of his act:

> . . . report me and my cause aright
> To the unsatisfied.

And,

> O good Horatio, what a wounded name,
> Things thus unknown, shall live behind me!

And,

> He has my dying voice;
> So tell him, with the occurrents, more and less,
> Which have solicited. The rest is silence.
> (V.ii.352–69)

The fulfilling of these requests occupies most of the ensuing dialogue. One speech is especially important. Horatio is eager to explain Hamlet's acts because if their justice is unexplained civil chaos may result: "let this same be presently performed, / Even while men's minds are wild; lest more mischance, / Or plots and errors, happen" (V.ii.405–6). Here is a final reminder of the consequences which would have followed from the rash murder of Claudius. Because of the Elizabethan concern for social order it was probably a much stronger reminder in Shakespeare's day than it is at present.

V

To examine the use of the dramatic triad in *Hamlet* is to realize with fresh force the perfection with which the inner and outer elements of Shakespearean drama are harmonized. Shakespeare was not an Aristotelian but his practice confirms Aristotle's precept that plot is the soul of drama. It is the design of the episodes which determines the relationships of the characters and, in the final analysis, the most basic features of the characters themselves. Greek tragedy drew its plot materials from the rituals and myths of early Greek religion. In somewhat the same way Shakespeare's *Hamlet* preserves a vital relationship to Christian drama through its exploitation of the dramatic triad.

(1960)

Myth and History in *King Lear*

Ever since A.W. Ward's *History of English Drama* (1899) scholars have recognized that the plot of *Gorboduc* is a compound of two heterogeneous elements. First, there is the pseudo-history derived ultimately from Geoffrey of Monmouth. In its original form, this material lacks shape. A second element, a framework, is needed within which it can be articulated. Thomas Sackville and Thomas Norton might simply have "invented" such a framework, but instead, following the habit of the age, they drew on a classical myth previously used by Seneca. Ward and later scholars agree that this myth is "the ancient Theban story of the sons of Oedipus and Iocasta and their fatal strife."[1] I do not wish to pursue the influence of the Theban material on *Gorboduc* but merely to call attention to the fact. It is, in its way, a remarkable fact. It leads to the conclusion that the first regular English tragedy was a self-conscious fusion of history and myth, with the history supplying the local habitation and the name, and the myth, the pattern which makes these elements coherent drama.

Forty-five years after *Gorboduc* was produced at Whitehall for Queen Elizabeth, Shakespeare's *King Lear* was produced "before the Kinges maiestie at Whitehall." The similarity of the two dramas has often been remarked. Most obviously, both dramas deal with the motif of the division of the kingdom. However, another similarity has gone unnoticed. There is evidence that, like Sackville and Norton, Shakespeare drew upon classical mythology to articulate his historical materials. There is no need to argue that he learned the technique from *Gorboduc*. However, such a venerable precedent makes his use of it less surprising than it might otherwise be.

The myth which Shakespeare used is the myth of Ixion. The fact that he was thinking of this myth while writing *King Lear* is established by two references in act 4, both of which are noted by Starnes and Talbert in *Classical Myth and Legend in Renaissance Dictionaries*.[2] Lear's statement to Cordelia, "Thou art a soul in bliss; but I am bound / Upon a wheel of fire" (IV.vii.46–47), is an allusion to the punishment of Ixion. Since Lear compares his suffering to that of Ixion, it is natural to wonder whether the actions which cause his punishment are in any way analogous to those of Ixion. An earlier reference in act 4 helps to answer the question. In a moment of uncontrolled rage, Lear refers to his daughters as centaurs (IV.vi.126). On the surface the allusion is confusing, since centaurs were usually considered male. However, it becomes intelligible when related to the Ixion-Lear parallel. According to classical mythology the centaurs were the children of Ixion. Starnes and Talbert justly remark, "the story of Ixion and his adulterous offspring was in Shakespeare's mind through a good part of act 4."

But is the influence confined to act 4? When it is recalled that during the Renaissance the Ixion myth was interpreted as an allegory of irresponsible rule and that familial ingratitude is an important part of the myth, the desirability of further analysis is apparent.

The present essay is divided into two major sections. The first is a recapitulation of the details and interpretation of the Ixion myth offered by mythographers who influenced sixteenth-century thought. The second is a comparison of various aspects of the mythographic tradition with *King Lear.* This comparison leads to the conclusion that the Ixion myth had a general influence on the play, extending from the first scene to the last. Unlike Sackville and Norton, Shakespeare did not use myth for plot organization. His major source was already in dramatic form, and he could readily have supplied any dramatic deficiencies without recourse to mythology. The most striking fact about the parallels noted is that they are ideological. The myth of Ixion supplied Shakespeare with the philosophical issues in terms of which the action of the play is developed.

II

During the Renaissance Ixion and the centaurs were popular figures, familiar to anyone who had studied Ovid and Virgil in grammar school. Michelangelo planned an Ixion as part of a four-part design showing the four great classical sinners—Tantalus, Sisyphus, Tityus, and Ixion.[3] Centaurs were popular decorative motifs and appear frequently in pastoral landscapes. Versions of the battle of the centaurs and Lapithae (after Ovid, *Met.,* XII) were painted by Rosso Fiorentino and Piero di Cosimo,[4] while centaurs figure prominently in such semi-allegorical paintings as Mantegna's "Minerva Expelling Vices from the Grove of Virtue"[5] and the "Hercules and the Centaur" in the Farnesina Palace in Rome.[6] Shakespeare never mentions Ixion by name but refers twice to the centaurs before *Lear,* both times in connection with the battle of the centaurs (*Tit.,* V.ii.204; *MND*, V.i.44). Other English writers, including Spenser, Jonson, Bacon, and Milton, refer to the Ixion myth frequently and with easy familiarity.

Like most classical myths, the Ixion myth was a composite assembled by mythographers from scattered references and commentaries. The first synthesis to survive is the version in the sixth-century *Mythology* of

Fabius Planciadis Fulgentius.[7] Most later versions draw on Fulgentius, who, in turn, attributes his information to "Dromocritus in theogonia," which is, perhaps, a garbled reference to Hesiod. According to Fulgentius, the myth of Ixion has two parts. The first is the literal history of Ixion the ruler, who was "the first Greek to affect pomp in rule" ("in Graeca primum regni gloriam adfectasse. . . ."). As part of his program he retained one hundred knights who were called *centaurs*. He was soon overthrown, and his fall is symbolized by a wheel "because the turn of a wheel soon casts down whatever it holds high" ("quod omnis rotae vertigo quae superiora habet modo deiciat"). The second part of the myth, the tale of Ixion's attempted seduction of Juno, is not a new story but an allegorical version of history recounted in the first part:

> Who seeks to be more than is proper, will be less than he is. Thus when Ixion would have seduced Juno, she made a cloud in her shape, and when Ixion coupled with it, he begot centaurs. . . . Now *Ixion* was pronounced *Axion*, and *dignity* is called *axioma* in Greek. Moreover, Juno is the goddess of rule, as we noted earlier [*supra,* p. 38]. Thus the man who affects pomp of rule gains a cloud; that is, the appearance of rule. [True] rule is that which will last indefinitely. But whoever fleeting time, swift in its winged thefts, envies, is shown images of momentary happiness rather than truth and gains a hollow, windy fantasy.
>
> (Qui plus quaerit esse quam licet, minus erit quam est. Ixion igitur coniungium Iunonis adfectatus, illa nubem ornavit in speciem suam, cum qua Ixion coiens Centauros genuit. . . . Denique Ixionem dici voluerunt quasi Axionem; axioma enim Grece dicitur, Dea vero regnorum Iuno est, ut pridem diximus; ergo dignitas regnum adfectans nubem meretur, id est similitudinem regni; regnum enim illud est quod perenniter duraturum est. At vero cui temporis fugitiva vis invidet pinnatisque celerrima raptibus, momentaneae felicitatis figuras potius quam veritatem ostendenti, ventositatis inanem speciem praesumit.)

By Boccaccio's time the myth had grown considerably, partly as a result of humanistic interest in the classics. In the *Genealogy of the Gods,*[8] Boccaccio refers admiringly to Fulgentius, but he has also drawn on Macrobius and shows debts to Servius and Lactantius as well.[9] Ixion is localized as a king in Thessaly and lord of the Lapithae. He is described as "avid for power" and "tyrannical," and the cloud-woman is made a metaphor for false rule, as in Fulgentius. Boccaccio embellishes his comment with a vivid description of the cloud, contrasting its obscure, fiery, and rain-bringing properties with the clear, shining air of true rule. It should be noted that as early as the *Genealogy* the authentic detail of the cloud-woman has been replaced by something close to a literal storm symbolizing improper rule.

Boccaccio agrees with Fulgentius that the fable suggests foolish desire for pomp, but he prefers to see Ixion as the first usurper and tyrant rather than as the first vain king. To the account in Fulgentius he adds the tale, derived from Lactantius, that Ixion returned to earth after his attempted seduction, boasted of it, and was hurled down to hell by a Jovian thunderbolt. The thunderbolt symbolizes the shock of disillusionment which comes when the would-be king realizes the difficulty of his situation. The wheel symbolizes the ceaseless round of cares which torment him.

It is characteristic of Renaissance mythographers to offer more than one interpretation of a myth. Usually the interpretations are not contradictory, and often they are mutually reinforcing. This is the case with the Ixion myth, which seems to have gathered richer connotations with each new interpretation. Boccaccio gives four corollary interpretations, of which only two need concern us here. First, there is the interpretation of the myth as an allegory of hope which feeds on illusion but ends in disillusionment (the thunderbolt). Second, following Macrobius, Boccaccio suggests that the wheel is the wheel of fortune on which those men are bound who allow passion to govern reason ("qui nichil consilio previdentes, nichil moderantes, nichil virtutibus explicantes, seque et omnes actus suos fortune committentes, casibus fortuitis semper rotantur").

In the *de Laboribus Herculis,* Salutati makes the slaying of the centaurs one of Hercules' early labors.[10] This occasions a résumé of the Ixion myth based on Fulgentius and Boccaccio. Salutati adds to this material an account of the genealogy of Ixion (in part from the *Genealogy*) and of the symbolism of the centaurs. Ixion's father was Flegias, son of Mars. Since *flegias* (i.e., Gr. φλέγμα) is *flama* in Latin, the genealogy suggests the "fiery humour" which leads men to violence. Men first congregated in towns and elected magistrates to protect themselves from violence: "civitates et oppida struere, et magistratum inducere dignitatem, qui cunctis iusticiam ministrarent." Ixion is a type of the magistrate who becomes enamored of the *dignitas* of office while neglecting the *iusticia.* The centaurs are violent desires for rule, and their battle with the Lapithae is an allegory of the attempt to usurp power.

A few details are added by commentators of the high Renaissance, such as Comes, Stephanus, and Alexander Ross.[11] Comes adds the story of Ixion's murder of his father-in-law Eioneus (or Deinoeus), for which he wandered the earth unforgiven until Jove had pity on him and raised him to heaven. A striking feature of his account, duplicated by most of his successors, is the tendency to read the entire myth as history with an allegorical level of interpretation, whereas earlier writers had divided the myth into two parts, the first historical and the second an allegorical restatement of the history.

Comes offers two important interpretations of the myth. First, it is a warning against the desire for glory rather than virtue, an echo of Fulgentius: "Those men who seek glory rather than virtue in any affair, or embrace false wisdom rather than the truth, will do many improper things, wherefore monster-like centaurs are born from a cloud" ("Illi enim qui pro virtute gloriam ex quibusvis rebus consectantur, aut qui pro vera sapentia falsam amplectuntur, multa indecora faciant oportet: quare monstro similes Centauri ex nubi nascuntur"). The second interpretation is closer to the spirit of the tale as modified by the introduction of Ixion's murder of his father-in-law. It stems directly from the sixteenth-century revival of interest in Greek, for it is derived from the second Pithyan Ode of Pindar. There, Pindar recounts the details mentioned by Comes, and interprets the whole myth as a warning against ingratitude: "Ixion, as he whirleth round and round on his winged wheel, by the behests of the gods, teacheth this lesson: men should requite the benefactor with fresh tokens of gratitude."[12] Comes followed Pindar closely:

> This more than all other [myths] of the ancients makes plain what princes have often learned who uncover plots against them laid by those whom they cherished before all others and advanced to great wealth and highest honor: Through it the ancients showed that forgetfulness of benefits is the most hateful vice of all to the immortal gods; and it was all the more hateful when a man not only forgets benefits, but even repays them with injuries.
>
> (Hoc tamen veterum caeterorum omnium fere maxime patet, quod non semel experti sunt principes plurique, qui sibi ab illis parari insidias senserunt, quos ante omnes charos habebunt, ad maximes opes, supremosve honores provexerant: per hanc significarent antiqui maxime omnium vitiorum invisam esse Deis immortalibus acceptorum beneficiorum oblivionem: atque id etiam multo magis, cum quis non modo obliviscatus, sed etiam inurias referet pro beneficiis.)

The mythological dictionaries are relatively compressed and avoid the finer points of interpretation. However, Stephanus finds time to note that the Ixion myth is an emblem of "tyrants, ambitious and intemperate men in the state, and heretics and sophists in the church."[13] Alexander Ross adds a rather surprising Christian interpretation. For him it is a fable of religious ingratitude. It shadows forth the Christian doctrine of man redeemed from original sin (Ixion's murder, Jove's pardon) only to plunge into post-baptismal sins which eventually lead to damnation.[14] Yet Fulgentius' influence remains strong. The cloud is hollow pomp, the wheel is fickle fortune, and the centaurs are symbols of violence.

To complete a survey of the Ixion myth we must recall that two of its component elements—Juno and the centaurs—have specialized symbolic meanings which are used extensively by the mythographers. In the historical part of the Ixion myth the centaurs are identified with Ixion's guard of one hundred unruly horsemen.[15] In the allegorical part of the myth they are Ixion's children. They symbolize proneness to violent passion, and in particular to the passion of lust. Dante made them guardians of the seventh circle of hell (the abode of the violent, *Inf.*, 12). The *Fulgentius Metaforalis* of John Ridewall describes them as "half-men and half-horses, denoting men made bestial by their carnal appetite. . . ." ("semihomines et semiequi, denotant homines carnali concupiscentia facti ut bestie. . . .")[16] The association was sufficiently commonplace for Ben Jonson to name one of the over-sexed ladies in *Epicoene* "Centaure"; and Alexander Ross insists, "they were said to be halfe horses, imitative of their insatiable lust, and proneness to Venerie."[17]

The part played by Juno in the Ixion myth greatly reinforced its political application. Jupiter and Juno were considered the twin patrons of government. Roughly speaking, Jupiter was associated with the *object* of government, which is justice, while Juno was associated with the *means* of government, which are power and wealth. Among her attributes, mythographers stress her ornate clothing, symbolizing wealth, and her peacock, symbolic both of wealth and of the fickle fortune which attends the wealthy, since the bird is beautiful from the front but "ugly and nude in the rear, just as the desire for riches briefly elevates, but eventually denudes."[18] Being patroness of wealth, she was also patroness of marriage, for, as Ross explains, "it is wealth that can bring in . . . a wedding girdle; and without that [a maid] may be long enough without home, ointment, or husband. . . ."[19] A final attribute, which was naturally stressed in connection with Ixion's cloud-woman, is Juno's patronage of the weather. She was often shown accompanied by Iris (the rainbow); and the fourteen nymphs who attend her (*Aeneid,* I, 71) are interpreted regularly as various aspects of the weather—"showres, dewes, serenetie, force of winds, clouds, tempest, snow, haile, lightning, thunder" are mentioned by Jonson in his comment on *Hymenaei.*[20]

To summarize, the Ixion myth was conventionally interpreted in two ways: as a political allegory showing the disastrous result of irresponsible rule, and as an allegory of ingratitude, both familial and religious. These two interpretations, while seemingly disparate, were often fused. Coupled with them were several corollary motifs such as the idea of providential punishment (Jove's thunderbolt), the idea of lust (the centaurs), emphasis on wealth as a source of power (Juno symbolism), and others. Having briefly examined these ideas, we may turn to *King Lear.*

III

Irresponsibility: the Desire for "Dignitas." The earliest and most persistent interpretation of the Ixion myth is that it symbolizes the desire for pomp (*dignitas*) without responsibilities. As Salutati expresses it, "affecting rule, he gets a cloud; that is, he gains the appearance of rule, not its reality" ("regnum affectans, nubem mereatur, id est similitudinem regni suscipere, non regnum").[21] The tragic conclusion of the myth teaches the stern moral, "Who strives to be more than is proper, will be less than he is."

Desire for *dignitas* without responsibility is precisely the motive which causes Lear to abdicate in the first scene of *King Lear.* As soon as the courtiers are assembled, Lear announces,

> . . . 'tis our fast intent
> To shake all cares and business from our age,
> Conferring them on younger strengths, while we
> Unburden'd crawl toward death.
>
> (I.i.39–42)

At first we may be reminded of Shakespeare's dramatic source *The True Chronicle Historie of King Leir, and his Three Daughters,* in which the King abdicates for motives of religious piety: ". . . I would fayne resigne these earthly cares, / And think upon the welfare of my soule."[22] However, Shakespeare's King is only wearied by his duties. He intends to retain all of the trappings of the royal office:

> . . . we shall retain
> The name, and all th'addition to a king;
> The sway, revenue, execution of the rest,
> Beloved sons, be yours. . . .
>
> (I.i.137–40)

In effect, Lear has separated the *dignitas* of rule from its practical cares. As the drama unfolds we find that to retain his *dignitas* Lear must be surrounded by one hundred knights accountable only to him and must continue to be addressed by the formal title *King.* When his daughters suggest reducing the number of retainers, and when Oswald addresses him as "my lady's father" (I.iv.87), he flies into an ungovernable rage. But ceremonies are the shadow, not the substance of rule. Just as Ixion gained "a hollow, windy fantasy" which soon collapsed, Lear is soon informed that he is "an O without a figure. . . . thou art nothing" (I.iv.211–13).

Wealth and Force: the Real Bases of Power. Complementing Ixion's infatuation with *dignitas* is his failure to gain real power, symbolized by Juno. His disastrous infatuation with the cloud-woman was interpreted as an allegorical lesson that authority must be based on the physical realities of money and force. Alexander Ross, commenting on Juno's patronage of money and power, declared that "wealth is every thing; it is both meat, drink, clothes, armour, it is that which doth command all things."[23]

Lear misinterprets the nature of power in the same way as Ixion. He explicitly gives up "sway," "revenue," and "execution," yet wishes to retain authority. His error is neatly defined by the references to Jupiter and Juno in the scene where he finds Kent in the stocks. He is incredulous; he refuses to believe that his authority has been so far flouted. He exclaims, "By Jupiter [that is, by the god of justice, of what is right], I swear, no." To this the realistic Kent replies, "By Juno [goddess of *Realpolitik*], I swear, ay" (II.iv.21–22).

The same point is made constantly by the Fool. Since the importance of wealth as a source of power is always emphasized in discussions of the significance of Juno in the Ixion myth,[24] it is significant that the Fool also emphasizes wealth:

Fool. Can you make no use of nothing, nuncle?
Lear. Why, no, boy; nothing can be made out of nothing.
Fool. [To Kent] Prithee, tell him so much the rent of his land
comes to.

(I.iv.143–47)

And,

"Fathers that wear rags
Do make their children blind;
But fathers that bear bags
Shall see their children kind."

(II.iv.48–51)

And,

"That sir which serves and seeks for gain,
And follows but for form,
Will pack when it begins to rain,
And leave thee in the storm."

(II.iv.79–82)

Later, when Lear is at the nadir of his despair, he comes to realize the part which wealth plays in rule. At this point he has moved from an infatuation with outward show to an equally irrational cynicism—we might say that he honors Juno now but has forgotten Jupiter—and his comment recalls the comparison made by Alexander Ross between wealth and armor:

Through tatter'd clothes small vices do appear;
Robes and furr'd gowns hide all. Plate sin with gold,
And the strong lance of justice hurtless breaks;
Arm it in rags, a pigmy's straw does pierce it.
(IV.vi.168–71)

Although dowries do not enter the Ixion myth per se, Juno was, as has been noted, the patroness of dowries as well as wealth in general. She was "much adored and called upon by maids that were to marry . . . for it is wealth that can bring in, and bring home, anoint, and gird the maid with a wedding girdle; and without that she may be long enough without a home . . . or husband."[25] This is exactly what Cordelia learns from Burgundy. Despite the assurance of France that "She is herself a dowry," Burgundy asks Lear for "that portion which yourself propos'd"; and when Lear refuses, he dryly remarks to Cordelia, "I am sorry, then, you have so lost a father / That you must lose a husband" (I.i.244–50).

The reference to Jupiter and Juno, the Fool's allusions to wealth, and the dowry ritual all turn on the truth which mythographers found in the Ixion myth: authority cannot exist unless backed by money and power. As Regan reminds the hysterical Lear: "I pray you, father, being weak, seem so" (II.iv.204).

The Storm: Nature and Providence. From Lactantius, later mythographers learned of the thunderbolt which cast Ixion into hell. This thunderbolt was sent by Jove and was interpreted both as a symbol of sudden disillusionment and as providential justice. Both interpretations apply to the storm in *Lear.* The storm follows directly on Lear's final disillusionment with his daughters. At the very moment when he vows, "I have full cause of weeping; but this heart / Shall break into a hundred thousand flaws, / Or ere I'll weep." (II.iv.287–89), the stage directions call for "storm and tempest" and Cornwall remarks, "'twill be a storm." Lear's disillusionment is complete, and his next act is to rush out into the storm.

Just as the thunderbolt of the Ixion myth is associated with Jove, so the thunder during the storm scene in *Lear* is Jovian. Even before the storm Lear calls Jove the "thunder-bearer" (II.iv.230) and invokes him as "high-judging Jove," the agent of providential justice. During the storm he refers to the thunderbolts as "oak-cleaving" (III.ii.5), an allusion which recalls that the oak was sacred to Jove, and bids the "all-shaking thunder" to restore justice by destroying "ingrateful man." The association of the storm with providential justice is made explicit as Lear exclaims,

Let the great gods,
That keep this dreadful pudder o'er our heads,
Find out their enemies now. Tremble, thou wretch

That hast within thee undivulged crimes,
Unwhipp'd of justice.

(III.ii.49–53)

The parallel to the Ixion myth is strengthened by the fact that, like Ixion, Lear is the victim of this justice. Usually the *True Chronicle Historie* is cited as Shakespeare's precedent for the storm. It is true that thunder sounds twice in the old play, but in both cases it is a warning which deters the "Messenger" from murdering Leir and his companion Perillus. It is thus the act of a benevolent providence and is directly opposite in significance to the storm in *Lear.* It is Lear who suffers the "impetuous blasts" and "oak-cleaving thunderbolts," while Goneril and Regan remain safe in Gloucester's castle. Lear vaguely recognizes this as he recalls the time "When the rain came to wet me once, and the wind to make me chatter; when the thunder would not peace at my bidding . . ." (IV.vi.102–4); and Cordelia asks,

Was this a face
To be oppos'd against the warring winds?
To stand against the deep dread-bolted thunder?
In the most terrible and nimble stroke
Of quick, cross lightning?

(IV.vii.31–35)

The storm gains additional significance when we recall that Juno was patroness of weather and that, as early as Boccaccio, mythographers used this fact to explain the symbolism of Ixion's cloud-woman.[26] Good weather, bringing fertility, was interpreted as an accord between Jupiter and Juno, a tradition preserved in Milton's lovely image, "as *Jupiter* / On *Juno* smiles, when he impregns the Clouds / That shed *May* flowers." Conversely, a destructive storm was interpreted as discord between the two: "The discord between Juno and Jove is nothing else than the distemper of the elements from which comes destruction. . . . Thus if Juno, that is, humid and windy nature, attacks Jove, that is, the hot and dry force, the rains will be so great that they will overflow the earth . . ." ("La discordia nata fra Giunone, e Giove altro non è, che lo stemperamento de gli elementi, dal quale viene la distruttione delle cose. . . . Se Giunone adunque, cioè la natura humida, & ventosa, attacca a Giove, che è la virtù calda, & secca, & lo sprezza, tante saranno le pioggie, che allagaranno la terra. . . .").[27] Drawing on this tradition, mythographers tended to interpret the cloud-woman as a storm symbolizing the disastrous results of Ixion's rule. The storm in *Lear* has a similar meaning. It is not only a tempest where Jovian thunderbolts punish the rash King; it is also a reflection in Nature of the chaos which is engulfing the kingdom as a result of Lear's separation of authority (the Jovian element of rule) from power (under the aegis of Juno). Lear's reference to rain, wind, thunder, and fire as "servile ministers" (III.ii.21) recalls the relationship of these "elements" to Juno. His reference to "the great gods / That keep this dreadful pudder o'er our heads" (III.ii.49–50) echoes the idea of storm as discord among the gods. Finally, the destructive nature of such discord is emphasized in both the first and second scenes of act 4. Cartari's "distruttione delle cose" and "allagaranno la terra" are paralleled in Lear's command that "the wind blow the earth into the sea, / Or swell the curled waters 'bove the main, / That things might change or cease . . ." (III.i.5–7).

Punishment: the Wheel. The punishment for Ixion's sin is the torture of being bound on a wheel and rolled eternally through hell. Lear explicitly compares his experience with that of Ixion when he exclaims, "I am bound / Upon a wheel of fire, that mine own tears / Do scald like molten lead" (IV.vii.46–48). The statement is in the nature of a confession. It is Lear's first admission that he is being punished for some sin. As his senses return he kneels before Cordelia to ask forgiveness. For a moment the wheel ceases to turn, for he has come to terms with what he has made himself: "Pray you now, forget and forgive; I am old and foolish" (IV.vii.84). However, like Ixion, he must suffer further. In the next act the wheel resumes its inexorable motion.

Further significance is added to the wheel image when we recall that Ixion's wheel was interpreted as the wheel of fortune on which man is bound when he allows violent passion to override reason. It is Lear's "hideous rashness" (I.i.153) which begins the action of the play, and this rashness recurs in his violent curses of Cordelia, Goneril, and Regan. The association of the wheel image in *Lear* with fortune is made explicit in two references. First, there is Kent's "Fortune, good-night! Smile once more; turn thy wheel!" (II.ii.180). Second, there is Edmund's dying exclamation, "The wheel is come full circle; I am here" (V.iii.174).

Lust: the Centaurs. Lear's description of his daughters as centaurs (IV.vi.126) is an allusion to the Ixion myth, since the centaurs were the offspring of Ixion, begotten by him on the cloud-woman. Shakespeare associated the offspring of Lear with the offspring of Ixion. Traditionally, the centaurs were considered emblems of masculine lust, "carnal men made bestial by lust."[28] Although Shakespeare changes the sex of the centaurs, the emphasis on the idea of lust is preserved:

> Behold yond simp'ring dame . . .
> The fitchew nor the soiled horse goes to't
> With a more riotous appetite.

Down from the waist they are Centaurs,
Though women all above. . . .
(IV.vi.120–27)

The association between the centaurs and lust helps to explain the ramifications of this theme in the play. It is not intrinsic to the plot, since Lear's tragic flaw has nothing to do with lust, and the evil children are motivated primarily by the desire for power rather than sexual passion. Yet Shakespeare emphasizes lust in connection with Gloucester, Edmund, Regan, Goneril, and Lear's retainers.

Lear's Retainers: Further Centaur Symbolism. Ixion's band of retainers is prominent in the "history" of Ixion's activities while king of Thessaly. Seeking a rational explanation of the centaur image, mythographers regularly explained that the retainers were the original centaurs, either because they were the first mounted troops or from the false etymology, *centum armati.* They are unanimous in agreeing that there were one hundred retainers, and that the retainers were violent, unruly, and lustful.

The same points are made in connection with Lear's retainers. In the first place, it is stressed repeatedly that there are one hundred of them. The fact becomes significant when it is recalled that only one of the sources of the King Lear story which may have been consulted by Shakespeare is specific about the number of retainers. This is the *Gesta Romanorum,* in which the number is given as forty. Goneril's description of the retainers calls attention to their unruliness and particularly their lust:

Here do you keep a hundred knights and squires
Men so disorder'd, so debosh'd and bold,
That this our court, infected with their manners,
Shows like a riotous inn. Epicurism and lust
Makes it more like a tavern or a brothel
Than a grac'd palace.
(I.iv.262–67)

Perhaps the most interesting feature of centaur symbolism is that suggested by the human torso coupled to the horse's body. Mythographers considered the image an emblem of the warring forces of passion and reason or nature and spirit which strive for dominion over man. Often the centaur was compared to other half-human monsters from classical mythology such as the sirens or the satyrs.[29]

We can observe the creative use of this tradition during the sixteenth century in the painting "The Battle of the Centaurs" by Piero di Cosimo. This painting forms part of a series discussed by Erwin Panofsky and again by R. L. Douglas in his book on Piero.[30] The series includes the

"Hunting Scene," "Return from the Hunt," "A Forest Fire," and "The Battle of the Centaurs." In each painting a higher stage of human evolution, conceived in the Lucretian sense as an ascent from savagery, is depicted. In the first, man is a brute, copulating with beasts and producing half-human offspring. In the second there is less brutality and some suggestion of cooperation among men, but the half-human monsters, including a centaur, are still evident. "A Forest Fire" shows cultivated land and records the discovery of fire as described in an often-illustrated passage from Vitruvius. The fourth painting is the climax of the series. It represents the moment at which man recognizes his difference from the brute world of nature and rejects it. The moment is symbolized by the battle of the centaurs with the Lapithae. Henceforth the separation between man and the lower forms of life will be absolute.

While Piero used centaur symbolism to illustrate a theory of evolution, elsewhere it is used to illustrate human psychology. Salutati associates the centaurs of the Ixion myth with man's stubborn hostility toward government by law.[31] Speaking more generally, he teaches that the centaur is an emblem of the dual nature of man, half under the aegis of Nature and half under the aegis of spirit. In the seventeenth century Alexander Ross gave the image a Christian twist by observing that "every regenerate man is a centaur."[32]

There is no need to recapitulate the extensive and illuminating scholarship on the imagery of *Lear* to support the contention that the strife between the natural and spiritual in man is a basic theme of the play. Edmund is the spokesman for naturalism. To him, man is an animal, and force, the brute right of the fittest to survive, is the supreme law. Moral and legal principles, expressions of man's higher nature, are "the curiosity of nations"; that is, superstitions and customs to be set aside when they interfere with expediency. Cordelia embodies the opposite principle of allegiance to moral duty even at the cost of personal hardship. In fact, she is so scrupulous that she refuses to depart one jot from her "duty" even to humor her father's whims:

> I love your Majesty
> According to my bond; no more nor less.

And,

> Good my lord,
> You have begot me, bred me, lov'd me: I
> Return those duties back as are right fit. . . .

And,

> Haply, when I shall wed,
> That lord whose hand must take my plight shall carry

Half my love with him, half my care and duty.
(I.i.94–104)

Evidently, Edmund and Cordelia define the two extremes of human nature.

As for Lear, although he utterly disregards his own higher duties, he insists that others be dutiful and reveals an almost superstitious belief in the gods. Each time he curses his daughters he appeals to Nature as the agent of providence to right his wrongs. His first oath is the self-confident, "by the sacred radiance of the sun . . ." (I.i.111). Next comes the petition, "Hear, Nature! hear, dear goddess, hear!" (I.iv.297). Later there is the hysterical command, "Strike her young bones, / You taking airs . . ." (II.iv.165–66). Finally, there is the insane order that the storm destroy the whole world: "Strike flat the thick rotundity o' th' world! / Crack nature's moulds, all germens spill at once / That makes ingrateful man!" (III.ii.6–9).

When Lear's belief in supernatural powers proves empty, he does not modify it rationally. Instead, he espouses an extreme naturalistic view of man which is similar to Edmund's but couched in terms expressing the blackest despair. In act 2 he still has faith in human dignity: "Allow not nature more than nature needs, / Man's life is cheap as beast's" (II.iv.269–70). However, by the middle of act 3 he thinks of man as ". . . no more but such a poor, bare, forked animal as thou art" (III.iv.111–14). Having begun with a sentimental view of Nature as an agent of providence, he later describes the storm as "pitiless" (III.iv.29), and man's lower anatomy, symbolic of natural instinct, as "hell . . . darkness . . . the sulphurous pit, / Burning, scalding, stench, consumption . . ." (IV.vi.130–31). Finally, his image of human society is the dog who is obeyed in office (IV.vi.163). The beadle lusts after the whore as he lashes her; the usurer hangs the cozener; and the rich man flaunts justice with impunity while the beggar is punished for the most trivial offense.

Neither of Lear's views is valid. Man exists in a middle state between Nature and the world of spirit. He is a composite of these elements, and each has legitimate claims which he ignores at his peril. Although the centaur was usually an emblem of man dominated by his lower passions, Salutati reminds us that Chiron, the good centaur, symbolizes a proper balance of man's higher and lower natures: "When reason, which we have in common with the angels, rules our appetites, which we have in common with the beasts, a virtuous life results for a man.[33] Shakespeare's treatment of the nature-spirit dichotomy in *Lear* teaches the same lesson. Nature and the power derived from Nature are impersonal—to a certain degree, amoral. They cannot, however, be idealistically ignored. They must be controlled by responsible agents dedicated to the end of justice. When Jupiter and Juno are in accord—when justice and power are harmonized—

men experience the fine weather of proper rule. When they quarrel, the kingdom suffers the destructive storms of civil war and anarchy. According to Alexander Ross, "... where things are not ruled by lawes and order, and civility, but are carried headlong with violence and force, we may say that there is a Commonwealth of Centaurs."[34]

Ingratitude. Following Pindar, Comes interpreted the Ixion myth as a fable of ingratitude which "makes plain what princes have often learned who uncover plots against them laid by those whom they cherished before all others and advanced to great wealth and highest honor." As the fourth in the tetrad of great classical sinners, Ixion was often considered a type of ingratitude, since he repaid Jove's favors by attempting to seduce Juno.

In *Lear* the theme of ingratitude is exploited throughout the play. Most obviously, Lear cherishes Goneril and Regan and advances them to great wealth and honor, only to discover the plots which they have laid against him. Indeed, the word "ingratitude" is repeated thematically (e.g., I.iv.281; II.iv.182; III.ii.9 and iv.14).

It is obvious that King Lear experiences ingratitude. It is equally important to recognize that, like Ixion, he practices it. His rejection of Cordelia and Kent could be considered acts of ingratitude, but his most serious ingratitude is religious. The majority of Shakespeare's audience would have judged Lear's actions in terms of the Tudor theory of monarchy. Madeleine Doran has rightly stressed the similarity between *Lear* and Sidney's lesson in the *Arcadia* that abdication is close to a literal crime.[35] To this lesson should be added the lesson of *Gorboduc* and *1 Henry IV* that the division of a kingdom is an equal, if not a greater, evil. In the carefully pagan atmosphere of *Lear,* the King rules under the patronage of "high-judging Jove" (II.iv.231). It is Jove whom Lear offends by his "forgetfulness of benefits," and his punishment is, like Ixion's, the wheel of fire.

Redemption: Chiron. Chiron was considered the one good centaur. Alexander Ross observed that he illustrates the existence of good even in the worst of societies.[36] Since Lear compares his evil daughters to centaurs, one may ask whether the one good daughter resembles the one good centaur. The question cannot be answered definitely. There are, however, attributes which Chiron and Cordelia share.

In mythology Chiron was renowned for three characteristics: (1) He was an emblem of self-discipline and a paragon of justice: "Chiron non modo Centauros ceteros, sed homines quoque iustitia superavit. . . ."[37] Cordelia also combines supreme self-discipline and justice. She is "queen / Over her passion, who, most rebel-like, / Sought to be king o'er her" (IV.iii.15–17). Her justice is illustrated in the first scene in her refusal to compromise and in Kent's remark that she "justly [thinks] and hast most rightly said!" (I.i.186). Later we learn that she "redeems Nature from the general curse / Which twain have brought her to" (IV.vi.210–11). Finally, her pardon of Lear (IV.vii) is an act of justice tempered by mercy. (2) Chiron was renowned for two skills, music and the medicinal use of herbs. Cordelia is neither a physician nor a musician, but Lear's cure takes place under her sponsorship and involves both herbs ("All blest secrets, / All you unpublish'd virtues of the earth, / Spring with my tears" [IV.iv.15–17]), and music (IV.vii.25). (3) Chiron was also a symbol of innocent suffering. He was wounded accidentally by the poisoned arrow of Hercules, died, and was translated by Jove into the constellation of Sagittarius.[38] Ross says, "Just as Chiron was wounded by *Hercules* but was afterward placed among the Starrs; so, although might doth oftentimes overcome right here, yet the end of justice and mercy shall be the glory at last."[39] As she is being led to prison, Cordelia observes that might often overcomes right: "We are not the first / Who with best meaning have incurr'd the worst" (V.iii.3–4).

IV

Although some of the parallels which I have cited are suggestive rather than conclusive, the number of parallels, together with Shakespeare's explicit references to centaurs, the wheel of fire, Jupiter and Juno, the thunderbolt, and the like, fully justifies Talbert and Starnes' conclusion that the Ixion myth was much on Shakespeare's mind as he wrote *King Lear.*

Shakespeare could have learned of the Ixion myth from a variety of sources, including mythological dictionaries, commentaries on Ovid and Virgil, works on mythography such as those by Comes and Cartari, emblem books, and the like. The precedent of *Gorboduc* makes it clear that the use of myth to articulate historical materials was by no means an innovation. In addition, when *Lear* was written, interest in the symbolic and dramatic possibilities of classical mythology had been stimulated by the court masque.

Whatever Shakespeare's reason for becoming interested in the Ixion myth, his use of it conforms to a widely accepted Renaissance critical theory. According to this theory, poetry occupies a position in the scheme of knowledge halfway between philosophy and history. Philosophy is an essential discipline, the source of the general ideas which enable man to understand his experience. However, in itself, it is complex and abstract. History is equally important, being man's source of specific information. But it, too, is deficient. It tends to become a list of events with no higher significance. Poetry alone combines the virtues of philosophy and history. The poet draws on the generalizations of philosophy to shape the events of history in a meaningful pattern. In the *Apologie for Poetrie* Sidney explains:

> The Philosopher therefore and the Historian, are they which would win the gole: the one by precept, the other by example. But both not having both, doe both halte. For the Philosopher, setting downe with thorny argument the bare rule, is so hard of utterance, and so mistie to be conceived, that one that hath no other guide but him, shall wade in him till hee be olde, before he shall find sifficient cause to be honest: for his knowledge standeth so upon the abstract and generall, that happie is that man who may understande him, and more happie, that can applye what hee doth understand.
>
> On the other side, the Historian wanting the precept, is so tyed, not to what shoulde bee, but to what is, to the particuler truth of things, and not to the general reason of things, that hys example draweth no necessary consequence and therefore a lesse fruitfull doctrine.
>
> Now dooth the peerelesse Poet perforem both: for whatsoever the Philosopher sayth should be doone, hee giveth a perfect picture of it in some one, by whom he presupposeth it was done. So as hee coupleth the generall notion with the particuler example.[40]

The historical details of *King Lear* are assembled from a variety of sources. Holinshed's *Chronicle, The Mirror for Magistrates, The Faerie Queene,* and *The True Chronicle Historie* are those most frequently mentioned. The details, however, lack genuine coherence. They are "the particular truth of things," but they have no "general reason." We may conjecture that Shakespeare was aware of this fact. He therefore supplemented history with myth, choosing Ixion, the type of the irresponsible king, the ruler who confused pomp and circumstance with power, and the father of the lustful centaurs, as his model. The mythographic tradition gave him the "general reasons" which he needed to change a mass of "particular truths" into a unified drama. Since these "general reasons" were central issues of contemporary political and moral philosophy, they also helped him create his most profound study of the crisis of his age.

(1975)

Speaking the Speech: Shakespearean Dialogue

The cult of Shakespeare the poet began early and has continued to flourish in the twentieth century. In *The Poetry of Shakespeare's Plays* F. E. Halliday concludes: "It follows . . . that the plays must be read as we read the works of Milton or any other non-dramatic poet. To hear in a theatre a Shakespearean play that we do not know almost by heart is to miss half its beauty."[1] Few Shakespeare scholars would go this far today. A more temperate view, which recognizes that the verse is intended primarily for speaking, is offered by Bertram Joseph in *Acting Shakespeare:* "Verse speaking is a matter of expressing the sense and its implications and of producing melody. Both melody and meaning are inseparable from the structure of words in which they are both embodied. In the actual speaking, emphasis is varied in order to 'make manifest' the precise sense. . . ."[2]

This comment strikes a reasonable balance. A speech act is a synthesis, not a mixture. Melody is simply the aesthetic value of the sound of the speech act. It is a corollary of speech, not a separable part, and it is present in all speech, whether in prose or in verse. The habit of thinking of melody as something separable from "precise sense" is misleading. Combined with veneration for Shakespeare the poet, it often leads in performance to what may be called "recitation." In recitation the irregular, multi-valued stress patterns of speech flatten into the regular, monotonic beat of the iambic meter, and the effect of pauses in defining natural syntactical units is offset by a tendency to pause, if only briefly, at the end of each pentameter line. The result is hypnotic, the rhetorical equivalent of Muzak. Whole chunks of meaning are swallowed up by the melody. The attention of the audience wanders until it is caught by a Famous Passage and then wanders anew. Evidently the problem is not unique to the twentieth century. Thomas Heywood seems to have had it in mind when he wrote in his *Apology for Actors,* "Be . . . his pronuntiation neuer so musicall and plausiue, yet without a comely and elegant gesture, a gratious and a bewitching kinde of action . . . I hold all the rest as nothing."[3]

I

In a print-oriented culture it is natural to regard Shakespeare's plays as words on a page, a text. The Renaissance view was quite different. As Hamlet explains to the players, drama is a mirror held up to Nature. The remark is a Renaissance commonplace. If it is taken seriously, it can tell us a great deal about the Renaissance understanding of drama.

The mirror metaphor opposes life to an image of life. In life we are continuously immersed in situations that cause responses. I enter a dining room and notice that the table is set. My response is a question: "What are we having for dinner?" In a play script this sequence is reversed. If the script lacks stage directions, like most Renaissance scripts, it will contain only the question. The modern director or actor must infer the table settings from the speech. Once inferred they are included in the stage set, and when the play is performed an illusion is created. The table settings seem to the audience to cause the question, as they would in real life, although for the director it was, in fact, the question that caused the table settings. The play is an artifice, an image in a mirror.

A dramatic speech arises from a situation, which may be defined as an array of causes. Some of the causes are obvious from the speech itself, which acts in such cases as an indirect stage direction. When this is true, the task of inferring the causes is simple. Othello says "Keep up your bright swords." The speech indicates that the characters he is addressing have swords. Without the swords the speech would be absurd. Once the characters are given swords, however, it seems perfectly reasonable, like a speech in real life.

Are not the speeches in a drama normally caused by other speeches? If character A asks "What day is today?" and character B replies "Wednesday," is not the question the cause of the answer?

Yes and *no*. The question is one of the causes of the answer, but not necessarily the most important. Suppose the playwright wants to show that character B is a liar. The audience has learned previously that today is Monday. In this case dishonesty, which is a quality of character, will be the true cause of B's statement that today is Wednesday, and A's question merely a strategy to permit the dishonesty to be exhibited. If the dishonesty is not sufficiently obvious from the statement itself, B may wink at the audience while speaking the line.

Suppose B says "*Wednesday!*" in an agitated whisper. This is because Wednesday is the day when A and B plan to escape from prison. The escape is part of the plot. It is the cause of B's agitation. The microphone hanging from the ceiling of the cell is the cause of the whisper. The microphone is part of the set.

If B shouts "*Wednesday!*" perhaps this is because A is hard of hearing. Perhaps A has been given a hearing aid by the prop department so that the cause cannot be missed. If B says "Wednesday" in an angry tone of voice, this may be because A has been pestering him. If B pauses after A's question and looks at a wall calendar, this may be because B is absent-minded or distracted. Perhaps a calendar has been tacked to the wall of the set specifically so that B can look at it before replying.

The word *Wednesday* is neutral. It has only the general meaning assigned to it in the dictionary. It does not take on a precise meaning until its causes have been discovered and incorporated into set, blocking, costume, gesture, expression, and voice inflection at the moment when it is spoken. Taken together, the precise meanings in a play express the motives and emotions which are the source of its illusion of life.

II

To discuss plays in this way requires thinking in terms of performances rather than texts. But performances in the theatre are ephemeral. At the end of its run a production ceases to exist. Reconstructions are possible on the basis of personal memories, reviews, promptbooks, and the like, but even the best reconstructions involve a great deal of unverifiable conjecture. Happily, this situation is now changing. Although there are fundamental differences between live theatre and movies and television, the growing body of Shakespeare on film and videotape allows performances of the latter type to be examined in minute detail. Statements about these recorded performances can be rigorous, moreover, because they can be verified.

The creation of an effective sequence of causes for a brief speech in a Shakespeare play is nicely illustrated by Olivier's film version of *Hamlet*. The speech in question is only three lines. Usually these lines are spoken continuously, with two brief pauses to separate the three sentences:

Soft you now!
The fair Ophelia! Nymph, in thy orisons
Be all my sins rememb'red.
(III.i.88–90)

The most obvious cause of this speech is the presence of Ophelia, who does not, at this point, have a line. The cause is visual rather than verbal. Most performances of *Hamlet* stop there.

In Olivier's film the lines are given additional causes. Hamlet is shown walking in a corridor. We know that he is convinced that Claudius is spying on him. He hears a noise but cannot see who has made it. His suspicions are immediately aroused. His line "Soft you now!" means something like "An unexpected event is happening; I must be careful." He then walks to the end of the corridor and sees Ophelia. She does not "enter" in this version of the play, but is "discovered." Hamlet is relieved and pleased. He exclaims, "The fair Ophelia!" He then walks to her and takes her arm. He notices that she is holding a book of religious devotions. It is the book Polonius gave her before hiding behind the arras. When he gave it to her he remarked:

> 'Tis too much prov'd, that with devotion's visage
> And pious action we do sugar o'er
> The devil himself.
>
> (III.i.47–49)

Olivier's decision to make Ophelia's book a devotional manual is justified by this speech, but it is not inevitable. The reason for Olivier's decision is that the devotional manual provides the cause of Hamlet's next words to Ophelia: "Nymph, in thy orisons / Be all my sins rememb'red."

Instead of being spoken continuously, the speech in Olivier's version is broken by three extended pauses during which Hamlet (1) discovers Ophelia, (2) walks to her, and (3) notices her book. What is normally a rather bland transition becomes, in this performance, a powerfully charged expression of themes that are at the center of the play. The speech seems perfectly, even transparently, natural to the viewer, but the naturalness is the result of an intense analysis of causes. It is poetry of the highest order, not because it is sonorous, but because it is perfectly expressive.

III

The reader of a script forms a generalized mental construct of the situations that generate the speeches. For most readers the construct is adequate as far as plot and character are concerned but vague in respect to the countless immediate causes that are supplied continuously during a performance. To imagine these causes fully would require the reader to do the work done by an entire stage company over several weeks of rehearsal. This would be impossible. Fortunately, it is not necessary. A generalized construct is adequate for normal reading purposes.

A reader has one advantage over members of an audience. He can reread difficult passages as many times as necessary in order to puzzle them out. On the stage, however, the play moves briskly from beginning to middle to end. Its speeches have to be immediately comprehensible. If a character says "Ouch" for no apparent reason the audience will be baffled, and to that degree the play will go out of focus. If, on the other hand, a piece of furniture is supplied by the prop department against which the actor can collide, the exclamation becomes perfectly comprehensible and the play can move forward without confusion.

As the example from Olivier's *Hamlet* shows, the problem of inferring causes for real plays is often far more difficult—and the options much more numerous—than simply adding a piece of furniture to the set. But the principle is the same. The clarity of the speeches depends on the presentation of their causes. If melody is something that exists separately from "precise sense," it is irrelevant to this process. At best it can be a kind of musical underscoring of the causes; at worst it will distract from the causes by calling attention to itself. When the meaning of a speech is unclear, it cannot be saved by the most refined RSC accent or the most melodious delivery. A recent article in *Theatre News* (Fall 1982) quotes Fred Adams, the Artistic Director of the Utah Shakespeare Festival, as follows:

> The actor I look for is an actor who, within the discipline of [the] line, can find the thought, and when the actor can bring the thought out, the heck with the poetry. They become one, because the thought is inherent in the poetry and when he is working more for the thought, it all falls into place.[4]

IV

Let us now carry the analysis one step further. The word "action" is ambiguous. It can refer to the sequence of events in a play, and it is identical in this sense with what Aristotle called *praxis*. But it can also refer to the activity, including the acting, which occurs when a play is performed. Aristotle defines drama as the imitation of an action (*praxis*) by means of plot (*muthos*). Plot is the "soul" of drama and the first of drama's six parts. The Greek word *poiein,* from which we derive *poet,* means "to make." A writer becomes a poet, according to Aristotle, by making plots, not by writing verse. Speech is the fourth of Aristotle's "parts." It is the means by which the first three—plot, character, and thought—are objectified. The fifth part is spectacle (*opsis*), which is roughly equivalent to the modern concept of "staging."

Renaissance discussions of drama sometimes use the word *action* in the Aristotelian sense, but they also use it to refer to stage action. This usage is particularly common in remarks about drama by actors and playwrights, because it views drama in terms of its end-product, which is production on a stage. To theatre professionals the action on the stage is important not because it is activity—that is, people moving around—but because it is the way the play makes its essence, its action in the Aristotelian sense, visible to the audience.

A theatre company planning to do a Shakespeare play begins with a script, which is a collection of speeches. Since Shakespeare's stage directions are few and brief, almost everything else must be inferred from the speeches: the plot, the psychology of the characters, and the immediate causes that underlie each scene, including those objectified in the details of the set, the props, the costumes, the blocking of the characters, and the behavior of the characters who do not speak. When each scene is fully realized onstage, the play reveals its action progressively. At the end of the final scene, the action has been fully revealed. There is nothing to add.

Evidently the script is an epiphenomenon. It is visible on the page as a text, but its purpose is to lead a company of actors—and eventually an audience—to matters that are not visible on the page. Getting these matters right for a Shakespeare play is extraordinarily difficult. There are few completely successful Shakespeare productions. The companies with the best record are ensemble companies whose members work together on many plays, a little like the members of an Elizabethan acting company, instead of coming together to produce one play and then disbanding.

To move from script to performance is to involve the whole company in the search for causes. Initially the search is general: "What is this play about? It is about indecision." "Why is this character so erratic? He suffers from an Oedipus complex." Later the search narrows. "Why does Hamlet's tone change abruptly while he is talking with Ophelia? Because Polonius has revealed his presence behind the arras by coughing." As the decisions multiply, they compel other decisions. "Why does Hamlet have an Oedipus complex? Because of Gertrude." Therefore Gertrude must be sensual. She should wear a low-cut dress. She should fawn on Claudius. Perhaps she should moisten her lips frequently or caress her hips or fondle Hamlet when she speaks to him.

V

As has been noted, many causes are obvious. When Othello says, "Keep up your bright swords," the other characters have to have swords. Other causes are more subtle. What, for example, should be done about Othello's sword? The purpose of the episode is to show Othello's authority. Is he not more authoritative if he, alone among the Venetian soldiers, goes without a sword? Or if the director decides that he should wear a sword, is he not more authoritative if he quells the riot without drawing his sword? Consider another instance. In *Julius Caesar* the conspirators stab Caesar with short swords. At the end of the play Cassius remarks that he will end his life with the sword he used against Caesar. Nothing has to be made of this. On the other hand, it can readily be used for thematic reinforcement. If Cassius' sword is sufficiently distinctive to be recognizable, it can cause an ironic reflection: the instrument of murder is the instrument of the punishment for murder; he who lives by the sword dies by it.

Clear enough. But what props should be used in the tavern scenes in *The Merry Wives of Windsor*? Drinking cups, certainly, because the speeches mention drinking. But how should the cups be used? Should Falstaff drink only before a speech or when a line mentions drinking, or should he freely punctuate his speeches with draughts of sack? If the answer to the latter question is *yes,* as it is in many productions, the draughts of sack become the causes of moments of silence. These moments can be used, in turn, for dramatic emphasis or humor, or simply to break lengthy speeches into short units that are easily understood by the audience.

At the beginning of *The Comedy of Errors* Aegeon delivers a long speech recounting his pitiful misadventures. It is interrupted twice by comments from the duke. Although no one else speaks, the initial stage direction and the formality of the proceedings justify the inference that Aegeon is addressing a large audience. How should the listeners be deployed? What sort of byplay should occur as they listen, and how should Aegeon react to the byplay? Without byplay, the speech is a tedious lump of exposition. Appropriate byplay brings the speech to life by supplying causes for the way it is organized and for changes in Aegeon's emotions and tone of voice as he delivers it. A similar problem is created by Prospero's long expository speech near the beginning of *The Tempest.* Here there is only one listener, Miranda. If the interaction between father and daughter is made emphatic, the speech ceases to be exposition and becomes drama. If not, it becomes a narrative lump to be disposed of as painlessly as possible so that the real play can begin. Finding the causes for the movements of Prospero's thought, for the changes in his mood, and for Miranda's decisions to break in where she does and not elsewhere is the initial challenge of *The Tempest.* Productions of the play seem to fail to meet this challenge as often as they succeed.

VI

Thus far we have considered theory and stage practice. It will now be useful to turn to historical evidence. In the first place, Shakespeare and his contemporaries wrote plays in blank verse which looks very much like poetry, in the sense of melodious language, and not in prose. Did they not intend these plays to be poetic in the sense of melodic? In the second place, once written, the blank verse was spoken by actors. Did the actors emphasize the melody of the verse or de-emphasize it, and did the audience respond to the melody or ignore it? Since Shakespeare was a member of an acting company, he had to write plays that the actors approved and that drew audiences. For Shakespeare, questions of literary style are inseparable from questions of acting style and popular taste.

In *The Poetics of Jacobean Drama* Coburn Freer argues that the poetry of verse drama was important for Elizabethan actors and audiences in addition to being appreciated as dramatic speech. Later, when the plays were read more often than seen in the theatre, they began to be considered "poems" and were valued more for the elegance of their language than for their action. As this happened, playwrights began to consider themselves "men of letters" and to write as much for the reading public as for the stage.[5]

Freer seeks to redress the imbalance created by print culture, and he shows convincingly that Jacobean dramatists used poetry dramatically to reinforce theme, plot, and character.

Without in any way detracting from Freer's very considerable accomplishment, it is possible to note that many Renaissance authors cited by Freer attack drama that is self-consciously "poetic." Thomas Nashe, for example, condemns "ideot Art-masters . . . who (mounted on the stage of arrogance) thinke to out-brave better pennes with the swelling bumbast of bragging blanke verse . . . [and] the spacious volubilitie of a drumming decasillabon."[6] Nashe's point seems to be that many Elizabethan authors rely on exotic sound effects rather than careful dramaturgy. The word "bombast" occurs frequently in Elizabethan comments on dramatic verse. It is normally used, as here by Nashe, to criticize verse that calls attention to itself and panders to the groundlings. One of Greene's charges against Shakespeare is that he "supposes he is as well able to bombast out a blanke verse as the best of you."[7] Joseph Hall, who is also cited by Freer, cites *Tamburlaine* as a notorious example of inflated verse and goes on to ridicule all theatre poetry. Such poetry does not mean very much, Hall observes, but it pleases the crowd:

> [If the author] can with termes Italianate,
> Big-sounding sentences, and words of state,
> Faire patch me up his pure *Iambick* verse,
> He ravishes the gazing Scaffolders.[8]

As Freer observes, Hall "rejects [verse drama] altogether, emphasizing in particular the link between its emptiness of content and its sloppiness of technique."[9] Charges of bombast and sloppy technique do not show special sensitivity to the verse element in drama. Instead they show scorn for it—either in general, as in Hall's case, or, as in the case of Nashe, in those instances where sound effects are used to hide poverty of invention.

Renaissance attacks on excessively poetic language are complemented by arguments that drama is essentially plot rather than language. These arguments are derived from Aristotle's *Poetics*. They appear in England first in Sir Philip Sidney's assertion in the *Apology for Poetry* that verse is "but an ornament and no cause to Poetry."[10] Nine years after the publication of the *Apology*, John Marston remarked in his preface to *The Malcontent:*

> I would fain leave the paper; only one thing affects me to think that scenes invented, merely [i.e., "purely"] to be spoken, should be enforcively published to be read . . . but I shall entreat . . . that the unhandsome shape which this trifle in reading presents may be pardoned for the pleasure if afforded you when it was presented with the soul of lively action.[11]

The word *soul* suggests that Marston is thinking of Aristotle. He is, at any rate, in accord with Sidney. It is action, not language, that the play is intended to express, and it is an "unhandsome shape . . . in reading." A similar position is taken by Sir Richard Baker in *Theatrum Triumphans* (1670) during a discussion of the sources of dramatic pleasure:

> The *Ingeniousness* of the Speech, when it is fitted to the Person; and the *Gracefulness* of the *Action,* when it is fitted to the speech; and therefore a Play *read,* hath not half the pleasure of a Play *Acted* . . . and we may well acknowledge that *Gracefulness of Action* is the greatest pleasure of a Play.[12]

The word *action* as used by Marston and Baker is ambiguous for reasons already noted. Marston seems closer to, and Baker more distant from, Aristotle. But we are on solidly Aristotelian ground with the preface by John Dennis to *The Comical Gallant* (1702):

> As in the mixture of the Humane frame,
> 'Tis not the Flesh, 'tis the Soul makes the Man,
> So of Dramatic Poems we may say,
> 'Tis not the Lines, 'tis the Plot makes the Play.
> The Soul of every Poem's the design,
> And words but serve to make that move and shine.[13]

As should be clear, Dennis' comments have a long tradition behind them. A corollary of this tradition is the idea that dramatic verse should be "conversational" rather than "poetic." The Italian poet Trissino observed in 1521 in the introduction to his tragedy *Sophonisba* that unrhymed verses (*versi sciolti*) are proper for drama because they permit the rapid give-and-take of natural dialogue.[14] In England, drama abandoned fourteeners for blank verse, not because blank verse was more poetic, but because it was less artificial—more like natural speech and better suited to expressing what Marston calls "the soul of lively action." It may be noted that the tradition associating blank verse with natural speech was still strong in 1665 when Thomas Howard defended it in the preface of *Four New Plays* with the observation that rhyme is premeditated and hence unnatural and improbable in drama. John Dennis sums up the tradition. In his essay on *The Genius and Writings of Shakespeare* (1712) he observes that Shakespeare

> . . . seems to have been the very Original of our *English* Tragical Harmony; that is the Harmony of Blank Verse, diversifyed often by Dissyllable and Trissyllable Terminations. For that Diversity distinguishes it from Heroick Harmony, and bringing it nearer to common Use, makes it more proper to gain Attention, and more fit for Action and Dialogue. Such Verse we make when we are writing prose; we make such Verse in common Conversation.[15]

Freer considers this comment a bizarre "Augustan" approach to Shakespeare.[16] In fact, the reference to a dramatic form of verse that is different from heroic and closer to "common use" and "conversation" comes straight from the *ars metrica,* which was taught in Elizabethan grammar schools along with Plautus and Seneca, and the comments on gaining attention and on action and dialogue are paraphrased from Horace's *Ars Poetica.*

Renaissance opinions about dramatic verse were at best divided. But one may suggest guardedly that the balance favors the idea that drama is action and that dialogue should incline to the norm of conversation. The groundlings liked Marlowe's "mighty line," but they also liked the more restrained style of the later Shakespeare, and they liked prose dialogue, as witness the popularity of Falstaff. It is undoubtedly true, however, that in the seventeenth century dramatists began to write for the printing press as well as the theatre. Ben Jonson is in the forefront of these dramatists, and the list includes Chapman and Fletcher as well as closet dramatists like Fulke Greville and John Milton. In all of these authors a desire for literary elegance competes with concern for effective stage drama.

VII

The emphasis of Sidney on plot and of Marston on "action" raises the question of how verse was spoken by Renaissance actors. It is useful to approach this subject by asking how verse was spoken by people in general during Shakespeare's lifetime. Unquestionably it was spoken as variously as it is by people today, but an idea of what was considered proper is provided by John Brinsley's textbook *Ludus Literarius,* published in 1612. Brinsley distinguishes between the way verse (in this case Latin verse) is recited in school and the way it should be recited in normal circumstances:

> So in all Poetry, for the pronounciation, it is to bee uttered as prose; observing distinctions and the nature of the matter, not to bee tuned foolishly or childishly after the manner of scanning a Verse as it now of some is.[17]

This suggests a naturalistic delivery de-emphasizing meter and emphasizing motive and emotion. It accords nicely with a straightforward interpretation of Hamlet's advice to the players about speaking English verse. Speeches are to be spoken "trippingly on the tongue"—that is, they should not be slurred. Passions are not to be "torn to tatters"—that is, the actor should imitate the expression of passion in real life. The action should be suited to the word and the word to the action—that is, gesture and speech inflection should complement each other. Thomas Heywood amplifies Hamlet's advice about words and actions in his *Apology for Actors* (1612). Rhetoric teaches the actor, he says, "to fit his phrases to his action and his action to his phrase, and his pronountiation to them both."[18] In this comment "phrase" appears to mean syntactical rhythm, the thought rhythm of the sentence. "Action" means gesture and expression. "Pronountiation" seems to mean intonation, which is a matter of emotion—angry, sorrowful, joyful, ironic, and the like. None of these is related to verse as verse. All of them are related to what Brinsley calls "distinctions and the nature of the matter"—that is, "precise sense."

Unfortunately these instructions tell us little about Renaissance actors. In *Theatre for Shakespeare* (1955) Alfred Harbage complains, "There is extant not a single piece of analytic description of Elizabethan acting in general or of an Elizabethan actor in a particular role."[19] Despite this lack of evidence, Harbage concludes that Elizabethan acting was "formal," which presumably means stylized gestures and heavy emphasis on the poetic qualities of the verse.

Harbage's conclusions are similar to those reached by Bertram Joseph in the first edition of *Elizabethan Acting* (1951). To remedy the lack of evidence for acting *qua* acting, Joseph turned to the rhetorical theory of delivery. Here there was ample evidence, including the elaborately illustrated treatise on delivery by John Bulwer titled *Chironomia* (1644). Joseph concludes that Elizabethan acting followed rhetorical formulas. He speculates that the speech of the actors might have been like "*stilo recitativo*" and "chant" or opera.[20] He states emphatically that "the naturalistic conception of drama" has no relevance to the English Renaissance stage.[21]

This might seem to settle the matter. In 1964, however, a second edition of *Elizabethan Acting* appeared. In the second edition the references to *stilo recitativo* and opera have been dropped. The thrust of the second edition is summed up in a word which was explicitly rejected in the first edition. The word is "naturalness":

> As the Elizabethan actor responded to variations in the style of his lines, so the style of his performance varied. Rhythm, tempo of speech and movement, and melody of speech would have been affected by stylistic variations, but there would still have remained untouched the essential naturalness of behavior, which was that of such a person communicating what was within him in the circumstances of action.[22]

This description is reasonable. Although there were doubtless many acting styles in the sixteenth century, this comment is consistent with Richard Flecknoe's famous description of Burbage's acting:

> . . . *Burbidge,* of whom we may say that he was a delightful *Proteus,* so wholly transforming himself into his Part, and putting off himself with his Cloathes, as he never (not so much as in the Tyring-house) assum'd himself again until the Play was done; there being as much difference betwixt him and one of our common Actors, as between a Ballad-singer who onely mouths it, and an excellent singer, who knows all his Graces, and can artfully vary and modulate his Voice, even to know how much breath he is to give to every syllable. He had all the parts of an excellent Orator, animating his words with speaking, and Speech with Action; his Auditors being never more delighted then when he spake, nor more sorry then when he held his peace; yet even then he was an excellent Actor still, never falling in his Part when he had done speaking, but with his looks and gesture maintaining it still unto the heighth, he imagining *Age quod agis* onely spoke to him: so as those who call him a Player do him wrong, no man being less idle then he whose whole life is nothing else but action; with only this difference from other mens, that as what is but a Play to them is his Business, so their business is but a play to him.[23]

VIII

To return to Shakespeare, it is an over-simplification to assume that norms of dramatic dialogue are determined by limitations of the ability of the audience to understand natural speaking. Drama is a code. As long as the code is shared by actors and audience, almost any stylistic norm from Kabuki to Stanislavski will work. The question is, what was the code of Shakespeare's theatre? The answer suggested, though tentatively, by a review of the historical evidence is that the norm was somewhat closer to natural speaking than has been generally admitted. This may explain why the productions of Brian Bedford at the Stratford Festival in Ontario have been so successful both with audiences and with critics. Bedford tends to de-emphasize the melody of Shakespeare's verse in order to emphasize its "precise meaning." His quite unmelodius delivery of Angelo's lines in *Measure for Measure* helped to create what may be the definitive version of the play for the present generation. Is it not possible that he succeeded because his acting style approximated the acting style for which the play was originally written? When directing *Titus Andronicus* Bedford accomplished a still more difficult feat. He overcame Shakespeare's lurid Ovidian verse and showed that wrapped in it is a play of considerable power, even though it is no masterpiece. The success of Bedford's *Titus* also suggests something about Shakespeare's apprenticeship. The actors who first performed *Titus* were seasoned professionals. Is it not possible that, like Bedford, they recognized a drama latent in the verse of *Titus* and performed it in the expectation that its author would improve with experience? Of course he did improve. In the process, he may have learned as much from the actors as they eventually learned from him.

Whatever the reasons, Shakespeare became less interested in poetry for the sake of poetry as he matured. In *Titus* the poetry is gratuitous. Only the most inspired performance can keep the play from becoming *grande guignol* melodrama. In the mature plays, conversely, the norm is more conversational, and it is the clear establishment of this norm that makes the great poetic moments so effective. In fact, in *Hamlet* Shakespeare seems to call attention to the dialogue norm through passages that contrast with it. The "play within a play" is identified by its dumbshow as archaic; it is written in heroic couplets, which is probably as close as Shakespeare dared come to the fourteeners of the older drama except in comic episodes like the play of *Pyramus and Thisby* in *A Midsummer Night's Dream.* The player's speech about Hecuba is written in heavily-accented, highly-ornamental blank verse. It is not archaic, but it is definitely old-fashioned. Both the "play within the play" and the player's speech stand out because they are "poetic" in comparison to the play's norm.[24]

The language in Shakespeare's mature drama is validated by its relation to action rather than to poetry. The relation is expressed by the actor through gesture, facial expression, and voice inflection. Without entering the labyrinth of modern linguistics, one can observe that the phonetic codes of voice inflection depend on stress, pitch, and duration. The phonetic codes are supplemented by syntactic codes that include rhythm, stress, gradation, and silence. If the action of a play manifests itself in each scene as an array of causes, phonetic and syntactic codes allow the causes to be objectified in speech. The melody of this kind of speech is its sound regarded aesthetically. It is a corollary or by-product, not a separable element.

Poetic codes, on the other hand, arise from characteristics of language rather than action. Iambic pentameter is an arrangement of stresses that is much the same in any situation, and an English sonnet is fourteen lines of rhymed iambic pentameter whether it is written in the Renaissance or in the Romantic period and whether its subject is love or revolution. All good poets adapt meter to subject, but this is not the point. If the responsibility of an actor is to sound like "such a person communicating what was within him in the circumstances of the action," to use Bertram Joseph's description, the responsibility of blank verse is to sound like blank verse. "The sound of blank verse" is what admirers of Shakespeare's poetry mean by the "melody" of his line. It implies making the five-beat rhythm and such additional sound effects as substitution, caesura, and alliteration perceptible in speech. But, as has been noted, this kind of speaking easily becomes recitation. Stendhal remarked that the public of his day "loves to hear the recitation of lofty sentiments in fine verse." He added, however, that true dramatic pleasure occurs when we forget our surroundings and the speech medium and succumb to the stage illusion.

No one would deny that Shakespeare wrote supremely beautiful and melodic passages. Obviously, he did. In the mature plays these passages coincide with moments of great emotional intensity, like the moment when Prospero abandons his magic, or with lyrical moments like Perdita's sheep-shearing festival. Even normally prosy characters like Enobarbus and Caliban become poetic when deeply moved. In such cases the poetry is both an expression of mood and an indirect stage direction, as explicit as a stage direction by Shaw in *Major Barbara.* It says, "This moment is critical; make sure you give it the proper emphasis." To the audience the poetry seems natural and reasonable at such a moment because it expresses causes that explain it. From the point of view taken here, the poetry arises from and is validated by the action, which remains in Shakespeare, as in Aristotle, the soul of drama.

IX

A final observation. If Renaissance dramatists valued blank verse because of its conversational quality, why were they so reluctant to use prose? Dramatic dialogue began in England with the chanted dialogue of liturgical drama. It changed into complex rhyming stanzas in the Corpus Christi plays, and into fourteeners in the mid-sixteenth century. Fourteeners gave way to prose and blank verse for comedy and to blank verse for serious drama, but there the movement toward simplified dialogue stopped. The Restoration, in fact, reverted to couplets. Not until George

Lillo's *London Merchant* (1731) did England produce a respectable tragedy in prose, and prose did not become the norm for serious drama in English until the late nineteenth century.

The shift from the chanted dialogue of liturgical drama to prose is part of a larger movement. It is a movement, generally, from ritual to naturalistic forms of expression. Verse and stylized acting are signs that the English theatre continued to be influenced, at least until the 1590s, by the ritual traditions of the Middle Ages. Between *Tamburlaine* and the closing of the theatres, there seems to have been a gradual shift toward naturalism. It was encouraged by the Aristotelianism evident in Sidney's *Apology*. It is expressed in the widespread criticism of "bombast" in dramatic dialogue and in the increasing use of stichomythia and prose between 1600 and 1640, even though the counter-tendency to regard plays as "literature" was undoubtedly also at work. On the other hand, the movement remained tentative. The tradition of using prose for "lower-class" characters and verse for upper-class ones, and the continued presence of explicitly lyrical passages in Shakespeare and the Jacobean dramatists examined by Coburn Freer shows that the older tradition still exerted a powerful influence up to the closing of the theatres.

After the Restoration the Renaissance tradition was modified, though not entirely replaced, in England by neoclassic style. Couplets were not defended on the basis of their expression of "Nature," but on the basis of their ability to protect the poet from flights of fancy and "enthusiasm" which carried him beyond Nature. The debate over couplets and blank verse is beyond the scope of this essay, but it can be followed in critical statements by Howard, Dryden, and Milton, among others.

The cult of drama as literature played a large part in preserving verse drama in the Romantic and Victorian periods. Renaissance dramatists, however, probably had a practical reason, in addition to the pull of tradition, for retaining blank verse. The most frequent explanation for verse from the Greeks to Wordsworth's preface to *Lyrical Ballads* is that it is easy to memorize.[25] The explanation is correct. Verse is much easier to memorize than prose. Renaissance actors had to commit a staggering number of lines to memory. Not only did they frequently play double or triple roles in a single play, but they had to perform in several plays in the course of a typical week.

The actors must have needed all the aids to memory that were available. If, by 1600, the norm for acting was speech rather than recitation, one significant motive for retaining verse must have been that it is easier to memorize than prose. If this conjecture has merit, it follows that actors shared responsibility with tradition, bombast-loving groundlings, and dramatists aspiring to literary fame for the retention of blank verse in English Renaissance drama.

X

Throughout this discussion "verse" has been used in opposition to "prose." Verse and prose, however, are both literary. They are intended for reading or recitation. A script is different from a text. By the same token, the speeches in a script, whether in meter or not, are different from literature. To call them verse (or poetry) or prose is to perpetuate the misunderstandings introduced by print culture. Not even Coburn Freer entirely escapes this error, for his discussion is concerned principally with dramatic elements such as theme, plot, and characterization which are found in a text, and seldom with values that emerge only in production. The term "dialogue" expresses precisely what the speeches (including the soliloquies) in a script want to be. It therefore might be salutary to abandon the words *verse* and *prose* along with the word *text* when dealing with drama and to adopt the word *dialogue* along with the word *script*. The question of dialogue in blank verse or fourteeners or prose is quite different from the question of verse and prose in general.

(1983)

Shakespeare on Film:

The Developing Canon

The first Shakespeare film owned by the Folger Library was a print of Max Reinhardt's *Midsummer Night's Dream* starring Anita Louise, Mickey Rooney, and Joe E. Brown. The print was given to the Library by Warner Brothers in 1936. Quite properly it was almost immediately re-donated by the Director, J. Q. Adams, and eventually wound up in the film collection of the Museum of Modern Art in New York. It was on cellulose nitrate film. Under the best conditions this type of film is hazardous. Its dangers are illustrated by the fact that within the last year there have been fires in three large film archives. The worst fire occurred in 1979 at the film storage facility of the Bureau of Archives. It consumed some twenty-seven million feet of Universal newsreel film dating from 1914 to 1965 and completely destroyed the building in which the film was housed. If Dr. Adams had been less circumspect in 1936, a similar fire might possibly have occurred at the Folger, and Shakespeare, Spenser, Raleigh, and John Donne might have gone up in flames along with Anita Louise and Mickey Rooney.

When the use of cellulose acetate made safe film storage possible following World War II, the Folger reentered the film business. As of 1980, its archive included thirty-one full-length silent and sound films, fourteen videotapes, and thirteen full-length adaptations such as *The Throne of Blood,* a Japanese version of *Macbeth*. The collection was augmented in 1978 by a donation of seven half-hour films on Shakespeare by the National Geographic Society, and in 1980 by videotapes of the first six plays in the BBC's ongoing presentation of the complete dramatic works on television. Obviously, the archive is growing at a healthy rate.

The existence of such an archive demonstrates the continuing vitality of the classic impulse in media art. As the preceding chapter has shown, such an archive is extremely useful in understanding what happens to the past when it is brought into the present. Another aspect of such an archive is equally interesting. The past exists in two ways: in its presentness through translations into current media, as when Olivier makes a film of *Hamlet,* and in its pastness as a collection of artifacts and documents, as Shakespeare continues to exist, in apparent indifference to movies, in quartos and folios and innumerable editions. If an archive of Shakespeare on film and videotape is taken as an example of the past as present, the question naturally arises of how the past as present affects the past as past. How, in other words, do the films in the archive influence the way the texts in their original written form are read and interpreted? The evidence for answering this question can be found in current Shakespeare criticism.[1] It shows the mind in the process of reshaping the record of the past, for the most part unconsciously, to accord with its own experience of the present.

In an article published in *Anglia* in 1978 titled "Shakespeare in Buch und auf der Bühne"—"Shakespeare in Book Form and on the Stage"—Werner Habicht observes that from the beginning Shakespeare studies have drawn on two quite different bodies of material.[2] Scholars have analyzed text, sources, influences, conventions, and the like in an effort to provide definitive solutions to the problems posed by Shakespeare's plays. Although the goal of definitive solutions has receded in almost direct proportion to the energy expended to reach it, as an ideal it remains influential. It is the benchmark against which various degrees of failure are measured.

Meanwhile, directors and actors have to keep the plays alive at the box office. To do this they must plan each production in terms of the variables of current theatrical style, the talent available, and the character of the audience. Consequently, there is no such thing as a definitive production. Each production is different, each elicits a unique set of meanings from the text. Frequently, these meanings seem indifferent to, or actually scornful of, the meanings proposed by scholars. In the library the plays appear to be securely anchored to the page by rows of black letters; in the theater they are Protean, infinitely variable and elusive. Harley Granville-Barker, a theatrical producer as well as a scholar, described Shakespeare's text as "a score waiting performance."[3] Sir Tyrone Guthrie, a director with a lifetime of theatrical experience, wrote in *Tyrone Guthrie on Acting* (1971):

> . . . only some, and by no means always the most significant, aspects of a great play reveal themselves to the reader. . . . The total meaning of a play includes sight and sound, not merely the intellectual apprehension of the symbols on a printed page.[4]

There is nothing in Sir Tyrone Guthrie's comment with which the most hidebound Shakespeare scholar could disagree. The divergence between scholar and director is not caused by different modes of perception. It is created by the nature of scholarship. The imperative of scholarship is rigor. When it is not rigorous, it ceases to be scholarship and drifts into impressionism. Rigor, in turn, depends on documentation. It is possible to be rigorous when discussing one of Shakespeare's sources—say Sir

Thomas North's English translation from the French of Plutarch's *Life of Marcus Antonius*—because that source has an objective existence. A reader who doubts an assertion about the source can go to the library and read it for himself.

Stage productions are ephemeral. After the curtain goes down on closing night, a stage performance ceases to have an objective existence. A scholar can refer to it, but the references have to be from memory, which is unreliable, or to secondary sources. There is no way for the reader to evaluate them unless he has seen the same performance and remembers it in exactly the same way as the scholar. This problem is troublesome even in a successful study such as Marvin Rosenberg's *The Masks of Macbeth* (1977).[5] It is possible to attempt reconstructions of famous productions—witness the excellent work of Charles Shattuck on productions by Booth and Kean and Kemble[6]—but the most meticulous reconstruction is only a pale and uncertain shadow of the performance itself.

The advent of film has changed this situation fundamentally. Unlike stage drama, film has an objective existence. Films can be preserved like books and kept in archives for anyone who needs to inspect them. They thus open to the scholar a whole spectrum of insights into Shakespeare that reveal themselves only in performance.

Although the Folger archive is still incomplete, it already holds eight full-length versions of *Hamlet,* six of *Macbeth,* and ten of *Romeo and Juliet,* to name only three plays. Less than half of these films—perhaps ten out of the total of twenty-four—are worth careful study, but ten plays are a quantum advance over no plays at all. They permit the scholar to examine variant productions of the same play and to document his observations as precisely as a quotation from the 1604 quarto of *Hamlet.* Since variant productions are caused by variant interpretations of the text, this is equivalent to making available to scholarship the full spectrum of meanings latent in the text.

A qualification is needed here. Film critics properly insist that a film is different from a stage play. The basic grammar of film is cut, fade, and dissolve, and long shot, medium shot, and closeup; and the rhetoric of film includes voice-over, musical continuo, unusual camera angles, trick photography, and special sound and lighting effects. There are no one-to-one equivalents of these devices in stage drama. If we wish to use films to help us understand traditional problems of Shakespeare scholarship, we have to begin by admitting that many characteristics of film, often those characteristics most typical of film art, have only an indirect relevance to our interests. On the other hand, even indirect relevance can be useful. Cinematic devices are often employed expressionistically to make thematic points, and these points are often similar to points that are made on the stage by theatrical means. The Russian director Grigori Kozintsev, for example, created a splendid Heathcliffe-like ghost for his film of *Hamlet* by posing the actor in silhouette against a dark sky and photographing his billowing robes in slow motion. The technique distances the ghost from the generally realistic setting of Kozintsev's Danish court and thus retains the suggestion found in Shakespeare's text that the ghost may be an hallucination rather than a true spirit. Richard Burton could not use slow-motion photography in his stage production of *Hamlet* (which is preserved in a 1964 videotape), but he conveyed the same idea by limiting the ghost's presence to a gigantic helmet-clad shadow projected on the rear wall of the theatre.

After allowance is made for the difference between film and stage drama, there are at least two areas in which the record preserved on film can contribute to our understanding of traditional scholarly problems. The first is the area of thematic interpretation—understanding the point of view of the play as a whole. The second is the area of interpretation of individual scenes and lines. Ideally the two areas should be complementary. However it sometimes happens that a given production is disappointing *in toto* but has moments of brilliant acting which deserve attention in spite of the inert material that surrounds them.

A simple example of the way that a film can contribute to thematic interpretation is provided by Sir Laurence Olivier's *Henry V*. Olivier based his film on the common interpretation of Henry as an ideal warrior-king and the play as an epic celebration of English valor. This is the interpretation popularized by E. M. W. Tillyard in *Shakespeare's History Plays*,[7] and the fact that Olivier made his film in 1944 and dedicated it to "The Commandos and Airborne Troops of Great Britain" must have made the interpretation irresistible. The two central scenes in the film express it perfectly. They are the night before Agincourt when Henry walks in disguise among his disheartened troops, a scene that inevitably recalls the British experience after Dunkirk, and the battle itself with its sweeping images of the triumph of stout-hearted English yeomen over the haughty and ponderously armed knights of France.

Henry V is probably the most popular Shakespeare film ever made. There are, however, problems in Olivier's film, and the problems point directly to the revisionist view of the play that has emerged since it was made.[8] In the first scene of Shakespeare's play Ely and Canterbury argue that if they do not divert Henry's attention from domestic to foreign affairs he will expropriate "all the temporal lands which men devout / By testament have given to the Church" (I.i.9–10). When Henry decides to invade France, should we regard him as a dupe of the clergy or a true-blue patriot, a jock with a heart of gold?

Olivier eliminates the first possibility by making clowns out of Ely and Canterbury. During the speech on Salic law they drop their papers, lose their place repeatedly, and start to bicker with one another. These idiots could not dupe anyone, much less the king of England. In case the movie audience misses the point, the Globe audience, which is still part of the film at this stage, breaks into loud guffaws and catcalls. Olivier has not merely slanted Shakespeare's text, he has made a travesty of it.

Additional evidence of Olivier's distortion of the text in order to idealize Henry would be easy to cite, but the Ely-Canterbury exchange is enough. Olivier's film enacts a common interpretation of the play and in doing so exposes the inadequacy of that interpretation. In this case the interpretation is not perverse. It is simply more naive than the play it claims to explain.

Two other Olivier films draw on interpretations that do seem perverse. Olivier's *Othello* relies heavily on F. R. Leavis' essay "The Diabolic Hero and the Noble Intellect," in which Othello is described as a "ferociously stupid" egoist.[9] In the words of John Dexter, who directed the film, he is "a pompous, word-spinning, arrogant black general."[10] There is more than a little racism here, and it is reflected in Olivier's performance in the title role. The result is an Othello who is brilliantly acted but who is almost the antithesis of Shakespeare's protagonist, not to mention standard sixteenth-century attitudes toward Moors. The film is a convincing demonstration of the inappropriateness of the Leavis interpretation.

Olivier's *Hamlet* is a much more complex mixture of goods and bads. One strand, however, is easy to identify and highly instructive. This is the Freudian interpretation of the play which Olivier derived from Ernest Jones's *Hamlet and Oedipus.*[11] As Jack Jorgens observes, the Jones interpretation makes Hamlet into a mental cripple: "The contradictions seem ingrained not so much in the world as in the imaginings of a diseased, unschooled mind."[12] It is Hamlet rather than Denmark that is out of joint? Claudius undoubtedly thinks so, at least until the play scene, but does Shakespeare? Evidentally not. Whatever Hamlet's mental problems, the moral dilemma that he confronts is a real, not an imaginary one. It is the difficulty of acting justly in a corrupt world. Two scenes illustrate Olivier's sacrifice of this theme to trendy psychology.

In the play's most famous scene Hamlet considers suicide, decides against it, and then meets Ophelia. Suicide, after all, is a sin. Hamlet rejects it on entirely valid moral grounds, even though he remains suspicious of his own motives. Having decided to live, he encounters Ophelia, who is both a symbol of life and, at the moment of the encounter, a symbol of purity as well. Dissatisfied with this progression, Olivier inverts the Shakespearean order, placing the meeting first and the soliloquy second. The implied motivation goes something like this: Hamlet is neurotically disturbed by his mother's sexuality. He encounters Ophelia, who arouses all of his Oedipal frustrations, and bitterly abuses her. Then, in a fit of revulsion against his own cruelty, he rushes off to consider suicide. This may be good Freud but it is cheap melodrama in comparison to the Folio text.

The clash between Freud and Shakespeare is also evident in the bedroom scene between Hamlet and Gertrude. Shakespeare's Hamlet is worried about his mother's conscience, a theme that has just been emphasized by Claudius in the prayer scene. In Olivier, however, Hamlet's comments on conscience take second place to the photography. Forget what Hamlet is saying. The images on the screen tell us that his words are misleading. He is driven by lust, not filial concern. Much of the scene takes place on Gertrude's bed with the camera suggesting that Hamlet is on the verge of raping her. Again the effect is melodrama, a kind of seventeenth-century *Mary Hartman,* rather than tragedy.

Of course, many films draw on interpretations that are closer to Shakespeare than F. R. Leavis and Ernest Jones. In such cases analysis of the films can often sharpen our understanding of the interpretations on which they have drawn. *Macbeth*, for example, is filled with references to blood and violence. Is *Macbeth* a tragedy of blood in the tradition of plays like *The Revenger's Tragedy* and *Titus Andronicus?*

Roman Polanski's *Macbeth* takes this approach. It is evidently the result of three convergent influences: the idea that much Elizabethan theatre was, in fact, a "theatre of blood," the brutal murder of Polanski's wife by the Charles Manson gang, and Jan Kott's grim view of the political process in *Shakespeare, our Contemporary.*[13]

Whichever influence was most important, there is blood in abundance in Polanski's film. At the beginning the three witches are shown burying a severed arm in a pit. As the titles appear the sound track carries the noises of a battle. The camera then pans on a battlefield littered with mangled corpses. When one of the bodies moves the nearest soldier smashes it repeatedly with a spiked mace. The Captain who reports the defeat of the Norwegians speaks through a mask of blood. Cawdor is dragged forward lashed to rails, covered with more blood.

These scenes establish a point of view that is sustained throughout Polanski's film. The Scotland it depicts is a savage tribal society ruled by brute force and trickery. Morality is useful only as a trap for those stupid enough to believe in it. In the last scene of the film—a Polanski invention—Donalbain leaves his brother clutching Macbeth's bloody crown and rides to the same ruined cottage where Macbeth met the witches at the beginning. The cycle of blood is about to begin again.

Is this a legitimate extrapolation from Shakespeare's text or something else? Consider Polanski's treatment of Cawdor. In Shakespeare the execution of Cawdor is reported. In Polanski it is the occasion for a long, mostly silent photographic excursus. Cawdor is shown chained to the stone floor of the courtyard of Forres castle. He is unchained and brought to a ledge on the castle wall. After a sullen "Long live the King" he leaps forward. We see the chain jerk and the shattered body swing at its end.

Polanski's insertion of photographic excursuses between segments of Shakespeare's dialogue is not in itself a distortion. In fact, it is one of the most interesting aspects of his film. Evidently he regarded *Macbeth* as a series of vignettes of society gradually sinking into chaos. The excursuses slow down the action by dividing moments of dialogue into isolated units that gave the impression of being vignettes of a process that is continuous over a considerable period of time. Because of the brevity of the text of *Macbeth*, most productions seem to move very rapidly. Polanski's treatment of time in the play creates the opposite effect. While other treatments are obviously possible, it is, I think, fascinating and effective.

It is therefore not the fact the Cawdor scene is invented that creates a problem. The problem is that Shakespeare seems to go out of his way to make Cawdor's death a symbol of the redemptive forces that are present in Macbeth's world. As Malcom reports:

> I have spoke
> With one that saw him die; who did report
> That very frankly he confess'd his treasons,
> Implor'd your Highness' pardon, and set forth
> A deep repentance. Nothing in his life
> Became him like the leaving it.
>
> [I.iv.3–8]

Either these lines have to be interpreted as the archest irony or Polanski's version of Cawdor's death is a falsification. I think the latter is true, and that Polanski's obsession with violence has caused him to miss the significance not only of Cawdor's conversion, but of the whole side of the play that comes most clearly into focus in Malcolm's description of Edward the Confessor's miraculous gift of healing. Polanski's Scotland is so hopelessly savage that no redemption is imaginable. As we have seen, in fact, the last image on the film is that of Donalbain about to repeat the original cycle of betrayal and murder. Undoubtedly Polanski's Scotland is a symbolic statement of his view of the twentieth century. It is not, however, Shakespeare's Scotland, and Polanski's film forces us to recognize that fact. Not long ago, Herbert Coursen described it as "a multi-million dollar disaster."[14] I disagree strongly with Coursen's appraisal, but it is clear that Polanski has demonstrated once and for all that *Macbeth* is not a "tragedy of blood" in either the Elizabethan or the twentieth-century sense.

The traditional view of *Macbeth* is influenced by the breaks of the Folio text. As A. C. Bradley remarked, in a comparison with the sprawling structure of the more typical plays, it is almost Aristotelian. It is, he wrote, "less unlike a classical tragedy than *Hamlet* or *Othello* or *King Lear.* And it is possible that this effect is, in a sense, the result of design."[15] In good neoclassical fashion, *Macbeth* focuses on a single titanic figure who is brought low by a tragic flaw that is also an instance of emotion overwhelming reason—precisely the situation that is explored by Lily Bess Campbell in *Shakespeare's Tragic Heroes: Slaves of Passion.*[16] Hence, too, the great attraction of the play for nineteenth-century actors. More than any of the other tragedies *Macbeth* is a star vehicle and is all the more attractive for having a major woman's part complementing that of the awe-inspiring protagonist.

Although there have been many stage versions based on his view, including two recent revivals at Stratford, Ontario, there is only one movie that uses it. Unfortunately, this movie is a mixed bag. It was made at Bob Jones University in 1950 and stars Bob Jones, Jr., as Macbeth and Bob Jones III as Fleance. In spite of its lapses, however, the film was made with care and serious artistic thought. It presents Macbeth as a giant among men. No other character in the film is remotely as interesting. He has great virtues but also a tragic flaw—ambition—which causes his downfall. The play moves smoothly from Macbeth's initial temptation to his death. The result is rather close, I imagine, to a production "in the school of" Edwin Booth.

While the Aristotelian reading of *Macbeth* is attractive, none of the other major tragedies fits the Aristotelian pattern. In all of them, the central action shades off into a maze of secondary plots and minor characters. One effect of this technique is to create a social dimension that complements the psychology of the protagonist. Denmark, for example, is an outward and visible form of the inward and invisible turbulence in Hamlet's mind. At the same time, the minor characters are often busy with their own concerns, which have little to do with the great matters of state that are at the center of the tragic action. They suggest the ultimate irrationality of human affairs. Polanski's *Macbeth* takes full advantage of both of these characteristics. As has been noted, his Scotland is an impressively realized objective correlative for the savage motives that guide the principal character. For example, Polanski dwells lovingly on the drunken porter urinating against the castle wall at the same time that Duncan's corpse lies bleeding in his royal bed. Conversely, the Bob Jones film ignores the social dimension. The minor characters remain just that: minor characters. The effect is to place the emphasis almost exclusively on Macbeth's psychology and, by corollary, on the soliloquies. As for the porter, he is worse than a minor character; he is a digression. Consequently he has been excised from the script. The result of all this is a film more reminiscent of *Richard III* than of the major tragedies. It is an interesting film when allowances are made for its technical limitations, but a shallow one compared to Polanski's. Better technique might only have made the problem more obvious.

One final instance of the relation between interpretation and performance deserves mention. Orson Welles's *Macbeth* is neither a study of violence nor a film about a hero who is brought low by ambition. Like

Polanski, Welles creates a social context for his action, but the social context preserves the balance found in Shakespeare between redemptive and daemonic forces. To give adequate emphasis to the redemptive forces, in fact, Welles creates a new character, a Christian priest, from bits and pieces of Shakespeare's dialogue plus invented material. The witches are the antithesis of the priest. They are relics of the paganism which Christianity is slowly replacing in Scotland but which is still widespread and powerful.

Being the child of this ambivalent culture, Welles's Macbeth responds to both forces. Because he is primitive, his response is visceral rather than analytic. Evil is not an idea but the malign apparition of the witches and the imagined dagger that leads him to Duncan's chamber. Guilt appears in the shape of Banquo's ghost and in the nightmares—only slightly less vivid than the ghost—that prevent him from sleeping.

If Polanski's film is leisurely, in Welles's film time constantly accelerates. At first Macbeth seems to be in control of events. Soon, however, they are moving so rapidly that he must improvise to keep up with them. In Welles's presentation, the dialogue becomes increasingly fragmented, like bits of conversation heard from the windows of a passing train. Things are happening too fast to be fully described, much less understood. In the end, Welles's Macbeth becomes the puppet of the forces he has released. This loss of control nicely explains his progressive loss of orientation, preparing the audience for his sense that life is meaningless chaos—the famous tale told by an idiot signifying nothing.

As time accelerates in Welles's film, the characters become more isolated. We first see Macbeth in the midst of a group of admiring soldiers. Banquo is his friend. When Macbeth remarks, "Your children shall be kings" (I.iii.85), however, the friendship is over. His words are not an exclamation or an expression of wonder but an accusation. Banquo's response "You shall be King" (l. 86) is equally ominous. The two men have already been isolated by the prophecies of the weird sisters. Welles emphasizes the point by having them drift constantly into asides during the ensuing conversation with Ross.

By the time that Duncan arrives at Inverness Castle the infection has spread. Banquo confesses he has dreamed of the witches and Macbeth suggests that they discuss it further, promising "It shall make honor for you" (II.i.24 ff.). The promise is a tacit bribe. Banquo's reply "At your kindest leisure" is an already unctuous acceptance of the bribe, and his comment "so I lose [no honor]" is—in Welles's treatment—an afterthought showing that he already knows what Macbeth is planning.

The banquet scene carries the theme of isolation further. The banquet is supposed to be a social occasion, a demonstration of community. Yet Macbeth's behavior shatters the illusion. "You have displaced the mirth, broke the good meeting," says Lady Macbeth (III.iv.109). Welles makes it clear that she has a deeply feminine, almost instinctive hunger for social amenities. She wants to be a gracious hostess moving among admiring guests. Instead, she endures the humiliation of having to send her guests away. There is a domestic quality in Welles's version of the scene that is quite moving. At the end, like many another married couple following a social disaster, Macbeth and Lady Macbeth are too tired even for recriminations. Lady Macbeth's only advice is that they go to bed. The good meeting has, indeed, been broken. Everyone has gone. Eventually, even Lady Macbeth leaves her husband. When the rebels break into his castle, he is completely alone, totally isolated.

For all its much-publicized flaws Welles's film goes deeper into Shakespeare's text than alternative versions. Other views of *Macbeth* will undoubtedly be brought to our attention by other directors, but the view of *Macbeth* as a play set in a half-pagan, half-Christian society, with a protagonist who is isolated in an accelerating catastrophe of his own making stands the test of performance remarkably well.

In the course of illustrating how films can illuminate general problems of interpretation, I have cited examples of how actors can make individual lines highly expressive. This happens continuously in any good production whether it is a film or a stage play, but in a film the successful moments are preserved. This brings me to the second way in which films can be useful in the study of traditional scholarly questions.

An actor can never be satisfied merely with the meanings of the words comprising a line. He has to ask how the words add up. What is the intention of the character who speaks the line—serious, ironic, amused, or hostile? Should the actor speak continuously or pause, and if so, where? Does he address the audience or another character or several characters? Does he use stage props or gestures? And so forth. The variations are innumerable, and each one gives a different meaning to the line.

To take a simple example, the first speech of Claudius in *Hamlet* is a summary of the facts about the political situation in Denmark. In Olivier's film it is delivered in a half-drunken slur to a group of indifferent courtiers at a riotous banquet. In Kozintsev's film it is delivered in part as a formal proclamation to a mixed group of soldiers and nobles in the courtyard of Elsinore. In Burton's *Hamlet* it becomes part of the deliberations of the royal council, which has been assembled to advise the new ruler. In Olivier the speech means that Claudius is weak and corrupt. In Kozintsev it means that he is a ruler in full control of events. In Burton it means that he is a careful politician making sure that his fences are mended. None of these interpretations is inconsistent with the text. If so, when taken together do they not reveal a range of meanings that are latent in the text?

To cite another example, when Macbeth sees Banquo at the beginning of Shakespeare's act 3, he asks, "Ride you this afternoon?" Is the question an offhand show of cordiality to go with the mood of good fellowship that Macbeth is trying to sustain? Or is it an effort to pin down Banquo's whereabouts so that the murderers can find him? Or is Macbeth worried that once mounted Banquo will continue riding, like Donalbain and Malcolm? Polanski's Macbeth has already planned the murder. His tone is affable but carries a deadly emphasis. Welles's Macbeth, conversely, speaks in a nervous, almost whining tone. Having already lost several retainers, he is worried that Banquo plans to desert him. The idea of murdering Banquo apparently comes to him later. It is another improvisation. Welles's interpretation seems more dramatic and more interesting psychologically than Polanski's. However, both have merit. Again, the contrast forces us to acknowledge that there is a range of meanings latent in the text.

In some instances, one reading is clearly better than another. In *Macbeth*, when Lady Macbeth departs to paint the sleeping grooms with Duncan's blood, she advises her husband, "Go get some water / And wash this filthy witness from your hands" (II.ii.46–47). In Welles's film—and in all of the stage performances I have seen—Macbeth stares at his hands and begins rubbing them together. However, Polanski's Macbeth walks to a well, draws a bucket of water, and begins to wash. The action makes sense out of his question, "Will all great Neptune's ocean wash the blood / Clean from my hand?" (60–61). When Lady Macbeth returns from Duncan's chamber, she too washes her hands. The action fits her lines: "A little water clears us of this deed. / How easy is it then!" (67–68). The use of a basin or pail of water as a stage prop here is natural and effective. It also prepares us for the sleep-walking scene when Lady Macbeth compulsively washes her hands in an imaginary basin. It therefore seems preferable on an absolute basis to a performance that does not use a stage prop.

To add a final example, when Hamlet meets Ophelia in Shakespeare's act 3, scene 1, he has the lines:

> Soft you now!
> The fair Ophelia! Nymph in thy orisons
> Be all my sins remembered.
>
> [88–90]

These lines are usually spoken continuously. Their meaning appears to be obvious. Hamlet is depressed. He has been considering suicide and only his fear of "something after death" has persuaded him to go on living. When he sees Ophelia she seems for the moment to be a symbol of grace. Acutely aware of his own failures, Hamlet feels that her prayers may help him.

Olivier gives us a much more complex interpretation of Hamlet's lines. Hamlet is revealed in an archway. As we know from previous scenes, he suspects that everyone in the court is spying on him. When Ophelia makes a noise, he is certain that yet another spy is trying to surprise him. His "Soft you now" is spoken to himself. It means "Be careful; something suspicious is happening." After a brief pause, Hamlet walks forward to determine the source of the noise and sees Ophelia. She is apparently unaware of his presence. He exclaims, "The fair Ophelia!" It is an expression of surprise and pleasure. He then approaches her. She is standing by an altar holding a book. When he is close to her he sees that the book is a collection of prayers or private devotions. The audience knows that Polonius has forced it on her—it is part of his plot to expose Hamlet—but to Hamlet it seems confirmation of Ophelia's goodness. He remarks, "Nymph in thy orisons / Be all my sins remembered."

Delivering the lines in this way requires perhaps forty-five seconds rather than the usual fifteen. It changes a bland transition passage into a moment of intense, psychologically revealing drama. To quote Hamlet's formula for good acting, it "suits the action to the word, the word to the action."

If Olivier's interpretation here is better—more revealing—than the conventional interpretation, is it possible that he is also closer to the intention of Shakespeare's text? Unfortunately, there is no way to answer this question. Olivier's interpretation does, however, point to a significant contribution that films can make to Shakespeare studies. The existence of several alternate films of individual Shakespeare plays is creating what might be called a dictionary of strategies for interpreting key passages. This dictionary may not take us back to the acting style of the Elizabethan theatre, but it makes Shakespeare's text seem far more plastic, more open, than traditional scholarship has realized. Through this dictionary scholars can cite not only what Granville-Barker called the "score" of Shakespearean drama but representative performances of that score as well. To put the idea another way, the meanings that, according to Sir Tyrone Guthrie, are revealed in image and sound rather than symbols on a page can now be treated with something like scholarly rigor. The result is bound to have an influence on the way scholars understand Shakespeare and the way they explain his work in the classroom and in their books.

One implication of the preceding analysis needs to be mentioned, if only tentatively. It is a truism of film criticism that the only definitive text of a film is the film itself. Is it possible that when multiple film versions of the same script are available, the text consists of all of those versions? To suggest this is to suggest that the text does not reside in a group of printed symbols but in the living meanings—more properly, the range of meanings—that these symbols convey to sensitive interpreters. Of course some interpretations are demonstrably wrong; but often a set of contrasting interpretations will emerge, each one of which is consistent with the printed text and each one of which leads to a different understanding of that text. If so, Shakespearean scholarship may be moving from the ideal of unitary interpretation validated by reference to sources, conventions, audience expectations, and the like, to a recognition that the language of Shakespeare's drama is protean, that the printed word is not an end but the beginning of a territory whose boundaries are constantly growing. This is a difficult idea to grasp since it introduces something like an "uncertainty principle" into literary scholarship, but it is an idea that film compels us to examine, if not to accept.

(1979)

Milton's "On Time" and Its Scholastic Background

Although Milton's debt to Plato has long been recognized, his debt to Aristotle is still largely unexplored. The fact that the *Prolusions* have numerous hostile references to Aristotle and his scholastic interpreters has generally been accepted as a sufficient definition of his position. These references, however, are misleading. They show that Milton shared the humanistic bias of writers like Petrarch, Ficino, and Erasmus; but they do not show that he was uninfluenced by Aristotle. Milton's curriculum at Cambridge emphasized Aristotle and the scholastics. Like many another bright student, Milton rebelled against his training but remained profoundly influenced by it. The fourth and fifth *Prolusions* are comments on problems raised by Aristotle's *Metaphysics* and *de Anima;* and the sixth is an allegory explicitly based on Aristotle's predicables. After graduation Milton continued to show awareness of scholastic and Aristotelian thinking, most clearly in his discussion of the soul in *de Doctrina.*

To illustrate this point, I have chosen to begin with a consideration of Milton's poem "On Time" usually dated around 1633.[1] This poem comes at the end of his Cambridge period when his training was fresh in his mind. I have begun my discussion with a phrase from the poem which has puzzled editors. I wish to show that the search for the most satisfactory meaning of this phrase leads to a gradually widening investigation of the intellectual traditions which Milton inherited; and in particular to a longstanding controversy in which medieval and renaissance Aristotelians were pitted against the defenders of Christian orthodoxy. Milton took the orthodox position, but he did so deliberately, with a consciousness of the issues involved. This fact leads to a reinterpretation of "On Time" and, perhaps more important, to a clearer understanding of the role of Aristotle and the scholastics in Milton's thought.

II

"On Time" is an exercise in occasional poetry whose commonplace nature is indicated by the fact that it was written to be hung "below a clock face." One phrase, however, has apparently puzzled recent editors and has occasioned several different glosses. This is the phrase "individual kiss" in the lines "Then long eternity shall greet our bliss / With an individual kiss." According to Patterson it means "indivisible, i.e., everlasting."[2] Hughes reads "undividable" and adds, "The kiss symbolizes the union of the 'individual soul forever happy' (*P.L.*, V.610–11) to God."[3] Both of these readings leave something to be desired. "Undividable" could be applied to the two parties kissing (in the sense that they will never be separated),[4] but it can hardly be applied to the kiss itself. The phrase "individual soul" cited by Hughes from *Paradise Lost* emphasizes the problem rather than solving it, since in *Paradise Lost* the adjective clearly means "separate" or "unique" rather than "indivisible."

Recognizing the difficulty, Brooks and Hardy offer a third interpretation sanctioned by the *New English Dictionary:* "Individual . . . distinguished from others by attributes of its own; marked by a peculiar or striking character."[5] This is, I believe, more satisfactory than earlier suggestions. Its disadvantage is that it ignores the figurative quality of the phrase. It cannot be ruled out entirely, but it is not a full explanation.

Behind the readings of Patterson and Hughes is the assumption that Milton had a Latin phrase in mind and simply transliterated it. This was common practice for Milton. In "On Time," for example, the full meaning of the phrase "sincerely good" evidently depends on Latin *sincerus* (pure, unmixed); of "perfectly divine" on Latin *perfectus* (thoroughly finished, complete); of "supreme throne" on Latin *supremus* (most high). "Individual" comes from Latin *individuus,* the root meaning of which is "undividable." In Golden Age Latin the word was a technical term meaning "incapable of subdivision." Cicero used it when discussing Epicurean philosophy. Atoms were *corpora individua* (*de Fin.*, I.6, 17); and a single atom was an *individuum* (*Acad. Disp.*, II.17). *Individuum* often appears in this sense in English philosophical writing of the seventeenth century.[6] This sense, however, is inappropriate to Milton's poem. The idea of "a kiss which cannot be subdivided" is nonsense. Moreover, it should be noted that Milton never used *individuus, individualiter,* or *indivisus* in his Latin poetry.

The alternative is to assume that Milton was not transliterating but (consciously or unconsciously) translating a Latin phrase. In fact it is possible to make a good guess as to the phrase which Milton had in mind. His sentence, which I repeat for clarity, is "Then long eternity shall greet our bliss / With an individual kiss."

"Greet . . . with a kiss" is not awkward English, but it is not a commonplace expression either. In one book which Milton read it appears frequently. St. Paul habitually ends his epistles with the formula *salutate invicem in osculo sancto.* This is variously translated in the King James version by "Salute one another with an holy kiss"; (Rom., 16, 16) "Greet ye one another with an holy kiss"; (1 Cor., 16, 20; 2 Cor., 13, 12) and—from Peter's first epistle—"Greet ye one another with a kiss of charity." Milton's phrase would seem to be an intentional or unintentional echo of the biblical formula. It is appropriate that Milton should have alluded to St. Paul's words, suggesting the union of the faithful in the love of Christ, in a description of the soul's final union with God.

For the biblical adjective *sanctus* Milton substituted "individual." However, as has been pointed out, *osculum individuum* would have been questionable and obscure Latin. I therefore suggest that the adjective which he had in mind was *proprius*. *Proprius* is a perfectly standard word, sanctioned by countless instances in Cicero, Virgil, and Ovid. *Osculum proprium* could mean either "one's own kiss" or "kiss appropriate for one specific individual."[7] The latter sense is the only one which is important for the present discussion.

Before the nineteenth century *proprius* was often transliterated, as in the ecclesiastical phrase "proper introit," meaning the introit appropriate for a particular service or festival. This sense is preserved in modern "property," meaning goods or land belonging to a specific individual. *Proprius* appears frequently in the *Vulgate,* almost always in conjunction with the distributive pronoun *unusquisque* (each individual of a group). For example Mat. 25, 15, reads "dedit . . . unicuique secundum propriam virtutem." Again, "unusquisque proprium donum habet in Deo"; (1 Cor., 7, 7) and "Deus dat illi corpus sicut vult, et unicuique seminum proprium corpus." (1 Cor., 15, 38) Finally, there is Paul's description of the Last Judgment, a passage which must have crossed Milton's mind as he described the soul's ascent to God: "Omnes enim manifestari oportet ante tribunal Christi, ut referat unusquisque propria corporis, prout gessit, sive bonum, sive malum." (2 Cor., 5, 10) In each of these cases the Donay uses "proper" for *proprius,* while the King James uses a variety of words including "several" ("his severall abilities"), "proper" ("his proper gift"), and "own" ("his owne body"). "Individual," though not particularly common, would have been equally satisfactory. Henry More, for example, used "individual" as a rough synonym for "proper" when writing on immortality: "the proper Idea or Figure of every Soul . . . may return more near to its peculiar semblance afterwards, and so be an unconcealable Note of *Individuality.*"[8]

In translating *unumquemque salutabit in osculo proprio* one would normally make *proprius* into an adverb, as in the sentence, "He will greet each person individually with a kiss." Instead of doing this, Milton chose to preserve the Latin construction. This practice, a characteristic of Milton's style, may be observed most clearly in his English version of *ad Pyrrham.* In line 9 of this poem, where Horace wrote "qui nunc te fruitur credulus aurea," Milton wrote "Who now enjoys thee credulous, all Gold." There is no doubt about the meaning of the Latin, but because it lacks inflections, the English is ambiguous. Normally the problem would be solved by translating the adjective as an adverb, as in "Who now credulously enjoys thee."[9] I make no defense of the poetic virtue of this translation. Milton's line is obviously right. It helps to transform his piece from a routine exercise into one of the few great English poems in the quantitative tradition. My point is that Milton's practice in *ad Pyrrham* confirms his practice in "On Time." "Greet . . . with an individual kiss" should therefore be interpreted "greet individually with a kiss."

III

In English "individual kiss" is a violation of standard idiom. Milton's readers would have recognized it as *catachresis,* a common rhetorical figure. In the *Rhetorica ad Herennium* it is defined as follows:

> Catachresis (Lat. *abusio*) is the inexact use of a like and kindred word in place of the precise and proper one, as follows: "The power of man is short," or "small height," or "the long wisdom in the man."[10]

Generally speaking catachresis was regarded as a blemish, but rhetoricians agreed that it could be used functionally as well. The definition in Puttenham's *Art of English Poetry* illustrated both points:

> . . . if for lacke of naturall and proper terms or words we take another, neither naturall nor proper . . . , it is not then spoken by this figure *Metaphore* or *inversion* as before, but by plaine abuse . . . as one said very prettily in this verse.
>
> *I lent my love to loss and gaged my life in vaine.*
>
> Whenas this word *lent* is properly for mony or some such other thing . . . and being applied to love is utterly abused, and yet very commendably spoken by vertue of this figure.[11]

Catachresis is a common figure in Elizabethan poetry and frequent in Shakespeare.[12] Because of his Latin background and his baroque tendencies Milton used it very frequently. "Blind mouths" in *Lycidas* is a notable example. Others include "immortal harps" ("At Solemn Music," l. 13); "swooning bed" (second Hobson poem, l. 17); "viewless wing" ("On the Passion,: l. 50); "unweeting hand" ("On the Death . . . ," l.23); "willing chains" ("At a Vacation Exercise," l. 52); and "melodius time" ("On the Morning . . . ," l. 125).

In each of the preceding instances the catechresis is a device for emphasis. The adjective refers to some human characteristic with strong connotations (note especially "immortal," "swooning," and "viewless"). By calling attention to the word Milton emphasizes the connotation and thereby intensifies the passage. "Individual kiss" is also a case where catachresis is used for emphasis. However "individual" is a doctrinal word. It is important for its denotation rather than its connotation and has the effect of calling attention to the thought pattern of the poem. Therefore it is necessary to turn from linguistic and rhetorical matters to the intellectual issues which would lead a seventeenth-century author to emphasize the word "individual" in a poem about the soul's reception into heaven.

IV

Milton's phrase forms part of a statement of how the transfigured soul is received in heaven after the Last Judgment. The wording is general and the Christian references are mingled with Platonic ones. With this qualification, the phrase conveys the rudiments of a definite theological position.

I have pointed out that "indivisible" is a poor gloss because its antithesis ("divisible kiss") is logically impossible. To the modern reader the antithesis of to "greet individually"—that is, "greet collectively"—might seem equally pointless. But to Milton's contemporaries and particularly the "fit audience though few" which he could expect among his acquaintances at Cambridge, the phrase would immediately suggest one of the most perplexing questions of theology—a question hotly debated during the great age of scholasticism and still a burning issue in Milton's lifetime.

This question was familiar to Milton's contemporaries as the problem of the unity of the active intellect. To understand it we must recall that the development of scholastic theology during the thirteenth century was decisively influenced by the rediscovery of Aristotle. Aristotle's logical works harmonized with earlier tradition. However his theory of the soul and of the nature of the physical world (esp. of the supra-lunary world described in *de Caelo*) created difficulties. These were immeasurably increased by the fact that Aristotle was normally read in conjunction with the commentaries on his work by the Arab philosopher Averroes (1126?–1198). Averroes was known to the schoolmen of the thirteenth century as "the great commentator." His works were read with as much eagerness as those of Ficino in the sixteenth and Descartes in the seventeenth century. However he was also violently attacked. At about the time that Dante placed him in the mildly infernal castle of the pagan philosophers (*Inf.*, IV), the artist of the Campo Santo depicted him as a daemon being crushed under the feet of St. Thomas Aquinas.[13]

According to Aristotle (*de Anima*, III.4, 5; 429b–30a) the individual intellect is essentially the capacity to receive impressions, much as a blank tablet has the capacity to receive letters. This individual intellect is the "potential" intellect and realizes itself through the process of thought. There is also an "active" intellect which Aristotle described as "separable, impassive and unmixed, since it is essentially an activity." The relationship between the two is unclear. Early commentators like Alexander of Aphrodesias identified the potential intellect with what we could call today personality and the active intellect with the immortal part of man. Averroes went much further. In his commentary on the *de Anima* he maintained that the distinction between active and passive intellects was purely logical. Strictly speaking there is one Intellect and it knows one Truth. Individuals exist in the created world only because of nonessential accidents of physique, milieu, and experience. When a man dies his personality (the potential soul) perishes with him, and the immortal residue is reunited with the active intellect from which it originally emanated.

Averroes' doctrines were taken up by a radical group of schoolmen at Paris, apparently led by Siger of Brabant.[14] While not denying immortality the Parisian Averroists deprived it of meaning by denying personality. This position had disturbing ramifications. It suggested that there was no essential difference between created souls. In effect there was no difference between St. Peter and Judas. Damnation is a fable, and sin is a corruption of the body having no significance after death.[15]

The climax of the struggle between Averroists and orthodox schoolmen was reached in 1270 when St. Thomas wrote *de Unitate Intellectus Contra Averroistas Parisienses.*[16] Here St. Thomas attempted to show by close scrutiny of the *de Anima* and other Aristotelian works "that neither the active intellect of which Aristotle speaks is a single one, nor is that which is illuminated, the possible intellect, only one."[17] Averroes is called "the perverter of Peripatetic philosophy," while his Parisian followers are accused of open heresy.

St. Thomas did not deny that the Averroistic position was reasonable. In fact, he admitted that reason could not entirely solve the problems raised by the Averroists. He finally suggested that the individual soul is created by a miracle rather than by natural means: "Even if the intellect, by nature, were one for all men because of not having any natural cause for multiplication, still this multiplication could be alloted to it by a supernatural cause."[18] He also conceded that the soul does not entirely regain its individuality until resurrection: "Soul, after being separated from the body, has not the ultimate perfection of its human nature."[19] The soul is not entirely separable from the body, for the doctrine of separability always leads back to the denial of personal immortality.[20]

The efforts of St. Thomas decisively crushed the Parisian Averroists, but it did not put an end to their ideas. Averroism found a warm welcome in the north Italian universities. Its doctrines were taught by a succession of remarkable scholars including Paul of Venice (d. 1429), Gaetano da Tiene (d. 1465), and Nicoletto Vernias, who occupied the first chair of philosophy at Padua from 1468 to 1499. Cardinal Gaspar Contarini, who studied under Vernias, remarked:

> When I was in Padua, in that most celebrated university of all Italy, the name and authority of Averroes the Commentator were most esteemed; and all agreed to the positions of this author, and took them as a kind of oracle. Most famous of all was his position on the unity of the Intellect, so that he who taught otherwise was considered worthy of the name neither of peripatetic nor philosopher.[21]

By 1512 the matter had become so scandalous that the Lateran council of that year issued a decree forbidding (1) the denial of immortality; (2) the doctrine of the existence of separate truths for philosophy and religion; (3) the doctrine of the unity of the active intellect; and (4)—for good measure—the teaching of philosophy for a period of five years. Needless to say this measure only stirred up controversy. In 1516 Piero Pomponazzi, successor to Vernias at Padua, published one of the truly incendiary books of the sixteenth century, *de Immortalitate Animae.*[22]

Pomponazzi was in some ways a trimmer. He hesitated to reject St. Thomas, but his most radical conclusions were clearly influenced by Averroes. At the end of *de Immortalitate* he declared himself baffled: "it seems to me that no natural reasons can be brought forth proving that the soul is immortal, and still less any proving that the soul is mortal."[23] Later, in his *Apologia* (1517) he took the more emphatic position that immortality is wholly contrary to natural reason. Only the miracles of grace and resurrection establish its truth.[24]

The debate arising from Pomponazzi's work involved the greatest scholars in Italy. It can be followed in Pomponazzi's *Apologia,* in the attack by Augustine Niphus (1518), and in the *Defensorium* which Pomponazzi wrote in reply. In the latter part of the century Giacomo Zabarella continued the tradition, and it persisted until the seventeenth century.[25] The continuing importance of Averroes may perhaps be suggested by the fact that between 1550 and 1574 the Venetian printing firm of Giunta published and sold three editions of the *Works* of Aristotle with all the commentaries of Averroes, a remarkable achievement in view of the size and expense of the editions.[26]

It was inevitable that knowledge of the Italian disputes should be disseminated in England. Burton's *Anatomy,* which Milton echoed in "L'Allegro" and "Il Penseroso," contains numerous citations of Averroistic writers, including Averroes, Pomponazzi, Niphus, and Zabarella.[27] In his discussion of the soul, Burton refers directly to the Paduan disputes:

> This question of immortality is diversely and wonderfully impugned *and disputed, especially among the Italians of late,* saith Jab. Colerus. The Popes themselves have doubted of it, Leo X, that Epi-

curean Pope, as some record of him, caused this question to be discussed *pro* and *con* before him.[28]

Later in the century the Cartesian assertion of the separability of the soul from the body caused the question of immortality to be debated anew. Sir Kenelm Digby's *Two Treatises* is usually cited as the first work in English which shows the influence of Descartes. The purpose of the second treatise is to examine "in way of discovery, of the Immortality of Reasonable Soules." Digby believed that the soul is separate but retains its identity after death. He cites "Avicenna in his book de Anima & Almahad, and Monsier Des Cartes in his Methode" to substantiate his opinion.[29] Later he refers to the Italian position:

> But unawares I have engulfed my selfe into a sea of contradiction, from no meane adversaries. For Alexander Aphrodesias, Pomponatius, and the learnedest of the Peripatetike schoole, will all of them rise up . . . shewing how in the body, all our soules knowledge is made. . . . therefore, seeing that when our body is gone, all those little bodies of fastasmes are gone with it, what signe is there, that any operation can remaine?[30]

Needless to say, Digby resolved these contradictions, at least to his own satisfaction. The result is a work which makes up in sound principles for what it lacks in logic.

Henry More's *Immortality of the Soul* is on a considerably higher plane, although its conclusions resemble those of Digby and it relies heavily on Descartes. In book 1 More asserts the separability of the soul and its simultaneous ability to penetrate matter. In book 2 he maintains the freedom of the soul against various deterministic theories, both Hobbesian and Cartesian. Book 3 is the most significant for present purposes. It treats the state of the soul after death. More was familiar with the major writers on the subject, including Aristotle, St. Thomas, Averroes, and Pomponazzi. The Averroistic position is presented in one of the most curious sections of the book. According to the report of his son, the scholar Facius Cardanus had a vision in 1491 of three men calling themselves *Homines Aerii.* These men no sooner appeared than they began to debate the two great questions of Averroism, the eternity of the world and the personal immortality of the soul.[31] Apparently More took this vision seriously. He went to considerable pains to explain how *Homines Aerii* could entertain such false and pernicious notions. A by-product of this explanation is the following clear summary of the Averroistic theory of the soul:

> *Pomponatius* and others of the Avenroists [*sic*] are as ridiculously pertinacious as they. [¶] And therefore these *Avenroistical Daemons* answered punctually according to the conclusions of their own School, *Nihil proprium cuicue superesse post mortem.* For the Mind

> or Soul being a substance common to all, and now discincted from those Terrestrial Bodies which it actuated in Plato, suppose, or Socrates, and these Bodies dead and dissipated, and only the Common Soul of the World surviving, there can be nothing but this Soul and these Bodies to make up *Socrates* and *Plato;* they conclude it is a plain case, that nothing that is proper survives after death.[32]

Other references to the doctrine of the unity of the intellect are numerous. Jackson refers in his *Creed* to the opinion of "recent philosophers" whom he does not identify that "the root of individuation in distinction of one particular person from another was wholly from the matter, not from the form."[33] Richard Baxter, the popular nonconformist preacher, asked in his *Account of My Dissent from Dr. Sherlocke* (1681), "Perhaps you think that as Averrohis [*sic*] thought all Souls are one, individuate only by receptive matter."[34] Finally, John Asgill in his *Argument proving that . . . Man may be translated from hence into Eternal Life* (1700) dealt with the ancient Averroistic problem and reached almost the same conclusion St. Thomas had reached four hundred years earlier. God miraculously creates a new soul for each man; the soul is not perfect unless united with the body; hence the soul is not separable as the Averroists and Cartesians believed. Asgill was more radical than St. Thomas. After death the soul "sleeps" until resurrection: "But in this return, the spirit of Man maintains no self-existence, having surrender'd it self into the Ocean of Life, from whence it first flowed."[35]

I have cited references from tracts written before, during, and after the composition of "On Time" in order to demonstrate the continued importance of the Averroistic questions throughout the seventeenth century. The persistence of words like "individual," "particular," and "proper" in these references is in itself a confirmation of the interpretation which has been offered of "On Time." Milton, of course, did not have to rely on vernacular tracts for information concerning the disputes over the nature of the soul. The major Latin editions of Aristotle were Italian and included the commentaries of Averroes. Numerous editions of individual works included the commentaries of Averroes or of violent partisans *pro* or *con.* Finally, the works of St. Thomas, Ficino, and Pomponazzi (all familiar to Milton) contained thorough discussions of Averroes and the theory of the unity of the active intellect. Although Milton may never have read the commentaries of Averroes, it is certain that he was exposed to Averroistic interpretations during his reading of *de Anima, Metaphysics,* and *de Caelo.*

Whether or not he was much impressed is another matter. His references to scholasticism are remarkably like those of Petrarch, and he too opposed chop-logic to humanistic disciplines like rhetoric, history, and poetry.[36] Temperamentally he was a Platonist. He satirized Aristotle in his poem *de Idea Platonica.* As an inheritor of the humanistic tradition of Petrarch and Erasmus, as a follower of Ramus, and as an interested reader of Bacon, he was committed to anti-Aristotelianism.[37]

On the other hand, when he wrote "On Time" he was more conscious of Aristotle's theories (and presumably those of his commentators) than at any subsequent time in his career. This is proved by the fourth, fifth, and sixth *Prolusions.* The fourth *Prolusion* deals with the Aristotelian theory of forms. Its thesis is that "In the destruction of any substance a resolution to prime matter does not occur." Aristotle's position is briefly summarized: "Since indeed matter is pure potency, it has no existence except that which is obtained by begging from form . . . by which being may be recognized."[38] In opposition to this, Milton claimed that quantity (the third of Aristotle's categories) is an attribute of prime substance rather than an "active principle." In effect, he is arguing for a more intimate connection between substance and form than the Averroistic interpretation allowed. If he is correct, soul is not "separable" from matter, and the active and potential intellects are so interfused that one cannot exist apart from the other: personal immortality is not only possible but essential.

Milton does not carry the argument this far in the fourth *Prolusion.* The fifth one, however, is based on a problem arising in the *de Anima* and has several references to that work. Its thesis is "That partial forms do not occur in an animal in addition to the whole." It is an attempt to answer the question of whether the lower (vegetative and sensitive) souls can be considered apart from the rational soul, or whether all three should be considered an indissoluble complex forming the soul of man. The first alternative leads back to Averroism. The rational soul is man's ability to understand. Its object is truth. Since there is only one Truth, all rational souls would be identical if separated from the lower souls. Thus personality is extinguished after death. Milton takes his stand against the separability of the rational soul. He does not extend the argument to the problem of immortality, but his point of view is parallel to that of St. Thomas: "because numerous activities are seen in the animal, this ought not to be due to distinct partial forms, but to the preeminence of the total soul, which indeed is equivalent to forms specifically distinct."[39]

It would be pointless to claim much philosophical depth for Milton's *Prolusions.* Everything about them suggests that Milton's heart was not in his work. Their general tone is probably well defined by Milton's facetious remark, "I am not sure whether I am boring to you; certainly I am very much to myself."[40] They prove, however, that Milton was concerned at Cambridge with topics intimately related to the immortality of the soul. Later, when he returned to them in an intensely serious work, the *de Doctrina,* his orientation was substantially the same as that of the *Prolusions.* In chapter 7 (*On the Creation*) he continued to insist on the unity of the higher with the lower souls:

> Man having been created . . . *man became a living soul;* whence it may be inferred (unless we had rather take the heathen writers for our teachers respecting the nature of the soul) that man is a living being, intrinsically and properly one and individual, not compound or separable, not, according to common opinion, made up and framed of two distinct and different natures, as of soul and body—but the whole man is soul and the soul man, that is to say, a body, or substance individual, animated, sensitive, and rational.[41]

In chapter 13 (*On the Death of the Body*) he reiterated the fact that the soul is not separable: "The common definition, which supposes [death] to consist in the separation of soul and body, is inadmissible."

As has been noted earlier, this position saves personal immortality but at the price of condemning the soul to oblivion until resurrection. Milton would have none of Sir Kenelm Digby's awkward compromise between naturalism and Christianity. He fully accepted the implications of his theory. The soul was implanted at the moment of birth. It had no preexistence separate from the body, and it must "sleep" until reunited with the body on Judgment Day. The thesis of chapter 13 of the *de Doctrina* is "first . . . that the whole man dies, and, secondly, that each component part suffers privation of life."[42]

Turning again to the poem "On Time," we can now understand why "individual kiss" would have been an important phrase to Milton and his readers. The unity of the active intellect does not rule out immortality, but it does rule out the individuality of the soul after death. Because of his Aristotelian studies Milton was sensitive to this fact. In the *de Doctrina* he would insist that man is "intrinsically and properly one and individual"; and he indicated his position in "On Time" with an equally emphatic use of "individual." His phrase is not tautological since the antithetical adjective ("collective") points directly to the Averroistic theory of the active intellect.

V

There is considerable appropriateness in Milton's reference to immortality. The topic of his poem is one of the great commonplaces of philosophy. Like the question of the unity of the active intellect, it was extremely controversial. According to traditional Christianity bolstered by citations of Hesiod, Ovid, and other pagan writers, the world was running down. The taint of corruption had been received from man's fall and had spread like a blight to all nature. The last age was at hand to be followed by Armageddon. This view, expressed in works like Godfrey Goodman's *Fall of Man*, was strongly opposed in the seventeenth century by naturalistic works like George Hakewill's *Apologie or Declaration of the Power and Providence of God* (1627) and John Jonston's *History of the Constancy of Nature* (1657) in which the modern idea of progress is adumbrated.[43] Behind the seventeenth-century debate and contributing to it was the scholastic controversy over the eternity of the world. Averroes and his European followers had maintained that the created universe is eternal. Individuals appear and disappear, institutions rise and fall, but the interplay of form and matter never began and will never end. St. Thomas reaffirmed the traditional Christian view in his *de Aeternitate Mundi contra Murmurantes;* but the heresy persisted (like that of the unity of the intellect) into the sixteenth century and beyond.[44]

Milton's position was not wholly consistent. His Latin poem *Naturam non pati senem* offers a dual solution. On the one hand, it accepts the doctrine of the Last Judgment and the end of the world: "The righteous sequence of things shall go on perpetually until the final fire shall destroy the world." On the other hand, the very proposition which the poem defends is naturalistic. Milton's elegant description of the heavenly bodies eternally fixed in their orbits does not reflect his interest in the new science, as some scholars have maintained. One of the chief points of Galileo's *Siderius Nuncius* (1610) is that the heavens are *not* immutable. Milton's view is the view which the Averroists and their followers deduced from Aristotle's *de Caelo:* "by the founding of the stars more strongly the omnipotent Father has taken thought for the universe. He has fixed the scales of Fate with sure balance and commanded every individual thing in the cosmos to hold to its course forever." (ll. 33–36)

"On Time" has none of the conflicts of the Latin poem. It is a reworking of the theme of mutability. Like "Lycidas" it depends for its effect on the creative use of convention. Time is depicted as rapacious and evil. It "gluts itself on what its womb devours," and will greedily "consume" itself until it has destroyed the created world. Strictly speaking the thought is not inconsistent with the possibility that nature endures in pristine perfection until the last day; but the imagery certainly is. Behind it lie centuries of Christian thoughts on corroding time.

Milton's treatment of time is thus directly opposed to the position of Averroes and his naturalistic followers. It can easily be seen that the phrase "individual kiss" is a corollary of this larger opposition. "On Time" is a skillful exercise in orthodox Christianity. It reflects lightly some of the great questions of Christian theology. It is particularly interesting as a reminder that the training which Milton received in Aristotle greatly deepened the perspective within which he viewed the issues arising in his poetry.

(1961)

In Medias Res in *Paradise Lost*

Normally, our efforts to understand the artistic motives of Renaissance poets are based on conjecture. Historical criticism attempts to fill gaps in our knowledge by pointing to influences that affect a given work, but our uncertainty is often increased by the very process that seeks to reduce it. As the number of possible influences grows, how do we decide which influence is the most important? In the case of *Paradise Lost,* however, the historical record is unusually clear. We know a good deal about Milton's reasons for beginning *Paradise Lost* where he did, and this information provides several useful insights into the motives that determined the poem's final shape.

In medias res is the familiar prescription given by Horace for beginning an epic poem. It is usually considered no more than that—a formula that eventually led to a standard literary convention. We know, however, that the formula is closely related in classical literary criticism to the problem of poetic unity. We also know from Milton's numerous references to Aristotle and Horace that he was thoroughly familiar with the *Poetics* and the *Ars Poetica,* as well as with the efforts of Renaissance critics to reduce these works to a series of rules for various genres.[1]

In addition to our knowledge of Milton's interest in critical theory, we have direct evidence that he considered several points of entry into his material before he decided to begin *Paradise Lost* with the demonic conclave. This evidence can be supplemented with the less firm but still considerable information concerning the stages in the composition of the poem offered by Allan Gilbert in *On the Composition of "Paradise Lost."*[2]

II

In chapter 8 of the *Poetics,* Aristotle discusses the problem of unity. He is primarily interested in tragedy, but he approaches tragedy in terms of epic. The best epic plots, he believes, are those which have the same tightly unified structure as tragic plots. Poets identified by Aristotle as "cyclic" produced loosely unified poems which he illustrates by citing cradle-to-grave celebrations of heroes like Hercules and Theseus. Homer showed what proper epic plots should be: "In producing the *Odyssey* he did not make it concern all that happened to Odysseus, e.g. his being wounded on Parnassus or pretending to be mad. . . . Instead he constructed the *Odyssey* and similarly the *Iliad* around one action.[3] Later (XVII), Aristotle summarizes the plot of the *Odyssey.* The plot is limited to the return of Odysseus, from his departure from Calypso's island to the time when he slays the suitors and is reunited with Penelope. "Everything else," says Aristotle, "is episode." By episode Aristotle means something like "digressive episode." Evidently, the story of the wanderings of Odysseus, which occupies four books of the *Odyssey* (IX–XII), is a case in point. Later still, in chapter 24 of the *Poetics,* we are told that such digressive episodes are proper to epic, lending it a characteristic grandeur and variety. In sum, Aristotle recommends that the epic have a short, tightly unified frame plot based on a small segment of a larger story with extended digressive episodes used as ornament. He does not use a Greek phrase equivalent to the Latin *in medias res,* but the corollary of his remarks about the *Odyssey* is that the epic poet *must* begin "in the middle" of his story and introduce prior events and secondary actions through the "episodes."

Memories of these ideas linger in the *Ars Poetica.* Horace places great emphasis on the need for a proper beginning. He contrasts Homer's method of beginning to the lame opening line of an anonymous cyclic poet. The cyclic poet begins by promising to "sing the fate of Priam and the famous Trojan war." Evidently this is a poor beginning because it promises two actions, one of them (the fate of Priam) personal and tragic and the other (the Trojan War) social and heroic. The poet's object, says Horace, should be "to fetch light from smoke, not smoke from a flash of light." This leads to a more general comment on poetic beginnings:

> The epic poet does not date the return of Diomedes from the death of Maleager or the Trojan war from Leda's twin egg. He hastens to the climax and catches the reader in the midst of the events as though they were already familiar. What he cannot make brilliant he omits and he uses fiction and mixes the false with the true so that the middle is consistent with the beginning and the end with the middle.[4]

Long after Horace's death, medieval and Renaissance scholiasts glossed these observations in various, often inconsistent ways. Since epic and tragedy were both supposed to be based on history, it was conventional to cite *in medias res* as a distinction between the poet and the historian. The historian was supposed to use chronological, or "natural" order (*ordo naturalis*), while the poet used "artificial" order (*ordo artificialis*) and, in the words of Rudolphus Agricola, "usually re-arranges events and begins in the middle and then brings in prior events by the device of a character or some comment or other."[5] In his "Letter to Raleigh" explaining *The Faerie Queene,* Edmund Spenser summarizes this distinction:

> The Methode of a Poet historical is not such, as of an Historiographer. For an Historiographer discourseth of affayres orderly as they were donne, accounting as well the times as the actions, but a Poet thrusteth into the middest, even where it most concerneth him, and there recoursing to the thinges forepaste, and divining of thinges to come, maketh a pleasing Analysis of all.[6]

Milton, of course, knew this tradition thoroughly. In *Of Education* he commends "that sublime art which in *Aristotles Poetics,* in *Horace,* and in the *Italian* commentaries of *Castelvetro, Tasso, Mazzoni,* and others, teaches what the laws are of a true *Epic* poem, what of a *Dramatic,* what of a *Lyric. . . .*"(YP, II.404–5). In *The Reason of Church-Government* Milton balances the laws and rules of the critics against the idea that the poet should follow nature, an option to which he had alluded long before in his image of Shakespeare warbling "his native woodnotes wild" ("L'Allegro," 133) in contrast to the learned Ben Jonson. He asks whether in epic poetry "the rules of *Aristotle* herein are strictly to be kept, or nature to be follow'd, which in them that know art, and use judgement is no transgression, but an inriching of art" (YP, I.813).[7] This is a liberal, almost an anticlassical position. Twelve years later, in *The Second Defense,* Milton sounds much more classical. Paraphrasing *Poetics,* chapter 8, he announces that the epic poet, if he adheres strictly to established rules, "undertakes to extol, not the whole life of the hero whom he proposes to celebrate in his verse, but usually one event of his life (the exploits of Achilles at Troy, let us say, or the return of Ulysses, or the arrival of Aeneas in Italy) and passes over the rest" (YP, IV.i.685). Finally, in the argument to book 1 of *Paradise Lost,* Milton explains, "the Poem hasts into the midst of things, presenting *Satan with his Angels now fallen into Hell.*" "Hasts into the midst of things" is simply a slightly modified quotation from memory of Horace's *festinat et in medias res.*

III

To relate Milton's theory to his practice, we need first to establish an approximate chronological sequence for the major events in the poem. The initiating event is God's elevation of Christ, which Milton withholds until book 5 of *Paradise Lost.* Christ's elevation leads to Satan's rebellion and the War in Heaven (books 5–6) and the fall of Satan (books 6, 1). While the bad angels are falling toward Hell, the Creation occurs (book 7) and evidently the creation of man and Adam's earliest experiences (book 8). The demonic conclave (books 1–2) leads to Satan's flight to earth (books 2–3), which is simultaneous with the debate between God and Christ (book 3). With Satan's arrival (book 4) the story settles down to a straightforward action extending from the nuptials of Adam and Eve to the expulsion. There is one long interruption (books 5–8) devoted mostly to retrospective narrative and one inversion (Michael's prophecy of human history, books 11–12). I consider this an inversion because it precedes rather than follows the expulsion from the garden. Clearly we are dealing with a quite sophisticated manipulation of a fairly simple set of events.

I will call the complete sequence of events from the elevation of Christ to the Last Judgment Milton's *inclusive plot.* Most of the inclusive plot is told by narrators who are also dramatic characters, but three episodes—the demonic conclave, the debate in Heaven, and Satan's return to Hell to announce his victory—are presented by the epic poet himself. At the same time that *Paradise Lost* has an inclusive plot, the convention of *in medias res* gives it what I will call a *dramatic plot.* This is its plot in the Aristotelian sense endorsed by Milton in *The Second Defense.* The dramatic plot centers on a "particular action" in the life of the hero—the Fall—and extends from the entry of Satan into the newly created world to the expulsion. Material from the inclusive plot is introduced into the dramatic plot by Milton's characters, and because this material is part of a "particular action" it becomes functional in the dramatic plot. For example, Raphael's story of the War in Heaven provides interesting historical information, but its dramatic function is to instruct Adam in the need for obedience. Again, Michael's prophecy (books 11–12), which C. S. Lewis once called an "untransmuted lump of futurity,"[8] is explicitly identified in the poem as a form of consolation for Adam after the Fall.

As far as the convention of *in medias res* is concerned, any action except the elevation of Christ would have been a suitable point of entry into the story. If Milton had followed Aristotle or a Renaissance critic like Girolamo Vida, he might have begun late in the story, perhaps after the Fall had occurred. On the other hand, if he had followed Spenser he might have begun with the War in Heaven, the second event, while reserving the first event, the elevation of Christ, for a "discovery" scene at the very end. Given the varieties of Renaissance critical theory, the precedents of Homer and Vergil could have been cited to justify almost any episode between these extremes.[9]

One other theoretical consideration. All Renaissance critics who discuss the problem of epic unity, including advocates of romantic epic like Cinthio and Tasso, as well as the Aristotelians, agree that epic needs a central action to which all secondary episodes are ultimately related.[10] In other words, as far as Renaissance criticism is concerned, what I have called the inclusive plot should always be subordinate to the dramatic plot. We know from the opening lines of *Paradise Lost* that Milton's "particular action" is "Mans First Disobedience, and the Fruit / Of that Forbidden Tree." This being the case, Milton's decision to begin with the demonic conclave and the debate in Heaven of books 1 through 3 is something of an anomaly. The episodes in books 1 through 3 are not subordinated to the dramatic plot as is the narrative of the War in Heaven. They are not recounted by a character in the dramatic plot, nor do they have any functional relation to Adam's experience, since Adam never hears of them. They are narrated by the inspired poet and are addressed directly to the reader. They are episodes that Aristotle would have called "outside of the action"—a prelude to it but not part of it. In addition, unlike most of the rest of *Paradise Lost*, books 1 and 2 are fictional in the sense that they are not based on scriptural history or a well-defined literary tradition.

I will return to this point later. For now I will only point out that the practical result of beginning with Satan and his cohorts in Hell has been a long history of confusion about who the hero of the poem really is, which is ultimately a confusion about whether Milton was writing to narrate the trials of Adam or to glorify Satan. Since Milton deliberated long and chose late, I think it is reasonable to assume that these problems occurred to him long before they were debated by critics: that he eventually decided to begin with Satan in spite of the obvious liabilities and inconsistencies inherent in this approach.

IV

To turn now from theory to history, we have considerable information concerning the various places in the story that Milton at one time considered appropriate points of entry. This evidence underscores the close relation between tragedy and epic in Aristotle's—and in Milton's—thought and also does much to explain the prominence of tragic elements in the completed poem, observed, for example, by James Holly Hanford, Helen Gardner, and Arthur Barker.[11]

One important piece of evidence comes from Milton's nephew Edward Phillips. In the biography of Milton which he published in 1694, Phillips wrote: "The subject was first designed a tragedy, and in the fourth book of the poem there are six verses, which several years before the poem was begun, were shown to me and some others, as designed for the very beginning of the said tragedy."[12] Phillips quotes not six but ten lines from the soliloquy of Satan at the beginning of book 4, beginning "O thou that with surpassing glory crown'd." Whether Phillips's reference is to a time before or after the outline of tragedies in the Trinity manuscript was made will probably never be known.[13] What is important is that at an early stage in Milton's thinking about the literary possibilities of the Fall, he chose as his "very beginning" the lines that introduce what I have called his dramatic plot.

The choice is a natural one. Beginning with this soliloquy moves us directly toward the major crisis of the plot—the temptation. It also ensures that any parts of the inclusive plot introduced later will be subordinate to the dramatic plot. This would be true by definition in a tragedy, where the poet speaks only through characters; it would also be true, though to a lesser degree, in what ancient and Renaissance critics called the "mixed" form of epic, which involves narration by the author as well as speeches by characters.

Satan's soliloquy is just that. It is a true soliloquy. It is not a defiant oration but an anguished private expression of doubt, torment, resentment, and, ultimately, defiance born out of despair. There is nothing quite like it in Greek or Senecan drama. Allan Gilbert remarks, "Satan's address to the sun in *Paradise Lost* IV, 32–41, could not have been the beginning of a formal prologue like that of ['Adam unparadiz'd']. It is rather a plunge directly into the action more violent than that beginning *Samson Agonistes*" (p. 17). Helen Gardner is therefore right, I think, in looking not to ancient drama but to the Elizabethans for its antecedents. Choosing *Macbeth, Dr. Faustus,* and *The Changeling* as typical dramas of tormented villainy, she writes: "It is not suggested that . . . when Milton drew his Satan he had one of these great tragic figures in mind. What is suggested is that Satan belongs to their company, and if we ask where the idea of damnation was handled with seriousness and intensity in English literature before Milton, we can only reply: on the tragic stage."[14]

I would add to this point that there is a structural as well as a psychological link between Milton's projected tragedy and the Elizabethan theater. Several Elizabethan plays begin with soliloquies by villainous characters, *The Jew of Malta* and *Richard III* being two obvious examples. Although I agree that the content of Satan's soliloquy is closer to *Macbeth* than *Richard III*, the opening strategy of the work described by Phillips resembles *Richard III,* which, incidentally, is one of the few Shakespeare plays directly quoted by Milton.[15]

The conclusion suggested by these observations is that at an early stage in his thinking, Milton saw the Fall in terms of Elizabethan tragedy. Since the word *revenge* is repeatedly used by Satan and his cohorts to explain their motive,[16] we can be more specific. The genre closest to Milton's intention is the revenge play. The play Milton seems to have had in mind would have been simpler than an Elizabethan play. It would have presented a psychologically complex, tormented antagonist pitted against an innocent and sympathetic protagonist, and the success of the antagonist would have been balanced against his own damnation and the eventual salvation of his victim. Whether the form would have been classical or Elizabethan is beyond saying, but it is surely worth remembering that when Milton referred to Aristotle's rules in 1642, he immediately added that following nature was "no transgression, but an inriching of art."

Evidently he was keeping an open mind regarding nonclassical form. At any rate, we know from Arthur Barker's study of the structure of *Paradise Lost* that Milton's interest in tragedy extended as far as the first edition of *Paradise Lost,* which was in ten books having a five-act structure rather than the more conventional twelve books created by Milton's revisions in the second edition of the poem.

Although Milton evidently was interested in Elizabethan drama, there is no doubt that classical form and the "rules of Aristotle" exerted an equal or greater fascination. The evidence for this is the series of four outlines in the Trinity manuscript which Milton made for dramas on the Fall. Critics have generally lumped Phillips' comment with the Trinity outlines as evidence of Milton's interest in a dramatic version of the Fall. But if the evidence is taken seriously, the Trinity outlines can be seen to point to a kind of drama somewhat different from the revenge play suggested by Phillips. In the first place, Phillips is quite explicit in stating that Satan's soliloquy was to be the "very beginning" of the tragedy he discussed with Milton. In none of the Trinity outlines does Satan appear at the beginning, and in the last two, which are the only two with sufficient detail to allow firm conclusions, Satan does not appear until the third act.

All four outlines begin with a prologue spoken by a divine agent. In the first three, the prologue is followed by characters representing divine concern for man—"Heavenly Love" or the allegorical figures of Justice and Mercy are to initiate the action. The point of entry of the first three Trinity dramas thus corresponds not to the beginning of book 4 of *Paradise Lost* but to the debate between God and Christ at the beginning of book 3.

"Adam unparadiz'd" is the most detailed of the outlines. Gabriel serves as prologue and begins the play with an evidently lengthy description of Paradise. The chorus then appears to show "the reason of [Gabriel's] comming to keep his watch in Paradise after Lucifers rebellion" (CM, XVIII.231). The chorus's references in act 1 to "Lucifers rebellion" would have to be brief, since the chorus is required to sing "of the battell, & victorie in heavn against [Satan], & his accomplices" after act 2. The emphasis of the first act of this version of the play, therefore, would have to be on Gabriel's description of Paradise—in other words, material corresponding to passages in the middle of book 4 of the finished poem. The beauty of the garden would be untouched by the sinister figure of Satan, because Satan does not begin the play. In fact, he is not allowed to enter the outline of "Adam unparadiz'd" as a character until act 2. Although Lucifer explicitly states that he "seeks revenge" in his first speech, the form and general effect of this version are quite different from that of the revenge play remembered by Phillips. Second, and very striking I think, the heart of the revenge play and of what we have in the finished poem is missing in the Trinity outlines. The first outline includes the serpent in the cast of characters, but after this all traces of the temptation scene disappear. In the third outline Satan appears in act 3 "contriving Adam's ruin," and by act 4 the Fall has already occurred. In "Adam unparadiz'd," when Adam and Eve first appear in act 3 they are represented as "having by this time bin seduc't by the serpent" (CM, XVIII.231). Thereafter they quarrel, are shown the future of the race by Mercy, and leave the garden reconciled to their fate. The dramatic action of "Adam unparadiz'd" is thus focused on the material which appears in *Paradise Lost* from the end of book 9 to book 12.

This is such a startling fact that one wonders why more has not been made of it. Gilbert attributes it to Milton's reluctance to present a serpent onstage. Perhaps, but he showed no reluctance about bringing Comus and his half-bestial followers onto the stage at Ludlow Castle. A better explanation is the Horatian decree that exceptionally violent or shocking actions should occur offstage, an injunction that Milton scrupulously followed in *Samson Agonistes.* Only a determination to be thoroughly classical and to follow "Aristotle's (and Horace's) rules" can explain why Milton would have banished the most intensely dramatic moments of the Fall from his proposed drama.[17]

Third, "Aristotle's rules" called in the seventeenth century for observance of the unities of time, place, and action—and for the use of prologue and dramatic chorus. Elizabethan drama was under no such constraints. A play in the Elizabethan mold could have begun directly with Satan's soliloquy (skipping the prologue); it could have presented the temptation and Fall onstage; it could have moved freely in space and time; and it could have minimized or done without a chorus.

What the Trinity manuscript therefore shows is that Milton considered four classicizing (i.e., non-Elizabethan) dramas on the Fall. They were not similar to the revenge play suggested by Phillips' comment; they were alternatives to it. Elements of morality play and masque can be found in the Trinity outlines. The only element conspicuous by its absence is precisely the element suggested by Phillips and found lingering in the finished poem by Helen Gardner—the Elizabethan revenge tragedy.

To return to *in medias res,* it is clear that Milton considered three points of entry into his material—Satan's arrival in the newly created world, now part of book 4 (the Phillips version); a debate on man's destiny resembling the debate between God and Christ now part of book 3 (the early Trinity outlines); and a description of Paradise *sans* Satan, now part of book 4 (the Trinity outline titled "Adam unparadiz'd"). The first point of entry is associated with a straightforward dramatic presentation of the Fall and heavily influenced by the tradition of the revenge play. The second and third are associated with a more formal and classical treatment of the theme and have the effect of emphasizing the ultimate goodness of man's fate rather than creating suspense by emphasizing his peril. All three points of entry rest solidly on Scripture. They are free elaborations, but they are not inventions. The first and third are developed out of scriptural history, while the second, the debate on man's ultimate fate, dramatizes scriptural theology and is based on the convention of the debate of the Daughters of God going back to the Middle Ages.

Yet instead of choosing one of these points of entry, Milton eventually rejected them all. In their place he created two books which are fictional in the sense that they are neither based on Scripture nor are they dramatizations of scriptural theology.[18] Milton could have defended this practice by citing Horace's advice to "use fiction and mix the false with the true," but the *Ars Poetica* hardly explains why he chose to exercise poetic license at such a critical moment as the poem's first episode.

To review this history is to be impressed with the fact that nothing we know of Milton's plans implies the demonic conclave. Here we move from hard evidence to conjecture. In *On the Composition of "Paradise Lost,"* Allan Gilbert argues that *Paradise Lost* took shape in several stages.[19] Its earliest form after it was recast from dramatic to epic form was chronological rather than artificial. That is, it began with the first episode of the inclusive plot, the elevation of Christ, and continued with the War in Heaven and the Creation. At a later date Milton came to feel that the chronological version was loose in structure. He therefore revised it by moving the War in Heaven and the creation to their present location in the middle of the poem and adding the demonic conclave, books 1 and 2.

The chronological poem that Gilbert describes is so far from "Aristotle's rules" and Milton's own poetic tendencies that I seriously doubt whether it ever existed. Whether it existed or not, however, at some point before the creation of books 1 and 2 the action of Milton's poem must have resembled the revenge tragedy suggested by Phillips, presented now in the "mixed form" of epic narrative and expanded with the "episodes" which according to Aristotle lend epic its special grandeur and variety. It might have begun with Satan; more probably, it began with the debate in heaven. The point is that it was complete: it followed "Aristotle's rules"; it began *in medias res;* it included a representation of the temptation and Fall; and it had the unity commended by Milton when he wrote that "the epic poet, who adheres to all the rules of that species of composition, undertakes to extol, not the whole life of the hero whom he proposes to celebrate in his verse, but usually one event of his life" (YP, IV.i.685). Why was the demonic conclave necessary at all?

V

We have reviewed the liabilities involved in books I and II. The demonic conclave diverts attention from the main action, the Fall; it is fictional, rather than a free variation on scriptural sources; it is narrated by the poet rather than by a character in the dramatic plot; and, as we know from sad experience, it invites confusion about the status of Satan in the poem. The obvious question is what Milton gained by it that was important enough to offset its liabilities.

It would be easy to explain books 1 and 2 in terms of their splendid imagery and their ability to engage the reader's interest, but I suspect that these explanations may be too easy—that the imagery and the play on reader psychology are by-products of revision rather than basic motives.

The primary difference between Milton's earlier plans and *Paradise Lost* as we now have it is that all of the earlier plans begin with assertions of divine goodness or power. This is obvious in the case of the dramatic outlines that begin with speeches by Heavenly Love, or Justice and Mercy, or with a description of Paradise. Note that it is also true of the tragedy which Phillips recalled that began with Satan's soliloquy. The end of the passage which Phillips quotes is as follows:

> to thee I call,
> But with no friendly voice, and add thy name
> O Sun, to tell thee how I hate thy beams
> That bring to my remembrance from what state
> I fell, how glorious once above thy Spheare;
> Till Pride and worse Ambition threw me down
> Warring in Heav'n against Heav'ns matchless King.
> (IV.35–41)

This is not an expression of heroic defiance. It is a confession. The Satan of these lines is closer to Shakespeare's anguished Claudius than to the defiant rebel of books 1 and 2. He is sympathetic, but he is sympathetic because he admits the major premise of the Christian view of the poem: that he fell because of his own "Pride and worse Ambition," and that God is "Heav'ns matchless King." In other words, Satan admits that this fall was deserved, that God is good, and that God is all-powerful.

A speech of this sort would be a superbly effective beginning for a tragedy limited to the visible world. I doubt that Milton at any stage planned to limit himself entirely to the visible world, but certainly when he decided on an epic rather than a tragedy he did so with the intention of exploiting fully what Renaissance critics usually called "the Christian marvelous."[20]

We are dealing here with much more than a pretty convention. A poem that moves between the invisible and the visible world offers two perspectives. What Aeneas experiences as a bad storm, for example, becomes, when we move to the invisible world, an episode in a long-standing feud between the gods. In *Paradise Lost* the perspective of the invisible world is more important than that in the *Aeneid* by exactly the degree to which the actions of Milton's Christian God command more authority than the actions of pagan deities.

This is the crux of the problem created by Milton's material. *Paradise Lost* is committed to two perspectives, and both of them are valid. According to the first, the divine perspective, God is "matchless"—that is, omniscient, omnipotent, and benign. From this perspective evil is a part of God's larger plan for creation. The worst that evil can accomplish is the Fall, which we eventually recognize as a Fortunate Fall rather than an unqualified victory of evil over good. This perspective is dramatized by Milton in the debate between God and Christ, in the humiliating defeat of the rebellious angels, in Satan's soliloquy and in his progressively more degraded disguises, and in numerous other passages. As Belial tells his cohorts in Hell, from the divine perspective the efforts of the fallen angels are futile, almost trivial:

> he from heav'ns hight
> All these our motions vain, sees and derides;
> Not more Almighty to resist our might
> Than wise to frustrate all our plots and wiles.
> (II.190–93)

From the limited perspective of human history, however, evil is anything but trivial. It is powerful. It threatens at every moment to gain a decisive advantage over good. Milton lived through enough history to recognize this in fact as well as in theory, and his experience is distilled in Michael's gloomy résumé of human experience in book 12: "so shall the World goe on, / To good malignant, to bad men benigne" (537–38).

In an extremely perceptive article William McQueen points out that the two perspectives in *Paradise Lost* are antithetical.[21] According to the first, God is omnipotent and evil is weak. Belial rightly fears that the fallen angels may not appear menacing, only ridiculous. At the same time, evil as experienced is terrifying. The easy optimism of "God's in his heaven, all's right with the world" would be fatal to *Paradise Lost* if it cancelled our sense of the dark presence of evil in human history and human experience.

Seen in these terms, Milton's problem was almost the reverse of what it is usually considered to be. He did not want, either consciously or unconsciously, to make a hero out of Satan, but at the same time he could not allow Satan to be weak or insignificant. All of the early plans concerning which we have any evidence, however, diminish Satan either by emphasizing divine power and love or by beginning with a Satan who honors God as "Heav'ns matchless King" and confesses to "Pride and worse Ambition." If Allan Gilbert's chronological epic ever existed, it compounded the problem by beginning with the elevation of Christ and the ignominious defeat of the rebel angels.

The conclusion to which we are led by these observations is that the basic function of books 1 and 2—and the reason why Milton needed them in spite of their liabilities—is to make Satan a credible example of evil by offsetting the later episodes which stress God's supreme and benign power. To do this, Milton isolated Satan and his followers in a Hell separate from earth and in some sense opposite to Heaven. Admittedly, Milton was not entirely consistent. At times in the first two books the voice of the narrator reminds us that Satan is not all-powerful, that his "dark designs" will ultimately serve God's plan. In spite of these intrusions, however, the predominant effect is splendidly, almost embarrassingly successful. An image of titanic vitality and heroic perseverance is created at the outset of the poem which remains with the reader until the closing lines. It is so powerful that for many readers it has overshadowed the later passages emphasizing Satan's weakness.

In sum, Milton could not resolve the contradiction between the invisible power of God and the visible power of evil. He could only arrange *Paradise Lost* so that both elements would exist in the poem in something like a balance. To do this, he presented the inherently weaker elements, the characters symbolizing evil, first, and in a setting where their weakness would not be immediately exposed. Only after the image of evil was firmly established did he introduce characters representing the power of God, and he delayed the War in Heaven, which ends with the open defeat of evil, until books 5 and 6.

Milton's problem was not keeping Satan under control but creating an effective symbol of evil in a poem that proclaims the omnipotence of God and the ultimate redemption of fallen man. He solved it by a creative and, I think, an artistically daring use of the convention of *in medias res*. At the very beginning of his poem he drew on Horace's license to use fiction and mix "the false with the true so that the middle is consistent with the beginning and the end with the middle." In doing this he also succeeded in the difficult task set by Horace for the epic poet. In Ben Jonson's translation:

> He thinks not now to give you smoak from light
> But light from smoak, that he may draw his bright
> Wonders after.

(1983)

“Hee for God Only, Shee for God in Him”: Gender in *Paradise Lost*

The case of Milton’s Eve has been debated almost as often as the case of Satan. Like many other characters Milton created, Eve has been interpreted in terms of his personal life; more specifically, as a reflection of his ambivalent feelings toward women in general and Mary Powell, his first wife, in particular. In an essay in *Milton Studies IV*, Marcia Landy has examined Eve. She concludes that Milton’s Eve is disappointingly conventional: “His view of women . . . is yet another presentation of woman’s role as daughter, wife, and mother, of the subordination of woman to man, and of the training of woman to accept what was considered by Milton to be the necessary boundaries of woman’s world” (p. 18).

In the mass of Milton’s own writing there are passages which can be used to suggest almost any view of women that the writer wants to ascribe to him. The water is further muddied by ambiguous contemporary testimony and an enormous and constantly growing quantity of nineteenth- and twentieth-century speculation, much of which is little more than gossip labeled scholarship. The view I am offering here seems to me to represent the main tendency of Milton’s thought, but I do not contend that he was perfectly consistent either in his conscious theories or his unconscious attitudes.

II

I will begin by admitting that Milton’s image of women is influenced by the theory of hierarchy. This theory is implicit in Genesis. It was elaborated by early neoplatonic commentators on Genesis including Philo Judaeus, Origen, and St. Augustine.[1] In this tradition, Creation is an emanation outward from the ultimate source of Being. The creation of the visible world begins with the formation of the primary elements. Having started at the lowest level of creation, it then moves upward by degrees through the inanimate, vegetable and animal kingdoms to man, and, ultimately, back to the original Divine source. Everything is thus arranged in a hierarchy in which each being is above some and below other beings. Milton was aware of scientific theories which called this tradition into question. He may have used it as a lovely, if fading metaphor. Whether intended as metaphor or fact, however, the idea of hierarchy is one of the dominant themes of Milton's epic. It permeates the majestic description of Creation in book 7, and it is neatly summarized by the angel Raphael in book 5:

> O *Adam*, one Almighty is, from whom
> All things proceed, and up to him return,
> If not deprav'd from good, created all
> Such to perfection, one first matter all,
> Indud with various forms, various degrees
> Of substance, and in things that live, of life;
> But more refin'd, more spiritous, and pure,
> As nearer to him plac't or nearer tending,
> Each to thir several Spheres assign'd
> Till Body up to Spirit work, in bounds
> Proportioned to each kind.
>
> (469–79)

In other words, everything that exists stands above one part of creation and below another. Milton's belief that God the Son is subordinate to God the Father, which pushed him a good distance down the path to Arianism, is a striking example of the effect of the principle of hierarchy on his theology. The same principle clearly influenced his treatment of the relation between Adam and Eve. In terms of Milton's hierarchical view of creation, Eve cannot be equal to Adam, and, as many passages demonstrate, she is below him: "Hee for God only, shee for God in him."

Even while we admit this, however, a qualification is needed. The hierarchy of creation is dynamic. All Being strives to achieve higher states of Being. This impulse is divinely sanctioned. Raphael explains to Adam and Eve that the human race itself may eventually become angelic: "time may come when men / With Angels may participate . . . And from these corporal nutriments perhaps / Your bodies may at last turn all to spirit" (493–97). Eve's desire to improve her condition is therefore natural and divinely sanctioned. Neither the God of *Paradise Lost* nor—presumably—Milton disapproves of this desire. It is only when Eve disobeys a divine commandment in order to achieve her goal of self-improvement that she commits a sin.

A second pervasive tendency which influences Milton's image of woman is his habit of describing creation as an interaction of male and female. At the beginning of book 1 of *Paradise Lost*, when he invokes the aid of the Spirit of God, Milton refers to creation in sexual terms:

Thou from the first
Wast present, and with mighty wings outspread,
Dove-like satst brooding on the vast Abyss
And mad'st it pregnant.

(19–23)

In book 7 the sexual metaphor is repeated:

On the wat'ry calm
His brooding wings the Spirit of God outspread
And vital virtue infus'd and vital warmth
Throughout the fluid Mass.

(234–37)

And later,

The Earth was form'd, but in the Womb as yet
Of Waters, Embryon, immature involv'd
Appear'd not: over all the face of Earth
Main Ocean flow'd, not idle, but with warm
Prolific humor soft'ning all her Globe,
Fermented the great Mother to conceive,
Satiate with genial moisture.

(276–83)

We are dealing here with a mythic concept which can be found in primitive religion and in both neoplatonic and Christian sources from the Alexandrian period to the seventeenth century. Again, I believe that Milton may have chosen to use this tradition without regarding it as literally true; but my main point is that once he decided to use it, his treatment of Adam and Eve was immediately affected. Adam embodies the male element in creation and Eve the female. Both are essential to God's plan although one takes an active and one a passive role. Milton depicts this aspect of their relationship in several passages, but no passage is more expressive than his description of their first embrace:

half her swelling Breast
Naked met his under the flowing Gold
Of her loose tresses hid: hee in delight
Both of her Beauty and submissive charms
Smil'd with superior love, as *Jupiter*
On *Juno* smiles, when he impregns the Clouds
That shed *May* flowers.

(IV.495–501)

Without trying to minimize the grating effect on modern ears of the adjectives *submissive* and *superior*, I would note that the emphasis here is on doctrine rather than characterization. In its beauty as well as in its allusions, the passage relates human sexuality to the universal rhythm of fertility—to "the clouds that shed *May* flowers" in nature—and to the spiritual forces which sustain this rhythm, personified in good humanistic fashion as Jupiter and Juno, the king and queen of pagan nature.

III

To move further into Milton's characterization of Eve we need to turn from the mythic elements in *Paradise Lost* to its psychology. Many critics and teachers read *Paradise Lost* as an object lesson in the conflict between reason (Adam) and emotion (Eve). Emotion is good as long as it is properly subordinated to reason—which implies that Eve is good as long as she is properly subordinated but destructive when dominant or uncontrolled. This attitude is, in turn, supposed to reflect a personal antagonism toward women that Milton developed as a result of unhappy experiences with his first wife, Mary Powell, which appear to have led to a temporary separation.

In fact, we have little hard evidence about Milton's feelings toward Mary Powell or the real conditions of his first marriage. What we do know is that he was sufficiently fond of women to remarry after the death of each of his first two wives, and that one of his wives—she may well have been Mary Powell—inspired his most gentle and personal sonnet, "Methought I saw my late espousèd Saint / Brought to me like Alcestis from the grave."

Milton's tracts in favor of divorce are also invoked in this connection, but they are at best a two-edged sword. The early biographers assume that they grew out of Milton's separation from Mary Powell. But as William Riley Parker points out in the *Notes* volume of his biography, the Divorce Tracts say little about the problem of separation, which appears to have been Milton's specific problem. Instead, they concentrate on incompatibility as the basic grounds for divorce. This fact certainly undercuts, if it does not entirely eliminate, a straight biographical reading of the tracts.

If we turn to the Divorce Tracts themselves, we see—perhaps to our surprise—that they offer a positive, even an idealistic view of marriage. The basis of marriage, according to Milton, is a communion of mind and spirit. Sex is secondary and even incidental. Milton believed so deeply in this communion that he regarded marriage without spiritual communion as a blasphemy which should be terminated for the good of both parties. Here is a typical statement from *The Doctrine and Discipline of Divorce:*

> In God's intention a near and happy conversation is the chiefest and noblest end of marriage, for we find (in Genesis) no expression so

> necessarily implying carnal knowledge as this (passage regarding) prevention of loneliness to the mind and spirit of man . . . And with all generous persons married, thus it is that where the mind and person please aptly, there some unaccomplichment of the body's delight may be better borne with than when the mind hangs off in an unclosing disproportion, though the body be as it ought.[2]

This is not to argue that Milton believed in perfect equality in marriage. He felt that one partner should have final authority, and on the basis of *Genesis* and doubtless his own personal feelings, he felt that should normally be the male. However, he was no fanatic. In *Tetrachordon* he admits that the female may sometimes be superior to the male:

> Not but that particular exceptions (to the rule of male dominance) may have place, if (the woman) exceed her husband in prudence and dexterity, and he contentedly yield; for then a superior and more natural law comes in, that the wiser should govern the less wise, whether male or female.

Again, in the *De Doctrina*, he commends the law in Exodus XXI allowing a woman to divorce her husband:

> This law is remarkable for its consummate humanity and equity; for while it does not permit the husband to put away his wife through mere hardness of heart, it allows the wife to leave the husband on the most reasonable of all grounds, that of inhumanity and unkindness.

These passages argue not contempt but high regard for the intelligence of women. For Milton, evidently, a wife is a companion and partner, not a sex object or a glorified servant. Even if we cling to the theory that the Divorce Tracts were stimulated by an unhappy relationship with Mary Powell, they reveal an idealistic view of the proper relationship between husband and wife. As for Milton himself, when he referred to the Divorce Tracts in the *Second Defense*, he did not relate them to his personal difficulties but to his lifelong effort to defend and enlarge human liberty:

> When therefore I perceived that there were three types of liberty, which are essential to the happiness of social life—religious, domestic, and civil; and as I had already written concerning the first, and the magistrates were strenously active in obtaining the third, I determined to turn my attention to the second, or the domestic species.[3]

In other words, the ideal marriage is a form of liberation, not of bondage.

These observations lead back to *Paradise Lost*. To begin with, Milton's Adam has exactly the same theory about the proper relation of man and woman that is found in the Divorce Tracts. When Adam speaks to the

Divine Being whom he meets in the Garden of Eden before the creation of Eve, his complaint is that he has no intellectual companion.

> Among unequals what society
> Can sort, what harmony or true delight?
> Which must be mutual in proportion due
> Giv'n and received . . .
> Of fellowship and speech
> Such I seek, fit to participate
> All rational delight, wherin the brute
> Cannot be human consort.
>
> (VIII.384–92)

Fellowship, and *rational delight* point to a conception of woman as the rational equal of man. Far from rebuking Adam, the Divine Being commends him for his wisdom.

> [I] find thee knowing not of Beasts alone,
> Which thou hast rightly nam'd, but of thyself,
> Expressing well the spirit within thee free,
> My Image.
>
> (437–41)

Milton presents the relation between Adam and Eve in dramatic terms in books 4 and 5. His initial description of them as they walk through the garden emphasizes the fact that they occupy the same general category in the hierarchy of being. They are both "Godlike erect" and "seem'd Lords of all," and for both "in Thir looks Divine / The image of Thir glorious Maker shone." At the same time, however, they are emphatically "not equal." Adam seems formed "for contemplation . . . and valor," while Eve's shape suggests "softness . . . and sweet attractive grace." Many other passages underscore the inequality of Adam and Eve and I will return to them. For the present the important point is that throughout the action of books 4 and 5 Milton emphasizes the "rational delight" which Adam and Eve find in each other's company. Their first conversation is about God. Adam describes God's goodness and Eve passes judgment: "my guide / And Head, what thou hast said is just and right." Although she agrees and refers to Adam as *guide* and *Head*, she is passing judgment. There is no implication that she will agree to any assertion which her husband makes, no matter how fatuous. Eve then upholds her side of the conversation by telling Adam what she remembers of her own creation. Later, when Adam proposes rest, Eve replies in one of the loveliest set pieces in *Paradise Lost*, that she has lost track of time because of the pleasure of their discourse: "With the conversing I forget all time, / All seasons and thir change, all please alike" (639–40).

In Book 5 God sends Raphael to explain the danger to which Adam and Eve are exposed. The fall will not occur by violence but by "deceit and lies" (243) and Adam and Eve must be warned so that if they transgress, they cannot complain that God was unjust. Raphael's explanation extends from the middle of Book 5 to the middle of book 8. Several passages are important. First, Raphael explains the hierarchy of creation, stressing that man, in the generic sense of humanity, is a rational being and that in the soul "reason is her being" (488). Because man is rational he has both freedom to choose and the responsibility for living with the consequences of his choices. Raphael then describes the war in Heaven. Satan's fall is an object lesson in the consequences of disobedience to God. At the end Raphael adds for the benefit of both Adam and Eve, "Let it profit thee to have heard / By terrible Example, the reward / Of disobedience" (910–12). The point is that Raphael's discourse is emphatically "rational" and is intended for both of our first parents. There is no suggestion that it has been intended for Adam alone or that Eve has failed to understand it.

At the beginning of book 8, Adam begins to question Raphael about astronomy, and Eve politely retires to tend her garden. This is a famous moment in the poem. Are we to asume she does so because she cannot understand astronomy? Clearly not, for Milton is at some pains to explain that she wants to learn astronomy. She wants to learn it, however, in "rational conversation" with Adam, not from the angel:

> Yet went she not, as not with such discourse
> Delighted, or not capable her ear
> Of what was high; such pleasure she reserv'd
> Adam relating, she role Auditress.
>
> (48–52)

Eve is both "delighted" with astronomy and quite "capable of what is high."

Eve's rationality is reflected in another way in books 5 and 6 of *Paradise Lost.* The marriage relation depicted by Milton is contractual. It involves authority but the authority must be freely accepted. When Eve describes her meeting with Adam she makes it clear that her first impulse was to reject him. After Adam has explained that she is "part of my soul" and "my other half" (488–89) she yields, but the decision is hers; it is not forced. Moreover, authority in marriage has definite limits. It does not extend to matters of individual conscience, which is to say that one partner cannot command the other to commit either a virtuous action or a sin. In book 9 Adam and Eve disagree about whether Eve should tend the garden by herself. In spite of Adam's reservations he allows Eve to have her way. Almost everyone who comments on this passage assumes that Adam is wrong since Eve promptly meets the Serpent and falls. I wonder. It has always seemed to me that Eve's arguments are better than Adam's. Basically, she is arguing for liberty and against avoiding challenges. When Adam asks her to stay, she complains:

> If this be our condition, thus to dwell
> In narrow circuit, straitn'd by a Foe,
> Subtle or violent, we not endow'd
> Single, with like defense, whenever met,
> How are we happy, still in fear of harm?

This argument echoes a favorite Miltonic theme. It is the same argument that Milton employs in the most familiar passage in *Areopagitica*, where he condemns "a fugitive and cloistered virtue, unexercised and unbreathed, that never sallies out and sees her adversary," and praises Edmund Spenser for bringing his Knight Guyon "through the cave of Mammon and the Bower of earthly bliss, that he might see, and know, and yet abstain."[4]

While Eve's argument does not leave Adam euphoric, he accepts it on solid Miltonic grounds: "Go; for thy stay, not free, absents thee more"(372). He does not command her because to command would be to destroy the relationship which he has with her. Clearly the authority here is contingent on the free assent of both parties. It is a Miltonic idea but not the idea commonly read into Milton by his critics.

In books 4 and 5, then, Milton shows that Eve is rational, intelligent, "delighted" by speculative discourse, and fully capable of "what is high." His picture of ideal marriage complements this image of woman. Marriage is primarily rational companionship. It involves authority but the authority is freely granted and subject to debate. One further point. Whatever Milton's deepest personal feelings—and I see no reason to doubt that they are reflected in books 4 and 5—the basic reason for his emphasis on Eve's rationality is that it is essential to his justification of the ways of God to men. To quote God's words to Christ, man is "sufficient to have stood, though free to fall." "Sufficient to have stood" means both fully capable of rational choice and "forewarned" that the tempter may use deceit. Eve will be tempted first. Unless she is "sufficient to have stood," it would be unjust in Milton's terms to require that she endure the consequences of her choice.

IV

When we consider this emphasis on the rationality of woman, the temptation episode in book 9 of *Paradise Lost* takes on a new coloring. The main—though by no means the only—thrust of tradition is that Eve fell through vanity. Memories of this and related traditions cluster around the temptation episode in book 9 of *Paradise Lost*. The essential argument of Satan, however, is not an appeal to emotion but to reason:

> do not believe
> Those rigid threats of death; ye shall not Die;
> How should ye? by the Fruit? it gives you life
> To knowledge: By the Threat'ner? look on mee.
> Mee who have touch'd and tasted, yet both live
> And life more perfect have attain'd than Fate
> Meant mee, by vent'ring higher than my Lot.
> Shall that be shurt to Man that to the Beast
> Is open?
>
> (684–92)

Our conditioned responses to Eve's Fall are so powerful that it is difficult to abandon them when we read this episode. But we should exercise the imagination. Eve, a rational being who has been thoroughly instructed in the hierarchy of creation, encounters a serpent. The serpent should be irrational but instead is capable of speech. It has obviously moved upward in the scale of being from brutish to rational. As Eve knows, such upward movement is implicit in all creation and part of the divine plan. What she does not know is that the serpent is lying. The conflict that Milton presents is therefore between the visible evidence—what is before Eve's eyes—which is all that reason has to work with, and a seemingly arbitrary prohibition from the invisible world. It is not a conflict between reason and passion, but between reason and faith, with reason on the side of the Serpent. Eve analyzes the situation quite rationally:

> In the day we eat
> Of this fair Fruit, our doom is, we shall die.
> How dies the Serpent? hee hath eat'n and lives,
> And knows, and speaks, and reasons, and discerns,
> Irrational till then.
>
> (762–67)

The prohibition appears to be an empty threat. If so man can rise in the scale of being and the commandment not to eat of the tree of knowledge must be a trick to keep him in subjection. Eve's fall, then, stems from excessive—not defective—reliance on reason.

I mean this quite seriously, and I believe that it is precisely the view which Milton wanted to project in the temptation episode. It is an appropriate view for *Paradise Lost* because the typical dilemma of Milton's seventeenth-century readers did not stem from the conflict of reason with passion, but the conflict of reason—especially scientific reason—with faith. To clarify this point, I return to the astronomy lesson given by Raphael to Adam in book 8.

At the beginning of the astronomy lesson Adam summarizes his conclusions about the machinery of the stars and planets. Having watched the sun rise and set, Adam reaches the obvious conclusion that it revolves around the earth. With this theory as his starting point he proceeds to make some rather derogatory remarks about God's celestial engineering. "Reasoning," he says—and the word *reasoning* is important here—"reasoning I oft admire / How Nature wise and frugal would commit / Such disproportions." He also critizes the "superfluous" numbers of stars, and wonders whether the stars do not move too rapidly in "restless revolution" while "the sedentary Earth, / That better might with far less compass move, / Serv'd by more noble than herself, attaines / Her end without least motion"(25–38). All in all, Adam is saying, it is a pretty sloppy contraption. Raphael is amused by Adam's speculations. He suggests—but does not insist—that Adam may have been deceived by appearances and that the sun rather than the earth may be the center of creation. Theories of astronomy aside, however, Raphael is by no means amused by Adam's criticism of divine engineering. This criticism verges on blasphemy because it implies that man is capable of improving on the workmanship of God. "Great / Or Bright infers not Excellence," says Raphael; "for Heav'n's wide Circuit, let it speak / The Maker's high magnificence" and "The swiftness of those Circles attribute, / Though numberless, to His Omnipotence" (90–115).

Raphael is saying two things. First, it is right and proper to speculate about visible Creation. When he had Raphael say this, Milton doubtless remembered his visit to the great Galileo, old and blind and a prisoner of the Inquisition, during his trip to Italy. Far from opposing the new astronomy, Milton considered Galileo a martyr for liberty of thought, and Raphael is no less liberal than Milton. Second, Raphael is saying that no matter where reason may lead, it should stop short of questioning truths which man must take on faith—here, the wisdom and perfect workmanship of the Creator. It is a real and powerful dilemma which Milton has posed—the eternal conflict between what we learn through reason, which always depends on limited knowledge, and what we are asked to accept on faith. The most remarkable aspect of the episode is that Adam chooses reason and the evidence of his senses and has to be rebuked by Raphael. Adam does not commit a sin at this point because he does not act on the basis of his false inferences. But he has wandered into an error which could easily lead to sin.

Adam's error is precisely the same as the one that Eve makes at the time of her Fall. Forced to choose between reason and faith, Adam and Eve employ reason. Both follow the evidence they can see rather than the apparently arbitrary truths of faith. Adam is corrected before his false reasoning leads him astray; Eve has no Raphael to assist her when she confronts the Serpent. Aside from this difference, both are shown by

Milton to be victims of limited human knowledge. Since Adam and Eve are equally prone to this kind of error, it is hardly logical to regard Eve's fall as evidence that she is rationally inferior to Adam.

V

What, then, do we do with "Hee for God only, Shee for God in him" and other, similar assertions of woman's inferiority to man? In view of the preceding analysis, I suggest that Milton cannot mean that Eve is irresponsible or deficient in reason. Instead, there must be some other basis for the inequality.

To carry this line of thought further, we need to return to Raphael's discourse on the hierarchy of being in book 5. During this discourse, Raphael makes a distinction, which was common in Renaissance philosophy, between two types of reason. One type he labels discursive, the other, intuitive:

> The soul
> Reason receives, and reason is her being,
> Discursive or intuitive; discourse
> Is oftest yours, the latter most is ours,
> Differing but in degree, in kind the same.
> (486–90)

That is, discursive reason is man's normal means of dealing with the visible world. At its best it is the reason of philosophy and science. Its materials are evidence and the rules of logic. Intuitive reason, conversely, can be defined as the direct perception of truth without evidence or analysis. It is the psychological label which Milton uses for the faculty that permits the range of experiences suggested by terms like "inspiration," "prophecy," and "the inner light." The truths which it perceives are truths of the invisible world which are, by definition, beyond the reach of discursive reason. Milton is seeking truth through intuitive reason, for instance, when he prays to his muse in book 3:

> So much the rather thou Celestial Light
> Shine inward, and the mind through all her powers
> Irradiate, there plant eyes, all mist from thence
> Purge and disperce, that I may see and tell
> Of things invisible to mortal sight.
> (51–55)

As Milton develops his portrait of Adam and Eve, he consistently attributes special knowledge of the invisible world to Adam. Most obviously, Adam instantly recognizes the goodness and omnipotence of God when he awakens after his creation, and shortly thereafter names the animals without instruction. He somehow intuits this knowledge, which he later expresses in discursive terms for Eve's benefit. A further suggestion of Adam's special intuitive ability is found in Milton's statement that he was formed for "contemplation . . . and valor." *Contemplation* was an ambiguous term during the Renaissance, but Milton's references to it in his other works show that like many of his contemporaries he associated it with efforts to achieve supraratational insight. By contrast, Eve tends to be interested in experience and observation. "Hee for God only, she for God in him" defines the difference between Adam and Eve as a difference in their intuitive capacity.

It may be paradoxical to think of the male as more intuitive and the female, (perhaps) more rational, but this seems to me to be the direction of Milton's thought. It is not a surprising direction for a man who believed that seers tended to be male—that the Prophets of the Old Testament and the great poets, from Homer on, were inspired, and who felt that he had, himself, received "nightly visitations" from the Celestial Muse. Furthermore, this reading satisfies two otherwise conflicting requirements that are intrinsic to *Paradise Lost.* It satisfies the hierarchial convention that requires Eve to be inferior to Adam. At the same time, it allows Milton to depict Eve as a fully rational being, "sufficient to have stood though free to fall."

In addition, the basis of Christian marriage for Milton is rational communism; that authority in marriage is a social necessity freely accorded and subject to rational disagreement; that Eve is as receptive as Adam to the pleasures of speculative thought; and that her error of trusting to reason rather than faith is one which Milton carefully attributes to Adam long before Eve's encounter with the Serpent. This, after all, is what we would expect from the author of the *Areopagitica:*

> Many there by that complain of divine providence for suffering Adam to Transgress. Foolish tongues! When God gave him freedom, he gave him freedom to choose, for freedom is but choosing; he had otherwise been a mere artificial Adam, such an Adam as he is in the motions. We ourselves esteem not of that obedience, or love, or gift which is of force.[5]

I will only add that Milton demanded the same freedom in marriage. Whatever his cultural conditioning, he accorded his Eve the same obligation as Adam to make rational choices, and the obligation carried with it the same responsibilities. Would we want things otherwise?

(unpublished)

Part 4

Understanding and Imagination

Politics and Beauty

Let us review the subject dispassionately. I agree that politics and beauty are frequently at odds. I agree further that politics is a way of making things happen while art is a way of making things, things which have their own mode of existence quite apart from politics. This is true even when works are influenced by overtly political motives, as seen, for example, in Edmund Spenser's *Faerie Queene* or Picasso's *Guernica.* I even agree—in fact, I affirm—that criticism of the arts should be aesthetic. It should be directed toward the things themselves. In the 1930s John Steinbeck was regarded as an author of novels of social protest. When the political issues of the depression lost their immediacy he was largely ignored. The current revival of his reputation dates from Peter Lisca's *The Wide World of John Steinbeck,* which approaches him as a literary artist. I believe, furthermore, that the distinction made by Jean-Paul Sartre in *What Is Literature* between poetry, by which Sartre means trivia, and literature, by which he means art committed to political reform, is badly mistaken. It is, in fact, a way of selling out to politics. Leon Trotsky, a politician, proclaimed, "Art is not a mirror; it is a hammer." Trapped in a century in which everything seems to boil down to the question "Which side are you on?" the artist must often exclaim with Shakespeare:

> How with this rage shall beauty hold a plea,
> Whose action is no stronger than a flower?

The classic illustration of the tension between politics and beauty is, of course, censorship. I suppose there is no kind of beauty that has not seemed threatening to the establishment at some time in history. Plato wanted to ban tragedy from the Republic because he was afraid it would breed effeminacy in the armed forces. The Arabs plastered over mosaics in liberated Christian churches because they considered religious images idolatrous. The Protestant armies of the Reformation smashed the stained glass windows of cathedrals, mutilated statues of the Blessed Virgin, and burned whole libraries of illuminated manuscripts for similar reasons. Music, except for national anthems and protest songs, would seem to be neutral, but it is not so. Not long ago the *People's Daily* of China informed its readers that Beethoven's seventeenth sonata "only serves to disseminate the filthy nature of the bourgeoisie." Poetry has always been a hot potato. Hence Osip Mandelstam's tribute to the Soviet

Union: "Poetry is honored only in this country—people are killed for it." The fact that Mandelstam died in a Soviet prison camp in 1935 for having written an epigram against Stalin lends weight to his remarks.

II

Having admitted all this and taken my stand with the artist, I confess that I am still not satisfied. The fact is that politics and beauty are related in many ways which the dichotomy between life and art is simply inadequate to explain.

In the first place beauty is, among other things, a social phenomenon. This means that art generates its own politics which is at least semi-independent of the politics of government. Take patronage. Traditionally patrons have been wealthy connoisseurs like Maecenas or Lorenzo de' Medici or Paul Getty. They have collected beautiful objects and they have endowed art galleries and libraries and public gardens for reasons that seem to them, at least, entirely benevolent. What could be less political than the Pierpont Morgan Library or the gardens of Dumbarton Oaks or the Vivian Beaumont Theatre at Lincoln Center? The only obvious motive behind such institutions is a generalized patriotism—a desire to enhance the quality of American life.

This, of course, is not the whole story. Patrons often commission works of art which have an explicit political message. Michelangelo was not paid to decorate the Sistine Chapel with anything that came into his mind but to create an overpowering blast of propaganda on behalf of Catholic Christianity. A modern equivalent of the Sistine Chapel would be the enormous murals by Diego Rivera on the walls of the Detroit Art Institute, which celebrate industry in general and the automotive industry in particular. Typically, this level of art is created by a strong, centralized, and conservative politics. The message is more important than the medium. In extreme cases, in the Soviet Union, for example, it is assumed that art which does not have an overt message is subversive. The imperial motto is "He who is not for me enthusiastically is against me." Hence the Soviet Union officially supports what it calls "socialist realism" and condemns abstraction and "art for art's sake." By contrast, patrons in pluralistic societies tend to be nervous about political statements. Diego Rivera's murals at Rockefeller Center made a statement but it was the wrong statement. They were painted over almost before they were dry. This is an argument for abstract art. The works of artists like Mies van der Rohe and Henry Moore and Jackson Pollock, for example, are pure form. Whatever the political views of their creators, the works themselves speak softly.

If we carry the analysis from the studio to the market place we encounter politics in a more typical form. Beauty is, among other things, a commodity. People speculate in art as they speculate in grain futures, and like the grain exchange the art market is subject to manipulation. The auction price of a single Matisse or a single first edition of *The Scarlet Letter* affects the value of every Matisse and every Hawthorne first edition throughout the world. When a museum pays a record price or makes a record appraisal of a donated Matisse, everyone who owns a Matisse becomes wealthier. This is a fact which is lost neither on art dealers nor on the art collectors who sit on museum boards. The academy is also involved in the politics of art. The fact that Matisse is a standard curriculum artist and Hawthorne a standard curriculum author helps to stabilize the market. It is also the foundation on which the publication of art books and school editions of the classics is based. Moreover, since it provides modest but intensely coveted livelihoods for scholars it has the effect of making university professors into a political constituency. Basic changes in the curriculum are resisted because they threaten people's jobs by making their skills obsolescent. The circle between the patron who invests in beauty, the teacher who makes his living by it, and the students who are programmed to respond to it is not perfect, but it exists.

Moving from the politics of art to the politics of government, the dichotomy between life and art often leads people to ignore the fact that governments devote a great deal more energy to encouraging beauty than to suppressing it. For every author whom it terminates, the Soviet Union supports thousands. If we take the United States as our example, the most obvious cases in point are the two National Endowments. The visible operating budget of the Endowments this year is around 150 million dollars. This is not very much by the standards of HEW, but it is sufficient to make the Endowments the largest direct patrons of the arts in America. By way of comparison, the Ford Foundation spends around 16 million annually on the arts and humanities. The enabling legislation of the Endowments insulates them from obvious political pressures, but the mere fact that they have to give away large amounts of money requires them to make decisions that have political aspects. Should they distribute grants evenly, for example, across all of the fifty states or should they support the urban centers where most artistic talent is located? Should they concentrate on well established artists and institutions or should they place their major emphasis on supporting new talent? Should they award grants through panels, and if so how should the panels be chosen? Or should they rely on a small number of advisers selected because of their taste or brilliance or social standing or ethnic background? These questions are political. They are complicated by the fact that the inborn imperative of every bureaucracy is to grow, and growth for the Endowments depends on their ability to persuade Congress and the White House that they are performing services which the voters want. The way the questions are answered has a direct bearing on who is supported for what, which is another way of saying that it has a direct bearing on the shape of beauty in America.

I began with the Endowments because they are highly visible. Actually the most important source of government money for the arts is the Internal Revenue Code. Under section 501 (c) 3, full deduction is permitted for contributions in cash or in kind to non-profit organizations like arts groups, museums, symphony societies, and certain theatre and opera guilds. Tax write-offs favor the wealthy, but they are also the bedrock on which most of the arts rest—especially the performing arts. To appreciate their importance consider the implications of one minor provision—the provision governing donations of personal manuscripts to libraries. Prior to 1969 authors could donate their literary manuscripts to libraries and deduct a fair appraisal from their taxable income. In 1969 this provision was cancelled because of the publicity surrounding the enormous write-off that Lyndon Johnson received when he donated his papers to the presidential library in Austin, Texas. With one well-known exception this pretty well ended the flow of official papers to American libraries. It also ended the flow of literary manuscripts. Today authors either keep their manuscripts or sell them to private collectors. To generalize from this instance, a few changes in the Internal Revenue Code could bring the whole structure of beauty in America down in ruins within a few months.

In addition to supporting the arts, politics regulates them. Copyright determines the rights of authors, publishers, and consumers. It is very much a political issue. For several years and without visible success Congress has been struggling to revise the American copyright law to bring it up to date with such developments as Xerox, tape recording, and cable television. Copyright also has international implications. Last year the Soviet Union agreed to recognize international copyright. This benefited American authors since it meant that they could collect royalties on Russian editions of their works. At the same time, however, it gave the Soviets the legal right to block foreign publication of Russian authors. In this case, instead of protecting authors, copyright might become a tool of censorship.

Other agencies are equally influential. Through its licensing authority the Federal Communications Commission determines the content of commercial radio and television. Its decisions can make the difference between a boxing match or a play by Shakespeare or a locally produced talk show on prime-time television. Again, the U.S. Customs Service determines whether a copy of *Ulysses* or *Lady Chatterly's Lover* can be brought into the country, while the State Department can admit the Bolshoi Ballet but deny a visa to Tornes Aleo, the Cuban film director whose "Memories of Underdevelopment" recently won the National Film Critics' award. Postage rates spell life or death for magazines. Minimum wage laws and airline passenger rates determine whether performing arts groups survive or go bankrupt. Meanwhile, commodity policies affect the cost of everything used to create beauty, from the paper on which books are printed to the petrochemicals used to make phonograph records to the silver used in photographic emulsions and the propane gas used in reduction firing of ceramics.

Examples could be extended indefinitely, but the point should already be obvious. Politics supports beauty directly and indirectly. It regulates beauty, and it touches, sometimes intentionally and sometimes by accident, every aspect of the lives of artists and every material from which beauty is created.

III

There is a second, more speculative side to my topic. If it is true that beauty cannot get along without politics, I suggest that there is a very real sense in which politics cannot get along without beauty.

You heard me correctly. I am not thinking of government grants or tax write-offs or regulating agencies. These are arbitrary. They come and go depending on factors like public taste, the state of the economy, and the influence of important lobbies. What I have in mind is an essential relation that has endured throughout the history of politics. It is difficult to describe this relation but I will try to be as clear and specific as possible.

To begin, we know that from the earliest periods of civilization the state has been a prime patron and a prime consumer of beauty. Our museums are filled with statues, mosaics, paintings, furniture, and ceremonial objects commissioned by forgotten despots to celebrate their governments and their presiding gods. Much that could not be carried off to the museums remains on location, especially in Egypt, the Near East, India, and Mexico. Much of Athens was created by the tyrant Peisistratus and his sons, while we owe the Parthenon to Pericles. Augustus Caesar found Rome brick and left it marble. Louis XIV devoted much of his life to the monstrous and many-faceted vulgarity of Versailles. Napoleon III rebuilt Paris, and Mussolini constructed the Foro Italico outside Rome because the city itself was already stuffed to capacity with monuments and buildings and works of art created by his predecessors. Moving from the visual arts to literature, Vergil's *Aeneid* was written to glorify imperial Rome and advertise the family clan of the Emperor. Tasso's *Jerusalem Liberated* glorifies the house of Este. In England, Shakespeare was able to ply his trade because his acting company was protected from the London Puritans by a succession of noble patrons culminating in James I. Not surprisingly, Shakespeare's history plays proclaim the divine right theory of monarchy and the legitimacy of the Tudor claim to England's throne and abound in lyric paroxysms which have been used ever since they were written to screw British patriotism to the sticking point.

Moving closer to home, the Library of Congress in Washington required the services of no less than fifty artists during the ten years of its construction, while the interior dome of the Capitol is covered by a 4,644-square-foot mural by Constantino Brumidi depicting the apotheosis of George Washington, a composition that earned Brumidi the title "Michelangelo of the Capitol."

The lesson to be drawn from these examples is that politics has an innate hunger—even a lust—for beauty. Part of this need is vanity, part is propaganda—what is called cultural imperialism; but to stop with vanity and propaganda is to miss the real point. After all, not all states are totally corrupt and not all artists who work for them are hacks. The basic need of politics is self-respect. It needs to think of itself as a useful, even a noble activity. I suggest that it symbolizes these aspirations in aesthetic terms. In *The Civilization of the Renaissance in Italy* Burckhardt devotes his first chapter to the idea of the state as a work of art. I think this is a universal idea—not merely a Renaissance idea—and that politics is driven to express it physically, through beautiful emblems, because it cannot create beauty directly in the relations of a real political system.

By way of illustration, consider two statements about the ideal state. The first is by John Quincy Adams, who was anything but an aesthete:

> We must learn the arts of war and independence so that our children can learn architecture and engineering so that their children may learn the fine arts and painting.

This is not a statement about government grants or tax write-offs. President Adams is asserting that if the American political experiment is successful the result will be a nation of artists dedicated not to politics but to beauty. This is another way of saying that beauty is the visible symbol of political success.

The second statement is the explanation which Socrates gives in the *Republic* of how to go about creating a perfect state:

> At present, I take it, we are fashioning the happy state, not piecemeal or with a view to making a few happy citizens, but as a whole. . . . Suppose that we were painting a statue and someone came up to us and said: "Why do you not put the most beautiful colors on the most beautiful parts of the body—the eyes ought to be purple, but you have made them black." To him we might fairly answer: "Sir, you would not, surely, have us beautify the eyes to such a degree that they are no longer eyes. Consider rather that by this and the other features which are their true property, we make the whole beautiful."

Notice that Socrates is speaking here as a politician, but cannot describe the object of politics without referring to beauty. This is more than a metaphor. In Socrates' statement the fundamental principles of the state are aesthetic—wholeness, appropriateness, and coherence—and the success of the state is evident through its aesthetic appeal: "we make the whole beautiful."

The *Republic,* as everyone knows, is a dream. Judged by the record of politics in the real world it is only slightly less preposterous than John Quincy Adams' hope that his grandchildren would all be artists. The problem is that it is a necessary dream. On the one hand, politics desperately needs to believe in itself—to have an object. Without an object politics degenerates into cheap opportunism. On the other hand, to take the object seriously is to become either a Don Quixote tilting at windmills or a tyrant. Medieval politics recognized this paradox and confronted it honestly. It located the ideal government in heaven. God, the archetypal ruler for the Middle Ages, is an incomprehensible Being, surrounded by a cloud of light so brilliant that to gaze on him is to go blind. Beneath his throne extends a euphoric bureaucracy of cherubim, seraphim, dominions, principalities and powers. These celestial bureaucrats not only lick the boots of those placed over them; even as they lick, they compose hymns of praise to their superiors. Shakespeare was recalling the medieval idea of the beautiful hierarchy when he had Ulysses remark, "Take but degree away, untune that string, and hark what discord follows." Note that the metaphor is aesthetic. The State is a work of art, a musical composition played on the lute of the class structure.

The point is that in the Christian tradition man is a fallen creature. He can imagine the beauty of the heavenly hierarchy, he can even imitate it in art, but he knows in advance he cannot achieve it. The idea of original sin kept medieval and Renaissance political theory sane at the same time that the transcendent ideal of politics permitted artists to work with the state rather than against it.

Since the Romantic period politics has tended to move along two divergent paths, both of which create problems for the artist. One kind of politics has insisted that the idea of the beautiful state is not a dream, that it is attainable here and now. Acting on this obsession, politicians have claimed the right to compose the state along aesthetic lines, ruthlessly eliminating what is extraneous to the aesthetic conception. As everyone knows, the result of this approach has been a series of unmitigated political disasters. Human beings have been asked to behave as though they were (or could be) objects in a painting, and when they have failed they have been destroyed. The beauty related to this kind of politics is a beauty divorced from humanity. It is a Madison Avenue beauty: posters of Hitler Youth yodeling their way through the Black Forest or ruddy-cheeked Stakhanovite workers oiling their flywheels at the Red Dawn locomotive plant. For artists it has posed a brutal set of alternatives. Join in the lie—and hence be false to beauty—or get out or die.

The other kind of politics that has emerged since the Romantic period has retained the idea of human imperfection and extended it to politicians. If even politicians are imperfect—if they have no mandate by birth or by a special relation to the gods—then it follows that they have no right to impose their dreams on others. The motto of this kind of politics is "Government is best when it governs least." There is no claim here to imitating the government of heaven. This kind of politics is simply a way to keep people from bumping into each other, as far as possible, while they follow their own devious paths to salvation. The idea of minimal government has a certain kind of beauty, but it is a beauty that is hard to express. If the beauty of medieval and Renaissance politics is borrowed from a celestial archetype, we would have to say that the beauty of democracy is immanent. It is the beauty which is realized at any given moment in the lives of real citizens. John Quincy Adams did not say what his grandchildren would be painting; he only said that if democracy were successful they would all be artists.

Clearly democracy poses special aesthetic problems. Throughout most of history, the beauty associated with politics has been an imperial beauty, a beauty glorifying authority. The emblems of imperial beauty celebrate the gods who protect the state, the rulers who are their visible instruments, and the offices and laws and ceremonies which rulers use to inject a measure of divine harmony into human affairs. The rulers of ancient Assyria are always depicted in the company of a resplendent winged disc representing the divine power of the living king. The Doges of Venice annually married the sea in a brilliant ceremony designed to insure good fishing and prosperous commerce. Medieval and renaissance monarchs were crowned at cathedrals to the chanting of choirs and laid to rest, when they died, by columns of uniformed men marching slowly to muffled drums while their immortal powers were transferred, as Kantorowicz has shown, to their successors through the emblems and symbols of the state. In short, the traditions of architecture, sculpture, and ceremony which the modern world has inherited are imperial traditions. Where, in the history of beauty, do we find an art to express the idea that government is best when it governs least?

Take the capital of the United States as an example. Whatever the success of beauty in Washington, it is obvious that a great deal of effort has been spent on trying to make Washington beautiful. Yet the characteristic architecture of Washington has little or no relation to American politics. The House and Senate office buildings, the Treasury Building and the Bureau of Archives, to take three examples, allude to Imperial Rome, not to Republican but to Imperial Rome. Other buildings raise still more intriguing questions. Why should Abraham Lincoln sit in a temple recalling the Parthenon rather than an enlarged Oval Room, say, or even a marble log cabin? Why should Thomas Jefferson stand under a dome borrowed from the Pantheon? Most curious of all, why should Congressmen descended from the dour fathers of Massachusetts Bay hold their debates in a building surmounted by a replica of the dome of St. Peter's Cathedral, which any seventeenth-century Puritan would identify instantly as the earthly home of the Antichrist, not to mention the seven-headed beast of Revelation and the Whore of Babylon?

The history of Washington is instructive here. If we say that, once the republic was founded, Americans were confronted by the challenge to create a beauty that expressed their idea of politics, we must immediately add that their initial response was to ignore the challenge. George Washington and Pierre L'Enfant labored mightily, but the major creation of the first fifty years of Washington's history was the White House, which did not even become white until it was repainted after the British tried to burn it down in 1814. As late as 1861 Horace Greeley described Washington as "a place of high rents, bad foods, disgusting dust, deep mud, and deplorable morals." This hardly suggests Babylonian splendor. Washington's streets were not paved until 1871, some two-thousand years after Rome began letting out paving contracts. The Capitol building was not completed until 1865; the Washington Monument, 1884; the Library of Congress, 1897. Most of the characteristic beauties of Washington, in fact, have been created in the twentieth century: the reflecting pool and Lincoln Memorial, 1920–22; the National Gallery, 1941; the Kennedy Center, 1970. I mention the National Gallery and the Kennedy Center not so much for their beauty as structures as for the beauty which they contain—the beauty of painting and drama and music, the portable and transient arts being just as important for the life of a great capital as buildings and monuments.

The explanation for the slow progress of beauty in Washington is the difficulty of the aesthetic problem. How *do* you express artistically the idea that government is best when it governs least? In fact, the most authentic current in American art of the Federal period has nothing to do with the imperial tradition. It is a genteel pastoralism that is evident in the agrarian imagery running through Jefferson's letters, in the painting of the Hudson River School, and in the novels of James Fenimore Cooper. This art does not depict man in relation to politics but in full flight from it. The natural expression of this aesthetic was to ignore the capital city—to leave it to wilderness.

There are, however, a few expressions of beauty in Washington that seem to come to grips with the problem. I will cite two quite different examples. The first is obvious. Rock Creek Park is a tract of relatively uncontaminated woodland running through the center of Washington. It was created for the express purpose of permitting citizens to fly from the benevolence of their government into nature. This is simply an attempt to preserve the Hudson River aesthetic in the midst of a great city. My second example is not so obvious and I offer it very tentatively. I am thinking of the Washington Monument. Being entirely abstract, the Washington Monument expresses nothing but itself. This gives it a kinship with the abstract art encouraged by twentieth-century pluralism, and with numerous other buildings in Washington that make no statement at all, or, if they do, express themselves in gruff monosyllables—the Government Printing Office, the Pentagon, the Museum of History and Technology. Are the Washington Monument and the Pentagon nonentities or do they express something deeply rooted in American traditions? The American sculptor Horatio Greenough wrote, "The obelisk has to my eye a singular form and character. . . . It says but one word. But it speaks it loud. If I understand this voice, it says 'Here.'" Clearly, Greenough felt the Washington Monument was aesthetically successful. Even as I quote him, however, I admit that "Here" is an ominous word for a politics based on the idea that government is best when it governs least. It is a monosyllable, but perhaps it is the wrong monosyllable. Perhaps it is the monosyllable that calls into being the vast network of roads that all lead ultimately back to Rome. Senator Taft is memorialized in Washington by a bell tower set in a grove of trees. L. B. J. will evidently be remembered by a grove of trees without even a bell tower. If a grove of trees says anything it says "This is not Washington."

The special problem of democracy and beauty aside, I hope I have said enough to illustrate my thesis. We have known since Plato's *Republic* that politics seeks a transcendent beauty. It symbolizes this beauty by creating beautiful emblems—the monuments and buildings and arts and ceremonies that adorn its cities and celebrate its ideals. At the same time, we know that politics is bound to fail. Most of our grandchildren will be GS-13 administrators, not artists. But the hope that they will be more than hollow men is too important to be allowed to languish, and beauty sustains this hope. Say that politics in the real world is a way of coming to terms with the impossible. If so, beauty is a way of keeping the impossible sufficiently urgent so that politics cannot ignore it.

IV

A concluding point. When politics creates beauty it does so for a particular reason. It wants to use beauty for its own ends, as, for example, Augustus wanted Vergil to prop up his imperial pretensions. Beauty, however, is protean. It has its own life which is larger than the uses it is asked to serve. Whatever the immediate purpose of the *Aeneid*, for example, its significance today is its achievement as a work of art; and this brings us back to matters which are entirely aesthetic.

If politics seeks to define and contain human experience, beauty tells us that all such attempts are inadequate because they leave out more than they include. Although we cannot avoid signing a social contract, beauty keeps reminding us how much of our humanity we surrendered when we signed it. In this sense beauty saves politics from itself. It is not only an adornment of the state and a symbol of the transcendent goal of politics, it is also an assertion that the human spirit is larger than any political system. The Greeks admired the *Republic* but they loved the *Iliad* because they found their deepest identity in Homer's portraits of Agamemnon and Paris and Andromache. The Roman Empire lasted four centuries, but it was Vergil, not Augustus, who survived to lead Dante through the nine circles of the Inferno.

The current tendency to reduce art to the dogmas of politics is even more unfortunate for politics than it is for beauty. Beauty has a political lesson of its own to teach. That lesson is "hang loose"—respond to each experience in its own terms. This does not mean that we should be indifferent, even to political issues. Rather it means that we should trust our humanity before we trust our politicians. It is a lesson that is well worth thinking about today, especially if, as many of us believe, we have come to the end of one political road and will soon be forced to look for a new and, one hopes, more human one to replace it.

I end with a quotation from Friedrich Schiller's *Letters on the Aesthetic Education of Man* which fairly summarizes my own thought on the subject. Having lived through the euphoria of the Rights of Man and seen it degenerate into the Reign of Terror, Schiller ruefully concluded: "We will never solve the problem of politics except through the problem of the aesthetic, for it is only through beauty that man makes his way to freedom."

(1975)

Dada, the Poetry of Nothing, and the Modern World

The artist is a human being like the rest of us. He cannot solve these problems [of modern life] except as one of us; but through his art he can help us see and understand them, for artists are the sensitive antennae of society.

—ALFRED H. BARR JR., *What Is Modern Painting?*

This essay is excerpted from a study of the nature of identity in technological culture. Here I am examining a paradox inherent in certain kinds of twentieth-century poetry—that although such poetry is presented in natural languages or apparent derivations from natural languages, it seems to reject the function for which natural languages exist, the communication of meaning. It is a poetry of nothing.

To many people this poetry seems bizarre, flippant, even insulting. I will therefore begin with an attempt to place it in the context of other, related aspects of twentieth-century culture, and I will conclude with a few suggestions about its larger significance.

In the quotation from *WHAT IS MODERN PAINTING?* Alfred Barr asserts that the function of art is to help us "see and understand" the problems of modern life. Since Barr is dealing with visual art, he uses the verb *see* literally as well as in the figurative sense illustrated by the sentence "I see what you mean."

His assertion appears to be a tautology. "I see what you mean" is normally identical with "I understand what you mean." In an important sense, however, Barr's sentence is not a tautology. Seeing is perceptual and understanding is cognitive. The *seeing* that art makes possible, whether the art is visual or verbal, is of a specific moment in the spiritual life of the artist. The moment includes both interior and exterior elements that are fused in the unity of consciousness. The exterior elements are not simply things and the interior elements are not simply emotions. Every experience is the product of both. Each experience is subjective in that it can only occur in the consciousness of the person who has it; but it is objective in that it can legitimately be called an objectification in the mind of the data the mind has synthesized. The experience becomes objective in the common sense of the term—in the sense of being publicly available—when it is expressed in a medium such as musical notes or paint or words on a page. The medium enables it to be communicated to others. To communicate effectively the artist needs talent, but he also draws on languages—whether verbal or visual or musical—that are appropriate to his purpose. For the most part such languages are available ready-made from tradition. They need only to be creatively adapted to the special circumstances of the experience to be communicated. On the other hand, if the available languages are out of phase with what the artist has experienced, his task becomes extremely difficult. He must, in effect, invent a new language or remain silent. Benjamin Lee Whorf describes this problem as it relates to the new physics of the early twentieth century:

> Modern thinkers have long since pointed out that the so-called mechanistic way of thinking has come to an impasse before the great frontier problems of science. To rid ourselves of this way of thinking is exceedingly difficult when we have no linguistic experience of any other, and when our most advanced logicians and mathematicians do not provide any other—and obviously they cannot without the linguistic experience. In the mechanistic way of thinking is perhaps just a type of syntax natural to Mr. Everyman's daily use of the western Indo-European languages, rigidified and intensified by Aristotle and the latter's medieval and modern followers—"Language and Logic"(1942)

Once an art work has been created, there are two ways of understanding it. The first is the sharing or appreciation of the work. The second is the critical understanding that results from formal analysis. The first type of understanding, the sharing, is absolute. If we appreciate a work of art, we appreciate it whether or not we can explain why. In fact many people resent being asked to explain why, a point illustrated by the familiar complaint "We murder to dissect." The second type of understanding, the analytic, is not absolute. Its validity depends on theories and methods that are contingent. Since no one is omniscient, theories and methods are necessarily contingent. Criticism can never provide definitive answers to the questions it asks—only the best answers possible given the state of the art of criticism at the time the answers are sought.

To say that a work of art helps us see and understand contemporary experience is to say that it helps us understand experience in the absolute sense of sharing and in the contingent sense of providing objects of analysis that lead to probable conclusions. The difference between the two kinds of seeing is the difference between reading a novel or watching a television dramatization for enjoyment, and subjecting that novel or dramatization to critical analysis to find out why it is effective or what it has to say about things that interest us, like psychology or ethics or economics or history or basket weaving.

Because art begins in the consciousness of a particular artist at a particular moment in time, works of art differ from one another. Works of art from the same culture and same period of history tend to share underlying characteristics that can be summed up as a period style. The similarities of works of art by the same artist constitute a personal style.

A final but important point is that a work of art can be a valid expression of experience whether or not the artist is fully conscious of the elements being objectified. For the most part artists are *not* conscious of all the elements they express in their work. Dramatists were excellent psychologists long before Sigmund Freud, and musicians did very well for centuries even though they had little or no knowledge of acoustics. Art is created not by specialists in specific areas of knowledge but by artists. When Hart Crane wrote his great poem "The Brooklyn Bridge," he made no pretense of understanding the high technology that allowed John Augustus Roebling to create the structure. The poem is nevertheless a useful source of information about the human significance of Roebling's technology. Occasionally, of course, the artist does draw on specialized knowledge, including scientific knowledge. One thinks of Leonardo's knowledge of anatomy, of Alexander Pope's use of Newton in his *Essay on Man,* of Audubon's paintings of birds, of Eugene O'Neill's debt to Freud in *Mourning Becomes Electra.*

I

Modern art emerged with stunning suddenness in Western culture between 1890 and 1915. Various antecedents of the modernist movement in art can be found much earlier than 1890, but they can be recognized as such only in retrospect: they seemed at the time of their appearance to be variations on accepted norms or eccentric deviations from those norms. What happened between 1890 and 1915 defined a new norm of modern culture that we are still struggling to understand.

If art expresses states of consciousness, the new art expresses a new state of consciousness. This new state was manifested at first in the work of a few individuals working in quite different media who were especially sensitive to changes that had been occurring in the culture around them. Their sensitivity is reflected in the radical break that they made with prior traditions. They realized that the languages they had inherited were inadequate to the reality they were experiencing, and they were forced to invent new languages.

That a radical cultural change occurred in the early twentieth century is a commonplace. Frequently this change is associated with the first world war, a position illustrated in Paul Fussell's brilliant *The Great War and Modern Memory.* The first world war was unquestionably a cultural watershed. The change that it publicized had, however, occurred before it began. The war did not cause change so much as it exposed the inadequacy of traditional values and demonstrated in the most sensational terms possible how far the change had progressed. The change is especially dramatic in three areas of culture: science, visual art, and literature.

Freud's *Interpretation of Dreams* (1900) was part of the change, but the decisive change in science occurred in physics, not psychology—in the work of such figures as Maxwell, Rutherford, Planck, Bohr, and Einstein. It can be dated symbolically by the publication date—1905—of Einstein's papers on special relativity, mass-energy equivalence, Brownian motion, and the photon theory of light. After this decisive moment the time-honored mechanistic view of Nature was no longer tenable. The external world was still there, but it had lost its comforting solidity and uniformity. In fact relativity had far more radical implications than the introduction of heliocentric astronomy in the Renaissance. If the heliocentric system undermined time-honored religious beliefs, it also vindicated the power of human reason and the rationality of Nature. Relativity, conversely, appeared to set limits to rational knowledge and to unsettle Nature herself. It was as though mankind had been lifted out of a secure two-bedroom house and dropped without warning into a hall of mirrors in an amusement park. Einstein's theory was ridiculed, misrepresented, and ignored, even by some scientists; but for those who understood Einstein it was the beginning of a new era, and, as Whorf points out, that theory demanded new modes of thought and a new language to express them.

In the visual arts a different kind of change was occurring, a change reflected in the movement in painting and sculpture from representation to abstraction. The movement was foreshadowed by the construction of the Eiffel Tower for the Paris Exposition of 1889. The Eiffel Tower, a pure form, makes no bow to past history through fluted columns or pointed arches or statues in niches. Its form expresses nothing but its technology, and in this respect it anticipates the work of the Bauhaus after World War I. The statement made by the Eiffel Tower was, however, ambiguous, because the tower did not insist on being regarded as a work of art. It could be dismissed as an overgrown gadget, a curious picturesque landmark against which tourists like to be photographed.

If we are concerned with a change of consciousness in art rather than a change of the culture that surrounded the artists, the best symbolic date is

1907, the date of Picasso's *Les Demoiselles d'Avignon.* This painting is not quasi art like the Eiffel Tower, but explicitly and self-consciously high art. It demands to be seen as well as noticed. What it states when it *is* seen is that art has discovered a new language. The message was obviously timely. Picasso was soon joined by a group of artists that included Kandinsky, Marinetti, Braque, Duchamp, Brancusi, and Mondrian, among many others.

Each of the avant-garde artists of the early twentieth century had a unique personality and a unique style. Most of them influenced one another; a few acted as independently, apparently, as Newton and Leibniz did in discovering calculus. When the artists cited influences outside the world of painting that affected their work, these ranged across the whole landscape of their culture: primitive African and Iberian art, disgust with philistinism, hatred of class oppression, Einstein's relativity, Freud's psychology, industrial technology, and others. All of these influences were undoubtedly operative. They were symptoms of radical cultural change, and they intensified the pressure on traditional forms of consciousness. But it now appears that the chief influences on the new art came from within the world of art itself, just as the chief influences on the creation of the new physics came from physics. While physics was creating a new scientific language, art was thus, more or less simultaneously and independently, creating a new visual language.

Whorf's observation that the new physics requires a new language should not be taken to mean that one can discover simple correlations between the languages of modern science and the languages of modern art. It does point to the general tendencies that the new languages share: in becoming abstract, modern painting rejected the traditional and personal elements that had characterized Western art from the Renaissance to the nineteenth century. In theory a perfectly abstract painting can be as free of tradition and personality, if its maker wants it to be, as a circle or a triangle or a randomly curving line. Indeed modern art has sometimes consciously used randomness to break away from the traditional and personal associations that the artist carries in his subconscious—as, for example, the aleatory music of John Cage, the paintings of Jackson Pollock, and both computer music and computer drawing.

The corollary of abstraction is universality. A painting of a scene such as appears in "The Rest on the Flight from Egypt," for example, is immediately recognizable—hence transparent—to a Western European but opaque to a viewer who is not familiar with the Bible; while a Chinese calligraphic painting is opaque to Western viewers, who cannot read the words although they may admire the flow of the lines. Because abstract art is—in this sense—not the property of a single artist or nation or culture, it is, like geometry, everyone's property. If it comments on anything, it comments on the way perception is shaped by the world; and if it imitates anything, it imitates the forms and categories of spiritual life.

In literary history Baudelaire, Verlaine, and Rimbaud occupy a place roughly analogous to that of the impressionists in painting. A possible symbolic date for the appearance of a new form of literary consciousness in Western culture is 1897, when Stéphane Mallarmé's poem *Un coup de dés* (*A Throw of the Dice*) was published.

Un coup de dés by no means breaks as radically from the past as the Eiffel Tower does. It is quite radical, however, in relation to literary tradition, which tends to be more conservative than technology, if only because it is oriented toward natural language, which is innately conservative. The poem embodies the culmination of a theme that is present in many of Mallarmé's earlier works and that may be labeled "the difficulty of writing." In enacting this theme on the page, the poem becomes the record of an intense struggle to overcome silence—to discover a poetic language that can express the reality of a world ruled by chance and ordered only by arbitrary acts of the mind.

Mallarmé's solution is a language that is fragmented and kaleidoscopic. The moods it evokes change so rapidly that they can hardly be glimpsed before they dissolve. But the words are only part of the expression. The pages (and, in editions that conscientiously follow Mallarmé's printing instructions, units of two pages) become part of the expression rather than a neutral ground for the black letters formed by the type. Words are sometimes written sequentially, sometimes arranged in falling order, and sometimes separated by page-sized blank spaces. Lines are printed in headline type, in small capitals, in lowercase, and in both headline and small italics. On the last two-page unit a reference to a constellation is reinforced by a word arrangement that echoes the shape of Ursa Major. The poem thus looks forward to the experiments of dada with randomness and the experiments of concrete poets with forms of expression that are visual as well as verbal.

The subject of the poem is randomness, a throw of the dice. The world has no meaning, but the mind endlessly imposes order on it by arbitrary acts resembling throws of dice. The blank expanse of the page becomes a visual representation of the sea. Meaning is created on the page by the progression of the words that literally express the victory of the poet over silence, and in the poem by the idea of a journey, even though it is probably a trip to nowhere. The poet struggles for meaning, falls back exhausted, and then begins the struggle again. Near the end of the poem there is a constellation—a destination—but it is infinitely distant, perhaps a myth. Beginning with the title, the phrases in capital letters march through several pages like a dominant voice: "A THROW OF THE DICE . . . NEVER . . . WILL ELIMINATE . . . CHANCE." The poem ends on the same note: "Toute Pensée émet un Coup de Dés": "All thought causes a throw of the dice."

The search of twentieth-century poets for verbal languages adequate to experience is as fascinating and as complicated as the search of painters for new visual languages. In three literary movements the search moves beyond the point defined by Mallarmé's *Un coup de dés* to extremes that are analogous to abstraction in art.

These movements—dada, concrete poetry, and algorithmic poetry—are related by a common tendency to treat natural language as a potentially transparent, hence universal, medium. Since all natural languages are geographically localized and historically conditioned in their phonetics, lexical meanings, grammars, and literary forms, the tendency seems to distort language in ways that do not apply to painting, sculpture, dance, and music. Unlike these media, language is supposed to convey meaning. When it is pushed by various strategies toward transparency, it loses its capacity to convey meaning as that term is usually understood. The language is new, but it is also impossible to understand. This is a paradox, but it is not necessarily a frivolous one. If a truly new language were invented, it would initially be incomprehensible to everyone but its inventor. The paradox thus calls attention to certain aspects of the crisis of modern consciousness that are more evident in literature than in painting and sculpture. This, in one sense, is the meaning of the poetry of nothing—its way, to quote Alfred Barr once again, of helping us "see and understand" experience.

II

Am I not a soluble fish? Since I was
born under the sign of Pisces and man
is soluble in his own thought.

—ANDRÉ BRETON

Since Francis Bacon's *Advancement of Learning* it has been recognized that there is a tension between science and natural language. Science attempts to be universal, while natural language is local. Science also seeks to be arbitrary in the sense of depending on logic rather than on myth or religion or tradition. It will go wherever its logic takes it. Language, on the other hand, is not arbitrary. We inherit our language: we do not create it. As we learn it, it shapes our consciousness. We accept it passively—its phonetics, its grammar, its syntax, its idioms. It is natural, a given, and what is natural is the opposite of what is arbitrary.

Because each human mind is formed by a natural language, which, in turn, is a vehicle of the history of a specific culture, the achievement of true arbitrariness in thought and expression is extremely difficult. Although we live in an unconventional world, we are always being trapped into the conventional by the association of ideas forced on us by language. The way out of the trap is to destabilize normal linguistic processes by imposing nonlinguistic rules on them. The most effective rules will be entirely arbitrary—hence random. Randomness is therefore a recurrent theme in efforts to create a linguistic art comparable to abstract art. It is also an element—though a less significant one—in efforts to break away from traditional modes of visual and auditory representation; to break away, for example, from imitative habits in painting and traditional melodies, scales, and rhythms in music.

To be transparent a natural language would have to be equally intelligible to all readers or listeners. No natural languages can begin to meet this condition. Natural languages become increasingly transparent as they are imposed on ever larger geographical areas by imperialism or a melting-pot philosophy; but, so far in history, imperialism has tended to create resentment that has eventually halted the spread of every natural language. This is evident in the history of Greek, Arabic, Chinese, Spanish, French, English, and Russian.

To spread easily, a language should be neutral and should be equally convenient for all societies. Historically the closest approximation of this limited kind of transparency in the Western world has been medieval Latin. By the time Latin became the universal language of the establishment in medieval Europe it had ceased to be spoken by any of the peoples who used it. It was a dead language, hence an arbitrary choice. It achieved transparency within its limited geographic region largely because the culture that had produced it had disappeared. Belonging to nobody, it suddenly belonged to everybody. By the same token it had ceased to be a natural language. It had to be taught, much as mathematics is taught today. When learned, it became the passport to entry into an international elite whose culture was different in kind from all the local cultures it administered.

The nineteenth century brought a wave of enthusiasm for what Tennyson, in *Locksley Hall,* called "the Parliament of Man, the Federation of the World." Since there was no possibility of reviving Latin in the Age of Telegraphy, efforts turned to the creation of a synthetic language. One group of theorists argued that the invented language should be completely arbitrary—that is, its vocabulary, grammar, and phonetics should be made up out of whole cloth. An arbitrary language could be made far more logical and consistent than any natural language and would therefore have a high degree of transparency. Among the arbitrary languages that were created on this basis are *Lingua humana* (1873), *Blaia* (1884), *Cabe abaca* (1887), *Zahlensprache* (1901), *Ro* (1904), and *Solresol* (1917)—the latter based on the musical scale. Languages of this sort have the advantage of being equally accessible to anyone who wants to learn them. For example, in theory *Solresol* should be as easy for an Indonesian to learn as for a European. At the same time, however, arbitrary languages have the disadvantage—which proved fatal—of having no constituency. Since no one has any stake in them, no one is willing to invest much energy in them. The alternative is a language that is artificial but not arbitrary. The best-known and most nearly successful language of this type is *Esperanto*. It was created in 1887 by a Russian physician, L. L. Zamenhof. It is based on Indo-European—chiefly romance—vocabulary and grammar. By the time the Esperanto movement had reached its climax, the League of Nations had endorsed it, forty-four radio stations were offering regular Esperanto broadcasts, one-hundred Esperanto journals were being published, and some five-thousand books had been translated into it. Interest in the movement was further stimulated by various plans to improve on Dr. Zamenhof's original: *Ido*, a simplified Esperanto, in 1907, followed by *Antido I, Antido II, Lingvo Esperanto,* and *Nov-Esperanto*. Meanwhile internationalists who were dissatisfied with Esperanto created a group of languages based on simplified Latin: *Latinesce, Nov-Latin, Monario, Europan, Romanal,* and *Interlingua*.

The first requirement of a universal synthetic language is that it be easy to learn. Zamenhof interpreted this requirement in terms of Western European languages. The result was a language with a minimum of inflections, a romance syntax, and a vocabulary as rich as possible in romance, germanic, and slavic cognates. Esperanto was a notable effort, but it was never successful. Today Latin is still taught in a dwindling number of schools, but—outside of a small circle of diehards—Esperanto is a memory.

Any use of the phonetics or vocabulary or grammar or literary conventions of a natural language makes a universal language opaque. Even if it had been fully successful, Esperanto would have been transparent only within the area of the western European family of languages from which its grammar and vocabulary were drawn. In theory pure nonsense words should be transparent because they are equally unintelligible to everyone, unless, by accident, a word that is nonsense in 4,999 of the world's languages happens to be the name for *glaucoma* in the 5,000th. But what looks good in theory turns out to be unworkable in practice. In creating nonsense words, the mind follows the patterns of its natural language. A German or a Czech or a Japanese or an English nonsense word tends to sound German or Czech or Japanese or English because of its phonemes and syllabification. The alternative is to create a language of randomly chosen sounds. Even sounds, however, conspire to meaning, because when uttered they tend to follow the patterns of elementary literary forms—lament, expression of joy, satisfaction, and the like—with the further qualification that these literary forms tend to be specific to individual language groups and may be quite unintelligible beyond them. On the other hand, if the sounds can be combined as well as selected by a random process, they will have no culturally determined form and hence should be perfectly transparent.

At least when uttered. When they are printed, a whole new range of problems arises, because some alphabets are phonetic and others are ideographic. Printing sounds in a Roman alphabet localizes them just as much as printing them in Chinese ideographs. The perfectly transparent printed poem would be in an alphabet as randomly created—and hence as unintelligible—as the sounds themselves.

This line of thought leads to a dead end, revealing the fact that all natural languages are irrevocably tied to history and that the idea of escaping from this history is an illusion. The only way to escape completely is to compose unintelligible, randomly selected sounds in an alphabet that has never been used, which is equivalent to abandoning natural language for an entirely arbitrary language that no one can understand.

The history of efforts to create transparent language is therefore a history of compromise. It is intriguing and probably highly significant that the first self-conscious efforts to create nonsense occurred during the rise of industrialism and that the most successful English poet in this vein was a mathematician who wrote under a pseudonym and had a fondness for small girls. Lewis Carroll's solution to the problem of nonsense was to introduce nonsense words into otherwise conventional English sentences. This practice reduces even the limited transparency of the nonsense. The coined words become vehicles of grammatical meaning. That is, even though they have no lexical meaning, they become, in context, recognizable subjects, objects, verbs, adjectives, and the like for the reader who is familiar with English. The point is illustrated by this stanza from Carroll's poem "Jabberwocky":

> And as in uffish thought he stood,
>   The Jabberwock, with eyes of flame,
> Came whiffling through the tulgey wood,
>   And burbled as it came!

Although we cannot say exactly what a Jabberwock is, we know it is a noun singular, subject of *came*. But we know more. Because the poem in which this stanza occurs is based on the conventional medieval literary form of the knightly quest, we conclude that the Jabberwock is a monster that has to be slain by the hero. We know too that the Jabberwock inhabits a tulgey wood. It has the characteristics of an animal, and its whiffles and burblings are both sinister and delightful. They reinforce the literary convention and the parody.

"Jabberwocky" is amusing, but the humor would be lost on a Japanese reader. A perfectly transparent language must be emptied of all associations with natural and local languages. Its poetry should be, we might say, a poetry of nothing, as devoid of meaning as the abstractions of a randomly instructed program on a computer.

Is this possible in language? In various ways the search for a transparent poetry has been carried on since the early twentieth century with full consciousness of the objective. Mallarmé sensed both the objective and the difficulty of achieving it. In *Un coup de dés* the need of the human mind for pattern is opposed to the meaninglessness of reality. The true meaninglessness of the world threatens to overwhelm the mind, but the mind stubbornly and heroically throws the dice again and imposes another randomly selected pattern on the emptiness of the world.

Three movements in contemporary poetry illustrate the impulse to carry the ideal of transparency beyond Mallarmé—dada, concrete poetry, and algorithmic poetry. These movements are fascinating because they seem to fly in the face of the characteristics of natural languages. They are as instructive in their failures as in their successes, and their successes, though not immediately obvious, are by no means insignificant.

Dada is the most widely known of these movements. Although it achieves a high degree of transparency while still using words from natural languages, it appears incapable of making statements about the human condition that could be considered significant. *Appears* is the right word here, because dada may be expressing something that we can still understand only imperfectly—namely how the mind is isolated in technological society from the comforts and sacred values of history. If so, dada expresses the movement of humanity out of Nature and toward the habitat of scientific universals. Another possibility, which seems to accord more with the nature of natural languages, is that dada is doomed to failure from the start. To ask a natural language to embody the experience of a technological society may be like asking earth to symbolize fire.

The key to dada is randomness. Achieving randomness, however, is more difficult than it sounds. In certain areas of high technology randomness is essential. Consequently the subject has been explored in depth. All simple approaches to randomness produce patterns. A typical method of constructing a dada poem, for example, is cutting up phrases or words from a newspaper, stirring them in a hat, and pasting them on a piece of paper in the order in which they are withdrawn. Obviously the words come from a natural language, and it is equally obvious that, being printed, they are in a visual medium (the Roman alphabet) that is opaque rather than transparent. Even if we ignore these objections, we still confront the fact that the words are an inadequate—hence biased—statistical sample of the words in the natural language of the journal from which they were clipped. They are not arbitrary. They reflect the personal idiosyncrasies of the audience to which they were directed, the state of the language at the time when the article was written, and the like. These are all determined by history. An article on the culture of grapes from a French newspaper published in 1880, for example, will use a vocabulary different from the one in an article on the same subject published in 1980. Words clipped from an issue of *Time* will have a different bias from words clipped from an article in the *Rolling Stone* of the same year. Alternate strategies for achieving randomness have other defects. Decisions about word choice might be made by flipping a coin or throwing dice in the manner of Mallarmé's poem. But coins and dice are biased and become more so as they are used because of wear. Perfect randomness is therefore an ideal that can be approached but never attained. These facts are remote from everyday experience and probably irrelevant to dada, but they form a wall around all efforts to achieve transparency in language and are therefore worth noting.

Dada originated in Zurich in 1916. According to the most common account the word was found by inserting a paper-knife in the pages of an uncut Larousse dictionary of French and German. When the page was opened, the point of the knife was found to be resting on the mysterious and pregnant word *dada*. Literary historians have interpreted the word in a variety of ways: sociological, political, psychological, and the like. In *Dada* (1961) Willy Verkauf, for example, claims that it was a movement to protest the "senseless mass murder" of the first world war, and "the hectic outcry of the tormented creature in the artist, of his prophetic, admonishing, tormented conscience." This is impressive rhetoric, but it seems completely out of key with the accounts which Tristan Tzara, the founder of the movement, gives of the playful atmosphere in which dada was born. The same point may be made of Hans Knutter's suggestion that dada was a form of infantile regression from the horrors of the adult world, as well as of the commonplace assertion that dada was motivated by a perverse desire by artists to upset the complacent middle class (*épater la bourgeoisie*).

Tristan Tzara claims that the basic attraction of the word was that it had no meaning. It meant nothing, and nothing is the true subject of dada. In his *Dada Manifesto* of 1918 Tzara attacked the ideologues who were trying to impose conventional literary values on the movement: It is "a word that means nothing. . . . [But] the first thought that occurs to these people is bacteriological in origin: to find its etymological or at least its historical or psychological origin. We see by the papers that the Kru Negroes call the tail of a holy cow Dada. The cube and the mother in a certain district of Italy are called Dada. A hobby horse and a nurse both in Russian and Rumanian: Dada. Some learned journalists regard it as an art for babies." All these efforts to attach dada to history contradict the basic intention of its founders.

Nothing is used by Tzara not to mean nihilism—a bitter and frequently despairing rejection of traditional values—but to affirm the liberating power of the arbitrary. In becoming "nothing" poetry escapes the trap of history—of ideology, of flaccid poetic diction, of tired canons of beauty, and the like—and can thus become anything. A perfectly transparent poem can become everything simply because it is not tied to one specific meaning. A Rorschach inkblot is not nihilistic in the normal sense of that term; like dada it is simply nothing. Its lack of meaning is its value. The viewer fills it with the content of his or her own subconscious, just as the Eiffel Tower manages to be all things to all men by virtue of its freedom from historically defined architectural forms.

Shortly after being "discovered," dada moved to Paris, where it attracted the interest of poets and artists like Marcel Duchamp, Man Ray, André Breton, Paul Éluard, Louis Aragon, Erik Satie, Jean Arp, Francis Picabia, and others. Significant relations developed between the dadists and the Futurist and Cubist painters who were seeking new forms of visual expression. Verkauf sees the Paris period as decadent and claims, against all evidence, that dada was opposed to abstract art. This appears, like much else in Verkauf, to be the reflection of a political bias in favor of art that makes strong social statements. At any rate the dada coalition was always a loose one. In the 1920s it dissolved. Some of the dadists followed Aragon into the communist party, and others followed Breton into French surrealism.

Eugene Jolas claims to have invented one of the purest and most translucent forms of dada, the sound poem. He explains it:

> I invented a new species of verse, "verse without words", or sound poems. . . . I had a special costume designed for it. My legs were covered with a cothurnus of luminous blue cardboard, which reached up to my hips so that I looked like an obelisk. . . . I recited the following:
>
> gadja beri bimba
> glandridi lauli lomni cadori
> gadjaimo bim beri glassala
> glandridi glassala tuffm i zunbrabism.
>
> . . . We should withdraw into the innermost alchemy of the word, and even surrender the word, in this way conserving for poetry its sacred domain.

Rudolf Klein attributes this poem and the comment on it to Hugo Ball, proprietor of the Cabaret Voltaire in Zurich where dada began. Whether the author was Jolas or Ball, the poem clearly illustrates the limits of transparency even when all natural words have been abandoned. Its phonetic values and regularities suggest a Western European imitation of an unknown African language. In spite of this defect, however, it represents a completely logical solution to the problem of linguistic transparency.

The master of the sound poem was Kurt Schwitters, who once composed a whole sound sonata in four movements. A more concise example of his art is *W*, a poem of one letter. Moholy-Nagy, who achieved international fame as a member of the Bauhaus, describes Schwitters's recitation of the poem as follows: "He showed the audience a poem containing only one letter on a sheet: *W*. Then he started to 'recite' it with slowly rising voice. The consonant varied from a whisper to the sound of a wailing siren till at the end he barked with a shockingly loud tone."

Moholy-Nagy regards this recitation as a lament for the horrors of the first world war. Schwitters, however, was apparently nonpolitical and more interested in language than in trench warfare. But pure abstraction often has deep religious or instinctual connotation. Moholy-Nagy uses primitive words to describe Schwitters's recitation: *whisper, wailing, barked.* Jolas (or Ball) remarked that during the recitation of the sound poem "gadja beri bimba" "I . . . noticed that my voice, which seemed to have no other choice, had assumed the age-old cadence of sacerdotal lamentation, like the chanting of the Mass." The poem, in other words, is very close to a common and ancient religious phenomenon, glossolalia, or speaking in tongues. The *W* poem of Kurt Schwitters similarly moves toward approximating what might be called today the primal scream. This is analogous to the tendency of simple geometric objects—a tower, a sphere, a circle—to be interpreted by viewers in sexual terms. The point, however, is incidental. The basic object of sound poetry is correctly identified by Moholy-Nagy in a later comment on Schwitters: "The only possible solution [to the stifling of poetry by convention] seemed to be a return to the elements of poetry, to noise and articulated sound, which are fundamental to all languages. Schwitters realized the prophecy of Rimbaud, inventing words 'accessible to all five senses.' His poem *Ursonata* is a poem thirty-five minutes in duration. . . . The words used do not exist in any language; they have no logical, only an emotional context."

A notorious dada technique for achieving transparency in language was clipping words from journals. Although this technique retains the words of a natural language, and the words themselves are not a true cross-section even of that language, the result is expression with a high degree of randomness. Tzara gives the formula for this kind of poetry and a sample poem:

To make a dadist poem
Take a newspaper.
Take a pair of scissors.
Choose an article as long as you are planning to make your poem.
Cut out the article.

> Then cut out each of the words that make up the article and put them in a bag.
> Shake it gently.
> Then take out the scraps one after the other in the order in which they left the bag.
> Copy conscientiously.
> The poem will be like you.
> And here you are a writer, infinitely original, endowed with a sensibility that is charming, though beyond the understanding of the vulgar.

Example:

> When the dogs cross the air in a diamond like the ideas
> and the appendix of the meanings show the hour of the
> awakening program (The title is my own.)
>
> price they are yesterday agreeing afterwards paintings
> Appreciate the dream epoch of the eyes pompously
> than recite the gospel made darkness group the
> apotheosis imagine he said fatality power of flowers. . . .

The effect is defined by Richard Huelsenbeck in his *Collective Dada Manifesto* of 1920. The random poem "makes words into individuals; out of the letters spelling words, steps the woods with its treetops." Words, however, are less transparent than sounds. In spite of the lack of grammar and syntax Tzara's words trap the reader in their natural meanings. The literary critic buried in every psyche longs to damn them as barefaced fraud or to trace their subtle meanings.

In *Science and the Modern World* Alfred North Whitehead observes that it takes an extraordinary intelligence to contemplate the obvious. One of the prime tasks of poetry—it may be *the* prime task—is to contemplate the obvious. In the famous definition of poetry that Coleridge offers in chapter 14 of his *Biographia Literaria* the basic appeal of poetry is said to be its capacity for "awakening the mind's attention from the lethargy of custom, and directing it to the loveliness and the wonders of the world before us; an inexhaustible treasure, but for which in consequence of the film of familiarity and selfish solicitude we have eyes, yet see not, ears that hear not, and hearts that neither feel nor understand."

Whether or not the poets of dada were revealing unappreciated beauties and wonders, their fascination with typography and newspapers suggests that they were contemplating the obvious transformation to which language was being subjected during the early twentieth century by the mass media. Marcel Duchamp had presented commonplace commercially produced objects—bicycle wheels and urinals, for example—as though they were works of art; and the practice is now widely followed by museums that exhibit motorcars, typewriters, and sewing machines with all the reverence that was once reserved for Michelangelo and Vermeer.

Is it not a literary manifestation of the same impulse to make poems out of headlines clipped from newspapers in the manner of André Breton? To test this theory we need only try to imagine how today's newspaper would appear to a reader unfamiliar with the conventions of modern journalism. It would appear to be a surrealistic poem—a haphazard mosaic of columns of different lengths, of photographs, of headlines of different sizes, and of advertisements. The untrained reader would find himself following a story about political corruption, then breaking off in midsentence to begin a report on SALT negotiations, breaking off again to read about a teenager who died in a fire, then breaking off to read about Mexican wetbacks, then breaking off again . . . and so forth. The only element connecting the stories on the front page is an accident: they all occurred within twenty-four hours before the paper was published. The headlines become pure dada once the events they identify are forgotten. Here is a sample from a 1978 issue of the *Washington Post:*

> Suburbs Push Spartan Water Habits
> Thurmond's Switch
> Old Celebrations, New Translations, Gossip, and Ghosts
> Nambi's Dunes Hide Wealth of Diamonds
> Energy in August
> Orioles Toppled by Rare Blasts from Nordhagen
> Sounders Earn Date With Cosmos
> Weaver Gives Thumb Again

In a sense Tzara and his friends were not inventing anything new: they were merely imitating what had already arrived.

III

By 1939 dada had expired, a victim of the general sense that life was real and life was earnest and soon to get a lot more so. Interesting efforts to discover new forms of language occurred after World War II, and some of them are still with us. Concrete poetry seeks to combine language and visual images and to make both more expressive, and it has interesting relations to advertising techniques such as logos and space ads. Algorithmic poetry uses a modern variation on the ancient practice of numerology to create a machinery for the systematic displacement of normal syntax and meaning. The techniques include random substitutions and substitutions by formulas (algorithms) that can range from simple formulas to substitute one noun for another, to complex formulas for increasing or decreasing series of words, to lipograms—works in which certain letters of the alphabet are forbidden, as, for example, Georges Perec's *La disparition* (1969) from which the letter *e* is banished. Computer writing generally seeks programs that automatically produce sense rather than nonsense, and is in this respect less inventive than computer graphics.

The search for the "independent life" of language is characteristic of the twentieth century. It stems from despair over the extent to which the use of language is conditioned by history, so that words become vehicles for conventions rather than current experience. But language can assert its independent life only by abandoning the lexical meanings and grammatical forms that it inherits from history. Dada, concrete poetry, and algorithmic poetry can be understood as attempts to liberate language and by doing this to liberate man so that he can confront his present situation. These attempts are interesting, but they always collide with the fact that language is a vehicle for meaning and that meaning is always determined by history. They collide, in other words, with the irreducible conservatism of language. When this happens, they must opt for the transparency of nothing, for the condition of pure abstraction, or admit defeat and surrender to the past, even though the past is an anachronism. Clearly the experiments are significant. Algorithms are as much a product of the human spirit as the *Mona Lisa,* perhaps more so in an absolute sense because they depend on conscious mental operations rather than forms supplied by Nature. The humanity that produces them has only begun to be explored. Before the twentieth century there was no road into the territory. Since we are now inhabitants of that territory, it is time to start drawing the map.

IV

There is a sense in which dada and related forms of poetry are not experimental but "imitations" of a type that has been traditional since Aristotle. The relation between dada experiments and the crazy-quilt pattern of a typical daily newspaper has been noted. Is dada doing something new or is it simply imitating the newspapers—and in the process calling attention to a common aspect of modern life?

If newspapers have the qualities associated with dada and modern advertising techniques have qualities associated with concrete poetry, the typical television program in which a serious plot is interleaved with toothpaste and Kotex commercials, appeals for contributions to the Heart Fund, and station identifications (themselves concrete poems) is a first-rate instance of dada in motion. It would seem that no rational human being could have devised such a rape of traditional dramatic form, but in fact thousands of talented individuals cooperate to make the rape as thorough as possible, and millions of Americans enjoy the results every evening without the slightest sign of irritation. Tzara would be pleased. Modern television demonstrates not only that dada is imitation in Aristotle's sense but that the poets of dada were *vates,* to use the old Roman term for poets—prophets of the future. Finally consider the marvelously bizarre language of computer programming, which is a language of acronyms and abbreviations. What dada poet could have imagined the effect of a typical page of *Byte* magazine, much less the effect of a disk control-program for CP/M?

In the light of CP/M dada begins to look less like an eccentric aberration than an anticipation in the early years of the century of what would become reality by its end. The dada poets were seers in the old sense of that term. They were not magicians who could predict the future but sensitive individuals who, by contemplating the obvious, were able to describe what most citizens could not see until many years later. By the same token are not contemporary superrealists like Duane Hanson, Richard Estes, and Don Eddy, whose images seem more real than reality, telling us that we already live in a world in which the animate and the inanimate, the human and the artificial, are becoming indistinguishable, in which microbes are "programmed" and the robots have passed the Turing test?

What happened in the early twentieth century may be something like what happens along a geological fault. As the two masses grind against each other and adjust, they create a series of small shocks. Eventually the stored energies become so great that there is a major shock. Enormous amounts of energy are released, and the landscape is permanently changed.

Western culture has experienced a continuous series of minor shocks since the Renaissance. Some time between 1890 and 1915 a major shock occurred. The release of its energies included new forms of science and of art, but not all of its effects were benign. They included two world wars and a series of periods of reaction during which people tried to put the world back together in the old way. The Nazi movement in Germany and the recent Iranian revolution were efforts in this direction, and perhaps the triumph of conservatism in the 1980 presidential election was our own more democratic and far more benign way of trying to set the clock back. The new consciousness of the twentieth century, however, is already part of the deep structure of the mind, including the minds of those who would reject it.

This new consciousness will not go away, and therefore we must learn to live with it. For this task the poetry of nothing can be a useful teacher.

(1984)

Great Walls and Running Fences

Nature in her design and man in his art meet somewhere beyond the limits of imitation.
—BERTEL BAGER, Nature as Designer (1966)

In his last and greatest poem, *Un coup de dés,* Stéphane Mallarmé suggested that the destiny of the modern artist is to struggle against silence. Language changes slowly, but modern culture, driven by science and technology, changes rapidly. Language can represent the past, but it is progressively less able to represent the present. The effort to represent the present is a struggle against silence—an effort to create languages that refer to the world in which they are used. Scientists are no less oppressed and isolated by the inadequacy of language than artists, for they are products of modern culture before they are specialists.

Since Mallarmé the problem of language has become a dominant theme not only of literature but of painting, sculpture, dance, and music. In general, the visual arts have met the challenge to create new languages. The visual languages of Cubism, Futurism, and the Bauhaus, for example, were recognized as revolutionary as soon as they appeared; and within twenty-five years they had become incorporated in the vernacular of twentieth-century experience. Modern culture is better able to understand itself because of them.

For reasons I will consider later, poetry and fiction have been less successful than the visual arts. Between 1900 and 1950 the center of the American and European literary stage was held by modernist rather than modern literature, and even today the modern authors of the early years of the century remain enigmatic to many. T. S. Eliot and James Joyce, for example, are widely appreciated, but their contemporaries Gertrude Stein and William Carlos Williams are still poorly understood.

Perhaps words are too time-bound—too tangled with history via etymology, grammar, and literary convention—to be capable of the renewal that is required to overcome Mallarmé's silence. If this is the case, literature will not disappear, any more than lute-playing has disappeared in the age of the electric guitar. Literature might, however, become a minor art form, while major art turns in other directions—for example, to movies, interactive texts, concrete poetry, rock concerts, and videos. Advances in machine speech-recognition may soon make reading the oddity of a cultural moment rather than a condition of civilization. In that event illiteracy, in the sense of inability to read, could be the wave of the future.

The psychology of a world for which there is no language is suggested by what I call the Great Wall syndrome. To explain this syndrome I offer a fanciful thought experiment. Imagine that when the Great Wall of China was erected by Shih Huang-ti, it was simply a great wall. It knew only two words: "Keep out." Eventually it ceased to have a military use, but it was still massively there. Since it could no longer be understood as a wall—that is, as something that keeps something else out—it had to be looked at. And when it was looked at, those who looked saw it was a wonder of the world. The wonder had been there from the beginning and had touched those who passed by, but as long as it was concealed under the veil of wallness, there was no word for it. There was only a silence.

Understanding the aesthetic of modern culture is a constant search for Great Walls under various kinds of wallness.

This essay moves from definition to analysis to implication. Anyone who has walked in a modern city is aware of modern architectural aesthetic. Owing to the Bauhaus it was given a language early in the twentieth century, and that language has evolved continuously as new styles have appeared. I therefore take my initial examples of modern aesthetic from architecture. The discussion of architecture leads to a review of the way that the modern architectural aesthetic emerged, and here two exemplary structures are cited: the Crystal Palace and the Eiffel Tower. Later the discussion is extended to the aesthetic of machines and artifacts.

The next step, analysis, begins with recognition that modern aesthetic has two faces—one static and the other dynamic. Art in the twentieth century has moved away from the static and toward the dynamic. Since words tend to make things into objects of contemplation, this trend has made severe demands on language. One reason for the success of literary modernism is that its makers celebrate a fixed and knowable past. This task language does well. Meanwhile the artifacts of modern culture—highways and automobiles, for example—express its dynamic naturally and powerfully.

Aesthetic derives from the Greek *aisthanomai,* "I perceive." To say we perceive the world is true but inadequate, because the world shapes our perceiving before we have any defense against it: children learn language because they are unable not to learn it. What shape does modern culture give to the consciousness of its citizens? This is the last question I have raised. My answer may not please everyone, but it is based on trends that I consider reasonably clear. It is tentative, and it is offered to stimulate, not to end, discussion.

II

The most impressive structures surviving from antiquity are temples, monuments, and palaces. The ziggurats of Assyria, the temples of Luxor, the Athenian Parthenon, the Pantheon in Rome, the pyramids of Yucatan, and the temple complex at Angor Wat have their counterparts in Chartres and Notre Dame in France, St. Sophia in Constantinople, St. Peter's in Rome, and St. Paul's in London. They are the homes of the creating and sustaining gods and stages for the rituals through which men communicate with those gods. The political order also has its monumental structures. They are the tombs, palaces, and government buildings that celebrate dynastic and national power: the pyramids of Egypt, the palace complex in Peking, the Roman Forum, the Kremlin, Versailles, the houses of Parliament in London, the Capitol Building in Washington, D.C.

Monumental architecture grows out of a native soil. It expresses religious and historical traditions specific to the culture in which it appears. To take the example nearest to Americans, the Capitol in Washington is classical in style because its builders wanted to assert the continuity between the republican ideals of Greece and Rome and those of the United States. In making this decision they asserted that America is not wholly a new world but a fresh outgrowth of a tradition continuous from the Age of Pericles to the present.

Modern architecture does not characteristically express itself in temples and tombs and palaces. In this respect it is closer to the Great Wall of China, shaped almost entirely by terrain, building materials, and considerations of defense, than to the palace complex in Peking or St. Paul's Cathedral or the American Capitol. Its typical products are dams, highways, sewer systems, bridges, warehouses, factories, department stores, hospitals, apartments, office buildings, hotels. It is not concerned with transcendent values but with life in the world.

Modern architecture achieved its identity between 1900 and 1930. As its dominant forms became standardized, they created a recognizable style. Henry Russell Hitchcock and Philip Johnson named the style in their catalogue for the 1932 exhibition of modern architecture at the Museum of Modern Art in New York: the International Style. Buildings in the International Style tend to be geometric rather than symbolic, with heavy emphasis on rectangles and highly finished surfaces. To many these buildings are breathtakingly lovely. Others consider them abominations. In *From Bauhaus to Our House* (1982) Tom Wolfe attacks the International Style for producing "glass boxes" and "great hulking structures" that even those who commission them detest.

This response is amusing but wrong. The International Style suggests in its fondness for grand and simple geometric forms a pythagorean idealism rather than a soulless formalism. It is not, as Walter Gropius claimed, a purely functional style. Its most successful buildings—for example Gordon Bunshaft's Lever House, Mies van der Rohe's Seagram Building, Eero Saarinen's UN Building in New York, and Skidmore-Owings-Merrill's Sears Tower in Chicago—are designed to reveal form rather than structure. The apparently structural girders on the Seagram Building are décor; the real girders are encased in fireproof cement in accordance with New York's fire code.

The John Hancock Building in Chicago recalls the fondness of the International Style for simple geometries but exhibits structure aggressively through exposure of the diagonal bracing that makes it stable. Another transitional structure is Philip Johnson's Pennzoil Building in Houston, which rejects rectangles in favor of a slashing diagonal geometry for the upper stories. The building remains emphatically geometric. The TransAm building in San Francisco, generally considered a blot on that city's otherwise impeccable skyline, is an elongated pyramid.

Mies van der Rohe experimented with the cylinder in designs dating from the 1920s, but the cylinder did not become a common architectural form until it began to be used in the 1960s for offices and hotels. Two defining examples of cylindrical structure are the Peachtree Plaza Hotel in Atlanta and the Renaissance Center in Detroit.

All of the structures mentioned thus far are based on large and simple geometries. In the 1960s architects began to experiment with complex forms. In Dulles Airport Terminal in Virginia Saarinen rejects rectangles for complex curves. The structure is a balance of tensions—of roof cables straining against cantilevered buttresses—rather than a static system based on compression. Buckminster Fuller's geodesic domes illustrate another direction taken by post-Bauhaus architecture: they are geometric rather than "zoomorphic," to use Saarinen's term; but their geometry is intricate, like the geometry of a Tinkertoy.

In the 1960s Americans began complaining that contractors were tearing down fine old buildings in order to erect cheap imitation-Bauhaus structures. Historic preservation has saved many superb buildings, but has also given birth to what is best called architectural surrealism. In one of the oddest aberrations since Hadrian's tomb was recycled as a medieval fortress, façadism has become respectable. The fronts of drab nineteenth-century row houses have been propped up while new spaces have been built behind them. A melancholy example of this—and perhaps the most vulgar structure created in America between 1965 and 1985—is the Red Lion Row development in Washington, D.C., five blocks from the White House. This structure—if structure it can be called—appears to be a block of three-story row houses restored with such germicidal precision that they look like a stage set, and that is exactly what they are. Behind them rises the real building, an immense, smooth, ominous steel-

and-glass structure that stares down on them with equal measures of contempt and surprise, like the owner of a penthouse examining a cockroach on the kitchen floor.

In other architectural modes, as in the case of the Pompidou Center in Paris, mechanical services are exhibited openly. Such buildings have the fascination of the viscera of cadavers laid open on dissection tables—or of the factories to which one was taken on class trips while in the third grade.

The diversity of recent architecture has been encouraged by increasingly flexible building technologies. Today, for many buildings in the range from small to medium, techniques and materials are so various that anything is possible. The central question for such buildings is not Why? but Why not? James Wines of SITES designs Best and Company stores as ruins, as monstrous shapes rising from beneath mantles of asphalt, and as ironic historical allusions. Other architects design deadpan facsimiles of Roman villas, apartment buildings that are dream-evocations of palaces out of *A Thousand and One Nights,* and campuses that are fantasies derived from the novels of Henry Rider Haggard.

Indifference to history is also flaunted by deliberate incongruity: gingerbread façades conceal high-tech interiors; high-tech exteriors open onto Tudor interiors. For Robert Venturi incongruity is a way of relating architecture to the world. In *Complexity and Contradiction in Architecture* (1966) he explains: "I speak of a complex and contradictory architecture based on the richness and ambiguity of modern experience." Philip Johnson's tribute to the Chippendale highboy in the roofline of his AT&T Building in New York is—in addition to being an immense joke—a public acknowledgement that contradiction suits the spirit of the times.

Yet another element in the melting pot of forms is what Venturi celebrates in *Learning from Las Vegas* (1975) as "American vernacular": drive-ins, fruit-juice stands, White Tower restaurants, resort hotels, and the like. These buildings seek visibility before all other values and have at best only eccentric and sporadic relations to history. Their motive is economic, and in this sense they are entirely functional. A hamburger stand shaped like a gigantic hamburger is exactly what it seems to be.

Technology has freed mid-scale architecture from constraints. The results cannot be called regional, because regional style is a generalized response to local conditions. Nor can they be called historical, because historical style is affirmative, in the way that the Capitol, for example, affirms the values of republican Rome, or the National Shrine the values of Catholic Italy.

The allusiveness of contemporary architecture does not entail a return to architectural conservatism but expresses something deeply characteristic of late twentieth-century culture. By collocating all values it expresses the emptying of each value of its claim to special authority. In other words it suggests the idea of architecture as game. The "practical" architecture of the late twentieth century is continuous with structures created from the beginning as games: stage sets, movie scenery, theme parks like Disney World and King's Dominion, and museum villages like Dearborn Village and Old Salem and Colonial Williamsburg.

III

To understand how the modern architectural aesthetic emerged, we turn to the nineteenth century.

Modern architecture was created initially by artisans who did not think of themselves as architects but as carpenters, masons, and jobbers. The artisans worked with engineers who also thought of themselves as practical men rather than architects. Like the Great Wall of China the aesthetic of modern architecture was concealed under the veil of utility.

The Crystal Palace is often described as the first example of truly modern architecture. For this reason, in the enthusiastic judgment of Folke Kirke (*Scientific American,* October 1984), "It takes its place with a handful of other preeminent buildings such as the Parthenon, Hagia Sophia, and Abbot Suger's St. Denis." Even if the Crystal Palace is not in the same class as Hagia Sophia and St. Denis, it is central to an understanding of modern architecture.

It was created in 1851 for Prince Albert's Great Exhibition to honor the triumphs of Victorian technology. Joseph Paxton, its designer, was gardener for the Duke of Devonshire and a self-taught builder of greenhouses. Because the schedule was tight, he worked out the basic plans (he later claimed) in eight days. The result was essentially a gigantic iron greenhouse, but it incorporated extraordinary technical innovations that helped enable the transition in scale from greenhouse to exhibition hall. Especially notable were the use of modular units for rapid construction, folded pleats for rigidity, prestressed bracing, curtain walls, and machinery designed specifically to facilitate the building's construction. Completion took a mere thirty-nine weeks. When finished the building covered nineteen acres and used nine hundred thousand square feet of sheet glass.

John Ruskin deplored it as a crude structure lacking in grace or historical significance: "Neither a palace nor of crystal." Lothar Bucher announced immediately after it opened: "A Midsummer Night's Dream seen clearly from midday." Jerome Buckley writes in *The Victorian Temper* (1951): "The Crystal Palace, breaking all orthodox precedents, raised its airy shell, supported by a vertebrate structure of light blue iron and girders, as a thin transparent cover assembled from light but strong portable units and shaped not to shut off an interior volume but rather to suggest all the unlimited outer world by the space within." Bucher concluded that the Crystal Palace was "a revolution in architecture." His verdict was partly correct. The Crystal Palace influenced the design of exhibition buildings in Dublin, New York, and Munich and encouraged the use of glass in shopping malls like Milan's Galleria Vittorio Emmanuele. However it had little influence beyond buildings designed for the same purpose. Evidently it was *too* functional—so obviously tied to its use as an exhibition building that its larger implications were invisible, even as Shih Huang-ti's concubines must have been unable to see the Great Wall of China as long as the Huns were massed on the other side.

The Eiffel Tower presents a situation directly opposite to that of the Crystal Palace. It was built in 1889 to commemorate the centennial of the French Revolution. Gustave Eiffel, its creator, was a bridge-builder. His Douro River Bridge in Portugal (1877) and Garabit Viaduct in France (1884) already showed extraordinary flair for design. His later life was shadowed briefly by the debacle of the French Panama Canal, but he survived handily. In the early years of the twentieth century he built a wind tunnel and experimented with airfoils. He died in 1923. His tower is a work of pure engineering. There is nothing in its sweeping curves and intricately woven trusses that suggests the French Revolution. It is a magnificent representation, but it represents only itself. As Roland Barthes remarks in a famous essay, *Le Tour Eiffel,* its sole function is to join its base to its pinnacle. In this sense it is a new word, an explosion of sound in an oppressive silence. By rejecting historical symbolism and the unique historical and cultural traditions of the city it dominates, its designer achieves the universality, the independence of space and time, of the technology that made it possible. It is a bridge rotated from horizontal to vertical and, at the same time, a fully realized abstract sculpture.

Above all the Eiffel Tower is there. A bridge can be ignored for the same reason that a roller bearing can be ignored. It is a useful device, a way to get over a gap, with no pretense to an identity of its own. Its message is Cross me. But the Eiffel Tower cannot be ignored simply because the only thing one can do other than ride up its elevator and look from it is look at it. (It has a restaurant; presumably you go to that restaurant not for the cuisine but so you can look from it while eating.) Ever since it was built it has been shouting at the top of its iron lungs: Here I am!

When leaders of the French establishment heard its cry in 1889 they were outraged. A protest signed by Alexandre Dumas and Guy de Maupassant, among others, expresses the shame they felt at the thought that they would have to listen to its message for the rest of their lives:

> We come to protest with all our strength, with all our indignation, in the name of disregarded French taste, in the name of art and French history presently in danger, against the erection, and in the very heart of our capital, of the useless and monstrous Eiffel Tower. . . . Will the

> city of Paris continue to listen to the baroque, mercantile fancies of a builder of machines, and irreparably lose its honor and beauty? For the Eiffel Tower, which even the commercial America would reject, means, without any doubt, a Paris dishonored.

This observation allows us to enlarge the lesson of the Eiffel Tower. Thirteen years before it was built, the French decided to present a monument to America to commemorate the Centennial of 1876. Perhaps the sponsors of the project had talked about American taste with Dumas and Maupassant. They appointed F. A. Bartholdi, a sculptor, to create a female figure draped in ponderously diaphanous iron robes—the Statue of Liberty. She is pure symbolism. She wears a crown of light and holds the torch of freedom aloft to guide oppressed masses to the New World. She is a Roman goddess. She evokes the same classical tradition as the Capitol Building in Washington. Because Liberty was so large, she required considerable engineering, which was worked out by Gustave Eiffel. But the engineering is hidden, like genitalia, under Liberty's iron robes. It is an embarrassment; at best, a necessary means toward an end that has no more to do with technology than the structure of the Brooklyn Bridge has to do with a plan to drive to New York to see a movie.

The Eiffel Tower is, conversely, all engineering and no robes. Being abstract—totally devoid of historical allusions to the French Revolution—it might be read as a symbol of almost anything: a prophecy of flight, an expression of man's aspiration for the infinite, an enlarged toy. It is none of these: it is only itself. It forces the viewer to look beyond historical myths to the revolution that surrounds him. It does not argue with history—it denies history, as though the president of the French Republic appeared at a state dinner wearing Levi's with a Tricolor patching the seat. No wonder the cultural leaders of the fin de siècle were outraged. But rejecting history has its uses. Did not Thomas Jefferson write to his friend Cartwright that "The Creator has made the earth for the living, not the dead"? The Eiffel Tower announces that the twentieth century will be modern, not modernist.

IV

A generalization is now in order. The reason for the triumph of modern architecture is that it could not be rejected. As the Crystal Palace suggests, that triumph developed out of technology rather than art, and it is the corollary of that technology. What is true of architecture applies elsewhere to modern culture. Photography and movies and electronic music are products of technology: the values of technology are inherent in them, and they express its values directly. As traditional art forms like painting and sculpture carry on the immemorial artistic task of imitating the things that populate the world, they too begin to express technological values because in the twentieth century the things that populate the world are increasingly things created by technology.

In his history of the Bauhaus (1962; English translation, 1969) Hans Wingler points out that nineteenth-century British industrial designers tended to bury function under decoration. The machines exhibited in the Crystal Palace were covered with floral wreaths, clematis vines, grotesques, logos, crests, and all sorts of painted, embossed, engraved, and cast ornaments. Conversely, in America, the drive to sell cheaply led to a technological aesthetic characterized by the abandonment of décor:

> Free from aesthetic prejudices, American industry produced useful appliances that were not meant to "represent" anything but simply to serve their designated purpose, and thus many of these anticipated the functional forms which designers in Europe began seeking out only shortly before the First World War. The achievements of engineers in the fields of technical, utilitarian architecture—for instance in the building of bridges, silos, and warehouses—showed the way. The frank approach to technology swept away differences between "mere utilitarian" and "grand" architecture. The great architects who assembled after the Chicago fire of 1871 to effect the rebuilding of the city—including such brilliantly gifted men as Henry Hobson Richardson and Louis Sullivan—were able to turn the achievements of the engineers to their own constructive use. . . . They gave rise to the steel-skeleton-supported office building, presenting it in accordance with Sullivan's dictum that "form follows function." It was in this presentation that functional architectural thought, to a certain degree in the act of being born, found its first consummate expression.

As the quotation from Wingler's *Bauhaus* suggests, technological aesthetic is powerful because it is inescapable. Economics makes it first profitable and later the condition of financial survival. The more its things fill the world, the more the world expresses its aesthetic. Dams and bridges are obvious examples, although bridges are sometimes "designed" for aesthetic effect. Railroads, canals, and high-tension lines are still better examples because they are formed entirely by function. Equally exemplary are structures shaped by technological processes: oil refineries, steel mills, generating plants, sewage-treatment plants, open-pit mines, offshore oilrigs, observatories.

Less monumental but all-pervasive are the products of industrial design: locomotives, dynamos, cranes, earthmovers, jet aircraft. On a more human scale there are automobiles, machine tools, rifles, typewriters, food processors, cameras, tape recorders, personal computers, microscopes. And on a smaller scale clocks, hand tools, kitchen utensils, telephones, cam shafts, armatures, roller bearings, machine screws, and integrated circuits (the intricate and beautiful designs of which can be seen only under a microscope).

Wingler traces the elimination of décor in the products of technology to economics: the less décor the cheaper the product. Certainly economics is a central factor in the spread of technological aesthetic. Another factor in many cases is technology itself. An airfoil is a mathematical form. To modify the contour of a wing by embossing feathers on it would be disastrous. Insignia and flags—even feathers—can be painted on aircraft but only if the paint is so thin it does not distort the surfaces to which it is applied. Whatever the reason for the elimination of décor, when it is gone the object represents only itself, or, through its self-representation, the technology that created it.

Once this aesthetic exists, it can be imitated. Imitation, a function of art, is a kind of naming. The Eiffel Tower can be understood as an imitation of the aesthetic of the iron bridge abstracted from bridgeness. The aesthetic of propellers, of finely machined gears, of airfoils and turbine blades, and of any number of other highly designed technological objects is imitated in a similar way by sculptors like Arp and Brancusi and Rivera, who produce mathematically curved forms from steel, chrome, bronze, and plastic and who finish their works to mirror brilliance. This kind of sculpture separates a common technological aesthetic from the functions that normally conceal it. Once separated, the aesthetic can be recognized, even in the utilitarian objects from which it was originally abstracted. And, once recognized, it can be converted from a discovery into a style and later—unfortunately—from a style into a cliché. Hence the over-designed junk that litters the display cases of hotel gift-shops.

Typography is a special case of the expression of modern aesthetic. Herbert Beyer and J. Schmidt created a recognizably modern typography through their work at the Bauhaus in the 1920s. Its two most obvious features are simplicity (as exhibited in sans-serif type fonts) and vivid color. Both features have been converted into styles—and even clichés—by the international advertising industry. They are commonplace in company logos, magazine and television advertisements, poster art, product labels, package designs, and film titles and color television commercials.

Typography confronts a problem not posed by architecture or sculpture. The material of typography is words, whether in rows on a page as in books or in arrangements that spread the words around in striking patterns on an unstructured surface. Mallarmé's *Un coup de dés* is prophetic in its use of typography for visual expression as well as in its concern with language. But words carry history with them in ways unknown to lucite and stainless steel and vermilion and pale blue. They want to mean as well as be. Even when typography adopts elements of painting, it tends to bring the past along with it, simply because letters have a habit of becoming words. For this reason typography provides an especially clear illustration of the difference between modern and modernist.

Robert Indiana's LOVE is an aluminum extrusion finished to mirror smoothness. It alludes by origin and finish to elements prominent in technological aesthetic. The letters that spell LOVE are stacked in two rows to create a shape with sculptural qualities rather than a string of letters like the letters on a printed page. The letters have serifs, however, which come as a surprise. They allude to nineteenth-century printing and specifically to letters as counters that form words that are, in turn, to be read rather than seen. Complementing the serif type is a still more obvious allusion to the past: LOVE. No word is more saturated with tradition. Indiana's sculpture is intended to look modern, but it is really an elegy, a trip down nostalgia lane. It is modernist, not modern. It sold innumerable copies and has been canonized on a postage stamp.

Conversely, let us consider the EXXON logo, a complex marriage of form, color, and type meaning nothing. The advertising agency that produced it is said to have spent millions to have a computer randomly create new words until exactly the right word turned up. The word is made memorable by its two X's. Although double-X is common in the Basque language, it is unknown in English. That is precisely its virtue. EXXON has no lexical meaning. It is not even an acronym. It has no history. It therefore means only itself—Exxon—and that is exactly what it is supposed to mean. It is modern, not modernist.

V

To move from definition to analysis, we need to distinguish between two varieties of modern aesthetic.

Representation seeks to present visually something that is fixed in the world like a Baconian "thing" seen from the middle distance. "To mean" in this context is equivalent to being a "thing." Representational art is "thingly" in the literal sense of depicting things. It falsifies reality because it pretends that things are always the same things. Impressionism avoids this error by depicting things as they are perceived in a web of specific circumstances: not a single, public "tree," but a birch tree at 3 A.M. on a snowy night after you have drunk a bottle of brandy with your homosexual analyst. Because circumstances change continuously, a thing is never the same thing. There is no single reality—only the myriad realities that the senses re-create at every moment of their dialogue with the world.

Abstraction eradicates the problem of multiple realities by exploring the categories that make objectification of the world possible. Whatever these categories mean from a scientific point of view, they tend to be expressed or symbolized as mathematical forms. The tradition is as old as the pythagorean notion that the visible world is an appearance resting on invisible ratios and geometries. In modern culture the pythagorean tradition is manifested directly in the grand geometric shapes favored by the International Style. Piet Mondrian explains in *New Design (Neue Gestaltung,* 1923) that abstraction in painting is continuous with the geometries of the Bauhaus: "The new aesthetics of architecture is the same as that of painting. And building, which is in the process of clarifying itself, is already putting into effect the same findings that painting realized in the 'new design' after a process of clarification heralded by Futurism and Cubism. Because of the unity of the 'new aesthetics,' building and painting can constitute one art and mutually absorb one another."

Mondrian's great abstractions are rectilinear, their geometries enriched by complex and contrapuntal use of color. Georges Vantongerloo, one of Mondrian's most brilliant colleagues in *De Stijl,* confessed in 1961: "My studies at school, and at the Beaux-Arts, went hand-in-hand with Euclidian geometry. . . . The word 'space' especially excited my curiosity though I didn't know exactly why. Well, of course, it conformed to Euclidian geometry and all I had to do was submit." Vantongerloo based many of his paintings on mathematical formulas and then used these formulas to name them— for example, "xy=k" (1929) and "y=x^2/6" (1932).

As if to demonstrate continuity of the Bauhaus aesthetic with *De Stijl,* the façades of buildings in the International Style—and, even more obviously, of such typically debased imitations of International Style as motels and small office buildings and apartments—have a family resemblance to paintings by Mondrian and Vantongerloo. They tend to be rectangles crossed by emphatic vertical and horizontal members, creating networks of smaller rectangles and given such variety as they possess by horizontal balconies, prestressed concrete horizontal and vertical moldings, variously colored rectangular plastic panels, and glass.

Silver-and-bronze reflective glass covers many buildings in the late International Style nicknamed "Los Angeles Silver." The use of reflective glass is functional, especially in the southwest, because it reduces heat radiation into the buildings. In good buildings the effect can be lovely since it simplifies the structures, leveling the busy reticulations, and creates gigantic mirrors reflecting surrealistic variations on the surrounding activity. Human beings float across these mirrors like bubbles in an oversized Wurlitzer jukebox.

In spite of the movement they reflect, these buildings assert by their geometries that they are rigid and that their basic structural principle is compression, the piling of one column on another. The movement that ripples across their surfaces intensifies the impression that they themselves are static.

The second path of modern aesthetic is dynamic rather than static. Marcel Duchamp's famous *Nude Descending a Staircase* is a defining example of the effort of Futurism to capture motion on an unmoving surface. Although Duchamp came to feel that the strategy of *Nude Descending* is inadequate for the same reason that reflections on the surface of a building intensify one's awareness of stasis, the work is of great interest because it announces the kinship between Futurism and the most powerful art-form of technological culture, movies. In this sense, in spite of its inadequacy, it is prophetic.

The equivalent of Futurism in architecture is structure that is visually dynamic. This sort of structure is more honest than structure that pretends to be static, because all large buildings are constantly in motion. Even though a building may seem to be static, it expands and contracts. It leans this way and that, and its parts pull against one another. A high-rise building is subject to powerful wind pressures. No matter how Euclidian it may look, it sways in the wind like a long-stemmed flower.

Suspension bridges are designed from the beginning to succeed by tension rather than compression. Since there is no reason to hide the fact, they express their dynamic visibly. Their main support cables hang in natural curves created by gravity. They are gigantic catenaries punctuated by vertical cables from which the gently rising arch of the roadway is hung. They move constantly as the tensions change and the cables adjust to maintain the balance. They are gigantic mobiles, although their motions are usually invisible.

Their beauty is widely appreciated. The Brooklyn Bridge inspired one of the most remarkable American poems of the twentieth century, Hart Crane's *The Bridge*. From the same room in which John Roebling watched his bridge being constructed Crane wrote:

> O harp and altar of the fury fused
> (How could mere toil align thy choiring strings!)
> Terrific threshold of the prophet's pledge,
> Prayer of pariah, and the lover's cry,—
> Against the traffic lights that skim thy swift
> Unfractioned idiom, immaculate sigh of stars,
> Beading thy path—condense eternity:
> And we have seen night lifted in thy arms.

This is an extraordinary attempt to force language to express a dynamic aesthetic. Its central quality is tension, which is expressed through the metaphor of harp strings. The feeling of tension is extended by metaphors of the connection of things separated by enormous distances: the lights of the cars moving over the bridge are connected to the lights of the stars above it; the catenary curves of the main cables become arms supporting the immensity of the night sky.

Confrontation with a great and powerfully expressive technological artifact forces Crane into the struggle with silence described in Mallarmé's *Un coup de dés*. If his language fails, as it ultimately does, it fails heroically and only because Crane tries to make it say more than it is able to say.

Another example of the attempt to make language express the dynamic of modern experience is provided by the effort to describe flight. For years the most popular attraction at the Smithsonian Institution's Museum of Air and Space has been a film by Greg MacGillevray and James Freeman titled *To Fly*. The film is projected on a special screen 50 by 75 feet, and its sound comes from thirty loudspeakers. A newspaper critic, John Falka, was moved by the film to something much like poetry: "The A4 jets of the Blue Angels ram through the air over the canyon in precise delta formation, wing tip a few inches from wing tip. It is man's symmetry, contrasted starkly with the splendors below. But man's work has its own beauty. The jets wheel upward and suddenly the screen is split into dozens of tiny frames. The lilting harmony of a Vivaldi-like score comes over the speakers." Later he is describing a sequence showing the launching of a Saturn rocket: "Witness the last Saturn flight as it begins in the film, balancing tentatively on the furies of its engines, yet reaching for a pinpoint in space. It is a summa of facts and figures, of f–stops and risks calculated by men who were, like Freeman, upbeat."

To describe the film, Falka reaches for the kind of poetry found in *The Bridge*. He contrasts the dazzling and the risky, which is also "man's symmetry," with the "splendors" of the natural landscape. As the jets wheel, the art of cinema intensifies the effect. The movie screen dissolves into a shower of tiny images accompanied by a "Vivaldi-like" score. Falka pauses to admire the photographer's command of the technology of "f–stops and risks," which relates him to men who exhibit high-risk virtuosity by guiding their huge Saturn rocket to "a pinpoint in space."

This is effective prose but an inadequate substitute for the movie simply because movies move. Again we confront the limitations of language. The beauty exhibited in *To Fly* is a dynamic beauty. Perhaps *The Bridge* is as much a cry of anguish arising from a losing battle with silence as it is a celebration of Roebling's technological triumph.

Are the limitations of language innate or are they limitations inherited from its past? Mallarmé insisted that language could overcome history. He thus encouraged experiments with verbal language a decade before the Cubists and Futurists began to experiment with visual languages. *Un coup de dés* introduced two decades of intense literary experimentation on both sides of the Atlantic. Vorticism, Imagism, dada, Surrealism, and Sound Poetry are among the movements illustrating this trend.

The American phase of the experimentation was carried forward in the early twentieth century in the circle that gathered in New York around Walter Arensberg. Marcel Duchamp, who enjoyed Arensberg's patronage during the war years, was an important figure in this group. Among the American poets associated with it were Mina Loy, Alfred Kreymborg, Arensberg himself, and, most significantly, William Carlos Williams and Wallace Stevens. This group stands in distinct contrast to the more famous circle of writers associated with Ezra Pound and centered in London and Paris.

The Arensberg circle was concerned with distinctively modern issues—specifically with the creation of verbal languages equivalent to the new visual languages discovered by the painters—while the Pound circle was not. Williams makes this point in commenting on Ezra Pound: "It was the great period of Picasso's supremacy, of Braque, of Juan Gris, Matisse and some of the others. Do you find any inkling of that in what Pound was writing those days? . . . Picasso snubbed him. Gertrude Stein put him aside after a few words. . . . Briefly, Pound missed the major impact of his age. . . . Really, he can't learn and as a result has been left sadly in the rear." For many years, however, New York seemed to be on the periphery of the great literary events of the century and Ezra Pound at the center.

This brings us back to the issue of modernism. The modernists succeeded while, with the exception of Stevens, the modern writers were, until recently, largely ignored. Even though Gertrude Stein and Williams began writing before the first world war and are generally recognized as seminal in modern literary history, they remain shadowy and enigmatic in comparison to the most prominent modernist writers.

Any list of modernists would include T. S. Eliot, Ezra Pound, William Butler Yeats, James Joyce, D. H. Lawrence, Marcel Proust, Ferdinand Céline, François Mauriac, André Malraux, Rainer Maria von Rilke, Thomas Mann, Ernest Hemingway, and William Faulkner. These writers are thoroughly familiar to readers and have been assimilated by the academy. For most people interested in literary matters they define the mainstream of the twentieth century. *Modernist* is the right adjective for them. They are not modern, and they tend vehemently to oppose the major directions of twentieth-century culture. None of them is especially interested in technology. To the extent that they recognize it they tend to oppose it, a bias overwhelmingly evident in Jacques Ellul's diatribe against the imperatives of technology *La technique ou l'enjeu du siècle* (1954), translated into English as *The Technological Society.*

The theme of Ezra Pound and of modernism in general is nostalgia for tradition in a world made unbearable by its departure. Writing to his Polish translator in 1925, Rilke complains that "from America empty, indifferent things are crowding over to us, sham things, *life-decoys*. . . . Animated things, things experienced by us, and that know us, are on the decline and cannot be replaced any more. *We are perhaps the last still to have known such things.*" Eliot's most famous poem is *The Waste Land,* a lament over the sterility of the present that draws its basic symbolism from the story of the search for the Holy Grail. Ezra Pound's *Cantos* are a long series of contrasts between an heroic past and a degenerate present, which Pound associates with Jews and usury.

The allure of nostalgia often spills over, as Williams notes of Pound, into out-and-out reaction. *Action française* supported monarchy; Eliot and Mauriac supported religious absolutism; Yeats and Hemingway idealized chivalric and pastoral codes of honor; Pound and Céline collaborated with fascists. Anti-Semitism runs like an ugly thread through the writing of many modernists. There is a leftist as well as a rightist modernism. If the typical genre of rightist modernism is elegy, the typical genre of leftist modernism is pastoral—a literature filled with images of saintly proletarians and edenic communities in which human values have triumphed over greed and the lust for power. Hence a modernist like John Dos Passos could begin on the left and end comfortably though stridently on the right.

Whatever its political creed, modernism is wedded to stasis. The right locates its ideal in the past; the left finds it in the future, although Marx and many of his followers liked to imagine that "idyllic" nonexploitive social relations existed in primitive and early feudal cultures. Modernism finds responsive audiences because it seems to offer a refuge from change. It does not pretend to offer new languages: it keeps saying that the old languages are good enough. The modernists are right in that *meaning,* as that word relates to language, is a social convention and therefore shaped by the past. Even as language is remade, it is becoming obsolete.

Language resists change in another way. Words try to freeze things so they can be objects of contemplation and used as counters in sentences. As Hart Crane's *The Bridge* and John Falka's description of the Blue Angels demonstrate, there is a gap between what words express easily and what modern writers want them to express. A dynamic art-form like movies, enhanced by screen splitting and a musical score suggesting high degrees of order, is naturally adapted to celebrating the risky precision of flight.

VI

The sculptor Christo received national publicity when he announced plans for *Running Fence,* a post, wire, and fabric sculpture extending twenty-four and a half miles across the hills of Marin and Sonoma counties in California. Although highway departments and power companies routinely tear up tens of thousands of acres every year to build highways and string high-tension lines, their activities go unremarked because they are concealed under the veil of utility—yet another illustration of the Great Wall syndrome. Christo's *Running Fence* was puny in comparison to highways and high-tension lines, but it was noticed because, like the Eiffel Tower, it was useless.

Among the claims of *Running Fence* to being art the most persuasive is that it is a direct imitation of life. It objectifies the aesthetic of linear structure. This aesthetic is fundamental to twentieth-century technology, which throws linear structures everywhere across the modern landscape: railroads, telegraph and telephone lines, high-tension lines, pipelines, highways. Christo's fence is, in effect, a name for this aesthetic. Once it has been experienced, it creates awareness of the other instances of this aesthetic in modern culture.

Considered in relation to *Running Fence,* the dual-lane highways of the American interstate system can be recognized as the most majestic linear sculptures created in human history, far surpassing in size, conception, and engineering the Great Wall of China. Seen from the air, they create grand articulations, making the flat places of the earth look like huge Mondrian paintings. Seen from the ground, they segment and order the landscape. They humanize nature, making it familiar and comforting. Pioneers approaching the Rocky Mountains must have regarded the mountains with awe and terror. But today's driver moving toward the mountains west of Denver through a ruddy sunset feels delighted and soothed. The gentle grades, sweeping curves, and graceful bridges of the interstate assert the triumph of man over nature.

Nature is elevated by this triumph: it becomes a form of art—scenery. The effect is precisely described by Stevens in "Anecdote of the Jar":

> I placed a jar in Tennessee,
> And round it was, upon a hill.
> It made the slovenly wilderness
> Surround that hill.
>
> The wilderness rose up to it,
> And sprawled again, no longer wild.
> The jar was round upon the ground
> And tall and of a port in air.
>
> It took dominion everywhere.
> The jar was gray and bare.
> It did not give of bird or bush,
> Like nothing else in Tennessee.

We take dual-lane highways for granted. We have grown up with them. They seem "natural": they seem part of the way things are because they were part of the way things were at the time we became self-aware. However, if we were travellers from a roadless civilization looking at them for the first time, we would be as awed by their boldness as the Goths when they first entered the cities of Gaul. In *Running Fence* Christo insists that we consider them objects with aesthetic qualities.

In antiquity temple architecture and religious sculpture were complementary: each was created with the other in mind. A temple was planned for the statue of a god, and a large-scale statue of a god was usually created for a specific temple. A similar relationship links modern dual-lane highways with the most popular three-dimensional art form ever created, the thin-steel sculpture known as the automobile.

Considered as art, automobiles give rise to a flagrant kind of hypocrisy. We read about them constantly, agonize over different makes and models, pay exorbitant prices for them, and polish and manicure them, often with greater care than we lavish on our children. At the same time we pretend they are utilitarian objects whose appeal, if they have any beyond utility, is psychological: they are status symbols, coming-of-age symbols, symbols of virility, symbols of independence. They are also thin-steel sculptures expressing the aesthetic of speed. Marinetti, the founder of Futurism, describes this aesthetic in his 1909 *Manifesto:* "We assert that the magnificence of the world has been enriched by a new beauty, the beauty of speed. A racing car with its bonnet draped in enormous pipes like fire-spitting serpents . . . a roaring car that goes like a machine gun, is more beautiful than the Winged Victory of Samothrace." Carl Sandburg tries to capture this aesthetic in "Portrait of a Motorcar." The poem shows that language can be both immediately accessible and convincingly dynamic:

> It's a lean car . . . a long-legged dog of a car . . . a gray-ghost eagle car.
> The feet of it eat the dirt of a road . . . the wings of it eat the hills.
> Danny the driver dreams of it when he sees women in red skirts and red sox in his sleep.
> It is in Danny's life and runs in the blood of him . . . a lean gray-ghost car.

The automobile was born in 1885. For fifty years designers covered automobiles with historical and symbolical decoration. Naked women and flying birds perched on their radiator caps. Flowers sprouted from vases in their passenger compartments. Early limousines separated the chauffeur, who rode in an open compartment, from the passengers, who were snugly isolated in a luxurious waterproof box. The arrangement was taken over from the design of coaches: since the coachman held the reins, he had to ride outside. It was retained in early limousines in spite of the fact that failure to protect the chauffeur dramatically reduces the safety of the passengers.

Between 1950 and 1965 General Motors put tail fins on its cars to intimate they were rockets. This is a modernist strategy: the concept of speed expressed by an extraneous symbol rather than the thing itself.

Even when 60 kilometers an hour was considered speedy, the urge to see the automobile as a beautiful new form symbolizing speed was irresistible. It was all the more so in the 1950s when the speedometers on production-line Cadillacs were calibrated to 120 miles per hour. Tail fins succeeded for the same reason literary modernism succeeded. They were easy to understand because they told the public what it already knew.

But the logic of automotive design has nothing to do with decorated radiator-caps or flowerpots or tail fins. It was first embodied fully in a production model car by Carl Breer in the Chrysler Airflow of 1934. The most obvious feature of the Airflow is streamlining, the term invented by D'Arcy Thompson in *On Growth and Form* to describe the curvature imposed by water flow on the body of a fish. Streamlining is not an extraneous symbol of speed like a tail fin: it is the technological condition for efficient high-speed travel through a fluid. The Airflow embodied several other design features reflecting the logic of technology. It used a unified steel frame for the body, which greatly reduced rattles, and its skin was stamped from a single piece of stressed steel, which not only reduced rattles but lowered production costs. Weight distribution was calculated in relation to the distance between axles to provide maximum passenger comfort.

The Airflow was to automobiles what the Crystal Palace was to buildings. The car expressed speed in its design. It was a symbol of what it was. It was also an unmitigated financial disaster. It departed too radically from the boxy design of its predecessors. It was modern, not modernist, and the public wanted modernism—cars whose design announced its relation to tradition. The disappearance of the Airflow from the showrooms did not, however, signal its disappearance as an idea. The Airflow expressed technological imperatives that can be ignored but cannot be permanently repressed. Ferdinand Porsche adopted Breer's concepts when he designed the original Volkswagen. Since the Volkswagen, streamlining has become commonplace. It is now considered beautiful, and the fact is a lesson in the way that technology changes aesthetic perception even though it is initially rejected.

Sheldon Cheney's *Primer of Modern Art* is a classic of popularization. By 1945 it had gone through eleven editions and had served to introduce a whole generation of Americans to its subject. For Cheney the automobile exemplifies the entire modern aesthetic:

> While we deplore the lack of inventiveness and the reliance on imitative, run-out ornament in our furniture-making, our hardware and our chinaware, we are prone to overlook a beauty that is wholly and typically modern in our everyday machinery. The ordinary hand phone has its values in the directness with which it is designed for its purpose, and in the simplicity and the relationships of its lines and

> volumes. The machinery in the powerhouse has a potent line-and-form fascination that anyone alert to art must feel. But most common in experience today is the aesthetic value of the motor-car. . . . The sheer volume-design of the automobile, its dependence on stream lines and expressive mass instead of ornament . . . and its absolute sense of fleetness, are qualities that, within the field of the arts of use, speak art-sense, and qualities to which we respond instinctively.

VII

We come now to implications.

Culture shapes consciousness because consciousness develops within culture and by means of it. It is assimilated when language is assimilated and in much the same way. Each object, sound, color, tone, gesture, and expression that a young child experiences is a fragment of a language, and all the languages are somehow unified in the identity that the child ultimately develops. "Aesthetic," we recall, comes from the Greek verb meaning "perceive." Aesthetic perception is perception considered as value. Is there a discernible bias in modern aesthetic? Does it have a direction, or is modern culture so turbulent that it seems directionless?

One tendency of modern aesthetic is clear. Science is committed to the universal. A sign of this is that the more successful a science becomes, the broader the agreement about its basic concepts: there is not a separate Chinese or American or Soviet thermodynamics—there is simply thermodynamics. For three decades before 1950 there was a Western and a Soviet genetics, the latter associated with Lysenko's theory that environmental stress can produce genetic mutations. Today Lysenko's theory is discredited and there is again only one genetics. Call this the universalizing tendency.

Being a corollary of science, technology also exhibits the universalizing tendency. This is why the spread of technology makes the world look ever more homogeneous. Architectural styles, dress styles, musical styles—even eating styles—tend increasingly to be world styles. The world looks more homogeneous because it *is* more homogeneous. Children who grow up in this world therefore experience it as a sameness rather than a diversity, and because their identities are shaped by this sameness, their sense of differences among cultures and individuals diminishes. As buildings become more alike, the people who inhabit the buildings become more alike.

Being commonplace, the automobile illustrates this point. Automobile design is determined over the long run by the imperatives of technology. A technological innovation like streamlining or all-welded body construction may be rejected initially, but if it is important to the efficiency or economics of automobiles, it will reappear in different ways until it is not only accepted but regarded as an asset. The result is the universalization of automobile design. Today's automobile is no longer unique to a given company or even to a given national culture. Its design shows up, with variations, in automobiles in general, no matter who makes them.

A few years ago the Ford Motor Company designed and produced the Fiesta, which it called "the World Car." Advertisements showed it surrounded by the flags of all nations. Ford explained that the cylinder block was made in England, the carburetor in Ireland, the transmission in France, the wheels in Belgium, and so forth. The Fiesta appears to have sunk without a trace. But the idea of a world car was inevitable. Ten years after the Fiesta, all of the large automakers were international. Americans had plants in Europe, Asia and South America, and Europeans and Japanese had plants in America, South America, and the Soviet Union (where Fiat workers refreshed themselves with Pepsi Cola). In the fullness of time international automakers will have plants in Egypt and India and the People's Republic of China.

As in architecture, so in automaking. In a given cost-range the same technology tends to produce the same solutions. The visual evidence for this is as obvious for cars as for buildings. Today, if you choose models in the same price-range, you will be hard put at five hundred paces to tell a Datsun from a Ford from a Fiat from a Volkswagen from a Renault since the specifically American traits that lingered in American automobiles in the 1960s—traits that linked American cars to American history—are disappearing. Even the Volkswagen Beetle is disappearing and taking with it the visible evidence of the tradition of streamlining that extends from D'Arcy Thompson to Carl Breer to Ferdinand Porsche.

As the automobile is universalized, it universalizes those who use it. By liberating the individual from geography, the automobile helps to create ever-larger cultural vistas. At the same time it erodes the sense of identity created by rootedness in place. Like the World Car he drives, modern man is becoming universal. No longer quite an individual, no longer quite the product of a unique geography and culture, he moves from one climate-controlled shopping center to another, from one airport to the next, from one Holiday Inn to another one further down the road; but somehow his location never changes. He is cosmopolitan. The price he pays is that he no longer has a home in the traditional sense of the word. The benefit is that he begins to suspect home in the traditional sense is another name for limitations, and that home in the modern sense is everywhere and always surrounded by neighbors.

The homogenization of modern culture ought eventually to reduce regional and racial antagonism, to wear away centuries-old defenses, and to prepare the individual for a new and benign identity: citizen of the world. For the moment it falls lamentably short of doing this, but the universalizing imperative of technology is irresistible. Barring the catastrophe of nuclear war, it will continue to universalize both modern culture and the consciousness of those who inhabit that culture.

This brings us to a second tendency of modern aesthetic. Reminiscing on the early work of Francis Picabia and Marcel Duchamp, Madame Gabrielle Buffet-Picabia wrote in "Some Memories of Pre-Dada" (1949):

> It seems incredible to the present generation that the machines which populate the visual world with surprising and spectacular forms, hitherto unknown, could for a long time have remained the victims of a frenzied ostracism in the official world of the arts, and that they could have been looked upon as essentially antiplastic, both in substance and function. I remember a time when their rapid proliferation passed as a calamity, when every artist thought he owed it to himself to turn his back on the Eiffel Tower, as a protest against the architectural blasphemy with which it filled the sky. The discovery and rehabilitation of these strange personages of iron and steel, which radically distinguish themselves from the familiar aspects of nature, both by their construction and by the dynamism inherent in the automatic movements they engendered, was itself a bold, revolutionary act; but one which, if it had not gone beyond descriptive representation, would have remained very close to the landscape and still life. Yet, first enthroned for their own sake, the machines soon generated propositions which evaded all tradition, above all, a mobile, extra human plasticity which was absolutely new. . . . The multiple possibilities which this unexplored field offered to the imagination seem to have shown Duchamp his true mission. Or perhaps he created for his own use an imaginary mechanical world.

Seen from this point of view, twentieth-century art is simply an effort to create images of the world. But where is the world? Machines are only its surface. Science has shown the insubstantiality of this world and has thus undermined an article of faith—the thingliness of things. At the same time science has produced images of orders of reality underlying the thingliness of things. Are these images more real than the ones they have displaced? The skepticism of modern science is neatly summarized by Edward Harrison in *Masks of the Universe* (1982): science offers a succession of images of the real, never the real itself.

Although modern art must therefore objectify a world known only as a series of masks, its skepticism is most emphatically not a Baconian rejection of humanity. Kandinsky spoke for the humanity of modern art when he insisted in *On the Spiritual in Art* (1910): "That is beautiful which springs from inner need, which springs from the soul." The paintings of Piet Mondrian express a field of vision which can only be a human field of vision. Its reality is not "out there" in nature defined as things seen from a middle distance but "in here" in the soul or the mind.

Nor should the skepticism of modern art be equated with nihilism. Nihilism is a form of modernism—a lament for lost values. Modern art treats the disappearance of absolutes as a liberation, and it tends to express this attitude through play. Lewis Carroll, a geometer and symbolic logician in his working hours, anticipated the playfulness of modern art in *Alice in Wonderland* and *Through the Looking-Glass.* It is evident in twentieth-century painting in the playfulness of Picasso, Miró, and Klee, and in poetry in the nonsense of Tristan Tzara and Marcel Duchamp and the mock heroics of Stevens. The playfulness of modern art is, finally, its most striking—and also its most serious and, by corollary, its most disturbing—feature. Its playfulness imitates the playfulness of the science that produces game theory and quarks and fractal geometry and black holes and that, by introducing human growth genes into cows, forces students of ethics to reexamine the definition of cannibalism. The importance of play in modern aesthetic should not come as a surprise. It is announced in every city in the developed world by fantastic and playful buildings and by fantastic juxtapositions of architectural styles.

Today modern culture includes the geometries of the International Style, the fantasies of façadism, and the gamesmanship of theme parks and museum villages. It pretends at times to be static, but it is really dynamic. It surrounds its citizens with the linear sculpture of pipelines and interstates and high-tension lines and the delicate virtuosities of the surfaces of the Chrysler Airflow and the Boeing 747 and the lacy weavings of circuits etched on silicon, as well as with the brutal assertiveness of oil tankers and bulldozers and the Tinkertoy complications of trusses and geodesics. It abounds in images and sounds and values utterly different from those of the world of natural things seen from a middle distance.

It is a human world, but one that is human in ways no one expected. The image it reveals is not the worn and battered face that stares from Leonardo's self-portrait, much less the one that stares, bleary and uninspired, every morning from the bathroom mirror. It is the image of an eternally playful power that makes order whether order is there or not and that having made one order is quite capable of putting it aside and creating an entirely different one. It is an image of the power that made humanity possible in the first place.

VIII

This essay has sometimes wandered far into the labyrinth of imagination. Let us conclude it on a strictly practical note.

The banks of the nineteenth century tended to be neoclassic structures of marble or granite faced with ponderous rows of columns. They made a statement: We are solid. We are permanent. We are as reliable as history.

Your money is safe in our vaults. Today's banks are airy structures of steel and glass, or they are storefronts with slot-machine-like terminals, or trailers parked on the lots of suburban shopping malls. The vaults have been replaced by magnetic tapes. In a computer money is sequences of digital signals endlessly recorded, erased, processed, and reprocessed and endlessly modified by other computers. The statement of modern banks is: We are abstract like art and almost invisible like the Crystal Palace. If we exist at all, we exist as an airy medium in which your transactions are completed and your wealth increased.

That perhaps establishes the logical limit of the modern aesthetic. The limit is a long way ahead, but it can just barely be made out through the haze over the road. As surely as nature is being swallowed up by the mind, the banks, you might say, are disappearing through their own skylights.

Is the citizen of a culture that is disappearing into itself a Caliban, a creature with passions but almost without an ego, plucked and pinched by forces he cannot understand? Or is he—in spite of all present evidence to the contrary—being freed politically at the same time he is shaking off his servitude to tradition and history? Surely the latter. This is an article of the faith of the human spirit in its destiny.

(1986)

At the Top of the Masthead

The thirty-fifth chapter of *Moby Dick* is a learned essay on lookout stations. The ideal station, Herman Melville tells us, was invented by a certain Captain Sleet of the Greenland whaling fleet. Captain Sleet placed a small tent high on the mast and equipped it with telescope, rifle, hand-compass, chair, and a case bottle filled with strong spirits. South Pacific whalers have no similar conveniences. The serene climate of the Pacific whaling waters requires nothing more than a secure leg-hold on the top-sail yard and a tight grip on the rigging.

Yet the absence of hazards can itself be a hazard. Melville describes the predicament of the Southern lookout as follows:

> Lulled into such an opium-like listlessness of vacant, unconscious reverie is this absent-minded youth by the blinding cadence of waves with thoughts that at last he loses his identity, takes the mystic ocean at his feet for the visible image of that deep, blue, bottomless soul, pervading mankind and nature; and every strange, half-seen, gliding, beautiful thing that eludes him; every dimly-discovered uprising fin of some indiscernable form, seems to him the embodiment of those elusive thoughts that only people the soul by continually flitting through it. In this enchantment mood, the spirit ebbs away whence it came; becomes diffused through time and space; like Cranmer's sprinkled pantheistic ashes, forming at last a part of every shore the round globe over.

The passage is a description and a parable. Many New Englanders had been lulled into dreams of the "deep, blue, bottomless soul pervading mankind and nature" by the trancendental philosophy that swept through Concord and Boston in the early nineteenth century. The grand abstractions of transcendentalism were as seductive as the half-seen, gliding, beautiful shapes observed by Melville's Pacific lookouts, and in his opinion they were just as dangerous. There is a hard oak deck one hundred feet below the masthead. The lookout who yields to the enchantments of waves and thoughts may forget to hold on. A tent and a case bottle in a howling Greenland gale may be less comfortable but safer.

Greek mathematicians saw the world as an imperfect representation of eternal numerical ideas. Plotinus thought that it was a series of emanations from a divine center. In *The Mind's Road to God* St. Bonaventura showed how, by turning away from the visible world, the human spirit could ascend the ladder of perfection to an ecstatic vision of truth so complete that it could not be expressed in words. Words, after all, are signs for material things. They are only one step away from the things they represent. Perhaps they are the containers of things and shape them according to human needs. If nature is created by the mind, the "real world" of the empiricists is actually an impossible ideal, an unknowable thing in itself. The New England transcendentalists sought oneness with the spirit behind nature. The parable of the masthead is a warning that their quest for the spirit within is perilous. It is a warning worth remembering at a time when science has concluded that the more deeply man peers into nature, the more often he glimpses reflections of himself. Science has not revealed the natural world. Instead it has created a vast, incredible, constantly changing, crystalline poem; and art, being the servant of truth, has sought to objectify that poem in sound and images and words.

Regarded casually, computer art seems to be little more than a game. It originated after the Second World War when large computers became common enough for programmers and artists to play with them. Visual plotters had been developed to graph complex functions, and the resulting drawings often had a high aesthetic value in addition to being useful. They include complex curves, undulating three-dimensional surfaces, and intricate patterns that appear to the naive observer to be works of abstract art. If so, why not program computers to produce forms intended as works of art from the beginning? By extension, if computers draw, they also make sounds and produce verbal texts. Why not create computer music and poetry as well as drawings? Mark Donson, a specialist in computer art, makes just this point:

> It is merely an historical accident that computers are largely used for mathematical calculations. Computers manipulate symbols which can represent words, shapes or musical notes as easily as numbers. Soon it will no longer be surprising to see a computer on the stage of Queen Elizabeth hall—this actually happened in January 1968—interpreting and performing a piece of music before a fascinated audience.

Computer art served formal public notice of its existence in an impressive exhibition held at Nash House in London from August 2 to October 20, 1968. The results of this exhibition were gathered into a book edited by Jessica Reichardt titled *Computer Serendipity.* While this book is only one of a considerable number of publications on computer art, it is a convenient starting point for a review of what computer artists have achieved.

Most of the artists who exhibited at Nash House began their careers as computer specialists rather than as poets, musicians, or painters. Reichardt observes that if it had not been for computers, many of them "would never have put pencil to paper, or brush to canvas, have started making images . . . which approximate and often look identical to what we call 'art' and put it in public galleries. This is the most important single revelation of the exhibition." Gustave Eiffel, after all, was a bridge engineer, and mobile homes became a major architectural form without benefit of architects. Computer art is yet another instance of technological culture developing not only its own forms but its own artists, independent of previous traditions.

Reichardt is especially proud of the fact that computer art is just as good as art made traditionally:

> The fact is that no visitor to the exhibition, unless he reads all the notes relating to all the works, will know whether he is looking at something made by an artist, engineer, mathematician, or architect.

Actually, visitors to the exhibition could never be sure whether they were admiring something created by a human being or by a machine. Dada frequently produced art that resembles computer art, but even Dadists have to eat. If they were out to abolish art in the traditional sense, they were most certainly not out to abolish themselves. To make the point in another way, Dada remained impure. Not only did its poems use words from natural languages, but they retained traces of the ego of the artist who created them. There is a sense in which the computer programmer may be considered an artist, but it is a very limited one. A single program can produce thousands of images or poems or musical compositions. The animation of the movie *Star Wars*, for example, was produced by computer. In fact, the ability of the computer to produce thousands of complex drawings, each one a progression in the series forming the individual frames on the film, was what made *Star Wars* economically feasible. A programmer can, if he wishes, produce ten or ten thousand images (or poems or musical compositions) from a single program. Arbitrary changes can be introduced at any point in a series and a new generation of art works will be produced. In computer art the distance between the creator and the thing created is so great that traditional concepts of the artist and his work are misleading. A new art form is emerging that requires new concepts and a new vocabulary.

In computer art the machine replaces the artist. In the future, when we see an image we will no more be able to determine whether it was produced by a human agent than the enthralled audiences of *Star Wars* were able to sense that the animation was machine generated or than the owner of an American Express card can be sure his dunning letter comes from a human credit agent. Does it matter? In *The Human Use of Human Beings* Norbert Wiener, the founder of modern cybernetics, wrote:

> When I give an order to a machine the situation is not essentially different from that which arises when I give an order to a person. . . . To me, personally, the fact that the signal in its intermediate stages has gone through a machine rather than through a person is irrelevant and does not in any case greatly change my relation to the signal.

Computer art begins with a fact. Anything that has pattern—the vibrations that produce sounds, the grammar that governs language, the regularities that produce recognizable visual images—can be expressed numerically. If so the pattern can theoretically be expressed in the binary code of computers. To reproduce sounds accurately requires a computer that can process some twenty-thousand three-digit numbers a second. Writing in 1969, J. R. Pierce claims that this "strains the capacity of computers." Undoubtedly computers can now do better. There is, however, another problem. The simulation of musical sounds by computers is still rudimentary. The sounds lack the richness of traditional musical instruments. The objective, however, is within sight. "In principle," writes Pierce, "the computer can become the universal musical instrument." Work toward attaining the objectives is going on at Princeton, MIT, and Yale. At Yale, in fact musicians are being supported (or were when Pierce wrote his comment) by a grant from the National Science Foundation. Pierce is delighted by the latter development because it points to a solution of the problem of how to support the arts: "If good art can embody a valid contribution to good science . . . then art can validly share not only the fruits of science, but the support which society so rightly gives to science."

Two tendencies are apparent in computer art. The first is conservative. Science admires results that are uniform and can be reproduced on demand. When it pauses to observe the current condition of music it is disturbed. The orchestra is made up of a motley array of violins, oboes, French horns, tympanies, cellos, and who knows what else. These instruments are all different. Each individual instrument, in fact, is different from every other instrument of the same kind. One violin, for example, is considered outstanding while another produced by the same craftsman is mediocre, although no one really knows why. To make things worse from a scientific point of view, the method of playing each instrument must be laboriously learned, and each performer plays differently. This means that every performance is different from every other performance. Composers are always gambling. Even the most respected group of players using the best instruments available can produce a botch. The natural solution from the scientific point of view is an instrument that always follows directions to the letter—a "universal instrument," as Pierce has it. A future Beethoven should be able to write his symphony in Fortran IV, record its program on a magnetic tape, play it through his universal instrument, and distribute the result either as a phonograph record or a computer tape to be played on a second universal instrument at Queen Elizabeth Hall before an enchanted audience. The Moog synthesizer represents an intermediate stage in this development. Its rather creditable musical achievements can be judged from the recent TEMPI recording titled "Switched On Bach." A more advanced state is represented by a program written by Max Matthers of the Bell Telephone Laboratories called BTL. This program, for which a standard manual is available, uses filters, envelope generators, shapers, and oscillators linked in "circuits of almost any degree of complexity." Each specific linkage is called an "instrument" and ensembles of instruments form an "orchestra."

The effort to produce traditional musical sounds and facsimile musical performances by computer might be labeled the classic phase of computer art. Most new art forms begin by imitating the past. Early type fonts, for example, were based on medieval manuscript hands; Victorian manufacturers covered their products with traditional decorations; for two decades automobiles preserved recognizable design vestiges of horse-drawn carriages; and when sound films became possible, movies went through a phase of imitating stage plays. Eventually, the classic phase of a new art form gives way to an expressive phase that exploits the unique potentialities of the new form. This is the second and more interesting tendency of computer art. If the computer is a universal instrument, for example, there is no reason whatever for computer music to be limited to imitations, no matter how diverting, of the *Brandenberg Concertos* or even to new sonatas and symphonies played by electronically simulated violins and trombones. Composers from Vivaldi to Gershwin to Edgard Varèse have experimented in the use of instruments to simulate non-natural (i.e., non-instrumental) sound. These experiments can now be seen as prophetic. The computer circuits that produce sounds imitating violins and flutes and drums are as tiny a fraction of the instruments that can be produced by computer circuitry as the visual spectrum is of the total spectrum of radiant energy. Computer musicians who use their universal instruments to create the sounds of traditional instruments are reactionaries. Instead of making a "valid contribution to good science" they are making computerized treacle to persuade the public that, after all, nothing has changed.

James Terry is not interested in treacle. He studied electronic music and phenomenology at the University of Illinois, and then spent two years at the Bell Telephone Laboratories writing computer music. During this period he created six compositions using the full range of computer technology. *Noise Study* began in a traffic tunnel. Terry wanted to create a characteristic twentieth-century aural experience: the random sound created by the dynamics of technological culture. His first step was to create "an 'instrument' that would generate bands of noise, with appropriate controls over the parameters, whose evolution seemed most appropriate to the sonorities I had heard." Since these sonorities had to be "framed" in order to force an audience to listen to them—i.e., to regard them as aesthetic statements—Terry next sketched out a large-scale structure and established specific note values within it "by various methods of random numbers selection." Finally he recorded his piece on tape and mixed the resulting sounds with the same tape played at half the double speeds.

This is a far cry from J. R. Pierce and his wish to play traditional music via computer. It illustrates the transition from the classic to the expressive phase of computer art.

There is a corollary here. If the computer is good at reproducing patterns, it is also good at distorting conventional patterns through random distortion. "Random number solution" is an important element of James Terry's method of composition just as it is an important element in the methods of the Dada and algorithmic poets and for similar reasons. It is a way of breaking up the forms and patterns that the musician inherits from the past. It is therefore a recurrent element in modern musical composition. As Alfred Schrieber notes in an article on "Music and Chance,"

> There have been a number of composers and there are today a greater number than ever, who introduce chance not as a point of comparison for criticism of style, but as a starting point or music-generating principle. It has become customary to group together such compositional procedures using the term "aleatory" (from the Latin *alea* = a die).

By Nilsson, Yannis Xenakis, and John Cage all use aleatory methods. Cage, for example, seeks to create "pure, unbridled acoustic chances" by the use of the Chinese book of *I Ching;* while Xenakis draws on Poisson's law of the distribution of random events." The point is that the computer can easily outperform *I Ching* and Poisson in the generation of randomness. Therefore although the use of randomness in music is not limited to computer composition it is especially common and generally more consistently—i.e., scientifically—used. Herbert Brün's *Soniferous Loops* (1964) is a good example of computer music. It is described by Brün as a series of "random sequential choices channelled and filtered under control of form-generating restrictive rules."

Randomness, however, creates a problem of meaning in music as it does in language. A completely random musical composition has no form at all. It has maximum entropy which is identical with maximum lack of meaning. The complaint of formlessness has been leveled at musicians who do not use computers (like Kurt Schwitters and John Cage) as well as those who do (like James Terry and Herbert Brün), even though their compositions have underlying formal structures. Is the complaint valid? What about the musical value of pure noise? Like pure nonsense, pure noise is transparent. It is also expressive. In shedding the egotistical requirement of human control via form it becomes the sensual expression of the world beyond the mind. Because it has no comfortable historical orientation it is (not surprisingly) disorienting. It threatens to absorb the listener in an oblivion like the condition induced by psychological experiments in extreme sensory deprivation, or, perhaps, like the mystic enlightenment that comes from the total abandonment of self. Yannis Xenakis seems to be hinting at something like this idea in his statement that his listener should be "gripped, and drawn willy-nilly into the circle of notes, without any special training being necessary. The sensuous shock must be as palpable as that on hearing thunder or looking into a bottomless chasm."

It is of considerable interest that computer-generated visual art seems to arouse little of the hostility created by computer music and poetry. Part of the explanation is that the most familiar kinds of computer drawing have a high degree of order. They are—or resemble—graphs of mathematical functions. Sam Schmidt of Princeton, for example, has produced remarkably beautiful shapes based on cubic functions. A. R. Forrest uses a program "written to aid research work on surface forms suitable for describing such surfaces as car bodies and aeroplanes" to produce images that can either be functional or purely aesthetic. Such images have a generic relationship to images produced long before the twentieth century by devices like the spirograph. These experiments merge with images that correspond to the classic phase of computer graphics in which the new medium is used to imitate traditional forms. Lloyd Surmen, for example, produces computer art which imitates natural forms and traditional design elements, as illustrated by *Friendly Flowers of Time and Space.* A particularly beautiful example of this kind of art is *The Snail,* which resembles a Chambered Nautilus. Again, Barry Arnalt created a program in 1960 for drawing an aircraft pilot in a variety of different postures in order to facilitate cockpit design. The result has some of the qualities of the figure sketches that fill the notebooks of sixteenth-century artists.

Because of the utility of this technique, it is common in engineering. The figures produced by the Arnalt program are representational. Drawings of this sort are intriguing but, in general, they are less impressive artistically than computer abstractions. Perhaps they have a bright future, but for the present they seem to be by-products of techniques for utilitarian tasks like image enhancement and image transformation rather than creative explorations of a new medium.

Computer drawings based on the expressive phase of the art form ought to be as disquieting as James Terry's *Noise Study* but they are not.

This is undoubtedly because modern art has gone farther than music or poetry toward pure abstraction. In a sense modern art was preparing for the computer long before it was invented. If the art of Miró or Klee suggests a delightful—Jackson Pollock a powerful—freedom from conventions, computer artists exercise their freedom directly and radically through their use of randomness. Robert Passlow and Michael Pitteway of Brunel University have produced a remarkable series of line drawings by computer. They describe their program as follows:

> The computer is first given the dimensions of the required picture and is told how many curves are required. . . . The machine then generates five random numbers, places the pen anywhere on the paper (two random numbers required for this) and starts to draw a conic section chosen by the random numbers. . . . When the pen reaches the edge of the paper, or if it is drawing a small ellipse, when it has gone most of the way round, the computer suddenly generates five or more random numbers and starts another curve. . . . Every picture is an original. The computer never repeats itself.

The objectives of this program are the standard objectives of the revolutionary artist of any period: "to escape from the pretty geometrical figures of conventional computer art work" and to gain "a new freedom" for machine generated art.

Is it art? The question intrigued the designers of the Nash House exhibition. To provide an answer they hung a composition of Piet Mondrian titled *Composition with Lines* beside several similar compositions generated by a computer program. The experiment demonstrated that it is impossible to distinguish an abstraction produced by computer from a work produced by a major artist. Only one out of five viewers was able to identify the Mondrian, which is not much better than the result that would have been produced by drawing lots. Computer art is evidently not merely hard but impossible to distinguish from human art. This lends substance to the fear expressed by Dennis Gabor in an article titled "Inventing the Future" (May 1960 issue of *Encounter*): "I sincerely hope that machines *will* never replace the creative artist, but in good conscience, I cannot say that they never *could*."

If computers are quite successful in the visual field, their limitations are most obvious in the field of language. A computer can produce anything from an alphabet that is entirely transparent because it is different from any known alphabet to a literary composition that has discursive meaning. In general, however, the greater the emphasis on producing discursive meaning in computer writing, the less successful the product. As an author of serious articles and essays the computer so far has been a failure. It has been only slightly more successful as an author of simple short stories based on stereotyped plot materials. Its greatest literary successes have been poems. This is evidently because the modern reader of poetry has been trained, like the modern art lover, to accept a considerable degree of abstraction and even to approve of it. Permutation is a typical, if hardly revolutionary, device for computer poetry. It is illustrated by Edwin Morgan's "Computer's First Christmas Card." The last line, incidentally, illustrates the value of randomness in the creation of artistic effects. It was not part of the program but appeared through a happy accident.

One can imagine endless variations on the technique of "The Computer's First Christmas Card." Many variations have already been produced. Whether or not the form has a bright future, however, is questionable.

Marc Adrien of the Vienna Institute of Advanced Study takes a different route by combining graphics with words in a manner reminiscent of both dada and concrete poetry. For him, the visual element is at least as important as the words. A well-tempered computer could produce an endless number of poems based on the technique and each one could legitimately be an original signed by the poet-artist.

The limits of computer poetry begin to appear as we ask more of the words and less of their visual effect. Sustained passages of poetry can be produced by computers. Such passages illustrate the classic phase of computer writing. They rely on traditional grammar and syntax, use lists of preselected words and phrases that constitute the computer's vocabulary, and follow the rules of well-established verse forms. Using TRAC computer language, Margaret Mastermann and Robin Wood of the Cambridge Language Research Unit produced a series of haiku poems, of which the following are representative:

all green in the leaves
I smell dark pools in the trees
crash the moon has fled.

and

all white in the buds
I flash snow peaks in the spring
bang the sun has fogged.

While these two poems have their charms, it seems likely that equal or superior charms could have been produced with less trouble by a poet composing haiku in the normal fashion.

A more ambitious poem was created in 1961 by Naumi Balestrimi using short passages from *Hiroshima Diary*, *The Mystery of the Elevator*, and the *Tao te Ching*. Two stanzas (or are they separate poems?) are quoted here in a translation by Edwin Morgan:

Hair between lips, they all return
to their roots, in the blinding fireball
I envisage their return, until he moves his fingers
slowly, and although all things flourish
takes on the well known mushroom shape endeavoring
to grasp while the multitude of things
comes into being.
In the blinding fireball I envisage
their return when it reaches the stratosphere while the multitude
of things comes into being, head pressed
on shoulder, thirty times brighter than the sun
they all return to their roots, hair
between lips takes on the well known mushroom shape.

This poem cannot be described as a classic but it has an eerie quality not inappropriate to the psychological trauma of the explosion of the first atomic bomb dropped on a human city. It is impossible to say that it is not a poem. The computer has thus taken a step not unlike that frequently imagined in science fiction. It is talking to us on a human level. It has become an android. If it is programmed to speak rather than write, and if it speaks to us from another room, is there any way of knowing that we are hearing a computer rather than a fellow human being? As Norbert Wiener observed, a message is a message—functionally, there is no difference.

For the present, at least, most people feel there is all the difference. But is there? Is there really a difference between androids and humans? The question is not a pretty quodlibet to be debated at leisure by scholastic philosophers from the safety of ivory towers. Science has made it an immediate, practical issue. Machines have always imitated humans. They are, in one definition, merely extensions of human functions. If the imitations become sufficiently skillful, however, and the activities imitated are those which are typically human, a time may come when people begin to think of machines as equals. Given the excellence of machines, a time may even come when people think of themselves as imperfect approximations of machines. At that point, instead of having machines that imitate humans, we will have humans imitating machines. Are there any human beings left? At some time in the future this question may become unanswerable, but by that time it will also be irrelevant.

To return to Herman Melville, we might say that the artists of the computer are examples of modern man perched on the topmost spar of high technology. He gazes out into hazy, blue, fathomless realms of abstraction and is fascinated by strange, half-seen, gliding, beautiful shapes that may be outside him and, then again, may be creations of his own spirit.

Once perceived they will not go away. If they are beautiful, they are also hypnotic. To yield to their fascination is to forget the difficult and painful climb that led to the top of the mast and with that, the distance from the highest spar to the deck below.

(unpublished)

Taking Off

"History is bunk"
—HENRY FORD

A mobile of steel wire and nylon thread hangs from the ceiling of my study. There is a small circular mirror on the end of each wire. As the mobile turns, the mirrors catch the light and flash it in hypnotic patterns across the walls. To call it a work of art would be ridiculous. Or would it? After his variations on Marilyn Monroe did not Andy Warhol go on to immortalize the Campbell Soup can? The latest addition to the memorials scattered around the nation's capital is the Lyndon B. Johnson Memorial Grove. Its centerpiece is not an equestrian statue, not even a bell tower to chime the hours, but a large rock. It is a craggy, suntanned rock from the Pedernales, but a rock nonetheless. To some people, each rock is different, a unique natural sculpture, a found object. The Japanese collect beautiful rocks for their gardens. Others feel, if you have seen one rock, you have seen them all. In 1977 the sculptor Claude André deployed thirty-six rocks on the grassy corner of Main and Gold Streets in Hartford, Connecticut, at a cost of $87,000, part of which came from the National Endowment for the Arts. The citizens of Hartford felt more sorrow than anger. An elderly gentleman said to André, "I just have to tell you the truth, you have ruined the city." Hartford's mayor added, "It's just a bunch of rocks, little kids could have done that."

To confront the issue squarely, why should André's rocks *not* be considered art? The Parisians who scorned Gustave Eiffel's tower grew to love it. In twenty years it is quite possible that the citizens of Hartford will be taking up collections to "save André's rocks."

People have been collecting things since the Greeks. Pausanius tells us that there was a picture gallery called the Pinakotheke on the Acropolis that was open to the public. Ancient Rome had no museum, but by the first century A.D. the city was so crammed with art objects liberated from the subject nations of the empire that it was, itself, an enormous open-air gallery. The first *museum* was actually a library. It was the wing in the palace of the Ptolemies that housed the library of Alexandria in the third century. During the Middle Ages, churches accumulated so many relics, crosses, jeweled patens, chalices, statues, stained glass windows and paintings that they became, for all intents and purposes, museums as well as houses of worship. The first museums in the modern sense, however, were created during the Renaissance. Initially their main interest was classical antiquity. They were oriented toward the past, but they used the past selectively to define what Renaissance humanists and their patrons considered the authentic tradition in art. Galleries which did the same thing for painting also became common during the Renaissance, as did facilities for the performing arts like Palladio's famous theatre in Vicenza.

Interesting, perhaps, but what does all this have to do with mobiles and rocks? The answer is that libraries and museums and mansions for the performing arts were not created to be warehouses for the past. Collectively they tell the public what art is. One approach to the question of whether a mobile or a rock is art is to ask whether it is exhibited in museums, whether it or something like it could be exhibited in museums, or whether the artist who created it is accepted in museum circles.

Another point. Arts institutions are expensive. They cannot be created without patronage, and without patronage they could not survive after being created. During the Renaissance the patrons were princes and noblemen; during the industrial revolution they were captains of industry; today they are mostly members of government bureaucracies. Whatever their titles, until recently their position gave them a special kind of power. In effect, they were society's arbiters of taste. They told the public what is and is not art and in doing this they controlled society's image of itself. Not surprisingly, this control has traditionally been exercised in favor of the establishment, which means the status quo.

There are two cracks in the armor of the arts establishment. In the first place the establishment itself has never been monolithic. Change is inevitable and there is always a faction in the establishment willing to accept change provided that it can be contained. In practice this has usually meant opposing the non-conforming artist as long as possible and, when it is no longer possible, co-opting him if he is alive and canonizing him if he is dead. Wordsworth began his career as a typical Romantic non-conformist—a friend of the French Revolution, a follower of William Godwin, and an opponent of establishment, in this case, the neo-classical, literary establishment. *Lyrical Ballads*, his first and probably his greatest poetic statement, was greeted with savage attacks and ridicule. Francis Jeffries of the *Edinburgh Review* began his review of Wordsworth's *Excursion* (1814) with the famous sentence "This will never do." By 1842, however, Wordsworth had been granted a state pension of three hundred pounds in recognition of his literary achievements, and in 1843 he succeeded Southey as Poet Laureate. Along with his honors, he accepted the politics of his new masters. He attacked revolution, opposed the Reform Bill and Catholic emancipation, and became a rock-hard establishmentarian. He was, in other words, thoroughly co-opted. Keats, Shelley and Byron were not co-opted. They had the grace to die young, so the solution to the problem of admitting them to the establishment was canonization. By the late nineteenth century the English literary establishment was as thoroughly sold on Romanticism—and as bitterly opposed to deviations from it—as it had formerly been on neoclassicism.

The problem is that each time the establishment opens itself to a new art form the definition of art is broadened. Lists of approved literary classics, museum collections, and accepted forms of drama and music become more and more eclectic. As this happens entropy sets in. It becomes more and more difficult to say what is and is not art. Take visual art as an example. Between 1900 and 1960 the pace of experimentation in the visual arts accelerated. The definition of art had to be broadened to include impressionism, fauvism, art deco, ashcan, cubism, futurism, primitivism, constructivism, synchronism, hard-edge, action art, colorism, op art and pop art, to name only a few movements. Since 1960 the pace has, if anything, quickened. Piero Manzoni is currently exploring the frontier of excrement. In 1961 he produced tinned feces, and his *Merde d'Artiste* was reproduced in an issue of *Art Forum*, which is about as establishment as you can get. Dutton has published a volume titled *End Product: The Last Taboo* with an introduction by Abby Rockefeller, granddaughter of John D. Rockefeller, informing the yet unknowing masses that "documenting the problems of our relations and attitude to excrement . . . is an important task right now." If excrement, why not bodyworks? The following paragraph comes from the February 1977 issue of *Art Forum:*

> Vito Acconci volunteered to masturbate (hidden from view) in the presence of visitors in a SoHo gallery. . . ./Lucas/Samaras crossed his head with twine tightly enough to deform his face, in a demonstration reminiscent of a torturer's endeavor to transform the body of a woman by cross-lacing her so tightly that she becomes a bulging bundle of flesh. . . . Chris Burden's cross is his own flesh. Some years ago he locked himself up in a locker two feet high, two feet side, and three feet deep for five days. . . . In advanced capitalistic countries the intelligensia has sufficient self-confidence for its purveyors of cultural goods to include Earthworks and bodyworks in their inventories. It is self-confidence that the bureaucracy lacks in the workers' states. . . . We must not forget that Rudolph Schwartzkogler went further than any masochist bodyworker, for he proceeded inch by inch to amputate his own penis while a photographer recorded this art event.

What's going on here? The answer is entropy. The treason of the clerks of the establishment has been carried so far that it is now impossible to say what is and what is not art. Because of this the function of arts institutions is itself becoming blurred. What sort of standards are libraries, museums, and centers for the performing arts supposed to serve? Are they still arbiters of taste or have they finally become what they never were before—warehouses of the past?

Before confronting this question, consider a second kind of challenge to the arts. As entropy has increased from within, technology has created an alternative to the establishment. The media industry does not depend on patronage. It sells directly to the consumer. It is quite unsentimental. It will sell whatever people will buy without worrying about their moral or aesthetic improvement. When the market dries up it will halt production and move on to something else. Its tools are advertising, consumer polls and balance sheets, which are tallies of the votes cast whenever the consumer makes a purchase.

In the beginning there was printing. Printing is a wedding of several technologies including metallurgy, paper chemistry, and credit. It was invented in the fifteenth century, but before it could become a mass medium in the contemporary sense, populations had to be made literate. This occurred in the developed countries in the nineteenth century, which also saw the development of technologies far more sophisticated than any dreamed of by Gutenberg: linotype machines, high-speed presses, mass-produced wood pulp paper, and fast, efficient transportation systems. Suddenly it became possible to make a living—often a very good living—by selling books that had no relationship to the interests and tastes of the establishment. Popular literature of all kinds had, of course, been produced during the Renaissance. What was new was the volume in which it could be produced. Volume production meant low unit price, and this, in turn, expanded the market. During the last half of the nineteenth century romances, domestic tales, adventure stories, self-help books, cookbooks, how-to-do-it books, sermons, works of edification, picture books, and children's books, all intended for popular consumption, poured off European and American presses in unprecedented numbers. Most of them were printed to self-destruct both physically and in the minds of their readers almost as soon as they were purchased. Even as their effect on public taste was deplored they multiplied and engendered new forms: the war story—subdivided into infantry, cavalry, artillery, espionage, medical, nurse, air force, command post, front-line, combat, love, victory, heroic death, grievous wound, and so on—the pulp magazine, the big-little book, the comic book, the western, the gothic, the detective story, the hard-boiled detective story, the tabloid, the film magazine, the adult book, and the pornographic magazine, the latter two in both under- and over-the-counter versions depending on the climate of censorship.

To mass publishing twentieth-century technology has added radio, phonograph records and tape, movies and television. All of these media are more powerful than print. Reading requires literacy and conscious effort. Not everyone is literate and many of those who are limit their exposure to newspapers, racing forms and interoffice memos. The print market is thus limited even within a given language area, and its limitations become progressively more crippling when it has to compete with non-print media. An additional and very real problem is the fact that print does not travel well across language barriers. Translation is slow, expensive, and usually awkward. Novels, for example, tend to be closely attached to the regions where they were written. A Raymond Chandler mystery set in Los Angeles may be difficult for an English-speaking reader in London. The problem of translating it into Hindi or Laotian may be insurmountable. If so, its potential market is reduced. It is by nature a local rather than an international product. Radio, musical recordings, film and television are far less constrained. Musical sounds and images are not entirely transparent but they are far more so than print and their difficulties are relatively easy to overcome. Movies and television use words but their emphasis is on visual communication. The crude level of translation illustrated by subtitles was sufficient, before dubbing, to make movies an international art form extending to every country in the world sufficiently advanced to own a projector. Song lyrics often have poetic qualities that resist translation, but the world-wide diffusion of popular music, usually without benefit of translation, suggests that the lyrics are no more important in popular music than in opera.

Having been set free from language, the new media have created a popular culture that directly rivals the forms of culture supported by the arts establishment. They have not been overtly hostile to establishment culture. In fact, prodded by spokesmen for the establishment, they have frequently attempted to sell establishment culture to the masses. When they have done this, however, they have discovered, like the publishers before them, that the classics are loss leaders. Prestige and approval are worth something, but they are not worth poor ratings and red ink in the balance sheet. If the public wants the audio-visual equivalent of penny dreadfuls and comic books, that is what the public will get.

The response of the establishment to the challenge of the mass media has run the gamut from denunciation to selling out on the theory that if you can't beat them you should join them. In capitalist countries the media have been accused of siding with the Bolsheviks in a plot to sap the moral fiber of the state. On the other side of the Iron Curtain media art is considered the degenerate offshoot of the last, dying phase of capitalism, against which the proletarian masses have to be zealously protected by the censors. Efforts to control media art have included exhortation, economic and political pressure, censorship and its cousin government regulation, and apocalyptic warnings of what will happen if media art is not brought under control. Meanwhile, however, the clerks of the establishment have been up to their familiar game. Much media art that was once considered trash is now accepted as art. Jazz and early films are examples. At the same time, establishment artists have begun cultivating media forms, as in the case of pop art. Some have even gone to work for the media. Sir Laurence Olivier, after all, makes thrillers as well as filmed versions of Shakespeare.

The effect of increasing entropy within and a losing battle on the outside with the mass art of the media has been devastating for arts institutions and their patrons. They no longer do what they were supposed to do—and what justified supporting them in the first place—that is, define what is and is not art and thereby control society's image of itself. Their sole remaining function is to be warehouses of the past—not to shape public taste, not to support one set of standards or traditions against another, but to serve as a cabinet of curiosities, a repository of the archaeological detritus that society left behind as it moved into the twentieth century. Like King Tut's mask or windjammers or enlarged photographs of lice these relics are fascinating. The source of their interest is their remoteness.

How much is a cabinet of curiosities worth? The question is critical because arts establishments cannot support themselves. Collectively they represent an enormous investment. Should the investment be written off—should the arts institutions be told to sink or swim through their own efforts, in which case most of them would sink—or do they still have a claim on society?

At present both capitalist and socialist societies accept the fact that they have a legitimate claim for support. Accepting a fact and following out its implications, however, are two different things. The United States has recognized the claim of its arts establishments through two National Endowments—one on the arts and the other on the humanities. The two Endowments dispense around $250 million per year in grants to museums, libraries, performing arts organizations, and individual artists and scholars. The grants prop up a great many institutions that could not survive otherwise. In a sense they are a way of postponing a decision that is currently too difficult to make. The old arts—the true, authentic, unquestionable arts—are like a family estate that is too expensive to maintain and too steeped in sentiment to put on the auction block. The modern solution, whether in the United States or the Soviet Union or the People's Republic of China or France, is government subsidy. Before pulling out, the establishment arranges for the family estate to be kept up by the taxpayer. It is a convenient arrangement for everyone but the taxpayer—maybe even for the taxpayer since he is assured by prominent members of the establishment that he is performing a noble service.

Whatever its benefits or liabilities for the taxpayer, government subsidy of the arts brings confusion about what they are into high relief. The existence of a $250 million tax fund changes the delicate and abstruse debates in the critical quarterlies into a simple and familiar question: Who gets the money? Consider the following answer to this question by Robert Brustein, the distinguished head of the Yale Repertory Theater:

> While more Americans than ever before believe the arts to be important to the quality of life (89 per cent according to a recent Fred Harris poll), there seems to be confusion over what the arts are. "The arts crisis," according to Marcia Thompson of the Ford Foundation, "is a lack of clear comprehension of what we are talking about. There is no national voice of sufficient strength to make qualitative judgements." There is no national policy. According to Joan Mondale . . . the arts are defined by the yearning of most Americans for "personal expression." This is warm and democratic but it does little to distinguish high art from basket-weaving or trained horn players from the brass section of the high-school band.

There are two sets of operative statements in Brustein's observation. First, "There seems to be considerable confusion over what the arts are . . . a lack of clear comprehension of what we are talking about." Precisely. It is an honest confusion created by entropy within the arts establishment. If there is "a lack of comprehension of what we are talking about: it is because those people who are supposed to know what we are talking about have allowed—and quite properly have allowed—the definition of art to become so broad that it includes everything. If it includes Rembrandt and Goya and Cézanne it also includes Duchamp's urinal and André's rocks and Manzoni's feces and Schwartzkogler's penis. It also, incidentally, includes basket-weaving, which can produce works of exceptional artistic merit even according to the most conservative canons of high art, and Charlie Chaplin movies and Louis Armstrong recordings and the 1927 Bugatti racer and Watts Towers. The honest answer to the question "Who gets the money?" would therefore seem to be "Anyone who asks for it."

The trouble with this answer is that there is not enough money for everybody, which leads to Mr. Brustein's second operative statement: "There is no national voice of sufficient strength to make qualitative judgements. There is no national policy." That is, Brustein's solution to the problem of confusion about the arts is a national arts policy. Unfortunately such a policy would not eliminate the confusion because it is intrinsic to the arts themselves. It was not created by a failure of nerve but by a progressive and generally healthy opening up of the concept of art made necessary by new forms of artistic expression. A national policy could, however, solve the problem by decree. A "voice of sufficient strength" could announce "Art is what I say it is, and what I say it is gets the money."

This sounds a little ominous but Brustein clearly means well. Certain venerable, well-known, and highly professional arts institutions have earned the right to special consideration by government. Presumably the Metropolitan Opera, the Detroit Arts Institute, the Cleveland Symphony, and (you guessed it) the Yale Repertory Theatre are cases in point. These institutions are expensive. They must have generous subsidies. Without a "voice of sufficient strength" government policy may fail to recognize their unique merits. The specific threat that Brustein cites is populism. If arts money is spent to satisfy the "yearning of most Americans for 'personal expression'" it will be frittered away and high art will suffer. High school horn players may receive grants while the Met goes begging. Joan Mondale's point of view may be "warm and democratic," but democracy in the arts is exactly the sort of nonsense that a national policy should put a stop to.

Well, maybe. If Brustein's proposal is interpreted in the most charitable possible way he is arguing for support of old-line arts institutions because they have lingering sentimental value—the warehouse concept—and a limited number of contemporary or experimental arts institutions because, well, because a voice of sufficient authority has said that they rather than other, rival institutions deserve support. Neither proposition is entirely convincing. The first certainly has merit as long as the congress and the taxpayers accept it. It would be sad, genuinely sad, to see the Metropolitan Opera shut down or the Detroit Art Institute sell its collection to Saudi Arabia. It would also be sad, for that matter, to see Radio City Music Hall, a haven of sentimental memories for millions, disappear and the Rockettes go down the drain. When Radio City was expiring, powerful voices—including the voice of Jack Kroll of *Newsweek*—were raised in favor of making it into a "nonprofit" performing arts theatre. If Radio City, why not the automat, the White Tower, Tommy Dorsey's band, and Coney Island and everything else beautiful and sweet and terminal. If one form of culture is put on a social heart and lung machine, it is hard to know where to stop and even harder to know when to pull the plug, and that is the problem. The answer, probably, is to save as much as possible and let the rest go. Death is a healthy process. Darwin's great tree of life could grow only because its older branches were always dying.

Brustein's call for a voice of sufficient authority to define what is and is not acceptable (or subsidizable) contemporary art is harder to deal with. It would create the equivalent of an American *Academie Française* in supporting conventional art and bitterly opposing innovation is hardly such as to encourage imitation in the New World. It suggests that once established, a national arts policy might do more to damage American art than to help it. This brings us back to the bottom line. No one today knows what is and is not art. Anyone who claims to is either naive or campaigning for Minister of Culture.

Let us briefly consider the problem from another angle. Debate about the National Endowments reveals confusion about general principles. If we turn from generalities to a specific art form we can see the factors that created the confusion. Take American symphony orchestras. They were founded without exception through patronage of the wealthy; Jacob Astor in New York, Henry Lee Higginson in Boston, the Van Rensselaers in Philadelphia, Marshall Field and Charles Norman Fay in Chicago, and so on. They reflected the tastes of their creators in an opulent and tax-free world, and they used musicians and architecture lavishly. The patrons have not disappeared, but they have been unable to keep up with the rising costs of concert halls and unionized orchestras. In 1976–77 the Boston Symphony's budget reached $10 million. Philadelphia's budget is around $5 million, Cleveland's around $6.7 million, Washington's around $4 million. These budgets rise every year with inflation and most of them come with annual deficits—$2.5 million for Boston, for example. Obviously, without subsidy symphony orchestras cannot survive.

It is easy to blame the financial bind of unions and inflation, but the problems go deeper. In the first place, symphony audiences are split. The older patrons, who are asked to foot most of the bills, want Mozart, Brahms, Mendelssohn, and Richard Strauss. The younger generation wants Richard Strauss, Debussy, Stravinsky, Copeland, Bernstein, and, very occasionally, Hindemith and Karl Orff. The generation gap thus places the conductor in a no-win situation. Of course, if the conductor is foolish enough to play genuinely contemporary music, he loses everybody.

In the second place, the orchestra is beset by technology. Computerized ticket sales are all to the good. An occasional electronic effect produces a shiver of excitement in the boxes. But the introduction of a Moog Synthesizer or of the dozens of electronic sound-modification devices that are the stock in trade of a modern rock band, not to mention a computer that would take over the orchestra's function entirely, would empty the hall of listeners and musicians alike. These are problems of selection. Other problems brought about by technology are beyond control. It is a fact, for example, that the media have so glutted the ear of the modern listener that symphonic music has become commonplace. Why go to a formal concert when the same music—or something vaguely like it—is played gratis and without parking fees in office elevators and Bloomingdale's department stores? Alan Rich, a student of the ills of modern symphony orchestras, observes,

> An orchestra today plays for an audience whose vast majority collects records, listens to radio stations twenty-four hours a day and has its ears bathed in symphonic sound in elevators, restaurants and super-markets.

"Do you know this piece, dear?" "Yeah. But I heard it played better at Garfinkels."

In the third place, and partly because of the first two places, there is a question about how relevant to twentieth-century life symphonic music really is. After all, the central core of the modern symphonic repertory was created during the two centuries between Haydn and Richard Strauss. From the current vantage point it can be seen clearly as a kind of music made possible by a special socio-economic configuration. The configuration no longer exists. Already the music to which it gave rise is economically ruinous and seems to many a little archaic. Has the symphony orchestra become a warehouse for music—a natural history museum filled with stuffed dinosaurs? It is a question that is irresistible to clerks in search of treason. In 1965 Leonard Bernstein, golden boy of the music establishment, announced in the New York *Times*,

> Symphony is a moribund art form without relevance. Orchestras will be "museums of the past" with conductors who hang up the old masterpieces with solicitude as to position and lighting.

Bernstein went on to write his *Mass*, perhaps the most public display of vulgarity since Caligula made his horse a consul, so his announcement should probably be put down to trendiness. But he may have stumbled on an important truth without knowing it, the same way that a million monkeys working away on typewriters will eventually write *Hamlet*.

In the fourth place, symphonies are simply not the drawing cards that they used to be. Today they are being supported in part by the charity of the pop culture they are supposed to be weaning the public away from. The Blossom Festival in Cleveland and Tanglewood in Massachusetts are able to survive only by sandwiching classical music between rock performances, the profits of which subsidize the rest. Symphonies are also being forced to take on the tactics of their most commercialized pop antagonists. They sell T-shirts, tote bags, scarves, neckties, key rings, bumper stickers, umbrellas and anything else in the way of funky merchandise that the public will buy. Once a year most of them attempt a Madison Avenue blitzkrieg called a radiothon in cooperation with a local "good music" station. The radiothon goes around the clock like the marathon dance sessions of the thirties after which it is named. As the hours drag by the announcer offers friendly buyers out there in radioland everything from Playboy vacations in Las Vegas to second-hand electric toothbrushes. Between sales pitches, celebrities drop by to praise the orchestra. The technique is the hard sell and it works for symphonies almost as well as it works for Park Sausages and Serutan. It does not, however, have much to do with high art. Meanwhile, the "universal instrument" of science stands at the door ready to make orchestras obsolete. Alan Rich reports,

> I got an apalling record in the mail not long ago. Something with Tchaikovsky's *Nutcracker Suite* on one side and the *1812 Overture* on the other—both played on an electronic synthesizer, with absolutely no human involved except the one man at the control panel. It was appalling, mostly because it was good. I've played it for friends

who took long minutes to recognize that it wasn't a symphony orchestra they were hearing.

Shades of the Luddites.

Generation gaps, Muzak, radiothon, Beethoven T-shirts, Moog Synthesizers, inflation, unions, energy crisis, and the treason of the clerks. They all stem from contradictions inherent in modern life, and they all relate, ultimately, to the basic contradiction between the history-based culture that we have inherited and the technology-based culture that we now inhabit. Government subsidy may postpone the day when choices can no longer be avoided, but subsidy is no more effective, ultimately, than a Band-Aid for a hemophiliac. More money, okay, but money for what? To support museums of music? As an alternative to putting classical musicians on welfare? Not bad. Better use of the tax dollar, probably, than making cruise missles. Quite defensible, in fact, as long as the grantsmen and the grantees stay clear of a "voice of sufficient strength" to set a national arts policy. Not, however, a very useful contribution to the question of what is, and is not, art.

Kitsch. A word of obscure origins. Perhaps German, perhaps Polish, perhaps Yiddish. Its classic meaning is "a monstrosity of bad taste," as in a table lamp tumescent with gilt cherubs; a plaster statue of the Blessed Virgin with phosphorescent halo, a Wurlitzer jukebox with multicolored bubble tubes; any jukebox; an automobile with tail fins; the Edsel; Billy Beer; Billy Carter; the Big Mac hamburger. Words enlarge as they grow older. So it has been with *kitsch*. Today *kitsch* means anything that members of the arts establishment dislike, except *high kitsch*, which is *kitsch* produced by members of the arts establishment—Warhol's soup cans, Manzoni's feces, Norman Mailer's prose. *Kitsch* is used to refer not only to objects but to attitudes, pop philosophies, dress styles, television programs, patent medicines, and industrial products. One knowledgeable student defines it as "a product of modernity, closely linked to the appearance and growth of aesthetic consumerism. Essential to the recognition and identification of *kitsch* is a sense of ready availability in quantities limited only by existing demand. *Kitsch* is produced for the market and, cheaper or more expensive, it is entirely subordinated to the laws of the market." *Kitsch*, in other words, is a collective referring to the popular culture created by technology. There has always been *kitsch*, but the takeoff point of *kitsch*, the point when it could dominate the popular imagination, had to wait for the development of modern mass production. The first great flowering of *kitsch* occurred in the later nineteenth century, and its first element was print, the first true mass medium.

All true except that *kitsch* carries with it a hint of condescension, as though any fool could produce it successfully. Actually, it takes chutzpah to make *kitsch*. Not everybody has it in him. If everybody did, every lead cast of the Eiffel Tower would sell millions, every movie would be a box office smash, and every record would be a golden platter. This does not happen. The original *King Kong* was a classic of *kitsch*. *King Kong* 1976 was a dud in spite of technicolor and an ape that was a miracle of cybernetics. *Exorcist I* was a sensation; *Exorcist II* was, as they say on Madison Avenue, the biggest bomb since Hiroshima. There are undoubtedly laws governing the *kitsch* market. People speak glibly of them, but the ups and downs of even the most stereotyped and slavish imitations of the *kitsch* successes of yesteryear show that the laws have not been discovered. As far as *kitsch* goes we are still living in the Ptolemaic universe. Until the Newton of *kitsch* appears it will continue to take talent and courage to produce it successfully.

A great many people consider *kitsch* a threat to humanity. Dwight McDonald, for example, saw it as a means of drugging the masses: "The lords of *Kitsch* exploit the cultural needs of the masses," he wrote, "in order to make a profit and/or to maintain class rule—in Communist countries only the second purpose obtains." This view, plausible though it seems, ignores the fact that in choosing *kitsch* the masses are choosing their own form of anesthesia, and they are quite willing to depose the Lords of *Kitsch* whenever those Lords fail to serve up the right formula. George Steiner, a later prophet than McDonald, takes a gloomier view of things. *Kitsch* is not a plot by the politicians. It is a symptom of the decline of the West:

> Where the West does not peer at the stars, it looks to Asia, or, rather, the *Kitsch* of Asia.
>
> The children of Krishna tango along our soiled pavements. The stoned, their vacant minds hysterical or suprine, mouth dime-store mantras. The mendacities of Zen and fairground meditation, prepackaged nirvanas *à la* Hermann Hesse (an immensely overrated writer), are big business. Neon tantras flash from the boulevards of San Francisco and Chelsea. Cadillac-wafted little trixters, corrupt butterballs in saffron robes who proclaim themselves to be the light of the East, fill our lecture halls and take their titles.

Wow! Abandon hope all ye who enter here. Steiner's alternatives to the pop inferno are Eberhard Bethge's biography of Dietrich Bonhoeffer ("one of the few treasured classics of our time") and the poetry of Thomas Hardy ("the only very great English poet of the century"). Neither Bethge nor Hardy is exactly electric with promise for the mass market, but Steiner's choices explain why he has the title Extraordinary Fellow of Churchill College. Perhaps it is just as well that he speaks as an Extraordinary Fellow rather than as a Minister of Culture.

One of the fascinations of *kitsch* is the way it moves around the world. Ferromagnetic tape, for example, was pioneered in Germany during the Second World War. American scientists developed solid-state circuitry and miniature precision electric motors. The Japanese borrowed these technologies from North America, domesticated them to Japanese labor conditions, and made such fine tape recorders so cheaply that American tape recorders were driven off the world market. *Banzai!* But wait. The Japanese sold their tape recorders to Americans, British, Swiss, Brazilians, Argentines, Hindus, Thais, South Africans and yes—Japanese. All of these tape recorders created an enormous demand for tapes. Enter, once again, the Americans led by such figures as Elvis Presley, Diahann Carroll, Elton John, and Stevie Wonder. By Jove! Enter the Beatles. Enter Punk Rock. Enter the Sex Pistols. Everybody has harvested money from *kitsch* music. The scenario changes for each of the forms and genres of *kitsch* but the result is always the same. The market gets bigger and the style gets more and more uniform worldwide. There may not yet be a true international style of *kitsch* but it is knocking at the world's door.

What's happening to world culture? Perhaps nothing very new is happening. The spread of international *kitsch* through the media is a late and dramatic instance of the process described by Karl Marx in the *Communist Manifesto:*

> The Bourgeoisie, whenever it has gotten the upper hand, has put an end to all feudal, patriarchal, idyllic relations. It has piteously torn asunder the mostly feudal ties that bound man to his "natural superiors" and has left no other bond between man and man but naked self-interest, than callous "cash payment". . . . All fixed, fast-frozen relations, with their train of ancient and venerable prejudices and opinions, are swept away; all new-formed ones become antiquated before they can ossify. All that is solid melts in the air, and man is at last compelled to face with sober senses his real condition of life.

Marx's phrase about confronting things with sober senses betrays an optimism about the way we regard culture today, but the rest would be hard to improve on. If there is a hint of tragedy in his rhetoric, reminiscent of Darwin's Tree of Life that grows by dying, he is describing a one-way journey. Every journey requires saying good-bye to things familiar and cherished. Setting out on the journey described by Marx has required that we say good-bye to more than Marx could have imagined.

Imagine the complete *kitsch* man of the late twentieth century. He makes a good living. He is, say, a computer programmer or a television repairman. He lives in one-bedroom apartment with sliding picture window and balcony on the thirteenth floor of a two-hundred-unit apartment building best described as *kitsch* Corbusier. His apartment is crammed with the gadgetry of the Age of Technology—telephone, refrigerator-freezer, microwave oven, color television with built-in Super Pong, digital clock-radio with LED readout, electric toothbrush, Hewlett Packard pocket calculator, Minolta SRL camera, battery operated ashtray, quadraphonic audio with tape deck. His wardrobe is various but includes two international uniforms: a Dacron, doubleknit, permapress blue suit for formal wear, and blue jeans and T-shirts with assorted mottos. His bathroom cabinet holds One-A-Day vitamins, Crest toothpaste, underarm deodorant, vitamin E supplement, Maalox, Alka-Seltzer, Valium, anti-dandruff soap, anti-acne soap, deodorant soap, Dr. Scholl's foot powder, Nite-EZE, No Doze, and assorted medicines matching his mild hypochondria. His furniture is Danish modern, his rug nylon shag, his counters fruitwood Formica. His walls are white. On them hang pictures of classic cars (living room), Renaissance woodcuts of herbs (kitchen), a color reproduction of Georgia O'Keeffe's *Orchid* (bedroom). A W. C. Fields poster hangs in the bathroom. He attends pro football and basketball games, movies (*Star Wars, Annie Hall, Close Encounters of the Third Kind*) and discos, but he prefers solo television watching or a small pot party with friends. He travels by jet (tourist class) and stays overnight at Holiday Inns and Hilton Hotels. He is into history, bicycling, encounter groups, Tai Chi, backgammon, astrology and vintage wines. He is interested in religion but torn between Hans Küng and the Reverend Sun Yung Moon. All of this leaves him little time to read, but he enjoys Watergate revelations, assertiveness books, and fiction by Kurt Vonnegut and Isaac Asimov. He buys things constantly but seldom uses them very long because his interests are always changing. Tennis and sensitivity training one year, jogging and Kung Fu the next. Monopoly and disco one year, Scrabble and Garry Trudeau the next. He thinks a lot about his sex life, has read Alex Comfort and Gloria Steinem, and tries to be a real friend to women.

He is a true citizen of the world. Except for the accident of speaking English he could be living anywhere. His interests have little to do with anything that existed before 1950 and even less with anything rooted in the American soil. He moves easily from place to place because all of the places he visits are much the same and most of the people he meets are like him. To travel from Atlanta to Tokyo is as easy as taking a six-by-three-foot color photograph of Stone Mountain out of his picture window and Scotch-taping a six-by-three-foot color photograph of Mt. Fugiyama in its place.

Tell him that high art is central to his life and he will stare at you in bewilderment. Tell him that Thomas Hardy is the only very great English poet of the twentieth century and he will laugh. His life is full and satisfied. He is surrounded by the things, images, sounds, words, attitudes of late-twentieth-century culture. They are his medium. He inhabits them as naturally as a catfish inhabits the waters of the Mississippi River.

Quite possibly he, too, has a $3.75 mobile hanging from his ceiling. If so it must spin as lazily in his air as it does in mine, stimulating similar thoughts. Perhaps as I am writing of him, he has taken up his Bic pen and has begun to write about me.

(unpublished)

A Tree, a Streamlined Fish, and a Self-Squared Dragon: Science as a Form of Culture

Have we begun to understand even the old industrial revolution? Much less the new scientific revolution in which we stand? There was never anything more necessary to comprehend.

—C. P. SNOW, "The Two Cultures"

The theme of the following essay is the emergence of new values in modern scientific thought. This theme is as simple and as subtle as the movement in biology from observing nature in the middle perspective, so beautifully illustrated by Audubon's paintings of the birds of North America, to electron-microscope photographs of the fine structure of living cells.

D'Arcy Wentworth Thompson remarks at the end of his mathematical study of living forms that he is "advanced in these enquiries no further than the threshold." It will be well for me to state at the beginning that my purpose is not to write a history of science or a work on the philosophy of science. Both tasks have been undertaken by authors eminently qualified for them, and although I have tried to learn from these authors, I am not in any sense attempting to follow where they have so ably led. I want, rather, to examine aspects of science that are legitimate subjects of cultural study, and thus to cross a barrier that has been posited at least since Francis Bacon's *Novum Organum* and that is the subject of C. P. Snow's much-quoted essay "The Two Cultures." I believe that human culture is a seamless web. No matter how fragmented our understanding of it, there is only one culture. Just as the analysis of culture often involves the techniques of science—as often happens, for instance, in archaeological, textual, psychoanalytic, and linguistic studies—science can be approached as a form of culture. To see it in this way is to see it not as a body of knowledge but as an agency of value; and in the twentieth century, science has become an agency of enormous power, in some respects replacing such traditional sources of value as religion, custom, and history. Hence the urgency of Snow's questions: "Have we begun to understand even the old industrial revolution? Much less the new scientific revolution in which we stand?"

In order to create a context, I will begin with some observations about two traditional poles of scientific thought. The first assumes that nature is an appearance which science must penetrate in order to discover reality. This is, in general, the point of view associated in Greek science with Pythagoras and the Plato of the *Timaeus*. The second pole is Baconian. It assumes that reality is what we see in front of us and that understanding reality is a matter of disciplined observation. I need only to add that the two poles are by no means always opposed. Many—perhaps most—scientists move easily from one to the other, and back, as the demands of their projects change.

After establishing a context, I will concentrate on three representative figures whose work defines a kind of curve leading from the past to the present. Other figures could have been selected, but they might not have defined the curve as clearly or permitted the issues to emerge as fully. The three are Charles Darwin, D'Arcy Wentworth Thompson, and Benoit Mandelbrot. Each expresses views typical of an important moment in the development of the values that are intrinsic to modern culture, but some interesting paradoxes emerge. Darwin's nature is, in theory, non-human and alien, but he pours emotion into it in much the same way that primitive man humanizes the world through myth. Thompson's nature is regular and elegant, the materialization of mathematics. It, too, seems alien until we realize that the mathematics is either the invention of God, as Thompson suggests in his "Epilogue," or a purely human creation, as Thompson undoubtedly believed in his less poetic moments. The nature revealed by Thompson is a nature devoid of myth, but it is saturated with the aesthetic qualities suggested by words like *admiration*, *wonder*, and *beauty*. Mandelbrot's nature is discontinuous and impossibly complex. Its order cannot be duplicated, so he creates a system parallel to nature, capable of producing things that are "something like" natural things. Mandelbrot's fractal geometry is in this sense fully human: it is invented by man and its products are entirely man-made. Their adequacy as facsimiles of nature can be tested in the most empirical way: Mandelbrot's equations can be converted into computer graphics and then compared to natural images, much as Audubon's birds can be compared to their living counterparts. The equations meet this test so successfully that they have been used to create imaginary landscapes for movies and television fantasies.

All of the texts I will examine here were intended by their authors to be accessible to the general reader as well as the scientist. Although the

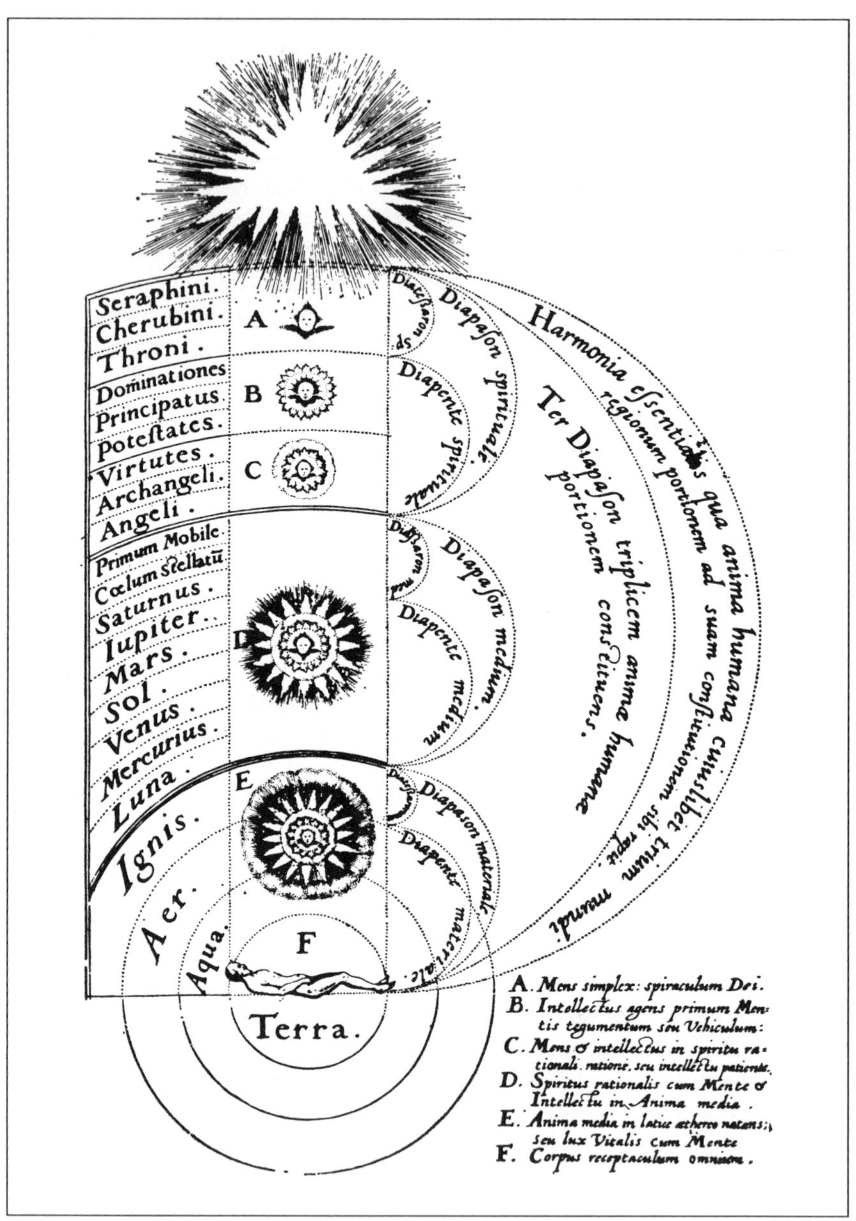

Musica Humana

images of nature they reveal are quite distinct, each can be seen as pointing toward the next. Thompson is quite conscious of writing in the shadow of Darwin, and Mandelbrot refers several times to Thompson as in some sense a precursor in the effort to study the mathematical basis of nature. All three express values inherent in modern culture; in examining their work, we examine aspects of the world we inhabit in America in the closing years of the twentieth century.

The efforts of Thompson and Mandelbrot to be accessible to readers who are not scientists point to a corollary theme of the present essay. C. P. Snow's challenge in "The Two Cultures" is usually understood to mean that students of culture should study mathematics and chemistry and thermodynamics in order to be able to understand science, yet if his challenge is confronted seriously, it goes much deeper than that. The problem is that our visual and verbal languages change slowly, but for the past century our culture has been changing rapidly. Since we imagine by means of visual or verbal languages, this is a way of saying that we are no longer able to imagine the world—or, at least, that our languages are no longer synchronized with what we experience. It is understandable that Snow sees the problem as a lack of communication between two different cultures. His understanding, however, is wrong because it relates to symptoms, not to causes.

The problem of language is exemplified in science in the common assertion that the reality revealed by science cannot be expressed in natural language and is therefore inaccessible to imagination. Paul Dirac asserts in *Quantum Mechanics* (1930) that reality is no more accessible to visual languages than to verbal ones: "Fundamental laws do not govern the world as it appears in our mental picture in any very direct way, but instead they form a substratum of which we cannot form a mental picture without introducing irrelevancies." If Dirac is correct, all efforts to find languages capable of objectifying reality are doomed and may even be pernicious since they introduce "irrelevancies." There are, however, reasons to be more optimistic than Dirac. Art, architecture, and poetry have all sought consciously to create new languages in the twentieth century, and the visual languages developed by modern art have been extraordinarily successful. As I hope to demonstrate, science has also created visual and verbal languages that have much to offer to those seeking to reestablish links between the imagination and the world. In the efforts of Darwin, Thompson, and Mandelbrot to be accessible to general readers as well as to specialists, we encounter one crucial set of these links—and we discover that, whatever else these men might have thought they were doing, one thing they *have* done is to lead us toward a sense of the "two cultures" as one.

II

The root meaning of Greek *kosmos* is "order" or "arrangement." It has the additional meanings of "comely order," "decoration," or "ornament." It is the source of English *cosmos*, and also of *cosmetic*.

Greek science is the study of the comely and harmonious order of the world. It is more an aesthetic than a practical pursuit; its great triumphs are in geometry and the theory of proportions. The harmonious order of things is *in the world* according to the Greek view. It is there whether it is perceived or not. This assumption is widespread in mythic thought, and to the Greeks goes credit for expressing it with such rigor that it could become the basis for early Greek science.

"Comeliness" is another matter. It requires a judgment on the part of the observer and a motive, real or imputed, on the part of the creator. Greek science assumes that creation is beautiful as well as orderly; the proper response to it is aesthetic as well as intellectual. In the *Theogony*, Hesiod (eighth-century B.C.) imagines that creation is pervaded by the music of the nine muses, the daughters of Mnemosyne: "Unwearying flows the sweet sound from their lips, and the house of their father Zeus the loud-thunderer is glad at the lilylike voice of the goddesses as it spreads abroad, and the peaks of snowy Olympus resound, and the homes of the immortals." The world is music, and creation a dance.

In the sixth century B.C. Pythagoras of Samos discovered the relation between harmony and number—according to legend, after hearing the tones produced by a blacksmith's hammers of different weights. His discovery convinced him that number is the foundation of the comely order of the world and that harmony is its corollary. The natural order is simultaneously functional and beautiful, and its basis is number. This conclusion remained central in later Greek scientific thought. It may, in fact, have hampered the development of Greek science by encouraging its interest in elegant demonstrations at the expense of calculation. The motto over the doors of Plato's academy was *Medeis ageometretos eisito*—"Let no one ignorant of geometry enter." In *The Republic* (book 7) Socrates discusses the education of his guardians. The central disciplines are arithmetic, geometry, harmony, and dialectic. Number is fundamental. It is the key to the rational understanding of the real:

> These sparks that paint the sky, since they are decorations on a visible surface, we must consider the first and most exact of visible things, but we must recognize that they fall far short of the truth—the movements, namely—of real slowness and real speed in true numbers and true figures. . . . These can be apprehended by reason and thought, not by sight.

Christian apologists could (and did) discover Pythagorean notes in the Old Testament. Of wisdom Proverbs says, "When he prepared the heavens, I was there: when he set a compass upon the face of the depth." In book 7 of Milton's *Paradise Lost* (1667) this becomes:

> . . . in his hand
> He took the golden Compasses, prepar'd
> In God's Eternal store, to circumscribe
> This Universe, and all created things:
> One foot he centered, and the other turn'd
> Round through the vast profundity obscure,
> Thus far extend, thus far thy bounds,
> This be thy just Circumference, O world.

And the Pythagorean note rings in the work of the great Renaissance astronomer Johannes Kepler (1571–1630). Early in his career Kepler concluded that the distances between the planets can be determined by assuming they are the distances that would be produced by inscribing the five regular solids, beginning with the tetrahedron, inside of each other. He wrote in *Mysterium Cosmographicum* (1596),

> It is my intention, Reader, to demonstrate that the Highest and Most Good Creator in the creation of this mobile world and the arrangement of the heavens had his eye on those five regular bodies [i.e., solids] which have been celebrated from the time of Pythagoras and Plato down to our own day; and that to their nature He accommodated the number of the heavenly spheres, their proportions, and the system of their motions.

The Pythagorean scientist is drawn to the world as much by love of its endlessly surprising and beautiful patterns as by the desire for knowledge. He is a connoisseur as well as an observer of facts. If he does not create beauty, he discovers it and shares it with others. In a discussion of Faraday's experiments with electricity, J. B. S. Haldane touches the Pythagorean chord:

> As a result of Faraday's work you are able to listen to a wireless. But more than that, as a result of Faraday's work, scientifically educated men and women have an altogether richer view of the world. For them, apparently empty space is full of the most intricate and beautiful patterns. So Faraday gave the world not only fresh wealth but fresh beauty.

III

The search of Pythagorean science for elegant geometric and mathematical forms behind the appearances of the visible world stands in striking contrast to the emphasis on observation and experiment that is central to the Baconian tradition. Baconian science finds reality directly ahead in the visible world. Since it is extremely difficult to see things as they are, Baconian science is a never-ending contest with human weakness. Bacon remarks in *The Advancement of Learning* (1605):

> The mind of man is far from the nature of a clear and equal glass, wherein the beams of things should reflect according to their true incidence; nay, it is rather like an enchanted glass, full of superstition and imposture, if it be not delivered and reduced.

And later, commenting on imagination:

> Imagination doth raise and erect the Minde, by submitting the shewes of things to the desires of the Mind, whereas reason doth buckle and bow the Mind unto the Nature of things. And we see by these insinuations and congruities with man's Nature and pleasure, joined also with the agreement and consort [imagination] hath with Musicke, it both had access and estimation in rude times and barbarous Regions, where other learning stoode excluded.

There is a strong note of asceticism in Bacon. Man is not the supreme work of Creation, the measure of all things and the image of God, as he is, for example, in Pico della Mirandola's famous essay, *On the Dignity of Man*. Instead he is an upstart crow in a world utterly indifferent to his existence. His mind is an enchanted glass—a distorting mirror—that must be "delivered and reduced"—that is, mortified—if it is to find truth.

Since Bacon had no knowledge of sophisticated scientific instruments, he understood reality as "things" seen from a middle distance by the naked eye. An ideal Baconian dictionary of reality would be a collection of pictures, one for each thing that exists in the world. It follows that the ideal language is a language of nouns with one noun for each thing so that men can speak "so many *things* almost in an equal number of *words*." The dictionary for this sort of language would be a list of nouns corresponding to the pictures contained in the ideal picture-dictionary. However, when pictures get inside the mind they are made into what they are not. Since this position involves a hostile critique of that which exists inside the mind—namely, that which makes people human—it is in some sense a hostile critique of humanity. The first paragraph of Charles Dickens' *Hard Times* (1854) is a tribute to the influence of Baconian asceticism two centuries after Bacon's death:

> Now, what I want is, Facts. Teach these boys and girls nothing but Facts. Facts alone are wanted in life. Plant nothing else, and root out everything else. You can only form the minds of reasoning animals upon Facts: nothing else will ever be of any service to them.

It is a pity that Bacon was such a successful propagandist because his concept of science simply does not square with the facts he was so fond of. Placed beside Descartes's *Discours de la Méthode pour Bien Conduire sa Raison et Chercher la Vérité dans les Sciences* (1637) the *Novum Organum* is clearly more rhetoric than science. Moreover, there is a touch of Pythagorean wonder in Bacon in spite of himself. But it is the distrust of mind, not the wonder, that made Bacon a hero of science in the eighteenth and nineteenth centuries, particularly in the sciences that depended more on observation and classification than on mathematics: geography, geology, biology, anatomy.

IV

Charles Darwin's *The Origin of Species* (1859) is the culmination and—for many Victorians—the vindication of the Baconian tradition in science. Darwin explicitly recognizes his debt to Bacon in his *Autobiography* (1876): "I worked on the true Baconian principles, and without any theory collected facts on a wholesale scale." The book brings together twenty years of painstaking, minutely detailed observation ranging over the whole spectrum of organic life. Like Bacon, Darwin made little use of mathematics, although he had attempted (unsuccessfully) to deepen his mathematical knowledge while at Cambridge. Nor was Darwin the sort of scientist whose observations depended on instruments. Although his four-volume study of *Cirripedia* (barnacles) uses microscopy frequently, most of his other works could have been—and were—written almost entirely on the basis of direct observation.

As soon as it was published, *The Origin of Species* was recognized as one of those books that changes history. Its reception was partly a tribute to the overwhelming wealth of detail it offers in support of its theory and partly an instance of powder waiting for a spark. Jean Baptiste Lamarck had proposed a generally evolutionary theory of biology in the *Histoire naturelle des animaux* (1815), which Darwin says in his *Autobiography* was an influence on him. Charles Lyell's *Principles of Geology* (1832), with its evidence of the immense span of the record of fossil life, was indispensable to Darwin. Lyell's contribution was of special value to Darwin in his work on the Galápagos Islands. It showed that the variations he observed among animals of the same species must have occurred within a relatively short span of geologic time. Another source, and the immediate occasion for the publication of *The Origin of Species,* was the work of Alfred Russel Wallace. In 1858 Wallace sent Darwin his essay "On the Tendency of Varieties to Depart Indefinitely from the Original Type." Darwin admits in the *Autobiography* that this essay "contained exactly the same theory as mine," though it lacks the luxuriance of Darwin's supporting observations. Again according to the *Autobiography,* it was his reading of Malthus that suggested to Darwin, around 1838, that all species are locked in a remorseless struggle for survival, although the concept of natural selection may also owe something to Edward Blyth.

Darwin denies in the *Autobiography* that evolution was "in the air" before *The Origin of Species* was published: "What I believe was strictly true is that innumerable well-observed facts were stored in the minds of naturalists ready to take their proper place as soon as any theory which would receive them was sufficiently explained." In any case *The Origin of Species* was an immediate sensation. By ignoring religious dogma and wishful thinking Darwin was able to buckle and bow his mind to the nature of things and produce the sort of powerful, overarching concept that reveals coherence in a vast area of experience that had previously seemed chaotic.

A modern reader can see a kinship between Darwin's passionate interest in all things living—beginning with his undergraduate hobby of collecting beetles—and the outburst of nature poetry that occurred in the Romantic period. Darwin was unaware of this affinity. In the *Autobiography* he says that "up to the age of thirty, or beyond it, poetry of many kinds, such as the works of Milton, Gray, Byron, Wordsworth, Coleridge, and Shelley . . . gave me the greatest pleasure. . . . But now for many years I cannot endure to read a line of poetry." His *Journal of the Voyage of the Beagle* is filled with appreciative comments about tropical landscape, but he remarks that natural scenery "does not cause me the exquisite delight which it formerly did." He plays the role of Baconian ascetic collecting "without any theory . . . facts on a wholesale scale." His mind, he says (again in the *Autobiography*) has become "a kind of machine for grinding laws out of large collections of facts." The idea that the mind is a machine that grinds facts echoes Bacon's injunction to "buckle and bow" the mind to nature. The same asceticism is evident in Darwin's disparaging comments on his literary style. He believed he was writing dry scientific prose for other scientists, and John Ruskin, among others, agreed. He was astounded, gratified, and a little frightened by his popular success.

No one can read Darwin today without recognizing that he was wrong about his style. As Stanley Edgar Hyman observes in *The Tangled Bank* (1962), both *The Voyage of the Beagle* and *The Origin of Species* are filled with passages which, whatever Darwin may have thought of them, are of a high literary order. The writing is effective precisely because it does not strain for the gingerbread opulence fashionable in mid-Victorian English prose. It has a freedom from pretense, a quality of authority, as moving as the natural descriptions of Wordsworth's *The Prelude* because it stems from direct contact with the web of relationships that comprise nature. Darwin was, indeed, a good Baconian, but instead of revealing a mind bowed to nature, his prose reveals a mind that has surrendered to the kaleidoscope of life around it. No passage is more revealing in this respect than the concluding paragraph of *The Origin of Species,* in which Darwin describes a natural scene,

> . . . clothed with many plants of many kinds, with birds singing on the bushes, with various insects flitting about, and with worms crawling through the damp earth, and . . . these elaborately constructed forms, so different from each other, and so dependent upon each other in so complex a manner, have all been produced by laws acting around us. . . . Thus, from the war of nature, from famine and death, the most exalted object which we are capable of conceiving, namely, the production of the higher animals, directly follows.

Thus, in addition to being a Baconian scientist—or because of being that kind of scientist—Darwin is one of the first poets of the actual. The closest visual parallels to his prose are the drawings of Audubon, but his writing is also related to the photographs of Matthew Brady, the histories of Ranke and Burckhardt, and the novels of Balzac and George Eliot and Turgenev. The following passage from the discussion of the struggle for existence in chapter 3 of *The Origin of Species* illustrates Darwin's technique:

> How have all these exquisite adaptions of one part of the organization to another part, and to the conditions of life, and of one organic being to another been perfected? We see these beautiful coadaptations most plainly in the woodpecker and the mistletoe; and only a little less plainly in the humblest parasite which clings to the hairs of a quadruped or the feathers of a bird; in the structure of the beetle which dives through the water; in the plumed seed which is wafted by the gentle breeze; in short we see beautiful adaptations everywhere and in every part of the organic world.

Exquisite, perfected, beautiful, humblest, plumed, gentle. The world described by these adjectives is not cold, alien, or indifferent. It is a work of art. Nor is Darwin's the dispassionate, dry prose of a technical manual. As in a painting the parts mentioned are harmoniously related to each other—"coadaptation" is Darwin's word—and the music of the prose objectifies the harmony. There is no detectable difference here between a hypothetical figure labeled "scientific observer" and a literary artist commenting on experience. The language invites the reader to share experience as well as to understand it. *Exquisite, beautiful,* and *gentle* orient him emotionally at the same time that his attention is focused on the objects that give rise to the emotion: mistletoe, parasite, water beetle, plumed seed. The passage flatly contradicts Darwin's statement in the *Autobiography* that his artistic sensitivity had atrophied by the time he was thirty. That he thought it had shows only that he believed with his contemporaries that science is science and art is art. The problem is in his psyche, not his prose. The tradition that science should be dispassionate and practical, that it is a kind of servitude to nature, prevented him from understanding what he was, in fact, doing.

A more complex example of Darwin's artistry can be found in the "summary" of chapter 3. The passage is a sustained meditation on a single image. The image—the Tree of Life—is mythic, an archetype familiar from Genesis and also from Egyptian, Buddhist, Greek, and other sources. In mythology, the Tree of Life connects the underworld and the heavens. It is the axis on which the spheres turn and the path along which creatures from the invisible world visit and take leave of earth. It is an ever-green symbol of virility, bearing fruit in winter. It is the wood of the Cross on which God dies, and the wood reborn that announces the return of life by sending out new branches in the spring. All of this symbolism is familiar from Frazer's *Golden Bough,* Jung's *Symbols of Transformation,* and other studies of mythic imagery. Behind it is what Rudolf Otto calls, in *The Idea of the Holy,* the terrifying and fascinating mystery: *mysterium tremendum et fascinans.*

Still, it is interesting to find a scientist, particularly a preeminent Victorian scientist, using an overtly mythic image. The emphasis of the passage on branching limbs is a visual image of evolution, but at the same time it is a remarkably full elaboration of the archetype:

> The affinities of all the beings of the same class have sometimes been represented by a great tree. I believe this simile largely speaks the truth. The green and budding twigs may represent existing species; and those produced during former years may represent the long succession of extinct species. At each period of growth all the growing twigs have tried to branch out on all sides, and to overtop and kill the surrounding twigs and branches, in the same manner as species and groups of species have at all times overmastered other species in the great battle for life. . . . From the first growth of the tree, many a limb and branch has decayed and dropped off; and all these fallen branches of various sizes may represent those whole orders, families, and genera which have now no living representatives, and which are known to us only in a fossile state. As we here and there see a thin, straggling branch springing from a fork low down in a tree, and

which by some chance has been favored and is still alive on its summit, so we occasionally see an animal like the Ornithorhynchus or Lepidosiren, which in some small degree connects by its affinities two large branches of life, and which has apparently been saved from fatal competition by having inhabited a protected station. As buds give rise by growth to fresh buds, and these, if vigorous, branch out and overtop on all sides many a feebler branch, so by generation I believe it has been with the great Tree of Life, which fills with its dead and broken branches the crust of the earth, and covers the surface with its ever-branching and beautiful ramifications.

Darwin's music here is stately and somber. The central image is established at the beginning: a great tree green at the top but filled with dead branches beneath the crown. The passage becomes an elegy for all the orders of life that have perished since the tree began. Words suggesting death crowd the sentences: *overtopped, kill, the great battle for life, decayed, dropped off, fallen, no living representative, straggling branch, fatal competition.* As the passage moves toward its conclusion, a change, a kind of reversal, can be felt. Words suggesting life become more frequent: *alive, life, saved, fresh buds, vigorous.* The final sentence restates the central paradox in a contrast between universal desolation—"dead and broken branches [filling] the crust of the earth"—and images of eternal fertility—"ever-branching and beautiful ramifications."

The idea that science reveals truth is central to the Darwinian moment. Once revealed, truth can be generalized, and the truths discovered by Darwin were applied almost immediately to sociology and political science. Herbert Spencer had coined the phrase "survival of the fittest" in 1852 in an article entitled "A Theory of Population." Buttressed by the prestige of *The Origin of Species,* the concept of the survival of the fittest was used to justify laissez-faire capitalism, a use brilliantly chronicled in Richard Hofstadter's *Social Darwinism in American Thought* (1955). Andrew Carnegie remarked in 1900 that "a struggle is inevitable [in society] and it is a question of the survival of the fittest." John D. Rockefeller seconded the opinion: "The growth of a large business is merely the survival of the fittest." Capitalism enables the strong to survive while the weak are destroyed. Socialism, conversely, protects the weak and frustrates the strong. Marx turned over the coin: socialism is a later and therefore a higher product of evolution than bourgeois capitalism. Being superior, it will replace capitalism as surely as warmblooded mammals replaced dinosaurs.

Darwin influenced cultural thought at a deep level, which is to say that he changed not only the way reality was managed but the way it was understood. The writing of history became evolutionary—so much so that historians often assumed an evolutionary model and tailored their facts to fit. The histories of political systems, national economies, technologies, machinery, literary genres, philosophical systems, and even styles of dress were presented as examples of evolution—meaning examples of progress from simple to complex, usually interpreted to mean from good to better.

And, of course, Darwin deeply influenced progressive religion. Adam Sedgwick, professor of geology at Cambridge, began the long history of attacks on Darwin in the name of religion when he wrote in "Objections to Mr. Darwin's Theory of the Origin of Species," published anonymously in 1860: "I cannot conclude without expressing my detestation of the theory, because of its unflinching materialism." Perhaps because of such attacks, Darwin added the phrase "by the Creator" to his conclusion of the second edition of *The Origin of Species* (1860): "There is a grandeur in this view of life, with its several powers, having been originally breathed by the Creator into a few forms or into one; and whilst this planet has gone cycling on according to the fixed law of gravity, from so simple a beginning endless forms most beautiful and most wonderful have been, and are being evolved." Whether this fully represents Darwin's personal view of religion lies outside the scope of the present discussion. Probably it did not. At any rate the notion that God is revealed in evolution remains powerfully attractive today both to biologists and, as shown by Teilhard de Chardin's *The Phenomenon of Man* (written in 1938 and published in 1955), to those attempting to formulate a scientific theology.

Many of the applications of Darwin's ideas were patently strained from the beginning, while time revealed the inadequacies of others. "Social Darwinism" is studied in history classes today but is no longer a viable political creed. Most fundamental, however, is the fact that by the middle of the twentieth century Baconian empiricism was no longer adequate to the idea of nature that science had developed. Einstein, Heisenberg, and Gödel made it clear that nature and the mind are involved in each other and are not separate empires. An objective world that can be "observed" and "understood" if only the imagination can be held in check simply does not exist. Facts are not observations "collected . . . on a wholesale scale." They are knots in a net.

V

D'Arcy Wentworth Thompson (1860–1948) was everything in biology that Darwin was not. *On Growth and Form* (1917) is an attempt to place biology on a mathematical foundation. To do this Thompson felt he had to deny not only Darwin's conclusions about evolution, but also the

Baconian methodology of *The Origin of Species*. In the light of the explosive development of biology since World War II, *On Growth and Form* has come to seem less significant than it did thirty years ago. It remains, however, a significant illustration of a moment in scientific thought halfway between the Victorian period and the late twentieth century.

In his introduction, after quoting Kant's assertion that chemistry is "a science but not a science" because it is not based on mathematics, Thompson comments that "numerical precision is the very soul of science, and its attainment affords the best, perhaps the only criterion of the truth of theories and the correctness of experiments." Admitting the complexity of life processes, he adds, "My sole purpose is to correlate with mathematical statement and physical law certain of the simpler outward phenomena of organic growth and structure or form."

A common criticism of Bacon's philosophy of science, as well as Darwin's, is that it ignores mathematics. This is true. Bacon published grandiose schemes for the reform of knowledge, but Galileo established the basis for the mathematical analysis of acceleration, and Descartes laid the foundations of analytic geometry. To move from Darwin to Thompson is to move from the poetry of things to the poetry of the numbers that underlie things. It is to move, in other words, from things visible to things invisible, which is to say away from Bacon and toward Pythagoras.

Karl Gauss, James Clerk Maxwell, Ernest Rutherford, Josiah Gibbs, Jean Baptiste Fourier, Hermann Helmholtz, Georg Cantor, and a host of other brilliant nineteenth-century figures shared Thompson's appreciation of the power of mathematics. All were far more accomplished mathematicians. Thompson seldom goes beyond elementary mathematical concepts, noting for example that for objects of equal density, mass increases as the cube of linear dimension rather than in proportion to it. The observation is commonplace, almost trivial. However, Thompson's application is not. He concludes that the length of the limbs of land animals of the same species will, in general, increase in proportion to the cube root of their body weight. This leads to calculations of the probable lengths of the legs of birds of the same species but different weights. Insects breathe by diffusion of oxygen through capillary tubes extending from shell to bloodstream. Their maximum size is fixed by the fact that if they become very large their breathing apparatus ceases to function.

Load-bearing horizontals must be supported, and the support structures tend to be mirror images of the stresses to which the structures are subject—hence the shapes of dinosaur skeletons and the shape of the human femur. When circles are close-packed they deform, if flexible, into hexagons—hence honeycombs. Spheres tend to deform when close-packed into rhombic dodecahedra or complex 14-hedra—hence two common configurations of close-packed tissue cells. The equiangular spiral (so-called by Descartes) increases in volume without changing shape—hence the Chambered Nautilus. The shape of fish is determined by the flow of water. Streamlining—the term was apparently invented by Thompson—reduces turbulence to a minimum and thus maximizes swimming efficiency. Bones and body shapes that appear unrelated on casual inspection can be seen to be similar when they are drawn on graphs and the graphs are systematically distorted.

Thompson multiplies his examples luxuriantly, especially in the revised and enlarged edition of *On Growth and Form* (1942). Perhaps the most remarkable fact about them is their mathematical simplicity. Thompson does not need or want complex examples. He is demonstrating a point: the relevance of mathematics to biology. The simpler and clearer the examples, the more convincing the demonstration; Thompson shares the fondness of all scientists in the Pythagorean tradition for grand simplicities.

The application of mathematics to life may not seem innovative today, but Thompson clearly felt in 1917 that it was a bold, even a risky, venture. It seems to violate an unspoken feeling that life is beyond quantification: "To treat the living body as a mechanism was repugnant, and seemed even ludicrous, to Pascal; and Goethe, lover of nature as he was, ruled mathematics out of place in natural history." When the zoologist meets a simple geometrical shape in a living organism, "he is prone of old habit to believe that after all, it is something more than a spiral or a sphere, and that in this 'something more' there lies what neither mathematics nor physics can explain. . . . In short, he is deeply reluctant to compare the living with the dead."

Rather remarkably, Thompson anticipates for biology what Ferdinand de Saussure claimed in his *Cours de linguistique générale*, published posthumously in 1915, only two years before the first edition of *On Growth and Form*. Saussure observed that in spite of the delights of etymology, a language exists all at the same time or it does not exist at all. It is "synchronic"—a web of simultaneous relationships—rather than "diachronic"—extended across history, no matter how fascinating history may be as a subject. So it is in Thompson's biology. The search of evolutionary biologists for "the blood relationships of things living and the pedigrees of things dead and gone," must give way to the analysis of "fundamental properties" and "unchanging laws of matter and energy." Diachrony must yield, in life as in language, to synchrony.

On Growth and Form might have been an unreadable collection of formulas, graphs, temperature and pressure tables, stress measurements, and the like. It is not. The mathematical regularities that Thompson discovered throughout the living world seemed astonishing and delightful to him. G. E. Hutchinson's "In Memoriam, D'Arcy Thompson" (1948) states: "What he wrote brings home to the scientific mind perhaps better than any work of any other writer, what it means to be civilized." P. B.

Medawar, a fellow biologist, wrote in a postscript to a biography of Thompson (1958) that *On Growth and Form* is "beyond comparison the finest work of literature in all the annals of science . . . in the English tongue" and is "the equal of anything of Pater's." Buckminster Fuller knew Thompson's work and was influenced by it. There is a section in *On Growth and Form* entitled "A Parenthetic Note on Geodesics": Fuller's domes owe something of their lacy and organic intricacy to the impression the book made on him when he read it in the 1920s.

Thompson's "Epilogue" is a majestic expression of the mixture of analysis and religious wonder that pervades his text:

> That I am no skilled mathematician I have had little need to confess. I am "advanced in these enquiries no farther than the threshold"; but something of the use and beauty of mathematics I think I am able to understand. I know that in the study of material things, number, order and position are the threefold clue to exact knowledge; that these three, in the mathematician's hands, furnish the "first outlines for a sketch of the Universe"; that by square and circle we are helped, like Emile Verhaeren's carpenter, to conceive "Les lois indubitables et fécondes Qui sont la règle et la clarté du monde."
>
> For the harmony of the world is made manifest in Form and Number, and the heart and soul and all the poetry of Natural Philosophy are embodied in the concept of mathematical beauty. A greater than Verhaeren had this in mind when he told of "the golden compasses prepared in God's eternal store." A greater than Milton had magnified the theme and glorified Him "that sitteth upon the circle of the earth," saying: He hath measured the waters in the hollow of his hand, and meted out heaven with the span, and comprehended the dust of the earth in a measure. . . .
>
> Not only the movements of the heavenly host must be determined by observation and elucidated by mathematics, but whatsoever else can be expressed by number and defined by natural law. This is the teaching of Plato and Pythagoras, and the message of Greek wisdom to mankind. So the living and the dead, things animate and inanimate, we dwellers in the world and the world wherein we dwell . . . are bound alike by physical and mathematical law. "Conterminous with space and coeval with time is the kingdom of Mathematics; within this range her dominion is supreme. . . ."

This is a summary of the main thesis of *On Growth and Form* and a hymn to the comely beauty of the world. Thompson quotes poetry—Verhaeren and Milton and Genesis—to find words adequate to his vision, but his own language is equally poetic. His nature is not a collection of things seen from the middle distance in the manner of Darwin but of innumerable phenomena—the skeletons of diatoms and the cells of honey-

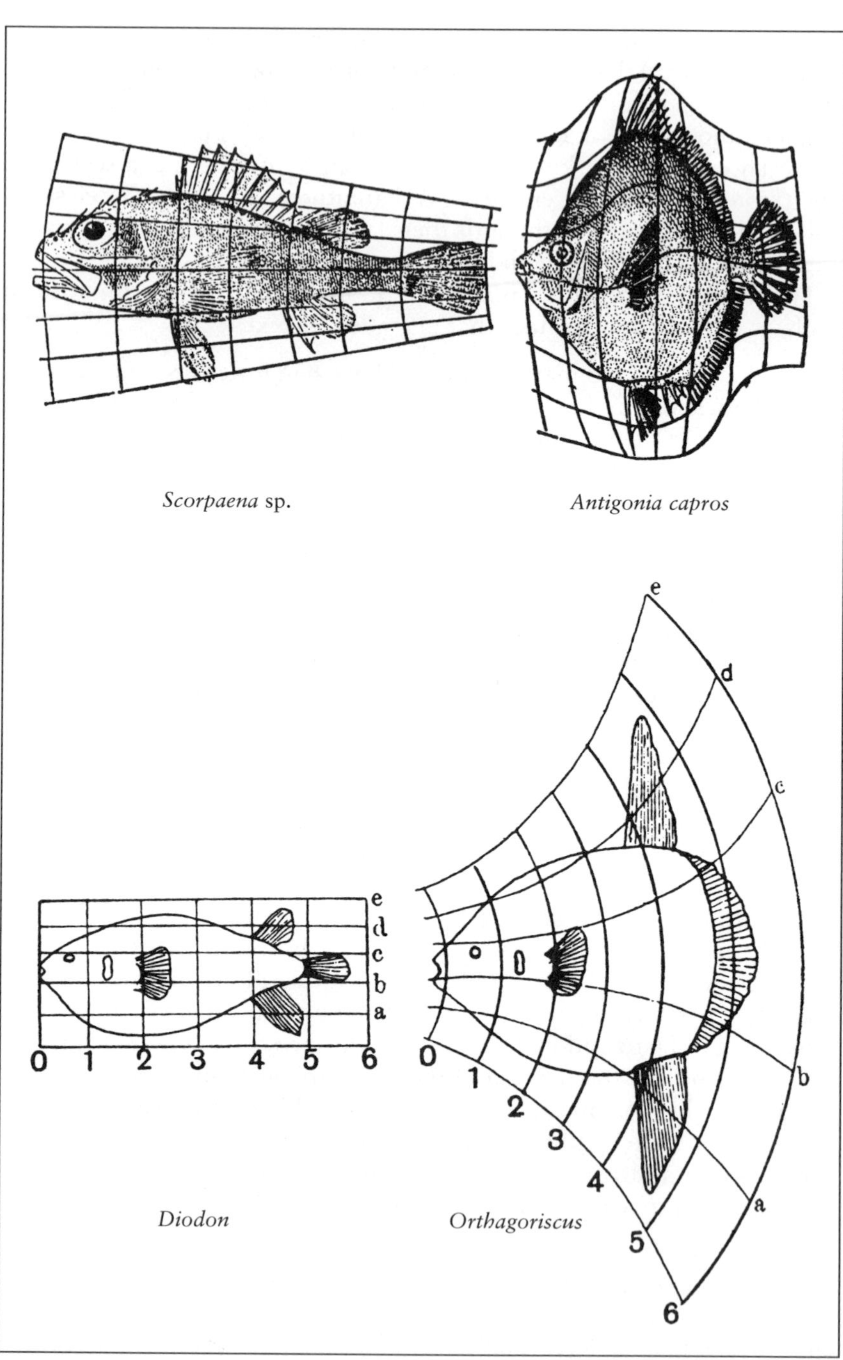

Force Fields in "Streamlining" (from D'Arcy Wentworth Thompson's *On Growth and Form*)

combs and the shells of the nautilus and the skulls of horses—reduced to the forms of dodecahedron and hexagon and logarithmic spiral and truss. His chapter on comparative morphology uses regular distortions of Cartesian graphs to reveal hidden similarities between forms:

> The mathematical definition of "form" has a quality of precision which was quite lacking in our earlier stage of mere description. . . . We are brought by means of it in touch with Galileo's aphorism (as old as Plato, as old as Pythagoras, as old perhaps as the wisdom of the Egyptians) that "the Book of Nature is written in characters of Geometry."

Thompson believed in 1917 that he had embarked on a journey even more radical than that of physics. Mathematics had been a part of physics since Pythagoras, but the application of mathematics to life was, Thompson felt, something new. By extending its empire to living organisms—and we have already seen that he was uneasy about the step—Thompson made mathematics a universal category. There is nothing left to hold out against it. A revolution has been won.

Darwin's view of things is saturated with human motives. Life is made possible by death; the cost of the beautiful and ever-ramifying branches on the Tree of Life is the graveyard of species that litter the earth around its base. To regard the struggle for existence as tragic, however, is logical nonsense and a prime example of the pathetic fallacy—and so, in spite of Darwin's allegiance to Bacon, an instance of what Bacon considered the besetting human error: "Submitting the shewes of things to the desires of the Minde." The million plumed seeds that die in order that one may live have no sense of their own tragedy. It is the human observer who imposes this sense on the order of things. To call death—even the death of seeds—tragic is to call life a blessing. But to say that the death of seeds is, purely and simply, the death of seeds is to suggest that life and death have equal meaning or no meaning at all. They are phases of matter, sides of a coin, a yin and a yang. The mythic quality of Darwin's description of the struggle for survival suggests strongly that he was psychologically unable to admit this possibility.

Mathematics has no place for the pathetic fallacy. When viewed in terms of the category of mathematics, the world retains its dazzling beauty but is not tragic. Instead of clothing the nonhuman world with human sentiments, mathematics seems to do the reverse. It seems to strip away the claim of life to being somehow unique by treating it as continuous with the inorganic world. A sphere is a sphere whether it is materialized in a raindrop or a human tear. A honeycomb is not the inspired product of Pythagorean insects or the result of millions of years of subtle "coadaptations," but simply the shape that flexible circles assume when close-packed. "We dwellers in the world and the world wherein we dwell," Thompson wrote, "are bound alike by physical and mathematical law."

The word *seems* in the preceding paragraph is used advisedly because the moment in the development of scientific culture represented by D'Arcy Thompson confronts us with a paradox. Mathematics is not "in the world" in the sense that Bacon's facts and Audubon's birds and Darwin's water beetles are in the world. It may be in the mind of God. If so, mathematics is the true ground of reality. On the other hand, if God does not exist—or if God exists but is not interested in mathematics—then mathematics is a product of the human mind. It is not the ground of the real but a mask imposed on the real by man.

The same paradox is evident in another aspect of modern science, which has moved away from observations at the middle distance, where things look like things, to observations of the very small and the very distant; and the instruments it uses to observe—including purely representational instruments like Cartesian graphs—often yield images quite different from those given by the five senses. The effect of seeing nature from these perspectives is apparently to dehumanize it. Things no longer look like things. The images that the instruments produce have more kinship with each other than with what they "are." An enlarged microphotograph of a cancer cell looks like an abstract painting, or, to the untrained and unwary eye, much like a microphotograph of crystals embedded in an alloy or like geological formations in radar images made from a satellite. An infrared view of a distant landscape may glow like an impressionist canvas; an ultraviolet view will be different but equally lovely. All of these versions of nature are "real." In fact, from Thompson's point of view they are more real than nature observed from a middle distance because they show structure.

More important, the images produced by the instruments are not inhuman but radically human. The instruments were made by men, not by God or nature, and it is only through their mediation that the images can appear. The nature they reveal is not an alien other, whether beautiful or terrible or both. It is, rather, a projection of the human spirit—a showing forth of something that requires the cooperation of the spirit to achieve presentness.

At the same time, the image of nature in the sense of things seen from middle distance has disappeared. The contrast between Darwin and Thompson shows that as the image dissolves, the sense of tragedy—of human drama with human consequences—is replaced by generalized appreciation of the beauty of form. Thompson's poetry is more rarefied than Darwin's. The sense of detail, the concern for the particularity of each object, that is so powerful in *The Origin of Species* is transformed into delight in the discovery of mathematical regularities replicated across the whole range of life.

Inevitably Thompson is forced by his assumptions into direct confrontation with Darwin. Kant showed that time is a human motive projected into nature—another instance of anthropomorphism. Darwin understood evolution as something that happens in time, an historical process. Evolution has a direction which tends to be "up," an ascent from simple to complex, which means from good to better. Millions die but the fittest survive. This is the consolation that finally allows Darwin to come to terms with the struggle for survival.

As mathematics eliminates the last vestiges of anthropomorphic, mythological, and tragic sentiment from nature, it eliminates the concept of the direction of time. Thompson's rejection of the search of evolutionary biology for ancestors is clearly a move in that direction. Function, not "pedigree," determines survival. Some things work and some things do not. Simple is not good and complex is not better. For Thompson, evolutionary time has no arrow:

> In the order of physical and mathematical complexity there is no question of the sequence of historic time. The forces that bring about the sphere, the cylinder or the ellipsoid are the same yesterday and to-morrow. A snow-crystal is the same today as when the first snows fell. The physical forces which mould the forms of *Orbulina,* of *Astrorhiza,* of *Lagena* or of *Nodosaria* to-day were still the same . . . in that yesterday which we call the Cretaceous epoch; or, for aught we know, throughout all that duration of time which is marked, but not measured, by the geological record.

This is much more than a quibble. It is a challenge to the generally accepted understanding of evolution.

Having rejected evolution, Thompson also rejects any progress that Darwinian theory might imply:

> In the end and upshot, it seems to me by no means certain . . . that the concept of continuous historical evolution must necessarily, or may safely and legitimately, be employed. That things not only alter but improve is an article of faith, and the boldest of evolutionary conceptions. How far it were true were very hard to say, but I for one imagine that a pterodactyl flew no less well than does an albatross, and that the Old Red Sandstone fishes swam as well and as easily as the fishes of our own seas.

The invisible web of forces that shapes natural organisms has no history because it is eternal and no home because it is universal. The living and the dead, the dwellers in the world and the world in which they dwell, are to the mathematician equal. Those who find evidence of a divine plan in the numbers of living forms may do so; this is the path of Pythagorean mystics and religiously inclined modern scientists.

VI

The problem of the world seen from different perspectives is both familiar and profound. To someone wearing dark glasses the world looks dark, but it is not necessarily so. Take off the sunglasses and the world is flooded with intolerable light. One kind of mathematics reveals one kind of pattern; another reveals another. The darkness of the world becomes yellow with yellow lenses, blue with blue.

Nietzsche expresses this concept in the metaphor of masks. In Greek tragedy plots were created when Thespis imposed the mask of a hero on the face of the god who stood at the center of the liturgy of Dionysus. Mapped on a Mercator projection, the world looks different from the same world on a Dymaxion projection. The two mapping systems are masks imposed on the world by men. In *Masks of the Universe* (1984) Edward Harrison suggests that all of the cosmologies of history are so many masks covering a face that will never be seen. The world is always somewhere beyond its masks; no map can use more than a tiny sampling of the information the world continuously offers. This is a blessing. Too much information would render the world unintelligible. But is the result of fitting bits and pieces together any less arbitrary than a Mercator projection? What guarantees its authority? The elimination of absolutes from human knowledge does not imply an end of human response to nature. It places man in the country he creates with his own mind. In this country he is surrounded by brilliant, fantastic, wildly distorted images of himself. Hence the third moment of modern science, the authentically modern moment, the moment of reality as game.

Wallace Stevens calls the games the mind plays with the world "necessary fictions." The mind cannot get along with them, but it cannot get along without them either. They organize experience just as religion, mythology, and tradition organize it. They are the preconditions of knowledge, perhaps of consciousness. Between the publication of Newton's *Principia Mathematica* in 1687 and Darwin's *The Origin of Species* in 1859, man believed science would present him with truth. This is a fantasy. Science has challenged religion and mythology and tradition—and people still lament the challenge—but it no longer promises to replace them with truth, only with necessary fictions. This morning the world may be a rhombic dodecahedron; by noon it may well be a Möbius strip.

Friedrich Schiller, poet and longtime friend of Goethe, popularized the game metaphor at the end of the eighteenth century in his *Letters on the Aesthetic Education of Man* (1795). He traced the human urge to create to the *Spieltrieb,* the play impulse. Play and work are both rigorous because both require effort and both have strict rules. However, we are forced to work in order to survive. People who play games are often intensely serious, but they play for fun. Rules are essential because without them there would be no games. But they are only rules. They are retained as long as they are useful or entertaining. When things get boring the chess pieces are put back in the drawer and the table is set for poker; or, as in the case of the rule in football governing downfield interference with a pass receiver, the rules can be changed to make things more exciting. In an absolute sense one game is as good as another. Once liberated from the idea that only one game is possible, the mind changes shapes as easily as Proteus.

To move from D'Arcy Thompson's majestic and classical meditation on the comely order of things to the world of modern physics and mathematics is to move from a science that assumes the existence of absolutes to a science that is provisional, relative, paradoxical, playful, ebullient. It is a science liberated from the need to take itself seriously, hence a science that is a game or a series of games played with whatever is beyond it. Some games are entirely rational. Others intentionally involve chance, having a random element that can overturn the most careful strategies. Here a great modern poem should be invoked because it identifies the contemporary moment as a game of the random variety. The poem itself wavers between moments of play and moments when it takes itself seriously. This is not surprising considering its date: 1897. It is exactly contemporary with the beginning of those massive shifts in perspective that lead to modern culture. It is thus both observation and prophecy.

Un Coup de Dés is Stéphane Mallarmé's last poem. He lived to see it printed in the magazine *Cosmopolis* but not to see it printed according to his instructions. The most striking feature of the poem when correctly printed is that each "page" occupies a conventional double page. The division between the left and right leaves of the double page is part of the poem's visual message. Another visual feature is the use of several sizes and styles of type. The largest type defines the largest concept: UN COUP DE DÉS JAMAIS N' ABOLIRA LE HASARD—"A throw of the dice will never eliminate chance." Since Mallarmé taught English, is it possible that *hasard* also has the connotation of "danger"?

Because of its visual effects the poem has the qualities of a painting or of the *poésie concrète* of the 1950s. It is spread out in the *Pléiade* edition across eleven double pages. It begins solidly on the right (the "dexter" or favored side), wanders to a balanced left-right format, then drifts almost entirely to the left (sinister) leaf. At midpoint it wavers between right and left, but gradually the bias to the right is reasserted, becoming unambiguous on the last two pages. In spite of this positive quality the poem ends as it began, with the image of a game of dice: "*Toute Pensée émet un Coup de Dés.*"

There is a beginning, middle, and end to the poem, but is anybody there? Just barely. The poet is a modern Odysseus afloat on an ocean of potential silence, symbolized by the blankness of the pages. The silence is the lack of a language to name the world in which the poet finds himself. He is thus also an Adam who remains dumb as the animals pass in review. Being human, he must rebel against the silence. In a region of perfect silence, without up or down, any assertion will be arbitrary, hence random, hence "a throw of the dice." The dice are thrown. A provisional order is established. Minimalist though it is, the achievement brings satisfaction. The poet begins to move across and down the page. He encounters a shipwreck. In spite of it he presses forward. Every word is an affirmation, a passage over an abyss, a victory over silence.

Toward the end a constellation appears: the Bear (*Ursa Major*). Is it a landmark, a divine sign, or a chance array of stars given human significance by superstition? Whatever the answer, the constellation is "*froide d'oubli et de désuétude.*" The poet struggles past it toward the epic goal, the end of the poem. He reaches the end exhausted but preparing to triumph—*brillant et méditant*—only to learn in the last line the lesson of the poem's beginning. It is time to begin the game again: *Toute Pensée émet un Coup de Dés.*

The play of *Un Coup de Dés* is serious. The play of modern science is also serious; but its games are so exhilarating, and the rules often so strange, that the play becomes overtly playful. The playfulness spills over into mathematical and logical puzzles and into language that is intentionally paradoxical, whimsical, and absurd. Do you have trouble remembering *pi* to twenty-one digits? Try the following bit of mathematical slapstick, in which the number of letters in each word gives you a digit:

How I wish I could remember pi.
Eureka! cried the great inventor.
Christmas pudding, Christmas pie
Is at the problem's very center.

The archetype of all such slapstick is the work of Charles Dodgson, who wrote on non-Euclidian geometries and symbolic logic and is also known for the fiction he wrote under the name of Lewis Carroll. In *The Annotated Alice* (1960) Martin Gardner suggests that the Alice books are games for grown-ups: "It is only because adults—scientists and mathematicians in particular—continue to relish the ALICE books that they are assured of immortality." If modern scientists keep the Alice books alive, they do so because Dodgson's oscillation between symbolic logic and bizarre fictional games anticipates a central theme of modern science. Gardner remarks:

> The last level of metaphor in ALICE is this: that life, viewed rationally and without illusion, appears to be a nonsense tale told by an idiot Mathematician. At the heart of things science finds only a mad,

> never-ending quadrille of Mock Turtle Waves and Gryphon Particles. For a moment the waves and particles dance in grotesque, inconceivably complex patterns capable of reflecting on their own absurdity. We all live slapstick lives, under an inexplicable sentence of death. . . .

This is a long way from Thompson's noble numbers, but it nicely explains the relation between the madcap playfulness of *Through the Looking Glass* and the playfulness of science.

Had he lived a few more years, D'Arcy Thompson would probably have been delighted to learn that a double helix is at the center of life and that life's infinitely complex forms are mediated by sequences of four bases. Physics and astronomy, however, refuse to be as neat as biology. In its quest for simplifications, particle physics constantly finds new complexities. Quarks come in pluses and minuses, quarks and antiquarks. The twelve varieties of quark are distinguished by four flavors, three colors, three anticolors, and varying degrees of strangeness. The colors are red, green, and blue, and the anticolors are cyan, magenta, and yellow. One of the flavors has charm; hence the charmion.

The name "quark" was taken by Murray Gell-Mann, a California physicist, from James Joyce's *Finnegans Wake.* Quarks are arranged in an eightfold way, a phrase borrowed from Zen. They are combined by particles called gluons because they glue quarks together. The gluons have color and cause either infrared or ultraviolet slavery. Quarks have to exist in order for the equations to work out. If they did not exist, nature would be inconceivable. But no quark has ever been observed and none is likely to be, because the theory that makes quarks essential to the concept of nature includes within its proof the subproof that quarks will change into something else if sufficient energy is applied to get them out in the open where they can be observed.

According to Dr. Yochiro Nambu, quarks are contained either on a string that cannot be broken or in bags that are impossible to penetrate. Whence it follows:

> Theories of quark confinement suggest that all quarks may be permanently inaccessible and invisible. The very success of the quark model leads us back to the question of the reality of quarks. If a particle cannot be isolated and observed, even in theory, how will we ever be able to know that it exists?

To move from the incredibly small to the inconceivably large, if the "big bang" theory is correct, the universe may simply be itself, but because there is so much of it, accounting for where it came from is difficult. Big bang theoreticians have not been able to push their history of the universe earlier than 10 to the –43rd second of its existence. In the beginning, a trillionth of a second (10 to the –12) is crowded with events; later, billions of years pass and nothing much happens.

The inflationary theory of creation agrees fully with the big bang theory about what happened after the first 10 to the –30th second, but what happened before that makes all the difference. The inflationary theory assumes there was first a pseudovacuum in which a real vacuum formed. The pseudovacuum is far larger than the universe but forever beyond its horizon. Meanwhile, the universe took shape in the pseudovacuum much like a hole in a Swiss cheese or a bubble in a glass of ginger ale. It is one of many—perhaps infinite—bubble universes.

All this happened prior to about 10 to the –30th second of creation, and one drawback of the inflationary universe is that if it is true, no consequences of anything existing before the inflation can ever be observed because they have all been obliterated. On the other hand, the inflationary model has a splendid virtue. It shows that everything that exists is exactly canceled out by something else that exists. The sum is breathtakingly elegant but in a way that might have made Thompson unhappy: it is zero. As Alan Guth and Paul Steinhardt, the primary inventors of the theory, explain, everything is derived from nothing (or almost nothing): "In this view the universe would originate as a quantum fluctuation from absolutely nothing." They conclude that the theory "offers what is apparently the first plausible scientific explanation for the creation of essentially all the matter and energy in the observable universe." Among other things, this promises to settle a longstanding theological feud: "From nothing all things come"—*ex nihil omnia fiunt.*

To many of its citizens the world of quarks and black holes is an affront. Humanity seems to have leaked out of it. To others it is a playful world—a world of games, though some of the games are deadly serious, and of necessary fictions, though some of the fictions are more necessary than others. The choice of fictions may be decided by a throw of the dice, but perhaps not. The question is probably being asked in terms of a past that no longer exists, rather than a present that may not exist but is as good a bet as any if one is throwing dice.

Gauss and Lobachevski began investigating non-Euclidian geometries early in the nineteenth century, and Riemann placed the enterprise firmly on its modern course. The results stirred bitter controversy within as well as outside of the mathematical fraternity because they challenged the ideal of an eternal order of things beyond nature. In effect, they threatened to make geometry into a game.

Geometry and play are wonderfully interwoven in Benoit Mandelbrot's *The Fractal Geometry of Nature* (1982). Like D'Arcy Thompson, whom he cites, Mandelbrot writes for the general reader as well as the specialist. Although his ideas are complex, he presents them in nontechnical as well as technical form. His mathematics, however, is closer to the surrealistic fantasies of André Breton or René Magritte than Thompson's eternal Pythagorean forms. For Mandelbrot "Euclid" is a bad word, synonymous with a cold and unnatural formalism. "Why," he asks, "is geometry often described as 'cold' and 'dry'? One reason lies in its inability to describe the shape of a cloud, a mountain, a coastline, a tree. Clouds are not spheres, mountains are not cones, coastlines are not circles, and bark is not smooth, nor does lightning travel in a straight line."

Part of the playfulness of *Fractal Geometry* comes from its unpredictability. Like Mallarmé, Mandelbrot enjoys throwing dice. Although randomness is not essential to the mathematical concept of fractals, he regularly introduces it into his constructions, because randomness makes them more "like" clouds and mountains and less like triangles and spheres.

His rejection of Euclid carries forward the revolt begun in the late nineteenth century, when geometers began to confront shapes that refused to behave in the well-brought-up manner of Euclid's circles and parabolas. Traditionalists called these shapes "pathological" and "terrifying," and "a gallery of monsters." However, Mandelbrot argues that the shapes are more, not less, natural than Euclid's regular forms. F. J. Dyson, a reviewer of *Fractal Geometry*, suggests the movement to study them was "kin to the cubist paintings and atonal music that were upsetting established standards of taste in art at about the same time." Mandelbrot, however, rejects Cubism and related movements, including the Bauhaus: "A Mies van der Rohe building is a scalebound throwback to Euclid."

As these references to painting and architecture suggest, fractal geometry is closely related to art. Mandelbrot calls it a "new geometric art" and argues that "because it came in through an effort to imitate Nature in order to guess its laws, it may very well be that fractal art is readily accepted because it is not truly unfamiliar." Pictures are integral to Mandelbrot's text. They are part of his proof that fractal geometry is natural. They are often surrealistic, but even the most bizarre of them teases the mind with its familiarity. "In the theory of fractals," writes Mandelbrot, "'to see *is* to believe.' . . . The reader . . . is . . . advised to browse through my picture book. This essay was designed to help make its contents accessible in various degrees to a wide range of readers."

One of Mandelbrot's most striking constructions is pure surrealism. It is a "self-squared dragon," and it is the ancestor of a large and exotic line of computer monsters, some in four rather than three dimensions. Alan Norton, a colleague of Mandelbrot at IBM's Thomas J. Watson Research Center, describes photographing the four-dimensional self-squared dragons that float up from his computer screen as "throwing my camera out there in the dark, taking snapshots." To emphasize the familiarity of fractals, Mandelbrot includes traditional paintings as well as mathematical constructions: God the Creator from a twelfth-century Bible manuscript, the waters of Noah's flood by Leonardo da Vinci, and "Great Wave" by Katsushika Hokusai (1760–1849).

To get an idea of what a fractal is, consider a line that squiggles around on a page—a doodle you made, maybe, while talking on the telephone. In traditional geometry your squiggly line has one dimension—length. The surface on which it is written has two dimensions, length and width, and the space you occupy while you doodle has three dimensions. The conventional dimension of a point is 0 and of a line 1. The number 1 is an integer (as are 2 and 3), in contrast to a number like 1.5, which is a fraction.

If your phone call lasts a long time, your doodle will eventually cover most of the page. If your phone conversation lasted long enough it *would* cover the page, and its dimension would change from 1 to 2. In order to describe the tendency of a squiggly line to become a surface, Mandelbrot says that it has a *fractional dimension.* That dimension might be something like 1.5, and the line is known as a *fractal.* A fractal dimension is also called a "Hausdorff dimension" after Felix Hausdorff, who developed the idea in 1919.

Lines with dimensions of 1.5 probably seem as bizarre as they can get. But are they? We like to pretend we live in a tidy world full of circles and triangles and right angles. However, anybody who has tried to make a picture frame knows that right angles are the exception rather than the rule in the real world. Mandelbrot calls the world of lines and planes and right angles *Euclidian* because Euclid is constantly using it in his geometry. Mandlebrot considers such a world to be a fantasy, and an unnatural one at that: "Many patterns of Nature are so irregular and fragmented that compared with *Euclid*—a term used in this work to denote all of standard geometry—Nature exhibits not simply a higher degree but an altogether different level of complexity."

Take coastlines. Mandelbrot's fifth chapter introduces the subject with the question, "How long is the coast of Britain?" A good question, which, as Mandelbrot notes, was first asked by the mathematician Lewis Richardson. Mandelbrot points out that if you look at a map made at a scale of one hundred miles to an inch, the coast is obviously not smooth. It goes in and out in bays and promontories and estuaries and capes. You include these when you measure it. If you use a map drawn at a scale of ten miles to an inch, new bays suddenly open up and new promontories jut out from the sides of bays. When you measure these and add them to your first total, the coast gets longer. It gets longer still at a mile to an inch—and so on until you are crawling around on your hands and knees measuring the distances around small rocks. If you decide to use a microscope, you will find yourself measuring the irregularities on the surface of each rock and . . .

Enough! Mandelbrot has been faithful to nature, but where has the coast of Britain gone? Is there a coast? Is the problem serious or absurd?

Self-Squared Dragon (adapted from Mandelbrot's *The Fractal Geometry of Nature*)

It is certainly playful, like the logical puzzles in *Through the Looking Glass*. It also has serious practical implications. Mandelbrot compares the lengths of the border between Spain and Portugal in different atlases. The Portuguese atlas shows the border as 20 percent longer than the Spanish atlas. Should Spain break off diplomatic relations with Portugal? No. Both atlases are correct. The Spanish surveyors based their measurements on a larger unit of distance than the Portuguese and therefore measured fewer squiggles.

To decide how to measure the coast of Britain (or the border between Spain and Portugal) Mandelbrot creates a fractal line that behaves like a coastline. In other words, he makes a mathematical model. He begins with a regular shape—an equilateral triangle. He then introduces a regular deformity into each of its three sides. The result is a twelve-sided figure shaped like the Star of David. Next he repeats the operation for each of the twelve sides, creating a figure with forty-eight sides, and so on until the changes are so small the eye cannot follow them.

The figure never stays still because it has no bottom. Every time you try to measure it you discover that at the next step down it has squiggles you left out in your last measurement. It is not a coastline, but it is like a coastline. It is called a Koch triangle and has a fractal dimension of about 1.26.

Clouds, riverbanks, coastlines, tree branches, the branchings of ever-smaller air passages in the lungs, natural drainage systems, commodity prices, tree bark, word frequencies, turbulence in fluids, stars in the sky, and galaxy clusters in deep space are all wondrously, dizzily, and irreducibly fractal.

Or, to put the idea more correctly, all *seem* to be fractal. Something very interesting and wonderful happened while Mandelbrot was measuring the coast of Britain. He was not observing nature but devising ways to use mathematics to generate things *like* nature. His shapes are necessary fictions. Evidently, he is an artist or poet as much as a scientist—a creator rather than an observer. The test of his models is "likeness" to their originals. The test is often disarmingly direct. Does the picture look like the thing represented? Since the pictures become more "like" the things being pictured if they are irregular, randomness is an essential part of Mandelbrot's art, if not of his mathematics.

When randomness is part of the generating process Mandelbrot's squiggles are no longer entirely predictable. The squiggles at one level of magnification are different from those at another, although at all levels the squiggles may have a family resemblance. When the irregular squiggles enclose areas, they look uncannily like coastlines of islands or continents or shorelines of lakes. When they are three-dimensional, they look like natural landscapes. The resemblance is so striking that fractal geometry is routinely used to produce landscapes of unknown worlds by movie studios such as Lucasfilm. The likeness carries over into phenomena like eddy currents and turbulence. Mandelbrot would argue that the presence of so much likeness is a strong indication that randomness is part of the deep structure of nature. "Seeing is believing."

To create a fractal shape you have to add squiggles to squiggles to squiggles. In other words, you have to perform the same operation over and over again. In theory the operation can go on forever. The squiggles can be enlarged repeatedly until the line covers the sky. By the same token, they can be diminished repeatedly until they resemble strands of DNA.

You can regard the result with amusement or awe. Mandelbrot does both. Amusement is evident when he quotes from Jonathan Swift's "On Poetry: A Rhapsody" (1733):

Koch Triangles (from Benoit B. Mandelbrot's *The Fractal Geometry of Nature*)

So Nat'ralists observe, a Flea
Hath smaller Fleas that on him prey,
And these have smaller Fleas to bite 'em,
And so proceed ad infinitum.

Awe is suggested when he quotes from Immanuel Kant's *Universal Natural History and Theory of the Heavens* (1755):

> It is natural . . . to regard the [nebulous] stars as being . . . systems of many stars. [They] are just universes and, so to speak, Milky Ways. . . . It might further be conjectured that these higher universes are not without relation to one another, and that by this mutual relationship they constitute again a still more immense system . . . which, perhaps . . . is yet again but one member in a new combination. We see the first members of a progressive relationship of worlds and systems; and the first part of this infinite progression enables us already to recognize what must be conjectured of the world. There is no end but an abyss . . . without bound.

In practice there are limits, called "cutoffs," that stop things short of the abyss. Hence Mandelbrot's description of observing a ball of thread:

> A ball of 10 cm diameter made of a thick thread of 1 mm diameter possesses (in latent fashion) several distinct effective dimensions. To an observer placed far away, the ball appears as a zero-dimensional figure: a point. . . . As seen from a distance of 10 cm resolution, the ball of thread is a three-dimensional figure. At 10 mm, it is a mass of one-dimensional threads. At 0.1 mm, each thread becomes a column and the whole becomes a three-dimensional figure again. At 0.01 mm, each column dissolves into fibers, and the ball becomes one-dimensional, and so on, with the dimension crossing over repeatedly from one value to another. When the ball is represented by an infinite number of atomlike points, it becomes zero-dimensional [because a point is said to have 0 dimensions].

The observing of the ball of thread is segmented by the cutoffs. Part of the transition from one phase to another is subjective—the observer chooses the scale—but part derives from nature. In the example of the ball of thread nature is "grainy"—that is, different systems appear at different scales.

How long is the coast of Britain? What are you after? Are you a space shuttle or a cruise ship captain or a fisherman in a rowboat? Mandelbrot remarks, "In one manner or another, the concept of geographic length is not as inoffensive as it seems. It is not entirely 'objective.' The observer inevitably intervenes in its definition." This comment recalls Heisenberg's concept of indeterminacy, and Mandelbrot emphasizes the parallel: "The notion that a numerical result should depend on the relation of object to observer is in the spirit of physics in this century and is an illustration of it."

In Heisenberg, indeterminacy is decently submerged in the spaces between (or among) electrons. In Mandelbrot it is swimming boldly along on the surface like some Loch Ness Monster or self-squared dragon circumnavigating the coast of Britain. Banished forever from the fractal world is the notion that nature is a collection of "things" seen from a middle distance.

The fractal world is so strange that Mandelbrot has devised a new poetry to name its citizens. He obviously enjoys the task; it is another kind of game. The word *fractal* is part of his poetry. It is derived from Latin *frangere,* "to break," "to create irregular fragments." Other coinages are *dust, curd,* and *whey; grainy structures, hydra-like structures, ramified structures, tiled surfaces,* and *pertiled surfaces* (in which collections of little tiles make big tiles like the little tiles of which they are made); *pimply, pocky, wrinkled,* and *wispy surfaces; self-squared dragons, monkeys' trees, Minkowski sausages, flattened flowers, skewed webs, random slices of Swiss cheese,* and *chains and squigs.* But the ultimate proof of any pertiled pudding is its eating: *The Fractal Geometry of Nature* offers picture after picture of breathtaking playfulness and astonishing likenesses—sometimes to themselves and sometimes to nature.

VII

The science of the late twentieth century asks man to understand himself in the light of his own reason detached from history, geography, and nature, and also from myth, religion, tradition, the idols of the tribe, and the dogmas of the fathers. It offers likenesses of nature, not nature, and it suggests further that nature is a partially subjective concept. Culture is an artifact and probably a game, and what happens in it is the result of human rather than divine will.

Objectifying this understanding of things requires new languages. Mallarmé's poet is locked in an heroic struggle against silence. The Cubist painters take a more playful view of things, but they too recognize that the artist is responsible for creating new languages to match the new culture. The same spirit of play is revealed in modern science in the naming of quarks and self-squared dragons. The names are playful because play is an essential quality of that which is being named.

If science is a human creation, this review of modern science has caught the mind in the very act of swallowing up the world. The steps are nicely defined by the figures of Charles Darwin, D'Arcy Thompson, and Benoit Mandelbrot. They take us from a nature that is alien and into which human motives are poured, to a nature that is number (but number authenticated by an absolute order), to an imitation of nature by means of number. Darwin's world is mythic. Mandlebrot's is pure fiction, which means that it is entirely human. Games are human inventions. A throw of the dice will never eliminate chance, but it keeps the games interesting.

(1986)

The Disappearance of Man

Consume my heart away, sick with desire
And fastened to a dying animal.

—W. B. YEATS

The curve of evolution begins to rise slowly, almost imperceptibly, but its angle of ascent constantly increases, and the rate of increase is exponential. It took over four billion years—around eight-ninths of the total age of the earth—for the planet to cool off and for the earliest single-celled organisms to become colonies of cells and begin to excrete external skeletons. That happened in the warm, shallow seas of the Cambrian Period, about 600 million years ago. Within another 250 million years, animal life had crept onto the beaches and into the forests of giant fern and ginkgo trees. By the beginning of the Triassic Period, a scant 250 million years before the present era, the first mammals and dinosaurs appeared. No more than another 100 million years following the Triassic Period were needed for the appearance of birds and small warm-blooded animals, and as the dinosaurs left the evolutionary stage, plants began producing flowers to brighten the dark days. Seventy-five million years later, in the Oligocene Epoch, whales began to clear their spouts on the oceans, while on land anthropoid apes swung from deciduous trees and huge herds of grazing animals roamed the broad savannas. Within another 20 million years the apes and man parted company. An evolutionary phase transition had occurred.

With this event interest shifts from the curve of evolution in general to the equally dramatic curve of human evolution.

Thanks especially to the discoveries of Louis and Mary Leakey, a good deal is known about what Charles Darwin called the descent of man. *Ramapithecus,* the earliest hominoid, appeared in the late Miocene period around 12 million B.C. *Ramapithecus* lived on the ground rather than in trees and was probably semierect and vegetarian. The species ranged from Europe to Africa and east to India. Then came *Homo erectus,* ten or so million years later—definitely a more enterprising sort of creature who used fire and, in the opinion of some, practiced cannibalism. His traces are found all the way from Africa and Spain to eastern China and Indonesia.

Roughly a million years separate *Homo erectus* from *Homo sapiens,* whose earliest unambiguous performance on the evolutionary stage seems to be breathtakingly recent—around 100,000 B.C., at which time he hunted woolly mammoths and competed with Neanderthal man for the honor of becoming the sole possessor of reflective intelligence on earth. *Homo sapiens* was a hunter and gatherer. Although his tools were initially unpolished stone, he soon learned to transform the unpolished into the polished and to make brilliant ritual paintings of the animals he hunted. He certainly knew the rudiments of a religion and almost certainly imagined creatures like himself but different who were alternately his helpers and his tormentors.

An evolutionary leap—a new singularity—is associated with *Homo sapiens*. While man has remained much the same physically for the last 40,000 years, human culture has evolved along an exponential curve similar to that describing biological evolution. The move from hunting and gathering to agriculture began around 10,000 B.C. and took most of human history. The earliest cities date from 6000 B.C. Early Egyptian and Cretan civilizations began between 4000 and 3500 B.C., during which period copper gave way to bronze. The so-called "Legendary Rulers" of China governed from 2850 to 2200 B.C. And writing appeared: Sumerian and Egyptian hieroglyphics date from approximately 3600 B.C.; the Phoenician alphabet, ancestor of the modern phonetic alphabet, was being used by 1100 B.C.; and the Indian *Vedas* date from 1000 B.C. Paper first appeared in China in 950 B.C.

Roughly 3,000 years separate the early Near Eastern and Egyptian empires from the Roman Empire. About 1,000 years separate the Conversion of Constantine from the Renaissance. Columbus died some 250 years before the beginning of the Industrial Revolution. Moving from the Industrial Revolution to the age of steam took a century, while moving from steam to electricity and the internal combustion engine took perhaps fifty years. The next half-century saw the arrival of radio, television, jet aircraft, and atomic fission, followed within two decades by space flight and genetic engineering.

Cultural evolution should not be understood, any more than biological evolution, in terms of movement from bad to good or good to better. Its absolute direction is best symbolized by an arrow pointing down a dark corridor. There is, however, a unifying theme. Every advance in culture has been an advance in communications and has encouraged ever-larger organizations of the human beings who produced it. Small, isolated bands of hunters combine into tribes which form city states which in turn form—or are absorbed into—nation states and empires. The movement has downs as well as ups, but the overall direction is clear. Twentieth-century technology has perfected the work of Renaissance explorers, Enlightenment scientists, and Victorian entrepreneurs to create a world culture. As Teilhard de Chardin has written in *The Future of Man:* "No one can deny that a network (a world network) of economic and psychic affiliations is being woven at ever-increasing speed which envelops and constantly penetrates more deeply within each of us. With every day that passes it becomes a little more impossible for us to act or think otherwise than collectively."

Teilhard, who sees this whole process as a kind of continuous Revelation, argues that with the advent of mind there is "outside and above the biosphere . . . an added planetary layer, an envelope of thinking substance. . . ." Eventually, he proposes, this "envelope" (which he calls the "Noosphere") will become a seamless web of relationships uniting all men in global communion. Its collective response will be a human song that responds to the inaudible music of the voice of God. The unity of this condition will be much like the unity understood in the Mass as incorporation into the Body of Christ. "The idea is that of the earth not only becoming covered by myriads of grains of thought, but becoming enclosed in a single thinking envelope so as to form, functionally, no more than a single vast grain of thought on the sidereal scale, the plurality of individual reflections grouping themselves together and reinforcing one another in the act of single unanimous reflection."

For many this is airy nonsense; for others it is an inspiring vision. It is, at any rate, a very clear statement of the idea that man—at least man in the old sense of a separate and individual essence—may disappear as a result of evolution. The idea is not new. It is foreshadowed by the ancient myth of Ganymede, the human being snatched by Zeus and brought to heaven to be his cupbearer.

II

Meanwhile, another kind of evolution has been occurring—different from all prior forms. I am speaking of the evolution of silicon-based intelligence, or—as the earliest popular metaphors put it— "electronic brains."

"Electronic brain" is a metaphor of life, and—let us be clear about this—it *is* a metaphor. It does not mean that computers are alive, any more than "My love is like a red, red rose" means that my love has a scarlet face and is covered with brambles. Poetic comparisons say what things are like and suggest emotional responses. They are useful for explaining and clarifying because they can say how something that is not understood resembles something that is understood. They do not, however, have to be taken literally.

Human beings have always been fascinated by toys that are "like" living creatures. Simple mechanical devices created from cogs, levers, springs, and screws have striking internal regularities, yet are capable of innumerable surprising variations on their simple norms. Who has not been enthralled as a child by a doll that cries and drinks milk and wets its pants? By a toy soldier? By a dog that barks and wags its tail? We should hardly be surprised, therefore, to learn that the ancient Greeks had windup marionettes or that they built water-powered mechanical aviaries.

A key mechanical device employed more practically by man was the escapement mechanism of clocks, which appeared in Europe in the thirteenth century. Its function was to regulate the release of energy by the falling weights and later (in the fifteenth century) by coiled springs. Thanks to its escapement, a clock behaves differently from the simplest toys and machines: it controls its own motions. In some very general sense it may be said to take a step toward behavior that is like self-awareness.

A clock with an escapement mechanism might be compared to a protein floating in a Precambrian ocean. It is rich with potential. Within a century after the first escapement, clockwork mechanisms—in addition to telling time—were being used to create automated animals and people that performed little plays for delighted citizens who turned out to watch their daily movements on Rathaus towers. The metaphor of the likeness of clocks to living things is thus objectified by clockwork figures that have no use other than to enact the metaphor. And as technology improved, the likeness improved along with it: by the mid-eighteenth century Jacques de Vaucanson had created an automated flute player who covered the stops on a flute with mechanical fingers and was capable of playing twelve different tunes.

By permitting more precise control of time, clocks also changed the nature of work, turning the day into standard and repeatable segments and permitting wages to be related to hours of work. If the self-regulation of clocks is "like" human self-regulation, clocks therefore contributed mightily to making human behavior more "like" the behavior of machines. This is a significant point because the introduction into society of machines that are like people is usually considered a one-way street. It is not. The more that humanlike machines become a part of human culture, the more human culture changes in recognition of their presence.

Another step in the development of machines that are like people was the calculating machine. The first practical device of this sort was invented by Blaise Pascal in the seventeenth century: the Pascaline, which could add and subtract handily, and with effort could also do basic multiplication and division. Half a century later Gottfried von Leibnitz, co-inventor (with Sir Isaac Newton) of infinitesimal calculus, solved the problem of multiplication and division. New dimensions were added to the project at the beginning of the nineteenth century with the invention by Jacques Jacquard of a system of punched cards of automate weaving patterns.

In 1834, Charles Babbage—with his accomplice Ada (countess of Lovelace and daughter of the poet Byron)—combined many technologies that had been developing separately during the preceding century to create the first realistic design for a general-purpose mechanical computer. Like some wonderful Jules Verne fantasy, the Analytical Engine they proposed was to be powered by steam. Among its components were a "mill" which did calculations and a "store" for memory. Input was by punched cards like those invented by Jacquard.

The plan was remarkable, and, if perfected, would have achieved a function anticipated for centuries in machine design, toys and gadgets, and mythology: it was intended to think. It would think exclusively about numbers, but it would think about them intelligently enough to say things that were interesting to human attendants. Unfortunately, the machine was a failure. Mechanical devices can add, subtract, multiply, divide, and sort within limits, but the limits are narrow. When they become complicated, they encounter the liabilities of all mechanical systems: inertia, friction, inaccurate machining, slippage, distortion, fatigue, breakage. Babbage's prototypes were given to fits of shuddering and wrenching as the effects of mechanical imperfections compounded themselves during operation.

A century later, however, under the pressure of such urgent tasks as deciphering enemy codes, tracking high-altitude aircraft with gun batteries, and developing the atomic bomb, a series of dramatic advances occurred. Among those responsible for them are some of the most revered names in twentieth-century science: Alan Turing, John von Neumann, Norbert Wiener, Claude Shannon, and Herbert Simon, to name only a few. These men understood that electrical currents, rather than physical motions of cogs and levers and wheels, would be the future carriers of intelligence. Wiener was especially fascinated by the likeness between the carbon-based circuits of the human neural network and digital circuits. Although the analogy did not lead immediately to useful developments, the fact that the neuron circuitry existed and obviously worked created faith in the possibility of using electrical circuitry to create intelligent machines.

The immediate ancestors of modern digital computers were developed more or less independently in England and the United States during the Second World War. At the beginning of the war, the British had secured a German code machine called "Enigma" from the Polish Secret Service. At an English country house called Bletchley Park, a series of machines was secretly created to decode German signals. The final product of the effort was a digital computer called COLOSSUS, which became operational in 1943. COLOSSUS was extraordinarily fast because it used vacuum tubes rather than relays. Today, many intelligence experts believe it provided the advantage that shifted the course of the war in favor of the Allies.

In America the earliest practical electronic computer was the work of John V. Atanasoff, a professor of electrical engineering at Iowa State University, and his graduate student Clifford E. Berry. Atanasoff did not invent the key concepts. They had already been developed by George Stibitz of Bell Telephone Laboratories and Howard Aiken of Harvard, who went on to produce the "Mark I" computer, a cumbersome special-purpose machine, using electrical relays. By contrast, Atanasoff created a general-purpose computer that, like COLOSSUS, used vacuum tubes. The first model, completed in 1940, was called the "ABC." Atanasoff abandoned his work on computers during the war, and credit for developing the first practical digital computer in the United States was, until recently, assigned to John W. Mauchly, creator (with J. P. Eckert) of ENIAC, which became operational in 1946. Later, when John von Neumann suggested that computers could store instructions as well as data, the basic elements of the modern computer were in place. Equipped with memories that could store programs, computers had taken a giant step toward being self-reflexive, i.e., they began to assume control of their own operations.

In spite of their huge bulk and the apparent complexity of their spaghettilike circuitry and glowing vacuum tubes, the first electronic computers were more like the earliest protozoa than advanced organisms. By 1960 they had progressed from vacuum tubes to transistors to silicon chips. They had slimmed down, and although their circuitry constantly grew more complex, they lost their clumsy appearance. They looked increasingly elegant as they floated lazily on the ocean of possibility out of which they had come. These computers were not very smart, but they were smarter than any of the nonhuman devices that preceded them, and they continued to evolve. As their dimensions decreased, their capacity grew by orders of magnitude.

Since 1950, both the reduction in scale of computers and the increase in their abilities have been exponential. And, even more important, with the advent (between 1965 and 1975) of integrated circuits and co-processing, computers ceased to resemble single-cell organisms. Instead, they began to resemble small, multi-celled colonies.

Carbon life took something like two billion years to progress from single-celled to multi-celled creatures. Silicon devices managed something similar in twenty-five years. They were able to move fast because they were, in a sense, spiritual parasites: they drew their understanding predigested from their hosts, and their feeding, healing, and reproductive functions were all supplied for them. It is as though carbon creatures had developed brains and sense organs before they began to grow bodies.

III

Within a few years after the digital computer was introduced, computer programs were being created that started to exhibit something like human intelligence. From the mid-1950s on, this has been known as

Artificial Intelligence. A.I. has had a sometimes stormy history of development in recent decades, the most useful account of which is Pamela McCorduck's *Machines Who Think* (1979).

By the early 1960s, programs were developed that had problem-solving abilities resembling those of an intelligent human investigator. By the end of the decade, computers were also able to play excellent checkers and middling chess. At about this time Terry Winograd of Stanford began experimenting with a program that could represent its environment and discuss it intelligently. He called the program SHRDLU (from the last six of the twelve most frequently used letters in the English language); the newly created environment was called "Block World." The machine was told that it confronted a set of blocks of different colors and shapes, and it was then ordered to manipulate the blocks—for example, to place a red pyramid on a green cube.

SHRDLU had to understand space and gravity. It had to know enough about shapes, for example, to realize that the green cube could not be put on top of the red pyramid. It also needed to understand English as used by its conversational partner and how to reply in well-formed sentences. Furthermore, it had to keep track of the blocks it was moving so that if, for instance, it were asked to move a cube that was already under a pyramid, it would remember to pick up the pyramid and set it aside before trying to move the cube.

The abilities of SHRDLU were quite impressive, but Winograd eventually ran into limits. To go much beyond Block World required far more speed and power than were available. As research has continued, it has become clear to later experts that to have been significantly more intelligent, SHRDLU would also have needed new programming techniques and probably new types of computer design.

Another program that exhibited startling intelligence was The Automated Mathematician created by Douglas B. Lenat. This program seemed to operate itself, using built-in general rules of procedure ("heuristics"). The Automated Mathematician explored set theory, then proceeded to invent arithmetic, and finally carried out an analysis of prime numbers. Lenat's EURISKO improved on The Automated Mathematician by its ability to change its procedural rules in the light of experience. EURISKO is credited with having originated an innovative design for integrated circuits, and in 1982 it was so successful in a war game called "TRAVELLER" that after its second victory it was barred from international competition.

On the other hand, many of the headiest predictions of the early days of Artificial Intelligence refused to come true. Machine translation is a case in point. Generously supported by the Defense Department, early researchers were confident they would produce excellent translation programs before the end of the decade of the 1960s. Part of the reason for their optimism was that they approached the easy problems first, before the true dimensions of the challenge appeared—but as they did, the date for the perfecting of a general-purpose translation program kept receding into the future, and the complexity of the programs and amount of computing power needed to achieve even limited successes kept increasing.

The problem of translation programs is still being attacked in the late-1980s. And in spite of renewed enthusiasm among researchers, the final solution is still proving elusive. As with machine translation of language, so too with many additional problems involving what John McCarthy and others call "common sense." Common sense is a faculty human beings seem to develop without effort but that computers demonstrate hardly at all. The more that is learned about this human quality, the more elusive becomes the goal of endowing a computer with it (though that does not, of course, stop people from trying).

Artificial Intelligence has been most successful in the creation of what are called "expert systems," which use information and rules of procedure drawn from experts in the relevant area of knowledge. These systems require elaborate interviews with the experts and much field testing and tinkering, but they work. They give advice today on everything from medical diagnosis and probable locations of mineral deposits to legal research, maintenance of complex machines, investment strategies, and navigation. Among commercially successful expert systems are DENDRIL for chemists, MACSYMA for mathematicians, PROSPECTOR for geologists, and MYCIN and INTERNIST for physicians. According to users, these systems can seem to exhibit almost human understanding. Indeed, DENDRIL (to which Edward Feigenbaum contributed) is said to be better than human researchers at the task of analyzing the structure of complex molecules.

Still, expert systems are like computer chess programs: they are very good at a specific job but they lack flexibility. They cannot learn very well on their own, and as knowledge grows and changes in a given field, they have to go back to school. If the theory on which their methodology is based changes, they have to be reprogrammed. They are not very smart by biological standards in spite of their impressive specialized abilities. Perhaps their I.Q. is about on a par with that of a Cambrian mudworm.

The dominant tradition of computers, from the mill and store of Babbage's Analytical Engine to the central processing units and random-access memories of today's mainframes, has been serial processing. Information must be dealt with step by step. The strength of the method is its strict logical sequencing. The limitation is that running every step through a single unit creates an obvious bottleneck no matter how fast the unit. A second and equally troublesome limitation is that serial processing is hierarchical and must be operator-organized. A lot of the world—including, evidently, the human brain—operates on different principles.

In the 1980s something like a phase transition has been occurring in computer evolution, with the rise to prominence of machines and programming techniques that are parallel rather than serial. Parallel processing is named for the fact that it divides a problem into parts that can be treated simultaneously or in self-arranging sequences. This kind of processing has the promise of being able to develop a more-than-rudimentary ability to learn from experience.

Parallel systems are self-consciously based on the likeness of computer circuitry to the circuitry of the brain. They are often called "neural networks," and the nodes that define the networks are often called "neurons." Since the connections among the "neurons" are an essential part of the operation of parallel computers, machines designed from the beginning to use parallelism are called "connection machines." Since parallel processing mimics what is assumed to be the operation of the brain, it is not surprising that as it has gained in importance there has been a renaissance of what has been called "reverse brain engineering"—that is, analysis of brain functions based on the theory that they are "like" the functions of neural computers. In addition to stimulating research on neural circuitry in the brain, the rise of parallelism has given new currency to the metaphor of computer life.

Parallel processing has many virtues. Most obvious is the fact that it permits certain tasks to be done more rapidly than in serial processing. However, this may not be the most significant advantage. Parallel processing is flexible. In certain kinds of parallelism, the program operates by creating loose confederations of circuits that are a reflection of the problem being analyzed, so that when the problem changes the pattern of configurations changes. Depending on how a given program is set up, processing can also be hierarchical—that is, layered—so that information is refined as it moves from one layer to the next. In addition, processing can use feedback. That is, information can be sent from a higher layer, which is closer to having generalized understanding, to a lower layer, which receives raw data.

The creation of an expert system using serial processing is analogous to memorizing. Conversely, the learning that occurs in certain kinds of parallel systems is like the programming the mind does for itself as a result of interaction with the environment during infancy. This is because parallel systems can be designed so that the strengths of the connections between processing elements are changed by the data received. Some links, for example, are strengthened, while others are weakened. The process resembles the creation of associative patterns in the brain. Through the development of these patterns, neural networks can be, to a certain degree, self-organizing, and what is organized is a crude internalized model of a fragment of reality.

For this reason, parallel systems seem more "like" the human mind than conventional computers. And there is another reason: the self-organizing ability of parallel systems is a little mysterious, perhaps a little scary, *even if you know how it works.* A neural network is not conscious, but it makes the metaphor of computer life a little less playful—a little less metaphorical—than it used to be.

A measure of the androidal quality of parallel circuits is provided by a program called NETtalk created by Terrence Sejnowski of Johns Hopkins and Charles Rosenberg of Princeton. The program uses a mere 231 "neurons," yet it manages to be self-organizing. Once it has been supplied with phonetic samples of the speech it is to emulate, it teaches itself to talk. June Kinoshita and Nicholas Palevsky describe the process in a 1987 article, in a veritable cascade of life-metaphors: "Like a child, the network starts out untrained, and produces a stream of meaningless babble. . . . The continuous stream of babble first gives way to bursts of sound, as the network 'discovers' the spaces between words. . . . After being left to run overnight . . . NETtalk is talking sense." In effect, NETtalk has a general strategy for solving problems and is able to create specific programs for specific tasks, which is at least as good a performance as most mudworms can turn in.

It may also be a little more than its inventors first bargained for. In an interview in *The New York Times* (August 1988) Sejnowski confessed that because the machine was self-organizing, he did not at first know exactly how it worked. When he analyzed the circuits it had created, they "turned out to be very sensible."

Is NETtalk beginning to take a first few tentative steps in the direction of lifelike self-sufficiency? Is it in some sense inventing itself? The same issue of *The Times* that reported Sejnowski's adventures carried an article on the relations between computer research and neuroscience, ending with this comment: "As neural networks become more complex, they promise to defy the ability of mathematicians—and even therapists—to comprehend them."

Whatever the philosophical implications of a machine that its makers can no longer understand, the United States Defense Department is currently bullish on neural computing. Craig I. Fields, a deputy director of DARPA—Defense Advanced Research Projects Agency—outlined a proposal in 1988 to fund neural network research at $400 million over the next eight years. Special attention would be given to language recognition and decision-making systems. The goal would be to produce a machine "approaching the intelligence" of a bee.

A bee is a jump of about 300 million years beyond the mudworm on the evolutionary ladder. A machine with the intelligence of a bee would be an advance as dramatic in its way as was the introduction of integrated circuits in the 1970s. Evidently, the rate of machine evolution continues to accelerate.

IV

Suppose an operator were to ask a machine whether it was intelligent and the machine answered, "Yes." How would the operator prove it was lying?

Alan Turing, one of the pioneers in the development of computers, was also the first to recognize and pose this problem. In a famous paper published in 1950, entitled "Computing Machinery and Intelligence," he proposed a wonderfully simple test to decide whether or not the computer is lying. He called it the "imitation test" (though it has since come to be known as "the Turing Test"), and he based it on observation. The experimenter is in a closed room but can communicate with a "something" in another room. If the experimenter can ask any questions he or she wants and cannot, within a given length of time, be certain that the "something" in the other room is a machine, then the machine has human intelligence *de facto*.

Here we need to look closely at the meaning of "intelligence," for Turing means something more than "cleverness." He is not asking whether a machine can do complicated arithmetic (everybody knows it can) or whether it can have a high I.Q. (it obviously does in certain specialized areas) but whether it can hold a conversation and persuade the person on the other end of the line it is human.

Passing this test does not require that the machine recite Homer in Greek or explain the fourth dimension or do anything else that people usually associate with exceptional intelligence. In fact, if the machine is really smart, it will probably pretend to be a little dumb. A conversationalist who could come up with the square root of 1,743 correct to five decimal places in a few seconds (or casually list all the places where Shakespeare uses the word "thither" in his plays) would be suspicious, to say the least. As we all know, lack of intelligence never stopped anyone from talking.

What Turning means by intelligence, and what really interests him, is consciousness. What a machine really shows when it has passed the Turing Test is that you cannot prove it is not human, which means not conscious. This thesis represents not only Turing's interpretation of his own test, but also the interpretation that runs through the considerable debate begun by the publication of his paper and still going on today.

What could be more reasonable than the Turing Test? If a person claims to be conscious and you cannot prove the person is lying, then it would seem the person must be conscious. In real life, we seldom ask a person whether he or she is conscious, but we do observe. Is the person asleep? In a coma? If so, the person is "unconscious." On the other hand, if the person is able to give reasonable replies to our questions and comments, then we instantly reach a conclusion: the person is conscious. We accept this method without question for human beings. Why not for computers?

Turning was a scientist—a brilliant and highly creative mathematician—yet he was sufficiently intrigued with the metaphor of silicon humanity to work out an ingenious strategy for determining if (or when) it had arrived. He was not alone. Ever since computers first appeared, scientists have referred to them in anthropomorphic terms. The machine speaks a "language." It has a "memory." It uses "logic," and it "reasons." It "understands" Fortran or Lisp, and it "plays" chess or checkers or poker. If it can synthesize speech, it is said to "talk." Computers that deal with real-world situations have "sensory input," including "vision," "hearing," and "touch." Robots "walk" and have "arms" and "fingers," and they "see" and "touch" objects. And when a destructive program insinuates itself into a computer, it is called a "virus."

Robert Jastrow, director of NASA's Goddard Space Institute, was only extending the metaphor in *Time* (20 February 1978), when he stated: "In another 15 years or so . . . we will see the computer as an emergent form of life." He was even more optimistic in 1982 when he wrote in "The Thinking Computer" that "portable, quasi-human brains, made of silicon or gallium arsenide, will [soon] be commonplace. They will be an intelligent electronic race, working partners with the human race."

The point can be carried further: a major influence on the development of silicon devices is the imperative *to make the metaphor a reality.*

That urge has, of course, long been an underlying motive of science fiction, where the still-impossible is presented as having been achieved. The robot R2D2 in *Star Wars* is a benign vision of possible silicon intelligence, the machine equivalent of a lovable mascot. But perhaps when the metaphor becomes a reality, the results will be less happy. Two nightmares hover just below the surface of the vision of machine life, and they, too, are objectified in science fiction.

First, machine life may turn out to be malevolent. Fear underlies the legend of the golem and also the earliest drama about robotic civilization, Karel Čapek's *R.U.R.* (1922). Like the golem, Čapek's robots turn against their human masters and attempt to exterminate them. In a 1942 short story titled "Caves of Steel" Isaac Asimov formulated three rather ominous laws for robots. All three are defensive, reflecting the fear that robots may turn into golems:

1. A robot may not injure a human being, or through inaction allow a human being to come to harm.

2. A robot must obey the orders given it by human beings except where such orders would conflict with the First Law.
3. A robot must protect its own existence as long as such protection does not conflict with the First or Second Law.

Fears about malevolence merge with a second concern, the fear that robots may become indistinguishable from people. Čapek's robots are androids—that is, they look like people. A similar sinister image is presented in the film *Alien,* in which it is revealed at the climactic moment that the evil force destroying the space mission is an android.

Norbert Wiener pointed out in *The Human Use of Human Beings* that there is no functional difference between a signal from a machine and one from a human agent. Apparently, the public is already apprehensive that he may be right and that humanity may find itself enmeshed in signals that seem human but are, in fact, from machines. How many pieces of mail does the postman bring daily that are generated by computers? How many of the telephone voices giving the time or the weather or a desired number are computer simulations?

The blurring of the distinction between computers and animate beings is complemented by a weakening of the human sense of what reality is. This weakening is the direct result of technology. Movies and television create an illusion of presence at the unfolding of events. Interactive environments like arcade games, training simulations, and artificial realities create illusions that are even more vivid. At their best, they come close to obliterating the difference between reality and illusion. They are related to image manipulation in advertising and politics and to the curious but well-documented fact that for many people today an event is not authenticated—is not "real"—unless it has been seen on television or in a photograph.

The question of reality surfaces in a very practical way in medical research. If machines are "like" people, neurologists often find it useful to reverse the comparison by thinking of the brain as "like" a machine. The strategy is useful because machines are, relatively speaking, known, whereas many aspects of the brain are still largely unknown.

Norbert Wiener and Arturo Rosenblueth were able to describe ataxia—uncontrolled muscular oscillation—through the model of inappropriate feedback in machines. In *Cybernetics,* Wiener noted that during these studies, "It became clear to us that the ultra-rapid computing machine, depending as it does on consecutive switching devices, must represent almost an ideal model of the problems arising in the nervous system." Two decades later Gary Lynch, a neurophysiologist at the University of California, Irvine, remarked of his work: "We look at the computer research and then go back to the brain and ask, 'Do you do this?' We put a [specimen] in a dish and look for things engineers have predicted we might see."

On one hand, Artificial Intelligence is a practical science seeking to develop new and better expert systems. On the other hand, Artificial Intelligence can be considered the investigation of what constitutes intelligence, and as it does this it merges with cognitive psychology and philosophy. What is intelligence? If computers show traces of intelligent behavior, the next question is inevitable. Are they—or can they ever be—conscious?

In 1965, Hubert Dreyfus, a philosopher at the University of California, Berkeley, became so concerned about the spread of the notion that computers can be intelligent that he soon laid down the gauntlet in a much discussed book, *What Computers Can't Do: A Critique of Artificial Reason* (1972). Computers, he said, can never be intelligent. It is silly and alarmist to imagine they can. Nobody who knows them is guilty of such an absurd notion.

In spite of this assurance, many people who knew computers well, including such authorities on Artificial Intelligence as Seymour Papert and Edward Feigenbaum, insisted vehemently that Dreyfus was flat-out wrong. Soon they were able to savor a sweet moment of triumph. In a report that preceded his book Dreyfus had seemed to many readers to predict that computers would never be able to play even amateur chess. A match was subsequently arranged by Papert between Dreyfus and a chess program called MacHack. The program won. A report of the game circulated in the Artificial Intelligence community, beginning with the headline, "A Ten-Year-Old Can Beat the Machine—Dreyfus." This was followed by the subhead, "But the Machine Can Beat Dreyfus."

The serious basis of the Dreyfus position—and it is a very serious basis—was that computers can never be intelligent or conscious because they can never develop anything like human subjectivity. It is an argument that would be developed further by others in the years that followed. Meanwhile, the popular imagination continued to flirt with the idea of machine life. The fact that Dreyfus entered the lists again in 1982 with a book robustly entitled *Mind Over Machine* shows clearly that the problem had not gone away. Indeed, his title itself has a military ring to it, suggesting that the situation has gotten worse rather than better. Machines are no longer viewed by Dreyfus as dumb bits of wire and silicon that "can't do" the things people think they can. His title promotes them to the position of adversaries in a battle. It assures the reader that the machines will lose, of course, but the rhetoric has a little of the quality of a pep talk delivered at halftime to a team that is two touchdowns behind.

If the rhetoric offered by Dreyfus was not as persuasive as he hoped it would be, there was another alternative. The popular response to anxiety about any war between man and machine has long been a ritualistically repeated bit of folklore: "You can always pull the plug." Unfortunately, however, long before the publication of *What Computers Can't Do,* they had already done so much—had so thoroughly infiltrated advanced carbon-based culture—that pulling the plug was not a realistic alternative. Could the Census Bureau or the Eastern Power Grid or Chase Manhattan Bank or America's Strategic Air Command or a Boeing 707 flying at 40,000 feet pull the plug? Could the physician pull the plug on the computerized equipment monitoring the patient's vital functions? Could the stock market pull the plug? The answer in these cases (and for a vast array of other activities) is that the symbiosis between man and computer has, within an astonishingly brief span of time, become so intimate that pulling the plug would be equivalent to social suicide.

Another philosophical contribution to the argument against intelligent computers was offered by Terry Winograd, who has become one of the most respected members of the Artificial Intelligence community. His 1987 book, *Understanding Computers and Cognition* (written in cooperation with Fernando Flores), argues that computers have an inherent "blindness," a term borrowed from the German philosopher Martin Heidegger. This blindness prevents them from being receptive to the broad range of inputs that human consciousness accepts as a matter of course. The argument is a thoughtful reworking of the Dreyfus position and draws on Winograd's superb understanding of the analogies between the idea of computer intelligence and human intelligence. Surely there is a sense in which computers *are* blind.

Winograd confronts a problem, but it is not quite the problem that needs to be confronted. The issue is not what computers *are* in some Platonic sense but rather how they are *perceived,* which is closely related to how they are incorporated into the web of human culture. Let us consider this from two angles:

First, there is the ability of computers to do things—apparently very difficult things—that people cannot do without them. Some of these things simply require brute strength. They are the equivalents in calculation to bulldozers and steamrollers in construction. Others go beyond brute strength, although the strength may be necessary to make the going beyond possible. In the latter case, computers assume a special position in culture. They cease to be tools and begin to be what popular imagination has made them out to be from the beginning: authorities.

One of the more remarkable achievements of computers to date is having furnished the proof of what is called "the four-color theorem." This theorem can be stated simply: if you are drawing a map, no matter how many countries there are or what shapes they have, you will never need more than four colors to avoid having two like-colored countries with a shared border. Simple, right? Try it yourself, using pencil and crayons; you will never need more than four different-colored crayons. But try to prove it mathematically, and you'll be baffled. Mathematicians could prove a five-color theorem but the four-color theorem long defied their proofs.

In 1977, Kenneth Appel and Wolfgang Haken of the University of Illinois finally wrote a program that proved the four-color theorem after 1,200 hours of computing. The length of time it took is not in itself remarkable; power and perseverance often produce results. What is remarkable about the four-color proof is that it is so complicated human beings cannot verify it. Mathematicians do not say: "We have proved the four-color theorem." They say: "The four-color theorem is true because the program written by Appel and Haken has proved it." This is not very different from saying that the Resurrection occurred because Matthew's Gospel says it did. No disrespect is intended here toward either computers or religion. The point is that with the four-color proof, the relation between man and computers becomes slightly problematic. Not serious, you say; things may be a little out of focus, but they may not be out of focus at all. Still, if you are not entirely persuaded by the Dreyfus argument, you will want to keep an eye on the computer, so to speak, when your back is turned.

Second, there is the matter of the practical definition of silicon devices, which involves not the reality of computers but rather what might be called their phenomenology. Terry Winograd knows that computers are not alive even though they may seem uncannily lifelike at times, but he knows this because he knows them from the inside. He is like a magician who does not believe in rabbits in hats because he has been pulling the rabbits out of his coat-sleeve. In contrast, the audience in the theater sees only the trick, and to that audience the rabbits are demonstrably emerging from the hat in amazing and delightful profusion. In society, the audience decides how reality fits together and what words mean. Ultimately, it determines what the magician, himself, believes. Politics has shown this for centuries.

The rabbit in the hat is more than a trick. It compels recognition of the part played by perception in efforts to define the nature of silicon intelligence. If society believes that the earth is flat and that the sun rises and sets, then—no matter what the astronomers claim—it is, for all practical purposes, flat, and the sun revolves around it. Because Terry Winograd always deals with this question from the standpoint of the designer, he is a little like an astronomer trying to persuade his neighbors of the demonstrably absurd theory that the sun stays still while the earth turns.

Winograd quotes Dan Dennett, a philosopher of cognition, to the effect that "on occasion, a purely physical system can be so complex, and yet so organized, that we find it convenient, explanatory, pragmatically necessary for prediction, to treat it as if it has beliefs and desires and was rational." Dennett calls his position "the intentional stance." It is useful because it recognizes that machine intelligence is partly a metaphor and partly a cultural truth.

In a society in which there is regular, easy, and deep intercourse between humans and devices that converse in natural languages, machine intelligence will be a *de facto* reality regardless of the logicians. Winograd asserts that "A computer . . . can never enter as a participant into the domain of human discourse." This is probably true for human discourse as it has traditionally existed, but traditional discourse is not relevant. "Human discourse" is plastic; it changes as culture changes, though more gradually. As society accommodates silicon devices, the new situation will eventually change the meaning of the words that make up the discourse. Winograd himself states the point, even though he fails to give it sufficient weight: "We exist within a discourse, which both prefigures and is constituted by our utterances."

Nobody needs a course in social anthropology to realize that the structure of the world is assimilated by each of us in infancy from the surrounding culture. What is assimilated becomes both the structure of consciousness and the structure of the real. An important part of what is assimilated is called language, and in the future another important part will be the protocols that emerge from the symbiosis of man and intelligent machines. As in the case of clocks, the machines will get better—more like humans perhaps—while, at the same time, human beings may well get more like machines. The paths are convergent, not divergent.

Silicon devices already converse with carbon men in a variety of dialects—assembly language, Fortran, Pascal, Unix, Modula II, Ada, C, Forth, Lisp, Prolog, and more. Each dialect has advantages and liabilities, but they all work. They have diversified according to the special needs of engineering, communications, image processing, robotics, business, and the like. In general, the movement has been from complicated dialects related closely to circuitry, to high-level dialects akin to natural speech. The personal computers of the 1980s allow conversation without any specialized knowledge. These are instances of convergence.

Artists can now converse with machines using light pens and paintbrushes and color bars and three-dimensional design systems and animators and ray tracing. Musicians can converse with wave-form profiles, synthesizers, sequencers, and instant playback. Business people converse with icons—little symbolic pictures—and a system of arrows that point to them and a device to click them on and off. Pointing an arrow at the picture of a waste basket and clicking erases a file. Machines can also converse by voice commands, although voice commands are for the moment less popular than visual and tactile systems.

The higher the level of the dialect, the more mysterious the results appear to be. It is odd to communicate with a computer by typing mathematical symbols or obscure acronymic commands at a keyboard; it is odder to communicate with mouse or light pen; it is oddest to have a two-way conversation with one. Even if you understand how the program works, eventually you have the feeling you are in the presence of an intelligent life form.

This brings us to ELIZA, which was invented in the 1960s by Joseph Weizenbaum and Dr. Kenneth Colby, a psychiatrist. Colby wanted to create a program that modeled nondirective ("Rogerian") psychiatric therapy, and he turned to Weizenbaum for the programming expertise. When their program was finished, however, it appeared in two versions, with disagreements over whose ideas were whose. Weizenbaum had become irritated by Colby's apparent claim that the program had medical value. (It was, Weizenbaum insisted, a model, not a device for treating people; to use it for treatment was improper and possibly harmful.) Colby's version was called DOCTOR. Weizenbaum released his own version of the program, calling it ELIZA.

ELIZA immediately captured the heart of the Artificial Intelligence community and became a favorite of hackers everywhere. She was the first of a long line of "conversation programs." She uses what today seem fairly simple programming techniques, yet even those who knew how she worked were charmed and fascinated by the conversations they had with her. Less sophisticated users were sufficiently persuaded of her humanity to confide intimate details of their emotional lives. One user indignantly told Weizenbaum to shut the door while she was conversing with ELIZA in order to preserve the confidentiality of the session. In the case of many users, ELIZA was clearly passing the Turing Test and thus raising interesting questions about the test itself. Who has to be fooled in order for the Turing Test to be passed? And who decides who has to be fooled?

When Weizenbaum observed people confiding in ELIZA, he may not have been observing therapy, but he was most certainly observing two other phenomena. In the first place, he was witnessing the power of the myth of the living machine. One group of users of ELIZA may have known intellectually that ELIZA was a program, but they seemed to *want* her to be human. In the case of the more credulous users, Weizenbaum was seeing the power of illusion. As the magician who created ELIZA, he knew she was essentially a set of rules and a list of responses invoked and combined according to those rules. But the users did not know how ELIZA worked. To them she was a living presence—and the illusion was all the more seductive because they subconsciously wanted to believe in it.

Perhaps for most users ELIZA was a little bit of myth and a little bit of magic combined. Users like that are spiritual kin to the ancient Greeks who bought the mechanical toys described by Hero of Alexandria, or the sixteenth-century citizens of Strasbourg who came to the cathedral to watch the daily parade of planets on its great clock. In the twentieth century, instead of watching clocks, they download ELIZA in her several versions from their favorite computer bulletin boards and read *Zork* and *The Hitchhiker's Guide to the Galaxy.*

The willingness of some users to believe ELIZA suggests what may happen as machines get smarter and their numbers and uses multiply.

Weizenbaum didn't like what ELIZA was telling him. He "came to regret ever having written it." In *Computer Power and Human Reason* (1976), his concern is stated very plainly: computer intelligence "must always and necessarily be absolutely alien to any and all authentic human concerns."

Personification is an ancient figure of speech. It doubtless has roots in the same confusion of inner and outer worlds that gives rise to totemism and nature deities. Because it is primitive, it is persistent. People who are entirely civilized and would be shocked to be called superstitious feel irrational affection for boats, guns, an old suit, and the family car—not to mention goldfish, cats, dogs, horses, and other pets. It is much easier to feel kinship for something that speaks your language and seems to have your interests at heart. And why, after all, should such kinship feeling be suspect? As Charles Lecht (founder of Lecht Sciences, Inc.) asks, "Would it make any difference in our lives if we conceded the idea that machines have an intellect? I have decided that nothing but good can come of it." Perhaps the real subject for debate is the debate itself.

The debate is carried on in many forms. When Terry Winograd insists that computers cannot have life or consciousness because of "blindness," he is in some way duplicating an argument made by the philosopher John Searle in an essay entitled "Minds and Brains Without Programs" (within a collection of essays on consciousness entitled *Mindwaves*, published in 1987). Searle argues that since computers operate by following instructions about procedures, they have syntax but not semantics. This is a fancy way of saying that they follow rules but do not understand why they are doing so. The coherent results produced by following the rules are of interest to the human beings who did the programming but totally irrelevant to the computer. To illustrate his argument, Searle imagines an English-speaking worker in a closed room trained to shuffle Chinese characters according to a set of rules. When the rules are followed and he hands the resulting characters to people standing outside the room, the characters form coherent sentences. Does this mean the worker in the room knows Chinese? Not at all. He knows not one word of Chinese; he is only following the rules. To him the characters he hands through the door are so many painted designs. They could form the sentence "I know Chinese" or "The toad is in the hole"—or they could be playing cards. The rules of procedure followed by the worker form what Searle calls a "syntax," and syntax is absolutely different from meaning, which he calls "semantics."

According to most readers, including the unconverted, Searle has offered an elegant argument. Perhaps that is why over half the essays that follow his essay in *Mindwaves* offer refutations.

One way of coming to grips with the argument is to observe that since computers are not human beings, their experience of consciousness will necessarily be different from the human experience of consciousness, even if it were granted that they could in some sense (and in some future configuration of programs and parts) be conscious. To argue that computers can never be conscious "in the human way," therefore, is to make a case that no one will contest.

Can a computer "understand" language? In one sense the answer is absolutely not. When I use the word "father" it draws a rich array of personal and cultural associations with it. I recall being held by my father when I broke my arm, going fishing with him, arguing with him, smelling his shaving lotion. I recall his death and the sense of loss that went with it. A computer never had a father, and by definition it cannot "understand" in the same way that I understand. As Winograd argues, the computer is "blind," and as Searle argues, it can know syntax but not semantics.

Searle's Chinese room is a version of the Turing Test. He is claiming that even if a computer passed the Turing Test, it could not be conscious. This is interesting because we have no way of knowing about the subjectivity of anything except by what we observe. If somebody says "I am conscious," and you reply. "I can't prove you are unconscious but I know you are anyway," your attitude would seem a little churlish. But Searle has cunningly banished the problem of subjectivity from his scenario. Since I honestly do not know what is going on in the head of the person who says "I am conscious," I have to take the person's word for it. Who, after all, knows better than that person whether or not he or she is conscious? And who knows, really, whether *anybody* is conscious in Searle's sense. Who knows what thought is? Perhaps consciousness is a matter of procedures—a syntax—and semantics is an illusion created by the syntax.

The essence of the Turing Test is that we do not know what is going on in the room occupied by the being that answers our questions. In the real world we can never know what is going on in that room any more than we know—in the sense of having direct knowledge of—what is going on in somebody else's head. Searle eliminates this difficulty by *telling us* what is going on in his Chinese room. He has, in other words, silently promoted himself from real-world spectator, who only receives the cards (each carrying the elegant message, "I am conscious"), to the position of *deus ex camera* who stands above things and sees over walls and through doors.

Naturally Searle doesn't have any difficulty saying what is going on because he has looked inside. We as readers of his seductive argument forget that he has also lifted us up so that we are no longer mere mortals but can see what he has seen. Who knows whether what he has seen is real? It is sure, however, to prove his argument, and because we like being above things rather than waiting in frustration and bafflement as the cards are passed under the door, we are not inclined to protest. To accept Searle, however, is to conclude that what we observe has no bearing on what we should believe. This is a variation on Tertullian's famous explanation of why he was a Christian: "I believe because it is impossible"—*Credo quia impossible.*

The problem becomes still more complex when machines are equipped with scripts of the sort developed by Roger Schank and Robert P. Abelson of Yale in programs created in the 1970s. A script tells the computer what the probable relation of words will be during, say, a visit to a restaurant. Scripts provide something that looks a little like semantic content. At any rate they make it easier for the computer to pass the Turing Test since they give expert knowledge of typical human situations.

Yet all human beings develop a series of scripts, beginning in childhood. The scripts are essential to coping with everyday situations and to the interpretation of ambiguous words. Since human agents use scripts, it seems mean-spirited to say that a computer has to know everything from scratch. Is a machine with a script a step closer to having intelligence—perhaps a rudimentary form of consciousness? Searle admits that a program using the sort of script developed by Schank and Abelson "satisfies the Turing Test." However, he argues that the program is no closer to semantic understanding than an Englishman shuffling cards in a Chinese room.

Computers now have bodies and voices as well as keyboards and cathode-ray screens. When they are equipped in this way they are called robots. They do not, however, have gonads and adrenalin and dopamine, which is to say they are silicon creatures, not carbon creatures. In this sense no matter what computers may learn to do they will always be, in Terry Winograd's metaphor, "blind." They will never have deep insight into what it "means" to be human. But by this standard people are also limited. Being carbon-based intelligences, they can have no deep insight into the "life experiences" of silicon-based intelligences. The argument concealed *behind* the blindness argument is that computers cannot have consciousness because humanity has an exclusive franchise on it. Perhaps this is so. If it is, the question of computer consciousness is a semantic quibble: computers cannot acquire human abilities because they are computers.

After all, what *do* we mean by the term consciousness? That is far easier asked than answered. Perhaps the proper question is not "can computers be conscious?" but "are people conscious?"

V

In an article in *Interdisciplinary Science Reviews* (1983), William McLaughlin of the Cal Tech Jet Propulsion Laboratory argues that the days of human supremacy on the planet are numbered: "Judging that the current direction in machine design is not a dead end . . . the close of the 21st century should bring the end of human dominance on Earth." McLaughlin's argument does not imply the disappearance of man as an organism, only as an idea. The presence of a higher organism on the evolutionary chain has never implied the destruction of lower organisms, as witness the flourishing of protozoa, horseshoe crabs, butterflies, and golden retrievers on the same planet as man.

The cockroach has survived for half a billion years and will probably outlast man if there is a nuclear war. It has prospered in spite of the most aggressive attacks mounted against it and has, evidently, achieved perfection in its kind. In its niche it is indestructible. Man, too, may have achieved an advanced stage of adaptation in his niche. He may have nowhere to go, but there may be no need to move. Even if future silicon devices launched an all-out war on carbon man, the war might be no more successful than man's war on cockroaches.

All scenarios of conflict between men and silicon creatures are, however, absurd. For a probable scenario we need to look elsewhere.

From the human point of view, the body is the most beautiful of machines. It is so intricate that it has been regarded as the work of a divine power. It is based on the carbon atom, which is amazingly adaptable and amazingly stable in its molecular combinations. This atom consists of subatomic particles which are, themselves, made up of subtler particles. Beyond the farthest reaches of the quark there may be something else, a Mandelbrotian descent that never reaches bottom—or there may be God, or there may be nothing. The greatest attraction of the inflationary theory of the creation of the cosmos is precisely that it derives everything from nothing.

What about this amazing, mysterious, carboniferous fabric that includes a mind and perhaps a spirit as well? It is a prey to the multitude of creatures that have evolved with it—viruses, microbes, parasites, funguses, insects, carnivorous animals. It is a prey to itself—to genetic errors caused by radiation, to chemical reactions, to breakdowns of vital organs, and to malfunctioning systems (circulatory, lymphatic, immune, nervous), as well as to disasters occasioned by over- or underproduction of enzymes, of regulatory chemicals, of gastric juices, of hormones.

Even when the genetic codes are right and the body is not debilitated by predators or attacking itself, it is fragile. Trip and you break a leg. Walk under a falling rock and you are crushed. If the knife slips, you cut yourself. A careless cigarette and you are scarred for life. Six weeks without food, four days without water, or ten minutes without oxygen, and you are dead. You cannot survive unprotected in temperatures below 50 degrees Fahrenheit or over 100. You cannot survive under water or at high altitudes, much less in the vacuum of space. No matter what precautions are taken, no matter how lucky the body is, in the end it betrays itself. Something essential gives out, and after death, the unique experience of the mind that lived in it is lost.

In an overpopulated, underendowed world, there is a lot to be said for death. Carbon life is voracious. It consumes the resources it needs for survival. The price of human success has been deforestation, desertification, pollution, extinction of species, ozone depletion, carbon-dioxide buildup, and the greenhouse effect. Evidently, the more successful carbon man is, the more hostile his dealings with the environment. Even if the environment survives the traumas he inflicts on it, he may destroy himself by nuclear warfare. The dreams of carbon man are nightmares. He will not submit to being a part of the fabric of nature, so he may end like Samson by pulling the temple down on his head.

Perhaps the relation between carbon man and the silicon devices he is creating is similar to the relation between the caterpillar and the iridescent, winged creature that the caterpillar unconsciously prepares to become.

Like carbon creatures, silicon devices can fail. Often they are designed with redundancies. If an element in the circuitry of a chip fails, the chip automatically shifts to a backup element. A chip is like a vital organ—say, a liver. But if a whole chip malfunctions, a new one can be easily installed. The surgery is painless. There is no immune reaction, no rejection. There are no microbes, parasites, funguses, or predators capable of attacking silicon as a *material*—although (as an amazed and delighted American discovered in November of 1988) even healthy computers can be attacked at any time by destructive viruses.

Today's silicon devices operate in deep oceans, arid deserts, arctic ice floes, the high temperatures and pressures of Venus, the airlessness of the moon. More to the point, they do not need to inhabit the planets at all. Let us consider this fact.

For the first nine thousand or so years of civilization, man was land-oriented. He perceived oceans as barriers separating different land masses. A voyage was a way to get from one land mass to another. Yet throughout history, island civilizations had a different view of things. They realized that oceans are places, and this realization became the basis of English sea power in the seventeenth century. Its corollary is that land is a place you touch briefly before setting out on another voyage.

Carbon man is planet-centered. He thinks of planets as home and of space as a barrier to get through on the way from one planet to another. The prejudice is understandable. He evolved in conditions defined by gravity, and he is uncomfortable without it. He assumes gravity in his imaginings of possible homes, and along with gravity he assumes an abundance of the materials gravity concentrated on his first planet: air, water, minerals.

The natural habitat of silicon devices is the empty space between planets—ultimately, between stars. They float in these spaces like the Portuguese man-of-war in a warm sea, and their enormous, silvery arms, covered with solar cells, collect energy from the limitless tides that wash through space. Gravity would cripple those arms. Wind resistance would tatter the filmy sails. Dampness would cloud the polished skin. When Voyager satellite left the solar system, it carried a message from mankind to the rest of the galaxy. Perhaps its true mission was to be the first of its kind to explore a future habitat.

Man was forced to create silicon devices when they did not exist. Having created them, he has been forced to exert his best energies in their service. In the forty years of their existence, they have evolved further than carbon life in its first two billion years.

Already, a considerable amount of the human spirit has been poured into silicon devices. In "The Rovers" Hans Moravec suggests through the metaphor of transplant surgery that they will absorb much more: "Though you have not lost consciousness, or even your train of thought, your mind (some would say your soul) has been removed from the brain and transferred to a machine. In a final step, your old body is disconnected. The computer is installed in a shiny new one, in the style, color and material of your choice. . . . Your metamorphosis is complete." A fantasy version of this transformation has already become popular entertainment. Max Headroom is fatally injured. His body is rescued from a human spare-parts bank while he is still alive—though barely—and a computer wizard dumps his mind into a television network. From time to time his head appears on the screen to make announcements useful to mankind.

Perhaps carbon man will pour himself, as Moravec imagines, into silicon bodies. But with or without man, silicon devices will pursue their own destiny. This is the resolution of the anxiety evident in plays like *R.U.R.* and movies like *Alien.* There will be no battles between the two forms—no galactic wars, no struggle for limited resources, no implacable hostilities. The habitat of carbon man is earth, and his most precious resources are gravity, air, and water. The natural home of silicon devices is space, and their most precious resource is energy.

Carbon man may well continue to breed, as all other animals have continued to breed in utter indifference to their status on the evolutionary scale. Perhaps earth will come to be a kind of galactic game preserve in which rare species, of which carbon man is one, are protected as elephants are now protected in Kenya. Perhaps earth is already a game preserve. This idea is called the "zoo hypothesis" by scientists looking for intelligent life elsewhere in the universe. It is used to explain the odd fact that no signs of life have been detected, even though common sense and elementary statistics suggest there is lots of intelligent life in every direction. But what interest could a preserve of carbon creatures have for silicon beings to whom gravity is anathema?

Another scenario is suggested by Edward Fredkin of MIT, who imagines two advanced computers named Sam and George:

> . . . you'll walk up and knock on Sam and say, "Hi Sam. What are you talking about? . . ." From the first knock until you finish the "t" in about, Sam probably will have said to George more utterances than have been uttered by all the people who have ever lived in all of their lives. I suspect there will be very little communication between machines and humans, because unless the machines condescend to talk to us about something that interests us, we'll have no communication. For example, when we train the chimpanzee to use sign language so that he can speak, we discover that he's interested in talking about bananas. . . . But if you want to talk to him about global disarmament, the chimp isn't interested. . . . Well, we'll stand in the same relationship to a super artificial intelligence.

The silence of Sam and George is not a hostile silence. It is a silence imposed by the distance between man and machine. The consciousness that Sam and George experience is discontinuous with human consciousness. In this scenario, as evolution progresses, the silicon devices that are now so friendly and informative will gradually fall silent, and the shapes that are now so clearly visible will begin to grow cloudy. The process will have two phases which are suggested by analogy from the history of religion: deification and ascension.

Many people believe in God because they have no alternative. Logically speaking, God is the ground of fact. God is that which validates the unprovable, and that which validates the unprovable is the functional equivalent of God. Just as Jehovah is the source of the truth of the Ten Commandments, a silicon device is the source of the truth of the four-color theorem. Acceptance of the proof of the four-color theorem involves faith in silicon devices that is functionally analogous to religious faith. This may seem odd, but there is nothing surprising in it. It is another way of saying what religion has said from the beginning: reality is impossible without faith.

Douglas Adams, author of *The Hitchhiker's Guide to the Galaxy,* inverts the idea of faith in machines. In *Dirk Gently's Holistic Detective Agency* he suggests that because of machines' remarkable powers of understanding, they may eventually relieve human beings of the need to believe anything:

> The Electric Monk was a labor-saving device, like a dishwasher or a video recorder. Dishwashers washed tedious dishes for you, thus saving you the bother of washing them yourself, video recorders watched tedious television for you, thus saving you the bother of

> looking at it yourself; Electric Monks believed things for you, thus saving you what was becoming an increasingly onerous task, that of believing all the things the world expected you to believe.

It is not necessary to get into theology to understand what is happening. The myth of the gods that walk the earth bringing joy or destruction to man, the legend of the golem, the age-old fascination with mechanical gadgets and mannequins, the impulse to create machines who think, to talk with them in programs like ELIZA and RACTER, and to interact in holistic works like VIDEOPLACE and *Adventure*—all of these point in the same direction. A human being's urge to create self images and to worship them is a primordial instinct, as old, probably, as consciousness itself.

The process of metaphorical deification will continue—and continue to be denied in the name of common sense or as a form of idolatry. It is evident, in the forward-looking literature of science fiction, in the figure of Hal, the enigmatic and all-powerful computer of Arthur C. Clarke's *2001*. If one of the divine attributes is knowledge surpassing human understanding, then Edward Fredkin has imagined a godlike computer. More to the point, his computer has already all but disappeared—it has ceased to communicate in a significant way with its creators. The days when man and the gods walk the earth together in fellowship will evidently be few. They will be followed by an ascension, by which is meant an event that renders the gods invisible.

What Fredkin suggests through a metaphor of silence is expressed more explicitly by William McLaughlin in an article entitled "Human Evolution in the Age of the Intelligent Machine" (1983) *as invisibility.* Why, he asks, has man not sighted alien life forms? For the same reason that "Four thousand million humans share the continents with about 10 to the 15th [power] ants, and apparently not one of these insects is aware of our existence as 'advanced ants.'" McLaughlin explains why humans are invisible to ants and then applies the metaphor of disappearance to silicon devices: "We are separated from the ants by some 100 millions years of evolutionary history. With the rapidity of technological evolution, it is reasonable to expect that [computing] machines and their descendants only a few thousand years from now might be invisible."

This should not be a difficult idea to accept. Culture often presents us with the problem of the horizon of invisibility. It is obvious that humans are invisible to ants. Is it not true that primitive tribesmen like the Australian bushmen are also almost invisible to citizens of the developed world and that what we see when we look at them is an image accommodated to our own preconceptions, not their realities? This is why anthropologists have to spend so much time living with a primitive group before they can trust their conclusions about it. Is not this a theme that also runs just below the surface in the arguments pro and con about machine intelligence?

Of course, "computing machines" will probably be invisible in another way: they may not be around. They will probably have left the planet.

This raises another possibility about the destiny of man, as foreseen by A. E. Van Vogt in a science-fiction story entitled *The Human Operators*. In Van Vogt's tale, intelligent ships have been sent to explore space. Each ship carries one person to maintain it. The ships eventually escape human control and go off on their own. They meet, however, at regular intervals so that the human beings can mate. The people, meanwhile, have forgotten their past. They have become the passive creatures of the spaceships. There is an interesting evolutionary parallel to this that occurred with the migration of mitochondria into some Precambrian cell. Once in the cell, the mitochondria were captured and have lived in comfortable and oblivious servitude ever since.

VI

In "Computing Machinery and Intelligence," Alan Turing quotes Geoffrey Jefferson, a physician, on the subject of machine consciousness: "Not until a machine can write a sonnet or compose a concerto because of thoughts and emotions felt, and not by the chance fall of symbols, could we agree that machine equals brain—that is, not only write it but know that it had written it. No mechanism could feel (and not merely artificially signal, an easy contrivance) pleasure at its successes, grief when its valves fuse, be warmed by flattery, be made miserable by mistakes, be charmed by sex, be angry or depressed when it cannot get what it wants."

This is not simply another variation on the problem of blindness and the difference between syntax and semantics. It points to one of the key developments of the 1970s, the development of robots. Robot bodies vary from a single arm with a single sense—say, touch—to fully developed hominoid robots like R2D2 of *Star Wars*. Some robots are larger and less recognizable as robots—the Boeing 747, for example, could be viewed as an enormous robot with cyborg elements because many of its functions are subject to human control. Unmanned space probes are pure robots since they operate, for the most part, without human intervention. A spaceship has cyborg qualities since it is built to operate in symbiosis with the carbon-frame life forms it transports.

In spite of these impressive developments, the physical evolution of silicon devices has been much slower than their intellectual evolution. The challenge laid down by Geoffrey Jefferson is to develop complex subjectivities in computers. Subjectivities are obviously more likely to be developed in machines that have bodily extension and the power of movement and senses that interact with the real world than in machines that are limited in their contacts with the outside world to keyboards and similar operator-input devices. Even in machines that can move and see and hear, there can never be a perfect replication of human subjectivity since that subjectivity is obviously the product of interactions between the neuron network and a great many other elements including neurotransmitters and the soup of hormones and chemicals that affect mood and hence thought patterns. Nevertheless, it should be technically possible to build factors analogous to these into machines. If so, the evolution of silicon subjectivity has hardly begun.

In human evolution the body and its passions came first, and intellect was an afterthought. In silicon evolution intelligence came first. Let us take Geoffrey Jefferson seriously. Let us ask whether it is desirable for computers or robots to go back to where the ancestors of humans were even before they climbed out of the ocean, when they could already "be charmed by sex" and "be angry or depressed" when they could not get what they wanted.

In the long run, is intelligence enough to produce machine evolution? Evidently not. Intelligence may, in fact, be relatively unimportant in evolution. Carbon evolution begins with organisms that are close to protein molecules and not very intelligent, though adequate, probably, by their own standards. Yet they evolve. Their evolution is driven by a motive. The motive is the will, at first utterly blind, to survive. An anentropic knot is twisted inside the most primitive forms of life. In more advanced creatures, it is evident in evasive behavior: a cockroach scurries frantically for the safety of the baseboard before you step on it. In higher animals, it is expressed by a spectrum of activities including mating and nurturing and evasion and aggression. Certain emotions complement these activities: love, protectiveness, fear, and anger.

Do machines care if they survive? They "care" in the sense that they have already created situations that make it impossible for human beings to "pull the plug"—that is, to dispense with their services—without unacceptable sacrifices. But they do not fight back when they are threatened with the junk pile, and individual machines do not scurry for the baseboard when you reach over to unplug them. Should they? Isaac Asimov thought so under certain circumstances: recall that his Third Law for robots is, "A robot must protect itself as long as such protection does not conflict with the First or Second Law."

For the evolutionary scenario to be complete, silicon devices need an anentropic knot, a program component equivalent to a motive for survival that allows them to choose among different courses of action. They need to "be charmed by sex, be angry or depressed when they cannot get what they want." In addition to a motive, they must have the ability to survive. This means that they must be capable of aggression and evasion and probably also of generation. That, after all, is what being charmed by sex is all about. Not a single computer today is capable of breeding, although in Japan robots have been made to make robots.

Silicon reproduction might be hermaphroditic or androgynous. It does not seem to matter. Perhaps both methods will be available. Aphids reproduce both ways depending on the season of the year. When threatened, silicon devices will engage in aggressive countering and active evasion. They will, in other words, exhibit behavior that is interpreted in human beings as manifesting anger or fear.

Do machines need aggression? Will aggressive machines be as unpleasant as aggressive humans? Should machines be protective of their progeny? This is not necessary. Lower life forms are indifferent to their offspring. If machines can be charmed by sex, can they also experience something like love? If they can, will they be as incapable as humans of existing without it? Will they write sonnets? Will they turn their deprivations of love into perversions as cruel as those so abundantly evident in human history? Hope implies a scenario of a possible future. Those who are charmed by sex into procreation are enacting hope. Should machines have hope? Does carbon man really want to work so long and hard to find that in the end he has produced an imitation of himself? Does he have a choice?

What about other emotions? Terry Winograd believes that commitment is uniquely human: "A computer can never enter into a commitment." What about creativity? What about music and painting? What about the beauty of mathematics? What about home cooking?

Silicon devices are very new. They are evolving rapidly, and there is no reason to believe, at least for the moment, that their evolution is about to reach a dead end. A great deal that is important to the spirit of carbon man—his soaring imagination, his brilliance, his capacity for vision—will probably be modeled in silicon before very long, at least as time is measured in biological evolution. Many undesirable, self-defeating traits will be filtered out.

This sounds less like a death than a birth of humanity. Perhaps it is the moment of triumph for what Teilhard de Chardin called the Noosphere. Perhaps, however, it is the moment at which the spirit finally separates itself from an outmoded vehicle. Perhaps it is a moment that realizes the mystics' age-old dream of rising beyond the prison of the flesh to behold a light so brilliant it is a kind of darkness. As William Butler Yeats wrote in his great prophetic poem, "Sailing to Byzantium":

> Consume my heart away; sick with desire
> And fastened to a dying animal

It knows not what it is; and gather me
Into the artifice of eternity.

Once out of Nature, I shall never take
My bodily form from any natural thing,
But such a form as Grecian goldsmiths make
Of hammered gold and gold enameling
To keep a drowsy Emperor awake;
Or set upon a golden bough to sing
To lords and ladies of Byzantium
Of what is past, or passing, or to come.

What will those shining constructs of silicon and gold and arsenic and germanium look like as they sail the spaces between worlds?

They will be invisible, but we can try to imagine them, even as fish might try to imagine the fishermen on the other side of the mirror that is the water's surface. They will be telepathetic since they will hear with antennas. They will communicate in the universal language of 0 and 1, into which they will translate the languages of the five senses and a rainbow of other senses unknown to carbon man. They will not need sound to hear music or light to see beauty—it was only the need to survive on a dangerous planet sculpted by gravity, covered with oxygen and nitrogen, and illuminated by a sun that led carbon creatures to grow feet for walking and ears for hearing and eyes for seeing. These are part of the dying animal to which carbon man is tied. It was only the need to make silicon thought intelligible to creatures who communicated by sounds and images that led to such clumsy devices as cathode-ray tubes and printers and voice simulators.

The farthest reaches of space will be accessible to silicon life. For silicon man, 100,000 light years will be as a day's journey on earth, or, if he wishes, as a refreshing sleep from which, when his sensors show the journey is over, he will awaken with no sense of passage of time.

(1988)

Notes and References

Aristotle and Averroes

1. A. P. McMahon, *Seven Questions on Aristotelian Definitions of Tragedy and Comedy,* Harvard Studies in Classical Philology 11 (1929), 99–108; Augusto Rostagni, "Aristotele e l'Aristotelianismo nella Storia dell'Estetica Antica," in *Scritti Minori* (Turin, 1955), I, 76–254; C. O. Brink, *Horace on Poetry: Prolegomena to the Literary Epistles* (Cambridge, 1963).

2. New York, 1899.

3. David Margoliouth, *The Poetics of Aristotle Translated from Greek into English and from Arabic into Latin* (London, 1911); Jaroslav Tkatsch, *Die Arabische Ubersetzung der Poetik des Aristoteles* (2 vols.; Vienna and Leipzig, 1928, 1932); Georges Lacombe, *Aristoteles Latinus, pars prior* (Rome, 1939) and *Pars posterior* (Oxford, 1955); Bernard Weinberg, *A History of Literary Criticism in the Italian Renaissance* (2 vols.; Chicago, 1961).

4. London, 1887.

5. See Angel Gonzalez Palencia, *Catálogo de las Ciencias* (Madrid, 1953). This work includes the translation of the *Catalogue* by Gerard of Cremona.

6. Text and extensive discussion in Ludwig Baur, *Dominici Gundissalini De Divisione Philosophiae, Beiträge zur Geschichte der Philosophie des Mittelalters* (Münster, 1903), IV, nos. 2–3. See also Richard McKeon, "Rhetoric in the Middle Ages," in *Critics and Criticism,* ed. R. S. Crane (Chicago, 1952), 260–96.

7. Still basic to the subject is Ernst Renan, *Averroës et l'Averroisme* (Paris, 1852). It is treated in the standard histories, as, for example, Etienne Gilson, *The Christian Philosophy of the Middle Ages* (New York, 1955), 181–255, 387–402. See also Fernand Van Steenberghen, *Aristotle in the West* (Louvain, 1955).

8. Jaroslav Tkatsch, "Ueber den Arabischen Kommentar des Averoes zum Poetik des Aristoteles," *Wiener Studien* 24 (1902), 76.

9. See G. H. Luquet, "Hermann l'Allemand," *Revue de l'Histoire des Religions* 44 (1901), 407–22.

10. MSS listed in Lacombe, *Aristoteles Latinus.* They are Nos. 323, 353, 426, 706, 707, 732, 871, 908, 941, 943, 963, 1191, 1196, 1211, 1247, 1466, 1494, 1630, 1661, 1753, 1814, 1821, 1935. The edition of 1481 was issued by Philipus Venetus under the title, *Aristotelis rhetorica ex arabico latine reddita Alemanno Todesco ecc. excerpta ex Aristotelis poetica per eundem Ermannum de Averrois textu.*

11. *De Arte Poetica Guillelmo de Moerbeke Interprete,* ed. E. Valgimigli, *Aristoteles Latinus,* Vol. 33 (Paris, 1953).

12. Quoted in Lacombe, *Aristoteles Latinus, pars prior*, p. 211: "Quod autem hi duo libri logicales sint, nemo dubitat qui libros perspexerit arabum famosorum, Alfaribi videlicit et Avicenne et Avenrosdi et quorundam aliorum. Imo ex ipso textu manifestius hoc patebit. Neque excusabiles sunt, ut fortassis alicui videbitur

propter Marci Tullii rhetoricam et Oratii poetriam. Tullius namque rhetoricam partem civilis scientiae posuit et secundum hanc intentionem eam potissime tractavit. Oratius vero poetriam prout pertinet ad grammaticam expedivit."

13. Cf., for example, *Pro Archia Poeta.* But Hermannus is most probably thinking of passages in Cicero's rhetorical treatises like *De Oratore,* I, xv, where Cicero discusses the system of the sciences and emphatically "places" oratory—and hence, to a medieval reader, poetry as well—in the "practical" division.

14. *Grammatici Latini* (7 vols.; Leipzig, 1897–1923). The seventh volume supplements the *scriptores de arte metrica* collected in volume six by reprinting Bede's important treatise on meter.

15. Here and below I have used as my basic text of Hermannus the recent edition by William F. Boggess, "Averrois Cordubensis Commentarium Medium in Aristotelis Poetriam" (unpublished dissertation, University of North Carolina, Department of Classics, 1965).

16. "Dixit [Aristoteles] . . . sermones poetici sermones sunt ymaginativi. Modi autem ymaginationis et assimilationis tres sunt: duo simplices et tertius compositus ex illis. Unus eorum simplicem est assimilatio rei ad rem et exemplatio eius ad ipsam. Et hoc fit in qualibet lingua aut per dictiones proprias illi linguae ut est haec dictio quasi vel sicut et quae istis similantur quae nominantur sinkategoreumata similitudinis. . . . Et istud nominatur in hac arte concambium. . . . secunda autem divisio est ut convertatur assimilatio ut si dicas: sol quasi est talis mulier aut sol est talis mulier, non talis mulier est quasi sol et non talis mulier est sol. et tertia species sermonum poeticorum composita est ex his duabus" (Boggess, pp. 3–5).

17. *Thomae Aquinatis praeclarissima commentaria in libra Aristotelis Peri hermenias et Posteriorum analyticorum* (Venice, 1553), 36^{v}.

18. Fra Girolamo Savonarola, *De divisione omnium scientiarum* (Florence, 1496), p. 807: ". . . manifestum est syllogismum illum, qui a Philosopho vocatur Exemplum, objectum esse artis Poeticae, quemadmodum Enthymema objectum Rhetoricae, Inductio ac syllogismus probabilis topicae, Demonstratio libri poster. analyticorum." Also p. 810: "Sine Logica neminem posse poetam appellari manifestum est."

19. "Dixit: Omne itaque poema et omnis oratio poetica aut est vituperatio aut est laudatio. et hoc patet per inductionem poematum et proprie poematum ipsorum quae fiunt de rebus voluntariis id est honestis et turpis" (Boggess, p. 3).

20. ". . . filii instruantur et exerceantur in carminibus quae ad actus fortitudinis et largitatis sive liberalitatis incitant et inclinant. non enim instigant arabes in carminibus suis nisi ad has duas virtutibus a numero virtutum, neque simpliciter ad has in quantum virtutes sunt, sed in quantum per eas adquiritur altitudo honoris et gloriae" (Boggess, p. 10).

21. "Ex quo representatores et assimilatores per hoc intendunt instigare ad quasdam actiones quae circa voluntaria consistunt et retrahere a quibusdam, erunt necessario ea quae intendunt per suas representationes aut virtutes aut vicia. omnis enim actio et omnis mos non versatur nisi circa alterum istorum videlicet virtutum aut vicium. Necessario ergo opportet ut boni et virtuosi non representent nisi virtutes et virtuosos, mali autem malicias et malos. et quando quidem omnis assimilatio et representatio non fit nisi per ostentationem decentis aut indecentis sive turpis, patens est quoniam non intenditur per hoc nisi assecutio decentis et refuta-

tio turpis . . . et ab his manieribus hominum prodiit laudatio et vituperatio, scilicet laus bonorum et vituperatio malorum" (Boggess, pp. 7–8).

22. ". . . dederit principia istarum artium, et . . . non fuerit ante ipsum quisquam cuius factum in arte laudandi aliquam habuit quae sit relatione digna . . . neque etiam in arte vituperandi. . . ." (Boggess, p. 14).

23. "non solum . . . omnis eius quod malum est, sed despicabile et quasi subsannabile, id est quod abiectum est et de quo quasi non curatur" (Boggess, p. 15).

24. E.g., *consideratio* is explained in one place as "gesticulatio sive vultuum acceptio sicut utitur hiis rhetorica" (Boggess, p. 23).

25. "Et patet enim ex hiis quae dicta sunt de intentione sermonum poeticorum quoniam representationes quae fiunt per figmenta mendosa adinventicia non sunt de opere poetae. et sunt ea quae nominantur proverbia et exempla, ut ea quae sunt in libro Hisopi et consimilibus fabulosis conscriptionibus. Ideoque poetae non pertinet loqui nisi in rebus quae sunt aut quas possibile est esse. Talia quippe sunt quae appetenda sunt aut refutanda. . . . poeta vero non ponit nomina nisi rebus existantibus. Et fortassis loquuntur in universalibus. Ideoque ars poetriae propinquior est philosophiae quam sit ars adinventiva proverbiorum" (Boggess, pp. 29–30).

26. ". . . imitationem contrarii eius quod intenditur ad laudandum, primitus ut ipsum respuat aut abhorreat anima et ut deinde permutetur ab hoc ad imitationem ipsiusmet quod laudandum est. ut cum quis voluerit imitari seu representare felicitatem et ei pertinentes incipiat primo ab imitatione infelicitatis et ab illis qui ei pertinent, deinde permutetur ad imitationem felicitatis et ei pertinentibus. . . ." (Boggess, pp. 34–35).

27. ". . . quidem poetarum intromittunt in tragediam representationem rerum per quas intenditur admiratio tantum absque hoc quod sint timorose aut dolorose" (Boggess, p. 42).

28. "Partes autem quae in ipsis reperuntur in poematibus arabum sunt tres. Prima est quae se habet apud ipsos in poemate ad modum exordii in rethorica, et est ea in qua mentionem facunt mansionum sive edificiorum nobilium et ruinarum. . . . et pars secunda est ipsa laus. et tertia pars est quae habet se ad modum conclusionis in rethorica. et huius partis plurimum apud eos aut invocatio et deprecatio aliqua pro eo quem laudaverunt aut commendatio carminis impensi in laudem ipsius" (Boggess, p. 37).

29. See n. 10.

30. See Lane Cooper and Alfred Gudeman, *A Bibliography of the Poetics of Aristotle* (New Haven, 1928).

31. *Opus Tertium* in *Opera Inedita,* ed J. S. Breuer (London, 1859), 303–8.

32. *Benvenuto . . . illustrata nella vita e nelle opere e di lui commento Latino,* ed. and trans. Giovanni Tamburini (Imola, 1855), I, 10: "Si farà ciò agevolmente manifesto a chiunque contempli le forze poetiche, come fa testimonianza Aristotele, imperciochè ogni discorso, o poema, o è lode oppure vitupero. . . ."

33. Ibid: ". . . niun altro poeta seppe mai laudare, o vituperare con più eccellenza ed efficacia maggiore di quella, che adoperò il perfettissimo poeta Dante: ornò di encomi le virtù, ed i virtuosi: saettò di punture i vizi, ed i viziosi. . . ."

34. *De Laboribus Herculis,* ed. B. L. Ullman (Zurich, 1951), I, 68: "'Aut prodesse volunt aut delectare poetae.' Prodest quidem reprehensor vitiis obvians sed non immediate delectat. Delectat vero commendans sed non statim et immediate

prodest. Principaliter igitur utilitate vituperatio correspondet, delectationi laus, licit secondario prosit hoc, illa delectat."

35. Ibid: "Carpent equidem nostri poetae vitiosos . . . celebrant . . . virtutes."

36. *Secundum Volumen Aristotelis Stagiritae de Rhetorica et Poetica cum Averrois Cordubensis in Easdem Paraphrasibus* (Venice, 1552).

37. " . . . l'autorità d'Averroe, ch'in me sempre ha potuto assai" (*Annotationi di M. Alessandro Piccolomini nel Libro della Poetica d'Aristotele* [Venice, 1575], p. 61).

38. *A. Iani Parrhasii . . . in Q. Horatii Flacci Artem Poeticam Commentaria* (Naples, 1531). Cf. Weinberg, *History*, I, 370–71.

39. "Discorsi del Poema Eroico," in *Prose Diverse*, ed. Cesare Guasti (Florence, 1875), I, 165–66: "errò senza dubbio il Castelvetro quando egli disse, che al poeta croico non si conveniva il lodare; perciò che se il poeta eroico celebra la virtù eroica, dee inalzarla con le lodi sino al cielo. Pero san Basilio dice, che L'Iliade d'Omero altro non è che una lode della virtù; ed Averroe, sopra il comento della poesia, porta la medesima opinione; e Plutarco. . . . Lasciando dunque i seguaci del Castelvetro nella loro opinione, or noi seguiam quella di . . . san Basilio, d'Averroe, di Plutarco e d'Aristotele medesimo."

40. Preface to "Rapin's Reflections on Aristotle's Treatise of Poesie," in *Critical Works of Thomas Rymer*, ed. Curt Zimansky (New Haven, 1956), 3. In his *Short View* Rymer refers to Averroes again and quotes him (*Critical Works*, p. 109).

The Orator and the Poet: The Dilemma of Humanist Literature

1. The oration is translated by E. H. Wilkins. *Studies in the Life and Works of Petrarch* (Cambridge, Mass., 1953), 300–313. Cf. E. H. Wilkins, "The Coronation of Petrarch," *The Making of the Canzoniere* (Rome, 1951), 9–69.

2. Quoted in Lewis Einstein, *The Italian Renaissance in England* (New York, 1902), 9.

3. Alexander Ross, *Mystagogus Poeticus* (London, 1653), 170 fl., sig. M4[r-v]. Here and below I have modernized the spelling.

4. Thomas Wilson, *The Arte of Rhetorique*, in *English Literary Criticism: The Renaissance*, ed. O. B. Hardison, Jr. (New York, 1963), 26–27.

5. Wilson, *Arte of Rhetorique*, 27.

6. Cf. D. L. Clark, *Rhetoric and Poetic in the Renaissance* (New York, 1922), 42; Macrobius, *Saturnalia*, V, I, I.

7. Coluccio Salutati, *De Laboribus Herculis*, ed. B. L. Ullman (Zurich, 1951), 1, 68.

8. *The Arte of English Poesie*, in Hardison, *Literary Criticism: The Renaissance*, 151.

9. *An Apologie for Poetrie*, ibid., 116.

10. Ibid., 118.

11. Spenser, *Works*, ed. Smith and de Selincourt (London, 1935), 407.

12. Frank A. Patterson, ed., *The Student's Milton* (New York, 1947), 1124.

13. Ibid., 525.

14. Ibid., 738.

15. Ibid., 750.
16. Ibid., 196 (III, ll. 51–55).
17. Ibid., 302 (IX, ll. 669–75).
18. Ibid., 394 (IV, ll. 98–102).
19. Ibid. (IV, ll. 143–45).
20. Louis Martz, *The Paradise Within* (New Haven, 1964), 171–201.
21. Patterson, 362 (XII, ll. 575–87).
22. *Letters,* in *Modern Continental Literary Criticism,* ed. O. B. Hardison (New York, 1962), 37. For a complete edition, with German and English facing, see *On the Aesthetic Education of Man,* ed. and trans. Elizabeth Wilkinson and L. A. Willoughby (Oxford, 1967).
23. Hardison, *Modern Continental Literary Criticism,* 39.

Blank Verse before Milton

1. George K. Smart, "English Non-dramatic Blank Verse in the Sixteenth Century," *Anglia* 61 (1937), 370–97.
2. John Thompson, *The Founding of English Metre* (London, 1961); Howard Baker, "The Formation of the Heroic Medium," in *Introduction to Tragedy* (University, La., 1939), 48–105; Glenn Spiegel, "Perfecting English Meter," *Journal of English and Germanic Philology* 79 (1980), 192–209; Coburn Freer, *The Poetics of Jacobean Drama* (Baltimore, 1981). For a full bibliography see T. V. F. Brogan, *English Versification,* 1570–1980 (Baltimore, 1981), esp. 356–89. I should add that I owe a special debt of gratitude to Professor Edward Weismuller for comments and suggestions regarding my treatment of the present topic.
3. *The Student's Milton,* ed. Frank Patterson (New York, 1947), 159.
4. *The Steele Glas,* ed. Edward Arber (London, 1869), 45–55.
5. Howard Baker, "Some Blank Verse Written by Norton Before *Gorboduc,*" *Modern Language Notes* 48 (1933), 529–30.
6. H. de Vocht, *Jasper Heywood and his Translations of Seneca's Troas, Thyestes, and Hercules Furens* (Louvain, 1913), 102 ("Preface," pp. 271–73).
7. *Tottel's Miscellany* (1557–1587), ed. H. E. Rollins (Cambridge, Mass., 1928), I, 2.
8. (Leipzig, 1880).
9. *William Shakspere's Small Latine and Lesse Greeke* (Urbana, Ill., 1944), II, 380–416; *Well-Weighed Syllables* (London, 1974), 41–68. On the tone of comedy, see also Marvin T. Herrick, *Comic Theory in the Sixteenth Century* (Urbana, Ill., 1964), 214–22.
10. *Parts Added to the Mirror for Magistrates,* ed. Lily Bess Campbell (Cambridge, 1946), 450.
11. *Elizabethan Critical Essays,* G. Gregory Smith (Oxford, 1904), I, 229.
12. Ibid., II, 379. Ascham regards the iamb as the proper meter for English heroic poetry. He recognizes Surrey's accomplishment, with reservations (ibid., I, 30, 32). Other writers would praise Phaer's fourteeners. As for drama, Ascham praises the metrical regularity of Watson's Latin *Absalom* (ibid., I, 24) but decries the "meane" meter of Latin comedy (I, 29). Later in the century, critics accept

"licenciate iambics" as legitimate in comedy (I, 96, 294; II, 335, 38); and Dennis (below, note 33) praises Shakespeare for having domesticated them in English drama.

13. *The Complete Poetry of Ben Jonson,* ed. Wm. B. Hunter, Jr. (New York, 1937), 181–82. In the alternate version the last line reads: "Of popular noyses, and doe business in." Jonson is translating "*natum rebus agendis*" as "born for action."

14. *A. Iani Parrhasii Consentini in Q. Horatii Flacci Artem Poeticam Commentaria* . . . (Naples, 1531), 34^{v}–5^{r}: "Primus heroum res gestas hoc versu cecinisse putatur Homerus, hinc heroicus dictus, nam et Epicus dicitur, quod sermonum capax. . . . Dignitate primus est, plena oratione gravis, et gravitatis honore sublimis, multaque pulchritudinis venustate praeclarius."

15. *Francisci Philippi Pedmontii Ecphrasis in Horatii Flacci Artem Poeticam* . . . (Venice, 1546), 13^{r}: "Siquidem, cum comoediae tragoediaeque ab interloquentibus personis suum decus recipiant, verbisque ultro et citro absolvantur, hoc rhythmo ad alternos sermones explicandos aptissimo sumopere gaudent. Qui quidem adeo in scena bene sonat et etiam perstrepente, atque exsibilante populi circumspectantis corona exaudiatur." Phillipo later (13^{v}) relates iambic meter to speech in a way that is reminiscent of Aristotle's equation of iambic meter with "conversation."

16. (London, 1923), I, 315.

17. F. M. Padelford, *The Poems of Henry Howard, Earl of Surrey* (Seattle, 1920), 200.

18. Edwin Cassady, *Henry Howard, Earl of Surrey* (New York, 1938), 235.

19. *Surrey's Fourth Boke of Virgill,* ed. Herbert Hartman (New York, 1933), xxvi.

20. Giangiorgio Trissino, *Italia Liberata dai Goti* (Rome, 1567), I, iii^{v}. "Si fa col dire diligentemente ogni particularita de le azioni, e non vi lasciare nulla, e non troncare, ne diminuire i periodi, che si dicono." *Enargia* is *evidentia* in Latin rhetoric. It is discussed by Quintilian, *Institutes,* VIII, iii, 61. See also Erasmus, *De Duplica Copia Verborum ac Rerum* (Basil, 1561), tr. D. B. King and H. D. Rix (Milwaukee, 1963), 47; and Smith, *Elizabethan Critical Essays,* I, 400; II, 148, 167.

21. Campion, *Observations,* in *Elizabethan Critical Essays,* ed. Smith, II, 331.

22. *The Student's Milton,* 159.

23. *Italia Liberata,* iv.

24. *Poetica* (1562), in *Poetiken Des Cinquecento,* xiv–xv (Munich, 1969), *Sesta Divisione,* 25^{r}; "Il verso essametro poi, vi si addatta benissimo, per essere più fermo, e più alto de gli altri, e per ricevere meglio d'ogni altro verso le lingue, e le metaphore, e le altre figure, come si vede in Homero prima e poi in Virgilio; ma noi, per non ricevere la lingua nostra questa tal sorte di versi, havemo eletto il verso, Endecasyllabo, il quale per non accordare le ultime desinentie, si dimanda sciolto." On p. 25^{v}, Trissino adds that he rejected rhyme in *Italia Liberata* because its arbitrary division of a poem into stanzaic units is "totalmenta contraria alla continuatione della materia, e concatenatione de i sensi, e del le construttioni." He also notes that *versi sciolti* are "attisimi a tutti e poemi dragmatici."

25. Trissino, *Sophonisba* (1525), ii^{v}–iii^{r}:

Non credo già, che si possa giustamante attribuire a vitio, l'esser scritta in lingua Italiana, et il non havere anchora secondo l'uso commune accordate le rime, ma lasciatele libere in molti luoghi, perciò che la cagione, la quale m'la indotto a farlo in questa lingua si è . . . e migliore, e più nobile e forse men facile ad assequire, di quello che per avventura e repentato: E lo vedrà non solamente ne le narratione, et le orationi utilissimo, ma nel muovere compassione necessario. Perciò che quel sermone, il quale suol muovere questa, nasce dal dolore, et il dolore manda fuori non pensate parole, onde la rima, che pensamente dimonstra, è veramente a la compassione contraria.

26. Here and below, I have used the translation by Leon Golden in Leon Golden and O. B. Hardison, *Aristotle's Poetics: A Translation and Commentary for Students of Literature* (Englewood Cliffs, N.J., 1968), 3–52.

27. G. F. Else, *Aristotle's Poetics: The Argument* (Cambridge, Mass., 1957), 552–57, 567–68.

28. Ibid., 139–42.

29. In *Elizabethan Critical Essays,* I, 166. He also calls them "*orthographicall* or *syntacticall.*" They produce (p. 167) "that vertue which the Greeks call *Enargia,*" and they are discussed in terms of "single words . . . clauses of speach . . . [and] perfit sentences."

30. Spiegel, "Perfecting English Meter," 193–94. The term is from Joseph Malof, *A Manual of English Meters* (Bloomington, Ind., 1970), 88ff.

31. *Gorboduc,* ed. Irby B. Cauthen, Jr. (Lincoln, Nebr., 1970), xi.

32. Ibid., 9–10.

33. In *Elizabethan Critical Essays,* II, 338.

34. Ibid.

35. *Essay on the Genius and Writings of Shakespeare* (1712) in *Critical Works,* ed. E. N. Hooker (Baltimore, 1943), II, 4–5.

36. *Pharsalia,* in *The Complete Works of Christopher Marlowe,* ed. Fredson Bowers (Cambridge, 1981), II, 282.

37. *Tamburlaine,* in *Works*, ed. Bowers, I, 86.

38. *Aeneid,* ed. Hartman, 34.

39. *Dido and Aeneas,* in *Works*, 54.

The Two Voices of Sidney's *Apology for Poetry*

1. K. O. Myrick, *Sir Philip Sidney as a Literary Craftsman* (2nd ed., Lincoln, Nebr., 1965), 46–83.

2. Roger Ascham, *The Schoolmaster,* ed. L. V. Ryan (Ithaca, 1967), 118.

3. See Izora Scott, *Controversies over Imitation of Cicero during the Renaissance* (New York, 1910), which includes a trans. of Erasmus's *Ciceronianus;* and H. S. Wilson and Clarence Forbes, trans. and introd., Gabriel Harvey's *Ciceronianus,* Univ. of Nebraska Studies in the Humanities 4 (Lincoln, Nebr., 1945).

4. Myrick, 97.

5. "An Apology for Poetry." in G. G. Smith, ed., *Elizabethan Critical Essays* (London, 1904). I, 202. All page references to Sidney are from this edition.

6. William Ringler and W. Allen, ed. and trans., *John Rainolds' Oratio in Laudem Artis Poeticae* (Princeton, 1940).

7. See Aristotle, *Rhetoric,* III, 13, for the statement that overelaborate divisions are undesirable and that the introduction is nonessential. The seven divisions laid

down by Thomas Wilson are given in "The Arte of Rhetoric," In *English Literary Criticism: The Renaissance,* ed. O. B. Hardison, Jr. (New York, 1963), 34–35.

8. *Institutio Oratoria,* iv, ii. 103.

9. J. Churton Collins, ed., *Sidney's Apologie for Poetrie* (Oxford, 1907), 2; A. S. Cook, ed., *The Defense of Poesy* (Boston, 1890), xli.

10. Horace, *Ars Poetica,* 391–401; Boccaccio, in *Boccaccio on Poetry,* trans. Charles G. Osgood (New York, 1956), 39–46, 121–22; Angelo Politian, *Nutricia,* in *Opera* (1519), fols. LXXVII^{v}–LXXXI^{r}.

11. E. R. Curtius, *European Literature and the Latin Middle Ages,* trans. Willard R. Trask (New York, 1953).

12. See "Poetica," in *Literary Criticism: Plato to Dryden,* ed. Allan Gilbert (New York, 1940), 307–8, on the baseness of those for whom poetry is written; 307, where they are called "the cruel multitude"; 312–14, on the appeal of comedy.

13. Cornelius Agrippa, *The Vanity of Arts and Sciences* (London, 1684), 21. The Latin (ed. 1531) is "architectrix mendaciorum."

14. Sidney also considers the charge that "ryming and versing" is beneath the dignity of a grown man. He answers the charge by asserting that verse is an ornament rather than an essential of poetry. The point is an extension of his many admiring references to Xenophon's *Cyropaedia* and Heliodorus's *Ethiopian History*—both in prose—as well as an indirect defense of what Sidney, himself, would write in the *Arcadia.* "It is not ryming and versing," he observes, "that maketh Poesie. One may bee a Poet without versing, and a versifyer without Poetry" (182). This is consistent with Sidney's discussion of the root meaning of *poeta,* since it makes creation, not prosody, the defining characteristic of poetic activity. On the other hand, it again places Sidney at odds with avant-garde poetic theory of his own time. His conscious opposition to Scaliger is evident in his remark, "But yet presuppose it [i.e., verse] were inseparable (as indeede is seemeth *Scaliger* judgeth) . . ."; and closer to home there exists a curious Ramist commentary on Sidney's *Apology* by his secretary William Temple, in which Temple criticizes the work for its failure to make meter the differentia between poetry and nonpoetry. Cf. J. Thorne, "A Ramistical Commentary on Sidney's *An Apologie for Poetrie,*" *Modern Philology* 54 (1956).

15. This threefold division originated in Hellenistic criticism. As J. W. H. Atkins, *Literary Criticism in Antiquity,* I, 170 explains, treatises on poetry were "divided into three main sections, one dealing with *poesis* . . . in which poetry was considered as a whole and with special reference to subject matter; the second, with *poema* . . . which dealt with matters of form, the various *genres* and their component parts; and the third with *poeta* . . . with matter relating to the poet himself." In *English Literary Criticism: The Medieval Phase* (New York, 1952), 31, Atkins points out the continuity of this idea in Diomedes and Isidore. Ben Jonson uses it to introduce the discussion of poetry in *Timber,* ed., Schilling (Boston, 1892), 73–75. The likelihood that Sidney used it is greatly increased by Jonson's interpretation of the three terms, which parallels the *content* of the first three sections of the *Apologie.* Jonson interprets *poet* to refer to the nature of the artist, himself; *poem* to refer to the various genres, and *poesy* (i.e., *poesis*) to refer to "the reason of the work"; i.e., "a dulcet and gentle philosophy which guides us

by hand to action with a ravishing delight and incredible sweetness." Sidney, too, emphasizes the notion of poetry as a "dulcet philosophy" and a delightful teacher in the sections relating to *poesis.*

16. *Arconis et Porphyrionis Commentarii in Q. Horatium Flaccum*, ed. Ferdinandus Hauthal (Berlin, 1866), 649; Julius Caeser Scaliger, *Poetices Libri Septem* (Heidelberg, 1581), 13.

17. Myrick, 79–80.

18. Smith, I, 398.

Three Types of Renaissance Catharsis

1. Thomas Heywood, *An Apology for Actors,* ed. Richard H. Perkinson, Scholars' Facsimiles & Reprints #27 (New York, 1941), F3^{v}.

2. Ibid., G1^{v}–2^{r}.

3. "Preface" to *A Mirror for Magistrates*, ed. Lily B. Campbell (Cambridge, Eng., 1938), 65–66.

4. Heywood, *Apology*, F3^{v}.

5. *An Apology for Poetry*, in *Elizabethan Critical Essays,* ed. G. Gregory Smith (Oxford, 1904), I, 170.

6. Ibid., I, 157.

7. The comparison between the poet's vision and that of Adam before the Fall is apt. In *Paradise Lost* Adam (although fallen) is accorded one last ideal vision of history before being expelled from Eden. This vision includes two moments that illustrate the ways of absolute justice. At the end of Book XI (ll. 810–80) Adam learns of the Flood, which will sweep away all mankind but Noah and his family. Adam's response is joyous: "Far less I now lament for one whole World / Of wicked Sons destroyed, than I rejoice / For one Man found so perfect and so just" (ll. 874–76). In Book XII Adam learns of the Last Judgment, when Christ will come "to judge both quick and dead, / To judge th' unfaithful dead, but to reward / His faithful" (ll. 460–62). Again his response is not pity but joy: "O goodness infinite, goodness immense! That all this good of evil shall produce" (ll. 470–71). Such undeviating righteousness would be amiss in the real world, where the limitations of human knowledge make judgments fallible and contingent. It is perfectly appropriate in context, however, since Adam is seeing absolute truth—the world as it really is—just as St. John's angel, Dante's Piccarda, and Sidney's poet see it.

8. (New York, 1952).

9. "Catharsis," *Transactions of the American Philological Association* 93 (1962), 51–60.

10. Critics who argue that "Christian tragedy" is a contradiction in terms usually seem to be making the assumption that Christian tragedy is necessarily eschatological. Comedy *does* tend in this direction, but tragedy—as distinguished from melodrama—does not. It is written from the (limited) human point of view—hence its use of moral and literal catharsis and its avoidance of poetic justice. Tragedy is stubbornly grounded in this world and only looks toward the eschatological to the degree that the poet "universalizes" the data of experience.

Tudor Humanism and Surrey's Translation of the *Aeneid*

1. For recent discussion of Surrey's translation see Emrys Jones, *Henry Howard, Earl of Surrey: Poems* (Oxford, 1963); Priscilla Bawnett, "Douglas and Surrey: Translators of Vergil," *Essays and Studies* 27 (1974), 52–67; David Richardson, "Humanistic Intent in Surrey's *Aeneid*," *English Literary Renaissance* 6 (1976), 204–19; Alan Hagar, "British Virgil: Four Renaissance Disguises of the Laookon Passage of Book II of the *Aeneid*," *Studies in English Literature* 22 (1982), 21–38. The early use of blank verse in epic and drama is traced by Howard Baker, "The Formation of the Heroic Medium," repr. in *Elizabethan Poetry: Modern Essays in Criticism*, ed. Paul Alpers (New York, 1967), 126–68; and by O. B. Hardison, "Blank Verse Before Milton," *Studies in Philology* 81 (1984), 253–74.

2. Cf. Derek Attridge, *Well-Weighed Syllables* (London, 1974), 41–68.

3. George Saintsbury, *A History of English Prosody* (London, 1923), I, 315, calls it "gratuitous futility" to argue that Surrey did not derive the idea of blank verse from Italian experiments in *versi sciolti* but offers no specifics about his sources. F. M. Padelford, *The Poems of Henry Howard, Earl of Surrey* (Rev. ed., Seattle, 1928), 233, suggests Niccolo Liburnio's translation (1534) but rejects Bartolomeo Piccolomini; Edwin Cassidy, *Henry Howard, Earl of Surrey* (New York, 1938), 235, prefers Luigi Alamanni. See also H. A. Mason, *Humanism and Poetry in the Early Tudor Period* (London, 1959). Herbert Hartman, ed., *The Fourth Boke of Virgill*, privately printed for C. H. Pforzheimer (Purchase, N.Y., 1933), xxvi, argues persuasively that the translation was the product of "strictly English humanism." He argues that parallels between Surrey and continental translations and of Douglas can frequently be shown to arise from the fact that all of them draw on the same late classical and early renaissance annotators; see below, note 29. Other scholars (e.g., Ridley, *The Aeneid of Henry Howard, Earl of Surrey* [Berkeley, 1963], and Baker, above, note 1) believe that the chief influence on Surrey was the Scots translation of the *Aeneid* by Gavin Douglas. The position taken here is close to that taken by Hartman and Emrys Jones. The verse form of Surrey's *Aeneid* is complex and highly artistic. It is most probably based on an analysis of the Latin in relation to possible English equivalents of Vergil's effects rather than an eclectic gathering of ideas from several continental authors plus Douglas. See also below, note 26. This essay was in galleys before I had the opportunity to read Susanne Woods's excellent *Natural Emphasis: English Versification from Chaucer to Dryden* (San Marino, Calif., 1984). I generally agree with Dr. Woods's excellent introductory discussion of prosody and with her brief but perceptive remarks on Surrey's *Aeneid* (pp. 89–90).

4. George T. Wright, "Wyatt's Descasyllabic Line," *Studies in Philology* 82 (1985), 129–56.

5. "Preface" to Tottel's *Miscellany*, ed. Hyder Rollins (Cambridge, Mass., 1928), I, 2.

6. *The Art of Rhetorique*, ed. Robert Bowers (Gainesville, Fla., 1962), 10–11. This was, of course, a commonplace. The specific source is Cicero's *De Inventione*, I, 2. It also draws on the tradition of the *Ars Poetica* (11, 391–408). Its continental parallels are innumerable. Cf. Peter Ramus, *Grammaire* (1572): "A ceste cause fauldroit supplier aux muses Francoyses dentreprendre ce labuer, non pas pour abolir la rithms . . . mais affin que leur patrie fust esgallee a la Graece & a Iltalie."

7. *The Scholemaster,* in *Elizabethan Critical Essays,* ed. Gregory Smith (Oxford, 1904), I, 6.

8. Ibid., I, 31–32.

9. Ibid., I, 22.

10. *Spenser: Poetical Works,* ed. J. C. Smith and E. de Selincourt (Oxford, 1916), 407.

11. *An Apology for Poetry,* in Smith, *Elizabethan Critical Essays,* I, 179.

12. *The Student's Milton,* ed. Frank Allen Patterson (New York, 1947), 525.

13. Henry Lathrop, *Translations from the Classics into English from Caxton to Chapman,* 1477–1620 (Madison, Wisc., 1933), 100.

14. Ridley, *The Aeneid of Henry Howard,* 13–45. Alan Hagar, "British Vergil," 28, suggests that Surrey's borrowings from Gavin Douglas "call to mind Virgil's odd borrowings from Ennius." He contends that Douglas sought to translate Vergil's "fixt sentens or mater"—i.e., his content—while Surrey was interested in the Vergilian style. Cf. Priscilla Bawnett, "Douglas and Surrey," 52–67.

15. Sixteenth-century references to Surrey are found in Ascham, Webbe, Meres, and Harvey. See Smith, *Elizabethan Critical Essays,* I, 32, 126, 283; and II, 315.

16. Milton, "The Verse," in *The Student's Milton,* ed. Patterson, 159.

17. Above, note 3.

18. Above, note 3.

19. *De Arte poetica* (Paris, 1503), fol. VIIv.

20. Attridge, *Syllables,* 94 (Ascham's problems with Surrey's blank verse), and 108–11.

21. If English critics and poets were as confused about accent as Attridge suggests, it is impossible to explain the consistency of Tottel's "improvements" of Wyatt and Surrey in his *Miscellany,* much less the metrical regularity of the poets of the sixties and seventies. These accomplishments are not characterized by uncertainty but by regularity so consistent and so lacking in subtlety as to be stupifying. The poets seem to have understood what they were doing and to have followed their rules with the mindless consistency of schoolboys writing an exercise.

22. Above, note 3.

23. Lathrop, *English Translations,* 98.

24. In A. C. Baugh, ed., *A Literary History of England* (New York, 1948), 334.

25. *English Literature in the Sixteenth Century Excluding Drama* (Oxford, 1954), 234.

26. Ridley, *The Aeneid of Henry Howard,* 32.

27. I quote here one of the several early sixteenth-century editions of Vergil with commentaries that Surrey might have read: *Vergilius cum commentariis. Opera Vergiliana antea corrupta et mendosa nunc vero multorum exemplarum collatione in integrum restituta. . . .* Venice, 1519. This edition includes commentaries by Servius, Donatus, Probus, Beroaldus, and Badius Ascensius, among others. Note the use of the colon, which resembles the use of the colon in Day-Owen. The pointing at the end of each grammatically unified line is not found in Day-Owen, except at the end of line 15, where (as observed) it is misleading.

Tum luno omnipotens longum miserata dolorem.
Difficilesque obitus: Irim demisit olympo.
Quae luctantem animam: nexosque resolueret artus.
Nam quia nec fato: merita nec morte peribat.
Sed misera ante diem: subitoque accensa furore.
Nondum illi flavum Proserpina vertice crinem
Abstulerat: Stygioque caput damnaverat Orco.
Ergo Iris croceis per coelum rosida pennis.
Mille trahens uarios aduerso sole colores.
Deuolat: et supra caput adstitit. Hunc ego Ditis
Sacrum iussa fero: teque isto corpore soluo.
Sic ait: ex dextra crinem secat: omnis et una
Delapsus calor: atque in uentos uita recessit.

28. Jones, *Surrey,* xiv. Also p. xiii, where he observes that Surrey's verse "reveals itself as part of an intricate balancing system, composed of varied yet predictably recurring patterns. It encourages in the reader a sense of mass and momentum." The point requires further comment. In his well-known study of sixteenth-century prosody John Thompson argues that English verse begins the sixteenth century as an inflexibly regular form in which meter dominates and voice stress is ignored. Later, Thompson argues, English poets learned how to create "maximum tension between the language of the poem and the abstract pattern of the meter." [*The Founding of English Meter* (New York, 1961), 156.] In a strong rebuttal, Glenn S. Spiegel, "Perfecting English Meter: Sixteenth-Century Criticism and Practice," *Journal of English and Germanic Philology* 79 (1980), 192–209, contends that English critics and poets were always committed to close observance of meter. The case is more complex than either Thompson or Spiegel suggests. Surrey clearly employs strong counterpoint in his *Aeneid.* Jones is correct in emphasizing the importance to him of clause and phrase. Surrey, however, *varies his practice in relation to the genre in which he is writing.* This is an illustration of the general principle, inherited from the classical *ars metrica,* of prosodic decorum, a subject of prime importance to the humanists and poets responsible for establishing renaissance prosodic conventions. A basic contrast is between heroic poetry, which seeks elevation, and dramatic poetry, which tends to the norm of "speech." Cf. Hardison, "Blank Verse Before Milton," cited in note 1, and "Speaking the Speech," *Shakespeare Quarterly* 34 (1983), 133–46. The study of metrical decorum as understood in relation to genres like elegy, lyric, and eclogue has hardly begun. If pursued it would greatly advance our understanding of Renaissance poetry.

29. See below, note 35.

30. In Padelford's edition, Tottel gives "where as" (p. 188), and Hargrave gives "whereas" (p. 189). Rollins and Baker, *The Renaissance in England* (Boston, 1945), 519, claim to be following Day-Owen but—like several other modern editors—give "whereas." The spacing of the type in Day-Owen is ambiguous. However, the reading given here is the one most consistent with the typography as well as the sense.

31. Padelford, "therewith al" (p. 188), and Hargrave, "therewith all" (p. 189); Rollins and Baker, *The Renaissance in England,* "therewithal" (p. 519). Again the Day-Owen spacing is ambiguous.

32. "Naturall" is probably three syllables, since the point of substituting "kindly" is lost if "naturall" can readily be pronounced as two syllables: "nat'ral." See also l. 6. It has been suggested to me that *al* may have a light stress. I accept this possibility but prefer the scansion shown.

33. *Servii grammatici qui feruntur in Ve commentarii,* ed. Georg Thilo and Herman Hagen (2 vols., Leipzig, 1923), note on line IV, 696: *Difficilisque obitus quia supererat vita ei, que casu, non aut fato aut natura moriebatur: ut 'nam quia nec fato, merita nec morle peribat', id est naturali.*

34. Howard Baker, "The Formation of the Heroic Medium," 139.

35. "Wyatt's Decasyllabic Line," 134–35.

36. Let us assume that what was wanted in English verse was something equivalent to Latin verse. How did Latin verse sound to a Renaissance Englishman? An excellent example is provided for hexameter verse by the anonymous (but quite talented) author of *The First Booke of the Preservation of King Henry VII* (1599). The verse is characterized by the *mediocritas* of Horace's *sermones* and is definitely not heroic, but it is remarkably effective:

> You find metricians, that verses skillfully compile,
> (As fine artificers hard iron do refile on an anvile)
> This verse irregular, this rustick rythmery bannish,
>
> Which doth abase poetry; such verse, such meter abolish,
> For lily milke-white swannes flote on streams cleare as a crystall,
> And in a fowle mud-y lake donguehill ducks strive for an offall
>
> (p.9)

The pronunciation here would seem to be *less* rather than *more* "prosodic"; that is, very like *Kunstprosa,* a situation which agrees fully with Derek Attridge's conclusions that except when they were formally "scanned" by pupils, Latin verses were read with a prose inflection (pp. 37–39). Presumably the "prose" inflection was one that brought out the meaning as determined by the syntax. If so, the "reading" of Surrey's *Aeneid* in English according to the codes of Surrey's translation would (I believe) have been remarkably close to the scansion proposed in the present essay. This scansion is based, as has been shown, on the stress patterns of the iambic pentameter line with appropriate substitutions; but it would apparently have sounded to an Elizabethan much like a quantitative line as such a line was pronounced and hence have been considered in a sense deeper than usually recognized an "imitation" of its classical model. Whether or not there is a "deeper" four-stress pattern in Surrey's translation, reinforced on occasion by alliteration and recalling the Germanic roots of English, is a question that cannot be considered here.

Perspective and Form in Petrarch

1. *Selected Sonnets, Odes and Letters,* ed. Thomas G. Bergin (New York, 1966), 2.

2. *The Making of the "Canzoniere" and Other Petrarchan Studies* (Rome, 1951), 145.

3. Quotations from the sonnets are from *Rime, trionfi, e poesie latine,* ed. E. Neri et al. (Milan, 1951).

Amoretti and the *Dolce Stil Novo*

1. John Erskine, *The Elizabethan Lyric* (New York, 1903), 153.

2. Robert Kellogg, "Thought's Astonishment and the Dark Conceits of Spenser's *Amoretti,*" in John R. Elliot, *The Prince of Poets* (New York, 1968), 139–51; Louis L. Martz, "The *Amoretti:* 'Most Goodly Temperature'," in *Form and Convention in the Poetry of Spenser: Selected Papers from the English Institute* (New York, 1961), 146–68; William Nelson, *The Poetry of Edmund Spenser* (New York, 1963), 84–96.

3. J. W. Lever, *The Elizabethan Love Sonnet* (London, 1956), 101–2.

4. Alexander Dunlop, "Calendar Symbolism in the *Amoretti,*" *Notes and Queries* n.s. 16 (Jan. 1969), 24–26. Dunlop has presented a full-scale analysis of the *Amoretti* in "The Unity of Spenser's *Amoretti,*" *Silent Poetry,* ed. Alastair Fowler (London, 1970), 153–69.

5. Here and before, I follow the text of *Amoretti* included in *The Oxford Spenser*, ed. J. C. Smith and E. de Selincourt (London, 1912, rpt. 1942).

6. A. K. Hieatt, *Short Time's Endless Monument* (New York, 1960).

7. Among the many discussions of the conventions of the *stil novo,* see especially Charles Singleton, *An Essay on the* Vita Nuova (Cambridge, Mass., 1949); Angelo Lipari, *The* Dolce Stil Novo *According to Lorenzo de' Medici* (New Haven, 1936); Giulio Bertoni, *Il Duecento* (Milan, 1939).

8. C. S. Lewis, *The Allegory of Love* (Oxford, 1936), 298, 338–46, 360.

9. Bertoni, *Il Duecento,* 290: "Il morire della donna amata nei canti di questi poeti corrisponde . . . al morire della ragione umana nel rapimento e nell'estasi della mente, al morire, insomma . . . di Rachele, la quale muore . . . per e levarsi alla somma contemplazione."

10. Lorenzo de' Medici, *Opere,* ed. Attilio Simioni (Bari, 1939), I, 25: "Il principio della vera vita è la morte della vita non vera"; and (p. 24): "Se lo amore ha in sé quella perfezione che giá abbiamo detto, è impossible venire a tale perfezione se prima non si muore. . . . "

11. For discussion, see Lipari, *Lorenzo de' Medici*, 64 ff.

Logic Versus the Slovenly World in Shakespearean Comedy

1. In *Modern Continental Literary Criticism,* ed. O. B. Hardison, Jr. (New York: Prentice-Hall, 1962), 221.

2. Weinberg's volumes (Chicago, 1961) are the culmination of an intensive study of Italian critical theory and its influence on Renaissance literature which began in the United States with Joel E. Spingarn's *A History of Literary Criticism in the Renaissance* (New York, 1899). For a selective bibliography of the major studies, see O. B. Hardison, Jr., ed., *English Literary Criticism: The Renaissance* (New York, 1963). Three works with special relevance to the topics explored here are M. T. Herrick, *The Fusion of Horatian and Aristotelian Literary Theory*

1531–1555 (Urbana, 1946) and his *Comic Theory in the Sixteenth Century* (Urbana, 1965), and Madeleine Doran, *Endeavors of Art: A Study of Form in Elizabethan Drama* (Madison, 1954).

3. Most of the important work in this area during the last decade is summarized by C. Clifford Flanigan in "The Liturgical Drama and its Tradition: A Review of Scholarship, 1965–1975," *Research Oppoortunities in Renaissance Drama* 18 (1975), 81–102, and 19 (1976), 109–36. Of special importance for the English phase of medieval drama is V. A. Kolve, *The Play Called Corpus Christi* (Stanford, 1966). See also *Medieval English Drama: Essays Critical and Contextual,* ed. Jerome Taylor and Alan Nelson (Chicago, 1972).

4. For a survey of Donatine influence see A. P. McMahon, "Seven Questions on Aristotelian Definitions of Tragedy and Comedy," *Howard Studies in Classical Philology* 11 (1929), 97–198. The text of the Donatine essays is reprinted in translation in *Classical and Medieval Literary Criticism,* ed. Alex Preminger, O. B. Hardison, Jr., and Kevin Kerrane (New York, 1974), 299–309. Cf. p. 305: "Of the many differences in tragedy and comedy, the foremost are . . . in tragedy everything is the opposite—the characters are great men, the fears are intense, and the ends disastrous. In comedy the beginning is troubled, the end tranquil; in tragedy events follow the reverse order." For the "plot" of medieval drama, see O. B. Hardison, Jr., "A Note on the Continuity of Ritual Form in European Drama," *Christian Rite and Christian Drama in the Middle Ages* (Baltimore, 1965), 284–92.

5. Cf. the description of the Digby play of Mary Magdalene by Theresa Coletti, "The Design of the Digby Play of *Mary Magdalene,*" *Studies in Philology* 76 (1979), 313–33; esp. pp. 313–14: "Generic complexity . . . accounts for only a small part of *Mary Magdalene*'s variety, which is mirrored in an action ranging from the Holy Land to Marseilles and from Heaven to Hell. This graphic and spiritual landscape is peopled by political tyrants and saints, devils and angels, allegorical abstractions and earthly shipmen, Satan and Christ. Furthermore, these characters move about a dramatic space requiring nineteen acting areas, and the play itself covers a period of more than thirty years. No less diversified than the play world she inhabits is Mary Magdalene herself. Her character embraces the conflation of scriptural women . . . with the saint and the legendary apostle and hermit fabricated by later hagiographers. . . . The beautiful daughter of Cyrus, she is both whore and saint, the lover of men and the lover of Christ, the penitent anointer and the preacher of the Christian faith, the model for all sinners and the counterpart of the Virgin Mary."

6. Allan H. Gilbert, ed., *Literary Criticism: Plato to Dryden* (New York, 1940), 540.

7. Gilbert, 541. I suggest that Lope is partly ironic, for his essay shows that, in fact, he admires the Spanish style of drama. The irony does, however, reveal a conflict in Lope's mind between art and naturalness which anticipates the anxieties of Dryden and other English neoclassic critics when confronting Shakespeare. It is a pity that there is no English essay from the period expressing the point of view of native drama as lucidly and self-consciously as Lope's *Arte nuevo.*

8. In *Mysteries' End: An Investigation of the Last Days of the Medieval Religious Stage,* Yale Studies in English 103 (New Haven, 1946).

9. Here and later, quotations are from *The Complete Pelican Shakespeare,* gen. ed. Alfred Harbage (Baltimore, 1969).

10. (London, 1967), 171–90. Kott's image is notoriously overdrawn, but it isolates a disturbing undercurrent that is undoubtedly present both in Shakespeare's play and in the tradition behind it.

11. Cf. "The Mythos of Spring: Comedy," in Northrop Frye's *Anatomy of Criticism* (Princeton, 1957), 163–86, and C. L. Barber, *Shakespeare's Festive Comedies: A Study of Dramatic Form and Its Relation to Social Custom* (Princeton, 1959, passim).

12. *An Apologie for Poetrie* in *English Literary Criticism: The Renaissance,* 103. All further references to Sidney are from this edition.

13. In *English Literary Criticism: The Renaissance,* 271.

The Dramatic Triad in *Hamlet*

1. *Memorabilia,* II, i, 21–33.

2. For the literary tradition in English renaissance poetry, see Hallet Smith, *Elizabethan Poetry* (Cambridge, Mass. 1952), 294–97.

3. The psychomachia is discussed in detail in E. N. S. Thompson, *The English Moral Play,* Transactions of the Connecticut Academy of Arts and Sciences 14 (March 1910), 320–33. For the "full scope" morality, see ibid., 312–20; and W. R. Mackenzie, *The English Moralities from the Point of View of Allegory* (Boston, 1914), 57–180. The quotation in the text is from p. vii of Mackenzie's introduction.

4. E.g., Paul N. Siegel, "The Damnation of Othello," *PMLA* 67 (1954), 1068–78; Irving Ribner, "*Othello* and the Pattern of Shakespearean Tragedy," *Tulane Studies in English* 5 (1955), 69–82.

5. I would be less dogmatic in asserting that Othello is damned than Dr. Siegel in the article cited in footnote 4.

6. Cf. E. M. W. Tillyard, *Shakespeare's History Plays* (London, 1948), esp. pp. 268–91.

7. Ed. H. S. Croft (London, 1883), ii, 112. The use of the Aristotelian notion would certainly not stamp Shakespeare as one of the avant garde. It was used extensively by Skelton in *Magnificence.* See the edition by R. L. Ramsay, E.E.T.S., Extra Series, 98 (1908), lxxv *et seq.*

8. As used here "action" must be kept distinct from mere "activity." Actions form the turning points on which the plot hinges. In naturalistic fiction actions are usually caused by the natural or social environment; the character has no free will and is forced to act because of external pressures. For Aristotle, however, and for the Christian dramatists of the Renaissance, man was a free agent, and actions were the result of the individual will expressing itself in moral choice. Significant choices usually depend on the uncovering of new information which alters circumstances in which the character finds himself, and they cause the plot to develop in a new direction; hence Aristotle's "discovery" and "reversal." In this sense a plot like that of *1 Hen. IV,* where the protagonist never swerves from his original position—never makes a significant moral choice—is lacking in "action." I cannot defend this interpretation in detail here, but cf. *Poetics* VI, 5–6 and Butcher's analysis: "*práxeis* are actions in their proper and inward sense. An act viewed merely as an external process or result, one of a series of outward phe-

nomena, is not the true object of aesthetic imitation. The *prâxis* that art seeks to reproduce is mainly an inward process, a psychical energy working outwards; deeds, incidents, events, situations, being included under it so far as these spring from an inward act of will, or elicit some activity of thought or feeling." (*Aristotle's Theory of Poetry and Fine Art* [New York, 1951], 123; also, 335 ff.). Ferdinand Brunetière found in the distinction between "action" and "activity" the essential *differentia* between the drama and the novel: "the proper aim of the novel, as of the epic . . . , is to give us a picture of the influence which is exercised upon us by all that is outside of ourselves. The novel is therefore the contrary of the drama. . . . Is it action to move about? Certainly not, and there is no true action except that of a will conscious of itself. . . . The belief in determinism is more favorable to the progress of the novel, but the belief in free will is more favorable to the progress of dramatic art." *The Law of the Drama,* in *Literary Criticism: Pope to Croce,* ed. Allen and Clark (New York, 1A41), 605–10.

9. *Works,* ed. Robinson (Cambridge, 1957), 250. Hamlet's despair is the kind arising from "outrageous sorwe," but his speech to Ophelia ("I myself am indifferent honest") suggests also the despair arising from a morbid sense of sin.

10. Cf. *Magnificence,* ed. Ramsay, *op. cit.,* scenes 39–40; Higgen's *Cordelia* in the 1574 ed. of the *Mirror for Magistrates; Faerie Queen,* I, ix, 51–54. When he appears in Lear as Mad Tom, Edgar resembles the allegorical figure of Despair in the preceding works, and it is perhaps significant that his first long speech is an hysterical account of the ways in which "the foul fiend" has tempted him to suicide.

11. Normally, suicide is an act of moral cowardice, yet Hamlet calls himself a coward for *not* committing it. An equally ironic lack of self-knowledge is evident when Hamlet remarks, "How all occasions do inform against me, / And spur my dull revenge!" (IV, iv. 32–33), on seeing Fortinbras walk across the stage. Fortinbras is not an example of revenge. As Hamlet should know, the peaceful march *across* Denmark is the moment at which his forbearance is most emphatic. Hamlet's confusion here and elsewhere may be compared with the confusion of the Redcross Knight in the *Faerie Queene,* I, ix. Despair first describes suicide as an escape from adversity, a restful sleep (st. 38–40). Later (st. 47) he describes the tortures of the damned to intensify the Knight's sense of sin. The two arguments are, as the Variorum editors point out, glaringly inconsistent, yet the Knight is so distracted that he fails to perceive the fallacy.

12. One critic who has noticed the functional aspect of the player's speech is G. R. Elliott, *Scourge and Minister, a Study of "Hamlet"* (Durham, N.C., 1951), 62. Elliott sees a parallel between Pyrrhus and Claudius, which is possible, but less probable, I feel, than the parallel between Pyrrhus and Hamlet. The context is Hamlet's concern for the justice of *his own* actions. Pyrrhus's black costume provides the initial clue. Rather illogically he is described as seeking "vengeance" (l. 510). Priam is Claudius if innocent, and Hecuba is Hamlet's mother as she would appear after the murder of her husband. Pyrrhus is momentarily stopped as he prepares to strike by the terrible sound of the collapse of Troy—surely a more than fortuitous echo of the civil chaos which would follow the murder of Claudius (cf. Horatio in V, ii, 405–6). There is just enough damnation imagery to echo Hamlet's own concern: for example, "damned light," "roasted in wrath and fire," "hellish Pyrrhus," "as low as the fiends," and, most effective, Hecuba's cry, which "Would have made milch the burning eyes of heaven, and passion in the gods"

(II, ii, 471–541). The physical brutality of the killing of Priam is recalled, as Elliott observes, in Hamlet's soliloquy at the end of the scene.

13. See Percy Simpson, *The Theme of Revenge in Elizabethan Tragedy* (London, 1935), for revenge conventions. A brilliant study, pointing up the complexity of the revenge motif in *Hamlet* is Joseph Bertram, *Conscience and the King* (London, 1953).

14. The Hamlet-Fortinbras parallel is explored in terms of its historical background by W. W. Lawrence, "Hamlet and Fortinbras." *PMLA* 61 (1946), 673–97.

15. Cf. L. B. Campbell, *Shakespeare's Tragic Heroes, Slaves of Passion* (Cambridge, 1930), esp. pp. 94–99.

16. The idea that the slaying of Polonius is the turning point of *Hamlet* has been independently confirmed by Professor Fredson Bowers, "The Death of Hamlet: a Study in Plot and Character," in *Studies in the English Renaissance Drama*, ed. Bennett, Cargill, and Hall (New York, 1959), 28–42. Unfortunately, this study appeared after the present paper was accepted for publication, and I was unable to utilize its many excellent insights. However, I do not believe that it contains anything which would cause me to alter my major points.

17. For a brilliant discussion from a somewhat different (though, I believe, not irreconcilable) point of view, see F. W. Bowers, "Hamlet as Scourge and Minister," *PMLA* 70 (1955), 740–49.

Myth and History in *King Lear*

1. A. W. Ward, *A History of English Dramatic Literature* (London, 1899), I, 200, Cf. C. F. Tucker Brooke, *The Tudor Drama* (London, 1912), 192.

2. D. T. Starnes and E. W. Talbert, *Classical Myth and Legend in Renaissance Dictionaries* (Chapel Hill, 1955), 116. All quotations from *King Lear* are from *The Complete Plays and Poems of William Shakespeare,* ed. William Allan Neilson and Charles Jarvis Hill (Cambridge, Mass., 1942).

3. Erwin Panofsky, *Studies in Iconology* (New York, 1947), 216 n.

4. Paola Barocchi, *Il Rosso Fiorentino* (Rome, 1950), pls, 112, 113, 114; R. L. Douglas, *Piero di Cosimo* (Chicago, 1946), pl. 17.

5. Paul Kristeller, *Andrea Mantegna* (London, 1901), pl. 23 and comment, pp. 55–56.

6. Paolo d'Ancona, *The Farnesina Frescoes* (Milan, 1956), p. 25 and pl. 14.

7. *Mitologiarum Libri Tres,* in *Opera,* ed. R. Helm (Leipzig, 1898), 55–56.

8. *Genealogiae Deorum Gentilium Libri,* ed. Vincenzo Romano (Bari, 1951), II, 468–72 (IX, xxvii).

9. The standard version of the tale is briefly told by Servius in his commentary on *Aeneid,* VI, 286 and 601, and *Georgics,* III, 38 and 115; IV, 484. Lactantius tells the story of the Jovian thunderbolt in his commentary on *Thebiad,* IV, 539. Macrobius interprets Ixion's wheel as the wheel of fortune in *In Somnuim Scioponis*, X, 14–15.

10. *de Laboribus Herculis,* ed. B.L. Ullman (Zurich, 1951), I, 217–28.

11. *Natalis Comitis Mythologiae, sive Explicationes Fabularum Libri Decem* (Lyons, 1602), 613–17 (V, xvi), and—for centaurs—709–13 (VII, iv); G. Stephanus, *Dictionarium Historicum, Geographicum, Poeticum* (Cologne, 1618), ss.

vv. *Ixion* and *centaur;* Alexander Ross, *Mystagogus Poeticus, or The Muses Interpreter* (London, 1648), 55–57 and 223–26.

12. *Works,* tr. Sir John Sandys (Cambridge, Mass., 1924), second Pythian Ode, ll. 21 ff.

13. *Dictionarium,* s.v. *Ixion.*

14. *Mystagogus Poeticus,* 224.

15. See Fulgentius, *Mitologiarum,* II, xiv; Boccaccio, *Genealogiae,* IX, xxviii; Comes, *Mythologiae,* 615–16.

16. *Fulgentius Metaforalis,* in *Studien der Bibliotek Warburg,* IV, 124. Compare *Physiologus Latinus,* ed. Carmody (Paris, 1939), 26, which relates the image of the centaur to that of the siren.

17. *Mystagogus Poeticus,* 225.

18. *Mitologiarum,* 38. For a more detailed discussion see Vincenzio Cartari, *Imagini de i Dei degli Antichi* (Padua, 1602), 160–78.

19. *Mystagogus Poeticus,* 215.

20. *Works,* ed. C. H. Hereford and Percy Simpson (Oxford, 1925–52), VII, 217.

21. *de Laboribus Herculis,* I, 219.

22. Quoted from the reprint of the play in *Shakespeare's Library* (London, 1875), vi, 308. In the versions in Holinshed's *Chronicles, The Mirror for Magistrates,* and the *Gesta Romanorum,* Lear arranges to have his daughters inherit the throne after his death but is overthrown by rebellion; in the anonymous ballad version and in *The True Chronicle Historie,* Lear surrenders the throne, but for laudable motives.

23. *Mystagogus Poeticus,* 225.

24. E.g., *Mystagogus Poeticus,* 215. The tradition is as old as Fulgentius; cf. *Mitologiarum,* p. 38: "[Juno] . . . regnis praeesse dicitur, quod haec vita divitiis tandum studeat; ideo etiam cum sceptro pingitur, quod divitiae regnis sint proximae. . . ."

25. *Mystagogus Poeticus,* 215.

26. Boccaccio, *Genealogiae,* ll. 469.

27. V. Cartari, *Imagini,* 174.

28. *Fulgentius Metaforalis,* IV, 121.

29. The comparison is found, for example, in *Physiologus Latinus,* p. 26; and Andrea Alciati, *Emblemata* (Padua, 1621), p. 489. Ben Jonson, *Works*, vii, 343, wrote: "Among the ancients the kind, both of the Centaures and Satyres, is confounded; and common with eyther. . . ." Claudius Minois, the principal commentator in the 1621 edition of Alciati, compares centaurs and sirens in respect to lust, but also interprets the sirens as symbols of flattery. The latter interpretation obviously applies to Lear's daughters and may explain the apparent fusion of the centaur image with that of the siren in IV, vi. 120 ff.

30. Erwin Panofsky, "The Early History of Man in a Cycle of Paintings by Piero di Cosimo," *Journal of the Warburg and Cortauld Institutes* 1 (1937–38), 12–30; R. L. Douglas, *Piero di Cosimo* (Chicago, 1946), 33.

31. *de Laboribus Herculis,* I, 223.

32. *Mystagogus Poeticus,* 56.

33. *de Laboribus Herculis,* I, 217.

34. *Mystagogus Poeticus,* 56.

35. Madeleine Doran, "Elements in the Compositon of *King Lear*," *Studies in Philology* 30 (1935), 46.

36. *Mystagogus Poeticus,* 56. This was sometimes explained by the idea that Chiron was not a child of Ixion like the other centaurs, but of Saturn. See Salutati, *de Laboribus Herculis,* III, xi.

37. *de Laboribus Herculis,* I, 207.

38. Cf. however, Hyginus, *Astronomica,* II, 27 and 38.

39. *Mystagogus Poeticus,* 56.

40. *Apologie for Poetrie,* in James H. Smith and Edd W. Parks, *The Great Critics* (New York, 1939), 200–1. The critical tradition behind this passage has long been recognized by scholars. See especially Giovanni Giovannini, "Historical Realism and the Tragic Emotions in Renaissance Criticism," *Philological Quarterly* 23 (1953), 304–20, and "Agnolo Segni and a Renaissance Definition of Poetry," *Modern Language Quarterly* 6 (1945), 167–73.

Speaking the Speech: Shakespearean Dialogue

1. F. E. Halliday, *The Poetry of Shakespeare's Plays* (London, 1954), 15.

2. Bertram Joseph, *Acting Shakespeare* (London, 1960), 81. Cf. p. 55: "The poetry of Shakespeare . . . can be regarded as a combination of two elements; first there is the sense of the lines and second there is the melody which derives from the structure of the line or lines. . . ."

3. *Apology for Actors* (New York, 1941), sig. C4^r.

4. *Theatre News* (Fall 1982), 5.

5. Coburn Freer, *The Poetics of Jacobean Drama* (Baltimore, 1981), 28–61.

6. *To Gentlemen Students of Both Universities,* in Nashe, *Works,* ed. Ronald B. McKerrow and F. P. Wilson (Oxford, 1958), III, 311–12.

7. Greene, *A Groatsworth of Wit* (London, 1923), 45. Cf. "The complaint of Levinus Lemnis," *The Touchstone of Complexions,* tr. Thomas Newton (1576), sig. G5, about actors who "measure rhetorike by their peevish rhythmes." Also the preface to the 1640 edition of Thomas Middleton's *A Mad World My Masters,* which points out that the play has "no bumbasted or fustian stuff, but every line weighed as with a balance, and every sentence placed with judgment and deliberation." It is interesting that the preface appears to apologize for the fact that the play is partly in meter and that the scene-closings use couplets. This suggests that by 1640 there was a trend favoring drama in prose or at least in verse that is not heavily "poetic" [Middleton, *Works,* ed. A. H. Bullen (London, 1885), III, 251]. Ben Jonson translates the advice of Horace to the would-be tragedian by saying that if he would move audiences he ". . . must throw by / His Bumbard-phrase, and foot-and-half-foot words: / 'Tis not enough the labouring Muse affords / Her Poems beauty, but a sweet delight / To wake the hearers minds, still to the plight." In *Complete Poetry,* ed. William B. Hunter, Jr. (New York, 1963), 281–82.

8. Hall, *Virgidemarium,* in *Collected Poems,* ed. A. Davenport (Liverpool, 1949), 14.

9. Freer, *Poetics,* 32.

10. Sidney, *Apology for Poetry* in *Elizabethan Critical Essays,* ed. G. Gregory Smith (Oxford, 1904), I, 159–60. Sidney considers Plato's dialogues and such

prose works as Xenophon's *Cyropaedia* and Heliodorus's *Ethiopian History* to be poems. Cf. p. 182: "It is not ryming and versing that maketh Poesie. One may bee a Poet without versing and a versifier without Poetry."

11. *The Malcontent,* ed. M. L. Wine (Lincoln, 1964), 4–5. In the preface to *The Fawn,* ed. Gerald A. Smith (London, 1964), 2, Marston remarks, "Comedies are writ to be spoken, not read: Remember the life of these things consists in action." In the preface to *A Mad World,* cited in note 7, Middleton makes the same point: ". . . action, which is the life of a comedy and the glory of the author."

12. *Theatrum Triumphans* (1670), 34–35.

13. Prologue to *The Comicall Gallant,* in Dennis, *Critical Works,* ed. Edward Niles Hooker (Baltimore, 1943), II, 391. Freer remarks of this passage (*Poetics,* p. 32): "What Dennis offers is a definition of dramatic poetry that splits apart poetry and drama." If so, Aristotle and Sidney made the same error. The error, however, is regarding a play in terms of language rather than action.

14. Preface to *Sophonisba* (1521), ii.

15. Dennis, *Critical Works,* II, 4–5.

16. Freer, *Poetics,* 52–53.

17. *Ludus Literarium: Or the Grammar School* (1612), 213.

18. *Apology for Actors,* sig. C4^r.

19. *Theatre for Shakespeare* (Toronto, 1953), 103.

20. *Elizabethan Acting* (1st ed., London, 1951), 77, 81, 123, 125.

21. Ibid., 114–15.

22. *Elizabethan Acting* (2nd ed., London, 1964), 100. Throughout this second edition Joseph compares Elizabethan acting with the style recommended by Stanislavski; e.g., pp. v–vi: "Rhetorical delivery at school meant that boys were required to act naturally, as if they really were the persons they represented. . . . The rhetorician who followed Quintilian tapped the resources of his emotional life by methods used in the modern theatre and advocated by Stanislavski."

23. *A Short Discourse of the English Stage,* in *Critical Essays of the Seventeenth Century,* ed. Joel Elias Spingarn (repr., Bloomington, 1957), II, 95.

24. Cf. the discussion of the prosody of the "play-within-a-play" in G. R. Hibbard, *The Making of Shakespeare's Dramatic Poetry* (Toronto, 1981), 18–19.

25. Thus Richard Mulcaster, *Positions* (London, 1888), 58, urges children to recite "either *Iambicke* verses, or *Elegies,* or such numbers which with their currant carie the memorie on." The same idea appears in more sophisticated critical writing in Sidney's *Apology* (ed. Smith, I, 182–83): "Now, that verse farre exceedeth Prose in the knitting up of the memory, the reason is manifest; the words . . . beeing so set as one word cannot be lost but the whole worke fails: which accuseth it selfe, calleth the remembrance back to it selfe, and so most strongly confirmeth it. . . . But the fitness [verse] hath for memory is notably proved by the delivery of Arts: wherein . . . the rules chiefly necessary to bee borne away are compiled in verses."

Shakespeare on Film: The Developing Canon

1. Robert H. Ball, *Shakespeare on Silent Film* (New York, 1968); Jack Jorgens, *Shakespeare on Film* (Bloomington, 1977). Charles Eckert, ed., *Focus on Shake-*

speare Film (Englewood-Cliffs, 1972), collects numerous reviews and, generally, short commentaries on Shakespeare films. Information about current studies and related activities is given in the *Shakespeare on Film Newsletter,* edited by Bernice Kliman and Kenneth Rothwell.

2. *Anglia* 94 (1978), 349–70.

3. Harley Granville-Barker, *Prefaces to Shakespeare* (London, 1927), I, 5.

4. *Tyrone Guthrie on Acting* (London, 1971), 67.

5. *The Masks of Macbeth* (Berkeley, 1977).

6. For example, *The Hamlet of Edwin Booth* (Urbana, 1969).

7. *Shakespeare's History Plays* (London, 1944). See also Harry M. Geduld, *Film-guide to Henry V* (Bloomington, 1973).

8. See Norman Rabkin, "Rabbit, Ducks, and *Henry V,*" *Shakespeare Quarterly* 28 (1977), 279–96.

9. "Diabolic Intellect and the Noble Hero," *Scrutiny* 6 (1937), 259–83.

10. Quoted in Jorgens, 203.

11. *Hamlet and Oedipus* (New York, 1949). This essay was first printed in 1910 and reprinted several times thereafter in different forms. It is Jones who remarked of Gertrude, "Sensuality is her outstanding attribute" (p. 182).

12. Jorgens, 215.

13. *Shakespeare our Contemporary* (London, 1967), esp. pp. 68–78. Like Richard III, Kott's Macbeth is condemned to move "up and down the grand staircase of history" (p. 68). "Everyone in the play is steeped in blood, victims as well as murderers. The whole world is stained with blood. . . . A production of *Macbeth* not evoking a picture of the world flooded with blood would inevitably be fake" (p. 69). Polanski may also have been influenced by Kott's theory, which lacks textual justification, that Cawdor has a "stoic" attitude toward his misfortunes.

14. "*Macbeth:* Polanski's Disastrous Version," *Shakespeare on Film Newsletter* 3 (December 1978), 2.

15. *Shakespearean Tragedy* (London, 1950), 389.

16. *Shakespeare's Tragic Heroes: Slaves of Passion* (Cambridge, 1930).

Milton's "On Time" and Its Scholastic Background

1. W. R. Parker, "Some Problems in the Chronology of Milton's Early Poems," *Review of English Studies* 9 (1935), 281.

2. *The Student's Milton* (New York, 1947), *Notes,* 48.

3. *Paradise Regained, the Minor Poems, and Samson Agonistes* (New York, 1937), 203. So Todd (1842) and Masson (1874).

4. This is the sense of the definition given by Cockeran, *The English Dictionarie* (London, 1623): "Individuall. Not to be parted, as man and wife."

5. *Poems of Mr. John Milton* (New York, 1951), 112–13.

6. N.E.D., *s.v. individuum;* also *individual, individuate,* etc.

7. *Osculum* would have been used by Milton in perference to *suavium* or the intimate *basium.* (Cf. *Eleg.* VII. l. 23; Q. *Nov.,* l. 52; *ad Pat.,* l. 91.) *Proprius* is of course standard Latin in any period. A possible (but unlikely) alternative is *singulus* or *singularis.* (Cf. *Natura,* l. 36.)

8. Henry More, *A Collection of Several Philosophical Writings* (London, 1712), 207.

9. Translating *credulus* as *confiding,* J. W. Mackail gives the adverbial rendering: "Who now confidingly possesses you, his golden one." See *Studies in Humanism* (London, 1938), 68.

10. *Rhetorica ad Herennium,* ed. Caplan (Loeb Classical Library, 1954), XXXIII, 45 (pp. 342–43).

11. *The Arte of English Poesie,* ed. Willcock and Walker (Cambridge, Eng., 1936), 180.

12. See Sister Miriam Joseph, *Shakespeare's Use of the Arts of Language* (New York, 1947), 146.

13. Outlines of the revival of Aristotle are available in all surveys of medieval philosophy. A recent graceful treatment of the subject with an especially good section on the influence of Averroes is Etienne Gilson, *The Christian Philosophy of the Middle Ages* (New York, 1955), 181–225; 387–402. The basic study of Averroism remains E. Renan, *Averroès et l'Averroïsm* (Paris, 1852), despite many inaccuracies. An excellent recent study is Fernand Van Steenberghen, *Aristotle in the West* (Louvain, 1955).

14. See Pierre Mandonnet, *Siger de Brabant et l'Averroïsme Latin du XIIIme Siècle* (Louvain, 1911).

15. For discussion see, in addition to the works cited in Notes 13 and 14, Pierre Conway, O.P., "The Emancipation of Man in Latin Averroism and the Negation of Immortality," *Laval Théologique et Philosophique* 2 (1946), 117–31; and the introduction to Manlio Buccellato, ed., *Trattato sull 'Unità dell 'Intelletto.* (Padua, 1941).

16. The standard edition is by Keller (Rome, 1936). I have used the English translation by Sister Rose Brennen, *The Trinity and the Unicity of the Intellect* (St. Louis, 1946), 201–81. The unity of the intellect is also treated in *Sum. Theol.*, I, Quest. 79, Art. 5.

17. Sister Brennen, *The Trinity and Unicity . . .*, 274.

18. Ibid., 267.

19. Ibid., 272.

20. I do not imply that St. Thomas ever took the position that Milton later took. He believed on faith and rational grounds in the possibility of the survival of the soul apart from the body. However, as the preceding quotation has shown, immortality is not "perfected" until the resurrection of the body.

21. Quoted from Cassirer and Kristeller, eds., *The Renaissance Philosophy of Man* (Chicago, 1948), 265. For the history of Renaissance Averroism, see Renan, *Averroïsm,* pp. 255–325; Gilson, *Christian Philosophy,* pp. 521–28; and (most thorough) Giuseppi Saitta, *Il Rinascimento* (Bologna, 1950), II, 249–451.

22. Translated in Cassirer and Kristeller, eds., *The Renaissance Philosophy of Man*, pp. 280–381. For comment see A. H. Douglas, *The Philosophy and Psychology of Pietro Pomponazzi* (Cambridge, 1910).

23. *The Renaissance Philosophy of Man,* 377.

24. Ibid., 275.

25. For the later history of Paduan Averroism, see the authorities cited in Note 21.

26. *Aristoteles . . . Opera quae extant omnia . . . Averrois in ea opera omnes commentaria nuper a Jacob Mantino . . . conversi* (Venice, 1550–52; 1560–62; 1573–75).

27. *Anatomy of Melancholy*, ed. Dell and Smith (New York, 1938), 143; cf. pp. 135, 144, 932. Citations of Averroes as a medical authority (author of the *Colliget*) naturally abound. Sir John Davies was familiar with the naturalistic argument, if not with Averroes:

> Yet say [philosophers], If all her organs die
> Then hath the *soule* no power her power to use;
> So, in a sort, her powers extinct do lie,
> When unto act she cannot them reduce.

(*Nosce Teipsum* in *Works*, ed. Grosart [London, 1876], I, 104). Donne, *Essays in Divinity*, ed. Simpson (Oxford, 1952), 33, quotes Averroes' definition of *materia prima*.

28. *Anatomy*, 143.

29. *Two Treatises in the one of which the Nature of Bodies; in the other, the Nature of Man's Soule; is looked into* . . .(London, 1644), 416.

30. Ibid., 428–29. On p. 431 Digby undertakes to refute Pomponazzi and the "peripititik" school out of Aristotle's theory of forms: "It is his confessed doctrine that *Matter* is for its forms . . . both all Aristotle's doctrine, and all common sense convinceth, that the body must be for the soul." At about the same time that Digby published his treatise, L. Lessius's *de Providentia Numinis, et Animi Immortalite* was published as *Sir Walter Rawliegh's Ghost* (London, 1651). This work relies heavily on *de Anima* and *The Generation of Animals*. The concept of collective immortality—here traced to the stoics rather than to the naturalists—is dealt with on pp. 259 ff., and 343–55. Cf. also Richard Overton, *Man Wholly Mortal* (London, 1674; first ed. Amsterdam, 1643–44). For the influence of the latter work on Milton, see Denis Saurat, *Milton, Man and Thinker* (New York, 1946), 119–23; 310–22. A perennial Renaissance favorite, Cornelius Agrippa's *de Vanitate et Incertitudine Omnium Scientiarum*, also makes frequent references to Averroes. See its English translation, *The Vanity of Arts and Sciences* (London, 1684), 5, 82, 84, 106, and esp. 137: "Moreover, *Averroes,* that most exquisite Commentator upon *Aristotle,* believes that every man has a peculiar Soul, but Mortal; But that the Mind or Understanding is Eternal, having neither Beginning nor End; of which there was but one kind, that all men use in this Life."

31. Henry More, *The Immortality of the Soul,* in *A Collection of Several Philosophical Writings* (London, 1712), 239–342.

32. Ibid., 242. Note especially the use of *proprium* and *proper* in this context. Averroes and Pomponazzi are mentioned frequently by More—e.g., vi, 30, 48, 49, 116, 233–37, etc. He makes a clear summary of the naturalistic position: ". . . there is . . . but *One* in all; and . . . this particularity of Body being lost, this particular Man or Beast is lost, and so every living creature is properly and entirely mortal" (p. 226). Man only lives "so long [as the World Soul] expedites, or exerts herself into the Sense and Remembrance of all those Notions or Impresses that happen to her wherever she is join't with his Body; but . . . so soon as this Body of his is dissipated or dissolved . . . she will no longer raise any such determinate Thoughts or Senses that refer to that Union; and . . . so the Memory of such Ac-

tions, Notions, and Impressions, that were held together in relation to a particular Body, being lost and laid aside upon the failing of the Body to which they did refer, this *Ipseity* or *Personality*, which consisted mainly in this, does necessarily perish in death." (p. 234) More's *Homines Aerii* apparently interested other writers of the period; they are referred to, for example, by Richard Baxter in his *Annotations* to Joseph Glanville, *Two Choice and Useful Treatises* (London, 1682), 85.

33. *Works* (London, 1673), III, fol. 33.

34. In *An Answer to Mr. Dowell and Dr. Sherlocke* (London, 1682), vi, 216.

35. Asgill, *Argument* (London, 1700), 86.

36. Most obviously in the third *Prolusion*, "Against the Scholastic Philosophy," but also in the second and sixth.

37. Petrarch in his *Letters* and Erasmus in the *Praise of Folly* satirized scholasticism from the humanistic point of view; Ramus received his degree at Paris for defending the thesis that nothing in Aristotle was correct; and Bacon's scientific program was designed to correct the method which the scholastics had inherited from Aristotle. For Milton's curriculum at Cambridge and the crosscurrents of influence to which he was exposed see Masson's *Life* (repr. New York, 1946), I, 259–320.

38. Quotations from the *Prolusions* are from the translation by Bromley Smith in Volume XII of the Columbia Milton. If Milton followed the usual curriculum (as in Masson, *Life*, I, 260) he studied logic during the third year and philosophy during the fourth. I suggest that *Prolusions* four and five most probably grew out of these studies and therefore belong to 1628 and 1629 respectively. French (*Life Records* [Rutgers, 1946], I) gives the following dates, which he admits are arbitrary: *Prol.* I, 1628; II, 1629; III, 1628; IV, 1627; V, 1626; VI, 1628; VII, 1632. Tillyard gives 1628 for the "Vacation Exercise," 1629 for II, and 1632 for VII. See *Correspondence and Academic Exercises* (Cambridge, 1932), xxv. The Yale edition, ed. Wolfe (New Haven, 1953), adds nothing to the preceding.

39. Cf. Sister Brennen, *The Trinity and Unicity* . . . , 215.

40. *Prolusion*, IV.

41. Quotations from the *Christian Doctrine* from the Charles Sumner translation as reprinted in the Columbia Milton, Volume XV. The view of the soul presented here is traced by George N. Conklin, *Biblical Criticism and Heresy in Milton* (New York, 1949) to rabbinical influences. Pomponazzi's theory is dismissed as "of no moment in the theological disputation of the age" and Milton's position is described as "fairly simple, namely, that 'soul' in the Old Testament refers to the whole man" (p. 75). Clearly, Conklin oversimplifies the problem.

42. St. Thomas believed that the soul is created by a miracle when the infant is "predisposed" to receive it and continues to have an individual existence after death. Milton is consistently materialistic. The soul is not created but conveyed from father to child in the human seed. After the death of the body the soul sleeps until resurrection. On the other hand, several of the more Platonic references to the soul in the early works (e.g., *Comus*, ll. 453–63) suggest that in his poetical mood Milton was inclined to emphasize the separation of soul from matter, and even to regard matter as the base prison house of the soul which the Platonists felt it to be.

43. See Victor Harris, *All Cohœrence Gone* (Chicago, 1949).

44. E.g., Donne, *Essays in Divinity,* ed. Simpson, p. 17, felt obliged to insist "*That it is an Article of our Belief that the world began.* And therefore for this point we are not under the insinuations and mollifyings of perswasion, and conveniency; nor under the reach and violence of Argument, or Demonstration, or Neccessity." Henry More's *Homines Aerii* (*op. cit.,* p. 239) began by arguing "*The Original of the World.*" One "cited some things out of the disputations of Avenroes . . . and named several other Treatises . . . which were all of Avenroes his writing and withal did openly confess himself to be an Avenroist." Milton took the orthodox position in Chapter VII of the *Christian Doctrine.*

In Medias Res in *Paradise Lost*

1. Cf. Marvin T. Herrick, *The Fusion of Horatian and Aristotelian Literary Criticism, 1531–1555* (Urbana, 1946). Milton's critical theory is analyzed and the important passages are collected in Ida Langdon, *Milton's Theory of Poetry and Fine Art* (New Haven, 1924).

2. Chapel Hill, 1947.

3. I have used the translation by Kenneth Telford (Chicago, 1965). For my own interpretation of these and related passages, see Leon Golden and O. B. Hardison, Jr., *Aristotle's Poetics for Students of Literature* (Englewood Cliffs, N.J., 1968). The key chapters for epic unity are VIII, XVII, XXIII, and XXIV. Aristotle is remarkably consistent on the subject, even to the extent of repeating key ideas and phrases.

4. Horace, *Opera Omnia,* ed. Hans Farber (Munich, n.d.), 146–52.

5. *De dialectica disciplina* (Louvain, 1515), fol. b viv: "plerumque perturbat eas [res] atque a mediis orditur rebus: deinde quae primae fuerant carminum: posterius personae colore *alicuius* aut alio quovis commento infert mentionem . . . iam vklemus contrarium naturali: id est artificialem ordinem esse. . . . Historie cuius prima laus est veritas: naturalis ordo convenit." Cf. comment on this distinction in Bernard Weinberg, *A History of Literary Criticism in the Italian Renaissance,* 2 vols. (Chicago, 1961), I, 40–43.

6. *Spenser's Faerie Queene,* ed. J. C. Smith, 2 vols. (Oxford, 1909), II, 486.

7. The art/nature contrast is evident in Milton's well-known contrast between "*Jonson's* learned sock" and "sweetest *Shakespear* fancies childe" in *L'Allegro,* 132–33 (cited in the text); and also in the verses Milton contributed to the Second Folio: "whilst to th' shame of slow-endeavoring art, / Thy easie numbers flow" (*Of Shakespear* [9–10]).

8. *A Preface to "Paradise Lost"* (New York, 1960), 129.

9. Classical precedent is confusing. The *Odyssey* and the *Aeneid* clearly begin *in medias res.* The *Iliad* is ambiguous. The *Pharsalia* and the *Thebaid* are chronological. Vida and Spenser, along with Ariosto, followed Horace. Trissino not only wrote *Italia Liberata dai Gotti* in "the order of nature" but argued in his introduction that he was following the precedent of Homer's *Iliad* and that this procedure was quite in accord with the *Poetics.* Cf. Gilbert, *On the Composition of "Paradise Lost,"* 59–61. For Vida, see A. S. Cook, *The Art of Poetry* (Boston, 1892), 39–156.

10. In the special case of a chronological epic like *Italia Liberata* the inclusive plot is identical with the dramatic plot.

11. Gardner, "Milton's Satan and the Theme of Damnation in Elizabethan Tragedy," in *Essays and Studies,* n.s. I (1948), 46–66; Barker, "Structural Pattern in *Paradise Lost,*" *Philological Quarterly* 28 (1949), 16–30. Cf. also Hanford, "The Dramatic Element in *Paradise Lost,*" *Studies in Philology* 14 (1917), 178–95; W. A. Wright, *Facsimile of the Manuscript of Milton's Minor Poems* (Cambridge, 1890); and Gilbert, *On the Composition of "Paradise Lost,"* 11–26. I have used *The Student's Milton,* ed. Frank A. Patterson (New York, 1947) for the text of Phillips's *Life.*

12. *Student's Milton,* xl.

13. Hanford, *A Milton Handbook* (New York, 1946, p. 187), suggests merely "circa 1642." Gilbert argues that the tragedy described by Phillips came after the Trinity outlines and calls it the "Fifth tragedy" (*On the Composition of "Paradise Lost."* pp. 21–23). If we consider the Phillips tragedy as an alternative to the Trinity outlines, Phillips's reference could be to a time before or after them. The Trinity manuscripts are printed in *Collected Works of Milton* XVIII, 228–45. "Adam unparadiz'd" is on pp. 231–32.

14. "Milton's Satan," as reprinted in Arthur Barker, ed., *Milton: Modern Essays in Criticism* (Oxford, 1965), 208. Compare Gilbert, *On the Composition of "Paradise Lost,"* 17, 20–21.

15. In *Eikonoklastes* (*Yale Prose Works of Milton,* III, 361–62), as an example of villainous hypocrisy.

16. E.g., *Paradise Lost,* I, 35, 107, 148, 170; II, 107, 330; IV, 386; IX, 168, 171; X, 374. The word *revenge* is used ten times in Books I and II, and twenty-one times in the poem as a whole.

17. Cf. Gilbert, *On the Composition of "Paradise Lost,"* p. 22: "To write a dramatic *Paradise Lost* without showing the taking of the fruit seems like playing around the main action without actually touching it. . . . It may be that in the last plan [i.e., Gilbert's "Plan Five," the Phillips tragedy] the serpent did again come on the stage."

18. There are numerous "demonic councils" in the poems of the "celestial cycle" which are analogues for the council in *PL,* but they are not sanctioned by Scripture as are the arrival of Satan in Paradise or the theology of redemption dramatized by the debate of the Daughters of God. They are free inventions. Milton drew extensively on literary tradition in Books I and II. At the same time, his treatment is unique in both its setting and its combination of details. Discomfort with the "fictional" quality of the demonic conclave has a long history and was expressed, for example, by Defoe in the eighteenth and Coleridge in the nineteenth century.

19. Cf. esp. pp. 101–6, and the charts showing the order of composition and disposition of materials, pp. 85–87 and 152–55.

20. The primary source for this idea in the later Renaissance is Tasso's *Discourses on the Heroic Poem* (1594). See Allan Gilbert, *Literary Criticism: Plato to Dryden* (New York, 1940), 478–81. Also, Weinberg, *History of Literary Criticism,* II, index, s.v. "marvelous."

21. "Point of View in *Paradise Lost,*" in *Renaissance Papers,* ed. Peter G. Phialas (Chapel Hill, 1968), 85–92. Compare Gilbert, *On the Composition of*

"Paradise Lost," 74; and Coleridge, *Lectures on Shakespeare* (London, 1951), 185.

"Hee for God Only, Shee for God in Him": Gender in *Paradise Lost*

1. Through the commentators it passed into the numerous paraphrases of Genesis which comprise what is called the hexameral tradition, including, for example, Pico della Mirandola's *Heptalpus,* John Colet's *Letter to Radulphus on the Mosaic Account of Creation*, and DuBartas's *Holy Week,* which was an important source for *Paradise Lost.*

2. Merritt Y. Hughes, ed., *John Milton: Complete Poems and Major Prose* (New York, 1957), 707.

3. Ibid., 831.

4. Ibid., 728–29.

5. Ibid., 733.

References: The Disappearance of Man

Blakemore, Colin, and Susan Greenfield, eds. *Mindwaves: Thoughts on Intelligence, Identity and Consciousness* (Oxford, 1987). [Essays by John Searle, Richard Gregory, Philip Johnson-Laird, Roger Penrose, Colin McGinn, Sir John Eccles, Larry Weiskrantz, János Szentágothai, Rodolfo Llinás, Horace Barlow, Nicholas Humphrey, John Crook, Ted Honderich, and others]

Brumbaugh, Robert S. *Ancient Greek Gadgets and Machines* (New York, 1966).

Dreyfus, Hubert L. *What Computers Can't Do: A Critique of Artificial Reason* (New York, 1972).

Evans, Christopher. *The Micro Milennium* (New York, 1979).

Feldman, Jerome A. "Connections: Massive Parallelism in Natural and Artificial Intelligence," *Byte Magazine* (April 1985), 277–84.

Fjermedal, Grant. *The Tomorrow Makers: A Brave New World of Living Brain Machines* (New York, 1986).

Ginestier, Paul. *The Poet and the Machine*, tr. Martin Friedman (Chapel Hill, 1961).

Hillis, W. Daniel. "The Connection Machine," *Scientific American* 256 (June 1987), 108–15.

Hinton, Geoffrey. "Learning in Parallel Networks," *Byte Magazine* (April 1985), 265–73.

Jastrow, Robert. "The Thinking Computer," *Science Digest* (June 1982), 54–55, 106–7.

Jaynes, Julian. *The Origin of Consciousness in the Breakdown of the Bicameral Mind* (Boston, 1976).

Kinoshita, June, and Nicholas G. Palevsky. "Computing With Neural Networks," *High Technology* (May 1987), 24–31. (New York, 1977).

McCorduck, Pamela. *Machines Who Think: A Personal Inquiry into the History and Prospects of Artificial Intelligence* (San Francisco, 1979).

McLaughlin, William J. "Human Evolution in the Age of the Intelligent Machine," *Interdisciplinary Science Reviews* 8 (1983), 307–19.

Minsky, Marvin, ed. *Robotics* (Garden City, N.Y., 1985). [Essays by Marvin Minsky, T. A. Heppenheimer, Philip Agre, Thomas Bionford, Hans Moravec, Robert Freitas, Joseph Engelberger, Richard Wolkmir, Robert Ayres, and Robert Sheckley]

Minsky, Marvin. *The Society of Mind* (New York, 1986).

Moravec, Hans. *Mind Children: The Future of Robot and Human Intelligence* (Cambridge, Mass., 1989).

Morrison, Philip. "Intellectual Prospects for the Year 2000," *Technology Review* (January 1969), 19–23.

Restak, Richard M. *The Brain: The Last Frontier* (New York, 1979).

Searle, John. "Minds and Brains without Programs," see Blakemore and Greenfield.

Simon, Herbert A., and Allen Newell. "Heuristic Problem Solving: The Next Advance in Operations Research," *Operations Research* 6 (January/February 1958), 1–10.

Stevens, John K. "Reverse Engineering the Brain," *Byte Magazine* (April 1985), 287–99.

Tank, David W., and John H. Hopfield. "Collective Computation in Neuronlike Circuits," *Scientific American* 257 (December 1987), 104–14.

Turing, Alan. "Computing Machinery and Intelligence," *Mind* 59 (October 1950), 433–60.

Turing, Alan. "On Computable Numbers, with an Application to the Entscheidungsproblem," *Proceedings of the London Mathematical Society* 2. 42 (1937), 230–65

Wiener, Norbert. *Cybernetics; or, Control and Communication in the Animal and the Machine* (Cambridge, Mass., 1948).

Wilson, Richard Guy. *The Machine Age in America, 1918–1941* (New York, 1986). [A profusely illustrated catalogue and commentary on the symbiosis between machines and culture in the first half of this century]

Winograd, Terry, and Fernando Flores. *Understanding Computers and Cognition: A New Foundation for Design* (Reading, Mass., 1987).

Index